SWEETPOTATO TECHNOLOGY FOR THE 21ST CENTURY

ABOUT THE BOOK

In 1981 the Asian Vegetable Research and Development Center convened many of the world's leading sweetpotato scientists at the first International Symposium on Sweetpotato in Shanhua, Taiwan. Ten years later, Tuskegee University hosted another such international meeting—under the same title as this book—in Montgomery, Alabama and at its campus in nearby Tuskegee. Because sweetpotato can play an important role in addressing growing world concern for food availability, diet, health and sustainable agricultural systems, both conferences had the same goal—to bring together the leading authorities working on sweetpotato to share the latest scientific and technical data on sweetpotato research, production systems and products.

This book describes the major developments in sweetpotato research and utilization as we face the next century. It contains all major papers delivered at this symposium organized under five headings: Genetic Engineering, Growing Systems, Developmental Physiology and Biochemistry, Food Technology/Human Nutrition and Interfacing New Technologies with Conventional Breeding. Each section ends with "Poster Presentations." Developed from symposium posters, they are informative on a wide range of research. A final section includes photographs taken and recipes served or disseminated at the symposium.

Tuskegee University dates its research on sweetpotato back to the turn of the last century and the internationally renowned George Washington Carver, teacher and first director of Tuskegee University's agricultural experiment station which now bears his name. His work with sweetpotato was only surpassed by his work with the peanut, and he labored untiringly that his research might improve the quality of life of "people furthest down."

In recent years, Tuskegee University has become engaged in specialized sweetpotato research for future space missions involving human life support over extended periods of time. Beginning in 1986, a team of Tuskegee University scientists, technicians, graduate and undergraduate students initiated sweetpotato research for CELSS, the National Aeronautics and Space Administration's acronym for Controlled Ecological Life Support Systems. In 1992 NASA established the Center for Food Production, Processing and Waste Management in Controlled Ecological Life Support Systems at Tuskegee University with a focus on sweetpotato and peanut. The editors of this book are the Center's directors. Walter A. Hill, an agronomist, is dean of the School of Agriculture and Home Economics and director of the G. W. Carver Agricultural Experiment Station; Conrad K. Bonsi, a plant breeder and pathologist, is associate director. Philip A. Loretan, an engineer (and a sweetpotato farmer), coordinates activities for the new Center.

About the word "sweetpotato:" the reader will note that it is spelled in this book as one word except in bibliographies when originally published as two words. Most of the English-speaking world still spells it as two words. However, in 1989 the National Sweetpotato Collaborators Group—the organization of sweetpotato scientists in the United States—officially adopted the one-word spelling of sweetpotato (*Ipomoea batatas*) to distinguish it from the potato (*Solanum tuberosum*). Following the lead of the Sweetpotato Collaborators, the U.S. Department of Agriculture and the American Society of Horticultural Science as well as the affirmative response to a polling of symposium participants, the editors have joined the two words within the body of each paper.

"There are but few if any of our staple farm crops receiving more attention than the sweetpotato, and indeed rightfully so—the splendid service it rendered during the great World War in the saving of wheat flour will not soon be forgotten. The 118 different and attractive products (to date) made from it are sufficient to convince the most skeptical that we are just beginning to discover the real value and marvelous possibilities of this splendid vegetable."

— George Washington Carver
Bulletin No. 38, November 1936

SWEETPOTATO TECHNOLOGY FOR THE 21ST CENTURY

WALTER A. HILL
CONRAD K. BONSI
PHILIP A. LORETAN
Editors

TUSKEGEE UNIVERSITY
Tuskegee, Alabama

Published in 1992 in the United States of America by Tuskegee University, Tuskegee, Alabama 36088.

Library of Congress Cataloging-in-Publication Data

Sweetpotato technology for the 21st century / edited by Walter A.
   Hill, Conrad K. Bonsi, Philip A. Loretan.
        p.   cm.
   Includes bibliographical references and index.
   ISBN 0-9625021-3-8 : $40.60
   1. Sweet potatoes--Congresses.   2. Sweet potato products-
-Congresses. I. Hill, Walter A., 1946-   . II. Bonsi, Conrad K.,
1950-   . III. Loretan, Philip A., 1940-   .
SB211.S9S95   1992
635'.22--dc20   92-61944
                                                        CIP

TABLE OF CONTENTS

Page

SECTION 2 — GROWING SYSTEMS

POSTER PRESENTATIONS

SECTION 3 — DEVELOPMENTAL PHYSIOLOGY AND BIOCHEMISTRY

POSTER PRESENTATIONS

SECTION 4 — FOOD TECHNOLOGY/HUMAN NUTRITION

POSTER PRESENTATIONS

SECTION V — INTERFACING NEW TECHNOLOGIES WITH CONVENTIONAL BREEDING

To Jill, Eunice, Marie

and

Shaka, Askia, Osei
Anibok, Akofa, Sesie
Dawn

For your patience, support and inspiration

Acknowledgments

The period of January 1990 to December 1991 was designated as a time for the celebration of the centennial year of the 1890 Land-Grant Colleges and Universities—those 17 institutions that have provided the principal means of access to higher education for African-Americans. They also provide outreach services for rural and neglected communities and conduct research of importance to the United States and the world community. For us at Tuskegee University, the commemoration included a proposal to the International Science and Education Council and the Office of International Cooperation and Development (OICD) within the U.S. Department of Agriculture (USDA) that Tuskegee University host an international conference on Sweetpotato Technology for the 21st Century. The objective would be to bring together experts and interested parties from around the world to envision and explore new methods and technologies for sweetpotato breeding, production, processing, storage, marketing and utilization as a food, feed and fuel source. State of the art presentations on genetic engineering, tissue culture, breeding, physiology, microbial/rhizosphere ecology, sweetpotato weevil and other pest management, storage techniques, promotion and marketing, new uses of roots and foliage, hydroponic production, multiple cropping systems and product development would be sought.

OICD accepted the proposal and additional support was granted from the USDA – Cooperative State Research Service and Agricultural Research Service, the National Aeronautics and Space Administration (NASA), the Association of Research Directors, and the U.S. Agency for International Development. We extend gratitude to each of these organizations for their support.

A committee was formed which included a distinguished group of sweetpotato scientists—Mel Hall, of the University of Georgia/Coastal Plains Experiment Station, Robert Jarret, USDA-ARS, Al Jones, on the eve of his retirement from USDA-ARS after many years of outstanding work in sweetpotato breeding, and Stan Kays of the University of Georgia; Ralph Prince and Yvonne B. Freeman from NASA; Henry Robitaille, Science and Technology for Epcot Center, J. Alton Coco representing sweetpotato processors, and Dwight H. Tilley, representing sweetpotato farmers. This group together with the editors and Richard J. Hughes of USDA-OICD formed the National Steering Committee. We met twice in Atlanta to discuss the concept of the meeting, set the agenda and propose names for invited papers. An International Advisory Committee gave constructive input: John Dodds of the International Potato Center headquartered in Lima, Peru; S. K. Hahn of the International Institute of Tropical Agriculture in Ibadan, Nigeria; and N.S. Talekar of the Asian Vegetable Research and Development Center in Taiwan. We thank these committee persons for their invaluable contributions in planning the symposium.

The symposium was held June 2 to 6, 1991 in Montgomery, Alabama and at Tuskegee University in Tuskegee. A special word of thanks goes to each contributor toward the symposium and this book. As Samson S. C. Tsou, deputy director general of the Asian Vegetable Research and Development Center and host of the first international symposium in 1981, noted: the presentations gave evidence of "the tremendous amount of new knowledge that has accumulated during the last 10 years and the many new technologies that are available to enhance research efficiency and provide new opportunities to improve sweetpotato."

Each of the papers in this book was reviewed by at least two peers in the subject matter. We thank the following people for serving as reviewers: A. M. Almazan, M. N. Alvarez, R. N. Beachy, P. K. Biswas, E. Bonsi, R. H. Brown, D. J. Cantliffe, M. L. D. Carelli, E. E. Carey, C. A. Clark, W. W. Collins, S. Crossman, J. Daie, E. S. Data, J. H. Dodds, J. O. Garner, Jr., D. Greene, M. R. Hall, J. H. M. Henderson, R. Jansson, R. L. Jarret, L. D. Johnson, D. Kamau, E. Karuri, S. J. Kays, W. M. Knott, Y. Kowyama, G. Kuo, J. Y. Lu, W. J. McLaurin, D. G. Mortley, S. N. Lyonga, T. Nagahama, K. Nakamura, G. G. Nayar, M. Oracion, G. Orjeda, G. O. Osuji, P. Ozias-Akins, R. D. Pace, J. K. Peterson, C. S. Prakash, R. Prince, E. Rhoden, H. A. Robitaille, R. Scheuerman, A. Susheela Thirumaran, N. S. Talekar, P. Thompson, A. A. Trotman, V.D. Truong, S. C. S. Tsou, T. Uewada, G. Varadarajan, W. M. Walter, Jr., J. Wargiono, R. Wheeler, L. D. Wickham, P. W. Wilson, J. A. Woolfe, Q. H. Xue and O. Yamakawa.

Those who presented posters at the symposium were also invited to develop papers for peer review and possible inclusion in this book. Those accepted are found at the end of each section under "Poster Presentations." They are presented alphabetically according to the last name of the first author.

We thank Peter Gregory, research director of the International Potato Center in Peru, for addressing the symposium banquet. We also thank Alabama Commissioner of Agriculture A. W. Todd, William K. Knott of NASA, McKinley Mayes of USDA/ CSRS, Henry Robitaille of Epcot Center, Richard Hughes of OICD and J. Alton Coco of the Sweet Potato Council of the U.S. for their words of welcome to the participants. An added note of thanks is extended to McKinley Mayes for his consistent support of research at the 1890 land-grant institutions and Tuskegee University for many years.

We cannot overlook in these acknowledgments one of the highlights of this gathering—the sweetpotato taste extravaganza which gave a festival spirit to the symposium. We thank Jack Tsay and his colleagues at the Tainan County Farmers Association (to which we are grateful for a beautifully designed sweetpotato recipe booklet) along with chefs Mei-chin Cheng and Chiu-O Chen who so ably demonstrated Chinese preparations of sweetpotato with the narration of Samson Tsou. Thanks are also extended to the Japanese chefs, Professor Machiko Ono, restaurateur Kyoko Hara and her able assistant Eriko Kanao for their artful demonstrations and the shared recipes. Special thanks to Barry Duell, their narrator and the chairman of the Kawagoe Friends of Sweet Potatoes, for leading an impressive Japanese delegation which included Eiji Yamada, artist and then curator of what is probably the world's first Sweetpotato Museum. We thank him for his original concept of "Supersweetpotato" and his posters—pictured on page 574. Thanks also to Aurea Almazan, Eunice Bonsi, Flora Gailliard, John Lu, Parico Osby and the Tuskegee students who assisted the chefs from Taiwan and Japan.

We thank all those who brought recipes and processed products (see Section 6) from around the world for display at the symposium banquet site. Some of these are pictured on pages 574 to 576. We appreciate Aurea Almazan's painstaking work in translating the metric measurements in the international recipes into those commonly used in the U. S.

We also thank all those at Tuskegee University who assisted in so many ways in making the symposium a success. The faculty and staff within the School of Agriculture and Home Economics, the George Washington Carver Agricultural Experiment Station, and the Cooperative Extension Program must be singled out for their hard work: Samuel Adeyeye, Ramble Ankumah, Ntam Baharanyi, Marva Ballard, P. K. Biswas, Velma Blackwell, Eunice Bonsi, Warren Buchanan, Sibyl Caldwell, Esther Carlisle, Pauline David, Nathaniel Ellison, Flora Gailliard, Jill Hill, William Hodge, David Kamau, Victor Khan, Judy Kinebrew, John Lu, Erskine McKinnon, Desmond Mortley, Mudiayi Ngandu, Parico Osby, George Paris, John Phillips, Channapatna Prakash, Larry Randolph, Errol Rhoden, Mattie Robinson, Charlotte Scott, Arthur Siaway, Joe Sparks, Clauzell Stevens, Audrey Trotman, Sherelle Williams, Patricia Young and Robert Zabawa. William Lester, our provost, Suchet Louis and Eloise Carter of International Programs and public relations officer J. J. Johnson III were other campus supporters. Students also helped; all are thanked.

Special thanks go to our president, Dr. Benjamin F. Payton, for his support and for identifying—in his opening remarks to the symposium—the challenge before us that "the discrepancy between our capacity to produce food to feed the world's population and the reality of millions of people who go hungry is a situation which we simply cannot tolerate."

Lastly, we thank all those who helped us in the preparation of this book: our technical editor, Marie Loretan, who worked creatively with us from start to finish and took responsibility for getting the manuscript ready for publication; Beverly Green, Sibyl Caldwell and Jill Hill who provided essential word processing and computer support at critical points; Marva Ballard for art work and consultation; and Louise Herron who skillfully handled all the financial matters associated with the symposium and this book.

Our hope is that this book will provide useful information to professionals, producers, processors, retailers and consumers about the latest sweetpotato technology and the capability of this crop to contribute significantly to the food and health needs of the world's peoples. Our hope is that this book will bring many to discover, as George Washington Carver put it, "the real value and marvelous possibilities of this splendid vegetable."

Walter A. Hill
Conrad K. Bonsi
Philip A. Loretan

Sweetpotato Research: Current Status and Future Needs

Significant change has occurred worldwide since the 1981 sweetpotato symposium in Taiwan that has increased interest in sweetpotato utilization in both developing and developed nations. Rapidly growing populations, particularly in developing countries, have caused concern over potential food shortages and hunger and, as a result, there is increased focus on root and tuber crops such as sweetpotato as sources of energy and nutrients. Growing awareness of sweetpotato's high nutrient content with its anti-carcinogenic and cardiovascular disease-preventing properties is reinforcing sweetpotato's role as an important health food. The inclusion of sweetpotato by the National Aeronautics and Space Administration (NASA) as a food for long-term space missions—because of its nutrition, versatility and growth habits—has created new opportunities for research in Controlled Ecological Life Support Systems and a new way to promote the crop. Biotechnology, including genetic engineering, is providing powerful new tools that, when combined with conventional breeding, hold great promise to improve sweetpotato yield, taste, nutrition, and resistance to insects and disease. The urgent need to halt environmental deterioration has led to increased study and application of sustainable agricultural systems including those with sweetpotato whose fast-spreading foliage serves as a protective ground cover. Priorities listed by the International Potato Center (CIP) serve to challenge sweetpotato researchers worldwide to stimulate the demand for sweetpotato by making it low cost and appealing and to fit sweetpotato into existing cropping systems. Expanding sweetpotato usage by developing acceptable processed food products and alternative-use non-food products are also challenges for the future.

The current status and future research needs of sweetpotato as presented and discussed during the symposium are summarized in Table 1 and are discussed below.

Nutrition, Taste and Versatility

Because of its high energy, dietary fiber, vitamin and mineral content, sweetpotato is a natural health food. Sweetpotato can be prepared in many ways—the leaves can be cooked like other greens and the roots can be baked, boiled, french fried or prepared as a salad, dessert, jam, condiment, beverages, cookies, candies, chips and other snacks. It can be mixed as a flour with other staples to make bread, pancakes, vermicelli, etc. or with other foods as in a casserole or stew. In order to establish a sweetpotato flour industry, varieties are needed that are low in crude fiber

Table 1. Status and needs of sweetpotato research.

Research Area	Status	Research Needs
General	✓sweetpotatoes are needed for diet diversity, health and, in some parts of world, survival.	✓enhanced interdisciplinary research efforts worldwide ✓germplasm, information and scientific data exchange ✓increased crop promotion and public policy support
Biotechnology	✓tissue culture used for germplasm maintenance, distribution, regeneration ✓method exists for somatic embryo production ✓RFLP's of 600 accessions of *I. batatas* and related species determined ✓binary Ti-plasmid vector system established for introducing foreign genes ✓shoot and root formation induced from callus	✓minimize reculturing requirement in tissue culture ✓development of RFLP, RAPD and isozyme analysis ✓RFLP mapping for genome characterization and selecting disease resistance genes ✓improved *Agrobacterium* co-cultivation and particle bombardment methods for gene transfer ✓promoters of sporamin and β-amylase genes ✓increased frequency of shoot regeneration ✓development of synthetic seed
Integrating Breeding and New Technology	✓major constraints in breeding are its hexaploid nature and limited seed production ✓partial genetic resistances are known for most insect pests and pathogens ✓availability of a broadened germplasm base ✓breeding for low β-amylase activity, low color degradation, high starch content, high flesh pigmentation (color) and flavor in Japan ✓methods include *in vitro* screening, somoclonal variation, transformation with recombinant DNA ✓capsid protein gene for SPFMV cloned and coat protein coding sequence isolated ✓cultivars available with multiple resistance to *Conoderus, Diabrotica* and *Systena* spp. ✓development of tetraploid lines completed ✓4x hybrids and *I. trifida* progenies obtained	✓survey world distribution and effects of diseases and insects ✓improved cultivar quality and insect resistance ✓work on Reniform nematode, Rhizopus soft rot, weevil, vineborers, and wireworms ✓combine resistance into horticulturally important cultivars ✓combination of strategies needed: screening under specific environments, identification/transfer of interspecific, non-preference, antibiosis resistance ✓isolation of genes for resistance to sweetpotato weevil ✓gene expression elucidated and technology developed ✓work on broad spectrum genes, e.g., wound healing ✓reliable regeneration system ✓more genetic research on close relatives of the sweetpotato ✓reconstruction of hexaploids from tetraploids ✓wider genetic background in the 4x population ✓isolation and characterization of additional genes

Research Area	Status	Research Needs
Nutrition, Taste and Versatility	√high in energy, dietary fiber, vitamins, minerals √sensory versatility: range of colors, flavors, sweetness, textures √a variety of products are available but have limited distribution √shochu by-products used as animal/fish feed, emulsion stabilizer, cultivation of mushrooms	√design culturally appropriate processing technology for developing appealing products using sweetpotato roots and greens √ensure processing methods that minimize nutrient losses √develop high quality frozen products √prevent postharvest loss due to insect infestation √develop non-food uses, e.g., fuels from starch √develop marketing strategies that are culturally specific
Physiology	√progress in stress metabolites, β-amylase and molecular genetics of sporamin √sink strength of roots is more important in affecting photosynthesis and translocation than the source potential of leaves and regulates dry matter production √low chilling tolerance is due to cell membrane injury and low linolenic acid	√integration of plant chemistry into breeding, pathology, processing, and other research programs √a better understanding of leaf canopy photosynthesis and respiration and partitioning of dry matter to storage roots √study of chemical defense systems in sweetpotato
Alternate Growing Systems	√research on wheat, soybeans, potatoes, cowpea, lettuce, and sweetpotato for space missions is on-going √1700-1800 g roots/plant have been obtained in hydroponic systems √mass education/entertainment value of food cropping systems established at Epcot Center √sweetpotato is grown in many cropping systems in Asia and Africa	√development of systems for sweetpotato production, processing and waste management for micro and hypogravity conditions √screening of more cultivars and breeding for growth in hydroponic systems √new ways to grow sweetpotato as an educational/entertainment food crop √further development of pheromones, other attractants and biological control methods √a global assessment of research and development of IPM strategies that take into account socioeconomic and cultural factors

and high in dietary fiber. For sweetpotato greens, the yield, quality and postharvest properties need improving (Tsou).

The recurring negative connotation of sweetpotato as being a poor man's food in some developing countries was challenged by Woolfe. She asked simply "what is wrong with something being low cost?" But if—as income increases—people want more variety and convenience, they will find sweetpotato has special traits: nutritional and sensory versatility in terms of its wide range of tastes, textures and colors. These traits make sweetpotato uniquely comparable not only to other root and tuber crops but also to vegetables and fruits. Thus, the potential for processing sweetpotato at the home, village or industrial level is great, but it is important that processing minimize nutrient loss.

Woolfe emphasized that sweetpotato (roots and greens) can support more people per unit hectare than any other food, and that there is a need to promote carotene-rich cultivars for children in many developing countries. Their protein and riboflavin content are also important. More starch and vegetable foods are now recommended in developing countries and sweetpotato provides both food types. Also, since antioxidant nutrients—β-carotene (vitamin A), ascorbic acid (vitamin C), and tocopherol (vitamin E) may protect against heart disease and cancer, there is renewed interest in sweetpotato in developed countries. Woolfe proposed that its fiber and vitamin content should be promoted starting with young people. She pointed out that up to 50% of sweetpotato flour replaces wheat in Peru, that fruity products, noodles, jellied blocks, yogurt, chips and ice cream are other acceptable products and that cultivars for processing must be synchronized with a particular use.

Duell's exploration of sweetpotato product development in Kawagoe, Japan illustrates how grass-roots promotional leadership sparked new interest in sweetpotato and encouraged the development of several small businesses. Building on the historical connections of the city with sweetpotato, that leadership increased the demand for and marketability of sweetpotato as a food.

McLaurin and Kays found a range of quality parameters—dryness, moisture and fiber content, 20 flavors, 15 odors and a range of non-sweet to sweet "sweetness" for 89 advanced sweetpotato clones. Their results substantiate the potential use versatility of sweetpotatoes and incidate that genetic diversity in sweetpotato germplasm allows for making substantial changes in the flavor of new cultivars.

The technology for processing sweetpotatoes for chips has been successfully developed by Data and Operario, but there is a need to develop technologies to prevent loss due to insect infestation. In the Philippines, fruity beverages and sweetpotato cocoa powder (for hot drinks) were highly acceptable (Van Den). The drinks are rich in vitamin A. A patent has been obtained by Visayas State College of Agriculture (ViSCA) and a joint project between ViSCA and the private sector is underway to upscale and market the products. For frozen product development freezing of sweetpotatoes should be done quickly and, after packaging, maintained at <-17°C. Walter and Wilson recommended the use of packaging with a low moisture vapor, gas barrier for a long shelf life ($\geq$6 months). They suggested that a high quality frozen product is needed to increase consumption in the U.S. pointing to numerous such products developed from sweetpotato in Japan. Johnson et al. presented data showing consumer acceptability of yogurts that incorporated sweetpotato with other fruits.

Non-food utilization of sweetpotatoes has been demonstrated by Nagahama et al. with waste product ("slops") from sweetpotato shochu distillation. Cellulase preparations have effectively degraded cellulosic components in sweetpotato shochu distillatory slops, permitting recycling of the shochu slops. The slops are highly nutritious and are used for hog and steer feed, production of yeast to feed fish, producing dietary fiber, emulsion stabilizers and cultivation of mushrooms.

Biotechnology

Considerable progress in biotechnology has been made in the last 10 years, but more research is required. More genes are needed that can be put into plants and gene expression technology and optimal gene delivery systems must be developed. In the future, the three different approaches to product development through biotechnology—use as a breeder's tool, addition of genes to enhance existing products, and development of entirely new products—will merge. Future progress in product development through biotechnology will occur in incremental steps—not in a big splash—and will require integration into mainstream industries and acceptance by the public (John Howard).

The sweetpotato breeding program at CIP has identified the hexaploid nature of the crop and limited seed production as major constraints (Dodds et al.). The major focus of the breeding program is to improve quality and obtain insect-resistant cultivars. Biotechnology-related research by CIP includes maintenance and distribution of germplasm, improvement of regeneration and transformation systems, restriction fragment length polymorphism (RFLP) mapping for genome characterization, and selecting disease resistance genes. The "comparative advantage" policy at CIP has resulted in nearly 30 contracts with other institutions—including eight in tissue culture (six countries), 14 in genetic engineering (nine countries), and seven in RFLP (four countries). CIP also has a decentralized breeding effort in response to regional differences and needs. This approach involves strong cooperation with national programs and universities.

A binary Ti-plasmid vector system to establish a method for introducing foreign genes into the sweetpotato has been developed. Several members of the sporamin multigene family and the gene for β-amylase have been characterized. Promoters of sporamin and β-amylase genes are expected to be useful to express desired proteins in sweetpotato to improve quality and yield (Nakamura). *Agrobacterium* co-cultivation and particle bombardment have also been used to introduce foreign genes into sweetpotato cells. Use of new techniques for DNA fingerprinting and RFLP using image analysis have been initiated (Prakash and Varadarajan; Carelli et al.).

Six hundred accessions of *I. batatas* and related species have been acquired by the U.S. Department of Agriculture and RFLP's have been used to assess genetic diversity (Jarret). Disease and insect resistance and other traits are being evaluated.

There is a need for improved germplasm storage methods to minimize the frequency of reculturing. Shoot and root formation has been induced from calli derived from sweetpotato petiole protoplasts, but there is a need to increase the frequency of shoot regeneration for useful application (Ozias-Akins and Perera). A method for somatic embryo production of sweetpotato has been developed (Cantliffe). This development suggests that automated production of synthetic seed could occur and in combination with fluid drilling technology could revolutionize sweetpotato production. Research needs on embryos include synchronization and singulation, induction of developmental arrest and the triggering of germination in the field.

Breeding and Molecular Genetics

In Japan, conventional breeding is focusing on developing cultivars with low β-amylase activity, low polyphenol content for low color degradation of snack foods, high starch content for processing, high flesh pigmentation (anthocyanins) for color production and high starch content and flavor for "shochu" (Komaki et al.).

An alternative route for resynthesis of hexaploid sweetpotato has been proposed by Oracion and Shiotani. The two-step approach includes crosses between sweetpotato and selected diploid gene sources to produce tetraploid breeding lines and utilization of the reduced and unreduced gamete pool of the tetraploid breeding population by controlled or open polycross to reconstruct hexaploid sweetpotatoes for conventional breeding. The development of tetraploid lines has been completed and reconstruction of hexaploids from tetraploids is in process. Over 25,000 hand pollinations were carried out by Orjeda et al. using five crossing combinations of sweetpotato and *Ipomoea trifida*. Of 1,374 hybrid progenies from $4x$ hybrids and *I. trifida* accessions, only 3.3% produced > 200 g storage roots per plant. Needed for further improvement is a wider genetic background in the $4x$ hybrid population.

A combination of strategies will be needed to control most insect pests and pathogens for which only partial genetic resistances are known (Hall et al.). These strategies include screening under controlled environmental conditions, identifying sources of resistance in related species and subsequent interspecific transfer, non-preference (antixenosis) and antibiosis. All of these approaches require added time and expense to ongoing breeding activities. As a result, the future must rely on germplasm exchanges and computer technology (data management) and must combine new and emerging technologies with conventional breeding programs.

The capsid protein gene for viral RNA for sweetpotato feathery mottle virus has been cloned and the coat protein coding sequence isolated. Ongoing work seeks to express these capsid protein genes and develop resistance for controlling viral diseases in sweetpotato (Beachy et al.).

There is a need to determine the distribution and effects of diseases and insects (*Cylas formicarius*) on sweetpotatoes in different parts of the world and enhance communication among pathologists and entomologists worldwide. Future work on the taxonomy of *Cylas* spp. should include biochemical, karyological and molecular analysis such as DNA fingerprinting. Use of sex pheromones in traps has shown good potential for integration into weevil management programs worldwide. Development of quality control standards for laboratory production and field testing protocols for synthetic pheromones are needed. Work is also needed on the identification and synthesis of host plant volatiles—as attractants—and on biological control methods using natural enemies—entomopathogenic nematodes, fungi, bacteria and parasitoids (Jansson and Raman). The greatest challenge in breeding sweetpotato is to combine resistance to all important diseases and insects into horticulturally acceptable cultivars. Methods to be used include *in vitro* screening, somoclonal variation, transformation with recombinant DNA in conjunction with traditional breeding for development of disease and insect resistant sweetpotatoes. There is a need for a new thrust in sweetpotato breeding since breeders have had access to a broadened sweetpotato germplasm base in the past few years. There is a need to work on the Reniform nematode, Rhizopus soft rot and *Cylas formicarius*. A challenge for the future is to transform sweetpotato with broad spectrum genes, e.g., genes that control wound healing, such as PAL synthesis (Clark and LaBonte; Carey et al.).

Problems to overcome include: not having a reliable regeneration system, the fact of multi-gene control of traits such as yield and limited genetic research on close relatives of the sweetpotato. Potential methods that need development include RFLP, RAPD (random amplified polymorphic DNA) and isozyme analysis. The key for the future requires cooperation between laboratories with capability to carry out RFLP and individual breeding programs (Collins).

Physiology

In addressing the question "why study sweetpotato chemistry," Kays comprehensively reviewed the chemical basis for sweetpotato traits. The review substantiates the fact that by better understanding the chemistry of the sweetpotato the more readily we can alter the plant and enhance the expression of traits deemed desirable, e.g., chemicals that control flavor or host plant selection decisions by insects. It was pointed out that the only areas in which research progress on sweetpotato chemistry has been notable is in the study of stress metabolites, β-amylase and the molecular genetics of sporamin. It was suggested that future research integrate plant chemistry into breeding, pathology, processing and other research programs.

Sweetpotatoes exhibit a remarkable allelopathic defense against weeds. Biological activity of secondary compounds from sweetpotato cultivars has been demonstrated, but their particular roles in allelopathy need to be further investigated (Harrison and Peterson).

Electrolyte leakage and chemical measurements by Garner et al. indicated that possible mechanisms responsible for low tolerance of sweetpotato genotypes to chilling are caused by cell membrane injury and low linolenic acid in mitochondria lipids. Studies of leaf and canopy photosynthesis and respiration and their relationship to partitioning of dry matter in storage roots were summarized by Brown. Evidence was presented by Kuo and Chen that the sink strength of roots is more important than the source potential of leaves in photosynthesis and translocation, and that the sink regulates dry matter production and yield in storage roots.

A lively debate occurred during the symposium after the presentation by Wilson and Wickham. The central question was one of terminology: "is the storage organ of the sweetpotato a root or a tuber?" Arguments were advanced for rethinking the definition and the use of "tuber" by Wilson and Wickham. Kays et al. defended the classical definition of sweetpotato as a "storage root" and argued that a change in terminology is unwarranted and a source of confusion in the literature. "Storage root" is the terminology used by the National Sweetpotato Collaborators Group, American Society of Horticultural Science and the U.S. Department of Agriculture, and it was used by the editors of this book.

Alternate Growing Systems

NASA's Controlled Ecological Life Support System (CELSS) program was described by Knott. The goal of the CELSS program is to produce food for long-term manned space missions. Such missions require hydroponic closed systems for crop growth. Past work in CELSS at Kennedy Space Center focused on wheat and soybean monocrop systems. Ongoing and future work will focus on the potato and multiple cropping systems. Two research groups—one in the United States (Bonsi et al.) and one in Japan (Uewada et al.) have developed methods that produce sweetpotatoes hydroponically with yields of 1700 to 1800 g/plant. Nutrient solutions, temperatures, photoperiods, relative humidity, light intensity and growing systems have been assessed. There is a need for screening and breeding more cultivars specifically for CELSS and for the development of systems for controlling environmental parameters of CELSS.

The mass education/entertainment value of food cropping systems has been clearly demonstrated at the "Land Exhibit" at Walt Disney World's Epcot Center. Previous attempts to grow sweetpotatoes there using systems designed for above-ground crops resulted in poor yields (Robitaille). New systems are being developed.

The sweetpotato is grown in many cropping systems in Africa. These systems include monoculture and intercrops with maize, cassava, banana and sorghum—to name just a few. Almost all sweetpotatoes grown in Africa are consumed by humans. Given the growing food needs in Africa, further neglect and lack of research on this crop is "no longer affordable" (Alvarez). Sweetpotato ranks fourth in China after rice, wheat and maize. China produces 80 to 85% of the world's sweetpotatoes which are used there mainly in the production of pork but also starch, alcohol and sugars. According to Sheng et al., research on sweetpotato in China will retain conventional breeding as the dominant approach—with a focus on developing multiple resistance and wide adaptability. It is expected that biotechnology and post-harvest processing may impact the future development of sweetpotato production in China.

There is a need for an integrated pest management (IPM) package to control the sweetpotato weevil. This has been done with moderate success in Taiwan (Talekar). These packages should be country- and ecosystem-specific with socioeconomic and cultural factors being considered in their development (Jansson and Raman).

Conclusion

It is important that national policies be influenced to increase funding on sweetpotato research (Gregory). For example, a farmer-scientist coalition has been formed by the National Sweetpotato Growers Association and the National Sweetpotato Collaborators Group and is seeking legislation to increase sweetpotato research in the United States (Collins).

An important point emphasized by many researchers was the need to enhance joint research efforts by sweetpotato scientists worldwide. Suggestions for enhanced cooperation included multidisciplinary and interdisciplinary research, exchange of germplasm, exchange of information and cooperative efforts on targeted problems. Regarding the latter, we all have a responsibility to let others know what we are doing. We need to share first of all the science by short notes or reviews of articles and books, and then we need to know about collaborative research opportunities, job opportunities, conferences, reports and announcements.

Developing a standard database and an electronic mailing system might be an important next step. CIP already has an electronic bulletin board system in biotechnology. The Philippine Root Crop and Training Center has an international sweetpotato newsletter, and they solicit our input. Marilyn Oracion, Truong Van Den or Emma Data at VISCA are the contacts. Tuskegee University has been funded by the U.S. Department of Agriculture to set up a National Sweetpotato Information Center, which will make information on sweetpotato readily accessible—nationwide—through electronic and print media. Current plans are to begin with data from the English-speaking world and to expand to include other languages. Several spoke at the end of the meeting of the importance of this networking. We should build upon the existing initiatives to optimize communication among sweetpotato researchers.

Speaking as a representative of the developing world, Simon Lyonga had this to say at the final session: "If sweetpotato is to contribute to the welfare of human beings, ...the linkages between the North and South or the developed laboratories with national programs has to be right, in order that there would be a steady transfer among programs.... Let's go from the technical to the social aspect—human beings collaborating for the developing world which really needs it for food."

The goal of all of us remains to serve people worldwide by working together as much as possible to enhance the quantity, quality and marketability of food (and nonfood uses) available from the sweetpotato. Fortunately, the versatility of sweetpotato lends itself to a wide array of tasty, nutritious preparations in fresh and processed forms to improve the diets of people around the world. What great opportunities are before us!

Walter A. Hill
Conrad K. Bonsi
Philip A. Loretan

Feeding Tomorrow's Hungry:
The Role of Root and Tuber Crops

Tomorrow's hungry include 80 to 100 million children now born each year. How will we feed them and provide secure provisions for a two-fold increase in our planet's population over the next two decades? How will we cope with the fact that nine out of ten of these children will be born in countries already short of good land to bring into agricultural production? Such land must furnish the world's food and fiber in the 21st Century. How will we intensify land use in these countries while sustaining their natural resource base and protecting their environment? What strategies can be used to complement extensively produced crops such as rice and wheat with intensively produced, nutritious crops? The global potential of root and tuber crops may provide some answers, if we take action now to exploit them.

Root and tuber crops are basic to the diets of millions in the temperate zones and in vast areas of the tropics and sub-tropics where most of the world's undernourished people live. These crops, such as potatoes, cassava, sweetpotato, yams, and cocoyams, are rich in energy and carbohydrates. In developing countries as a whole, they provide 9% of the total caloric intake. In some regions, particularly in parts of Equatorial Africa, they contribute almost half of the total calories consumed. Potatoes and sweetpotatoes contain substantial levels of protein. Although other root and tuber crops are relatively low in protein per plant, in some areas, such as in West Africa, Equatorial Africa, and semi-arid Africa, these crops are consumed in such large quantities that they contribute substantial amounts of protein to the diet. Root and tuber crops also provide substantial amounts of vitamins and minerals.

Several root and tuber crops—including sweetpotato—are fast growing and rapidly produce ground cover to prevent soil erosion. They are tolerant to severe weather and can be used as relay crops in various cropping systems. They not only play a vital role as food for millions of people, they are also widely used to feed animals and to manufacture industrial products such as starch and alcohol.

Although important now, root and tuber crops must play an even bigger role during the next two to three decades. As scientists, our challenge is to realize the massive potential of these crops. Research such as that reported in this book is, of course, a vital element that must be sustained. But we must complement our research efforts with strong efforts to help national governments to break away from policies that emphasize monocropping of cereals to meet soaring food needs. We must help them to realize that policies based solely on the strategy of the "Green Revolution" will not be enough for the 21st Century. We must better inform national policymakers of the technological advances in root and tuber crops made by such institutions as the International Institute of Tropical Agriculture (IITA), the Asian Vegetable Research and Development Center (AVRDC), the Centro Internacional de Agricultura Tropical (CIAT), the International Potato Center (CIP) and national institutions around the world. We must tell these policymakers and the international funding institutions that fuller exploitation of root and tuber crops can truly make a difference in a world facing the threat of hunger in the 21st Century.

It is not surprising that policymakers have waited so long to fully exploit root and tuber crops. Why? Because we researchers generally do a poor job of communicating, except with each other! Communication must become one of our improved technologies. We need a two-pronged attack: to continue our research while developing strong, widespread awareness of the human importance of our research.

We are moving in the right direction. I refer to the increased awareness among the international scientific community of the role that root and tuber crops can play. The case of sweetpotato is a good example. Recognizing that this crop has been seriously underfunded, sweetpotato recently has been given a higher priority within the Consultative Group on International Agricultural Research (CGIAR). In developing countries, sweetpotato is ranked fifth in economic value production, sixth in dry matter production, seventh in energy production, ninth in protein production, and it has tremendous flexibility of utilization as food, feed and industrial products. Yet, sweetpotato was only nineteenth on the CGIAR's priority list. So, in 1985, the CGIAR decided to put more resources into this valuable crop and encouraged CIP to include it in what had previously been a mandate only for potatoes. Now 40% of CIP's total resources go into sweetpotato research. We are building on the successes of the other international agricultural research centers, in particular IITA and AVRDC, and on National Agricultural Research Systems (NARS) around the world. We are also developing new initiatives in sweetpotato research and development, working with the international centers and the NARS to determine our research priorities. Present priorities include stimulating demand, developing new, low-cost processing techniques, and stimulating transfer of this technology. Genetic improvement using conventional and biotechnological techniques is also a high priority as we seek to lower production costs and increase consumer acceptance of the crop. A basic aim is to fit sweetpotato into cereal-based and other food systems.

Thus, research on sweetpotato already has a brighter future. But, for sweetpotato—as for the other root and tuber crops—we must remember that this research work is only one of the two prongs of the attack. We, the scientific community, have relatively little influence on national policies. Many national policymakers are unaware of the full potential of sweetpotato. In the future, we must improve the information flow about the enormous potential of this important crop.

I believe that root and tuber crops could fuel a broad-based industrial revolution in developing countries in the 21st Century. Let's keep doing the research that is so amply demonstrated in this fine book. But let's not be modest about it. We are doing valuable work. We have knowledge right now that would help to make this planet a better place to live. Let's shout about it for all the world's policymakers to hear. Perhaps our deeds as well as our words can help in feeding tomorrow's hungry.

Peter Gregory
Research Director
International Potato Center
Lima, Peru

SECTION 1

GENETIC ENGINEERING

Sweetpotato Technology for the 21st Century. W.A. Hill, C.K. Bonsi and P.A. Loretan (Eds.) 1992. Tuskegee University, Tuskegee, AL

John Howard

ABC'S of Biotechnology

There are three major issues that need to be addressed if biotechnology is to be successful in the future. First, in the past ten years there has been great technical progress. But even as successful as this has been, there still is a need for much more progress in technology development. Second, for those who are waiting for biotechnology to have its impact—the big splash that is going to happen when it hits agriculture, there is some very disappointing news. It may never happen. Biotechnology has already impacted agriculture, but in ways that are not highly visible. When people look back ten years from now they will say it has had a big impact, but it will be in incremental steps, not a big splash. Third, more time needs to be spent on integrating biotechnology into the mainstream of other industries. Most people think integration is having molecular biologists talk with plant breeders, and that is clearly part of the process. However, there is also need to think about integration in terms of the private sector and universities coordinating research in ways that have not been traditional for biologists. There are also the growers, the producers, the public sector, the regulatory agencies as well as the consumers. Public acceptance has to go along with the science.

Technology for product development can be categorized in three major areas: (1) breeders' tools, i.e., use of technology that allows breeders to do selections as usual but making it a more efficient process for them; (2) addition of genes to enhance existing products; or (3) development of entirely new products. Most of the media hype as been focused on this latter point, for example, pharmaceutical compounds in potatoes. However, most of the current applications exist in the category of breeders' tools, and in the future all three uses will merge together. Examples of these are given below.

Five years ago Pioneer Hi-Bred International started looking at a problem of viruses in plants from a laboratory perspective. When field scientists could not define the symptoms in a plant properly, they said it had a virus. Most plants are infected by viruses so this has some merit. However, which virus and how is it spreading? ELISA-based technology which uses antibodies was used to develop diagnostic tools that could specifically identify which virus was present in the plant. After the technology was developed, a new problem was created. Laboratory scientists could not go to all of the various locations around the world to do analyses, nor could

Pioneer Hi-Bred International, Inc., 7300 N.W. 62nd Avenue, Johnston, Iowa 50131, USA.

samples be sent in for analysis because of restrictions on transporting viruses. Therefore, the technology was further developed. The equivalent of the home pregnancy test kit for viruses was made (Townsend, personal communication). This was easy enough to use so agronomists, farm consultants or any type of field scientist could use it. Here is an example of how simple this could be : (1) Take a piece of leaf off the plant and rub it with sand paper, (2) mix with reagent A, (3) add reagent B, and (4) determine the color. A color reaction indicated the virus, lack of color was indicative of a virus free plant. A simple yes/no answer. This demonstrates the need to develop beyond the existing technology that is normally encountered and to integrate the technology into other areas. This has been used now for the last several years with farm consultants, university extension workers, sales agronomists, and it is routinely used in a number of states as well as overseas. This has been such a successful integration that no one thinks of this as biotechnology anymore.

If this is no longer biotechnology, what about other methods for the breeders? RFLPs or restricted fragment length polymorphism is another potential tool for breeders. In brief, this method can be used to characterize plants; for example, a short plant versus a tall plant can be empirically correlated with a set of molecular markers that match this phenotype. This can be done for any trait that can be measured in the plant. There are several potential applications for this technology one of which is to uniquely identify the germplasm so it can be put it into discrete pools for breeding or for legal descriptions (Smith and Smith 1989). This may not only be used as a supplemental tool to characterize germplasm but could be the primary tool. There is data which shows that this is more accurate than any other method today. In fact, one could actually predict yield based on this method better than by pedigree. While this is a very powerful tool, the industry has not yet accepted this. It is a case which technically has been successful, but the industry is lagging in acceptance. Also, the courts have not yet decided this is acceptable data. So this is another area which needs further integration.

Another way to use this technology is to actually map where the traits of interest are on the chromosomes. You can use quantitative or qualitative traits. More than 30 traits have been mapped in maize. While this approach will be an aid in breeding, this is a case where better technology is needed. Where it can be used today is in backcrossing programs (Grant, personal communication). Backcrossing programs can be cut down from three to two years using this method. Now that is a great advancement, and it is being used today. There is a limit in the methodology, however. The current methods only allow a very few traits per year to be analyzed economically. Therefore, more economical methods are needed to be able to use this approach across all the different traits breeders would like to use it for.

Some people define biotechnology as adding genes into plants. Therefore, they no longer want to count RFLPs as having an impact on agriculture from biotechnology. An example of adding new genes into a plant is the collaboration between American Cyanamid and Pioneer to develop herbicide-resistant corn. Through *in vitro* selection, a mutated gene was obtained that conveys herbicide resistance. This should be out next year. The corn has been tested for several years, and there is no detrimental effect at all in terms of the agronomic qualities. The material, however, is not competitive in the marketplace with other lines of corn, and farmers are unwilling to sacrifice older genetic material that has a higher yield potential for herbicide resistance. The registration for the herbicide will not be complete until 1992, so there is now a need to integrate seed company products with the chemical industry in a way that was never thought about several years ago. For a case like this in corn, it will take seven years before the product is on the market. The average life cycle of a corn hybrid on the market is only six years. So this product can be outdated before it gets to the market. Therefore, there is a need to figure out new ways to integrate product registration into the product development cycle.

Some people now say this is no longer biotechnology because it is *in vitro* selection. What they now want to define as biotechnology is recombinant DNA technology.

One of the advantages of recombinant DNA, at least in theory, is that you can deliver genes into any genotype and deliver to precise locations. The hope is to do it fast and economically. This is not available today. The *Agrobacterium* method for getting genes into plants can currently be used. While this does work for certain crops, it does not work at all in others. John Sanford and Ed Wolf at Cornell developed another method, the particle gun. Pioneer developed technology with this particle gun using cell cultures and were able to regenerate plants that were transformed (Tomes et al. 1990). Since these initial experiments on tobacco, others have used the method with other crops. This has not been reported with sweetpotato yet, but in theory it could work. Both of these methods provide ways of getting genes into plants; however, neither is genotype independent as most scientists would like.

In sunflower, either method should work. In practice, Pioneer scientists have not shown it to work. Instead both methods were combined (Bidney et al. 1992). This method allowed some but not all of the seed to be transformed. What this does for sunflower is increase the transformation frequency dramatically. It also reduces the tissue culture cycle tremendously to give much more freedom to work in the genotypes that scientists would like. This may have direct application in sweetpotatoes.

Now that some types of delivery systems are working in most crops of interest today, what genes should be put in? There are several examples. Herbicide resistance genes were one of the first examples. Dupont has shown resistance to sulfonyureas, Calgene - bromoximil resistance, and Monsanto - glyphosate resistance. These are just three examples of many. Today's standard is that, for most major herbicides important in agriculture, there are resistant genes.

What about agronomic properties? There are several cases that can be cited for virus resistance. Pioneer has been working with alfalfa plants that show resistance to alfalfa mosaic virus (Hill et al. 1991).

Another example is insect resistance. Monsanto has shown great progress in getting resistance in tomato plants as well as other crops using *Bacillus thuringiensis* protein. This is just a sampling of the things that can and are being put into crops.

There are also examples of traits for the processors. Calgene, for example, has introduced a gene into tomatoes that keeps them from getting soft after ripening.

Pioneer has genes which alter the composition of grain such as genes that increase the methionine content of the seed.

Biotechnology is here, but its definition keeps changing. Even though progress looks very good, there is still a need for much better technology. More genes are needed that can be put into plants. Gene expression technology is also very critical for the future. The optimal delivery system has not been developed. All of these areas need continued development if biotechnology is to realize its full potential in the future.

While some of this technology is used today, it is not fully integrated. The impact of this technology will change agricultural practices at least from the seed industry's point of view. For example, what about trademarks? Is a trademark needed to state the "active gene ingredient" on every bag of seed that is sold? Patents are becoming an everyday occurrence. How will government regulations work? Recombinant products will hit the market in the next several years, but there is no clear regulatory path today through USDA, FDA, or EPA. Which of these agencies is going to determine the regulatory policies? The impacts are far reaching in the sense that the seed industry, in general, has been nonregulated in the United States. In the future the seed industry will be regulated. Last, what about public acceptance of these products?

Life is getting more complicated. Seed companies used to look at taking a product from the breeders to the growers. Now they have all these other pieces—*in vitro* selection, tissue culture, molecular biology, RFLPs, diagnostics, and somehow this must all be integrated. In conclusion, biotechnology is really an artificial industry. That is, the real industry is the agricultural industry, and we need to figure out how to integrate these new technologies into it.

REFERENCES

Bidney, D.L., C.J. Scelonge, J. Martich, M. Burrus, L. Sims, and G. Ruffman. 1992. Microprojectile bombardment of plant tissues increases transformation frequency by *Agrobacterium tumefaciens*. Plant Molecular Biology 18:301-313.

Hill, R.K., N. Jarvis-Eagan, E.L. Halk, K.J. Krahn, L.W. Liao, R.S. Mathewson, D.J. Merlo, S.E. Nelson, K.E. Rashka, and L.S. Loesch-Fries. 1991. The development of virus-resistant alfalfa, *Medicago sativa* L. Bio-Technology 9:373-377.

Howard, John. 1990. Agri Tech paper. Agro-Industry Hi-tech 1:43-46.

Smith, J.S.C., and O.S. Smith. 1989. The use of morphological, biochemical, and genetic characteristics to measure distance and to test for minimum distance between inbred lines of maize (*Zea mays* L.). Presented at the UPOV Workshop, held in Versailles. 1-18 (1989) France, October, 1989.

Tomes, D.T., A.R. Weissinger, M. Ross, R. Higgins, B.J. Drummond, S. Schaaf, J. Malone-Schoneberg, M. Staebell, P. Flynn, J. Anderson, and J. Howard. 1990. Transgenic tobacco plants and their progeny derived by microprojectile bombardment of tobacco leaves. Plant Molecular Biology 14:261-268.

J. H. Dodds, J. Benavides, F. Buitron, F. Medina, C. Sigüeñas

Biotechnology Applied to Sweetpotato Improvement

The application of biotechnological methods to sweetpotato in order to improve valuable characteristics of this crop is relatively new at the International Potato Center (CIP) in Lima, Peru. It was only in 1987 that CIP assumed the worldwide mandate for this crop. Two major constraints for sweetpotato breeding programs are its hexaploid nature and limited seed production. The major problems have been identified and can be resolved by improving quality and obtaining insect resistant cultivars.

The use of biotechnology for maintenance and distribution of germplasm is a vital base for breeding/improvement activities. Transformation techniques offer a good alternative for resolving some classical breeding problems. Experiments carried out at CIP have shown that it is possible using *Agrobacterium* to introduce new characteristics into sweetpotato and more experiments are in progress for improving both regeneration and transformation systems. RFLP (gene mapping) techniques applied to sweetpotato may be important for genome characterization and for selecting pest and disease resistance genes.

This paper covers some of the sweetpotato biotechnology research of CIP and includes information on CIP's many collaborative projects.

Sweetpotato germplasm, collection, introduction and maintenance

CIP has been involved in the development of a sweetpotato gene bank in Latin America since 1985. Nearly 50% of the accessions have been received as donations to CIP from different institutions. The remaining accessions came from new collection expeditions.

There are many advantages to maintaining sweetpotato germplasm *in vitro* rather than in the field and these have been described previously (Wilkins and Dodds 1982). CIP's tissue culture laboratory maintains more than 3,000 sweetpotato accessions including material from CIP, the Asian Vegetable Research and Development Center in Taiwan and the International Institute of Tropical Agriculture in Nigeria. These materials were introduced into *in vitro* culture in the form of nodal cuttings. Propagation media for both meristems and nodal cuttings have recently been standardized for optimizing rapid *in vitro* growth. All the sweetpotato collec-

International Potato Center (CIP), P.O. Box 5969, Lima, Peru.

tion data have been introduced in a computer data base (using the potato collection as a model) to maintain continual records of the *in vitro* collection.

Because an *in vitro* sweetpotato germplasm collection may contain genetic duplicates, a few experiments are in progress for standardizing techniques for electrophoretic and RFLP analyses on these accessions.

Long-term storage of the sweetpotato germplasm collection is one objective that this laboratory is developing for obtaining a conservative medium that is widely applicable to a broad range of genotypes.

Pathogen elimination

The production of virus-free plants is important for the international exchange of clonal material to avoid all risks of introduction of new diseases to non-affected areas. Meristem culture combined with thermotherapy is being applied to sweetpotato for producing pathogen-tested plants. Before cutting meristems, plants are placed in a thermotherapy chamber with 38°C/16h-32°C/8h. This treatment has improved efficiency in the process of obtaining virus-free material.

In vitro plants obtained from meristem culture are assayed for the sweetpotato feathery mottle virus (SPFMV) and the potato spindle tuber viroid (PSTV). Two factors limiting the production of virus-free plants are: (1) few sweetpotato viruses are known; and (2) molecular methods for viral identification are established only for SPFMV. For this reason, CIP's virology laboratory is working on the identification of sweetpotato virus diseases and on the development of a virus indexing system for this crop.

Germplasm distribution

The international distribution of pathogen-tested sweetpotato germplasm by CIP began in 1990. Sixty pathogen-tested accessions have been produced to date and are now being distributed to both developed and developing countries. This material is sent together with a phytosanitary certificate indicating its virus-free status.

Transformation techniques

For molecular manipulations and plant transformation, the vector system using the soil bacterium *Agrobacterium*, is used to introduce foreign genes into plants. The ability of *Agrobacterium* to transform plants is determined by two regions of the Ti or Ri plasmid: the virulence region (*vir*) and the T-DNA region. Several plant vectors have been developed from Ti or Ri plasmid of *Agrobacterium*. Host specificity is determined by the nature of the Ti or Ri plasmid harbored by the bacteria and the plant chromosomal background (An et al. 1986).

The main limitation in using *Agrobacterium* at the present time is the host range. While many dicotyledonous plants are susceptible to *Agrobacterium,* monocotyledonous plants, especially cereals, are not susceptible to this infection.

Efficient gene transfer systems have been developed for tobacco, tomato, petunia, *Arabidopsis* and potato (Horsch et al. 1985, An et al. 1986, McCormick et al. 1986, Sheikholeslam and Weeks 1987). However, it has recently become possible to introduce foreign genes in other agronomically important species.

Preliminary assays on sweetpotato

Experiments carried out at CIP have shown that sweetpotatoes are amenable to infection with *Agrobacterium*. It has been able to improve the nutritional value of sweetpotatoes using a synthetic gene encoded for a protein high in essential aminoacids (HEAAE). In these studies, 24 varieties of sweetpotatoes were inoculated with the modified *A. rhizogenes* strain, and most responded by forming hairy roots at the site of inoculation (Table 1). These clones represent diverse origin and show differences in morphology, root shape, and color. No difference was observed in the root-forming ability between the wild type *A. tumefaciens* and *A. rhizogenes*

Table 1. Test of transformation and regeneration capacity of sweetpotato cultivars.

Name of clone	Code	Formation of hairy roots	Regeneration of transformed plantlets from cultured roots
Huachano Chico	1 - IN	+	-
Huachano	2 - IN	+	+
Tipo 3	3 - IN	+	-
Yema de Huevo	12 - IN	+	-
Blanco	14 - IN	+	-
Torre Blanca	17 - IN	+	-
Sanjuanino	23 - IN	+	-
Sanpedrano	28 - IN	+	-
Perotito	35 - IN	+	-
Bubu	38 - IN	-	ND
Copara N 1	39 - IN	+	-
Maleno	44 - IN	+	+
Llicuas RHB	46 - IN	+	-
Oreja de Galgo Negro	48 - IN	+	-
Ihuanco	52 - IN	+	+
Sambo	54 - IN	-	ND
Negro	55 - IN	+	-
Pata de Gallina	59 - IN	-	ND
Marimacho	61 - IN	+	-
Parendero Negro	62 - IN	+	-
Parendero Blanco	63 - IN	+	-
Japones Portuguez	64 - IN	+	-
Rinon	66 - IN	+	-
Japones Belleza	76 - IN	+	-

ND means not determined due to lack of "hairy root" formation.

strains (containing the HEAAE). Plantlet regeneration experiments were performed using clones that formed "hairy roots." Only three clones regenerated plantlets; however, many plantlets were obtained from each of the three cultivars that responded. Evidence for the integration of the HEAAE gene was provided by Southern analysis.

These results demonstrated that the *A. rhizogenes* transformation system functions for sweetpotato and illustrates the need to improve its capacity for regeneration to obtain transformed plants.

Transformation for characteristics of global importance

The major advantage of using genetic transformation for improving vegetatively propagated crops is the potential to add valuable characters to existing cultivars of proven value. Such characters include genes for improvement of quality and resistance to various diseases. Insect damage is the most important problem related to sweetpotato production worldwide. The sweetpotato weevil and sweetpotato butterfly are major contraints on the future development of the crop. The use of this biotechnology will provide a novel source of resistance in sweetpotato breeding, which would not be possible with conventional breeding approaches.

There is now great potential for use of biopesticides such as the bacterial insecticide *Bacillus thuringiensis* (Bt toxin) and proteins from relatives of some crop plants that confer insect resistance such as cowpea trypsin inhibitor (CpTI).

The *B. thuringiensis* toxins are proteins which are toxic to lepidopteran, dipteran and coleopteran insects (Brousseau and Mason 1988). The proteins are highly specific in that they are not toxic to other organisms.

Portions of a cloned protein gene have been used to construct a chimeric gene capable of expression in plant cells (Leemans 1987). Using an *Agrobacterium* binary vector system, Bt genes were transferred into tobacco cells and were regenerated. Transgenic plants produced sufficient levels of Bt toxin to either kill lepidopteran insects or inhibit their feeding (Barton et al. 1987).

Proteinase inhibitors are similarly of interest because of their function as natural protective compounds against herbivorous insects and their potent inhibitory activities against proteolytic enzymes of insects and microorganisms (Ryan 1989). As primary gene products, they have been recognized as ideal candidates for transfer to crop plants by genetic engineering. Several promising proteinase inhibitor genes such as CpTI have been isolated and characterized (Hilder et al. 1989). CpTI are small polypeptides that are found in the seeds of various species of the Leguminosae. Efficacy of the protein has been demonstrated by feeding studies. Tobacco plants were transformed using *Agrobacterium tumefaciens* infection of leaf discs. Several CpTI transformed plants gave a considerably higher level of resistance than the control (Hilder et al. 1987). CIP recently began a joint venture with AGC, a UK-based biotechnology company which holds the patent on the CpTI gene. CIP now has a free license to use this gene in sweetpotato.

Other proteinase inhibitor cDNAs and genes are being used to transform plants as inhibitor I and II genes from potato and tomato plants (Ryan 1989). The vectors presently available allow the incorporation of sweetpotato into the genome to obtain better cultivars.

Agrobacterium rhizogenes as a vector

In another series of experiments made at CIP, sweetpotato has been transformed using a binary plasmid containing a marker gene for kanamycin resistance, the neomycin phosphotransferase II (NPTII) and a chimeric glucuronidase (GUS) reporter gene. These inoculations resulted in rooting of the stem segments on hormone-free media. The hairy roots produced were placed on the regeneration media suplemented with respective antibiotics to select transformed plants. The first shoot regenerated after two weeks and the expression of CaMV 35S/GUS gene was evaluated.

In the fluorimetric assays, the GUS specific activity was quantified by measuring the rate of hydrolysis of the substrate 4-methylumbelliferyl β-D-glucoronide. A comparison of GUS related activities of the leaf tissue of a transformed plant and a non-transformed one is shown in Fig. 1. Leaves from transformed plants contained GUS specific activity value of 2400 pmol 4-MU/min/mg protein.

The GUS activity in leaves and stems was localized by incubating the affected tissue in the substrate X-gluc. Sections of stems from non-transformed plants did not stain blue when incubated with X-gluc, while sections of stems from putatively transformed plants revealed blue stained vascular cells and cambium tissue. Leaf sections from transformed plants were stained intensely blue whereas no blue color was seen in the leaves of non-transformed plants. These results confirm the use of this vector in both cointegrated and binary methods to obtain sweetpotato transgenic plants and also the possibility of obtaining other genes with higher expression.

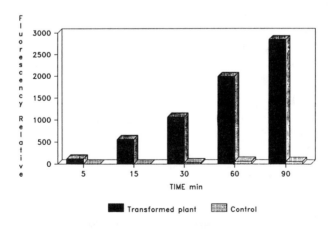

Figure 1. GUS kinetic activity.

Regeneration as an important factor for transformation

A successful regeneration of whole plants from transformed cells is an essential feature of plant transformation. Two conditions should be defined depending on which transformation system is employed. For *A. rhizogenes*-mediated transformation, a system employing roots as explants should be performed; if *A. tumefaciens* is used as vector, regeneration should occur at the wounded surface of the explant.

Reports of success in obtaining whole plant regeneration of sweetpotato are few and all of them occurred after a long period of culture and a large callus phase (Yamaguchi et al. 1973; Hwang et al. 1983; Carswell et at. 1984; Templeton-Somers et al. 1985; Murata et al. 1987). Experiments are being conducted in CIP's tissue culture laboratory to identify the appropriate culture conditions to achieve efficient regeneration with both vectors in a short period and with a minimum of callus production. Different explants, such as internode, root, leaf and petiole tissue of diverse genotypes, have been subjected to different culture media with the following growth regulators: auxins, cytokinins, gibberellins, polyamines, and antiauxins (Table 2).

Table 2. Growth regulators concentration (mg/L)

MEDIA	IAA	NAA	2,4-D	KIN	BAP	ZEA	GA$_3$	TIBA	Put
F1					1				
F2	0.2				1		10		
F3	0.2				1				
F4	0.5				1				
F5	0.5				1		10		
F6	0.2			1					
F7					0.2				
F8						2			
F9						0.2			
F10						2			20
F11						0.4			
F12	0.2					2			
F13		0.2			0.2				
F14		2			0.2				
F15			0.2			0.2			
F16			0.04			0.04			
F17						0.04			
F18						0.08			
F19						0.2		0.2	
F20						0.2		1	
F21	2			1					
F22	2			1			1		
F23	2			1			5		
F24	2			1			10		

IAA–indoleacetic acid; NAA–1-napthalene acetic acid; KIN–kinetin; BAP–6-bencilaminepurine; ZEA–zeatin (trans)ribose; GA3–gibberellic acid; 2,4-D–2,4-dichlorophenoxyacetic acid; Put–putrescine; TIBA–2,3,5-triiodobenzoic acid.

The physiological stage of donor plants have been shown to be relevant. Optimum conditions were obtained when the donor plant came from stem segments cultured in liquid medium with a high concentration of gibberellic acid (GA). Some genotypes need to be cultured in glass vessels while others grow well in either plastic or glass vessels.

Experiments carried out to date show that callus formation and shoot organogenesis are significantly affected by: genotype, culture media, explant age, explant size, pre-incubation of explants in dark, time of culture and position of explant during culture. Some genotypes show a high regeneration potential while others seen to be quite recalcitrant.

Adventitious (direct) or *de novo* (via callus) organogenesis can be obtained in sweetpotato depending on the culture media and explant. In both regeneration systems plant regeneration can be obtained by 20 days of culture.

It was noted that root regeneration is a very common process of any of the explants even without the addition of auxins to the medium. Shoot organogenesis was induced with the addition of cytokinins alone in leaves and roots, while petioles and internodes needed a balance of auxins and cytokinins. Use of putrescine and pre-incubation of explants by 2 to 3 weeks in the dark enhanced plant regeneration from roots and leaves. High concentrations of GA (5 to 10 mg/L) increased the regeneration frequency from internodes but not from roots, leaves or petioles.

Pre-culture of donor plants in a medium including antiauxins enhanced shoot organogenesis in some genotypes which were hard to regenerate in media including only hormones with or without polyamines. Shoot organogenesis from roots can be obtained without callus phase. This type of regeneration frequently shows the least somaclonal variation. These conditions are optimum in a transformation system employing *A. rhizogenes*. For efficient regeneration, large roots were absolutely necessary. Short roots produced large calli and were difficult to regenerate (Fig. 2).

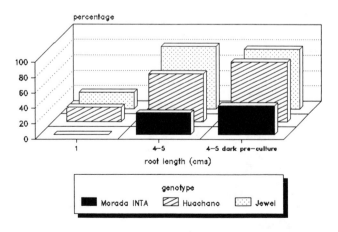

Figure 2. Plant regeneration from roots in medium with zeatin.

A significant difference was obtained between petiole explants cultured with or without the leaf lamina. Petioles without the leaf lamina were very hard to regenerate and large calli were most frequently obtained. A high frequency of plant regeneration could be obtained from petioles which included the leaf lamina. A small callus phase preceded shoot organogenesis (Fig. 3).

With leaf discs, shoot organogenesis occurred mainly from the midrib with a large callus phase and after a long period of culture. Depending on the media, plant and genotype, regeneration was also obtained directly from roots, which were formed previously by the callus produced in the wounded surface of the leaf.

In internodes, root and shoot organogenesis was obtained with high frequency and without a callus stage. Histological sections were made, and they showed that root initiation begins on cambium cells and shoot organogenesis begins on clusters of meristematic cells in the cortical parenchyma, at a distance from the wounded surface of the internode. Therefore, internode explants are not ideal explants to use in transformation employing *A. tumefaciens* as a vector. The use of petioles, which include the leaf lamina, is highly recommended.

RFLP techniques and their potential use in sweetpotato breeding

Restriction fragment length polymorphism (RFLP) techniques offer a new biotechnological tool for a better knowledge of the plant genome. These techniques have potential for manipulation of genetic variation including that of a polygenic quantitative nature. This class of genetic variation is of great importance in plant genetic improvement.

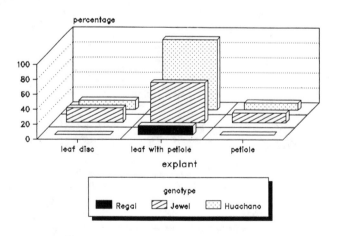

Figure 3. Plant regeneration from leaves in medium with 2,4-D and zeatin.

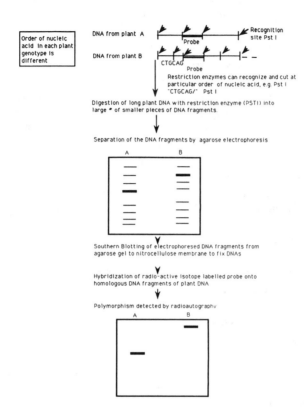

Figure 4. Schematic diagram of RFLP technique to detect DNA polymorphism among plants of interest.

Some of the advantages of their application would be (Dodds and Watanabe 1990): (1) determining genotype without progeny testing; (2) screening and selecting by "genotypes rather than phenotypes"; (3) monitoring quantitatively inherited traits; (4) increasing efficiency in monitoring introgression of desired genetic traits; and (5) facilitating breeding on polyploid crop species where selection is not really efficient and requires a larger size population, more labor and more logistics than diploids.

Steps of RFLP techniques involve (Fig. 4): (1) isolation of DNA from plant tissues; (2) DNA digestion by restriction enzymes; (3) agarose gel electrophoresis of the digested DNAs; (4) blotting; (5) hybridization with radioisotope labelled DNA probes; and (6) autoradiography. Details in RFLP techniques are described elsewhere (Beckmann and Soller 1986). These techniques can be used to generate saturated genetic linkage or RFLP maps utilizing genomic DNA from the plants and probes called RFLPs (obtained from cDNA clones) for this purpose. The develop-

15

ment of RFLP techniques can be useful for the knowledge and utilization of a wide range of genetic materials. RFLP maps are being analyzed for many important crop plants including rice, maize, wheat, sugar cane, tomato, peppers, potato and sweetpotato. RFLP analysis is being applied to potato for improving knowledge about its genome: improving nutritional quality, yield and disease resistance.

It is clear that RFLP techniques have the potential to improve productivity of the sweetpotato. There is significant genetic information about this crop. The exact origin of the cultivated sweetpotato has not been well established. Recent studies indicate that *I. trifida* and *I. batatas* are both products of autopolyploidy and have sets of genomes identical to those of 2x *I. trifida* (Orjeda et al. 1990). Studies of these characteristics using RFLP markers can help to resolve this question.

Wild species are known to be a pool of desirable traits that are not available in the cultivated sweetpotato. Studies of these species with RFLP markers will help increase the knowledge of characteristics like insect resistance and quality.

Collaborative research strategies at CIP

CIP's collaborative research with other laboratories over the last few years has made increasing use of biotechnology possible. CIP has always had a policy of "comparative advantage" by which its projects are contracted out with other institutions better able to do a particular piece of work. For example, the tissue culture laboratory at CIP now has nearly 30 contracts with different laboratories in both developed and developing countries. These contracts are easily divided into three groups: tissue culture, genetic engineering and RFLP techniques (Figs. 5, 6, 7).

Potato and sweetpotato germplasm, for example, are maintained *in vitro* in a specially constructed facility at CIP.

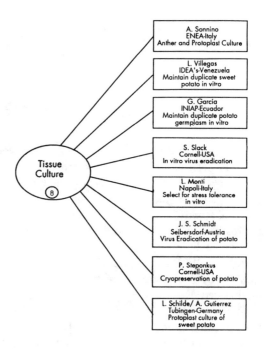

Figure 5. Collaborative projects related to tissue culture.

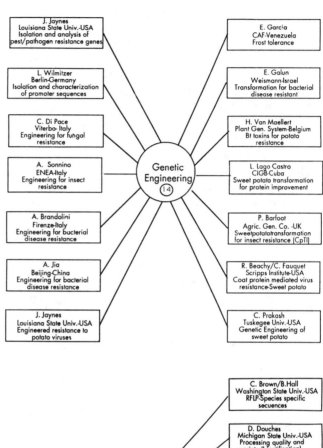

Figure 6. Collaborative projects related to genetic engineering.

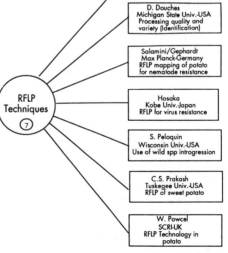

Figure 7. Collaborative projects related to RFLP techniques.

However, for security reasons, research contracts have been established with national programs in Ecuador and Venezuela to maintain *in vitro* duplicates of these collections.

In genetic engineering a contract with the biochemistry department at Louisiana State University (USA) has allowed the development of gene synthesis techniques for potato and sweetpotato. Using LSU facilities synthetic plasmids have been prepared for CIP. Promoter sequences have been obtained from a group from Germany. CIP has developed tissue culture techniques for inoculation, regeneration and selection of transgenic plants. Contracts made with laboratories have led to the utilization of these genetic constructions in Italy, China and Venezuela.

Transformation studies on sweetpotato are just beginning. A new collaborative project has been established with the University of Durham (Britain). With funds from the Overseas Development Administration (ODA), scientists of Agricultural Genetic Company (AGC), the University of Durham and CIP will attempt to incorporate AGC's insect resistance gene, CpTI, into the sweetpotato. Plans are also being developed to screen Bt strains against the sweetpotato weevil.

RLFP techniques are new for CIP and collaborative projects play a major role. New projects have been or are going to be established with laboratories from the USA, Germany and Japan to construct genomic linkage maps and produce specific sequences or genetic markers for improving knowledge of the potato and sweetpotato genome.

All the above techniques are integrated into the overall program activities at CIP. These activities lead to close collaboration with developing country national programs to deliver improved germplasm, technologies, information and training. The sweetpotato has much to gain from biotechnology when correctly channelled to address priority problems.

ACKNOWLEDGMENTS

CIP wishes to acknowledge the many institutions included in the collaborative networks described. Too many people are involved to be used as co-authors; however, all should receive the credit as co-authors of this collaborative approach.

LITERATURE CITED

An, G., B.D. Watson, and C.C. Chiang. 1986. Transformation of tobacco, tomato, potato and *Arabidopsis thaliana* using a binary Ti vector system. Plant Physiol. 81:301-306.

Barton, K.A., H.R. Whiteley, and N.S. Yang. 1987. B*acillus thuringiensis* d-endotoxin expressed in transgenic *Nicotiana tabacum* provides resistance to lepidopteran insects. Plant Physiol. 82:1103-1109.

Beckmann, J.S., and M. Soller. 1986. Restriction fragment length polymorphisms in plant genetic improvement. Oxford Surveys of Plant Molecular and Cell Biology. Vol. 3.

Brousseau, R., and L. Masson. 1988. *Bacillus thuringiensis* insecticidal crystal toxins: gene structure and mode of action. Biotech Adv. 6:697-724.

Carsweel, G., and R. Locy. 1984. Root and shoot initiation by leaf, stem and storage root explants of sweet potato. Plant cell, Tissue and Organ Culture. 3(3):229-236.

Dodds, J.H., and K. Watanabe. 1990. Biotechnological tools for plant genetic resources management. Diversity 6(3 & 4):26-28.

Hilder, V.A., M.R. Gatehouse, S.E. Sheerman, R.F. Barker, and D. Boulter. 1987. A novel mechanism of insect resistance engineered into tobacco. Nature 330:160-163.

Horsch R.B., J.E. Fry, N.L. Hoffmann, M. Wallroth, D. Eichholtz, S.G. Rogers, and R.T. Fraley. 1986. A simple and general method for transferring genes into plants. Science 227:1229-1231.

Hwang, L., R. Shirvin, J. Casyao, and J. Bouwkamp. 1983. Adventitious shoot formation from sections of sweet potato grown in vitro. Scientia Horticulturae. 20:119-229.

McCormick S., J. Niedermeyer, J. Fry, A. Barnason, R. Horsch, and R. Fraley. 1986. Leaf disc trasnformation of cultivated tomato (*L. sculentum*) using *Agrobacterium tumafaciens*. Plant Cell Rep. 5:81-84.

Murata, T., K. Hoshino, and Y. Miyaji. 1987. Callus formation and plant regeneration from petiole protoplast of sweet potato, *Ipomoea batatas* (L.) Lam. Japanese Journal of Breeding. 37(3):291-298.

Orjeda, G., R. Freyre, and M. Iwanaga. 1990. Production of 2n pollen in diploid *Ipomoea trifida*, a putative wild ancestor of sweet potato. Journal of Heredity 81:462-468.

Ryan, C.A. 1989. Proteinase inhibitor gene families: Strategies for transformation to improve plant defenses against herbivores. BioEssays 10:20-24.

Sheikholeslam S.H., and D.P. Weeks. 1987. Acetosyringone promotes high efficiency transformation of *Arabidopsis thaliana* explants by *Agrobacterium tumefaciens*. Plant Mol. Biol. 8:291-298.

Templeton-Somers, K., and W. Collins. 1985. In vitro growth and regeneration characteristics of diverse populations of sweet potato (*I. batatas* (L.) Lam). VII International Symposium on Tropical Root and Tuber Crops, July 1-6, Pointe-a-Pitre, Guadeloupe.

Vaeck, M., A. Reynaerts, H. Hofte, S. Jansens, M. De Beukelleer, C. Dean, M. Zabeau, M. Van Montagu, and J. Leemans. 1987. Transgenic plants protected from insect attack. Nature 327:33-37.

Wilkins, C.P., and J. H. Dodds. 1982. The use of *in vitro* methods for plant genetic conservation. Outlook on Agriculture. 11:67-72.

Sweetpotato Technology for the 21st Century. W.A. Hill, C.K. Bonsi and P.A. Loretan (Eds.) 1992. Tuskegee University, Tuskegee, AL

Kenzo Nakamura

Regulation of Expression of Genes Coding for Sporamin and ß-Amylase of the Sweetpotato

Expression of genes encoding sporamin and β-amylase, the two most abundant proteins of storage roots of the sweetpotato, can be induced concomitant with the accumulation of starch in various organs by exogenous supply of high concentrations of sucrose. Metabolic regulation by sucrose suggests that expression of these genes is closely associated with the expression of the metabolic sink function of the cells. In support of this idea, we observed tuber-specific expression of a chimaeric gene with a sporamin promoter in transgenic potato. Promoters of sporamin and β-amylase genes should be useful to express desired proteins in storage roots to improve their qualities and yields. In addition to several members of the sporamin multigene family, a gene for β-amylase was also characterized. Furthermore, we developed a novel reporter and binary Ti-plasmid vector system to establish a method for introducing foreign genes into sweetpotato.

In order to apply gene manipulation techniques for the improvement of the sweetpotato, especially for the improvement of both yields and qualities of the storage root, it is desirable to have promoters that can direct the expression of useful proteins in the storage root. A large proportion of protein in the storage root of the sweetpotato is accounted for by two major proteins, sporamin and ß-amylase, which specifically accumulate, concomitant with the massive accumulation of starch, upon formation of selected storage roots. In addition to understanding processes that occur during the development of the storage root, studies on the molecular mechanisms of the regulation of expression of genes that encode these storage root-specific proteins should provide us with tools to genetically improve the storage root.

A multigene family coding for sporamin

Sporamin with an apparent molecular weight of 25,000 Da accounts for about 60 to 80% of the total soluble protein of the storage root of the sweetpotato (Maeshima et al. 1985). Sporamin is identical as the antigenic component A of Uritani and Stahmann (1961; Li and Oba 1985), and it probably constitutes the major part of ipomoein, a name given to the globulin fraction of the storage root proteins by Jones and Gersdorff (1931). Sporamin is not detectable, or is present in only small amounts, in organs other than the storage root in normal field-grown plants

Laboratory of Biochemistry, School of Agriculture, Nagoya University, Chikusa, Nagoya 464-01, Japan.

(Maeshima et al. 1985; Hattori et al. 1985), and sporamin in the storage root is preferentially degraded in preference to other proteins during sprouting (Maeshima et al. 1985) and after wounding or fungal infection of the tissue (Li and Oba 1985). These results suggest that sporamin plays a role as a storage protein in the storage root. However, since the amino acid sequence of sporamin shows homology to Kunitz-type trypsin inhibitors of Leguminosae, sporamin may have some physiological functions other than as a storage protein.

Sporamin is actually a mixture of closely related proteins (Maeshima et al. 1985) encoded by a multigene family (Murakami et al. 1986). Structural comparison of many of the cloned cDNAs revealed that members of the sporamin multigene family can be classified into two major subfamilies, A and B, based on nucleotide sequence homologies among them (Murakami et al. 1986; Hattori et al. 1989). The hexaploid genome of the sweetpotato may contain as many as 60 copies of sporamin genes. Both the A-type and B-type sporamin genes are present in various diploid wild-species of *Ipomoea* (Y. Kowyama, T. Hattori, T. Kumashiro and K. Nakamura, unpublished results). A-type and B-type sporamin genomic clones, gSPO-A1 and gSPO-B1, respectively, have been isolated and characterized (Hattori and Nakamura 1988). These sporamin genes do not contain introns.

ß-amylase and its structural gene

Sweetpotato storage roots are unusually rich in ß-amylase, and it represents about 5% of the total soluble proteins of the organ. The sweetness of storage roots has been ascribed to the hydrolysis of starch to maltose by this abundant ß-amylase during cooking, and the taste of varieties of sweetpotato that have no or only low ß-amylase activities is only slightly sweet when storage roots of these varieties are cooked (Martin 1987; Kumagai et al. 1990). Like sporamins, ß-amylase is not detectable—or is present in only small amounts—in organs other than the storage root of the normal, field-grown plants (Nakamura et al. 1991). A precursor to the subunit of ß-amylase of the sweetpotato deduced from the cDNA nucleotide sequence (Yoshida and Nakamura 1991) does not contain a N-terminal transit peptide sequence suggesting that ß-amylase is localized outside of the amyloplast. ß-amylase cannot be detected by enzymological and immunological methods in some of the "non-sweet" varieties of the sweetpotato (K. Oba, personal communication), yet these storage roots accumulate normal amounts of starch and support normal sprouting of the next generation. Thus, in spite of extensive enzymological studies, the precise physiological role of β-amylase in the storage root is not known at present.

We isolated only one-type of β-amylase cDNA from the storage root cDNA library (Yoshida and Nakamura 1991). Genomic Southern blot hybridization of DNAs from several different varieties of the sweetpotato as well as diploid and tetraploid wild-species of *Ipomoea* with a cDNA probe showed simple patterns of hybridization and all of the seven independent lambda genomic clones of β-amylase showed overlapping restriction maps suggesting that there may be only one copy of β-amylase gene per haploid genome. In a cloned gene for β-amylase, gβ-Amy, 1880 bp-sequence that is completely identical to the cDNA was split into 7 exons by 6 introns (Yoshida et al. 1992).

In the highly diverged 5'-upstream regions of two of the sporamin genes, gSPO-A1 and gSPO-B1, two types of DNA sequence blocks of 20 to 30 bp, Box 2 and Box 3, were found to be conserved between them. Box 1 contains a TATA-box (Hattori and Nakamura 1988). Sequences similar to these conserved sequence blocks were also present in the 5'-upstream region of gb-Amy. In addition, we found that nuclear extracts from sucrose-treated petioles contain a factor that can bind to short sequence motifs present in either single or multiple locations in the 5'-upstream regions of gSPO-A1, gSPO-B1 and gβ-Amy (Ishiguro and Nakamura 1992). These sequences conserved among the genes coding for sporamin and β-amylase may play important roles in the coordinated regulation of their expression.

Sucrose-induction of expression of sporamin and β-amylase genes

In contrast to field-grown plants, sweetpotato plantlets cultured axenically on sucrose-containing agar medium store a large amount of sporamin preferentially in their stems (Hattori et al. 1990). The stems of these plantlets also contain a large amount of both β-amylase and starch. In addition to the stems of axenic plantlets, accumulation of large amounts of sporamin, β-amylase and starch also occurs in leaves and petioles when leaf-petiole cuttings from the plants were supplied with high concentrations of sucrose (Hattori et al. 1991; Nakamura et al. 1991). The accumulation of sporamin, of β-amylase and of starch in the petioles shows similar dependence on the concentration of sucrose; their accumulation can also be induced by other metabolizable sugars such as glucose and fructose. Sporamin, β-amylase and starch are accumulated within the same parenchyma cells of the storage root, and sucrose-induced accumulation of these components in leaves and petioles also occurs within the types of cells (S. Takeda and K. Nakamura, manuscript in preparation).

These observations suggest that expression of genes coding for sporamin and ß-amylase is linked to the metabolite storage function of cells, either as temporary sink or as long-term storage sink, and the apparent storage root-specificity of these proteins in plants is due to the concentrated flow of sucrose to the storage root. Genes coding for patatin of the potato tuber are also known to be regulated by sucrose (Rocha-Sosa et al. 1989; Wenzler et al. 1989) suggesting that a mechanism regulating the expression of certain genes in response to high concentrations of sucrose exists in a wide variety of plants.

Expression of a sporamin gene promoter in transgenic tobacco and potato

We have constructed fusion genes comprising the 1 kb 5'-upstream region of the gSPO-A1 gene coding for the A-type sporamin and the coding sequence of bacterial CAT (chloramphenicol acetyltransferase) or GUS (β-glucuronidase), and introduced them into tobacco by *Agrobacterium*-mediated transformation. Transgenic tobacco plants cultured axenically on sucrose-containing medium expressed CAT or GUS activity predominantly in their stems (Hattori et al. 1990; Ohta et al. 1991). Histochemical examination of expression of the sporamin promoter:GUS fusion gene in transgenic tobacco plants with a chromogenic substrate of GUS revealed a distinct spatial pattern of expression of the GUS activity in the stems that is similar to the spatial pattern of the accumulation of starch granules in the stems of the sweetpotato plantlets cultured axenically (Ohta et al. 1991).

The sporamin promoter:CAT fusion gene was also introduced into potato and the expression of the reporter activities was examined in transformed plants grown in the greenhouse. Although strong CAT activities could be detected in tubers from most of the plants, extracts from leaves, petioles, stems, and roots did not show significant levels of CAT activity (K. Nakamura, S. Ohta, T. Hattori, and T. Momma, manuscript in preparation). Histochemical examination of the expression of the sporamin promoter in the tubers of potato plants transformed with the sporamin promoter:GUS fusion gene showed strong expresssion in starch-accumulating parenchyma cells. These results strongly support the idea that the expression of the sporamin genes is closely related to the developmental stage or storage function of the cells rather than to factors that are storage root-specific per se.

Expression of sporamin in transgenic tobacco

Sporamin is synthesized on rER as a prepro-precursor with an N-terminal extra sequence (Hattori et al. 1987) and accumulates in the vacuoles of parenchyma cells of the storage root (Hattori et al. 1988). The N-terminus of the precursor contains a signal peptide and the adjoining propeptide of 16 amino acid residues is removed post-translationally. When the precursor to sporamin was expressed in transformed tobacco cells, the precursor was sequentially processed and correctly targeted to the vacuole (Matsuoka et al. 1990). However, when the propeptide was deleted from the precursor, sporamin was secreted into the culture medium with kinetics similar to those of proteins that are normally secreted by the host tobacco cells (Matsuoka and Nakamura 1991). These results indicate that the propeptide of the precursor to sporamin is required for correct targeting of sporamin to the vacuole and further suggest that the propeptide of the precursor to sporamin, together with the signal peptide, may be useful to target alien proteins into the vacuolar compartment of the cells by gene manipulation techniques.

An intron-GUS reporter gene and a binary Ti-plasmid vector with two selectable markers for use in transformation of the sweetpotato

Although the *Agrobacterium*-mediated transformation has been extensively used in some plant species, methods for transformation of many other important plant species, including the sweetpotato, have not been established. In order to develop a defined system to transform new plant species by using *Agrobacterium*, it is desired to establish optimum conditions for the transfer and expression of a foreign gene into plant cells and for the regeneration of a whole plant from the transformed cells.

We have developed a novel binary Ti-plasmid vector system in which the modified GUS reporter gene containing an intron within the GUS-coding sequence is placed between two selectable marker genes, kanamycin-resistance and hygromycin-resistance, within the T-DNA border sequences (S. Ohta, K. Matsuoka, and K. Nakamura, submitted for publication). Unlike the original GUS reporter gene, the Intron-GUS reporter gene (Ohta et al. 1990) does not express any detectable GUS activity in *Agrobacterium* cells. By using the Intron-GUS reporter gene fused downstream of the CaMV 35S promoter, one can monitor the transfer and expression of the fusion gene in plant cells at a very early stage of transformation even in the presence of *Agrobacterium* cells. The T-DNA is not always integrated into the plant genome in an intact form and a loss of part of the T-DNA in transformed plants occurs with certain fusion genes. The Ti-plasmid vector with two selectable markers and selection of transformed plants with two antibiotics enabled us to select plants that contain intact copies of the fusion gene with high frequency.

Using these Ti-plasmid vector systems, we could detect the transfer and expression of the Intron-GUS fusion gene in sweetpotato tissues as early as 5 to 6 days after co-culture with *Agrobacterium,* and almost all of the kanamycin- and hygromycin-resistant calli obtained expressed GUS activities. Northern blot hybridization of RNAs from these calli tissues suggested that splicing of an intron from the Intron-GUS gene in sweetpotato cells occurs in a similar manner as those in tobacco and rice cells (Tanaka et al. 1990).

ACKNOWLEDGMENTS

I gratefully acknowledge the participation of current and past associates and students in work from the author's laboratory, especially Dr. T. Hattori, and fruitful collaborations with other investigators, particularly Dr. Y. Kowyama of Mie University. Research in my laboratory has been supported by grants from the Ministry of Education, Science and Culture, Japan.

REFERENCES

Hattori, T., and K. Nakamura. 1988. Genes coding for the major tuberous root protein of sweet potato: identification of putative regulatory sequence in the 5'-upstream region. Plant Molecular Biology 11:417-426.

Hattori, T., T. Nakagawa, M. Maeshima, K. Nakamura, and T. Asahi. 1985. Molecular cloning and nucleotide sequence of cDNA for sporamin, the major soluble protein of sweet potato tuberous roots. Plant Molecular Biology 5:313-320.

Hattori, T., S. Ichihara, and K. Nakamura. 1987. Processing of a plant vacuolar protein precursor *in vitro*. European Journal of Biochemistry 166:533-538.

Hattori, T., K. Matsuoka, and K. Nakamura. 1988. Subcellular localization of the sweet potato tuberous root storage protein. Agricultural and Biological Chem. (Tokyo) 52:1057-1059.

Hattori, T., N. Yoshida, and K. Nakamura. 1989. Structural relationship among the members of a multigene family coding for the sweet potato tuberous root storage protein. Plant Molecular Biology 13:563-572.

Hattori, T., S. Nakagawa, and K. Nakamura. 1990. High-level expression of tuberous root storage protein genes of sweet potato in stems of plantlets grown *in vitro* on sucrose medium. Plant Molecular Biology 14:595-604.

Hattori, T., H. Fukumoto, S. Nakagawa, and K. Nakamura. 1991. Sucrose-induced expression of genes coding for the tuberous root storage protein, sporamin, of sweet potato in leaves and petioles. Plant and Cell Physiology 32:79-86.

Ishiguro, S., and K. Nakamura. 1992. The nuclear factor SP8BF binds to the 5'-upstream regions of three different genes coding for major tuberous root proteins of sweet potato. Plant Mol. Biol. 18:97-108.

Jones, D.B., and C.E.F. Gersdorff. 1931. Ipomoein, a globulin from sweet potatoes, *Ipomoea batatas*. Isolation of a secondary protein derived from ipomoein by enzymic action. Journal of Biological Chemistry 93:119-126.

Kumagai, T., Y. Umemura, T. Baba, and M. Iwanaga. 1990. The inheritance of β-amylase null in tuberous roots of sweet potato, *Ipomoea batatas* (L.) Lam. Theoretical and Applied Genetics 79:369-376.

Li, H-S., and K. Oba. 1985. Major soluble proteins of sweet potato roots and changes in proteins after cutting, infection, or storage. Agricultural and Biological Chemistry (Tokyo) 49:737-744.

Maeshima, M., T. Sasaki, and T. Asahi. 1985. Characterization of major proteins in sweet potato tuberous roots. Phytochemistry 24:1899-1902.

Martin, F.W. 1987. Non-sweet or staple type sweet potatoes. Horticultural Science 232:160.

Matsuoka, K., and K. Nakamura. 1991. Propeptide of a precursor to a plant vacuolar protein required for vacuolar targeting. Proceedings of the National Academy of Sciences of the United States of America 88:834-838.

Matsuoka, K., S. Matsuomoto, T. Hattori, Y. Machida, and K. Nakamura. 1990. Vacuolar targeting and posttranslational processing of the precursor to sweet potato tuberous root storage protein in heterologous plant cells. Journal of Biological Chemistry 265:19750-19757.

Murakami, S., T. Hattori, and K. Nakamura. 1986. Structural differences in full-length cDNAs for two classes of sporamin, the major soluble protein of sweet potato tuberous roots. Plant Molecular Biology 7:343-355.

Nakamura, K., M. Ohto, N. Yoshida, and K. Nakamura. 1991. Sucrose-induced accumulation of β-amylase occurs concomitant with the accumulation of starch and sporamin in leaf-petiole cuttings of sweet potato. Plant Physiology 96:902-909.

Ohta, S., S. Mita, T. Hattori, and K. Nakamura. 1990. Construction and expression in tobacco of a β-glucuronidase (GUS) reporter gene containing an intron within the coding sequence. Plant and Cell Physiology 31:805-813.

Ohta, S., T. Hattori, A. Morikami, and K. Nakamura. 1991. Stem-predominant expression of the sweet potato sporamin gene promoter:β-glucuronidase (GUS) fusion gene in transgenic tobacco is conferred by multiple cell type-specific regulatory elements. Molecular and General Genetics 225:369-378.

Rocha-Sosa, M., U. Sonnewald, W. Frommer, M. Stratmann, J. Schell, and L. Willmitzer. 1989. Both developmental and metabolic signals activate the promoter of a class I patatin gene. EMBO Journal 8:23-29.

Tanaka, A., S. Mita, S. Ohta, J. Kyozuka, K. Shimamoto, and K. Nakamura. 1990. Enhancement of foreign gene expression by a dicot intron in rice but not in tobacco is correlated with an increased level of mRNA and an efficient splicing of the intron. Nucleic Acids Research 18:6767-6770.

Uritani, I., and M.A. Stahmann. 1961. The relationship between antigenic compounds produced by sweet potato in response to black rot infection and the magnitude of disease resistance. Agricultural and Biological Chemistry (Tokyo) 25:479-486.

Wenzler, H.C., G.A. Mignery, L.M. Fisher, and W.D. Park. 1989. Analysis of a chimeric class-I patatin-GUS gene in transgenic potato plants: high-level expression in tubers and sucrose-inducible expression in cultured leaf and stem explants. Plant Molecular Biology 12:41-50.

Yoshida, N., and K. Nakamura. 1991. Molecular cloning and expression in *Escherichia coli* of cDNA encoding the subunit of sweet potato β-amylase. Journal of Biochemistry (Tokyo), 110:196-201.

Yoshida, N., K. Hayashi and K. Nakamura. 1992. A nuclear gene encoding β-amylase of sweetpotato. Gene 120:255-259.

Sweetpotato Technology for the 21st Century. W.A. Hill, C.K. Bonsi and P.A. Loretan (Eds.) 1992. Tuskegee University, Tuskegee, AL

C. S. Prakash, Usha Varadarajan

Genetic Transformation of Sweetpotato

Foreign genes have been introduced into the genome of sweetpotato using *Agrobacterium* vector and particle bombardment approaches. Transgenic shoots with stable expression of foreign genes have been recovered using the *Agrobacterium* cocultivation procedure. Plants inoculated with wild type *A. tumefaciens* developed crown galls confirming that sweetpotato could be potentially transformed using the Ti plasmid vector. Transgenic studies involved the use of disarmed *A. tumefaciens* strain LBA 4404 with a binary vector pBI 121 harboring *gus*A and *kan* genes. Explants of cvs. 'Jewel' and 'TIS-70357' cocultivated with this bacteria showed high frequency transformation as evidenced by the ß-glucuronidase (GUS) assay. Culture of these explants on kanamycin media produced calli from which shoots and subsequently plants were regenerated. PCR amplification of the *kan* gene and Southern analysis confirmed the presence of the introduced gene in the putative transgenic shoots. When 10 additional cultivars of sweetpotato were subjected to *Agrobacterium* cocultivation, all were transformed as visualized by the GUS assay. In the particle bombardment study, leaf and petiole explants were bombarded with tungsten microprojectiles coated with plasmid DNA carrying a *gus*A gene using a biolistic device. The GUS histochemical assay of the explants and calli showed the transformed nature of the tissues. Expression of the *gus*A gene was stable as the regenerated calli lines exhibited high GUS activity even after one year of sub-culture, and roots regenerated from transformed calli were positive for GUS. These studies thus show the potential of these approaches for future introduction of agriculturally useful genes into sweetpotato.

INTRODUCTION

Genetic engineering techniques have considerable promise in increasing agricultural productivity around the world because of their potential to genetically redesign crop plants. Gene transfer technology is already enabling introduction of many novel 'value-added' traits such as improved nutritional quality and resistance to pests, diseases, and other stress factors into a few crops (Goodman et al. 1987). Genetic transformation of plants also provides powerful means to study the fundamental biology of crop plants (Schell 1987).

When compared to other crop plants, sweetpotato [*Ipomoea batatas* L. (Lam.)] has received limited attention from molecular geneticists with only a few exceptions

Tuskegee University, Molecular and Cellular Genetics Laboratory, Milbank Hall, Tuskegee, AL 36088, USA.

27

(e.g., see articles by Nakamura and Beachy et al. in this volume). Nevertheless, many useful genes that are being increasingly identified have relevance to sweetpotato. Genes for resistance to plant diseases (Abel et al. 1986; Destéfano-Beltrán et al. 1990), tolerance to insect pests (Boulter 1989; Fischhoff et al. 1987), improved storage proteins with high essential amino acids (Yang et al. 1989) have been isolated and expressed in other crop plants. Introduction of such useful foreign genes into sweetpotato will augment current breeding programs by enabling accelerated development of cultivars with improved productivity and quality traits.

An essential prerequisite to the genetic engineering of any crop is the development of reliable techniques to introduce foreign DNA into its genome. While several innovative methods to insert genes into the plant genome have been developed (Weising et al. 1988), *Agrobacterium* Ti plasmid is the most versatile vehicle to introduce genes into dicotyledonous plants. *Agrobacterium tumefaciens* is a soil bacterium that causes crown gall tumors in plants by transferring a piece of DNA (T-DNA) from its tumor-inducing plasmid (Ti) into plant cells. The T-DNA integrates into the plant genome and directs the production of certain unique plant hormones called opines. Use of disarmed strains (devoid of tumor inducing genes) with selectable marker genes has permitted the production of transgenic plants in a number of plant species (Schell 1987). Another relatively recent approach to directly introduce DNA into plant cells is the particle bombardment or biolistic method (Sanford 1990). Foreign DNA is coated on microscopic metal particles and propelled at very high velocity into target tissues using a biolistic device. Many plant species including rice, corn, wheat, soybean, cotton and sunflower have been transformed using this 'gene gun' technique and transgenic plants have been developed in a few crops (Sanford 1990).

Sweetpotato improvement by conventional means is challenging because of its hexaploidy, sterility and incompatibility problems. Molecular genetic approaches circumvent many of these problems and permit the direct introduction of useful genes into the genome of adapted cultivars. When we initiated this study, a search of the literature failed to provide information on the susceptibility of sweetpotato to infection by *Agrobacterium*, and there were no published reports on development of transgenic sweetpotato plants. Since then, Al-Juboory and Skirvin (1991) have reported plant regeneration from callus cultures obtained by inoculation of sweetpotato plants with wild type *Agrobacterium tumefaciens*. This paper summarizes the results of our studies testing particle bombardment and *Agrobacterium* vector approaches to introduce foreign genes into the sweetpotato and our efforts to develop transgenic sweetpotato plants. Detailed results are published elsewhere (Prakash and Varadarajan 1992; Prakash et al. in preparation).

MATERIALS AND METHODS

Testing sweetpotato susceptibility to crown gall infection

The susceptibility of sweetpotato to crown gall infection was tested by inoculating oncogenic (wild type) strains of *Agrobacterium tumefaciens* (C58 and A281) on cvs. 'Jewel' and 'TIS-70357.' Single colony derived cultures of the bacteria were grown on LB agar medium. Sterile toothpicks scraped on the cultures were used to pierce the shoots of sweetpotato plants in the greenhouse. Control plants were treated similarly but using toothpicks dipped in sterile water. Shoot wounds were covered with petroleum jelly and observations on gall appearance taken periodically.

Description of *in vitro* grown cultivars

Leaf and petiole pieces from *in vitro* grown plants of 'Jewel' and 'TIS-70357' were used as target tissues for bombardment and as explants for *Agrobacterium* cocultivation. In addition, 10 other cultivars of sweetpotato representing a genetically diverse collection were also tested for their potential for transformation with *Agrobacterium* vector: 'Nemagold,' 'White Triumph,' 'Excel,' 'Cherokee,' 'PI 376945,' 'PI 344120,' 'PI 318856,' 'Q 24978,' 'PI 508531,' and 'PI 531173.' All accessions were obtained from the Regional Plant Introduction Center, Griffin, GA. *In vitro* plants were maintained on MS (Murashige and Skoog 1962) medium with BAP (0.5 mg/L) and sucrose (20 g/L), and solidified with Gelrite (2.0 g/L) (pH 5.6). Shoot cultures were maintained at 25° C under 16 h light (50 $\mu Em^{-2} s^{-1}$).

Source of exogenous DNA

The plasmids pBI 121 or pBI 221 were employed as sources of foreign marker genes (Clonetech Lab, Palo Alto, CA). Both plasmids have the screenable marker *gus*A gene, which encodes for the ß-glucuronidase (GUS) enzyme (Jefferson et al. 1987), fused chimerically to a CaMV promoter at 5' end and a terminator from nopaline synthase (*nos*) gene at 3' end. The pBI 121 also has an antibiotic resistance *kan* gene flanked by promoter and terminator sequences from the *nos* gene.

Agrobacterium cocultivation

The *A. tumefaciens* disarmed strain LBA 4404 containing the binary vector pBI 121 was grown overnight at 28°C in LB liquid medium with 50 mg/L kanamycin. The bacterial suspension (5 mL) was centrifuged for 10-12 min at 3000 g and resuspended in 5 mL of MS salt solution. Explants (4 to 6 mm) were shaken in a bacterial suspension for 20 minutes, blotted dry and cultured on an MS medium without antibiotics for three days. Subsequently, explants were washed with MS medium containing carbenicillin (100 mg/L) and cultured on MS-regeneration medium which consisted of MS basal salts and vitamins supplemented with NAA (1 mg/L), BAP (0.1 mg/L), sucrose (20 g/L), carbenicillin (100 mg/L), and solidified with Gelrite (2.0 g/L) and incubated at 25°C (16 h photoperiod). The explant with regenerated shoots and plantlets were subcultured on MS medium with BAP (0.5 mg/L) and transferred to a fresh medium every four weeks.

Microprojectile bombardment

Plasmid DNA was adsorbed onto tungsten microprojectiles (1.2 µm) as described (Klein et al. 1988). The biolistic device that uses a gunpowder discharge to propel the microprojectiles was employed (Sanford et al. 1987). The procedure for bombardment of microprojectiles on sweetpotato was similar to the published protocols (Klein et al. 1988). For bombardment, target tissues were placed on filter paper moistened with MS solution and carbenicillin (300 mg/L) and located in petri plates containing MS salts supplemented with MS vitamins, sucrose (30 mg/L), IAA (2 mg/L) and kinetin (2 mg/L). Control explants were bombarded with blank microprojectiles, i.e., not coated with DNA. Two days following bombardment, all explants including those in control were transferred to a MS-regeneration medium to promote cell proliferation.

Antibiotic selection

The plasmid pBI 121 contains a gene (*kan*) that confers resistance to an antibiotic in transformed cells. Explants exposed to this plasmid were subjected to antibiotic selection to specifically promote regeneration of transformed cells. A portion of treated and control explants were transferred to MS regeneration medium supplemented with the antibiotic kanamycin (50 mg/L). This dose was determined to be the minimum required to cause lethality in cultured sweetpotato explants by a titre study involving 0 to 1000 mg/L of kanamycin (Prakash, unpublished).

GUS histochemical assay

Bombarded and cocultivated explants, regenerated shoots, and plants were examined periodically for the expression of the *gus*A gene (Jefferson et al. 1987). Tissues were flooded with the GUS assay solution and incubated overnight at 37° C. The GUS assay solution (100 mL; pH 7.0) consisted of 100 mM ethylene diamine tetracetic acid, 100 mM sodium phosphate (pH 7.0), 0.5 mM potassium ferro cyanide, 0.1 % Triton X-100, and 5-bromo-4-chloro-3-indolyl-ß-D-glucuronic acid (X-Gluc) (50 mg in 1 mL DMSO) (NJ Lab Supply) (McCabe et al. 1988). For tissue assay of the transgenic plants, hand sections were made prior to the examination.

PCR and Southern analysis

DNA was extracted from the putative transgenic shoots obtained from the *Agrobacterium* study and from control shoots using a procedure developed recently in our lab (Varadarajan and Prakash 1991). The polymerase chain reaction (PCR) amplification was performed on a thermal cycler (Perkin Elmer Cetus) in 100 µl volume with 100 ng of template DNA, 0.2 µM of 3' and 5' primers corresponding to the *kan* gene, 50 µM each dNTP and 2.5 units of *Taq* polymerase with denaturation phase conducted at 92°C (1.5 min), annealing phase at 48° C (1 min) and extension phase at 72°C (3 min) with final extension lasting seven minutes (Innis et al. 1990).

RESULTS AND DISCUSSION

Susceptibility to crown gall infection

Sweetpotato cvs. 'Jewel' and 'TIS-70357' inoculated with virulent wild-type strains of *A. tumefaciens* developed characteristic crown galls 3 to 4 weeks after inoculation (Fig. 1). While both C58 and A281 strains produced galls, the C58 produced larger galls on both cultivars than A281. Control plants did not develop any conspicuous galls. This preliminary study was encouraging as it confirmed the susceptibility of sweetpotato to *Agrobacterium* infection and thus showed the potential of Ti plasmids as vectors for introduction of foreign genes into this crop.

Agrobacterium-mediated transformation and regeneration of transgenic plants

Sweetpotato explants cocultivated with *A. tumefaciens* pBI 121 exhibited signs of transformation as early as two days after cocultivation when tested by GUS histochemical assay. Distinct blue areas were observed in tissues closer to the cutends of both leaf (Fig. 2) and petiole (Fig.3), indicating the presence of ß-glucuronidase enzyme encoded by the introduced *gus*A gene. The control explants did not exhibit such expression (Fig. 4), and this also indicates the lack of detectable endogenous GUS in sweetpotato explants. The tissue area transformed in both cultivars in both petiole and leaf explants was extensive (Table 1). In a similar study conducted with 10 cultivars of sweetpotato representing considerable genetic diversity, all were positively transformed and there were no apparent differences in the rate of transformation among the cultivars. Thus, *Agrobacterium*-mediated gene transfer does not appear to be cultivar-specific in sweetpotato, and it should thus be possible to develop transgenic plants in a wide range of sweetpotato cultivars.

To promote selective regeneration of transgenic tissues, explants were transferred to a kanamycin-enriched medium immediately after cocultivation. Many explants exhibited symptoms of antibiotic sensitivity such as bleaching and eventual necrosis. However, a substantial number of explants developed microcalli which subsequently regenerated into either roots or shoots. Regenerated shoots were dissected, grown on a medium without kanamycin and regenerated into plantlets. The putative transgenic plants were tested for their antibiotic resistance by either growing them on a medium enriched with kanamycin or by spraying them with kanamycin (100 mg/L) (Weide et al. 1989). Most of these plants survived antibiotic challenge while control plants succumbed in 3 to 5 days. Various tissues of trans-

Table 1. Transformation efficiency and percent explant area transformed as evident by GUS histochemical assay in two cultivars of sweet potato cocultivated with *Agrobacterium tumefaciens* /pBI 121 vector.

	Jewel Leaf	Jewel Petiole	TIIS-70357 Leaf	TIS-703557 Petiole
Number of explants tested	42	33	24	22
Number and percentage* of explants GUS positive	42 (100)	30 (91)	24 (100)	20 (91)
Percentage of explant area showing *gus*A expression	9.6	18.4	9.5	9.9

*Figures in parenthesis refer to percentage

31

genic sweetpotato plants were assayed for GUS activity. CaMV directed *gus*A expression occurred throughout the plant and in all organs (Fig. 5), but considerable developmental and tissue-specific variation in the intensity of gene expression was apparent. For example, the most intense expression was localized in the vascular tissues of developing shoots and leaves (Fig.6).

To confirm the presence of the introduced DNA into the putative transgenic shoots, PCR analysis was performed by selective amplification of the *kan* gene. A ~1 kb fragment corresponding to this gene was seen in the DNA extracted from a few of the antibiotic resistant shoots, while the DNA from control plants did not show such a band (Fig. 7). The pBI 121 plasmid included as a positive control also clearly showed a band at this location. The authenticity of this fragment as corresponding to the *kan* gene was further confirmed by Southern hybridization of the PCR blot with a radiolabelled plasmid insert of the *kan* gene (Fig. 7).

Particle bombardment mediated gene transfer

Explants of sweetpotato subjected to bombardment with microprojectiles coated with plasmid pBI 121 showed isolated transformed cells two days after bombardment (Fig. 8). The control explants did not show such expression when subjected to the GUS assay. The extent of transformation was dramatically higher when plasmid pBI 221 was used (Fig. 9). When explants bombarded with pBI 221 were subcultured, many produced calli and roots that assayed positive for *gus*A expression. The transformation appears to be stable. Roots that arose from transformed sectors were also clearly positive for *gus*A expression (Fig. 10)

When explants bombarded with pBI 121 carrying an antibiotic resistance gene *kan* were cultured on a kanamycin-containing medium, a few of them survived and produced calli. Calli subcultured for several passages showed very strong GUS expression (Fig. 11). Indeed, we have maintained some transgenic callus lines of cvs. 'Jewel' and 'TIS 70357' for nearly a year that have high levels of *gus*A expression. These results cumulatively show that particle bombardment can be a useful approach for rapid introduction of foreign genes into sweetpotato and to develop transgenic tissues. Further research aimed at regenerating shoots from transformed calli and roots is underway.

CONCLUSIONS

Foreign marker genes have been successfully introduced and expressed in sweetpotato using *Agrobacterium* and particle bombardment mediated transfer procedures. Transgenic plants have been obtained that appear to be stable in their expression of introduced genes. It should thus be possible to introduce agriculturally useful genes into sweetpotato and to develop cultivars with useful agronomic and quality traits using these procedures.

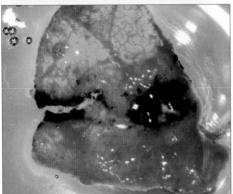

Figure 1. Crown gall developed on the sweetpotato cv. 'Jewel' four weeks after inoculation with an oncogenic strain (C58) of *Agrobacterium tumefaciens*.

Figure 2. A leaf explant of sweetpotato cv. 'Jewel' cocultivated with *Agrobacterium* pBI 121 showing transformed regions at cut-ends.

Figures 3 and 4. (bottom left and right): A petiole of sweetpotato cv. 'Jewel' subjected to *Agrobacterium* cocultivation showing transformed regions (*gus* A expressing cells) near cut-ends (Fig. 3) compared to control petioles (Fig. 4).

Figure 5. A transgenic sweetpotato plant cv. 'Jewel' developed through *Agrobacterium* cocultivation assayed for GUS activity.

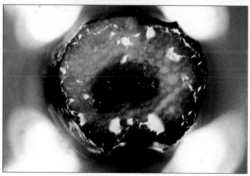

Figure 6. A cut-section of a transgenic sweetpotato plant showing tissue-specific expression of the CaMV directed *gus*A gene localized in vascular areas.

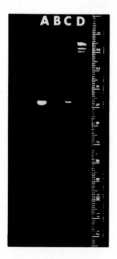
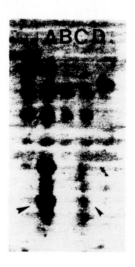

Figure 7. Polymerase chain reaction (PCR) and Southern analysis of the putative transgenic shoots from the *Agrobacterium* study. The figure on the left panel shows PCR products on an ethidium bromide stained gel. Lane A is sweetpotato transgenic plant of cv. 'Jewel,' lane B is negative control of an untransformed plant, and lane C is positive control (plasmid DNA containing *kan* gene, pBI 121). Bands show the localization of *kan* gene in the expected molecular weight region, ~1 kb of transgenic plant and the plasmid pBI 121. Lane D is l DNA restricted with *Hin* D III as a molecular weight marker. The figure on the right panel shows the autoradiographic results from the hybridization of DNA from the above PCR gel with a radioactively labelled *kan* gene. Arrows show the location of *kan* gene in the DNA from transgenic sweetpotato plant (lane A), and the positive control (lane C). The lane B has DNA from the control, non-transformed plant.

Figure 8. A leaf explant from sweetpotato cv. 'Jewel' exhibiting *gus*A expressing cells. Photo taken two days after the bombardment with micro-projectiles coated with plasmid pBI 221 and subjected to GUS histochemical staining overnight.

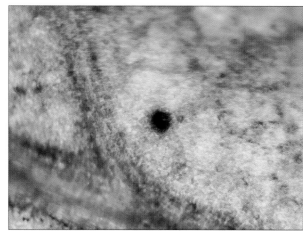

Figure 9. Control (right) and transformed (left) petiole explants of sweetpotato cv. 'Jewel.' The petioles were subjected to bombardment by micro-projectiles that were either coated with plasmid pBI 221 (left) or uncoated (right) and cultured for two weeks prior to staining for *gus*A activity.

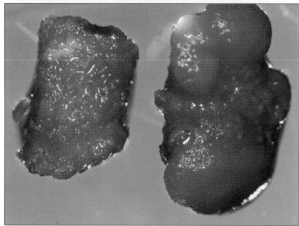

Figure 10. A petiole explant of sweetpotato cv. 'Jewel' subjected to bombardment with pBI 221 showing untransformed (left) and transformed sectors (right) when cultured on a non-selection medium.

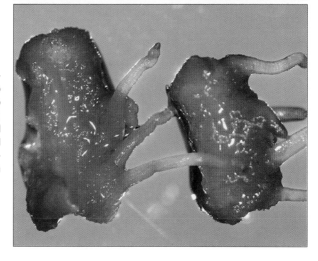

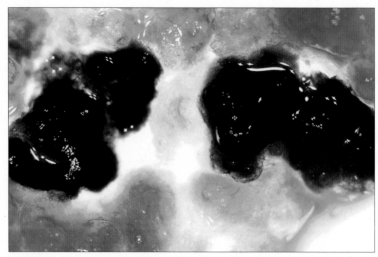

Figure 11. A callus isolate obtained after five cycles of subculture and tested for *gus*A activity. This callus was derived by bombarding of petiole explants of cv. 'Jewel' with pBI 121 and subsequently selected on an antibiotic medium.

ACKNOWLEDGMENTS

We gratefully acknowledge Dr. Karen Kindle (Cornell University) and Dr. A. S. Kumar (Hawaiian Sugar Planters Association) for their cooperation and technical assistance. Dr. Bob Jarret (USDA/ARS) supplied the accessions used in the study. We thank Dr. G. S. Varadarajan, Dr. John Williams and Mr. Ivet Thomas (Tuskegee University) for their assistance during the study. We thank Dr. John Dodds (CIP, Peru) for useful comments and input into the study. The research was supported by a grant from USAID (DAN-5053-G-00-0058-0C).

REFERENCES

Abel, P.P., R.S. Nelson, B. De, N. Hoffmann, S.G. Rogers, R.T. Fraley, and R.N. Beachy. 1986. Delay of disease development in transgenic plants that express the tobacco mosaic virus coat protein gene. Science 232:738-743.

Al-Juboory, K.H., and R.M. Skirvin. 1991. *In vitro* regeneration of *Agrobacterium* - transformed sweet potato (*Ipomoea batatas* L.). PGRSA Quarterly 19:82-89.

Boulter, D. 1989. Genetic engineering of plants for insect resistance. Outlook on Agriculture 18:1-6.

Destéfano-Beltrán, L., P.G. Nagpala, M.S. Cetiner, J.H. Dodds, and J.M. Jaynes. 1990. Enhancing bacterial and fungal disease resistance in plants: application to potato. Pages 205-221 *in* The molecular and cellular biology of the potato, edited by M.E. Vayda and W.D. Park. C.A.B. International, Wallingford, UK.

Dodds, J.H., C. Merzdorf, V. Zambrano, C. Siguenas, and J. Jaynes. 1991. Potential use of *Agrobacterium*-mediated tene transfer to confer insect resistance in sweet potato. Pages 203-220 *in* Sweet potato pest management, A global perspective, edited by R. Jansson and K.V. Raman. Westview Press, Boulder, CO.

Fischhoff, D.A., K.S. Bowdish, F.J. Perlak, P.G. Marrone, S.M. McCormick, J.G. Niedermeyer, D.A. Dean, K. Kusano-Kretzmer, E.J. Mayer, D.E. Rochester, S.G. Rogers, and R.T. Fraley. 1987. Insect tolerant transgenic tomato plants. Bio/Technology 5:807-813.

Goodman, R.M., H. Hauptli, A. Crossway, and V.C. Knauf. 1987. Gene transfer in crop improvement. Science 236:48-54.

Innis, M.A., D.H. Gelfand, J.J. Sninsk,y and T.J. White. 1990. PCR Protocols. San Diego, Academic Press. 482 pp.

Jefferson, R.A., T.A. Kavanagh, and M.W. Bevan. 1987. GUS fusions-ß glucuronidase as a sensitive and versatile gene fusion marker in higher plants. EMBO J 16:2901-2907.

Klein, T.M., T. Gradziel, M.E. Fromm, and J.C. Sanford. 1988. Factors influencing gene delivery into *Zea mays* cells by high-velocity microprojectiles. Bio/Technology 6:559-563.

McCabe, D.E., W. Swain, B.J. Martinell, and P. Christou. 1988. Stable transformation of soybean (*Glycine max*) by particle acceleration. Bio/Technology 6:923-926.

Murashige, T., and F. Skoog. 1962. A revised medium for rapid growth and bioassays with tobacco tissue cultures. Physiol. Plant.15:473-497.

Prakash, C.S., and Usha Varadarajan. 1992a. Foreign gene transfer into sweetpotato. (Abstr.) HortScience 26:492.

Prakash, C.S,. and Usha Varadarajan. 1992b. Genetic transformation of sweetpotato by particle bombardment. Plant Cell Reports 11:53-57.

Sanford, J.C. 1990. Biolistic plant transformation. Physiologia Plant. 79:206-209.

Sanford, J.C., T.M. Klein, E.D. Wolf, and N. Allen. 1987. Delivery of substances into cells and tissues using a particle bombardment process. Particulate Science and Technology 5:27-37.

Schell, J.S. 1987. Transgenic plants as tools to study the molecular organization of plant genes. Science 237:1176-1182.

Varadarajan, G.S., and C.S. Prakash. 1991. A rapid and efficient method to extract DNA from sweet potato and its related species. Plant Molecular Biology Reporter 9:6-12.

Weide, R., M. Koornneef, and P. Zabel. 1989. A simple, nondestructive spraying assay for the detection of an active kanamycin resistance gene in transgenic tomato plants. Theoretical and Applied Genetics 78:169-172.

Weising, K., J. Schell, and G. Kahl. 1988. Foreign genes in plants: transfer, structure, expression, and applications. Annual Review of Genetics 22:421-477.

Yang, M.S., N.O. Espinoza, P.G. Nagpala, J.H. Dodds, F.F. White, K.L. Schnorr, and J.M. Jaynes. 1989. Expression of a synthetic gene for improved protein quality in transformed potato plants. Plant Science 64:99-111.

Sweetpotato Technology for the 21st Century. W.A. Hill, C.K. Bonsi and P.A. Loretan (Eds.) 1992. Tuskegee University, Tuskegee, AL

D.J. Cantliffe

Somatic Embryos in Sweetpotato

A method for somatic embryo production of sweetpotato has been developed. The first step of somatic embryogenesis was to obtain embryogenic callus from 0.2 mm apical domes with 1-2 leaf primordia on medium containing 10 mM 2,4-dichlorophenoxyacetic acid (2,4-D). Selective proliferation of embryogenic callus was obtained on solid media containing 10 mM 2,4-D and 1 mM benzylaminopurine (BAP) and in liquid media containing 5 mM 2,4-D. Suspension cultures larger than 710 mm were commonly used to produce embryos. Cultures were recultured every 2 weeks in liquid media and every 6 weeks on agar media. The formation of embryos was triggered by transferring embryogenic calli or cell aggregates from nutrient media containing 2,4-D to fresh media without 2,4-D. Late torpedo and cotyledonary stage embryos had the highest potential for plant formation. The automated production of synthetic seed in combination with fluid drilling technology would make sweetpotato production using somatic embryos economically feasible.

Sweetpotato {*Ipomoea batatas* (L.) Lam.} is used as both a food crop and as a biomass crop because of its rapid quantitative production of convertible carbohydrates. Conventionally, sweetpotato is propagated asexually using stem cuttings. However, this propagation method is costly since high labor, large nurseries and storage facilities are required. The lack of resistance to virus diseases in commercial sweetpotato cultivars further complicates the maintenance and multiplication of virus-free stocks. Mass production of disease-free plant material can be expected using tissue culture. The production of synthetic seed, through somatic embryogenesis, and direct seeding would reduce the production cost of this vegetatively propagated crop.

In order to develop synthetic seed, induction of somatic embryogenesis and seeding techniques of embryo are required. Sweetpotato is a recalcitrant species with regard to somatic embryogenesis and, as such, has been difficult to work with. We have developed a method for somatic embryo production of sweetpotato, and now the focus is on singulation of embryos and synchronization of embryo development. Fluid drilling has been chosen as a direct planting method of somatic embryos to the field at this time. Automation of callus proliferation, embryo development and harvest is also under investigation by a team of agricultural engineers. The purpose of this report is to describe the method of sweetpotato somatic embryo production and seeding developed.

Vegetable Crops Department,University of Florida, Gainesville, FL 32611, USA.

SOMATIC EMBRYO PRODUCTION

Somatic embryo production is achieved through three major steps. Protocols and media, respectively, are shown in Tables 1 and 2, for each step. The first step of somatic embryogenesis is to obtain embryogenic callus from an explant under aseptic conditions. Embryogenic callus formation in sweetpotato has been reported from storage root (Liu and Cantliffe 1984), stem (Komaki and Kukimura 1988; Liu and Cantliffe 1984; Murata and Miyaji 1984), petiole (Komaki and Kukimura 1988), leaf blade (Komaki and Kukimura 1988; Liu and Cantliffe 1984), anther (Tsai and Tseng 1979), shoot tip (3-5 mm, Liu and Cantliffe 1984; 0.5-1.0 mm, Jarret et al. 1984) and apical domes (Cantliffe et al. 1987).

The most efficient explant is the apical dome (Cantliffe et al. 1987). The frequency of embryogenic callus formation declines from 90 to 30% as the numbers of leaf primordia attached to the apical dome explant increases from 1 to 3 (Cantliffe et al. 1987). The 2,4-dichlorophenoxyacetic acid content of the media was important. While explants on media with 0 or 4.0 mg/L 2,4-D either produce non-embryogenic friable callus or fail to survive culture, at 0.5-3.0 mg/L 2,4-D over 80% of the apical dome explants form embryogenic callus (Liu and Cantliffe 1984). In practice, embryogenic callus is initiated from 0.2 mm apical domes with 1-2 leaf primordia on medium containing 10 mM (2.2 mg/L) 2,4-D (Table 2). Two weeks after culture apical dome explants enlarge 2- to 3-fold in diameter. After 3-4 weeks the peripheral region of the apical dome produces smooth-surfaced tissue. After 4-8 weeks the surfaces are nodulated by the formation of numerous pro-embryos. Cell layers subjacent to apical domes produce a substantial amount of white to pale brown non-embryogenic friable callus. The characteristics of the two different type cells which compose embryogenic and nonembryogenic callus are listed in Table 1.

The second step is embryogenic callus proliferation. This is achieved either on agar solidified or liquid nutrient media (Table 1). The callus proliferation medium also has a high 2,4-D content (Table 2). Selective proliferation of embryogenic callus has been obtained on solid media containing 10 mM 2,4-D and 1 mM

Table 1. Characteristics of embryogenic and non-embryogenic callus in sweetpotato.

CALLUS	Embryogenic	Non-embryogenic
Growth rate	slow	fast
Structure, texture	nodular, compact	uniform, friable
Color	yellow, opaque	white, translucent
Density	1.15 - 1.19	1.03 - 1.11
CELLS		
Diameter	25 - 50 μm	75 - 200 μm
Shape	spherical	oblong-elongated
Nature	cytoplasmic	vacuolated
Type	meristematic	parenchymatous

Table 2. Protocol for somatic embryogenesis and plantlet production in sweetpotato.

Procedure	Step 1 Embryogenic callus induction	Step 2 Embryogenic callus proliferation Agar cultures	Step 2 Suspensions	Step 3 Embryo production Agar cultures	Step 3 Suspensions	Step 4 Conversion to plantlets
Explant, inoculum or propagule	Apical dome plus 1-2 leaf primordia (ca. 0.2-1.0 mm)	Embryogenic callus from stage 1,2; 1 mg cm^{-2}	Embryogenic callus from stage 1,2; 6-40 mg mL^{-1}	Embryogenic callus from stage 2; 1 mg cm^{-2}	Embryogenic callus from stage 2; 6 mg mL^{-1}	Somatic embryo from stage 3; 1 embryo cm^{-2}
Incubation condition	60X15 mm plastic petri dishes; 12.5 mL medium; dark; 27°C	100X15 plastic petri dishes; 25 mL medium; dark; 27°C	125 mL, 250 mL Erlenmeyer flasks; 20, 40 ml medium; rotary shaker 100 rpm; dark; 27°C	100X15 mm plastic petri dishes; 25 mL medium; 1st week in dark; 10 hrs photo period; 27°C	125 mL or 250 mL Erlenmeyer flasks; 20 or 40 mL medium rotary shaker 100 rpm; dark; 27°C	100X25 mm disposable plastic petri dishes; 25 mL medium; 10 hrs photo-period 25°C
Medium	CI medium	CP medium for Agar cultures	CP medium for suspension cultures	EP medium for agar cultures	EP medium for suspension cultures	EC medium
Recultures	-	Every 8 weeks	Every 2 weeks	-	-	-
Formation of embryo-genic callus, somatic embryo & plantlet	Within 4 weeks, non-embryogenic callus, within 8 weeks, embryogenic callus	-	-	Globular embryos within 8 days, first mature embryos in 12 days, mature embryos arrested at 21 days	Clusters of embryos in 21 days	Root growth 8-14 days, visible shoot growth 14-21 days

benzylaminopurine (BAP) and in liquid media containing 5 mM 2,4-D (Chée and Cantliffe 1988b). Growth habits of embryogenic cell aggregates from liquid media and calli from agar media are similar. Embryogenic units grow faster in liquid media than on agar media since the whole periphery is involved. When embryogenic callus is proliferated in liquid media, cell aggregate suspension cultures are obtained. Embryogenic calli larger than 355 mm make up 75% of the mass of suspension cultures (Chée and Cantliffe 1989). The 125 to 355 mm fraction of suspension cultures contains cell aggregates of which 20% are embryogenic. The cell aggregates smaller than 125 mm are mostly nonembryogenic. The proliferation of the embryogenic fraction of suspension cultures occurs through the fragmentation of the larger calli when the cultures approach their stationary phase of growth at 2 weeks. Embryogenic cultures are maintained by subculturing the 355 to 710 mm fraction of suspension cultures to liquid or solidified media. Since embryo formation occurs readily from larger calli the fraction of suspension cultures larger than 710 mm is used to produce embryos. The cell aggregates smaller than 355 mm are mostly non-embryogenic and thus discarded. Non-embryogenic cells and calli always appear as a by-product in embryogenic callus proliferation.

When embryogenic callus is maintained on solidified media, the protocol for subculture is as follows. The calli are collected into a small amount of liquid medium and fragmented mechanically into their component subunits. The resulting suspension culture is then sieved and the various fractions used for embryogenic callus proliferation or embryo production as indicated above. Cultures are recultured every 2 weeks in liquid media and every 6 weeks on agar media.

The third step is to produce embryos. In this step, the formation of embryos is triggered essentially by transferring embryogenic calli or cell aggregates from nutrient media containing 2,4-D to fresh media without 2,4-D. The patterns of embryo development from callus were studied and embryos capable of producing plants were described (Chée and Cantliffe 1988a). Late torpedo and cotyledonary stage embryos have the highest potential for plant formation (Fig. 1). Abscisic acid

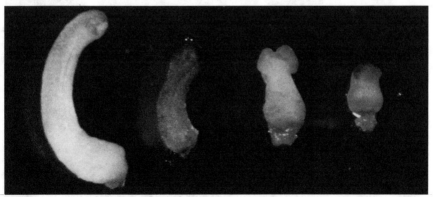

Figure 1. Various stages of sweetpotato somatic embryo development. The torpedo (second from right) and cotyledonary (far left and second to left) stage embryos have the highest potential for plant formation.

41

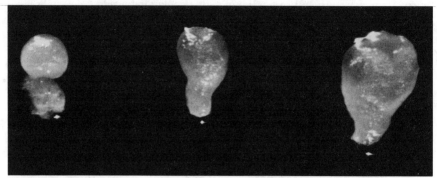

Figure 2. Globular (left), heart (center), and torpedo (right) stages of sweetpotato embryo formation.

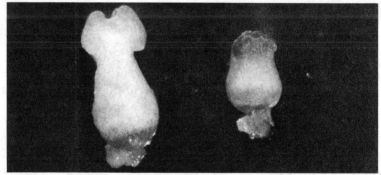

Figure 3. Somatic embryos of sweetpotato arrested growth after three weeks on embryo production media.

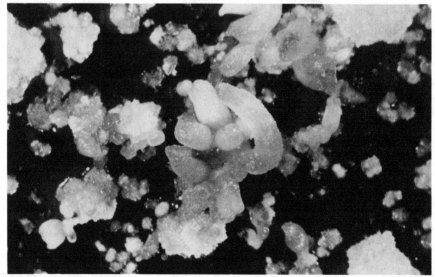

Figure 4. Embryogenic callus and embryos of sweetpotato in varying stages of development.

(ABA) was beneficial for the formation of embryos in those stages (Cantliffe et al. 1987). Eight days after transferring embryogenic calli to embryo formation medium, globular embryos are observed (Fig. 2) and after 2 weeks the first mature embryos are obtained (Fig. 1). At 3 weeks embryos are found arrested at all stages of development (Fig. 3). The incubation conditions are 27°C and dark for the first week; thereafter, they are kept in a 12 hour light/14 hour dark photoperiod. Transferred mature embryos resume growth and form plantlets upon subculture to fresh medium (Fig. 4).

Table 3 shows the composition of the media used for each culture stage in somatic embryo production of sweetpotato. The basic culture conditions and protocols of the three major steps have been worked out. However, many factors must be optimized in steps 2 and 3 for the production of synthetic seed to become a feasible reality. Such factors are concentrations and types of plant growth regulators, inorganic and organic media constituents, media pH, incubation conditions, illumination, vessel type and size, solidified versus liquid media, agitation speed, aeration,

Table 3. Composition of media used for each culture stage in somatic embryogenesis and plant production of sweetpotato.

	Culture stage			
	Embryogenic callus induction	Embryogenic callus proliferation	Embryo production	Embryo conversion to plantlets
Inorganic salt	MS[z]	Modified MS 30 mM KCl	Modified MS 10 mM NH_4NO_3 20 mM KNO_3	MS
Organic substances (μM)				
Thiamine HCl	5	5	5	5
Nicotinic acid	10	10	10	10
Pyridoxin HCl	5	5	5	5
Myo-inositol	500	500	500	500
Growth regulators (μM)				
2,4-D	10	10/5[y]	0/0,0.5	
BAP	-	1/0		
ABA	-	-	0,1,10/0,10	
NAA	-	-	-	0,0.1
Sucrose (%)	3	3	3	1.6
Agar (%)	0.6	0.6/0	0.8	0.8
pH before autoclaving	5.8	5.8	5.8	5.8

[z]Murashige and Skoog (1962).
[y]Concentration in agar solidified media/concentration in liquid media.

culture duration, sorting of embryogenic from nonembryogenic callus or cell aggregates, synchronization of embryo formation, and selection of embryos capable of producing plants must be considered.

SEEDING METHOD FOR SOMATIC EMBRYOS

The use of encapsulation of synthetic seeds has been limited by problems of embryo survival after desiccation and the costs of encapsulation. Fluid or gel drilling would reduce the handling cost and prevent embryo desiccation during direct field planting. Agricultural carrier gels, developed for planting primed and pre-germinated seed, were tested for their phytotoxicity or effect on somatic embryos (Cantliffe et al. 1987; Schultheis et al. 1990). The gels were supplemented with inorganic and organic nutrients (Table 2). Of the gels tested, Natrosol, which supported normal embryo growth (Cantliffe et al. 1987, Schultheis et al. 1990), has promise for use as a gel carrier for fluid drilling of somatic embryos.

Plantlet formation from embryos cultured in Natrosol gel was promoted by additions of 0.1-1.0 mM naphthaleneacetic acid (NAA) (Chée et al. 1990). Shoot growth was enhanced predominantly on media including BAP although plant formation was negatively affected by this hormone (Chée et al. 1990). Additions of these or other hormones in adequate ratios directly to the seeding gel could enhance early plantlet development in the fluid drilling system. Cooperative research is in progress with soil scientists working with mycorrhizae in order to enhance plantlet survival during emergence and incorporate the potential for using reduced amounts of inorganic fertilizer.

CONCLUSIONS

A method for the production of synthetic seed has been described. However, some problems need to be addressed before mass production of synthetic seed in sweetpotato is feasible. First, embryos need to be synchronized and singulated. The future experimental approach is to obtain, manage, and maintain suspension cultures of small cell aggregates that are embryogenic. Synchronization of development can then be studied using different incubation conditions and media factors. The rapid evaluation of liquid cultures using video image analysis has been computerized in cooperation with agricultural engineers (Grand d'Esnon et al. 1988; Harrell and Cantliffe 1991). This technology forms the basis for the automated mass production of synchronized and singulated embryos in bioreactors.

Secondly, developmental arrest must be induced at a desired stage to allow the storage of embryos until they are needed without damage or reduced growth of the embryo. This may be accomplished via hormonal control, possibly ABA or via some osmotic conditioning treatment. Dehydration is a preferred method to store embryos; unfortunately, embryo survival to date has been low after dehydration (Kitto and Janick 1985) and storage periods generally are for short duration (Gray 1989).

Finally, germination must be triggered in the field. The germination rate of encapsulated somatic embryos of alfalfa has been demonstrated to be much lower in natural conditions than *in vitro* (Redenbaugh et al. 1987). Liu et al. (1989) encapsulated carrot somatic embryos and then dehydrated the capsule to 8% moisture. They obtained 68% germination after 10 days storage at 4°C. Gray (1989) obtained more rapid and greater germination of grape somatic embryos after they were dehydrated. This approach to improved germination and prolonged storage of somatic embryos warrants further study.

REFERENCES

Cantliffe, D.J., J.R. Liu, and J.R. Schultheis. 1987. Development of artificial seeds of sweetpotato for clonal propagation through somatic embryogenesis. Pages 183-195 *in* Methane from biomass: a system approach. Edited by W.H. Smith and J.R. Frank, Elsevier Applied Science, New York.

Chée, R.P., and D.J. Cantliffe. 1988a. Somatic embryony patterns and planted regeneration in *Ipomoea batatas* Poir. In Vitro 955958.

Chée, R.P., and D.J. Cantliffe. 1988b. Selective enhancement of *Ipomoea batatas* Poir. embryogenic and non-embryogenic callus growth and production of embryos in liquid culture. Plant Cell, Tissue, and Organ Culture 15, 149-159.

Chée R.P., and D.J. Cantliffe. 1989. Composition of embryogenic suspension cultures of *Ipomoea batatas* Poir. and production of individualized embryos. Plant Cell Tissue Organ Culture, 17:3952.

Chée R.P, J.R. Schultheis, and D.J. Cantliffe. 1990. Plant recovery from sweetpotato somatic embryos. HortScience 25:795797.

Grand d'Esnon, A., R. Chée, R.C. Harrell, and D.J. Cantliffe. 1988. Qualitative and quantitative evaluation of liquid tissue cultures by artificial vision. International Journal of Agricultural Engineering Research. Paper no. 88, 395.

Gray, D.J. 1989. Effects of dehydration and exogenous growth regulators on dormancy, quiescence and germination of grape somatic embryos. In Vitro Cell. Dev. Biol. 25:1173-1178.

Harrell, R., and D.J. Cantliffe. 1991. Automated evaluation of somatic embryogenesis by artificial vision. Pages 178-195 *in* Cell culture and somatic cell genetics of plants. Vol. 8. Scale-up and automation in plant tissue culture, edited by I. Vasil, Academic Press, New York.

Jarret, R.L., S. Salazar, and Z.R. Fernandez. 1984. Somatic embryogenesis in sweetpotato. HortScience 19:397-398.

Kitto, S.L., and J. Janick. 1985. Hardening treatments increase survival of synthetically-coated asexual embryos of carrot. J. Amer. Soc. Hort. Sci. 110:283-286.

Komaki, K., and H. Kukimura. 1988. Varietal difference of embryoid formation from sweetpotato callus. Kyushu Agricultural Research 50.

Liu, J.R., and D.J. Cantliffe. 1984. Somatic embryogenesis and regeneration in tissue cultures of sweetpotato (*Ipomoea batatas* Poir.). Plant Cell Reports 3:112-115.

Liu, J.R., J. Jae-Heung, Y. Seung-Gyun, L. Haeng-Soon, J. Hyouk, and K. Jenog-Sook. 1989. Development of a model system for artificial seed reproduction: II A dry type of carrot (*Daucus carota* L.) artificial seeds. Korean J. Plant Tissue Cult. 16:165-173.

Murata, T., and Y. Miyaji. 1984. Regeneration of plants from stem callus of sweetpotato. Japan. J. Breed. 34 suppl. 1, 24-25.

Murashige T., and F. Skoog. 1962. A revised medium for rapid growth and bioassays with tobacco tissue culture. Physiol. Plant. 15:473-497.

Redenbaugh, K., D. Slade, P. Viss, and J.A. Fujii. 1987. Encapsulation of somatic embryos in synthetic seed coats. HortScience 22:803-809.

Schultheis, J.R., D.J. Cantliffe, and R.P. Chée. 1990. Optimizing sweet potato (*Ipomoea batatas* (L.) Lam) root and plant formation by selection of proper embryo developmental stage and size, and gel type for fluidized sowing. Plant Cell Reports 9:356-359.

Tsai, H.S., and M.T. Tseng. 1979. Embryoid formation and plantlet regeneration from anther callus of sweetpotato. Botanical Bulletin of Academic Sinica 20, 117-122.

Robert L. Jarret, Nicholas Gawel, Alan Whittemore

Sweetpotato Germplasm Conservation and Related Research at the Southern Regional Plant Introduction Station

The clonal repository for sweetpotato germplasm now holds approximately 600 accessions of *I. batatas* (maintained *in vitro*) and numerous additional accessions of *I. batatas*-related species. Related species have been acquired in cooperation with various national and international programs. Data relevant to the increase and maintenance of the wild related species has been compiled on a data base. The effects of chemical and environmental variables on "minimal growth" *in vitro* germplasm storage have been investigated.Taxonomic relationships of the various *batatas*-related species, and the extent of genotypic diversity within the wild and cultivated *batatas* clones, have been investigated using restriction fragment length polymorphisms (RFLPs). This presentation will discuss the present state of the U.S. sweetpotato germplasm collection and the research program at the clonal repository.

INTRODUCTION

A clonal repository for the acquisition and maintenance of sweetpotato (*Ipomoea batatas* L.) and related species germplasm was established in Griffin, GA in 1987. Since that time the collection has increased in size and diversity to include approximately 600 accessions of sweetpotato (maintained *in vitro*) and numerous additional *Ipomoea* species. In order to facilitate the entry of clonal materials into the U.S., for inclusion into the collection, virus indexing facilities have been established in Griffin. Various plant collecting trips have been planned and conducted in cooperation with other national and international agencies, most notably the International Potato Center (CIP). Collecting trips have emphasized the acquisition of wild *batatas*-related species and other *Ipomoea* storage-root-forming species from around the world. Data relevant to the increase and maintenance of the wild related species has been compiled on a data base. Taxonomic relationships of the various *batatas*-related species, and the extent of genotypic diversity within the wild and cultivated *batatas* clones, have been investigated using restriction fragment length polymorphisms (RFLPs) as detected with random genomic probes selected from a pUC 18 (cv. 'Centennial') library. This presentation will discuss the present state of the U.S. sweetpotato germplasm collection and the research program of the clonal repository.

USDA/ARS, Department of Plant Introduction, Georgia Station, 1109 Experiment Street, Griffin, GA 30223, USA.

47

RESEARCH ACTIVITIES

Defining systematic relationships in section *Batatas*

A number of *Ipomoea* species have been suggested as belonging to section *batatas* (Austin 1988). Unfortunately plant material or seed of many of these species has not been readily available for study. Two species, *I. gracilis* and *I. littoralis*, believed to be closely related to cultivated *I. batatas* were collected in Australia in 1989 in order to determine their taxonomic classification in relation to sweetpotato and other endemic Australian *Ipomoea* species.

In order to elucidate the taxonomic relationships of these two species, restriction enzyme digested DNA was transferred to nylon membrane and probed with ^{32}P-labelled low to moderate copy number randomly selected sequences isolated from an *I. batatas* EcoRI genomic library. Polymorphisms were scored as described by Debener et al. (1990), and the data were analyzed using BIOSYS-1 (version 1.7) and SAS (5.16) software to produce the principal coordinate analysis in Fig. 1. The results clearly indicate the affinity of *I. littoralis* with section *batatas* (as represented by *I. batatas*). These results are in contrast to *I. gracilis* which clusters closely with Australian endemic species *I. argillicola*, *I. muelleri*, *I. pescaprae*, and *I. graminea* members of section *Erpipomoea*.

I. gracilis produces a small (8 to 12 cm in length) tap root which is eaten by Australian aborigines. Our single accession of *I. littoralis* has not produced storage roots under greenhouse conditions over a period of one year. At the present time, the repository has only a single accession of *I. littoralis* from Hawaii. Our results indicate that additional accessions of this species should be targeted for future collection.

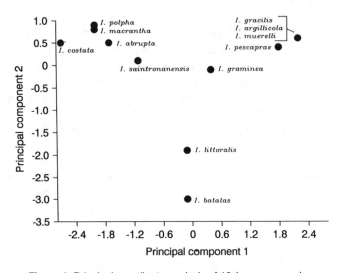

Figure 1. Principal coordinate analysis of 12 *Ipomoea* species.

In vitro germplasm storage of sweetpotato

Accessions in the U.S. sweetpotato germplasm collection are maintained as virus free tissue cultures (Jarret 1990). One of the most time-consuming aspects of managing an *in vitro* germplasm collection is the continual need to reculture accessions as the plantlets outgrow the culture vessel or deplete the nutrient media. We have evaluated the effects of various growth retarding treatments on *in vitro* growth inhibition of sweetpotato (Jarret and Gawel 1991a,b) in an effort to define those environmental variables that can be manipulated to prolong the time period between recultures while maintaining the genetic integrity of the individual accessions.

Culture incubation temperature is a variable that greatly influences the growth rate of sweetpotato plantlets *in vitro* (Jarret and Gawel 1991). Our studies have indicated that for a majority of genotypes tested, explant (axillary bud) survival and shoot development are inhibited at temperatures less than 18.3°C (Jarret and Gawel 1991). Explants of many plant introductions (PIs) rarely survive below 18.3°C for longer than 6 months. In addition, shoot development from surviving explants cultured continually at 18.3°C is greatly retarded. However, the deleterious effects of this temperature inhibition may be alleviated by incubating cultures initially for 2 to 4 weeks at 21.1 or 26.7°C. prior to maintenance at 18.3°C (Figs. 2a,b). This procedure allows curators to take advantage of the reduced growth which occurs at 18.3°C with less concern for loss of explant viability or failure of shoots to develop.

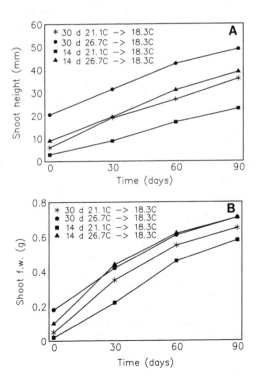

Figure 2. Increase in shoot height (A) and shoot fresh weight (B) of cv. 'Jewel' *in vitro* plantlets. Nodal explants, containing a single axillary bud, were incubated at either 21.1°C or 26.7°C for 2 to 4 weeks and then transferred to 18.3°C.

Table 1. Effects of ABA on growth inhibition of cv. 'Jewel' *in vitro* after 3 months.

ABA	Shoot fresh weight		Shoot height	
(mg/L)	(g)	% control	(mm)	% control
0.00	0.96	100	130.0	100
0.10	0.84	87	106.0	82
1.00	0.04	4	9.9	8
10.00	0.00	0	0.0	0

An alternative to "slow growth" germplasm maintenance is maintenance of germplasm in a state of "no growth" (Jarret and Gawel 1991). This procedure involves the culture of nodal segments containing a single axillary bud on a Murashige and Skoog (1962) media supplemented with abscisic acid (ABA). Axillary buds cultured in the presence of ABA remain quiescent (Table 1) for up to 2 years without loss of viability. When transferred to fresh media, in the absence of ABA, axillary buds develop normally from these nodes.

Germplasm evaluation

Considerable emphasis is still being placed on the collection of sweetpotato germplasm. However, there are continuing efforts to identify, within the collection, clones possessing useful or potentially useful agronomic characteristics or disease or insect resistance genes to support sweetpotato improvement programs. In order to promote the use of the collection to the fullest extent possible, individual accessions have been evaluated for their disease and insect resistance characteristics. Much of the germplasm characterization is conducted in cooperation with other federal and state sweetpotato improvement programs.

Examples of resistance genes currently identified among the collections' accessions include those listed in Table 2. In addition, variability for various

Table 2. Examples of disease and insect resistance genes identified in the collections accessions.

Pathogen	Source of resistance
Fusarium oxysporum	W-lines[z]
Internal cork	Jewel, W-lines[z]
Plectris aliena	W-119, W-w-125, W-154
Meloidogyne incognita	W-lines[z]
Chaetocnema confinis	W-lines[z]
Erwinia chrysanthemi	cvs. Sumor, Nemagold, PI 531116
Streptomyces ipomoea	PIs 286629, 531147, 531142, Travis
Fusarium solani	PI 508519
Diplodia gossypina	PI508518, cv. Hayman, W-51-19
Rotylenchulus reniformis	PIs 508519, 508514, 508518, 531146
Phyllosticta batatas	cv. Excel

[z]Jones et al., 1980; [y]Clark et al., 1989.

horticultural characteristics, i.e., plant growth habit, vine pigmentation, storage root color and sweetness, sprouting ability, etc. has been observed and recorded.

SUMMARY

The clonal repository for sweetpotato germplasm continues to emphasize conservation of genetic diversity in sweetpotato and its related species. All clonal materials are maintained *in vitro*. Research activities, utilizing RFLPs, are focused on determining the systematics of section *batatas*, quantifying genetic diversity within the collection and developing optimal plant collecting strategies. The effects of ABA, as a quiescence-inducing compound, are being investigated on long term *in vitro* maintenance. Sources of disease and insect resistance have been identified in the collection and efforts continue to characterize accessions for use in support of crop improvement programs.

REFERENCES

Austin, D. 1988. The taxonomy, evolution and genetic diversity of sweet potatoes and related wild species. Pages 27-60 *in* Exploration, maintenance and utilization of sweet potato genetic resources, edited by P. Gregory. Proc. 1st Plan. Conf., 23-27 Feb. 1987. Intl. Potato Center, Lima, Peru..

Clark, C.A., J.A. Wilder, and V. Duarte. 1989. Resistance of sweet potato to bacterial rot and stem rot caused by *Erwinia chrysanthemi*. Plant Disease 73:984-987.

Debener, T., F. Salamini, and C. Gebhardt. 1990. Phylogeny of wild and cultivated *Solanum* species based on nuclear restriction fragment length polymorphisms (RFLPs). Theor. Appl. Genet. 79:360-368.

Jarret, R.L. 1989. A repository for sweetpotato germplasm. HortScience 24:886.

Jarret, R.L., and N. Gawel. 1991a. Abscisic acid-induced growth inhibition of sweetpotato (*Ipomoea batatas* (L.) Lam.) *in vitro*. Plant Cell Tiss. Org. Cult. 24:13-18.

Jarret, R.L., and N. Gawel. 1991b. Chemical and environmental growth inhibition of sweetpotato (*Ipomoea batatas* (L.) Lam.) *in vitro*. Plant Cell Tiss. Org. Cult. 25:153-159.

Jones, A., P.D. Dukes, J.M. Schalk, M.A. Mullen, M.G. Hamilton, D.R. Paterson, and T.E. Boswell. 1980. W-71, W-115, W-119, W-149 and W-154 sweet potato germplasm with multiple insect and disease resistance. HortScience 15:835-836.

Murashige, T., and F. Skoog. 1962. A revised medium for rapid growth and bioassays with tobacco tissue cultures. Physiol. Plant. 15:473-497.

Sweetpotato Technology for the 21st Century. W.A. Hill, C.K. Bonsi and P.A. Loretan (Eds.) 1992. Tuskegee University, Tuskegee, AL

Carelli, M.L.D.[1]*, R.M. Skirvin*, D.E. Harry**

Transformation and Regeneration Studies of 'Jewel' Sweetpotato

Due to its hexaploid nature, low seed viability, problems of incompatibility and sterility, sweetpotato is difficult to improve by conventional breeding. To facilitate sweetpotato improvement, we are developing a system to introduce important agricultural characteristics into sweetpotato using *Agrobacterium tumefaciens* mediated transformation. Sensitivity of sweetpotato tissue to the antibiotics kanamycin, hygromycin and carbenicillin was studied. The presence of 50 mg/L kanamycin inhibited callus formation from leaf explants. Shoot and root formation was inhibited by kanamycin at 10 and 100 mg/L respectively. Hygromycin inhibited shoot formation at 1.0 mg/L and root formation at 5.0 mg/L. Carbenicillin added to the media at 300 mg/L induced abnormal root development from leaf explants and resulted in higher shoot and root regeneration of sweetpotato. 'Jewel' sweetpotato was transformed using *A. tumefaciens* strain NT-1 (pEHA101, pZA-7), which carries a T-DNA vector containing genes conferring resistance to the antibiotics kanamycin and hygromycin and ß-glucuronidase activity (GUS). Transformation studies were done using leaf disc explants. Among the regeneration media and protocols tested, limited regeneration from leaves was obtained on MS medium with 0.06 mg/L BAP and 0.25 mg/L NAA. Callus lines exhibiting kanamycin and hygromycin resistance as well as GUS activity were obtained.

INTRODUCTION

Sweetpotato is one of the world's major food crops (FAO 1986). Its culture requires few inputs such as the use of fertilizer and herbicides. For this reason sweetpotatoes are cultivated on subsistence farms of developing countries. Using conventional breeding methods specific cultivars have been developed with improved characteristics. However, the use of conventional breeding for sweetpotato improvement is especially difficult due to the hexaploid nature of its genome, low production of viable seeds, and problems of sterility and incompatibility. Also genetic variability of certain traits such as resistance to the sweetpotato weevil does not appear to exist in the sweetpotato. The use of genetic engineering procedures to introduce foreign genes into plants could be useful to complement conventional breeding programs for sweetpotato.

[1]Graduate student supported by the Conselho Nacional de Desenvolvimento Cientifico e Tecnologico (CNPq) - Brazil; *Department of Horticulture, University of Illinois, 258 PABL, 1201 W. Gregory Dr., Urbana IL 61801-3838; **Department of Forestry, University of Illinois, 110 Mumford Hall, 1301 W. Gregory Dr., Urbana, IL 61801-3838, USA.

The most commonly used vector for introduction of foreign genes into plant genomes is the soil bacteria *Agrobacterium tumefaciens* (see Zambryski 1989, for recent review). *A. tumefaciens* is the causal agent of crown gall disease on many dicotyledonous species. Following bacterial infection, a specific segment of the bacteria's tumor-inducing plasmid (Ti-plasmid), the T-DNA, is excised, transferred to the plant cell and integrated into the plant genome (Chilton et al. 1977). The transfer of the T-DNA is mediated by products of the genes located in the *virulence* region of the Ti-plasmid. The expression of T-DNA genes induces uncontrolled cell proliferation resulting in tumor formation. The *vir-* and T-DNA regions of the Ti-plasmid can be placed on separate plasmids to form a binary system for T-DNA transfer into the plant (Hoekema et al. 1983).

To regenerate plants from transgenic cells, the genes responsible for tumor formation must be removed from the T-DNA. The identification of transformed cells is possible by replacement of tumor-inducing genes by selectable marker genes in the T-DNA region (Horsch et al. 1985). The most common selectable markers used in plant transformation experiments are genes conferring resistance to the antibiotics kanamycin and hygromycin. It is thus important to determine tissue and species sensitivity to those antibiotics and to find an adequate concentration that will select transformants and still allow plant regeneration.

The first step in the development of a transformation system is to obtain a protocol for *in vitro* regeneration of whole plants. Several protocols have been described for sweetpotato regeneration (Sehgal 1975, Tsay et al. 1982, Chee and Cantliffe 1988) but percentages of regeneration are often low. A system for fast shoot regeneration was recently developed to obtain shoots from leaf explants (Dagnino, D.S., M.L.D. Carelli, R. Arrabal, and M.A. Esquibel, unpublished results). Details of this protocol are included in the materials and methods below.

In this study we report the sensitivity of sweetpotato leaves to the antibiotics kanamycin, hygromycin and carbenicillin, and we describe the effect of these antibiotics on callus growth, and regeneration of root and shoot. We also demonstrate the successful introduction and expression of foreign genes into sweetpotato tissue, using a binary *Agrobacterium* vector system.

MATERIALS AND METHODS

Agrobacterium tumefaciens strains

The T-DNA plasmid vector, pZA-7, was transformed into two *A. tumefaciens vir* helper strains: NT-1 (pC58Z707, Hepburn et al. 1985) and NT-1 (pEHA101, Hood et al. 1986). Both binary strains used in the experiments [NT-1 (pC58Z707, pZA-7) and NT-1 (pEHA101, pZA-7)] were provided by Dr. A. Hepburn (Department of Agronomy, University of Illinois at Urbana-Champaign). The T-DNA of these vectors (segment that is transferred and integrated into the plant genome) contained two selectable markers for expression in plant cells: the neomycin phosphotransferase gene (*npt* II) (Fraley et al. 1986), which confers kanamycin resistance, and the hygromycin phosphotransferase gene (*aph* IV), conferring hygromycin

NT-1 (pEHA101, pZA-7)

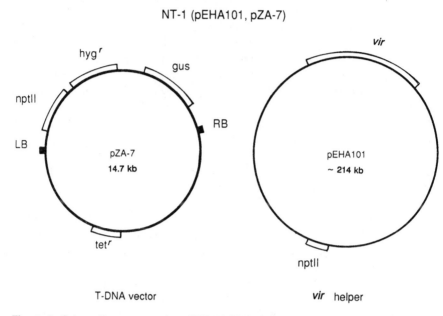

T-DNA vector   *vir* helper

Figure 1. Schematic representation of NT-1 (pEHA101, pZA-7) binary vector used in these experiments. The T-DNA vector pZA-7 carries genes for kanamycin resistance (*npt*II), hygromycin resistance (*hyg*ʳ) and ß-glucuronidase activity (GUS), for expression in plant cells. Plasmid ZA-7 also contains a gene conferring tetracycline resistance (*tet*ʳ), for bacterial selection. The *vir*-helper plasmids pEHA101 and pC58Z707 (not shown) contain the respective *vir* region and a kanamycin resistance gene (*npt* II) for bacterial selection.

resistance (Waldron et al. 1985). The plasmid ZA-7 also contains a screenable marker conferring β-glucuronidase (GUS) activity (Jefferson 1987) (Fig. 1).

A. *tumefaciens* strains were maintained in Luria broth medium (LB, Rodrigues and Tait 1983) containing: 1% tryptone (Difco), 0.5% bacto yeast extract (Difco), 1% NaCl, and 15 g/L agar at pH 7.0. LB media was supplemented with tetracycline 2.0 mg/mL and kanamycin 50 mg/mL to assure the maintenance of both T-DNA and *vir* helper plasmids, respectively. Prior to transformation experiments the strains were grown overnight in LB media.

Plant material and regeneration system
'Jewel' sweetpotato plants were introduced *in vitro* using axillary buds obtained from greenhouse grown plants. Shoots were maintained *in vitro* on shoot prolif-eration medium (SPM) composed of Murashige and Skoog (MS, 1962) high mineral salt medium supplemented with Staba vitamins (Staba 1969), myo-inositol 100 g/L, ascorbic acid 50 mg/L, sucrose 30 mg/L, agar 7 mg/L, 6 benzylaminopurine (BAP) 2.0 mg/L and naphthaleneacetic acid (NAA) 0.1 mg/L at pH 5.7. Discs were cultivated in 25 x 150 mm test tubes with 10 mL of medium. All plant cultures were

Figure 2. Sweetpotato leaf disc explants were obtained from the base of *in vitro* leaf blades and contained the mid-rib segment and petiole cut end.

maintained at $25 \pm 2°C$ under cool white fluorescent light bulbs (60 μEm^{-2}s^{-1}) with 16 h light photoperiod, unless stated otherwise.

Shoot regeneration from leaf explants was obtained on leaf regeneration medium (LRM) which was a modification of the medium used by Dagnino et al. (unpublished results). LRM was composed of SPM salts and vitamins supplemented with 0.06 mg/L BAP, 0.25 mg/L NAA, 30 mg/L sucrose and solidified with 7 mg/L agar. Leaf discs (1.5 cm diameter) were obtained from *in vitro* grown plants and cultured with the adaxial side in contact with the media. Leaf discs included the base of the leaf blade, mid-rib segment and petiole cut end (Fig. 2).

Antibiotic sensitivity assays

Tissue sensitivity to kanamycin, hygromycin and carbenicillin was independently tested in separate experiments. Sensitivity of sweetpotato tissue to kanamycin was determined by two experiments. Inhibition of callus proliferation was assessed by culturing leaf segments on SPM to which kanamycin was added at concentrations ranging from 0 to 500 mg/L. Cultures were maintained at $25 \pm 2°C$ in the dark and evaluated after 60 days. Kanamycin inhibition of adventitious shoot and root formation was determined by culturing leaf discs, as previously described, on LRM supplemented with kanamycin at concentrations of 5, 10, 25, 50, 100 mg/L. Hygromycin inhibition of shoot and root formation was determined by culturing leaf discs on LRM containing hygromycin at concentrations of 0.5, 1.0, 2.5, 5.0, 10, 15 mg/L. The effect of carbenicillin on organogenesis was tested by adding 300 mg/L of the antibiotic to LRM and culturing leaf discs as described. All antibiotics were added to the medium as powder after sterilization. In all experiments a control treatment lacking antibiotic was included. Twenty replicates were used in each treatment. After 60 days, the number of regenerated roots and shoots was recorded and callus proliferation was determined by visual evaluation.

Leaf disc transformation and selection

Leaf transformation was performed based on procedures described by Horsch et al. (1985). Cultures were pelleted by centrifugation and resuspended in $MgSO_4$

(10mM) solution. Leaf discs were precultured on LRM for two days. Precultured leaf discs were subsequently placed in the resuspended bacterial solution for about 1 minute and mixed by gentle swirling. Explants were blotted on sterile filter paper and cocultivated on LRM for two days. Leaf discs were transferred either to LRM containing carbenicillin 300 mg/L or LRM containing carbenicillin 300 mg/L and kanamycin 100 mg/L. Explants were transferred to fresh medium every two weeks or as required. Kanamycin selected callus tissue was later maintained on SPM, supplemented with kanamycin 50 mg/L, hygromycin 10 mg/L and carbenicillin 500 mg/L.

ß-glucuronidase assays

Callus lines exhibiting kanamycin and hygromycin resistance were tested for the presence of ß-glucuronidase (GUS) activity as described by Jefferson (1987). Callus material was cut into sections and placed in a solution of 5-bromo-4-chloro-3-indolyl ß-glucuronic acid (X-glu) in the dark at 37°C for 24 hours. GUS activity was visually indicated by intense blue color. Control explants, not cocultivated with *A. tumefaciens*, were also incubated in the presence of X-glu.

RESULTS AND DISCUSSION

Regeneration studies

'Jewel' leaf explants placed on LRM formed roots after 5 to 7 days in culture. Seventy five percent of the explants regenerated roots. Adventitious roots developed from the petiole cut end of the leaf disc. Twenty five percent of the leaf explants developed adventitious shoots which were visible after 4 to 6 weeks in culture. Regenerated shoots originated either from the petiole cut end or directly from adventitious roots (Fig. 3). In general, one shoot was regenerated from each explant. Multiple shoots occasionally (1%) developed from the same regeneration site or at different sites in the roots.

Figure 3. Sweetpotato shoot regeneration obtained directly from an adventitious root after 4 to 6 weeks of culture.

Table 1. Kanamycin inhibition of callus growth on sweetpotato leaf explants.

Kanamycin (mg/L)	leaf callus	
0	+++	- no callus
1	+++	+ scant callus
5	+++	++ localized callus
10	++	+++vigorous callus
20	+	
50	-	
100	-	
150	-	
200	-	
250	-	

Antibiotic sensitivity

Plant cells are known to be sensitive to a number of antibiotics including kanamycin and hygromycin (Pollock et al. 1983, Catlin 1990). To determine the sensitivity of callus development to kanamycin levels, leaves were inoculated in SPM containing different concentrations of kanamycin. Kanamycin concentration of 50 mg/L completely inhibited callus formation from leaf tissue (Table 1). Kanamycin inhibition of shoot and root formation was determined by culturing leaf discs on LRM supplemented with kanamycin as previously described. Shoot regeneration decreased at 5 and 10 mg/L kanamycin and was completely inhibited at 25 mg/L (Fig. 4a). To inhibit root development 100 mg/L kanamycin was required (Fig. 4a). A similar study, carried out to determine hygromycin effect on organ regeneration, showed that shoot regeneration was inhibited at 1.0 mg/L and root regeneration at 5.0 mg/L (Fig. 4b).

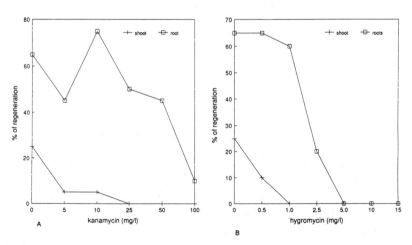

Figure 4. Kanamycin (A) and hygromycin (B) dose responses showing inhibition of shoot and root regeneration from sweetpotato leaf explants. Shoot and root percentages were obtained after 8 weeks in culture.

Carbenicillin is an antibiotic commonly used to suppress growth of *A. tumefaciens* after coculture with plant material (Christen et al. 1984). Sweetpotato leaf cultures inoculated on medium containing 300 mg/L carbenicillin produced abnormal roots which were short, thick and highly branched when compared to normal roots. Explants cultured in the presence of carbenicillin showed a higher percentage of shoot (30 vs 13%) and root formation (71 vs 60%) than controls. These results are different than those of Valvakens et al. (1989) and Colby and Meredith (1990) that reported an inhibitory effect of carbenicillin on root regeneration of *Arabidopsis* and *Vitis*. In contrast Roberts et al. (1989) reported increased growth of cell suspension cultures of *Bouvardia ternifolia* induced by carbenicillin and other β lactam antibiotics. This growth promoting effect was attributed to the presence of an auxin compound resulting from the decarboxylation of carbenicillin.

Transformation studies

An initial experiment to produce transformed sweetpotato plants was made by cocultivating leaf discs, precultured for two days in LRM, with *A. tumefaciens* for two days. Discs were then subjected to kanamycin selection. Kanamycin resistant calli were visible one week after placing the discs on selective media. Occasional roots were formed but failed to grow into the medium. No shoots were obtained in this initial experiment. Leaf discs became yellow before any shoots formed. The failure to regenerate shoots was probably due to the high concentration of kanamycin (100 mg/L) used for selection. Leaf discs cocultivated with NT-1 (pEHA101, pZA-7) gave rise to callus, which grew on selective media. However, no antibiotic-resistant callus was recovered from leaf discs inoculated with NT-1 (pC58Z707, pZA-7) (Table 2). Callus tissue selected on kanamycin was subsequently maintained on SPM containing kanamycin (50 mg/L), hygromycin (10 mg/L) and carbenicillin (500 mg/L). Putative transformed calli were assayed for GUS activity. Eighty-eight percent of the callus lines growing on antibiotic selection showed GUS expression indicated by the intense blue color when incubated in X-glu (Fig. 5).

Since no shoot regeneration was obtained using the first transformation protocol, a second experiment was devised. In this experiment, leaf discs cocultivated with *A. tumefaciens* strain NT-1 (pEHA101, pZA-7) were transferred to kanamycin free media. Shoot and root regeneration occurred at 6% and 45%, respectively. Regenerated shoots were then transferred to LRM supplemented with kanamycin (50 mg/L) and carbenicillin (300 mg/L). Regenerated shoots failed to grow or to produce roots under antibiotic selection, indicating that they were not transformed.

The results of both experiments suggested that a preliminary selection for transformants is necessary but concentrations of kanamycin lower than 100 mg/L should be used. In our experiments to evaluate kanamycin and hygromycin inhibition of shoot regeneration, we showed that 10 mg/L kanamycin and 1.0 mg/L hygromycin were sufficient to inhibit shoot formation from nontransformed cells. Antibiotic concentrations near those levels could be used to select transformed cells which have the ability to regenerate shoots. These studies are in progress.

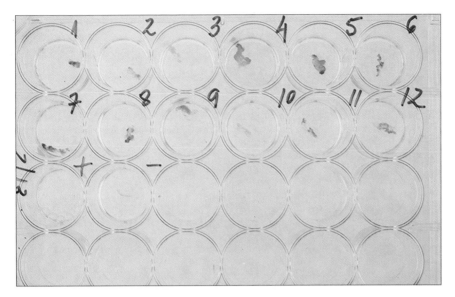

Figure 5. Histochemical GUS staining of sweetpotato callus grown under kanamycin and hygromycin selection. Ten out of 12 callus lines showed GUS expression, as indicated by the intense blue color. These lines had been transformed by *A. tumefaciens.*

ACKNOWLEDGMENTS

This research was paid in part by the University of Illinois Agriculture Experiment Station and by the Conselho Nacional de Desenvolvimento Cientifico e Tecnologico (CNPq), Brasil. We would like to thank Dr. A.G. Hepburn for providing the *Agrobacterium* strains and Dr. S.K. Dhir for helping with the GUS assay protocol.

REFERENCES

Catlin, D.W. 1990. The effects of antibiotics on the inhibition of callus induction and plant regeneration from cotyledons of sugarbeet (*Beta vulgaris* L.). Plant Cell Reports 9: 285-288.

Chee, R.P., and D.J. Cantliffe. 1988. Selective enhancement of *Ipomoea batatas* Poir. embryogenic and non-embryogenic callus growth and production of embryos in liquid culture. Plant Cell Tissue and Organ Culture 15: 149-159.

Chilton, M-.D., M.H. Drummond, D.J. Merlo, D. Sciaky, A.L. Montoya, M.P. Gordon, and E.W. Nester. 1977. Stable incorporation of plasmid DNA into higher plant cells, the molecular basis of crown gall tumorigenesis. Cell 11: 263-271.

Christen, A.A., M.A. Kirkpatrick, and P.F. Lurquin. 1984. Antibiotics and bacterial auxotrophic mutants in the co-cultivation of plant protoplasts and bacterial cells or spheroplasts. Zeitschrift fur Pflanzenphysiologie band 113, heft 3: 213-221.

Colby, S.M., and C.P. Meredith. 1990. Kanamycin sensitivity of cultured tissues of *Vitis*. Plant Cell Report 9: 237-240.

FAO (Food and Agriculture Organization of the United Nations). 1986. 1985 Production Year Book. Vol. 37, FAO - Rome, Italy.

Fraley, R.T., S.G. Rogers, and R.B. Horsch. 1986. Genetic transformation in higher plants. CRC 4:1-46.

Hepburn, A.G., J. White, L. Pearson, M.J. Maunders, L.E. Clarke, A.G. Prescott, and K.S. Blundy. 1985. The use of pNJ5000 as an intermediary vector for the genetic manipulation of *Agrobacterium* Ti-plasmids. Journal of General Microbiology 131:2961-2969.

Hoekema, A., P.R. Hirsh, P.J. Hooykaas, and R.A. Schiperhoort. 1983. A binary vector strategy based on separation of *vir* and T-region of the *Agrobacterium*. Nature 303:179-181.

Hood, E.E., G.L. Helmer, R.T. Fraley, and M.-D. Chilton. 1986. The hypervirulence of *Agrobacterium tumefaciens* A281 is encoded in a region of pTiBo542 outside of T-DNA. Journal of Bacteriology 3:1291-1301.

Horsch, R.B., J.E. Fry, N.B. Hoffmann, D. Eichholtz, S.G. Rogers, and R.J. Fraley. 1985. A simple and general method for transferring genes into plants. Science 227:1229-1231.

Jefferson R.A. 1987. Assaying chimeric genes in plants: the GUS gene fusion system. Plant Molecular Biology Report 5:387-405.

Murashige, T., and F. Skoog. 1962. A revised medium for rapid growth and bioassay with tobacco tissue culture. Physiologia Plantarum 15:473-497.

Pollock, K., D.G. Barfield, and R. Shields. 1983. The toxicity of antibiotics to plant cell cultures. Plant Cell Reports 2:36-39.

Robert, M.L., M.R. Flores, and V.M. Loyola-Vargas. 1989. Growth promoting effects of certain penicillins on cultivated cells of *Bouvardia ternifolia*. Phytochemistry 28:2659-2662.

Rodrigues, R.L., and R.C. Tait. 1983. Recombinant DNA. Benjamin/Cummings Publishing Co. 236 pp.

Sehgal, J.E. 1975. Hormonal control of differentiation in leaves of sweetpotato (*Ipomoea batatas* Poir.). Beitrage Biology Pflanzen 51:47-52.

Staba, J.E. 1969. Plant tissue culture as a technique for the phytochemist. Pages 75-106 *in* Recent advances in phytochemistry, Vol.. 2, edited by M.K. Seikel and V.C. Runekles Appleton Century Croft, N.Y.

Tsay, H.S., P.C. Lai, and L.T. Chen. 1982. Organ differentiation from callus derived from anther, stem and tuber of sweetpotato. Journal of Agricultural Research China 31(3):191-198.

Valvakens, D., M.V. Montagu, and M.V. Lijsebettens. 1989. *Agrobacterium tumefaciens* mediated transformation of *Arabidopisis thaliana* root explants by using kanamycin selection. Proceeding of the National Academy of Science USA 85:5536-5540.

Waldron, C., E.B. Murphy, J.L. Roberts, G.D. Gustafson, S.L. Armour, and S.K. Malcon. 1985. Resistance to hygromycin B. Plant Molecular Biology 5:103-108.

Zambryski, P. 1989. *Agrobacterium*-plant cell DNA transfer. Pages 309-333 *in* Mobile DNA, edited by D.E. Berg and M.M. Howe. American Society for Microbiology. Washington, D.C.

Peggy Ozias-Akins, Srini C. Perera

Regeneration of Sweetpotato Plants from Protoplast-derived Tissues

Protoplasts can be isolated in high numbers from petioles of *in vitro*-grown sweetpotato plants. Protoplasts cultured in Kao and Michayluk medium containing 1 mg/L 2,4-dichlorophenoxyacetic acid and 1 mg/L benzylaminopurine begin to divide within 2 to 3 days. Division frequencies, calculated as ratio of dividing cells at 7 days to total number of protoplasts at time of culture, ranged from 1.86-9.51% depending upon isolation date and other variables. Shoot and root formation could be induced directly from protoplast-derived callus; however, fewer than five shoots were formed from 'Georgia Jet' callus over several passages. Many more roots than shoots were formed initially; thus our strategy has been to secondarily regenerate shoots from these protoplast-derived roots. This second method for shoot regeneration has led to the production of numerous shoots over several subcultures using root segments.

INTRODUCTION

Sweetpotato tissue culture has a substantial history (Henderson et al. 1984); however, use of tissue culture as a tool for genetic improvement has been hindered by the difficulty of regenerating whole plants. Two pathways for regeneration, embryogenesis and organogenesis, are possible and have been explored in sweetpotato. Embryogenesis was reported independently by Liu and Cantliffe (1984) and Jarret et al. (1984). The limitations of an embryogenic system appear to be restricted to explant type and source plant genotype. Embryogenic suspension cultures may eventually provide a stable and readily available source of protoplasts that can be used for somatic hybridization and gene transfer (Chee and Cantliffe 1988). We have taken the alternative approach, organogenesis. Culture of leaf mesophyll or petiole protoplasts of sweetpotato has previously been accomplished (Bidney and Shepard 1980; Murata et al. 1987; Otani et al. 1987; Sihachakr and Ducreux 1987). We sought to combine the capacity of protoplast-derived callus to form roots with the capacity of *in vitro*-formed roots to initiate shoots (Templeton-Somers and Collins 1986).

MATERIALS AND METHODS

Two cultivars of sweetpotato (*Ipomoea batatas* (L.) Lam.), 'Georgia Jet' and 'Red Jewel,' were used. Plants were grown in culture vessels (Magenta GA-7)

Department of Horticulture, University of Georgia, Coastal Plain Experiment Station, Tifton, GA 31793, USA.

61

containing 50 mL of basal Murashige and Skoog (1962) medium (MS) with 1/5 the normal concentration of manganese, a total of 0.4 mg/L thiamine, and 1% agar. Shoot cultures were incubated in a 16-hour photoperiod at 27°C.

Experiments to ascertain conditions for adventitious shoot development from cultured root segments were conducted with root explants taken at the time of shoot subculture (University of Georgia clone GA-117). The distal 5 cm of each excised root was divided into 1 cm segments. In some experiments, the order of the root segments was labelled. Experiments were designed to test the effects of cytokinins (kinetin, N^6-[2-isopentenyl]adenine (2iP), and benzylaminopurine (BAP) each at 0.02, 0.1, and 0.5 mg/L), carbohydrate source (sucrose, glucose, fructose, and maltose) and concentration (1-6%), and gelling agents (Gelrite, Nolan/Kelly Bio Labs; agar, Sigma A-1296). Five root segments were cultured per 10 cm plastic dish (40 segments per treatment) at 27°C under a 16-hour photoperiod (50 $\mu Es^{-1}m^{-2}$ cool white fluorescent). Each treatment included 8 culture dishes for a total of 40 root segments. After 8 weeks of culture, root and callus growth were scored as absent, moderate, or extensive and the number of shoots was recorded.

Protoplasts were isolated from petioles of in vitro-grown plants. Two enzyme solutions used consisted of 0.5% Onozuka Cellulase RS, 0.5% Macerozyme R-10, 0.05% Pectolyase Y23, and 0.5M mannitol (enzyme 1) or 1% Onozuka Cellulase RS, 0.1% Pectolyase Y23, 5mM $CaCl_2.2H_2O$, and 0.5M mannitol (enzyme 2). Enzyme solutions were adjusted to a pH of 5.8-6.0 and sterilized by filtration. Petioles were chopped and incubated in enzyme solution for 4 to 5 hours with gentle shaking. Protoplasts were filtered through Miracloth (Calbiochem), washed once with 154mM NaCl, 125mM $CaCl_2$, 5mM KCl, 5mM glucose, pH 5.6 (Menczel and Wolfe 1984), purified by floating on 20% sucrose, and washed once with culture medium. Protoplasts were cultured at a density of 1 to 5 x 105 protoplasts/mL (2 mL in a 6 cm plastic dish) in Kao and Michayluk (1975) basal salts plus 0.5M glucose, 1 mg/L 2,4-D, and 1 mg/L BAP (dark, 27°C). Each plate containing small cell colonies was diluted with 0.5 mL culture medium with the glucose reduced to 0.3M. After 4 weeks, 2 mL of culture medium containing 0.3M glucose and 0.8% SeaPlaque (FMC) agarose was added to each plate. Resulting calli were maintained on MS medium modified to contain 800 mg/L NH_4NO_3, 1400 mg/L KNO_3, 0.5 mg/L 2,4-D, 0.5 mg/L kinetin, 1.0 mg/L abscisic acid, and 0.8% agar.

Several treatments were tested for their effect on protoplast yield, viability, and division frequency. These consisted of treating enzyme solutions before use with 1% activated charcoal, growing source plants in medium supplemented with 2 mg/L silver thiosulfate (STS), and culturing protoplasts in liquid vs. agarose (0.4%) solidified media, the presence or absence of 4 $\mu g/mL$ fluorescein diacetate (FDA), or the presence or absence of 2 $\mu g/mL$ 2,6-dichlorobenzonitrile (DB). Protoplast viability was measured by staining an aliquot of protoplasts with 4 $\mu g/mL$ FDA and counting the percentage of stained (viable) protoplasts. Division frequency was calculated after 7 days by dividing the number of dividing protoplasts by the total number of protoplasts cultured.

RESULTS AND DISCUSSION

Sweetpotato roots still attached to stock shoot cultures had been observed to occasionally form buds. It has previously been shown that adventitious roots growing from cultured leaf explants of sweetpotato will spontaneously form buds *in vitro* (Templeton-Somers and Collins 1986). The frequency of bud formation in sweetpotato could be increased by explanting root segments onto the surface of semisolid MS medium without growth regulators. Under these conditions, root segments thickened slightly and produced a small number of laterals after about two weeks of culture. Buds could be detected at the earliest after three weeks of culture. The first indication of bud formation was slight swelling of the root and frequent anthocyanin production in the vicinity of the swelling. Individual segments usually produced single buds, but as many as three buds were formed in some cases.

The most notable effect on bud formation occurred with a change in carbohydrate composition and concentration in the medium. Sucrose (1%) and fructose (1%) were the only sugars that allowed considerable bud formation with 0.12 and 0.25 average number of buds/segment, respectively, formed in the same experiment. Treatments with glucose (1%) and maltose (1%) resulted in 0 and 0.02 buds/segment, respectively. It has been known for some time that glucose is inhibitory to the growth of excised dicotyledonous root cultures (Butcher and Street 1964). Lazzeri and Dunwell (1984) and Sharma and Thorpe (1989) observed an inhibitory effect of glucose on both lateral root and shoot bud differentiation from cultured root segments of *Brassica napus*. Carbohydrate concentration also had a pronounced effect on bud formation. Higher carbohydrate concentrations (up to 6%) encouraged callus formation and this effect was more pronounced with sucrose than with fructose. The addition of 1% sucrose resulted in 0.51 buds/segment, whereas 5% sucrose inhibited bud production to 0.1 buds/segment. In a separate experiment, root segments cultured on 2% and 6% fructose produced 0.22 and 0.54 buds/segment, respectively. Media for the sucrose concentration experiment did not contain any growth regulators and those for the fructose concentration experiment contained 0.02 mg/L kinetin; thus the effect of the two sugars cannot be compared from these data. However, it is clear from three different experiments that both fructose and sucrose are suitable carbohydrate sources for bud-forming root cultures of sweetpotato. There was no difference in response between filter-sterilized and autoclaved fructose. The optimum sucrose concentration for bud differentiation from potato roots was 0.5 to 1.0% and high sucrose concentrations also were found to encourage callus formation (Espinoza and Dodds 1985).

Agar (0.8%) versus Gelrite (0.2%) was tested in two experiments. One comparison, made on MS plus 3% sucrose, indicated an inhibitory effect of agar on root formation (0.18 and 0.42 buds/segment, respectively, after 8 weeks). A second experiment compared the two solidifying agents in MS plus 2% fructose and 0.02 mg/L kinetin. No significant difference in bud formation was observed between the two treatments after 8 weeks in culture. Agar did, however, noticeably inhibit lateral

63

root growth compared with Gelrite. In addition, bud development on agar appeared to be somewhat delayed when compared with Gelrite.

Light versus dark was examined in one experiment. Light promoted vigorous lateral root growth and bud formation. Distance from the root tip (scored in 3 experiments) had little effect on the ability of a particular root segment from sweetpotato to form buds. In *Convolvulus arvensis*, distance of the root segment from the root tip did not affect frequency of bud formation (Bonnett and Torrey 1965); however, in *Brassica oleracea*, the capacity for shoot regeneration was strongly dependent on position (Lazzeri and Dunwell 1984).

Three cytokinins, each at three concentrations, were tested for their ability to promote or inhibit bud formation. Data in Table 1 indicate that kinetin and BAP were not as inhibitory to bud formation as 2iP at the higher concentrations, although analysis of variance indicated no significant difference between the three cytokinins. There was a significant difference between the three concentrations tested (P<.01). Media containing kinetin and BAP at the lowest concentration (0.02 mg/L) supported a higher frequency of bud formation than any of the other cytokinin-supplemented media. Lazzeri and Dunwell (1984) found that low concentrations of kinetin were optimal for bud formation in *Brassica*. Chi-square analysis of the degree of callus formation and root growth from the adventitious root segments did not show significant differences between either type of cytokinin or concentration. However, there was clearly a trend toward increased callus formation and decreased root growth at higher cytokinin levels.

A relatively pure protoplast preparation could be obtained from *in vitro*-grown sweetpotato petioles of 'Georgia Jet' and 'Red Jewel' by digestion with either of the enzyme solutions tested (Fig. 1a). First division of protoplasts could be observed after 2 to 3 days in culture (Fig. 1b). Several treatments affected protoplast viability

Table 1. Average number of buds per root segment of sweetpotato at three concentrations of BAP, kinetin, and 2iP (35 root segments per treatment).

Cytokinin type		mg/L	
	0.02	0.1	0.5
BAP	0.50	0.10	0.18
Kinetin	0.52	0.28	0.13
2iP	0.20	0.22	0.06
Significance of main effects			
Cytokinin type	NS		
Cytokinin concentration	*		

NS = Non-significant; *significant at P< .01.

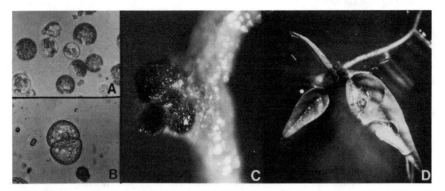

Figure 1. Sweetpotato protoplast culture and plant regeneration. (a) Freshly isolated protoplasts; (b) First division; (c) Bud formed on cultured root segment; (d) Shoot formed on cultured root segment.

and division frequency. A significant (P<0.05) improvement in protoplast viability and division frequency was observed after pretreatment of the enzyme solutions with activated charcoal. Growing the source plants in medium containing STS did not affect protoplast viability but did significantly increase division frequency. Perl et al. (1988) obtained a greater yield of protoplasts from *Solanum tuberosum* plants grown in the presence of STS, presumably due to the inhibition of ethylene generation by STS. Liquid medium was significantly better than agarose-solidified medium for protoplast division. Staining protoplasts with FDA or culturing them in the presence of DB for 24 hours did not have an effect on division frequency. In all of these experiments, protoplast yield ranged from 4.0 to 5.5 x 10^5 protoplasts per gram fresh weight of petioles, viability ranged from 70 to 98%, and division frequency ranged from 1.86 to 9.51%.

Protoplast-derived callus only formed shoots when cultured on the modified MS medium containing 0.5 mg/L 2,4-D, 0.5 mg/L kinetin, and 1.0 mg/L abscisic acid followed by MS plus 1.0 mg/L kinetin. A single cluster of shoots was obtained from 'Red Jewel,' and shoots from five calli were obtained from 'Georgia Jet.' As has been observed by others (Murata et al. 1987; Sihachakr and Ducreux 1987), the frequency of shoot formation directly from protoplast-derived callus is low, and roots can be formed at a higher frequency on a wider range of media (Murata et al. 1987). Our results show that 11 to 46% of the protoplast-derived calli subcultured onto MS plus 1 mg/L kinetin or MS basal medium formed roots during any one subculture. These roots were divided into segments and cultured on MS medium containing 2% sucrose and 0.02 mg/L kinetin to obtain buds as described above (Fig. 1c,d). The roots continued to form laterals from which segments were taken for additional passages. This strategy will allow a larger number of shoots to be derived from a finite population of protoplasts, particularly when direct shoot regeneration is not successful.

ACKNOWLEDGMENTS

This work was supported by state and Hatch funds allocated to the Georgia Agricultural Experiment Stations. Plant material was graciously supplied by Dr. Mel Hall, Department of Horticulture, Coastal Plain Experiment Station. The technical assistance of Evelyn Perry and Anne Bell and statistical advice of Ben Mullinix and Kaine Bondari are gratefully acknowledged.

REFERENCES

Bidney, D.L., and J.F. Shepard. 1980. Colony development from sweet potato petiole protoplasts and mesophyll cells. Plant Science Letters 18:335-342.

Bonnett, Jr., H.T., and J.G. Torrey. 1965. Chemical control of organ formation in root segments of *Convolvulus* cultured in vitro. Plant Physiology 40:1228-36.

Butcher, D.N., and H.E. Street. 1964. Excised root culture. Botanical Review 30:513-586.

Chee, R.P., and D.J. Cantliffe. 1988. Selective enhancement of *Ipomoea batatas* Poir. embryogenic and non-embryogenic callus growth and production of embryos in liquid culture. Plant Cell, Tissue and Organ Culture 15:149-159.

Espinoza, N.O., and J.H. Dodds. 1985. Adventitious shoot formation on cultured potato roots. Plant Science 41:121-124.

Henderson, J.H.M., B.R. Phills, and B.T. Whatley. 1984. Sweet potato. Pages 302-326 in Handbook of plant cell culture, Crop species, edited by W.R. Sharp, D.A. Evans, P.V. Ammirato, and Y. Yamada. Macmillan Publ. Co., New York.

Jarret, R.L., S. Salazar, and R. Fernandez. 1984. Somatic embryogenesis in sweet potato. HortScience 19:397-398.

Kao, K.N., and M.R. Michayluk. 1975. Nutritional requirements for growth of *Vicia hajastana* cells and protoplasts at a very low population density in liquid media. Planta 126:105-110.

Lazzeri, P.A., and J.M. Dunwell. 1984. In vitro shoot regeneration from seedling root segments of *Brassica oleracea* and *Brassica napus* cultivars. Annals Botany 54:341-350.

Liu, J.R., and D.J. Cantliffe. 1984. Somatic embryogenesis and plant regeneration in tissue cultures of sweet potato (*Ipomoea batatas* Poir.) Plant Cell Reports 3:112-115.

Menczel, L., and K. Wolfe. 1984. High frequency of fusion induced in freely suspended protoplast mixtures by polyethylene glycol and dimethylsulfoxide at high pH. Plant Cell Reports 3:196-198.

Murashige, T., and F. Skoog. 1962. A revised medium for rapid growth and bioassays with tobacco tissue cultures. Physiologia Plantarum 15:473-497.

Murata, T., K. Hoshino, and Y. Miyaji. 1987. Callus formation and plant regeneration from petiole protoplast of sweet potato, *Ipomoea batatas* (L.) Lam. Japanese Journal Breeding 37:291-298.

Otani, M., T. Shimada, and H. Niizeki. 1987. Mesophyll protoplast culture of sweet potato (*Ipomoea batatas* L.). Plant Science 53:157-160.

Perl, A., D. Aviv, and E. Galun. 1988. Ethylene and *in vitro* culture of potato: Suppression of ethylene generation vastly improves protoplast yield, plating efficiency and transient expression of an alien gene. Plant Cell Reports 7:403-406.

Sharma, K.K., and T.A. Thorpe. 1989. *In vitro* regeneration of shoot buds and plantlets from seedling root segments of *Brassica napus* L. Plant Cell, Tissue and Organ Culture 18:129-141.

Sihachakr, D., and G. Ducreux. 1987. Plant regeneration from protoplast culture of sweet potato (*Ipomoea batatas* Lam.). Plant Cell Reports 6:326-328.

Templeton-Somers, K.M., and W.W. Collins. 1986. Field performance and clonal variability in sweet potatoes propagated *in vitro*. Journal American Society Horticultural Science 111:689-694.

Poster Presentations

SHOOT REGENERATION FROM *AGROBACTERIUM*-TRANSFORMED SWEETPOTATO *IN VITRO*

Karim H. Al-Juboory
University of Baghdad, College of Agriculture, Department of Horticulture, Abu-Grahib, Baghdad, Iraq.

Robert M. Skirvin
Department of Horticulture, University of Illinois, 258 Plant and Animal Biotechnology Laboratory, 1201 West Gregory Drive, Urbana, IL 61801, USA.

Four lines of *Agrobacterium*-transformed sweetpotato (*Ipomoea batatas* L.) cv. 'Jewel' were tested for their ability to regenerate *in vitro* on media supplemented with combinations of 6-benzylamino-purine (BA) and alpha-naphthaleneacetic acid (NAA). Petiole sections and calli formed embryoid-like bodies only on Nitsch and Nitsch (NN) medium supplemented with various levels of both BA and NAA. Shoots were observed only on NN medium with both BA and NAA at 0.1 mg/L. Some of these shoots were rooted and moved to soil where they have grown for up to 2 years.

INTRODUCTION

The lack of a reliable regeneration system has limited the importance of biotechnological protocols for recalcitrant species such as the sweetpotato, *Ipomoea batatas*. For example, Eilers (1987) reported the production of *Agrobacterium*-transformed sweetpotato calli. Some of these calli differentiated sparingly on modified Murashige and Skoog (1962) medium to yield whole plants which later were confirmed to be transformants.

Roots and shoots have differentiated from repeatedly subcultured leaf-derived calli (Sehgal 1975), stem, leaf and root explants (Carswell 1981), tuberous root and petiole sections (Hwang et al. 1983), as well as leaf, stem and tuberous root explants (Carswell and Locy 1984). Somatic embryogenesis has been reported from leaf, shoot tip, stem and root tissues (Liu and Cantliffe 1984; Jarret et al. 1984). In this paper, we report reliable methods to produce shoots from transformed sweetpotato calli.

MATERIALS AND METHODS

Experiment 1. The effect of growth regulators and various media on callus growth. Uniform (ca. 1 mm diam.) clumps of TMR-338 transformed 'Jewel' sweetpotato calli initiated by Eilers (1987) were harvested 21 days after sub-culture from suspension cultures and grown on Skirvin and Chu's modification of MS medium (1979) supplemented with Staba vitamins (Staba 1969), BA (0.2 mg/L) and NAA (0.1 mg/L). These calli were transferred to various media (Murashige and Skoog 1962 [MS]; Nitsch and Nitsch 1969, [NN]; Gamborg and Eveleigh 1968 [B-5]; and White's 1943, [W], supplemented with various concentrations of BA (0, 0.1, 1.0, 2.0 mg/L) and NAA (0, 0.1, 1.0, 2.0 mg/L). Twenty-four callus pieces were transferred to each medium. All cultures were maintained in 25 x 150 mm culture tubes. The media were adjusted to pH 5.7, agar (6 mg/L) was added, and autoclaved 121°C and (1.06 Kg cm^{-2}) for 15 minutes. Cultures were maintained in a culture room at about 22°C with 16/8 hr photoperiod 40 μmol s^{-1}m^{-2}. The calli were transferred to fresh medium and their growth was assessed immediately and at one-week intervals for 8 weeks by determining their diameter with a Pickett No. 1200 circle template. Callus growth and differentiation were evaluated after 8 weeks.

Experiment 2. The effect of NN medium supplemented with BA and NAA on petiole-growth. Fully expanded leaves were harvested from a greenhouse-grown TMR338-transformed sweetpotato plant (Eilers 1987). Their petioles were removed and were disinfested by soaking for 20 min in 10% bleach solution (0.525% NaOCl) plus 5 drops of Triton X-100 as surfactant. The explants were then placed in liquid MS medium without growth regulators for either 24 or 48 hours. At the end of this time, the explants were removed from the liquid medium and redisinfested with 5% bleach for 20 minutes. The explants were rinsed 3 times with sterile distilled water. The petioles then were cultured on NN media containing the combinations of BA and NAA described in Experiment 1. Cultures were maintained in a culture room as described earlier. Cultures were examined for regeneration after 4 weeks. The experiments were repeated 2 times and the results were analyzed in a randomized complete design (RCD) with 24 petioles in each replicate.

Experiment 3. Growth and development of other transformed sweetpotato lines. Uniform clumps of calli from three other untested clones of Eiler's (1987) transformed 'Jewel' callus (AT 35-1, AT 35-2, R-1000) were moved to the regeneration medium identified in Experiments 1 and 2 [NN + BA 0.1 mg/L) + NAA (0.1 mg/L)].

The cultures were grown in the light as described above. Regeneration was assessed after 8 weeks.

RESULTS

In Experiment 1, BA significantly affected callus growth on all 3 media. It also interacted significantly with NAA and media to influence growth. NAA alone had no significant effect on callus growth, and it showed no significant interaction with media. However, NAA significantly interacted with BA and BA plus media to affect callus growth (Table 1). Shoot regeneration (40%) was observed only on NN medium supplemented with BA (0.1 mg/L) and NAA (0.1 mg/L) (Table 1).

In Experiment 2, some petiole segments formed adventitious shoots after 4 weeks on NN medium supplemented with BA at 0.1 mg/L and NAA (Table 2). The best regeneration (46.3%) and formation of embryoid-like bodies (60.2%) was

Table 1. Effects of NAA and BA and different media on growth and shoot differentiation of TMR-338-transformed 'Jewel' sweetpotato callus *in vitro*. (Original diameter = 0.1 cm) n = 24 [Experiment 1].

BA mg/L	NAA mg/L	NN media		B5 media		White's media	
		Diam.	% shoot regen.	Diam (cm)	% shoot regen.	Diam (cm)	% shoot regen.
0.0	0.0	1.00	0	0.65	0	0.25	0
	0.1	1.02	0	0.58	0	1.00	0
	1.0	0.83	0	0.45	0	0.25	0
	2.0	0.83	0	0.83	0	1.25	0
0.1	0.0	1.05	0	0.85	0	1.25	0
	0.1	0.78	40	0.55	0	1.00	0
	1.0	0.88	0	0.65	0	1.50	0
	2.0	0.38	0	1.12	0	2.00	0
1.0	0.0	1.02	0	0.70	0	1.75	0
	0.1	1.08	0	0.88	0	1.75	0
	1.0	0.80	0	0.88	0	2.00	0
	2.0	0.83	0	1.12	0	2.25	0
2.0	0.0	1.02	0	1.08	0	1.00	0
	0.1	0.88	0	1.20	0	1.50	0
	1.0	0.98	0	1.05	0	1.50	0
	2.0	0.98	0	1.50	0	1.00	0
Significance							
NAA		NS[z]		NS		NS	
BA		*		*		*	
NAAxBA		*		*		*	
NAAxMedia		NS		NS		NS	
BAxMedia		*		*		*	
NAAxBAxMedia		*		*		*	

[z]Nonsignificant; *significant at p=0.05.

observed on medium with both BA and NAA at 0.1 mg/L (Table 2, Fig. 1). Some of these shoots were later moved to soil and eventually into a greenhouse where they were grown for over 2 years.

In Experiment 3, embryogenic-like callus was observed on all three lines, but no shoot regeneration was obtained.

DISCUSSION

Callus clones used in the present study had been transformed by 2 strains of *A. tumefaciens* (338 TMR and AT 35-A 348 kan 2 [=A 35]) and 1 type of *A. rhizogenes* (R1000). The 338 TMR is an octopine producing "rooting" mutant whose T-DNA lacks the cytokinin biosynthetic gene. When the present study began, the cultures had been maintained as suspensions which had been subcultured monthly for about one year.

Table 2. Effects of Nitsch and Nitsch (NN) medium supplemented with various levels of BA and NAA on shoot regeneration from greenhouse-grown petiole explants TMR 338-transformed 'Jewel' sweetpotato petioles *in vitro* (n=24).

NAA mg/L	BA mg/L	% Shoot regeneration	% Embryogenesis[z]
0.0	0.0	0	0
	0.1	0	0
	1.0	0	0
	2.0	0	0
0.1	0.0	0	0
	0.1	46.3	60.2
	1.0	7.1	30.1
	2.0	2.5	37.8
1.0	0.0	0	0
	0.1	0	0
	1.0	0	0
	2.0	0	0
2.0	0.0	0	0
	0.1	0	0
	1.0	0	0
	2.0	0	0
Significance			
NAA		NS[y]	NS
BA		NS	NS
NAAxBA		*	*

[z]embryogenesis = formation of embryoid-like bodies.
[y]Nonsignificant; *significant at p=0.05.

Previous success with sweetpotato regeneration has been limited to organs or callused organ-derived tissue to which at least some parental tissue may have been attached (Carswell and Locy 1984; Hwang et al. 1983; Jarret et al. 1984; Liu and Cantliffe 1984a, b; Sehgal 1975). Regeneration from true callus clones has been less successful (Tsay et al. 1982).

In the present study, when 4 callus clones were transferred to NN medium supplemented with BA (0.1 mg/L) and NAA (0.1 mg/L), only TMR-338-transformed callus regenerated (Table 1). The other transformed clones (AT 35 and R-1000 [*A. rhizogenes*]) developed embryogenic-like callus only. There was no obvious reason why the TMR-338 line regenerated while the others did not.

It has been difficult to regenerate sweetpotato shoots from callus cultures of any type. In the present study, we report procedures whereby whole plants were obtained from long-term suspension cultures of *A. tumefaciens*-transformed sweetpotato cells. Some of these plants were rooted, acclimated, and are now growing in a greenhouse.

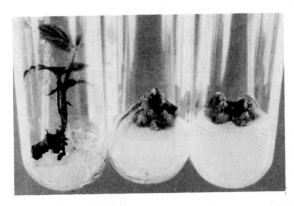

Figure 1. An adventitious shoot which has developed on a petiole of a TMR-338-transformed 'Jewel' sweetpotato clone *in vitro* (left). The middle petiole has formed embryoids and the other (right) has formed callus only.

LITERATURE CITED

Carswell, G.K. 1981. Plantlet regeneration from tissue cultures of sweet potato. M.S. Thesis. North Carolina State University, Raleigh, NC USA.

Carswell, G.K., and R.D. Locy. 1984. Root and shoot initiation by leaf, stem, and storage root explants of sweet potato. Plant Cell Tiss. Org. Cult. 3:229-236.

Eilers, R.J. 1987. Cell and tissue manipulations of sweet potato. M.S. Thesis. University of Illinois, Urbana, IL USA. 192 pp.

Gamborg, O.L., and D.E. Eveleigh, 1968. Culture methods and detection of glucanases in suspension cultures of wheat and barley. Canadian Journal of Biochemistry 46:417.

Hwang, L.S., R.M. Skirvin, J. Casyao, and J.C. Bouwkamp. 1983. Adventitious shoot formation from sections of sweet potato crown *in vitro*. Sci. Hortic. 20: 119-129.

Jarret, R.L., S. Salazar, and S. Fernandez. 1984. Somatic embryogenesis in sweet potato. HortScience 19:397-398.

Liu, J.R., and D.A. Cantliffe. 1984a. Somatic embryogenesis and plant regeneration in tissue cultures of sweet potato (*Ipomoea batatas* Poir.). Plant Cell Reports 1:112-115.

Liu, J.R., and D.J. Cantliffe. 1984b. Improved efficiency of somatic embryogenesis and plant regeneration in tissue cultures of sweet potato (*Ipomoea batatas* Poir.). HortScience 19:589.

Murashige, T., and F. Skoog, 1962. A revised medium for rapid growth and bioassays with tobacco tissue culture. Physiol. Plant 15:473-497.

Nitsch, J.G., and C. Nitsch. 1969. Haploid plants from pollen grains. Science 163:85-87.

Sehgal, C.B. 1975. Hormonal control of differentiation in leaf cultures of *Ipomoea batatas* Poir. Beitr Biol Pflanzen 51:47-52.

Skirvin, R.M., and M.C. Chu. 1979. *In vitro* propagation of 'Forever Yours' rose. HortScience 14:608-610.

Staba, J.E. 1969. Plant tissue culture as a technique for the phytochemist. Pages 75-106 *in* Recent advances in phytochemistry, Vol. 2, edited by M.C. Seikel and V.C. Runekles. Appleton-Century Croft, New York City, USA.

Tsay, H.S., P.C. Lai, and L.J. Chen. 1982. Organ regeneration from anther callus of sweet potato. Journal of Agricultural Research, China 31:123-126.

White, P.R. 1943. A handbook of plant tissue culture. Jacques Cattell Press, Lancaster, PA, USA.

Sweetpotato Technology for the 21st Century. W.A. Hill, C.K. Bonsi and P.A. Loretan (Eds.) 1992. Tuskegee University, Tuskegee, AL

RFLP AS PROBES FOR GENETIC VARIABILITY IN THE GENUS *IPOMOEA*

Yasuo Kowyama

Plant Breeding Laboratory, Faculty of Bioresources, Mie University, Tsu 514, Japan.

Tsukaho Hattori

Center for Molecular Biology and Genetics, Mie University, Tsu 514, Japan.

Tadasi Asahi, Kenzo Nakamura

Biochemistry Laboratory, School of Agriculture, Nagoya University, Chikusa-ku, Nagoya 460-01, Japan.

Restriction fragment length polymorphisms (RFLPs) of nuclear and cytoplasmic DNAs have been analyzed to reveal interspecific and intervarietal relationships in 9 *Ipomoea* species including 5 sweetpotato cultivars and 2 reference species from the distantly related genus, *Pharbitis* and *Calystegia*. Extensive RFLP variation has been found among species and even among cultivars, especially when cDNAs of nuclear genes were used as probes in Southern blot hybridization. Based on the RFLP data, a phylogenetic tree was generated using the UPG microcomputer program. Cytoplasmic DNAs of a hexaploid *I. trifida*—which was previously identified as an ancestral species—are almost identical with those of a sweetpotato cultivar, indicating that the hexaploid *I. trifida* is an extreme type of segregant in cultivated sweetpotato. Present results suggest that polyploidization of nuclear DNA played an important role in the genetic differentiation of the *Ipomoea* species throughout the evolutionary process.

Nishiyama et al. (1975) and Teramura (1979) classified the sweetpotato and its wild relatives of the genus *Ipomoea* section *batatas* into two groups, termed group A and B, based on morphological, physiological, and cytogenetical examinations, and they proposed that a hexaploid form of *I. trifida* (K123) in group B was an ancestral species of the sweetpotato. As pointed out by Jones (1967), it is still open to question whether the hexaploid plant, K123 is a progenitor or only an extreme type of segregant in cultivated sweetpotato.

Taxonomical identification of *Ipomoea* species is very difficult because of homologous variations in most morphological traits (Austin 1978, 1987). RFLP analysis has considerable potential for exploring the phylogenetic relationships among species and populations of the genus *Ipomoea*.

In the present experiment, RFLP analyses of nuclear and cytoplasmic DNAs have been carried out to reveal the phylogenetic relationships of wild species closely related to the sweetpotato.

MATERIALS AND METHODS

Twenty-one accessions including 5 cultivars of sweetpotato, 8 wild species of *Ipomoea* section *batatas* and two reference species from distantly related genera, *Pharbitis nil*, and *Calystegia hederacea,* were used in the present experiment I (Table 1). The wild *Ipomoea* species were collected in Mexico and the United States

Table 1. Plant materials used for RFLP analysis.

Plant No.	Species	Variety Accession No.	Ploidy	Taxonomic group
1	*I. batatas*	Minami-Yutaka	6*x*	B
2	"	Tama-Yutaka	"	"
3	"	Tsurunasi-Genji	"	"
4	"	Beni-Aka	"	"
5	"	Koukei No.14	"	"
6	*I. trifida*	K177	"	"
7	"	K123	"	"
8	*I. littoralis*	K233	4*x*	"
9	*I. tiliacea*	K270	"	A
10	*I. gracilis*	K134	"	"
11	*I. trifida*	K222	3*x*	B
12	*I. leucantha*	M73-3	2*x*	"
13	"	L109-51	"	"
14	"	L122-30	"	"
15	"	K221	"	"
16	"	L108-21	"	"
17	"	H3-18	"	"
18	*I. triloba*	K121	"	A
19	*I. lacunosa*	K61	"	"
20	*Calystegia hederacea*		"	
21	*Pharbitis nil*		"	

by Nishiyama (1961) and have been maintained by vegetative propagation. These *Ipomoea* species belong to groups A or B and exhibit a polyploid series from diploid to hexaploid.

Procedures for DNA isolation, restriction endonuclease digestion, electrophoresis, Southern blotting, hybridization and autoradiography were as described by Maniatis et al. (1982). Total plant DNA was isolated from lyophilized leaf tissue, and four restriction endonucleases, *BamHI, EcoRI, HindIII* and *XbaI*, were used to digest the DNA samples. Ten cloned DNA probes were used, as shown in Table 2, in which 4 probes were cDNA clones of gene encoded in nucleus of the sweetpotato (Hattori et al. 1989), and the remaining probes were obtained from mitochondrial genes of pea (Morikami and Nakamura 1987) and from chloroplast DNA of tobacco (Sugiura et al. 1986). These probe DNAs were labeled with 32P-dCTP using random oligonucleotide priming method. Based on RFLP data, a phylogenetic tree was generated using the UPG microcomputer program.

RESULTS AND DISCUSSION

As shown in Fig.1, various kinds of restriction fragment patterns were detected in the Southern blot hybridization depending upon the probes, restriction endonucleases and sample DNAs used. A high degree of RFLP was observed when nuclear

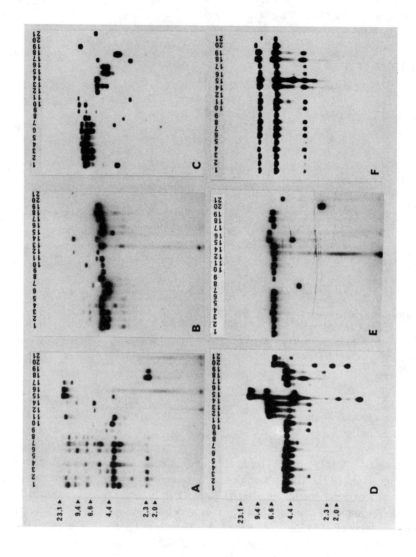

Figure 1. Southern blot analysis of *HindIII* digested total DNAs from different *Ipomoea* species with probes of sporamin B (A), COX Vc (B), β-amylase (C), ATPase (D), COX II (E) and chloroplast DNA fragment, pTBa 2 (F). Plant material number is given in the top of each panel.

Table 2. Probes used for RFLP analysis.

Probe	Probe source	Coding location	Plant source
pIMO 23	Sporamin A	Nucleus	*Ipomoea batatas*
pIMO 336	Sporamin B	"	"
pCOX 2	Cytochrome C oxidase II	"	"
pSP b A	β-amylase	"	"
pMTH 44	F1F0 ATPase	Mitochondria	*Pisum sativum*
pCOX 2	Cytochrome C oxidase II	"	"
pTBa 1	Cloned DNA fragment	Chloroplast	*Nicotiana tabacum*
pTBa 2	"	"	"
pTBa 20	"	"	"
pTS 6	"	"	"

gene probes were used, whereas probes from mitochondrial and chloroplast genes yielded fairly simple patterns of RFLP among plant materials. This indicates that genetic variation of restriction fragment alleles might have occurred more frequently in nuclear genes than in cytoplasmic genes throughout the evolutionary process of the genus *Ipomoea*. Among the nuclear genes used in the present experiment, sporamin A and B genes are members of a multigene family, while genes for COX-Vc and β-amylase are coded in a single locus of chromosome. The multigene probes such as sporamin exhibited a more abundant pattern of RFLPs among species and cultivars, as compared with the probes of a single copy gene. This shows that nuclear genes belonging to a multigene family are useful probes for the detection of RFLPs.

Phylogenetic trees of the genus *Ipomoea* generated from the RFLP data of nuclear and cytoplasmic DNA are shown in Figures 2 and 3, respectively. In the phylogenetic tree derived from RFLP patterns of nuclear DNA, diploid species of *Ipomoea* and distantly related diploid species (*P. nil* and *C. hederacea*) were clearly separated from tetraploid and hexaploid species of *Ipomoea*, suggesting that ploidy level plays an important role in genetic differentiation of the genus and species in Convolvulaceae.

In the phylogenetic tree of cytoplasmic DNA, a marked difference in RFLP pattern was observed among the *Ipomoea* species and the taxonomically distant species, *P. nil* and *C. hederacea*, suggesting that variation of cytoplasmic DNAs had occurred during the genetic differentiation of the genus in Convolvulaceae. Among the species of the genus *Ipomoea*, on the other hand, cytoplasmic variation in the RFLP pattern was rather small, when compared with nuclear variation in RFLPs. Diploid and triploid species of the group B were in a cluster and separated from sweetpotato cultivars and the other wild species belonging to groups A and B, suggesting that the diploid clones of *I. leucantha* used in the present experiment had made no contribution to evolutionary development of the sweetpotato.

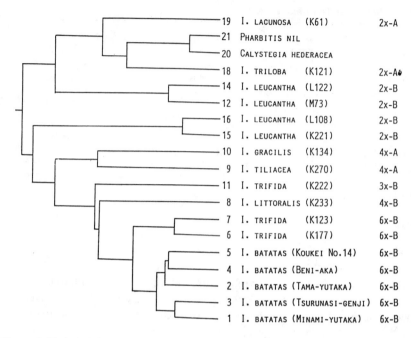

Figure 2. Phylogenetic tree of the genus *Ipomoea* derived from RFLP data of nuclear DNA.

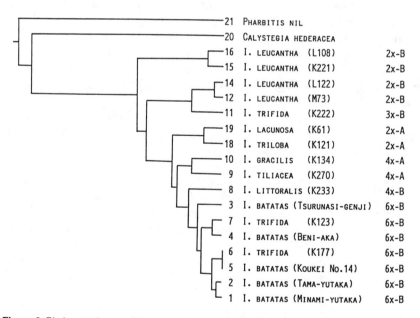

Figure 3. Phylogenetic tree of the genus *Ipomoea* derived from RFLP data of cytoplasmic DNA.

Furthermore, it is very noteworthy that cytoplasmic DNAs of the hexaploid form of *I. trifida*, K123 and K177, are almost identical with those of sweetpotato cultivars, and fall within a range of cytoplasmic variation in the sweetpotato cultivars. This finding strongly suggests that the hexaploid forms, K123 and K177, are extreme segregants of the sweetpotato rather than a different wild species, as pointed out by Jones (1967).

REFERENCES

Austin, D.F. 1978. The *Ipomoea batatas* complex. 1. Taxonomy. Bulletin Torrey Bot. Club 105:114-129.

Austin, D. F. 1987. The taxonomy, evolution and genetic diversity of sweet potatoes and related wild species. Pages 27-59 *in* Exploration, maintenance and utilization of sweet potato genetic resources, Report, 1st Sweet Potato Planning Conference, CIP, Lima, Peru.

Hattori, T., N. Yoshida, and K. Nakamura. 1989. Structural relationship among the members of a multigene family coding for the sweet potato tuberous root storage protein. Plant Molecular Biology 13:563-572.

Jones, A. 1967. Should Nishiyama's K123 (*Ipomoea trifida*) be designated *I. batatas*? Econ. Bot. 21:163-166.

Maniatis, T., E. F. Fritsh, and J. Sambrook. 1982. Molecular cloning: a laboratory manual. Cold Spring Harbor, N.Y., 545 pp.

Morikami, A., and K. Nakamura. 1987. Structure and expression of pea mitochondrial F_1ATPase a-subunit gene and its pseudogene involved in homologous recombination. Journal of Biochemistry 101:967-976.

Nishiyama, I. 1961. The origin of the sweet potato plant. Pages 119-128 *in* Proceedings, Tenth Pacific Scientific Congress, Honolulu, Hawaii, USA.

Nishiyama, I., T. Miyazaki, and S. Sakamoto. 1975. Evolutionary autopolyploidy in the sweet potato (*Ipomoea batatas* (L.) Lam.) and its progenitors. Euphytica 24:197-208.

Sugiura, M., K. Shinozuka, N. Zaita, M. Kusuda, and M. Kumano. 1986. Clone bank of the tobacco (*Nicotiana tabacum*) chloroplast genome as a set of overlapping restriction endonuclease fragments:Mapping of eleven ribosomal protein genes. Plant Science 44:211-216.

Teramura, T. 1979. Phylogenetic study of *Ipomoea* species in the section *batatas*. Memo. College of Agriculture, Kyoto University. 14:29-48.

THE BIOCHEMICAL BASIS OF N-CARBOXYMETHYLCHITOSAN-MEDIATED ENHANCEMENT OF THE STORAGE PROTEIN CONTENT OF SWEETPOTATO

Godson O. Osuji, Raul G. Cuero

Cooperative Agricultural Research Center, Prairie View A&M University, Texas A&M University System at Prairie View, P.O. Box U, Prairie View, Texas 77446, USA.

N-Carboxymethylchitosan (NCMC) was administered as 0.1% solution by soil application to sweetpotatoes growing on the farm. The soluble protein and the RNA contents as well as the activities of the NH_4^+ ion salvaging enzymes of the mature storage roots were determined by photometry. The sweetpotatoes from the NCMC-treated crop had 4% storage protein (fresh weight, FW) while the control had 2% storage protein. The RNA content of the NCMC-treated sweetpotatoes was 80% higher than the control. The glutamate dehydrogenase activities of the NCMC-treated and the control were 100 μmol min^{-1} g^{-1} and 50 μmol min^{-1} g^{-1} FW, respectively. The activities of the glutamate synthase/glutamine synthetase cycle were not altered by the NCMC-treatment of the crop. These results suggest that the NCMC enhanced the storage protein contents by enhancing the NH_4^+ ion salvage capabilities of the crop.

Sweetpotato production is an important industry globally because it is adaptable to a wide range of climatic and soil regimes (Henderson et al. 1984). It is the seventh largest food crop, and in the U.S. 85% of the crop is used as food (FAO 1981). The U.S. produced 0.5 billion kg of sweetpotato in 1987 (Walter 1988). However, sweetpotato is protein deficient, as it contains only about 2% protein on a wet weight basis (Huang 1982). It is also regarded in many countries as food for the poor (Tsou and Villareal 1982). Efforts have been made to increase its protein content (Walter et al. 1984). Breeding trials, especially in Asia from 1972 to 1979, produced high-protein (5 to 10% on dry weight basis) from hybrid progenies, but they had orange flesh color which was not acceptable to consumers (Li 1982). So far, it has not been possible to produce any high-protein sweetpotato with a white-flesh color. Although the enhancement of the protein content of sweetpotato would increase its nutritional and economic value, few attempts have been made to understand the biochemical basis of its protein-deficiency. Osuji and Ory (1986) reported losses of ammonia via purine catabolism by the roots during storage. The enhancement of the storage protein content of corn following the treatment of the crop with chitosan (Osuji and Cuero 1991) stimulated the expansion of the technology to the sweetpotato.

MATERIALS AND METHODS

Preparation of N-Carboxymethylchitosan (NCMC)

NCMC was prepared from native chitosan (Protan Lab., Redmond, WA. USA) by modifying the Vercellotti method (Cuero and Lillehoj 1990; Cuero et al. 1991).

Previous carboxymethylation of chitosan was done by reduction of glyoxylated chitosan with cyanoborohydride according to the method of Muzzarelli (1988). Sodium borohydride at pH 5 was used as a reducing agent with subsequent filtration through a 0.22 micron filter.

Treatment of sweetpotato with NCMC in the field

Field plot trials were carried out on the Prairie View A&M University farm in Waller County, Texas. A complete randomized block design (2 treatments x 3 replicates per treatment) was used on a total area of 1300 m^2. Sweetpotato (*Ipomoea batatas*, 'Gold Rush' cv.) slips were planted 0.6 m apart on ridges 25.4 cm high and 1.2 m apart in the last week of July and were harvested in the first week of December. They were hoed, weeded, and irrigated with water once per week.

Water and NCMC were applied at 30 and at 40 days after planting. Two hundred mL of distilled water or of 0.1% NCMC was poured slowly around the base of the plant to ensure even and complete soaking of the soil. No fertilizer was applied to the plants.

Four months after planting, 5 storage roots were harvested randomly from each plot, peeled carefully to minimize loss of peripheral tissues, cut into small cubes ca. 1 cm^3 and mixed thoroughly. Samples were removed for protein and other biochemical analyses.

Storage protein extraction and purification

The cubes of the storage roots (200g) were frozen and homogenized in 250 mL of ice-cold 0.05 M sodium borate buffer pH 8.4 containing 1% 2-mercaptoethanol for 3 min. The homogenate was centrifuged at 5000 g for 15 min; the pellet was rehomogenized in 250 mL of buffer and then recentrifuged at the same conditions. The first and second supernatants were combined and recentrifuged at 15,000 g for 15 min. An aliquot (50 mL) of the supernatant (storage protein extract) was then chromatographed through a column (10 x 2 cm) of DEAE-Cellulose which had been equilibrated with 0.05 M borate buffer pH 8.4. The void effluent was discarded. Non-storage proteins were washed out with 200 mL of 0.05 M Tris-HCl buffer pH 8.4. The pure storage protein was finally eluted from the column with 200 mL of 0.05 M Tris-HCl buffer pH 8.4 containing 0.15 M NaCl (Harvey and Boulter 1983).

Protein contents of the storage protein extracts, as well as the pure storage protein, were determined by the Biuret method using bovine serum albumin as standard (Gornal et al. 1949).

Polyacrylamide gel electrophoresis of storage proteins

Sodium dodecyl sulfate-polyacrylamide gel electrophoresis (SDS-PAGE) was done according to Laemmli (1970) using Tris-glycine buffer pH 8.9 containing 0.05% SDS. The sweetpotato crude protein extracts (50 μL) were added to an equal volume of sample buffer (Davis et al. 1986), heated in a boiling water bath for 2 min, then 15 μL aliquots (equivalent to proteins extracted from 3 mg storage root) were loaded into the wells of a 10% PAG. The purified storage protein of sweetpotato was also prepared and loaded into an adjacent well as a reference standard marker. A protein molecular weight marker mixture (sigma) consisting of bovine serum albumin (66,000), chicken egg albumin (45,000), bovine erythrocyte carbonic anhydrase (29,000) and bovine milk α-lactalbumin (14,200) was prepared and loaded into an adjacent well. Electrophoresis was at 100 v for 5 h, after which the gel was silver-stained according to Sigma technical bulletin (1989).

The storage protein bands in the PAG were quantified by densitometric tracing at 450 nm using Schimadzu densitometer.

Extraction of high molecular weight RNA

Total high molecular-weight RNA was extracted from 10 g of frozen cubes of sweetpotato by the method of Schuler and Zielinski (1989). After precipitating the RNA from potassium acetate solution, it was dried in vacuum, dissolved in 1 mL of distilled water and its concentration was determined by photometry at 260 nm.

Extraction and assay of enzymes of ammonium ion salvage

Glutamate dehydrogenase was extracted from 20 g sweetpotato storage root by homogenizing in a blender with 50 mL of extraction buffer for 3 min at 2°C (Loyola-Vargas and Jimenez 1984). The homogenate was frozen at -80°C for 30 min and after thawing at 0°C was centrifuged at 15,000 g for 15 min. The supernatant was used for enzyme determinations and for western blot analysis.

Glutamate dehydrogenase [GDH; EC 1.4.1.2] activity was determined by the method of Loyola-Vargas and Jimenez (1984) in Tris-HCl buffer pH 8.2 containing NH_4Cl (3-200 mM), α-ketoglutarate (10 mM), NADH (0.16 mM) and $CaCl_2$ (5 mM). Reaction was started by addition of 0.2 mL of the enzyme extract and followed by spectrophotometry at 340 nm. Final volume of the reaction was 3 mL.

Glutamine synthetase was extracted from 20 g sweetpotato by homogenization with 50 mL of extraction buffer (100 mM Tris-HCl pH 7.6 containing 1 mM $MgCl_2$, 1 mM EDTA and 10 mM 2-mercaptoethanol) (Lea et al. 1990) in a blender for 3 min at 2°C. The homogenate was centrifuged at 15,000 g for 15 min and the supernatant was used for activity determination. Glutamine synthetase (GS; EC 6.3.1.2) activity was determined in Tris-HCl buffer pH 7.8 containing hydroxylamine (3 to 80 mM), glutamate (32 mM), $MgSO_4$ (20 mM), ATP (20 mM). An aliquot (0.2 mL) of the extract was added to start the reaction. After incubation at 37°C for 30 min, 1 mL $FeCl_3$ reagent (Lea et al. 1990) was added, which brought the total volume of reaction to 3 mL. Precipitated protein was centrifuged out at 10,000 g for 5 min and the absorbance of the supernatant was determined at 540 nm. A calibration curve with authentic γ-glutamylhydroxamate was used to calculate the rates of the enzyme reaction.

Glutamate synthase was extracted from 20 g sweetpotato by homogenizing with 50 mL of extraction buffer (KH_2PO_4-KOH pH 7.5, 0.5 mM EDTA, 100 mM KCl, 0.1% 2-mercaptoethanol and 0.5% Triton X-100) in a blender for 3 min at 2°C (Lea et al. 1990). The homogenate was centrifuged at 15,000 g for 15 min and the supernatant was used for assay of enzyme activity.

Glutamate synthase (GOGAT; EC 1.4.1.13) activity was determined in KH_2PO_4-KOH buffer pH 7.5 containing glutamine (3 to 70 mM), α-ketoglutarate (16 mM), NADH (0.16 mM) and 0.2 mL of the enzyme extract (Lea et al. 1990). The absorbance of the reaction was monitored at 340 nm every min for 7 min in a Beckman DU-64 spectrophotometer. The final volume of the reaction was 3 mL. Controls without α-ketoglutarate and glutamine were also set up.

Immunochemical assay

Bovine GDH (Sigma type 1 no. 2501) was purified by ion exchange chromatography and Sephadex G-200 gel filtration (Yeung et al. 1981) and used as antigen for the production of antibody in goat (immunological properties will be published elsewhere).

For western blot analysis, the GDHs extracted from the sweetpotato were added to equal volumes of sample buffer containing SDS (Davis et al. 1986), incubated in a boiling water bath for 2 min and then 20µL aliquots (equivalent to GDH extracted from 4 mg storage root) were loaded into the wells of a 10% polyacrylamide gel (Laemmli 1970). The bovine GDH was used as control. Electrophoresis was for 4 hr at 100 v (Davis et al. 1986). Western transfer to nitrocellulose paper was done with a Bio-Rad trans-blot electrophoretic cell as described by Towbin et al. (1979) at 30 v, overnight. The buffer was 25 mM Tris, 192 mM gly, 20% methanol (pH 8.3). Immunochemical detection of the fractionated GDH was done according to the nitroblue tetrazolium and 5-bromo-4-chloro-3-indolyl phosphate method of Promega (1987), with goat anti-bovine GDH antibody and rabbit anti-goat immunoglobulin-alkaline phosphatase conjugate as second antibody. A similar denaturing polyacrylamide gel electrophoresis of the GDHs was performed, but 10µl aliquots of samples were loaded into the gel wells. Sigma molecular weight markers (bovine serum albumin, 66 KD; chicken egg albumin, 45 KD; carbonic anhydrase, 29 KD and α-lactalbumin, 14.3 KD) were loaded into adjacent wells. The gel was silver-stained after electrophoresis according to Sigma bulletin (1989).

RESULTS AND DISCUSSION

Figures 1 and 2 show that NCMC treatment increased two-fold the storage protein (ipomoein, mol. wt. 35 KD) content because in the electrophoretic fractionation (Fig. 1) the ipomoein band is thicker in the NCMC-treated than in the control crops; and in the densitometric trace (Fig. 2) the areas of the ipomoein bands were 60,000 and 30,000 for the NCMC-treated and the control crops, respectively. The Biuret assay of the protein content (Table 1) also shows that the NCMC treatment

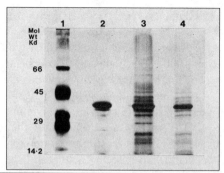

Figure 1. SDS-PAGE of the soluble protein extracts of sweetpotato. Lane 1 - molecular weight markers; Lane 2 - partially purified storage protein (ipomoein) and soluble protein extracted from 3 mg: Lane 3 - N-Carboxymethylchitosan (NCMC)-treated; and Lane 4, control sweetpotato storage roots. Electrophoresis was in 10% PAG then, after electrophoresis, the gel was silver-stained.

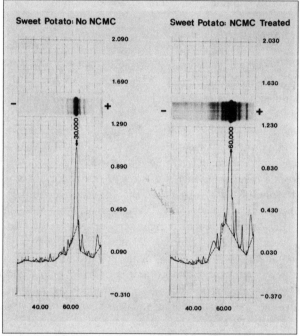

Figure 2. Densitometric traces of the electrophoretic storage protein lanes in Figure 1. Sweetpotato: NO NCMC is the trace of lane 4 while sweetpotato: NCMC Treated is the trace of lane 3 in Fig. 1. Aligned above each densitometric trace is the SDS-PAGE fractionation pattern, below which is the densitometric area of the ipomoein.

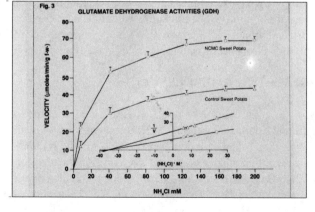

Figure 3. The effects of NCMC on the GDH activities of sweetpotato. The inset is the Lineweaver-Burk plot of the data. The concentrations of αKG and NADH were fixed at 10 mM and 0.16 mM respectively.

Table 1. The storage protein and RNA contents of sweetpotato storage roots.

Sweet potato	Protein[a](mg g^{-1})±SE	RNA[a](μg g^{-1})±SE
NCMC-treated	40.0 ± 2.0	0.123 ± 0.008
Control	20.0 ± 1.0	0.070 ± 0.005

[a]Protein and RNA concentrations are on fresh weight basis and are the averages of triplicate extractions from the sweetpotato.

doubled the storage protein content. Sweetpotato contains about 2% protein on a fresh weight basis (Huang 1982). The results in Table 1 show that the storage protein content of the NCMC-treated sweetpotato was 4.0%, while that of the control was 2.0%, giving a 100% increase in the storage protein content of the crop.

In the field, the NCMC-treated sweetpotato was not physically distinguishable from the control; neither were the storage roots different in size, shape, or color from the control.

The time during the growth of the sweetpotato at which the NCMC treatment was applied was also found to be important. In the preliminary studies, application at 2 months and at 3 months after planting did not result in higher protein levels. Double administration of the NCMC at 30 and 40 days after sweetpotato planting enhanced the protein content, possibly because storage root formation is initiated 2 to 8 weeks after planting of the crop (Wilson 1982, Hahn and Hozyo 1984). This result suggests that the deposition of storage protein in the sweetpotato storage root commences very early and that the NCMC interacted with the biochemical processes which control the accumulation of storage proteins. The above results stimulated a search for possible biochemical events that could be linked to the NCMC-mediated enhancement of the storage protein content of the sweetpotato. Table 1 shows that the NCMC-treated sweetpotato had about 80% more high-molecular-weight-RNA (mainly rRNA and mRNA) than the control. This result suggests that the NCMC increased the capacity of the sweetpotato to synthesize proteins.

Ammonium ion toxicity has been found to decrease the storage protein content of corn (manuscript in preparation). Therefore, we assayed for the activities of the ammonium ion metabolizing enzymes (GDH, GS and GOGAT) in extracts of the NCMC-treated and control crops. The initial velocities of the enzymes were determined and used for the construction of double reciprocal plots in order to derive the kinetic constants of the enzymes. Figure 3 shows that the apparent V_{max} of the GDH extracted from the NCMC-treated crop was double (100 μmol/min/g FW) that of the control crop (50 μmol/min/g FW); but the apparent Michaelis constant (K_m) was unaffected by the NCMC. Figure 4 shows that neither the apparent V_{max} nor the apparent K_m values of the GS were affected by the NCMC treatment.

Figure 5 shows that the apparent V_{max} of the GOGAT from the NCMC-treated and the control crops were the same but the NCMC treated crop had a higher apparent K_m (33 mM Gln) than the control (6 mM Gln). Ammonium ion is assimilated for amino acid synthesis mainly via the GS/GOGAT cycle (Lea et al. 1990). Although

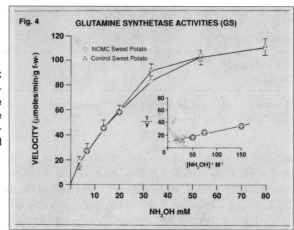

Figure 4. The effects of NCMC on the GS activities of sweetpotato. The inset is the Lineweaver-Burk plot of the data. The concentrations of L-glu and ATP were 32 mM and 20 mM respectively.

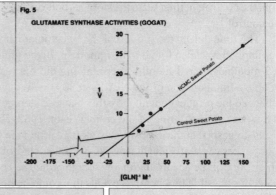

Figure 5. The effects of NCMC on the GOGAT activities of sweetpotato. The initial velocities of the enzyme were used to construct the Lineweaver-Burk plot. The concentrations of αKG and NADH were 16 mM and 0.16 mM respectively.

Figure 6 (left). Effects of NCMC on the GDH isoenzymes of sweetpotato. Western blot analysis of the GDH extracted from 4 mg of 1: untreated (control) and 2: NCMC-treated sweetpotato; 3: bovine GDH. Antibody to the bovine GDH was used as the primary antibody.

Figure 7 (right). SDS-PAGE of the GDH extracts of 2 mg of sweetpotato tubers: lane 2, untreated sweetpotato; lane 3, NCMC-treated sweet-potato. Lane 4 is the bovine GDH. After the electrophoresis, the PAG was silver-stained. Lane 1: the molecular weight markers.

84

GDH is no longer accepted as the major route for ammonium ion assimilation in plants (Rhodes et al. 1989), the doubling of its velocity in the NCMC-treated crop with the concomitant doubling of the storage protein content (Figs. 1 and 2) suggests that the enzyme is linked to protein storage metabolism in the crop. The isoenzymic patterns of the GDH extracted from the NCMC-treated and control crops were compared by immunochemical (Western blot) analyses. Figure 6 shows that both crops possess the same patterns of GDH isoenzymes, meaning that the NCMC did not induce synthesis of new isoenzyme forms of GDH. Therefore, the NCMC treatment increased the GDH activity probably by improving the catalytic conformation of the enzyme. This is one of the mechanisms by which enzyme activities are regulated (Fersht 1985). A comparison of the protein bands in Fig. 7 with the Western blot results in Fig. 6 shows that the GDH antibody was specific to the GDH; the other proteins of the sweetpotato, especially the storage protein (ipomoein, mol. wt. 35 KD), did not react with the GDH antibody.

We had earlier obtained high-protein corn by treating corn at the flowering stage with NCMC solution (Osuji and Cuero 1991). The successful expansion of the NCMC technology to double the storage protein content of sweetpotato suggests that it would be possible to apply it to other protein-deficient crops, e.g., yam tuber, cassava, and cocoyam, and thereby improve their nutritional and industrial values.

Sweetpotato is known to be inefficient in the salvage of NH_4^+ ion (Osuji et al. 1991). By doubling the velocity of the GDH (Fig. 3), the NCMC treatment possibly improved the NH_4^+ ion salvage capability, thereby doubling the storage protein content of the crop.

REFERENCES

Cuero, R.G., and E.B. Lillehoj. 1990. N-carboxymethylchitosan: algistatic and algicidal properties. Biotechnology Techniques 4:275-280.

Cuero, R.G., G.O. Osuji and E. Duffus. 1991. N-carboxymethylchitosan: uptake and effects on chlorophyll production, water potential and biomass in tomato plants. Food Biotechnology 5:95-103.

Davis, L.G., M.D. Dibner, and J.F. Battey. 1986. Polyacrylamide gels for protein separation. Pages 306-310 in Basic methods in molecular biology. Elsevier, New York.

FAO (Food and Agriculture Organization). 1981. Production Yearbook, Rome, Italy.

Gornal, A.G., C.J. Bardawill, and M.M. David. 1949. Determination of serum proteins by means of the Biuret reagent. Journal of Biological Chemistry 177:751-766.

Hahn, S.K., and Y. Hozyo. 1984. Sweet potato. Pages 551-566 in The physiology of tropical field crops, edited by P.R. Goldswort and N.M. Fiser, John Wiley, New York.

Harvey, J.P., and D. Boulter. 1983. Isolation and characterization of the storage protein of yam tuber. Phytochemistry 22:1687-1693.

Henderson, J.H.M., B.R. Phills, and B.T. Whatley. 1984. Sweet Potato. Chapt. 11 in Handbook of plant tissue culture: crop species, Vol. 2, edited by W.R. Sharp, D.A. Evans, P.V. Ammirato and Y. Yamada. Macmillan, New York.

Huang, P.C. 1982. Nutritive value of sweet potato. Pages 35-36 in Sweet potato. Proceedings, First International Symposium, edited by R.L. Villareal and T.D. Griggs. AVRDC, Taiwan.

Laemmli, U.K. 1970. Cleavage of structural proteins during the assembly of the head of Bacteriophage T_4. Nature 227:680-685.

Lea, P.J., R.D. Blackwell, F. Chen, and U. Hecht. 1990. Enzymes of ammonium assimilation. Pages 257-276 in Methods in plant biochemistry, Vol.3: Enzymes of primary metabolism, edited by P.M. Dey and J.B. Harbone. Academic Press, New York.

Li, L. 1982. Breeding for increased protein content in sweet potatoes. Pages 345-354 in Sweet potato, Proceedings, First International Symposium, edited by R.L. Villareal and T.D. Griggs. AVRDC, Taiwan.

Loyola-Vargas, V.M., and E.S. de Jimenez. 1984. Differential role of glutamate dehydrogenase in nitrogen metabolism of maize tissues. Plant Physiology 76:536-540.

Muzzarelli, R.A.A. 1988. Carboxymethylated Chitins and Chitosans. Carbohydrate Polymers 8:1-21.

Osuji, G.O., and R.G. Cuero. 1992. N-carboxymethylchitosan enhancement of the storage protein contents of maize seeds (Zea mays L.). Food Biotechnology 6(2):105-126.

Osuji, G.O., R.G. Cuero, and A. Washington. 1991. The effects of α-ketoglutarate on the activities of glutamate synthase, glutamate dehydrogenase and aspartate transaminase of the sweet potato, yam tuber and cream pea. Journal Agricultural and Food Chemistry 39:1590-1596.

Osuji, G.O., and Ory, R.L. 1986. Purine degradative pathway of yam and sweet potato. Journal of Agricultural and Food Chemistry 34:599-602.

Promega Technical Manual. 1987. ProtoBlot western blot AP system. Fish Hatchery, Madison, WI U.S.A.

Rhodes, D., D.G. Burnk, and J.R. Magalhaes. 1989. Assimilation of ammonia by glutamate dehydrogenase? Pages 157-189 in Recent advances in phytochemistry, Vol. 23: Plant nitrogen metabolism, edited by J.E. Poulton, J.T. Romeo and E.E. Conn, Plenum, New York.

Schuler, M.A., and R.E. Zielinski. 1989. RNA Isolation from light- and dark-grown seedlings. Pages 89-96 in Methods in Plant Molecular Biology. Academic Press, New York.

Sigma Technical Bulletin No. P3040. 1989. Silver-stain kits for polyacrylamide gels. Sigma Chemical Company, St. Louis, MO, USA.

Towbin, H., T. Staehelin, and J. Cordon. 1979. Electrophoretic transfer of protein from polyacrylamide gels to nitrocellulose sheets: procedures and some applications. Proceedings of the National Academy of Sciences, U.SA. 76:4350-4354.

Tsou, S.C.S., and R.L. Villareal. 1982. Resistance to eating sweet potato. Pages 37-44 in Sweet potato, Proceedings, First International Symposium, edited by R.L. Villareal and T.D. Griggs, AVRDC, Taiwan.

Walter, W.M. 1988. Sweet potato makes good french fries. HortScience 23 (6):959.

Walter, M.W., W.W. Collins, and A.E. Purcell. 1984. Sweet potato protein: A Review. Journal of Agricultural and Food Chemistry 32:695-699.

Wilson, L.A. 1982. Tuberization in sweet potato (Ipomoea batatas L.), Pages 79-94 in Sweet potato, Proceedings, First International Symposium, edited by R.L. Villareal and T.D. Griggs, AVRDC, Taiwan.

Yeung, A. T., K.J. Turner, N.F. Bascomb, and R.R. Schmidt. 1981. Purification of an ammonium-inducible glutamate dehydrogenase and the use of its antigen affinity column-purified antibody in specific immuno-precipitation and immuno-adsorption procedures. Analytical Biochemistry 110: 216-228.

EVOLUTIONARY BIOLOGY OF THE SWEETPOTATO: CURRENT KNOWLEDGE AND FUTURE RESEARCH DIRECTIONS

G. S. Varadarajan, C. S. Prakash
Plant Molecular and Cellular Genetics Laboratory, School of Agriculture and Home Economics, Tuskegee University, Tuskegee, Alabama 36088, USA.

INTRODUCTION

The sweetpotato [*Ipomoea batatas* (L.) Lam.] has been widely introduced into cultivation because of its successful growth under diverse ecological conditions. It is ranked seventh in production among world foods (Gregory 1988). By virtue of its economic importance historically, most biological studies on *Ipomoea* have been conducted on this cultivated species. Recently, research has been extending to its wild relatives as well.

The sweetpotato and nearly 15 wild species (McDonald and Austin 1990) are often classified in a taxonomic group *Ipomoea* section *batatas* in the Convolvulaceae family. In addition to the remarkable edible storage roots in sweetpotato, the *batatas* group exhibits several interesting but complex biological phenomena. These include polyploidy, self incompatibility, interspecific hybridization, sterility, and phenotypic plasticity. A number of researchers have worked on these aspects, which triggered some interesting questions on sweetpotato evolutionary biosystematics. In essence, discussions on taxonomic foundation, cytogenetic infrastructure, and the dynamic nature of reproductive compatibility among the members of this group provided a good insight into the evolutionary complexities within *Ipomoea* section *batatas*. The purpose of this work is to summarize the key evolutionary inferences gleaned from the existing literature and to develop testable, working hypotheses for future studies.

AN OVERVIEW OF EVOLUTIONARY BIOLOGY OF *IPOMOEA* SECTION *BATATAS*

Taxonomy, cytogenetics and reproductive characteristics afford the main sources of data for the evolutionary interpretations within *Ipomoea* section *batatas* (relevant references cited in Austin 1978; Nishiyama et al.1975; Nishiyama 1982).

Taxonomy
Previous studies based on field, herbarium, and experimental investigations suggest that *Ipomoea* section *batatas* includes closely related members, which may be frequently sympatrically distributed (e.g., Abel and Austin 1980; Austin 1978, 1988; Muramatsu 1980; van Ooststroom 1940). This group is almost entirely native to the New World with some regional endemics (e.g., *I. cynanchifolia, I. peruviana*) as well as geographically fairly widespread taxa. *Ipomoea littoralis* is the only exceptional member of the group confined to the South Pacific.

Interspecific hybridizations are evident in sympatric localities of several species (e.g., Abel and Austin 1980). A remarkably high degree of phenotypic plasticity presumably occurs in the wild populations. This, combined with an apparently free gene flow between species, obscures morphological discontinuities among several "diagnostic" characters causing uncertainties in the limits of several species (e.g., between *I. batatas* and *I. trifida*; *I. littoralis* and *I. batatas*). It has been generally agreed, however, that *I. trifida* or *I. trifida* and *I. triloba* together may be the closest relatives of *I. batatas* (Austin 1988).

Cytogenetics

Cytogenetic research has surveyed ploidy level variations over 50% of the species (Austin 1988), indicating a range from diploidy to hexaploidy. The basic chromosome number (x) is 15. Studies on meiotic chromosome behavior furnish evidence for the existence of at least two divergent genomes (A and B) within the group. Such studies independently conducted by various workers further suggest allopolyploidy as well as autopolyploidy to be the operative mechanisms for evolution of various taxa (e.g., Jones and Deonier 1965; Magoon et al. 1970; Nishiyama et al. 1975).

Reproductive aspects

Reproductive compatibility appears to be as plastic as the morphological traits, although three distinct levels of compatibility are frequently described (Nishiyama 1982). Reproductive criteria have also been the partial basis for the proposal of the autopolyploidy mechanism (Shiotani et al. 1970; Shiotani 1988). Together with artificial crossing experiments and fertility tests involving synthetic hybrids, this area of research has further substantiated the complexity of the genetic system within the section.

IPOMOEA SECTION *BATATAS*, A POLYPLOID PILLAR COMPLEX

Detailed analyses of taxonomic, cytogenetic, and genetic status of taxa suggest that the *batatas* group may fit in with a model of polyploid pillar, similar to a number of dicotyledonous weeds (*Phacelia*), sunflowers, and grasses (*Dactylis*) (references in Davis and Heywood 1973). The *batatas* polyploidy pillar, as visualized by us (Figure 1), is an array of phylogenetically closely related individuals with high variability between and among wild species populations. Morphological discontinuities among species are often weakly defined because of interspecific hybridization and introgression. Instances of hybridization have been documented to involve the members of the same or different ploidy levels. Natural hybridization events involving a polyploid (*I. batatas*) and one or more diploid species populations (*I. trifida*) have produced a series of apparently intergrading forms. Such forms have combined the characteristics of the diploid and polyploid taxa or even those not generally prevalent in the parental populations. Thus, for the evolutionary development of the superstructure of polyploid pillars in the *batatas* group, the diploid mem-

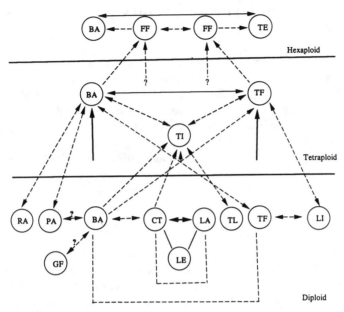

Figure 1. *Ipomoea batatas* and allies as representing a model of polyploid pillar complex. Interspecific hybridization is probably widespread among diploid species as well as between selected diploid and tetraploid species. Interspecific hybridization is apparently uncommon among tetraploids. At the hexaploid level, FF (feral forms) are the likely intermediate candidates for BA (*I. batatas*) and TF (*I. trifida*). For other details refer to text. Solid vertical lines – assumed instances of chromosome doubling; solid horizontal lines – documented instances of hybridization; broken lines – hypothesized instances of hybridization. CT - *I. cordatotriloba*, LA - *I. lacunosa*, GF – *I. grandifolia*, LE – *I. leucantha*, LI – *I. littoralis*; PA – *I. peruviana*, RA – *I. ramossissima*, TI – *I. tiliacea*, TL – *I. triloba*.

bers have provided a strong genetic foundation. This notion is further supported by the role of these diploid taxa as genome donors, as well as by their ability to be a source of morphological variability for polyploid populations by naturally hybridizing with them.

CONCLUSIONS

1. *Ipomoea* section *batatas* appears to be a monophyletic, polyploid pillar group.

2. Interspecific hybridization and polyploidy are the likely mechanisms in the evolution of the group.

3. Several fundamental issues need to be clarified in the evolutionary context of the group, which have a special significance in the improvement of the sweetpotato.

4. Molecular genetic tools that will reveal DNA variation have a great potential in addressing intriguing evolutionary issues in the group.

DIRECTION OF OUR FUTURE STUDIES ON *IPOMOEA* SECTION *BATATAS*

Our preliminary studies have shown that *Ipomoea* section *batatas* is probably monophyletic, with included members sharing the most recent common ancestral taxon. A detailed survey of literature undoubtedly provides a few interesting evolutionary inferences. Yet, it reveals some gaps in understanding the complexity of evolutionary biosystematics within the group. Of these, we are currently pursuing research in our laboratory (1) to reconstruct phylogenetic history of the section, (2) to identify the nearest diploid genome donor(s) for the polyploid taxa, and (3) to resolve the long existing controversy over the polyploidy mechanism. To investigate these issues, we employ selected molecular genetic tools.

SIGNIFICANCE

Several plant systems are characterized by evolutionary and genetic complexities similar to the sweetpotato (e.g., mustards, wheat). A clear understanding of these has enabled scientists to uncover issues of both basic and applied interests (e.g., Song et al. 1988; Tanksley et al. 1989; Wendel 1989). The use of molecular genetic approaches has helped these workers to precisely investigate or reinvestigate evolutionary and genetic aspects in the taxa. We are currently applying these approaches to *Ipomoea* section *batatas*. We foresee that our studies will help in broadening our understanding of parentage, polyploidy and genomic divergence of sweetpotato. Additionally, such studies will provide the much needed knowledge for developing specific crop improvement strategies (targeted introgression experiments, assembling various levels of polyploid populations utilizing molecular markers), and conservation of genetic resources in the wild.

ACKNOWLEDGMENTS

We sincerely thank D. Austin, R. Jarret, N. Sinha, and U. Varadarajan for their help and assistance during the course of development of this work. The research was supported by USDA (Grant No. 89-37263-4813) and USAID (DAN-5053-G-SS-906600) to CSP.

REFERENCES

Abel, W., and D. Austin. 1980. Introgressive hybridization between *Ipomoea trichocarpa* and *I. lacunosa* (Convolvulaceae). Bull. Torrey Bot. Club, 108: 231-239.

Austin, D. 1978. The *Ipomoea batatas* complex- I. Taxonomy. Bull. Torrey Bot. Club, 105: 114-129.

Austin, D. 1988. The taxonomy, evolution, and genetic diversity of sweet potatoes and related wild species, Pages 27-59 *in* Exploration, maintenance, and utilization of sweet potato genetic resources, International Potato Center, Lima, Peru.

Davis, P., and V. Heywood. 1973. Principles of Angiosperm Taxonomy, Krieger Publishing

Company, Huntington, NY.

Gregory, P. 1988. Sweet potato research at CIP, Pages 11-16 *in* Exploration, maintenance, and utilization of sweet potato genetic resources, International Potato Center, Lima, Peru.

Jones, A., and M. Deonier. 1965. Interspecific crosses among *Ipomoea lacunosa, I. ramonii, I. trichocarpa*, and *I. triloba*. Bot. Gaz. 126:226-232.

McDonald, A., and D. Austin. 1990. Additions and changes in *Ipomoea* section *batatas* (Convolvulaceae). Brittonia, 42:116-120.

Magoon, M., R. Krishnan, and K. Vijay Bai. 1970. Cytological evidence on the origin of sweet potato. Theor. Appl. Genet. 40:360-366.

Muramatsu, M. 1980. Main taxonomical characters in the close relatives of sweet potato, *Ipomoea batatas*, and their hybrid lines. Japan J. Breeding (supplement), 30:221-222.

Nishiyama, I. 1982. Autohexaploid evolution of the sweet potato, Pages 263-274 *in* Sweet potato, edited by R. L. Villareal and T.D. Griggs, Proceedings of the First International Symposium, Asian Vegetable Research and Development Center, Taiwan.

Nishiyama, I., T. Miyazaki, and S. Sakamoto. 1975. Evolutionary autoploidy in the sweet potato (*Ipomoea batatas* (L.) Lam.) and its progenitors. Euphytica, 24:197-208.

Shiotani, I., I. Nishiguchi, and S. Mitsuishi. 1970. Cytogenetic studies of basic genomes for producing sweet potato, Pages 36-68 *in* Studies on artificial synthesis of sweet potato plants, Mie Prefecture, Univ. of Mie, Tsu.

Shiotani, I., 1988. Genomic structure and the gene flow in sweet potato and related species, Pages 61-74 *in* Exploration, maintenance, and utilization of sweet potato genetic resources, International Potato Center, Lima, Peru.

Song, K., T. Osborn, and P. Williams. 1988. *Brassica* taxonomy based on nuclear restriction fragment length polymorphism (RFLPs). 1. Genome evolution of diploid and amphidiploid species. Theor. Appl. Genet. 75:784-794.

Tanksley, S., N. Young, A. Paterson, and M. Bonierbale. 1989. RFLP mapping in plant breeding: new tools for an old science. Bio/Technology 7:257-264.

van Ooststroom, S. 1940. The Convolvulaceae of Malaysia III. The genus *Ipomoea*, Blumea 3: 481-582.

Wendel, J. 1989. New World tetraploid cottons contain Old World cytoplasm. Pages 4132-4136 *in* Proceedings, National Academy of Science, USA. Vol. 86.

ANALYSIS OF GENOMIC VARIATION IN THE SWEETPOTATO THROUGH DNA FINGERPRINTING

G. S. Varadarajan, N. K. Sinha, C. S. Prakash

Plant Molecular and Cellular Genetics Laboratory, School of Agriculture and Home Economics, Tuskegee University, Tuskegee, Alabama 36088, USA.

INTRODUCTION

Polymorphic DNA markers provide powerful and precise means to investigate the genomic biology, construct genetic maps, and to elucidate evolutionary phenomena in several crop species (reviewed in Helentjaris 1989). Such investigations have applications in gene tagging, gene cloning, and marker-based breeding and in determining precise evolutionary changes (Bonierbale et al. 1988). In the sweetpotato [*Ipomoea batatas* (L) Lam.], a genetic map and a broad understanding of its evolutionary history seem to have enormous potential for the improvement of this crop. Prior to achieving these goals with a broad-based restriction fragment length polymorphism (RFLP) approach, we are interested in understanding the spectrum of genetic variation among the individual genotypes of *I. batatas* and some of its immediate allies.

DNA variation

A plant genome consists of several subsets but broadly includes low copy (unique), moderately repetitive, and multiple copy, hypervariable regions. Our long term goal is to study DNA polymorphism in hypervariable, multiple copy regions, and low copy and moderately repetitive regions of the sweetpotato genome. We apply DNA fingerprinting techniques to study variation in the multiple copy regions and RFLP techniques to study low copy and moderately repetitive regions of the genome. This paper describes our preliminary studies on DNA fingerprinting of the sweetpotato.

DNA fingerprinting approach

Variations in highly repetitive regions and multiple copy genomic sequences allow the recognition of characteristics that are specific to individuals (Jeffreys et al. 1985; Rogstad et al. 1989; Westneat et al. 1988). Such characteristics are often described as DNA fingerprints. Several workers (Dallas 1988; Nybom et al. 1990) have applied the DNA fingerprinting approach to estimate genetic relationships among individual members (genotypes) of a plant species/ population. We have used this technique to assess genetic similarity among various accessions of the sweetpotato, and it is being extended to some of the allied species. The studies outlined in this paper aimed to optimize the methodology in the sweetpotato system in order to identify informative probe-enzyme combinations and to develop DNA finger-printing data for assembling representative genotypes for RFLP studies.

MATERIALS AND METHODS

Developing autoradiographs of DNA profiles

DNA was extracted from various individuals (cultivars) of the sweetpotato and its related species (Varadarajan and Prakash 1991). Eight or ten µg DNA was enzymatically digested, the restriction fragments electrophoretically size fraction-ated by agarose gel electrophoresis, and vacuum transferred to nylon membranes (Gene Screen plus, Dupont; Hybond-N, Amersham). DNA bound to membranes was immobilized by UV crosslinking and baking (Ausubel et al. 1988) in an oven at 80°C for one hour. A human minisatellite repeat sequence 33.15 (Jeffreys et al. 1985) was radioactively labeled (Feinberg and Vogelstein 1983), hybridized to the target DNA of *I. batatas,* and the hybridized blots were washed in low stringency buffers (Sambrook et al. 1989) and examined by autoradiography.

Identification and evaluation of DNA fingerprints

Image analysis
Autoradiographs were subjected through an Image Analyzer (BIOSCAN) to detect DNA fingerprints. The image analyzing equipment consists of a videocamera (Dage, MTI 81), a fluorescent light source, and various diffusion filter attachments. First, a scannable image of the autoradiograph developed by the camera was transferred to the monitor of the Image Analyzer, where luminance was analyzed (OPTIMAS, 1990) for the autoradiograph. Luminance analysis involved screening each sample at equal, specified segments of the image. Luminant areas could be graphically reproduced for clear viewing after exporting the readings to Microsoft Excel (2.1d). The graphic representations portrayed luminant (which generally correspond to the "bands") as well as nonluminant areas. The intensity of luminance at each segment was averaged from the gray value scale along the specified sampling area. The scanned, analyzed image was frozen by TARGA Image board (M8, 1987) and stored in an 80386 based IBM compatible computer.

Statistical evaluation of DNA fingerprints
Luminance readings, peaks, and charts were closely examined to identify the band areas on the frozen autoradiographic image. The crude image consists of luminant points that represent both "signal" and "noise." From these many "definite" loci (=bands) were identified on the basis of band-sharing by at least 50% of the individuals in a population. The shared bands lacking significant (p>0.05) intralocus luminance variation were considered to represent the "actual" locus. Using luminance range (mean plus three standard deviations), the statistical signifi-cance of other "independent" bands was determined, eliminating some bands from

the crude image. Analyses of variation (ANOVA), population mean, and confidence limits of clusters (see below) were performed using the statistical package SAS (1985; fifth edition).

Estimation of genetic similarity among individuals of a population

Statistically significant bands were sequentially numbered from high to low molecular weight fragment sizes, and recorded as being present or absent in a data matrix. Unique and polymorphic bands were individually scored although, in some instances, such bands differed from the nearest, otherwise shared bands only by a few hundred base pairs. The data matrix was analyzed by the UPGMA clustering approach (Sokal and Sneath 1973), from which similarity coefficient for the population was determined.

RESULTS AND DISCUSSION

Autoradiographs of Southern blot analysis involving sweetpotato DNA, digested by *Dra* I, *Hae* III, and *Hin* f I enzymes, hybridized to the 33.15 probe, revealed multiple bands. Southern hybridization in several genotype samples produced a continuous smear of bands in which individual loci were difficult to discern and score for further analysis. The lack of demarcation of individual bands has been a common, major problem in several DNA fingerprinting studies involving multiloci probes (e.g., Demas and Wachtel 1991; Dallas 1988; Zimmerman et al. 1989). Apparently, this is primarily due to a very high copy number (usually in millions) of homologous sequences found in the adjacent restriction fragments and to some extent to a high radioactive background. Therefore, the DNA fingerprinting approach by itself needed a more powerful and sensitive detection component that would insure a clear identification.

Image analysis (Figure 1) provides a direct means to identify a band region much more clearly. Statistical tests performed on the luminant areas enabled us to objectively eliminate the "noise" level and enhance the "signal" level (Figures 2a and 2b) such that the phenograms (Figure 3) could be constructed exclusively on the basis of statistically significant bands.

The 33.15 probe revealed more polymorphic bands in *Dra* I and *Hae* III digests than in *Hin* f I digest. Polymorphism among the sweetpotato genotypes is evident in at least one locus. Cluster analysis suggests that a certain genotype (PI 531136) may be genetically more divergent than the remaining members of the population as revealed by Southern hybridizations in *Dra* I and *Hae* III digests (Figure 3).

Possible extensions of DNA fingerprinting technique

It is encouraging that each of the sweetpotato genotypes tested produced a clearly identifiable band pattern. Thus an extension of this technique with a much larger sample size would determine the applicability of the technique for unambigu-

SWP.CULT.33.15 HAE III

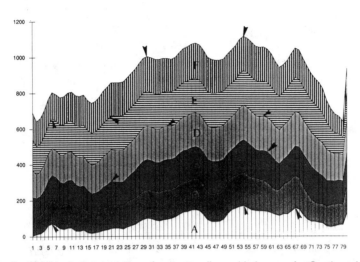

Figure 1. Graphical representation of an autoradiographic image of a Southern blot of six sweetpotato cultivars following image analysis. Genomic DNA of these cultivars were digested by *Hae* III and probed with a human minisatellite sequence 33.15. Vertical axis- range of luminance. Horizontal axis- (1 through 79) points of luminance readings. Arrows- Peak luminant areas (bands). A through F, sweetpotato cultivars: A- Jewel, B- PI 531143, C- NC 345, D- NC 312, E- NC 196, F- PI 531136.

Fig. 2. Autoradiographic image of Southern blot produced by the image analyzer. Genomic DNA of 6 cultivars of sweetpotato (A –F, Fig. 1), digested by *Hae* III, was probed with a human minisatellite sequence 33.15). Luminance records reveal high luminant areas (peaks, Fig. 1) in various sizes (kilobases) of DNA profile, marked by horizontal bars. 2a. Horizontal bars correspond to luminant areas that include "noise" and "signal," prior to statistical tests. 2b. Horizontal bars represent "signal" (statistically significant bands or restriction fragments) after statistical tests.

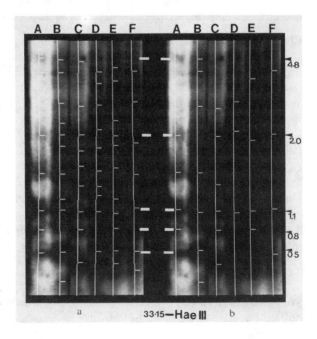

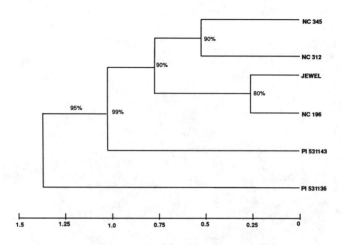

Figure 3. Phenogram of six sweetpotato cultivars based on 28 statistically significant bands identified from Southern blots. Genomic DNA of these cultivars were digested by *Hae* III and probed with a human minisatellite sequence 33.15. Similarity coefficient = 0.67.

ous identification of the cultivars. With the improvements that have been introduced into the methodology, we foresee the applications of DNA fingerprinting in the following areas: elimination of duplications of genotypes/ accessions in germplasm, identification of most divergent parental genotypes for crossing experiments, and assembling of genetically representative genotypes for RFLP studies.

SUMMARY AND CONCLUSIONS

1. The multilocus probe human minisatellite sequence 33.15 has revealed polymorphic, hypervariable restriction fragment lengths in the cultivar accessions of the sweetpotato.

2. Restriction enzymes *Dra* I and *Hae* III produced more hypervariable, polymorphic restriction fragments than *Hin* f I or other enzymes.

3. Image analysis and statistical tests on luminant areas facilitated precise and objective identification of individual bands in the Southern blots.

4. Each cultivar of the sweetpotato exhibits individual patterns of variation in the highly repetitive, multiple copy genomic regions.

ACKNOWLEDGMENTS

We greatly acknowledge A. Jeffreys and B. Ledwith for the generous supply of probes; Usha Varadarajan for her valuable assistance in DNA experiments; Jack

Kirkman for the Image Analysis; Roger Hagerty, Sue Loomis, and Arlington Weithers for their help in photography and image formatting; and W. Collins and R. Jarret for the supply of plant material of the sweetpotato cultivars and related species. Grants USDA # 89-37263-4813, USAID #DAN-5053-G-SS-906600, and RCMI - G 12 RRO 3059 01A1 have supported this research.

REFERENCES

Ausubel, F.M., R. Brent, R.E. Kingston, D.D. Moore, J.A. Seidman, J.A. Smith, and K. Struhl. 1988. Current Protocols in Molecular Biology. John Wiley & Sons, New York.

Bonierbale, M., R. Plaisted, and S. Tanksley. 1988. RFLP maps based on a common set of clones reveal modes of chromosomal evolution in potato and tomato. Genetics 120: 1095-1103.

Dallas, J.F. 1988. Detection of DNA fingerprints of cultivated rice by hybridization with a human minisatellite DNA probe. Proc. Natl. Acad. Sci. USA 85: 6831-6835.

Demas, S., and S. Wachtel. 1990. DNA fingerprinting in reptiles: Bkm hybridization patterns in Crocodilia and Chelonia. Genome 34: 472-476.

Feinberg, A.P., and B. Vogelstein. 1983. A technique for radiolabeling DNA restriction endonuclease fragments to high specificity. Analytic Biochemistry 132: 6.

Helentjaris, T. 1989. Future directions for plant RFLP technology and its applications. Pages 159-162 in Development and application of molecular markers to problems in plant genetics, Cold Spring Harbor Laboratory, New York.

Jeffreys, A., V. Wilson, and S.L. Thein. 1985. Hypervariable minisatellite regions in human DNA. Nature 314: 67-73.

Nybom, H., S. Rogstad, and B. Schaal. 1990. Genetic variation detected by the use of M 13 DNA fingerprint probe in Malus, Prunus, and Rubus (Rosaceae). Theor. Appl. Genet. 79: 153-156.

Rogstad, S., J. Patton, and B. Schaal. 1988. A human minisatellite probe reveals RFLPs among individuals of two angiosperms. Nucleic Acids Research 16: 11378.

Sambrook, J., E. Fritsch, and T. Maniatis. 1989. Molecular cloning. A Laboratory Manual, second edition. Cold Spring Harbor Laboratory Press, New York.

Sokal, R., and P.H.A. Sneath. 1973. Numerical Taxonomy. Columbia University Press, New York.

Varadarajan, G.S., and C.S. Prakash. 1991. A rapid and efficient method to extract DNA from sweetpotato and its related species. Plant Mol. Biol. Reporter 9: 6-12.

Westneat, D., W. Noon, H.K. Reeve, and C. Aquadro. 1988. Improved hybridization conditions for DNA fingerprints probed with M 13. Nucleic Acids Research16:4161.

SECTION 2

GROWING SYSTEMS

Sweetpotato Technology for the 21st Century. W.A. Hill, C.K. Bonsi and P.A. Loretan (Eds.) 1992. Tuskegee University, Tuskegee, AL

William M. Knott

Space Agriculture

As part of the Controlled Ecological Life Support System (CELSS) program, researchers are studying ways to make plants the central recycling component of a life support system for long duration space flights. Monitoring and control technologies, cultural methodologies, and physiological research data for selected crop species must be developed in order to make this possible. The development of these technologies and science data bases is concentrating on growing crops under controlled environmental conditions. This highly managed agricultural system must contain sensitive, reliable, and long lasting sensors and expert control systems and must be automated, light weight, miniaturized, and conservative in energy use. For systems that will be deployed in free space, all components must also be capable of operating in microgravity. The physiological data which must be collected on the crop species to be used in a CELSS differs significantly from those which have been developed for conventional agricultural situations. The CELSS crop physiologists are not concerned about field conditions, and therefore such problems as cold, drought, pests, wind, and salinity are of little concern to these researchers. The CELSS researchers can create any environment at any time; thus their challenge is to develop the scientific understanding and protocols that enable them to utilize this environmental control capability to optimize crop growth and productivity. Deployment of a CELSS in free space will require that we understand the influence of microgravity on the physiology of crop plants. Before plants will ever be used in space for life support, scientists must learn more plant physiology than we have ever known before and develop reliable monitoring and control systems for plant growth.

INTRODUCTION

At some unspecified time in the future, human beings will embark upon space voyages that are years in duration or possibly leave earth never to return. In order to undertake such pioneering voyages, life support systems that are different from any that have been used on earth or in space to date must be developed. These systems must operate under the driving principle that all or most of the mass on the space craft that the humans require for their life support must be recycled on some predetermined time frame. These trips will be initiated without sufficient reserves of life support constituents (oxygen, water, and food) to sustain the crew for the duration of the mission. Therefore, a life support system must be in place which will generate

National Aeronautics and Space Administration, Mail Code MD-RES, Kennedy Space Center, FL 32899, USA.

the oxygen, water, and food required by the crew and recycle CO_2 along with liquid and solid wastes, hereafter referred to as "resources" since this system cannot have wastes—only materials to be used to regenerate the life support constituents. One may think of such an activity as trying to consolidate many of the earth's life support processes into a medium size house. The central process by which the earth maintains its life support capabilities is photosynthesis, but several additional biological processes are essential for the maintenance of earth conditions conducive for human existence, especially those of microorganisms.

To date, all space crafts have taken sufficient stored materials to supply the life support requirements for the crew. Some minimal cleansing of the craft's environment by selected physical chemical processes (for example, atmospheric CO_2 is removed from the shuttle by lithium hydroxide cannisters) is routine. Recycling life support systems for long duration space flights, on the other hand, will not include sufficient supplies to complete the mission; therefore, at least some material must be recycled. These recycling systems will consist of both biological and physical chemical components united in a highly managed computer Controlled Ecological Life Support System (CELSS) which is specific to meeting the life support requirements of the crew. The actual components such a system will include are currently unknown and will probably differ depending on the mission for which it is being developed.

The research and technology development necessary for such systems will require several years of work. NASA's CELSS program is currently focusing on plants including agricultural crops and algae as the primary recycling component for these systems. An understanding of the physiology of these biological organisms being grown under controlled environmental conditions is essential for the operation of a CELSS. Environmental response surfaces for each crop species to be incorporated into a system must be determined and the necessary horticultural procedures to maintain the plant established. If the space mission is to occur primarily in free space, then the physiological effects of microgravity on plant growth and productivity must be determined. Technologies that will monitor the conditions within the controlled environment so that acceptable environmental conditions can be maintained for plant growth are required along with sensors that will monitor plant health. Expert computer control systems that will take inputs from these various sensors and maintain an acceptable environmental state in the system are crucial to the successful development of a CELSS. The primary purpose of this paper is to outline some of the research and technology required to develop the agricultural or biomass production component of a CELSS and to summarize some of the research already completed in this area especially that conducted as part of the CELSS Breadboard Project at the Kennedy Space Center.

CELSS Breadboard Project

The primary goal of the Controlled Ecological Life Support System (CELSS) Breadboard Project is to design, construct, and test a groundbased CELSS at a one person scale (Prince and Knott 1989). The successful development and operation of such a system will establish the feasibility of producing an operational CELSS that will meet the life support requirements for crews during long duration space flight. A plan for the CELSS Breadboard Project was written and approved in 1986 (Koller 1986). The project was initiated primarily because research results on certain crops suggested productivity was sufficiently high to allow a CELSS to be economically feasible (Salisbury and Bugbee 1989; Wheeler and Tibbitts 1987). However, productivity estimates based on small scale laboratory studies cannot always be relied upon to predict the production of a large scale operational system.

Biomass production is the central module of an integrated functioning CELSS. It is one of the four modules being developed for the Breadboard Project; the other three are food preparation, biomass conversion, and resource recovery. Biomass production activities involve the growth of crops under environmentally controlled conditions using thin film hydroponics in a sealed environment and under artificial lighting. Edible biomass produced in the Biomass Production Chamber is removed and transported to laboratories adjacent to the chamber for processing into food. Biomass conversion activities include various reactors, such as enzyme digesters, single cell protein reactors, and aquaculture which will process inedible biomass into usable products. The resource recovery module converts materials commonly referred to as waste to plant nutrients, inorganic elements to plant fertilizer and organic substances to CO_2 and water. The primary data sets collected during each trial run of the components of the Breadboard CELSS are documenting mass flows, energy use, and manpower requirements for the operation of each individual module or appropriate subcomponents.

A unique facility, the Biomass Production Chamber (BPC), was constructed as the biomass production module for the Breadboard Project in 1987. The BPC (Fig. 1) is a large steel cylindrical chamber approximately 3.5 meters in diameter by 7.0 meters high that was modified to grow plants (Prince et al. 1987). The chamber consists of two floors with eight stainless racks fitted into each floor. Each rack supports two lamp banks, one positioned approximately 1.5 meters and the other 3 meters from the floor. Under each lamp bank is an adjustable platform approximately 0.5 m^2 in area for growing plants. The two floors of the chamber, each with two growing levels, make a total chamber growing area of approximately 20 m^2. The lamp banks and platforms on the 16 racks are shaped like isosceles trapezoids. Three 400 watt high pressure sodium lamps are fitted into each lamp bank (96 total in the chamber) providing approximately 1000 $\mu m/m^2/sec$ PPF (photosynthetic photon flux) at approximately 5 centimeters below the lamp fixture. Two eight step dimmers for each growing level allow for manual and computer control of the lighting system for intensity and photoperiod. Monitoring sensors for irradiance, temperature, and humidity are positioned, one set on each of the four growing levels.

Two separate air handling systems are attached to the chamber, one per floor or chamber compartment. Each air handling system consists of a network of stainless steel ducts, blowers, cooling coils, filters, and one 15 ton chiller. This air handling system supplies ventilation air at the rate of .3 m/sec into the chamber between the lamp banks and the plant growing trays. The air exits the chamber through the lamp

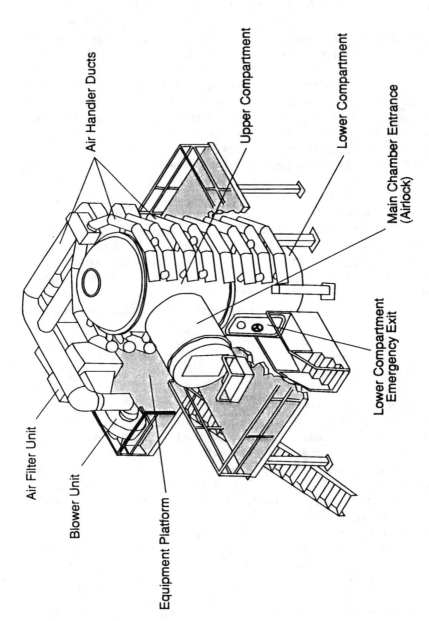

Air Handler Ducts

Upper Compartment

Lower Compartment

Main Chamber Entrance
(Airlock)

Air Filter Unit

Blower Unit

Equipment Platform

Lower Compartment
Emergency Exit

Figure 1. The Biomass Production Chamber

banks and returns to the ducting system for conditioning and filtering. Air exiting the chamber passes first through the blower, then across the cooling coils and finally through the roughing and absolute filters, before it returns to the chamber. The blowers move the sealed atmosphere of the chamber sufficiently to turn over the internal volume of the chamber approximately every 17 seconds or three times a minute. Temperature and humidity are controlled by the chilled and warm water system and through atomized water injection. Atmospheric carbon dioxide and oxygen are monitored continuously and carbon dioxide is controlled by a compressed gas delivery system (Sager et al. 1988).

Plants are grown in the BPC by a nutrient film technique (NFT). The isosceles trapezoid shaped plant growth trays cover about 1/2 of one rack platform or .25 m^2 (Mackowiak et al. 1990). Sixteen trays (4 m^2) occupy each growing level for a total of 64 trays in the BPC (16 m^2). A plastic winged plant support system holds the plants approximately 50 mm above the nutrient film. Once the seeds are placed in the tray, a germinating hood is placed over each tray for 4 days, removed, and then a support cage placed around each platform. A modified 1/2 strength Hoagland solution is supplied to each plant growing level from a 250 liter plastic tank. The nutrient solution is pumped to the back of each tray where an emitter supplies the solution in a thin film across each tray bottom. Solution flow from each tray is controlled at approximately one liter per minute. After the nutrient solution passes through the roots of the plants, it returns by gravity to the storage tanks and is then recycled to the tray system. The pH of each of the four systems is controlled continuously through the injection of nitric acid. Water is replenished daily from a dionized water tank, and the nutrient solution is replenished from concentrate stock solution as required. Each of the four nutrient delivery systems are monitored continuously for pH, conductivity, temperature, dissolved oxygen, flow rate, and liquid level. A sample is removed from each tank every three days for a total inorganic ion analysis.

The central controller for the BPC is a programmable logic computer (PLC) (Hilding et al. 1987). The PLC is programmed in ladder logic and each parameter is controlled through a PID loop system. An AT computer frontends the PLC and has a menu driven program for inputting control parameters for the BPC. A monitoring system totally separate from the control system is operated through a second AT computer. This monitoring system has sensors separate from the control sensors and the data are displayed on the computer screen in either tabular or graphic form. Most of the chamber parameters are monitored continuously and five minute averages are stored in the computer. Both control and monitoring data are archived in a central HP 9000 computer. The local AT computers and the central HP 9000 are equipped with statistical packages which allow for the analysis and summarization of the data.

PLANT STUDIES IN THE BPC

Three crop plants, wheat (*Triticum aestivum* L.) soybean (*Glycine max* L.), lettuce (*Lactuca sativa* L.), have been grown through entire life cycles in the BPC. The growout study for each crop species has been replicated at least three times. The entire BPC was planted at one time for each of the studies and harvested all at the same time at the conclusion of the growth period. Environmental conditions under which each crop was grown were determined by research conducted previously at various universities. At each harvest, the data collected on each crop include: fresh and dry weights of total biomass, fresh and dry weights of edible biomass, total leaf area, elemental analysis of the biomass, proximate analysis of the edible biomass, and ultimate analysis of elemental concentrations of the total biomass. During each growout, carbon dioxide exchange rates are calculated from the rate of carbon dioxide increase during the dark cycle and the rate of carbon dioxide decrease after the lamps are turned on each day. Oxygen and condensate water production are measured and recorded each day. At specified times in the life cycle, environmental conditions such as irradiance levels, relative humidity, and temperature are varied and carbon dioxide exchange rates and evapotranspiration rates are measured and recorded for each change in environmental parameter. Daily atmospheric samples are taken from the BPC for analysis to determine trace organic contaminants. One gas chromatograph is on line to the chamber and monitors continuously for low carbon hydrocarbons especially ethylene. The atmosphere, chamber surfaces, nutrient solutions, and condensate water are analyzed periodically for microbiological constituents. The nutrient solutions and condensate water are also analyzed for total organic carbon and selected trace organic contaminants that are expected to be present. The plant studies within the BPC allow us to characterize the growth of each crop through its entire life cycle, to determine gas and water exchange rates under various environmental conditions, to measure mass and energy fluxes through a growing crop community, and to identify any chemical or microbiological contaminants that may build up in a closed system.

The chamber has operated throughout each growout study with no major breakdowns. Results from growout studies for wheat and soybean in the BPC suggest that a facility of this type may produce enough edible biomass, water, and oxygen and recycle enough CO_2 to meet the life support requirements for one person (Table 1). Results from the soybean growout studies are similar to those given here for the wheat studies. The primary deficiency that resulted during BPC growout studies was the insufficient production of edible biomass. Research studies suggest that this deficiency can be overcome with proper manipulation of the environmental conditions under which the plants are grown. Many additional studies need to be conducted in the BPC, but these initial ones suggest that a life support system based on plants is probably feasible.

RESEARCH AND ENGINEERING ISSUES

Much research relative to growing plants in space for agricultural purposes needs to be completed prior to NASA making a commitment to the development of biological regenerative life support systems. Crop research questions include the identification of species and varieties best suited for controlled environment condi-

Table 1. Production of wheat in the Biomass Production Chamber (BPC)*

Parameter	Current Yield (g day^{-1})	Persons Supported by BPC	Area Rqmt. per Person (m^2)
Seed	310	0.4	40
Total Biomass	780	0.6**	28
Water (L day-1)	120	6.9	2.3
CO$_2$ (removed)	1300	1.3	12
O$_2$	960	1.2	14

*Area = 16 m^2; irradiance = 1/3 full solar.
**25% of inedible (straw and roots) converted to food.

tions and the documentation of growth and productivity for each species' growth and productivity over response surfaces for the major environmental parameters. This research will differ significantly from classical agricultural crop studies because the plant does not have to fit within established climatic conditions, but we must determine the best conditions under which the plant should be grown. What are the optimal environmental conditions for the growth and productivity of each crop, and do these conditions differ depending on the stage in the life cycle of the plant? What are the basic mechanisms which control formation of the edible biomass for each crop, and can we control the formation of these organs? Can we improve the basic processes of photosynthesis, respiration, and/or transport in the plant in order to enhance plant growth and productivity? Is the genetic potential, currently available in existing crop species, sufficient to maximize productivity under controlled environment conditions, or will genetic engineering be required in the future? Can we produce a nutritional and psychologically satisfying diet from a limited number of crop species? Can we efficiently convert inedible biomass into an edible product or should we concentrate on crops species which have a high harvest index? These and many additional questions need to be researched over the next several years before one may consider a CELSS as operational.

Several engineering issues unique to the growth of plants in controlled environments need to be studied. The principles which are important to the engineering of these systems are energy efficiency, miniaturization, reliability, and maintainability. Many of the sensors for monitoring the chamber environment are inadequate in sensitivity or maintainability. What are the best artificial irradiance systems for growing plants? Can lamps be manufactured which do not burn out? Can systems be developed which collect natural lighting, transport the energy to the appropriate location, and diffuse the irradiant energy over a growing plant canopy? On-line monitors are needed for the identification of ions within nutrient solutions, analysis of trace organic contaminants in the atmosphere, and identification of microorganisms in solutions. Can we develop noninvasive instruments which will detect plant stress before it impacts productivity? What type of robotic capability and/or automation is required for harvesting, planting, and maintaining crops in a controlled environment? An expert computer system must take all the environmental data, analytical results, and biological information and translate it into a control capability.

If a CELSS is operational in free space, then all systems must be engineered so that they will operate in microgravity. This fact introduces another level of complexity into the engineering requirements for this system. Nutrient solutions being supplied to plant roots must be contained in some manner. Liquid and gas interfaces in bioreactors, condensate collectors, and other components within the system must be properly controlled. Particles resulting from processing of the biomass must be properly contained.

Some research has been completed relative to development of microporous membrane systems for use in nutrient delivery in microgravity. The use of such systems to control the delivery of water and nutrients for plants in microgravity was proposed by Wright et al. (1988). These systems place the nutrient solution behind a barrier and under slight negative tension with the delivery of water and nutrients to the plant roots by capillary action through the membrane. A tubular membrane system of this type has been built and several species of plants have been grown on it for extended periods of time (Dreschel and Sager 1989). This system appears to have application to growing plants in microgravity and a flight test is currently being scheduled for 1992. Additional methods of delivering nutrient solutions to plant roots in microgravity need to be developed and tested over the next several years.

There are many questions related to the physiology of the plant in microgravity which must be studied. The response of plants to the microgravity of space are summarized in a recent article by Halstead and Dutcher (1987). Several of the responses that have been identified for plants being grown in microgravity will have direct effect on successfully utilizing plants for a CELSS under these conditions. Will a plant grow through an entire life cycle in space? Is photosynthesis, carbohydrate metabolism, and long distance transport affected adversely by microgravity? Is cell division and the basic genetic component of the plant altered in microgravity? These lists of engineering and physiological problems are not meant to be comprehensive, but it does indicate some of the issues that must be resolved prior to the development of a CELSS for long duration space flight.

CONCLUSION

Theoretically, there appears to be no reason that a biological system should not be able to function as a life support system during long duration space flights. Indeed, a biological system is the only means currently available to develop a truly recycling life support system. However, there are many scientific and engineering questions which must be answered prior to the development of a functioning CELSS. Many of these problems are unique to a controlled environment space system and have not been addressed by the agricultural research community. A primary difference in approach to crop research needed to develop a CELSS is that the plant does not need to fit into an existing environment; the environment needs to fit the existing plant.

The engineering and physiological questions raised by the inclusion of these systems in a microgravity environment are, of course, unique to the space environment. The Breadboard Project at the Kennedy Space Center is beginning to address a few of the questions related to mass flow, energy use, and manpower requirements that are needed to operate a CELSS at a one person scale. Initial data on gas and water exchange, biomass production, microbiological constituents and trace organic contaminants have been generated for three crops being grown at a community scale under sealed atmospheric and controlled environmental conditions. Trials with additional crops are scheduled for the future and multicropping studies will occur as the total CELSS becomes better defined. Sweetpotato is one of these crops.

Other modules of a CELSS will be developed and integrated with the biomass production facility over the next two years. During the next year, emphasis will be placed on the preparation of meals from the edible plant material produced from the Biomass Production Chamber and the conversion of unused material in the system to minerals, carbon dioxide, and water for plant growth. The development of a biomass conversion module, which should allow for the more complete use of biomass produced in the system, will be integrated into the Breadboard as data dictate. Testing of a complete Breadboard system is currently scheduled for 1993 and 1994. A larger integration test facility is planned for construction in 1995 to begin the integration and subsequent testing of a new improved CELSS at that time.

REFERENCES

Dreschel, T. W., and J. C. Sager. 1989. Control of water and nutrient using a porous tube; a method for growing plants in space. Hort Science. 24(6):944-947.
Halstead, T. W., and F. R. Dutcher. 1987. Plants in space. Annual Review of Plant Physiology. Vol. 38:317-345.
Hilding, S. E., R. Prince, E. Taylor, and W. Knott. 1987. Control and data acquisition system design for a sealed Biomass Production Chamber at Kennedy Space Center. Proc. of the ISA Int. Conf. Anaheim, CA. October.
Koller, A. M. 1986. CELSS Breadboard Facility Project Plan. Biomedical Operations and Research Office, National Aeronautics and Space Administration, Kennedy Space Center.
Prince, R. P., W. M. Knott, J. C. Sager, and S. E. Hilding. 1987. Design and performance of a KSC Biomass Production Chamber. Soc. Automot. Eng. (SAE) Paper No. 871437, Seattle, WA.
Prince, R. P., and W. M. Knott. 1989. CELSS Breadboard Project at the Kennedy Space Center. D.W. Ming and D. L. Henninger (Eds.), Lunar base agriculture: soils for plant growth. Amer. Soc. Agron., Madison, WI.
Salisbury, F. B., and B. Bugbee. 1988. Plant productivity in controlled environments. Hort. Soc. 23:293-299.
Wheeler, R. M., and T. W. Tibbitts. 1987. Utilization of potatoes for life support systems in space; III. Productivity at successive harvest dates under 12-h and 24-h photoperiods. Am. Potato J. 64:311-319.
Wright, B. D., W. C. Bausch, and W. M. Knott. 1988. A hydroponic system for microgravity plant experiments. Trans. ASAE 31:440-446.

Sweetpotato Technology for the 21st Century. W.A. Hill, C.K. Bonsi and P.A. Loretan (Eds.) 1992. Tuskegee University, Tuskegee, AL

Conrad K. Bonsi, Walter A. Hill, Desmond G. Mortley,
Philip A. Loretan, Carlton E. Morris, Esther R. Carlisle

Growing Sweetpotatoes for Space Missions Using NFT

The sweetpotato is one of the crops with subsurface edible parts that has been selected by the National Aeronautics and Space Administration (NASA) for growth in Controlled Ecological Life Support Systems (CELSS). If sweetpotatoes are to be used as a food source for future long-term manned space missions, then it is important that their growth and yield in a controlled environment be evaluated. There is the need, therefore, to study the appropriate systems and most practical means of growing sweetpotatoes for such missions. Since 1986, a team of researchers at Tuskegee University has been successfully growing sweetpotatoes using a nutrient film technique (NFT) system. Experiments have been conducted in NFT to determine the influence of such factors as relative humidity, light intensity, photoperiod, temperature regime, nutrient solution composition and frequency of application, pH requirements and channel size and shape on the growth and yield of sweetpotatoes. The research also includes screening various cultivars to determine their potential for use in the system as well as the appropriate frequency for cutting the foliage tip ends for use as a green vegetable. Nutritive qualities of storage roots and edible foliage grown in this system are also being evaluated. To date, the maximum storage root fresh weight produced per plant using the system has been 2800 g.

Sweetpotatoes rank very high among the four crops with subsurface edible parts initially chosen for CELSS (Hill et al. 1984). The sweetpotato is highly nutritious, with both edible storage roots and foliage, and can be prepared in many different ways. Developing systems for growing sweetpotatoes in controlled environments for high storage root and foliage yields with high nutrient content involves understanding the physiology of the plant grown under these conditions. Langhans and Dreesen (1988) and Salisbury and Bugbee (1988) described and summarized the progress and problems associated with growing plants in controlled environments for future space missions. Unlike above-ground crops (lettuce, cowpeas, wheat, and soybeans) selected for CELSS, sweetpotatoes and the other crops with subsurface edible parts require special below-surface conditions and growing systems to accommodate growth in the root zone (Hill et al. 1992). A nutrient film technique (NFT) system developed at Tuskegee University (Hill et al. 1989) has been used to successfully produce storage roots of up to 2800 g/plant. This paper reports the

George Washington Carver Agricultural Experiment Station, Tuskegee University, Tuskegee, Alabama 36088.

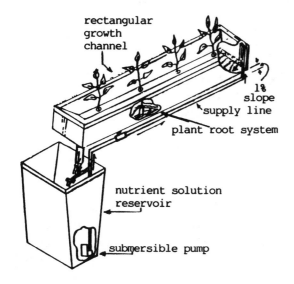

rectangular
growth
channel

1%
slope
supply line

plant root system

Figure 1. Standard NFT growing system.

nutrient solution
reservoir

submersible pump

results of the effects of several physical and environmental factors and cultivar differences on storage root and foliage yield of sweetpotatoes grown hydroponically using the NFT system.

THE STANDARD NFT GROWING PROTOCOL

A rectangular (0.15 x 0.15 x 1.2 m) growth channel (Fig. 1) was designed for growing sweetpotatoes and possibly other root and tuber crops using NFT. This channel includes a movable root contact pressure plate assembly (Morris et al. 1989a). Part of this assembly is a flat, rigid PVC plate in which four 2.5 cm holes are provided for inserting plants (15 cm vine cuttings) at 25 cm spacing. A flexible vinyl film is secured along the length of each side edge of the plate by means of pressure fit connections. The assembly is secured to the top edges of the growing channel by the same means. The flexible vinyl film suspends the plate near and parallel to the bottom of the growing channel with the flexibility of the film allowing upward movement of the plate within the channel as the plants' roots grow. The assembly provides contact and pressure to the plant roots inside the growth channel thereby promoting enlargement of the roots. This enlargement causes the assembly to move upward, thereby maintaining the desired pressure conditions during growth.

The plants are supplied nutrient solution from a 45 liter reservoir initially containing 30.4 L (8 gal). The solution, a modified half-Hoagland nutrient solution (Table 1), is changed every two weeks and topped with deionized water if the volume of nutrient solution falls below 8L prior to the two-week replacement interval. Nutrient solution is pumped from each reservoir to the upper end of each growing channel by small submersible pumps (Teel Model 1P680A, 1/200 HP). The channels

Table 1. Composition of modified half-Hoagland nutrient solution[1].

Stock solution mL/30.4L (8 gal)	Solution A g/L	Solution B g/L
$CaCl_2$ - 60.8[2]	H_3BO_3 - 2.86	EDTA Fe - 5
$NH_4H_2PO_4$ - 15.2[2]	$MnCl_2.4H_2O$ - 1.81	
KNO_3 - 91.2[2]	$ZnSO_4.7H_2O$ - 0.22	
$MgSO_4$ - 30.4[2]	$CuSO_4.5H_2O$ - 0.08	
Solution A - 15.2	MoO_3 - 0.09	
Solution B - 15.2		

[1]N:K ratio - 1:2.4
[2]One molar concentration

are graded with a 1% downward slope toward the reservoir. The nutrient solution spreads across each growing channel in a thin film as it flows back to the reservoir. A 1 L min^{-1} flow rate is set by using a bypass line back to the reservoir and a control valve. Plants are trained as they vine out by tying them to vertical strings dropping 1 meter from above each growing channel.

The greenhouse temperature used ranged from 24 to 33°C depending on the season of the year and weather conditions. The daytime irradiance level in the greenhouse varied with the season, the time of day and the weather conditions; however, the level ranged from 200 to 1700 µmol m^{-2}s^{-1}. The relative humidity (RH) ranged between 60 and 95%.

Plants were harvested 120 days after planting and yields were determined on a g/plant basis. All foliage was cut at the base, weighed fresh and dried for 72 h at 70°C and reweighed dry. A 25 g sample of randomly chosen storage roots from each plant was taken and dried at 70°C for 72 h to determine percentage dry matter (% DM) and storage root dry weight.

GROWING SYSTEM

A number of studies sought to determine the optimal physical and environmental conditions for sweetpotato growth in CELSS. The aforementioned NFT protocol was used in all of them with modifications only to the parameter under scrutiny.

Flat plate assembly
A study was conducted to evaluate the effect of the flat plate assembly on sweetpotato production in NFT. Rectangular channels of the same depth and length as the standard channels but 45 cm (18 in) wide were used. The wide channels were used in order to minimize the effects of the side walls of the channel on root growth. Two sweetpotato cultivars 'TI-155' and 'Georgia Jet' ('Ga Jet') were grown. Results indicate that storage root number, weight (fresh and dry) and percent dry matter (DM) as well as fibrous root fresh and dry weights tended to be higher (Table 2) for both cultivars with the flat plate assembly than without it.

112

Table 2. Effect of flat plate assembly on growth of 'TI-155' in 45 cm wide channels using NFT.

Treatment	Storage Roots				Foliage		Fibrous Roots	
	No.	Fr. Wt.	Dr. Wt.	DM	Fr. Wt.	Dr. Wt.	Fr. Wt.	Dr. Wt.
		------g/plant------		%	-----g/plant-----		-----g/plant-----	
				'TI-155'				
With Plate	3.0	1010	160	15.8	379	45	277	9.0
W/O Plate	1.5	911	135	14.8	406	45	213	7.5
				'Ga Jet'				
With Plate	5.8	973	177	18.2	495	60	365	32.3
W/O Plate	3.8	772	136	17.6	466	50	317	24.3

Channel size and depth

The Biomass Production Chamber (BPC) at Kennedy Space Center uses trapezoidal growth channels. An evaluation of the NASA BPC growing channel was initiated to determine if channel depth influenced the yield of hydroponically grown 'Ga Jet' sweetpotatoes (Morris et al. 1989b). Three channel depths were studied, 5 cm standard BPC channel, 10 cm channel and 15 cm channel. Results showed that the number of storage roots tended to increase with channel depth but not significantly (Table 3). The highest storage root fresh weight (659 g/plant) was produced in the channel with the least depth (5 cm). This value was significantly higher than the 318 g per plant produced in the 10 cm channel. The storage root dry weights followed the same trend as the fresh weight. There were no significant differences in fresh and dry foliage weight or fibrous root weight due to treatments. The results indicate no advantage to increased channel depth.

Standard rectangular growth channels with three different widths, 15, 30, and 45 cm were used to evaluate the effect of channel width on 'Ga Jet' sweetpotato growth and yield. The channel depth was 15 cm. The results (Table 4) indicate that, with the exception of the storage root number that significantly increased for the 45 cm wide trays, there were no apparent differences due to the channel width. Enlarged

Table 3. The effect of channel depth on growth of 'Ga Jet' sweetpotato plants in a greenhouse using NFT.

Channel	Storage Roots			Foliage		Fibrous Roots
Depth cm	No.	Fr. Wt.	Dr. Wt.	Fr. Wt.	Dr. Wt.	Dr. Wt. g/plant
		---------g/plant--------		---------g/plant--------		
15	5.5a	554ab	91ab	561a	73.9a	10.5b
10	3.0a	318b	51b	324a	50.3a	10.0a
5	2.5b	659a	109a	616a	89.3a	13.0a

*Means in a column followed by the same letter are not significantly different at 5% level according to DMRT; (from Morris et al. 1989b).

Table 4. The effect of channel width on growth of 'Ga Jet' sweetpotato plants in a greenhouse using NFT.

Channel		Storage Roots			Foliage		Fibrous Roots
Width	No.	Fr. Wt.	Dr. Wt.	Fr. Wt.	Dr. Wt.		Dr. Wt.
cm		--------g/plant--------		--------g/plant--------			g/plant
45	4.8a*	357a	78.9a	365a	60.0a		10.0a
30	3.0b	303a	68.5a	320a	48.0a		8.0a
15	2.5b	306a	65.5a	350a	46.3a		7.3a

*Means in a column followed by the same letter are not significantly different at 5% level according to DMRT; from Morris et al. 1989b.

roots formed near the center of the 30 and 45 cm wide channels. In the 15 cm wide channel, storage roots enlarged in the center and in contact with the side walls. Storage roots did not form in contact with the side walls in either the 30 cm or the 45 cm wide channels. Enlargement of the storage roots started at approximately the same distance (5 to 10 cm) from the plant stem in each treatment. These results indicate that growth channels with widths greater than 15 cm do not necessarily increase storage root production.

Plant density

Greenhouse experiments were conducted to evaluate the effect of spacing within and between growing channels on the yield of 'TI-155' sweetpotatoes grown hydroponically using NFT (Mortley et al. 1990b; 1991a). Spacing within growth channels were 13, 25 and 38 cm, and spacing between growth channels were 13, 25 and 38 cm. Storage root number, fresh weight and percent dry matter increased with increased spacing between plants within the channel (Table 5). Although the yield of fresh storage roots per plant was highest as the number of plants per channel decreased (wider spacing), the total yield per channel was slightly lower for the channel with the fewest plants. However, the closer the plant spacing, the lower the

Table 5. Effect of plant spacing within a growth channel on yield of 'TI-155' sweetpotatoes.

Plant		Storage Roots			Foliage		Fibrous Roots	
Spacing	No.	Fr. Wt.	Dr. Wt.	DM	Fr. Wt.	Dr. Wt.	Fr. Wt.	Dr. Wt.
cm		-----g/plant-----		%	-------g/plant-------		-------g/plant-------	
25	3.2	622	128	19.3	342	49.1	247	11.2
18	3.0	567	103	18.1	199	27.0	178	7.4
13	2.4	372	66	17.6	171	23.1	172	7.1
Sig. Y	NS	NS	NS	NS	L*Q**	L*Q**	NS	L*

Y=Linear (L), Quadratic (Q)
*Significant at P=0.05 and **Significant at P=0.01; from Mortley et al. 1991a.

Table 6. Effect of plant spacing between channels on yield of 'TI-155' sweetpotatoes.

Channel		Storage Roots				Foliage		Fibrous Roots	
Spacing	No.	Fr. Wt.	Dr. Wt.	DM		Fr. Wt.	Dr. Wt.	Fr. Wt.	Dr. Wt.
cm		-----g/plant-----		%		------g/plant------		-----g/plant-----	
38	3.9	452	57	12.7		289	34.6	143	5.1
25	2.1	286	36	10.7		280	34.4	143	4.9
13	1.5	124	19	13.2		144	18.4	99	7.2
Sig. Y	L*	L*	L*	NS		NS	NS	NS	NS

Y=Linear (L), Significant at P=0.05 (*); from Mortley et al. 1991a.

foliage yield per plant. The within-row spacing of 25 cm produced the highest foliage and fibrous root fresh and dry weights.

The number and weight of storage roots increased as the spacing between channels increased from 13 to 38 cm (Table 6). Differences in percent dry matter were not observed among treatments. Increasing the channel spacing from 13 to 25 or 38 cm had no significant effect on foliage and fibrous root yields. These yields, however, were higher than those for plants grown in channels spaced only 15 cm apart.

Nutrient solution application frequency

The standard time-interval used for changing nutrient solution in the NFT system has been once every two weeks. Experiments were conducted to compare a 2-, 14- and 28-day time interval between nutrient solution changes. The nutrient solution change interval treatments were initiated 28-days after planting. Results (Table 7) clearly indicate that storage root, foliage and fibrous root weights were higher for the 2-day change interval than for the 14- and 28-day intervals. The 2-day change interval produced the highest mean fresh storage root weight per plant to date (1688 g) as well as the highest single plant storage root yield of 2800 g. It should

Table 7. Effect of interval between nutrient solution changes on growth of 'TI-155' sweetpotatoes using NFT.

Change		Storage Roots				Foliage		Fibrous Roots	
Interval	No.	Fr. Wt.	Dr. Wt.	DM		Fr. Wt.	Dr. Wt.	Fr. Wt.	Dr. Wt.
days		------g/plant------		%		-------g/plant-------		-----g/plant-----	
2	3.8a	1688a	243a	13.8b		2078a	325a	388a	15.8a
14	2.5a	76b	75b	11.1b		350b	45b	179b	6.3b
28	3.0a	614b	119ab	19.4a		195b	25b	147c	5.4c

*Means in a column followed by the same letter are not significantly different at 5% level according to DMRT.

Table 8. Effect of two light intensities on growth and yield of sweetpotatoes.

Light		Storage Roots			Foliage		Fibrous Roots	
Intensity $\mu mol\ m^{-2}s^{-1}$	No.	Fr. Wt. -----g/plant-----	Dr. Wt.	DM %	Fr. Wt. -----g/plant-----	Dr. Wt.	Fr. Wt. -----g/plant-----	Dr. Wt.
480	3.5	756	103	13.4	603	69.7	143	5.7
960	3.5	1126	214	19.3	454	65.1	239	12.9
LSD (5%)	NS	295	60	3.8	NS	NS	45	2.9

be noted, however, that high foliage yield may be undesirable in a limited space environment. Also, the results implicate the need to assess nutrient solution change intervals in between 2- and 14-day intervals for producing optimum storage root yields and vegetable greens.

Nutrient solution flow rate and pH

The standard nutrient solution flow rate of 1L/min of the Tuskegee University NFT system was arbitrarily selected. Since flow rate can be expected to influence the availability of nutrients in the root zone and consequently yield, experiments were conducted to study the effects of different flow rates on yield of sweetpotatoes grown in the greenhouse using NFT. Similarly, studies were conducted to determine the effect of varying nutrient solution pH on yield and quality of sweetpotatoes (Martinez et al. 1990). Results of these studies are presented in detail in other papers in this volume (Martinez et al. 1992; Carlisle et al. 1992).

PLANT GROWING ENVIRONMENT

Light intensity

Experiments were conducted in environmental growth chambers to evaluate the effects of two light intensities, 480 and 960 $\mu mol\ m^{-2}s^{-1}$, on 'TI-155' sweetpotatoes grown in an NFT system (Bonsi et al. 1988; 1989). A modified half-Hoagland solution provided nutrients to the plants. Plants were exposed to a 14 h photoperiod, a 28/22°C temperature regime, 70% relative humidity (RH) and an ambient CO_2 level. Other growing conditions were standard. Results of these studies indicate no difference between the irradiance treatments for storage root number and foliage fresh and dry weights (Table 8). However, storage root fresh and dry weights, percent dry matter, fibrous root fresh and dry weights were higher for the 960 $\mu mol\ m^{-2}s^{-1}$ than for the 480 $\mu mol\ m^{-2}s^{-1}$.

Photoperiod

Environmental growth chamber experiments were conducted to investigate the effects of two photoperiods (PP)—12 and 24 h—on growth and storage root yield of two sweetpotato cultivars, 'TI-155' and 'Ga Jet' (Mortley et al. 1989; 1990a; Bonsi et al. 1992). Both treatments had temperature regimes of 12 h at 28°C and 12 h at 22°C. The light irradiance level was 400 $\mu mol\ m^{-2}s^{-1}$ at canopy level and 70 percent

Table 9. Effect of two photoperiods on growth responses of two sweetpotato cultivars.

| Cultivar | PP | Storage Roots | | | Foliage | |
| | | No. | Fresh wt. | Dry wt. | Fresh wt. | Dry wt. |
			------g/plant------		------g/plant------	
'Ga Jet'	12	2.5	296.8	51.9	459	56.7
	24	3.3	322.1	59.2	273	38.9
'TI-155'	12	1.3	221.1	37.9	417	51.4
	24	0.0	0.0	0.0	56	5.4
Sig.* (p>0.05)		*	*	*	*	*

RH was maintained throughout the growth period. Other growing conditions were standard for NFT. Results showed varietal differences in response to continuous light. 'Ga Jet' sweetpotato storage root fresh and dry weights and fibrous root dry weights were increased under continuous light (Table 9). 'TI-155' produced no storage roots and little foliage when plants were exposed to 24 h light.

Effect of relative humidity

Growth of sweetpotato in environmental chambers using relative humidities of 50 and 85% was compared (Mortley et al. 1992). Other conditions included a 14 h photoperiod and a diurnal temperature variation of 28/22°C.

GERMPLASM SELECTION

Effect of cultivar differences

Several sweetpotato genotypes were grown in NFT in an attempt to identify those with high yield potential for possible use in the CELSS program (Mortley et al. 1991b). Four vine cuttings of each cultivar were grown in the greenhouse using the standard NFT growing procedure. As expected, the sweetpotato genotypes responded differently in NFT (Table 10). High root yield and low foliage weight was obtained with several genotypes, suggesting their potential use for space applications. The percent edible biomass index (EBI) for the cultivars tested ranged between 30 and 82 percent with the majority above 70 percent EBI. There was a negative correlation between the storage root and foliage weight for many of the cultivars.

CONCLUSION

Results of several years of study have shown that sweetpotatoes can not only be grown hydroponically but can also consistently produce storage roots in an NFT system. These studies have also provided basic data on the physiological responses and growth of sweetpotatoes under artificial conditions. Yields of up to 2.8 kg/plant have been achieved. Light intensity, relative humidity, photoperiod, pH and plant density have been shown to affect the yield of storage roots in the NFT system. Cultivar differences in yield were also observed.

Table 10. Response of 14 sweetpotato genotypes to growth in NFT hydroponic system.

Genotype	Storage Roots				Foliage		EBI
	No	Fr Wt.	Dr Wt.	DM	Fr Wt.	Dr Wt.	%
		------ g/plant ------		%	------ g/plant ------		
W-221	6.5a**	332.4abc	44.5bcd	13.6d	527.4a	47.2bc	47.2bc
TI-2093	6.0a	322.6abc	79.4ab	24.5bc	188.4de	29.9cde	73.2a
TI-1892	5.6	234.4bcd	54.1bcd	23.3bc	136.0ef	17.7def	78.8a
Jewel	5.5ab	470.0a	103.4a	21.8bc	176.5def	32.6bcd	77.0a
Carver	5.5a	370.0ab	81.8bc	23.4bc	204.9cde	27.9cde	74.7a
TI-130	4.5abc	186.7bc	41.6bcd	21.9bc	322.4bc	38.7bc	51.7b
TI-70357	4.0a-d	186.9bcd	44.6bcd	24.0bc	86.8ef	14.6def	76.9a
Bunch	3.0a-d	126.8ad	23.2d	18.4cd	38.5f	58.8a	78.7a
TU-52 White	3.0a-d	384.0ab	99.1a	25.9b	366.4b	7.5f	64.3ab
TU-80 White	3.0a-d	305.9a-d	63.2a-d	21.0bc	74.8ef	14.1df	81.9ab
GA-122	1.8bcd	151.3cd	32.5cd	21.5bc	132.8ef	10.6ef	77.8a
Centennial	1.3cd	345.1abc	84.9ab	24.7bc	281.5bcd	41.7abc	64.2ab
Rojo Blanco	1.0cd	230.6bcd	74.3abc	32.3a	124.0ef	22.8c-f	77.1a
TU-50	0.5d	116.7d	24.3	12.1d	347.1b	50.7ab	30.8c

**Mean separation within columns by Duncan's Multiple Range Test. Means followed by the same letter are not significantly different (5% level); from Mortley et al. 1991b.

Optimization of environmental conditions, nutrient application protocol and selection of high dry matter, short-vining and early maturing cultivars are expected to increase yields of sweetpotatoes grown in the NFT system. Future research efforts are, therefore, focused on varietal screening and the determination of the optimum photoperiod, temperature regime, CO_2 level and nutrient application protocol for high storage root yield and nutritive quality of storage roots and foliage. These studies are necessary in order to ascertain optimum conditions for growing sweetpotato in CELSS for future space missions.

REFERENCES

Bonsi, C.K., P.A. Loretan, W.A. Hill, C.R. Ogbuehi, and C.E. Morris. 1988. Effects of photoperiod and light intensity on growth and storage root production of sweetpotatoes. Proceedings, 8th Symposium of the International Society for Tropical Root Crops, Bangkok, Thailand. Oct. 30-Nov. 5, 515-519 pp.

Bonsi, C.K., P.A. Loretan, W.A. Hill, C.R. Ogbuehi, and D.G. Mortley. 1989. Effects of light intensity on growth and storage root production of sweetpotatoes. HortScience 24:760.

Bonsi, C.K., P.A. Loretan, W.A. Hill, and D.G. Mortley. 1992. Response of sweetpotatoes to continuous light. HortScience. 27:471.

Carlisle, E.R., D.G. Mortley, P.A. Loretan, C.K. Bonsi, W.A. Hill, C.E. Morris, and A. Trotman. 1992. Effect of flow rate on hydroponically grown 'Ga Jet' sweetpotatoes. Pages 160-161 in Sweetpotato technology for the 21st century, edited by W.A. Hill, C.K. Bonsi and P.A. Loretan. Tuskegee University, Tuskegee, AL.

Hill, W.A., P.A. Loretan, and C.K. Bonsi (eds). 1984. The sweet potato for space missions, Tuskegee University, Tuskegee, AL.

Hill, W.A., P.A. Loretan, C.K. Bonsi, C.E. Morris, J.Y. Lu, and C. Ogbuehi. 1989. Utilization of sweetpotatoes in Controlled Ecological Life Support Systems (CELSS). Adv. Space Res. 9(8):29-41.

Hill, W.A., D.G. Mortley, C.L. Mackowiak, P.A. Loretan, T.W. Tibbitts, R.M. Wheeler, C.K. Bonsi ,and C.E. Morris. 1992. Growing root, tuber and nut crops hydroponically for CELSS. Adv. Space Res. 12(5):125-131.

Langhans, R.W., and D.R. Dreesen. 1988. Challenges to plant growing in space. HortScience 23:286-293.

Martinez, E., C.K. Bonsi, W.A. Hill, D.G. Mortley, and C.E. Morris. 1990. Effect of continuous vs periodic pH adjustment on growth of Ga Jet and TI-155 sweetpotato cultivars grown using NFT. HortScience 25:864

Martinez, E.R., C.K. Bonsi, P.P. David, D, G. Mortley, W.A. Hill, P.A. Loretan, and C.E. Morris. 1992. Effect of constant pH vs periodic pH adjustment of nutrient solution on yield of sweetpotato using NFT. Pages 171-173 in Sweetpotato technology for the 21st century, edited by W.A. Hill, C.K. Bonsi and P.A. Loretan. Tuskegee University, Tuskegee, AL.

Morris, C.E., P.A. Loretan, C.K. Bonsi, and W.A. Hill. 1989a. Movable root contact pressure plate assembly for hydroponic sytem. United States Patent No. 4,860,490.

Morris, C.E., E. Martinez, C.K. Bonsi, D.G. Mortley, W.A. Hill, C.R. Ogbuehi, and P.A. Loretan. 1989b. Effects of channel size on sweet potato storage root enlargement in the Tuskegee University hydroponic nutrient film system. Proceedings NASA-HBCU Space Science and Engineering Research Forum. Huntsville, AL. 15-19 pp.

Mortley, D.G., C.K. Bonsi, P.A. Loretan, W.A. Hill, and C. Ogbuehi. 1989. Effects of two photoperiod and temperature regimes on growth and storage root yield of sweetpotatoes. HortScience 24:760.

Mortley, D.G., C.K. Bonsi, P.A. Loretan, W.A. Hill, and E. Martinez. 1990a. Effect of photoperiod and temperature regimes on yield of sweetpotatoes grown using NFT. HortScience 25:858.

Mortley, D.G., C.K. Bonsi, P.A. Loretan, W.A. Hill, and C. Morris. 1990b. Effect of spacing on yield of sweetpotatoes grown using NFT. HortScience 25:857.

Mortley, D.G., P.A. Loretan, C.K. Bonsi, W.A. Hill, and C.E. Morris. 1991a. Plant spacing influences yield and linear growth rate of sweetpotatoes grown hydroponically. HortScience 26:1274-1275.

Mortley, D.G., C.K. Bonsi, P.A. Loretan, C.E. Morris, W.A. Hill, and C.R. Ogbuehi. 1991b. Evaluation of sweetpotato genotypes for adapability to hydroponic systems. Crop Sci. 31:845-847.

Mortley, D.G., C.K. Bonsi, P.A. Loretan, W.A. Hill, E.R. Carlisle, and C.E. Morris. 1992. Effects of relative humidity on sweetpotato growth in an NFT system. Pages 173-177 in Sweetpotato technology for the 21st century, edited by W.A. Hill, C.K. Bonsi and P.A. Loretan. Tuskegee University, Tuskegee, AL.

Salisbury, F.B., and B.G. Bugbee. 1988. Space farming in the 21st Century. 21st Century Science and Technology 1(1):21-41.

Sweetpotato Technology for the 21st Century. W.A. Hill, C.K. Bonsi and P.A. Loretan (Eds.) 1992. Tuskegee University, Tuskegee, AL

Tsutomu Uewada, Makoto Kiyota, Yoshiaki Kitaya, Ichiro Aiga

Hydroponic Cultivation of Sweetpotato

We have developed a hydroponic method for efficient cultivation of sweetpotato. In this method, nursery stock with roots developed in a sandy medium were set in a plastic box. A rockwool slab was set at the bottom of the box as a nutrient solution layer. The upper and middle parts of the roots formed storage roots in the aerial space above the solution layer. The lower part of the roots became absorbing roots in the rockwool slab. When the NH_4NO_3 concentration in the nutrient solution was doubled for about one month after planting, and the KCl and KH_2PO_4 concentrations were doubled from the 31st day until harvest, the yield increased. When the temperature in the root zone was lower than the air temperature, the foliage weight increased and root fresh weight decreased. The yield of fresh storage roots grown for three months was 4.5 kg/m^2. This yield was twice that found for conventional field cultivation at similar climatic conditions.

Hydroponic cultivation of plants permit their production in locations where the absence of adequate soil, water resources or climatic conditions would otherwise prohibit production. Previous studies on hydroponic cultivation of sweetpotato in Japan did not achieve root yields equivalent to yields from field studies. On the other hand, Hill et al. (1989) obtained relatively high yields per plant with a hydroponic system in greenhouse and growth chamber conditions. We have developed a simple hydroponic method in which sweetpotato can be grown easily and with large yields.

Cultural System and Procedure

A plastic box was used to cultivate sweetpotato hydroponically (Figure 1). Inside the box was a solution layer and an aerial layer. The depth of the solution layer was 2 cm, and the thickness of the aerial layer above the solution layer was 30 cm. The nutrient solution used was Kasugai's solution B whose composition is shown in Table 1 (Kasugai 1936). The box was covered with silver colored polyethylene film to avoid transmission of sunlight into the box since storage root formation of sweetpotato is inhibited by light (Uewada and Kawagishi 1980) and the temperature in the box increases considerably without shading.

Nursery stocks were from vine cuttings which had 5 to 6 nodes as follows. The cuttings were grown for about 20 days in a sandy medium (Figure 2-a). After the roots elongated to 30 to 40 cm in the sand, they were washed with water to remove sand (Fig. 2-b). This nursery stock was then set in holes in the cover of the box (Figure

College of Agriculture, University of Osaka Prefecture, 4-804, Mozu-ume, Sakai, Osaka, Japan.

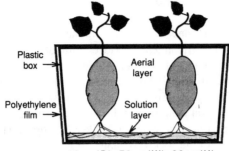

Figure 1. The box for hydroponic cultivation of sweetpotato.

40cm(D)x70cm(W)x32cm(H)

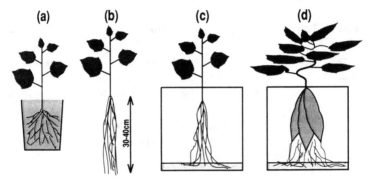

Figure 2. Procedure for hydroponic cultivation of sweetpotato.

2-c). The upper and middle parts of the roots developed storage roots in the aerial space above the solution. The lower parts developed into absorbing roots in the solution layer (Figure 2-d). Nutrient solution was added on a daily basis to maintain the solution layer at a depth of 2 cm.

Table 1. Composition of Kasugai's solution B.

	(mg/L)
NH_4NO_3	57.5
KCl	43.0
$MgSO_4 \cdot 7H_2O$	120.0
KH_2PO_4	38.3
$Ca(NO_3)_2 \cdot 4H_2O$	117.0
$MnCl_2 \cdot 4H_2O$	0.4
$FeCl_3$	150.0
Total N	40.0
NH_4-N	10.0
NO-N	30.0
P_2O_5	20.0
K_2O	40.0
CaO	40.0
MgO	40.0

Effect of Rockwool Set in the Solution Layer

Growth characteristics and yields of sweetpotatoes (cv. 'Kokei No.14') grown in the culture box under two treatments—with or without a 2 cm rockwool slab in the solution layer at the bottom of the box—were observed. The experiment was conducted outdoors during 102 days from July 10 to October 20. Mean air temperatures at the inside and the outside of the cultural box were both about 27° C, and the relative humidity at the inside of the box was always more than 85%.

Results of the experiment are shown in Table 2. The dry and fresh weights of the storage roots grown with the rockwool slab were 1.4 and 1.5 times higher than without it. The number of storage roots for both treatments were similar, but the size of each storge root grown with the rockwool slab was larger than that without it. There was no significant difference in the growth of shoots for the two treatments.

Effect of Modification of the Nutrient Solution

Sweetpotato (cv. 'Kokei No.14') was cultivated in the cultural box with the rockwool slab using Kasugai's solution B as the control. In treatment 1, NH_4NO_3 in the standard solution was doubled for the first 30 days after planting in order to accelerate the shoot growth, and KCl and KH_2PO_4 were then doubled from the 31st day to the harvest day in order to accelerate storage root development. In treatment 2, the three nutrients, as mentioned above, were modified on the same day as treatment 1, but these levels were tripled. The experiment was conducted outdoors during 148 days from June 10 to November 5.

The results are shown in Table 3. The fresh weights of the storage roots for treatments 1 and 2 were 1.3 times and 1.2 times higher, respectively, than for the control. There was no significant difference between treatment 1 and 2. The growth of shoots was also accelerated by modification of the nutrients.

Table 2. Growth of sweetpotatoes cultivated in nutrient solution with and without rockwool.

Treat-ment	Fresh wt (g/plant)			Dry wt (g/plant)			Water content (%)		Number of
		Storage			Storage			Storage	Roots
	Shoots	Roots	Total	Shoots	Roots	Total	Shoots	Roots	(per plant)
Without rockwool	456	430	886	46	78	124	89.9	81.9	3.0
With rockwool	470	650	1120	52	108	160	88.9	83.4	3.3
t-test (5%)	ns	s	s	ns	s	s	ns	ns	ns

Plants were harvested 102 days after planting.
s: significant; ns: nonsignificant.

Table 3. Growth of sweetpotatoes cultivated with modified nutrient solution.

Treatment	Fresh weight (g/plant)			Number of Storage Roots (per plant)
	Shoots	Storage Roots	Total	
Control	1250a**	1270a	2520a	3.5a
1	1400b	1600b	3000b	3.0a
2	1481c	1530b	3010b	3.6a

Plants were harvested 148 days after planting.
*Control: Kasugai's solution B was supplied during the experiment.
  1: NH_4NO_3 in Kasugai's solution B was doubled for 30 days after planting and, after that, KCl and KH_2PO_4 were doubled from the 31st day to the harvest day.
  2: The modification of the solution was carried out on the same day as treatment 1, but the level of each nutrient was tripled.
** Different letters within columns indicate significant difference at 5% level.

The results demonstrate that doubling the NH_4NO_3 level in Kasugai's solution B for 0 to 20 days after planting and subsequently doubling the KCl and KH_2PO_4 levels in Kasugai's solution B from the 31st day after planting until harvest increased the storage root yield.

Effect of Cooling the Root Zone

Sweetpotato was grown using treatment 1 as described above. In order to cool the root zone in the cultural box, the box was immersed in a cold water bath. The experiment was conducted outdoors for 134 days from June 10 to October 20.

Changes in the air temperature and the root zone temperatures for the cooled root zone and the control are shown in Figure 3. The temperatures shown are the mean values of maximum and minimum temperatures every day during the growing period. The root zone temperature for the control was similar to the air temperature, and the root zone temperature for the cooled treatment was 3 to 5°C less than the air temperature for the greater part of the experimental period.

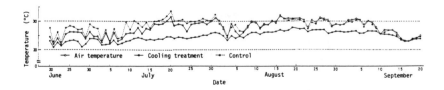

Figure 3. Changes in the air and root zone temperatures for cooled root zone and control treatments.

Table 4. Growth of sweetpotatoes cultivated hydroponically at different root zone temperatures.

Treatment	Fresh weight (g/plant)			Number of Storage Roots (per plant)
	Shoots	Storage Roots	Total	
Control	1350	1550	2900	3.1
Cooled root zone	1630	1250	2880	3.2

Plants were harvested 134 days after planting.
Temperatures for the control and cooled root zone treatments are shown in Figure 3.

The growth characteristics and the yields are shown in Table 4. The fresh weight of the shoots with the cooled root zone was 1.2 times higher than for the control. There was no difference between the number of storage roots for the two treatments. The storage root growth was suppressed by cooling the root zone.

Growth of Three Cultivars Grown Hydroponically

Three famous Japanese sweetpotato cultivars, 'Naruto kintoki,' 'Kotobuki' and 'Kokei No. 14,' were grown using treatment 1 as previously described. The experiment was conducted outside for 124 days from June 20 to October 20.

The results are shown in Table 5. The storage root fresh weight of 'Naruto kintoki' was 1.3 times higher than the other cultivars. The shoot growth showed a similar tendency.

Storage root yield of 'Naruto kintoki' was 1700 g/plant for a growing period of 120 days. The yield per square meter estimated from the planting density was 4500 g/m^2, which was twice as much as the yield by the conventional Japanese field method.

CONCLUSION

A new hydroponic method to cultivate sweetpotato was developed. In this method, the roots in the aerial space above the solution layer developed storage roots,

Table 5. Growth of three sweetpotato cultivars grown hydroponically.

Cultivar	Fresh weight (g/plant)			Number of Storage Roots (per plant)
	Shoots	Storage Roots	Total	
Naruto kintoki	1500a*	1700a	3200a	3.0a
Kotobuki	1400ab	1350b	2750b	3.2a
Kokei No. 14	1350b	1350b	2700b	3.5a

Plants were harvested 124 days after planting.
Different letters indicate significant difference at the 5% level.

and the roots in the solution layer where a rockwool slab was set were absorbing roots.

In order to increase the yield of the storage roots, it is desirable to double the NH_4NO_3 level in the Kasugai solution B during the first month of growth, and to double the KCl and KH_2PO_4 levels in the Kasugai solution B during the second and third months of growth.

The yield varied depending on sweetpotato cultivar used. 'Naruto kintoki' produced the highest yield, which was 4500 g/m^2—twice the yield using the conventional Japanese field method.

REFERENCES

Hill, W.A., D.G. Mortley, C.L. Mackowiak, P.A. Loretan, T.W. Tibbits, R.M. Wheeler, C.K.Bonsi,
and C.E.Morris. 1992. Growing root and tuber crops hydroponically. Advances in Space Research 12(5):125-131.

Kasugai, S. 1935. Studies on the hydroponic cultivation of sweet potato. Japan. Jour. Crop Sci. 7:12-18.

Uewada, T., and S. Kawagishi. 1980. Studies on the mechanism of tuberization of sweet potato. Japan. Jour. Crop Sci. 49:141-142.

Sweetpotato Technology for the 21st Century. W.A. Hill, C.K. Bonsi and P.A. Loretan (Eds.) 1992. Tuskegee University, Tuskegee, AL

Henry A. Robitaille*, Beth E. Lawrence**

Cropping Systems for Mass Education

The Land, presented by Kraft General Foods, represents agriculture in Future World at EPCOT Center, in the Walt Disney World Vacation Resort. Millions of guests are exposed annually to important agricultural crops, tools, concepts and technologies via a boat ride and walking tour through the pavilion, personal correspondence, direct telecasts to classrooms, special merchandising, and mass media opportunities. Entertainment value, important in The Land show, is often achieved by highlighting recognizable foods like bananas, tomatoes and rice. Sweetpotatoes have been only ineffectively showcased because the important and recognizable storage roots grow below ground. In order to effectively display these plants we attempted to grow them aeroponically for future inclusion on a very showy but shaded aeroponic plant conveyor. Although sweetpotatoes responded well to aeroponics, they did not produce storage roots at a conveyor environment light level of 547 μm/m^2/sec.

INTRODUCTION

The Land represents agriculture in Future World at EPCOT Center in the Walt Disney World Vacation Resort. The purpose of this large multi-show pavilion, sponsored by Kraft General Foods, is to impress on 10 million plus annual guests the importance of food and fiber production and good nutrition. These guests see the main show, food production and research greenhouses via a boat ride or walking tour hosted by agricultural staff scientists and students. More than 40 crops are grown at any given time, selected for their importance in world food or fiber production (e.g., sweetpotato), future potential (e.g., peach palm), or general interest value (e.g., tomato). Carefully chosen agricultural tools, concepts and technologies on display include integrated pest management, biotechnology, aquaculture, computerized environmental and irrigation controls, drip irrigation, hydroponics (several variations) and space agriculture. Although the goal is principally to produce an entertaining show for effective agricultural communications, large quantities of food are harvested for EPCOT Center restaurants. Research is ongoing to solve show problems, enhance the show and provide a creative outlet for a great professional staff who in turn leverage the whole international scientific community.

Sweetpotato has been a featured crop at The Land due to its worldwide importance in food production. It is not effective when traditionally grown, however,

*The Land, EPCOT Center, P.O. Box 10,000, Lake Buena Vista, FL 32830 USA;**Current address: Texas A&M University, College Station, TX 77843, USA.

because the distinctive storage roots are not visible. There is an aeroponic whole-plant conveyor in the show that would highlight the entire sweetpotato plant (Plate 1, p. 131). Due to many overhead obstructions, light levels at the conveyor are reduced by 50%. Sweetpotatoes have been produced in hydroponics (Lardizabal and Thompson 1988, Walker et al. 1988, Morris et al. 1988, Loretan et al. 1988, Hill et al. 1989), but not specifically in aeroponics, a variation that involves growing roots in air while misting them with a nutrient solution.

The mineral nutrition of sweetpotatoes has been reviewed in detail (Bouwkamp 1985). The greatest and most consistent responses were to potassium, where applications usually increased yields, often linearly (Geise 1925, Knavel 1971, Godfrey-Sam-Aggrey 1976, Zimmerley 1929, Duncan et al. 1958, Jones et al. 1979, Speights and Paterson 1961). The sweetpotato requirement for potassium is high (Scott and Bouwkamp 1974), and the involvement of that element in photosynthesis and translocation (Tsuno and Fujise 1965, Tsuno 1970) and starch synthesis (Tsuno and Fujise 1965, Murata and Akagawa 1968) has been documented.

The objective of this research was to study the effects of light intensity and potassium level on sweetpotato production in aeroponics.

MATERIALS AND METHODS

Large boxes were constructed of wood and lined with plastic film to support sweetpotato vines above, and hold nutrient solution in a 25 cm deep reservoir under the roots below (Plate 2, p. 131). The root and shoot zones were separated by a polystyrene board drilled to hold the rooted cuttings at equal spacing. A submerged pump supplied solution to continuously misting nozzles halfway up in the root zone. Plastic covered the bottom half to maintain darkness in the root zone and prevent the solution from splashing outside the box. Half of the upper part of each box was framed to hold shade cloth that reduced light intensity by 50%, resulting in 2 light treatments of 1147 $\mu m/m^2/sec$ (incident) and 547 $\mu m/m^2/sec$ (conveyor environment). Plants were grown in a standard Land nutrient solution, and in the same solution with double the potassium as potassium sulfate:

Potassium	117.240 mg/L	Phosphorus	19 mg/L	Zinc	0.20 mg/L
Nitrogen	116	Iron	2.50	Chlorine	0.14
Calcium	100	Boron	0.25	Copper	0.13
Sulfur	32.80	Manganese	0.25	Molybdenum	0.13
Magnesium	25				

The experiment was designed as a 2x2 factorial, with two levels each of light and potassium, two replications for each treatment combination, and four plants per replication (Figure 1). Potassium and light levels were randomly assigned to the boxes. The cultivar was MD320, vigorous but compact, and already being studied in hydroponic systems by NASA scientists. Small rooted cuttings were obtained

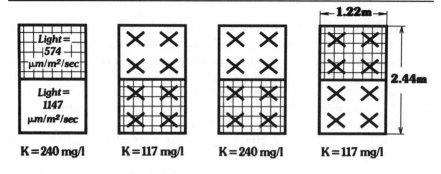

Figure 1. Layout of the factorial experiment showing two levels each of light intensity and potassium concentration, two replications, and four plants per replication.

from NASA researchers at the Kennedy Space Center Breadboard Project and inserted into the experimental aeroponic boxes.

Plants grew vigorously in all treatments and showed no visual nutrient deficiency symptoms. Aphids on shoots were successfully controlled with inundative ladybird beetle releases. Nutrient solution levels were maintained continuously with fresh water; solutions were replaced weekly as insurance against root disease problems. Temperatures and relative humidities were monitored using Campbell 107 and 207 sensors in the root and aerial environments, respectively, attached to a Campbell CR7 datalogger. Root temperatures averaged $25.2 \pm 0.5°C$, and shoot temperatures 32.9 ± 2.2 and $31.1 \pm 2.0°C$ for the 1147 and 547 $\mu m/m^2/sec$ light intensity treatments, respectively. The shade cloth did increase relative humidity in the shoot environment by almost 10%, with average readings of $52.3 \pm 6.7\%$ and $63.1 \pm 6.2\%$ at the high and low light levels, respectively. Light levels were read with a LI-190SB quantum sensor attached to the Campbell CR7 datalogger.

Plants were harvested at 90 days, blotted dry, and divided into shoots and roots. Total shoot lengths and weights were calculated for each plant. Roots were further subdivided into total, pencil and storage roots, and weighed by individual plant. There was a very clear distinction between fibrous, storage and pencil roots, the latter being characteristically elongated and thickened, but less than 1 cm diameter.

RESULTS AND DISCUSSION

The only potassium effect ($P=0.05$) was to increase total vine fresh weight at the higher light level (Figure 2). This may have been related to potassium's ability to counteract the effect of high nitrogen on excessive vine growth (Tsuno and Fujise 1964) since the nutrient solution nitrogen level was relatively high. Not surprisingly, total root ($P=0.01$), pencil root, and vine ($P=0.05$) fresh weights, and total vine lengths ($P=0.05$) were all increased significantly at the higher level of light (Figures 2, 3, 4 and 5). No storage roots formed at the lower light levels. Sweetpotato plants

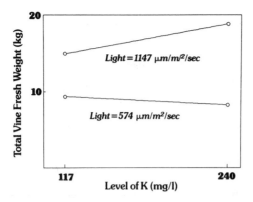

Figure 2. The effect of two light levels at two levels of potassium on total sweetpotato vine fresh weight. Increasing potassium at the higher light level increased (P=0.05) vine fresh weight.

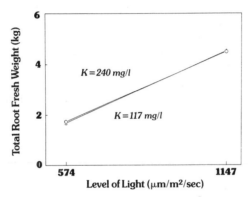

Figure 3. Doubling light intensity from 547 to 1147 μm/m^2/sec increased (P=0.01) total sweetpotato root fresh weight at both levels of potassium. This was because enlarged roots formed at the high but never at the low light level.

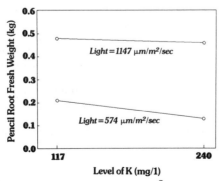

Figure 4. Doubling light intensity from 547 to 1147 μm/m^2/sec increased (P=0.05) sweetpotato pencil root fresh weight at both potassium levels.

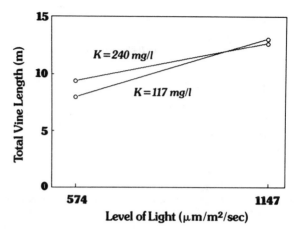

Figure 5. Doubling light intensity to 1147 μm/m^2/sec increased (P=0.05) total sweetpotato vine length at the two levels of potassium.

were successfully grown in aeroponics with excellent show and educational value potential (Plate 3). However, storage root formation for this cultivar would require a higher light level than that available in the area of the plant conveyor at The Land. These results indicate the need for additional research using different cultivars.

ACKNOWLEDGMENT

We are deeply grateful to Dr. John Bouwkamp for information on sweetpotato cultivars and nutrition.

LITERATURE CITED

Bouwkamp, J.C. 1985. Sweet potato products: a natural resource for the tropics. CRC Press, Inc., Boca Raton, FL.

Duncan, A.A., L.E. Scott, and F.C. Stark. 1958. Effect of potassium chloride and potassium sulfate on yield and quality of sweet potatoes. Proc. Am. Soc. Hortic. Sci. 71:391.

Geise, F.W. 1925. The influence of nitrogen, phosphorous and potash separately and in combination on sweet potato production. Proc. Am. Soc. Hortic. Sci. 22:363.

Godfrey-Sam-Aggrey, W. 1976. Effects of potash fertilizers on sweet potatoes in Sierra Leone. Exp. Agric. 12:87.

Hill, W.A., P.A. Loretan, C.K. Bonsi, C.E. Morris, J.Y. Lu, and C. Ogbuehi. 1989. Utilization of sweetpotatoes in Controlled Ecological Life Support Systems (CELSS). Adv. Space Res. 9(8):29-41.

Jones, L.G., R.J. Constantin, and T.P. Hernandez. 1979. The response of sweet potatoes to fertilizer phosphorus and potassium as related to levels of these elements available in the soil. La. Agric. Exp. Stn. Bull. No. 727.

Knavel, D.E. 1971. The influence of nitrogen and potassium nutrition on vine and root development of the 'Allgold' sweet potato at early stage of storage root development. J. Am. Soc. Hortic. Sci. 96:718.

Plate 1. Squash plants growing on the whole plant conveyor in the Creative House at The Land, EPCOT Center.

Plate 2. Experimental aeroponic production box designed to support sweetpotato vines above and hold 25 cm deep nutrient solution pool below. A submerged pump ran continuously to supply fogging nozzles suspended halfway up in the root zone.

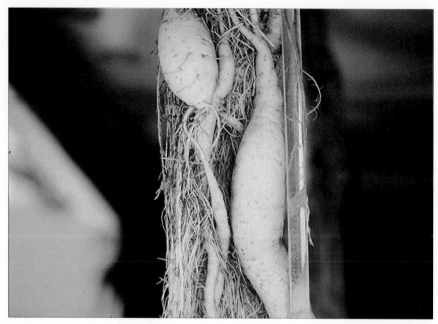

Plate 3. Close up of a sweetpotato root system after 90 days in the aeroponic production box.

Lardizabal, R.D., and P.G. Thompson. 1988. Hydroponic culture, grafting and growth regulators to increase flowering in sweet potato. HortScience 23:993-995.

Loretan, P.A., W.A. Hill, C.K. Bonsi, and C.E. Morris. 1988. Effect of aggregate, nutrient solution, and pot size on production of sweet potato roots. HortScience 23(5):828.

Morris, C.E., P.A. Loretan, W.A. Hill, and C.K. Bonsi. 1988. Experimental hydroponic system for growing sweet potato plants. HortScience 23 (5):828.

Murata, T., and T. Akagawa. 1968. Enzymatic mechanism of starch synthesis in sweet potato roots. I. Requirement of potassium ions for starch synthetase. Arch. Biochem. Biophys. 126:873.

Scott, L.E., and J.C. Bouwkamp. 1974. Seasonal mineral accumulation by the sweet potato. HortScience 9:233.

Speights, D.W., and D.R. Paterson. 1961. Sweet potato fertilizer and variety trials in northeast Texas. Texas Agric. Exp. Stn. Rep. No. 219.

Tsuno, Y. 1970. Dry matter production of sweet potatoes and yield increasing technics. Fertilite, 38:3.

Tsuno, Y., and K. Fujise. 1965. Studies on the dry matter production of sweet potato. Bull. Natl. Inst. Agric. Sci. (Jpn.), Series D, No. 13.

Tsuno, Y., and K. Fujise. 1964. Studies on the dry matter production in sweet potato. IV. The relation between the contribution of mineral nutrients in plant distribution ratio over dry matter produced. Proc. Crop Sci. Soc. Jpn. 32, 301.

Walker, D.W., K.J. Poche, and E.M Pouche. 1988. Evidence of differential nitrogen uptake in two sweet potato cultivars. HortScience 23 (5):828.

Zimmerley, H. H. 1929. Sweet potato fertilizers. Va. Truck Exp. Stn. Bull. No. 66.

M. N. Alvarez

Sweetpotato Cropping Systems in Africa

There are several ways in which the African farmer can address the continent's food crisis and increase his productivity. One way is to intensify the cropping system. The sweetpotato lends itself to this system. Besides being compatible with various farming practices, it also contributes significantly to meeting year-round food security needs. The sweetpotato, with its short growth cycle, has become popular in urban, peri-urban and other high density areas because of its efficiency in producing biological material for both human and animal food. Although new, higher yielding varieties are spreading, there are many more agro-ecological zones in Africa in which sweetpotato can quickly contribute to increased food production with minimum increase in inputs. In order to extend successfully the improved sweetpotato cropping system technology, strong government commitment must be ensured, seed production and technology transfer systems established and the chauvinism against the crop removed.

INTRODUCTION

The sweetpotato is among the root crops that play an important dietary role in many parts of tropical Africa (Hahn et al. 1989). While it is an important staple crop in only a few densely populated countries such as Rwanda, Burundi and parts of Uganda, it continues to be an important subsidiary food in other countries of Africa.

In an environment of declining per capita food production and increasing population, food self-sufficiency programs have gained priority in many parts of the continent. As population pressure increases and land cultivation intensifies, attention is focused on marginal land and on improving productivity with reduced inputs. Fortunately, the sweetpotato lends itself to these conditions.

The widespread distribution of the crop in Africa and the trend of increasing production is an indication of sweetpotato's growing importance. It is grown over a wide range of environmental conditions, from sea level to 2300 meters above and between 30 degrees north and south of the equator (Hahn 1989). It fits well into various crop combinations and cropping practices ranging from intensive nursery bed production to subsistence production during different seasons.

Sweetpotato growing will continue to have special relevance to Africa in the future. The areas where its production is most advanced and intensive are highly

International Institute of Tropical Agriculture, East and Southern Africa Root Crops Research Network, P. O. Box 158, Lilongwe, Malawi.

populated, of low resource and under low-input small farm operations. The successful spread of technology for improving its production will provide us with some of the greatest opportunities for African agriculture in the 21st century.

HISTORY OF CULTIVATION

It is believed that sweetpotato reached Africa in the sixteenth century (Yen 1976). However, there has been very little expansion of the crop as a major food crop (Table 1). The more intensive forms of cultivation are located in the highland areas between 1000 to 2300 meters above sea level (masl) of Central Africa (Rwanda, Burundi, eastern Zaire and western Uganda), which are also densely populated. Large scale production and intensity of cropping is also greatest in this area, where sweetpotatoes are a major staple. Average per capita production is well over 100 kg per year (Ewell 1990). Lower middle elevation (500-1000 masl) areas which are less intensively cultivated are found in Kenya, Madagascar, some parts of Tanzania and Malawi. Sweetpotatoes are also grown in lower (0-500 masl) coastal areas with high rainfall (>1500 mm) as in West Africa and low rainfall areas (600mm) as in coastal East and Southern Africa.

Although sweetpotato had an early introduction to the continent, its cultivation for commercial production is limited. Most of the production is in East and Southern Africa with 12 countries producing more than 90% of Africa's total (Table 2).

PRODUCTION PRACTICES

Throughout Africa, sweetpotato is grown primarily by women either as a sole crop or in combination with other crops, depending on ecological region. Most farmers grow it as a short season crop. Except in countries where sweetpotato is a major staple, it is usually grown as a subsidiary component of the cropping system (Alvarez and Ndamage 1985; Lyonga and Ayuk-Taken 1983; Mutuura et al. 1990; Norman et al. 1984).

In an intensive production system, as in Rwanda and Burundi, the crop occupies a significant portion of the arable land area. From a survey done in Rwanda (Alvarez

Table 1. Sweetpotato production compared to other major root crops in Africa.

Crop	All Africa Area (000 ha^{-1})	All Africa Mean Yield (t/ha^{-1})	All Africa Production (000 t)	E & S Africa Production	E & S Africa Output as % of Africa
Cassava	8,100	7.1	54,600	31,150	57
Yams	2,400	10.5	23,600	250	1
Sweetpotatoes	1,200	6.0	6,105	4,900	80
Potatoes	800	8.8	6,900	2,350	33

Source: Means 1986-88 from FAO figures.

Table 2. Sweetpotato production in Africa.

Country	Production (000 Tons, Mean 1986-88)
Angola	170
Burundi	426
Cameroon	154
Ethiopia	144
Kenya	104
Liberia	550
Madagascar	475
Nigeria	260
Rwanda	810
Tanzania	340
Uganda	1800
Zaire	372
Africa, Total	6105

Source : FAO 1989 Production Yearbook.

and Ndamage 1985), it was observed that all land preparation was done by hoe. More than 40 percent of farmers had their sweetpotato land in short term fallow in the previous season. The remaining farmers planted sweetpotato after another crop. Preplanting cultivation entails ridging, mounding or tillage on flat land depending upon the soil type and drainage. Most farmers plant the crop on raised beds 1 to 3 m wide in the valley bottoms and on large ridges, mounds or heaps 30-50 cm high when planting on the hills. A few plant on tilled flat ground in well drained areas. In Uganda, where sweetpotato production is equally intensive, more mounds are used. The mounds are 45 to 60 cm high and about 1m in diameter. Some areas also use very big mounds of up to 1 m in height planted with 20 or more vines. In this system, sweetpotato is also grown on small plots ranging from 0.2 to 1 ha both in valley bottoms as well as on hill slopes. When the land is in short term fallow, the weeds are plowed and buried in the soil and the position of the mounds usually shifts from season to season within the same plot.

In less intensive systems, sweetpotato is usually grown as a minor sole crop in small plots on the borders of fields of the main crop or in association with other food crops such as maize, cassava, beans, bananas and sorghum. There is a considerable amount of sweetpotato grown in small compound gardens and other sporadic forms of cultivation in plots along roadsides and any available open space in urban and peri-urban areas. Such areas range from .01 to .04 ha.

In rice-based cultures like Sierra Leone, Liberia, and some parts of Nigeria and Madagascar, sweetpotato plays an important role during the "hungry period." After harvesting rice from the valley bottoms, farmers normally grow a short duration upland crop to take advantage of the residual moisture. This period is usually the peak of the dry season. Similarly, during the peak rainy season in Sierra Leone, sweetpotato can be harvested and the proceeds from its sale pay for labor on the rice crop.

The various crop combinations observed in Rwanda are shown in Table 3 and the position of sweetpotato in the system in terms of area and time is shown in Figure 1. In some cases the crop occupies the land for 1.5 seasons where it is planted in the first season and harvested in the middle of the second season.

Table 3. Frequency distribution of intercropping patterns of sweetpotato in Rwanda.

Crops intercropped	Frequency (%)
Cassava	26
Beans	14
Sorghum	8
Maize	5
Banana	3
Combination with any two or all of the above	44

Source: Alvarez and Ndamage 1985.

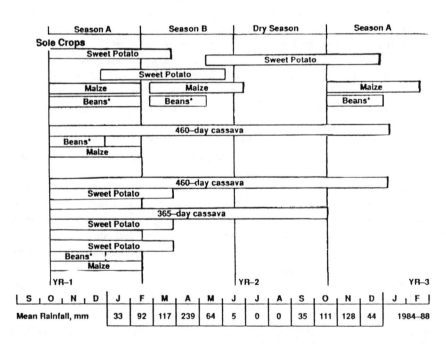

Figure 1. Cropping patterns for sole crops and multiseason intercrops in Rwanda (after Balasubramanian and Sekayange 1991).

Table 4. Yields of component crops in intercropping systems involving sweetpotato. Experiments were conducted across different intercrop periods varying from 165 to 460 days at Kagasa, Rwanda (1400 m altitude, 850 mm annual rainfall) 1985 to 1986.

Intercrop System	Growth Cycle (days)	Yield (t ha^{-1})	
		Sole Crop	Inter-Crop
Cassava - HC	460	49.1	25.3
Sweetpotato	165	17.3	16.5
Cassava - LC	365	36.6	10.5
Sweetpotato	165	11.0	11.0
Sweetpotato	165	17.3	13.8
Bean	80	0.6	0.5
Maize	120	1.3	0.3

HC = high cyanide; LC = low cyanide (after Balasubramanian and Sekayange 1991).

Under these circumstances, no other crop can be planted after the harvest of sweetpotato. In order to evenly distribute the labor demand over the season, farmers often plant the sweetpotato crop in the second half of a season and harvest at the end of the following season. The yield of these combinations when studied in Rwanda is shown in Table 4 (Balasubramanian and Sekayange 1991). These combinations apply similarly to the East African mid-elevation. Other cases of relay cropping with maize or intercropping with agro-forestry trees and other crops has also been reported (Mutuura et al. 1990).

Planting

Planting time is generally at the onset of rains. The months vary depending on the region. In Rwanda the first season planting is between October and March with a peak in November on the hills. Early planting is in October to November. In Uganda, planting is done at the first rainy season (April to May) or second rainy season (August to September). The extended planting time is influenced by availability of planting material, land and labor. Other crops usually get higher priority for labor at this time. May to June is the planting period in the valley.

Most farmers avoid obviously diseased planting material. However, most farmers do use physiologically old vines. The survey in Rwanda showed that more than 60% of planting material used were usually old vines. The planting method is similar across the regions. A mixture of old and young vines are cut at a length of 30 to 40 cm and planted two vines per hole at a very high density. The hole is dug with a hoe or by hand and the two vines planted so that a short tip of the vines would appear on either side after covering. With two plants per hole at close spacing, the density is very high with a median density of 17 plants per square meter. Only a few farmers,

Table 5. Effect of plant density on sweetpotato yield over two seasons for two years (1988-89) at Rubona, Rwanda (1650 m altitude, 1171 mm rainfall).

Density (ha^{-1}) (000)	Yield (t ha^{-1})	
	Rainy Season	Dry Season
27	13.5	7.9
33	14.6	8.7
44	13.5	7.7
50	17.7	12.8
67	17.1	13.1
88	17.1	13.5
100	18.2	14.2
133	17.9	12.5

Source: ISAR 1990.

less than 20%, used apical cuttings only as planting material. In Uganda the use of selected apical cuttings is the common practice. The apical vines 30 to 45 cm long are planted on mounds or ridges to give a population range of 20,000 to 30,000 vines per ha. The yield of sweetpotato at different densities when tested for two seasons for two years is shown in Table 5 (ISAR 1990).

Planting material at the beginning of the rainy season is a limiting factor on account of reduced growth and loss of plant vines during the dry season. Farmers who have access to hydromorphic plots can grow sweetpotatoes in the valley during the dry season and will have vines at the beginning of the rains. Some farmers do buy planting material from the market or from neighbors who grow sweetpotato in the valley. In the dry and cool areas farmers are sometimes forced to wait for roots to sprout in order to obtain material for planting.

This latter practice results in late planting and limits production. This is particularly so where the rainy season is short. In such areas, even when fields are ready for planting after the first good rain, planting is delayed by 2 to 3 months, due to unavailability of the planting material (Hahn et al. 1989). When planted late, the sweetpotato is monocropped or sometimes intercropped with cassava. The plots are grown without fertilizer and less than 5% used compost in sweetpotato fields. This is usually done when grown in association with another crop. The mean sweetpotato plot size in Rwanda is .12 ha with a range of .01 to .63 ha. In most parts of Africa where the crop is grown, the plots are similarly small. A few large plots may be found in peri-urban areas, where the crop is being grown for sale in the cities or towns.

Weeding

Sweetpotato plots usually need weeding at a time when there is a high demand on the farmer's time. It is a common saying in Rwanda that only those with nothing to do weed sweetpotato fields. Only 26% of farmers weeded their sweetpotato fields once and generally this weeding exercise involves the uprooting of only tall aggressive weeds. On account of the dense planting, it is not easy to weed any other way without injuring the plants. Another 10% weeded twice, generally when sweetpotatoes are grown in combination with other crops. The dense planting in Rwanda results in quick ground cover and thus requires little weeding. The Uganda system allows for proper weeding between mounds without damage to the plants.

Varieties Used

Of the more than 100 clonal names reported in Rwanda, only five were widely used and two were most popular. On an average, farmers will grow a mixture of three to five varieties. Some districts may register up to 30 different varieties. Other surveys have reported hundreds of clones in Africa (Alvarez 1985, Mutuura 1990). Most of the farmers' traditional varieties are of long cycle and disease infected; there is much interest in early bulking varieties. The mean yield of local lines compared with improved cultivars have shown that yields can be doubled (Alvarez 1987).

Harvesting

In Rwanda, Burundi and Uganda, more than 95% of farmers make their first harvest after four months or later with mean harvest time being 5.5 months with a range of three to 12 months. This extended period is due to the piecemeal harvest. The flexibility of the harvest time makes it an important food security crop at times of adverse conditions.

Because of differences in the length of growing seasons of the various varieties used, only a few early bulking ones will give a good yield at early harvest. Unlike the early ones, late bulking varieties tend to suffer less weevil attack as they progress into the dry season. All harvesting is done by hoe. Less than 20% of harvest goes to the market. Most sweetpotatoes grown are primarily for home consumption and are harvested at intervals when needed for home use or market. Harvested sweet-potato is usually consumed within the week. There is hardly any storage after harvest, although isolated cases of parboiling, chipping and drying for storage has been mentioned. Boiling and frying are the most common forms of preparation and occasionally it is used as a dessert.

The sweetpotato leaf, which has 13 to 28% crude protein (IITA 1980), is also an important vegetable in many parts of Africa, but in smaller quantities as compared to Sierra Leone and Liberia. Its use as an animal feed is minimal.

CONSTRAINTS AS SEEN ON THE FARM

From surveys made, the farmers have identified many of their main constraints. Many of these are interelated, but for the purpose of this paper they will be discussed separately.

Soil Fertility

Most farmers indicated that they would like sweetpotato varieties that could be harvested early and which are adapted to their soils. Although these soils are generally well prepared, they are usually poor and eroded. Some farmers deliberately plant in less fertile soils. Although farmers do realize the benefits of having good and well prepared soil for sweetpotato production, their knowledge of managing and improving the quality of their soils is a limiting factor. This situation is aggravated by the prohibitive cost or non-availability of resource inputs such as fertilizer.

Planting Material/Seed

In general, the farming system employed in producing sweetpotato whether in the valley or on the hillside and at different altitudes differs very little. In a few cases, this difference may be significant. For example, optimal use of healthy, good quality planting material is rare. This may be attributed to the lack of an adequate quantity at the time when it is most needed. On account of this, the entire length of sweetpotato vine, regardless of physiological age, is often used for planting. Despite this practice, most farmers still indicate that they lack enough planting material.

The use of high planting densities of 80 to 160 plants ha^{-1} is apparently a risk safety device that enables the farmer to obtain good establishment. Under unfavorable conditions, planting material that is of higher quality will stand a better chance to germinate. High planting density may also offer optimal utilization of limited land area and a reduction in the need for weeding.

Diseases and Pests

Farmers recognize the problem of pests (insects and rodents) and diseases but these problems are ranked differently in different locations. Furthermore, they do avoid the use of planting material that show severe virus or other disease symptoms; nevertheless, the risk of losing valuable lines due to diseases and pests continues to be high. Oftentimes, farmers speak of preferred varieties that they no longer have available because they succumbed to these biophysical constraints. Perhaps the practice of planting multiple varieties is the farmer's defense against risk of disease, drought and insects and allows for year-round production.

Storage

With increasing demand for sweetpotato in the cities, the concern for post-harvest quality during storage and transportation is now a problem for city suppliers. In areas where land is limited, storage in the ground is becoming costly because the land cannot be used.

OUTLOOK FOR THE 21ST CENTURY

Africa is experiencing an explosive population growth and accelerated environmental degradation (World Bank 1989). The production base is strained and the challenge is now to develop a strategy that will halt and reverse the trend. This situation has given rise to concern about sustainability in agricultural production (Okigbo 1989).

It is estimated that about one-quarter of sub-Saharan Africa's population—more than 100 million people—face chronic food insecurity (World Bank 1989). In order to reverse this, agricultural productivity must increase and urgent action is needed to improve food security. The sweetpotato is a crop that certainly has a role to play in meeting this need. Food processing and increasing its accessibility as an energy food will allow the sweetpotato to better play its role in guaranteeing food self-sufficiency and food security.

Rwanda is an example where intensive utilization of sweetpotato as a home garden and field crop has contributed significantly in meeting nutritional and year-round food security needs. Similarly, Cameroon and Sierra Leone are having an impressive impact from their research results on sweetpotato. With the release of improved high-yielding varieties, they are now close to overproduction. These programs have achieved this through collaboration with IITA, donor support and government commitment. The commitment from governments to include sweetpotato in addressing their policy for food security and nutrition is paying off. Many other countries can benefit from these experiences.

Genetic improvement for the optimal utilization of this crop in Africa is still relatively new and not yet fully exploited. The combination of biotechnology and traditional breeding can provide answers for the new challenges of rapidly evolving needs in post-harvest handling, stress tolerance and other alternate uses. It is in answering these problems that the great scope of the crop will be realized thus enabling it to contribute significantly to the continent's economy and sustainable agro-ecosystem for the 21st century.

CONCLUSION

The sweetpotato cropping system is predominantly a subsistence operation. It is a reserve food and almost all is consumed by humans in Africa. It is usually harvested when needed and when other food crops are out of supply due to drought.

The scale of sweetpotato production might be limited by labor needed for land preparation, availability of planting material at critical times, diseases and pests, weeding, bulk marketing, transportation costs and limited technological advancement in mixed cropping systems. Farmers have demonstrated the degree of compatibility of sweetpotato production with various farming systems with limited resources. Although this crop usually receives low priority in terms of inputs and time, the farmer perceives it as a reliable crop with very little risk involved.

The growing food needs of Africa will continue to be served by the small, limited-input farmer. Considering the potential of the crop, its further neglect by research is no longer affordable. The accelerated effort needed to facilitate its increased production in Africa will require a joint effort between various institutions around the world. We can all contribute to ensure its success.

REFERENCES

Alvarez, M.N., and G. Ndamage. 1985. Sweet potato in Rwanda: State of the art. Bulletin Agricole Du Rwanda 18(4):211-215.

Alvarez, M.N. 1987. Sweet potato and the African food crisis. Pages 66-69 *in* Tropical root crops: Root crops and the African food crisis, edited by E.R. Terry, M.O. Akoroda and O.B. Arene, Ottawa: IDRC.

Balasubramanian, V., and L. Sekayange. 1991. Area harvests equivalency ratio for measuring efficiency in multiseason intercropping. IITA Research 1 (2):16-19.

Ewell, Peter, T., and Roger A. Kirkby. 1990. Roots, tubers and beans in the food systems of Eastern and Southern Africa. Paper presented at the conference on Dialogue and training for the promotion of roots, tubers and legumes in Africa. November 26-30, 1990, Mombasa, Kenya.

Food and Agricultural Organization. 1989. Production yearbook. Rome: FAO.

Hahn, S.K., John C.G. Isoba, and T. Ikotun. 1989. Resistance breeding in root and tuber crops at the International Institute of Tropical Agriculture (IITA), Ibadan, Nigeria. Crop Protection 8:147-168.

ISAR (Institut des Sciences Agronomiques du Rwanda). 1990. Sweet Potato-Cassava Program. Biannual report for 1988-1989. Pages 5-28.

Lyonga S.N., and J.A. Ayuk-Takem. 1984. Comportment studies with sweet potatoes in the highland zone of Cameroon.Pages 193-196 *in* Tropical root crops: production and uses in Africa, edited by E.R. Terry, E.V. Doku, O.B. Arene, and N.M. Mahungu. Proceedings of the 2nd Triennial Symposium of the International Society for Tropical Root Crops-Africa Branch held in Douala, Cameroon, 14-19 August, 1983. International Development Research Centre, Ottawa, Ont., Canada. IDRC-221e.

Mutuura, J., P.T. Ewell, A. Abubaker, T. Munga, S. Ajanga, J. Irungu, F. Omari, and S.Maobe. 1990. Sweet potatoes in the food systems of Kenya: Results of a socioeconomic survey. Paper presented at the Fourth East and Southern Africa Root Crops Workshop, October 26-November 2, 1990, Mansa, Zambia.

Norman, M.J.T., C.J. Pearson, and P.G.E. Searle. 1984. The ecology of tropical food crops. Cambridge University Press. 245-346 pp.

Okigbo, B.N. 1989. Development of sustainable agricultural production systems in Africa. Roles of International Agricultural Research Centers and National Agricultural Research Systems. Based on the first lecture in Distinguished African Scientist Lecture Series delivered at the International Institute of Tropical Agriculture, Ibadan on April 26, 1989.

World Bank. 1989. Sub-Saharan Africa from crisis to sustainable growth. Washington, D.C.

Yen, D.E. 1976. Sweet Potato *Ipomoea batatas* (Convolvulaceae) Pages 42-45 *in* Evolution of crop plants, edited by N.W. Simmonds, London and New York: Longman.

Sweetpotato Technology for the 21st Century. W.A. Hill, C.K. Bonsi and P.A. Loretan (Eds.) 1992.Tuskegee University, Tuskegee, AL

N. S. Talekar

Insect Factors in Breeding and Cultivation of Sweetpotato

Among over 300 insect and mite species that feed on sweetpotato in the tropics and subtropics, only three species of root feeding weevils, *Cylas formicarius, C. puncticollis* and *Euscepes postfasciatus,* and one vineboring caterpillar, *Omphisa anastomosalis,* cause serious damage and yield loss over wide areas. *Cylas formicarius* is found throughout the tropics and subtropics, whereas *C. puncticollis is* confined to Africa and *E. postfasciatus* to Oceania, Hawaii, the Caribbean and Latin America. These weevils feed mainly in storage roots and, in their absence, inside vines. Vine infestation serves as an important inoculum source of weevil for infestation of roots. Availability of cultivars with resistance to weevils will be extremely useful in sustainable production of this crop. However, intensive search for sources of resistance within *Ipomoea batatas* germplasm has failed to find a suitable material with consistent resistance under varied environmental conditions. It may be necessary to introduce genes for weevil resistance into sweetpotato from other *Ipomoea* species. Thinner woody stems are always less damaged than the thicker fleshy ones by *C. formicarius.* Breeding sweetpotato cultivars with thin woody stems presents an opportunity to reduce weevil populations and thereby lessen the damage to sweetpotato roots. A simple and inexpensive integrated control method has been developed which involves crop rotation, using relatively tender planting slips, planting new crop away from weevil-infested sweetpotato and controlling alternate host *Ipomoea* species in the immediate areas. This IPM package has been successfully used on farmers' fields in Taiwan to combat sweetpotato weevils. Sweetpotato vineborer is important in Asia and the Pacific. Vineborer feeding in the vines adversely affects plant vigor and root yield. Sources of field resistance to vine borer are available and are being used in our resistance breeding program. Certain *Ipomoea* species that serve as alternate hosts of the weevils also harbor sweetpotato vine borer. Destruction of these alternate hosts will help to reduce damage by both weevil and vine borer to sweetpotato. Vine borer females produce a sex pheromone that attracts males for mating. Synthesis and utilization of this chemical will aid considerably in the IPM of this pest.

INTRODUCTION

A total of at least 270 species of insects and 17 species of mites are reported to feed on sweetpotato *(Ipomoea batatas* Lam.) in the field and in storage throughout the world (Talekar 1987a). All plant parts, namely, roots, stems, foliage, and even

Asian Vegetable Research and Development Center, Shanhua, Tainan 74199,Taiwan, Republic of China.

the seeds harbor insect pests. The pest species are taxonomically diverse and cause direct damage to the storage roots by feeding on them or indirect damage by defoliating or boring vines. Both reduce yield depending upon the severity of the infestation and the crop growth stage when such infestation occurs. Certain insect species, such as aphids, leafhoppers and whiteflies, in addition to feeding on foliage, transmit most of the virus and mycoplasma-like organisms that cause certain diseases.

Sweetpotato harbors an enormous number of pest species possibly because, in the tropics, it can be successfully grown throughout the year and under extremes of moisture conditions such as prolonged drought or flooding, where other crops cannot survive. If not harvested, sweetpotato can remain green in the field practically indefinitely. This survivability coupled with its habit of producing excessive foliage makes it an ideal niche for food and shelter for a variety of insect species.

The insects that attack sweetpotato can be classified—based on the phenology of the host plant—as defoliators, vine borers or root feeders. Except for one or possibly two species, none of the enormous number of defoliator species causes any significant yield loss over an appreciable area. There are only two major species of vine borers that cause significant yield loss. Since root feeders feed directly on the storage roots, their damage results in making the produce unfit for consumption which, at times, amounts to total loss. Among the more than 40 species that attack sweetpotato roots, however, only three are specific pests of sweetpotato, and at least one of them is present wherever sweetpotato is grown in the tropics. The discussion in this paper will focus on the importance of only one defoliator, two vine borers and three root feeders in breeding and cultivation of sweetpotato.

DEFOLIATORS

Although over 180 insect species feed on sweetpotato foliage, except for *Agrius convolvuli* (L.) and to some extent *A. cingulata* (F.) (Lepidoptera: Sphingidae), none appears to cause significant yield loss over an appreciable area. Other species such as those belonging to genera *Bedellia, Brachmia* and *Acraea* do, at times, cause yield loss; however, their infestation is highly localized and rarely endemic.

Agrius convolvuli occurs practically all over Africa and Asia. A related species *A. cingulata* damages sweetpotato in the West Indies and Florida (Edward 1937; Watson 1944), but it rarely causes as severe damage as *A. convolvuli*. In some parts of Africa, this pest can cause serious defoliation and there are reports of yield loss of between 20 and 50% (Faure 1914).

The insect lays eggs on the foliage and newly-hatched larvae start feeding on the leaves. Larva of this insect is one of the largest caterpillars and may reach 90 mm in length and 14 mm diameter when full grown. It feeds voraciously on sweetpotato foliage for 3 to 4 weeks before becoming a pupa. There are usually three overlapping generations during a cropping season.

No efforts have been made to develop *A. convolvuli* resistant cultivars. In small-scale planting, collection and destruction of the larvae and ploughing of an infested field soon after harvest to expose pupae are often suggested as routine control measures.

VINE BORERS

Although several insect species feed on sweetpotato vines, only two, *Megastes grandalis* Guenee and *Omphisa anastomasalis* Guenee (Lepidoptera: Pyralidae) cause any significant yield loss. *M. grandalis* occurs in Brazil, Guyana and Trinidad and Tobago; *O. anastomasalis* is widespread in Asia and the Pacific.

M. grandalis

Adults lay eggs in the axils or on leaf lamina. Soon after egg hatching, larva of this insect enters the vine and feeds inside the stem on the underground part that bears the storage roots. The frass is ejected outside from the larval entry hole or cracks in the stem; its presence indicates the presence of larva in the stem. During dry season, such damage causes stunted growth and shedding of leaves which results in failure of storage root formation. If roots are formed, the larva enters them via the stem and tunnels through the roots. Damage is visible only when such roots are cut open (Cowland 1926). Up to 95% of the sweetpotato roots may be damaged by the *M. grandalis* larvae in cases of severe infestation, which eventually results in large yield reduction (Parasram 1969).

O. anastomasalis

This insect is widespread in Asia and the Pacific. Adult females lay eggs on petioles, axils, stems and on major veins in the leaf lamina. Eggs hatch and caterpillars enter vines and tunnel through the vines for an average of 35 days before pupation. The major damage results from caterpillars boring into the main stem leading to storage roots. The frass collects at ground level around the larval entry hole, indicating the presence of larva inside the stem. Severely tunnelled vines show weak growth and poor foliage development that appears yellow and wilted during sunny days. Such plants show poor storage root formation. At times the caterpillars can also bore into the roots. In Hawaii, Chung (1923) reported serious damage by this pest, which resulted in the death of the sweetpotato plant. In Malaysia, this pest reduces yield by about 30% (Ho 1970). In Taiwan about 90% of unprotected plants sustain damage and the yield reduction is about 50% (Talekar and Cheng 1987).

Breeding for vine borer resistance

In a study of six West Indian sweetpotato cultivars, Lowe and Wilson (1972) found that cultivar '049' was free of *M. grandalis* damage, '03/62' had 7%, 'I62' had 10%, and '28/7' had 13% plants damaged. The most susceptible cultivar, 'C 9/9', had 40% plants damaged. Despite the damage, root yield of '28/7' was not reduced.

West (1977) found no significant difference in *M. grandalis* damage to vines of '049' and three other cultivars, 'A16/15,' 'A28/7' and 'Red vine' for up to 18 weeks after planting. He did observe, however, that '049' remained free of *M. grandalis* for six weeks after planting and was the least acceptable cultivar for oviposition by female *M. grandalis*. In further studies, Wilson and Lowe (1973) found that in '28/7', the plants damaged by *M. grandalis* developed extensive phloic vascular bundles which enabled uninterrupted translocation of assimilates from foliage to storage roots, which in turn allowed this cultivar to give normal yield despite the damage. Cultivation of such a tolerant cultivar will enable growers to obtain normal yields in areas where *M. grandalis is* endemic.

Screening of over 800 accessions of the sweetpotato germplasm of the Asian Vegetable Research and Development Center (AVRDC) in Taiwan has resulted in identification of three accessions; I 55, I 92 and I 789 which were consistently least damaged by *O. anastomasalis* in all field tests conducted at Penghu island where this insect is endemic. Preliminary studies indicate that these cultivars have a low level of antibiosis to *O. anastomasalis* (AVRDC 1990). Accession I 55 is now being utilized in AVRDC's sweetpotato vine borer resistance breeding program (Talekar and Cheng 1987).

ROOT FEEDERS

Root feeders, mainly weevils, are by far the most destructive pests of sweetpotato throughout the tropics and subtropics. In several areas, they are the major limiting factors in successful cultivation of sweetpotato. Their damage is especially significant because they attack the tuberous roots directly. The slightest damage by these pests can make the whole root unfit for human consumption because of the peculiar terpene odor it imparts in damaged roots.

Although several weevil species are reported to feed on sweetpotato roots, only two species belonging to genus *Cylas, C. formicarius* (F.) and *C. puncticollis* (Boh.), and one belonging to genus *Euscepes, E. puncticollis* (Fairmaire), (Coleoptera: Curculionidae) are significant in terms of severity of their damage over wider areas. Despite their taxonomic differences, their mode of infestation and nature of damage are quite similar. Hence, control measures devised to combat them are practically identical.

Cylas species

While *C. formicarius* is found in Asia, the Pacific, North and Central America and certain countries in Africa, *Cylas puncticollis* is confined to certain countries in Africa only. The two subspecies of *C. formicarius, C. formicarius formicarius* (F.) and *C. formicarius elegantulus* (Summers) which were often mentioned in past literature as independent subspecies, are now considered as synonyms of *C. formicarius* (Wolfe 1991). The mention of *C. formicarius* in this paper, therefore, includes both former subspecies.

Adults lay eggs in the older portions of vines near the crown or storage roots when the roots are exposed. Larvae bore into the respective plant parts where adults have oviposited. There is no tunnelling and movement of larvae from stem to the root or in other directions within the plant. Given the choice, the insect prefers to lay eggs and feed in roots rather than in stems. When roots are not developed, the insect lays eggs in the stem and the emerging adults search for exposed storage roots to lay eggs.

The major damage results from the larval feeding in the roots. The tortuous larval feeding tunnels become filled with frass that rots, giving the damaged tissue the characteristic terpene odor. Even the slightly damaged roots are rendered unfit for human consumption. Although larval feeding in the stems at times can be substantial, the role of this feeding in yield reduction has produced contradictory results (Cockerham et al. 1954, Talekar 1982a, Mullen 1984, Sutherland 1986a, Lema and Hahn 1987, AVRDC 1991, AVRDC unpublished results). Although the significance of weevil feeding in stems on the reduction of root yield is uncertain, it is certain that the weevils feeding in the stems act as the source of inoculum for infestation of roots that develop later. Adult weevils also feed on foliage. Such feeding is only occasional in the case of *C. formicarius,* but seems to be quite common in *C. puncticollis* (Hahn and Leuschner 1981). The influence of such defoliation on the root yield has not yet been documented in either species.

Euscepes postfasciatus

Although this species is confined to tropical and subtropical areas of theWestern Hemisphere, mainly in the Caribbean and South America, it is also found in Hawaii, Fiji, Tonga and Okinawa (Messenger 1954).

Like the *Cylas* species, *E. postfasciatus* adults lay eggs in vines and storage roots, and larvae feed in respective plant parts where eggs are laid and pupate. Adults of *E. postfasciatus* are very sturdy insects and can live without food under laboratory conditions for up to 45 days (Tucker 1937). If buried, they can survive in soil for several months. When provided with food, they can live for 10 months. Adults can also survive considerable periods of flooding (Sherman and Tamashiro 1954).

The damage caused by *E. postfasciatus* and *Cylas* species is similar. Adults feed externally on the vines or roots, mostly on roots. Damaged roots have a few small pits and numerous holes in which several weevil adults feed (Sherman and Tamashiro 1954). Larvae gnaw winding tunnels in roots and stems. These tunnels become packed with frass and the characteristic terpene odor similar to the one caused by *C. formicarius* is also found in *E. postfasciatus*-damaged tissues. Damaged vines darken from normal green to brown or black and damaged main stems become swollen, malformed and cracked.

Control of Weevils

Since the biology and the nature of damage of all three species are similar, it is possible to control these pests by adopting common control strategies. Indeed, the review of literature on this topic shows a common theme in combating these pest species.

Because of their concealed feeding habits, sweetpotato weevils can be difficult to control by conventional insecticide application. However, because of several factors—their limited flying activity which implies that the insect is carried from place to place via movement of plant material, their host specificity to genus *Ipomoea,* their preference for oviposition, in the absence of roots, in older vines and their characteristic mode of entry and damage to the plant, these weevils are vulnerable to effective control by integration of simple cultural practices such as rotation, clean cultivation, mulching and use of tender vine cuttings for planting a new crop. Utility of such inexpensive practices in controlling *C. formicarius* has been demonstrated in experimental fields and farmers' fields (Talekar 1983, 1987b; Talekar et al. 1989). Based on these results, an IPM package that is practical on small farmers' fields has been developed (Talekar 1988). Jansson (1992) discusses integration of new technology for the control of sweetpotato weevil on large-scale commercial plantings.

Breeding for sweetpotato weevil resistance

During the past 50 years, numerous attempts have been made to find sources of resistance primarily to *Cylas* species, and to incorporate resistance into agronomic cultivars. This line of research has been followed mainly at USDA laboratories and at the International Institute of Tropical Agriculture (IITA) in Nigeria and the Asian Vegetable Research and Development Center (AVRDC) in Taiwan from their establishment in the early 1970s until the latter two institutes discontinued their research on sweetpotato in 1989. Despite these efforts, not a single sweetpotato cultivar has been bred, using previously identified sources of resistance, and which is grown in any appreciable area to control *Cylas* species. Efforts to find sources of resistance have been thwarted by differences in weevil infestation among various trials, locations, seasons, and—at times—among replicates of a single cultivar in a trial (Talekar 1982b, 1987c) .

Environment plays a very important role in the interaction between the weevil and sweetpotato. Details of this interaction and its role in finding a source of resistance to the weevil are discussed elsewhere (Talekar 1987d).

It is believed that the sweetpotato weevil originated in South Asia (Kemner 1924; Wolfe 1991). However, sweetpotato was introduced to South Asia relatively recently, not more than 350 years ago (Yen 1982). Before the introduction of sweetpotato, the insect obviously survived on wild *Ipomoea* species feeding inside their woody stems. Indeed a large number of *Ipomoea* species harbor sweetpotato weevil in India (CTCRI 1983) and elsewhere (Sutherland 1986b). Even such woody plants as *I. pes-caprae* are attacked by this pest. Sweetpotato roots, by comparison, are much more nutritious and given the choice, the weevil prefers sweetpotato over all other *Ipomoea* species (Cockerham 1943) that have been tested so far. It is unlikely, therefore, that any sweetpotato cultivar would be developed that would have roots less preferred than the woody stems of *I. pes-caprae* and which would still be acceptable for human consumption.

Although, for reasons explained above, it appears difficult to develop sweetpotato cultivars with weevil resistance in the roots, it is possible to breed a cultivar with resistance to the weevil in the vines. Even though the influence of weevil feeding in vines on the root yield has not been consistent, the fact remains that in the absence of storage roots, the weevil feeds and multiplies in the vines. When the root develops, the weevil adults emerge from the infested vines and move to infest the roots. A sweetpotato cultivar with resistance to weevil in vine will suppress the weevil population and reduce the insect inoculum and subsequent damage.

Screening of AVRDC's entire sweetpotato germplasm has resulted in identification of six entries; two *I. batatas* accessions and four progenies from crosses between *I. trifida* and *I. batatas,* that are consistently less damaged by the weevil (Figure 1). A significant positive correlation was observed between vine diameter and weevil infestation (Figure 2) (AVRDC 1991). It implies that plants with thin vines are less likely to be damaged than the ones with thick vines. This fact presents an opportunity to breed sweetpotato cultivars with at least moderate levels of resistance which, if integrated with simple cultural control practices such as rotation, clean cultivation, and the use of tender stem cuttings, will give effective control of the sweetpotato weevil.

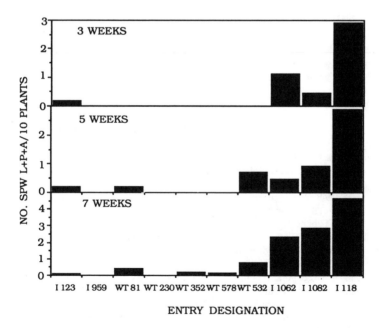

Figure 1. Number of weevils found in the crowns of various entries at 3, 5, and 7 weeks after weevil release. SPW = sweetpotato weevil, L = larvae, P = pupae, A = adults.

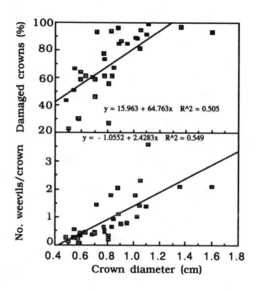

Figure 2. Relationship of sweetpotato crown diameter and infestation of sweetpotato weevil.

REFERENCES

AVRDC (Asian Vegetable Research and Development Center). 1990. 1988 Progress Report. Shanhua, Taiwan, 414 pp.

AVRDC (Asian Vegetable Research and Development Center). 1991. 1990 Progress Report, Shanhua, Taiwan, 313 pp.

Chung, H. L. 1923. The sweetpotato weevil in Hawaii. Hawaii Agricultural Experiment Station Bulletin No. 50, 20 pp.

Cockerham, K. L. 1943. The host preference of the sweetpotato weevil. Journal of Economic Entomology 36:471-472.

Cockerham, K. L., O. T. Deen, M. B. Christian, and L. D. Newsom. 1954. The biology of sweet potato weevil. Technical Bulletin, Louisiana Agricultural Experiment Station, No. 483, 30 pp.

Cowland, J. W. 1926. Notes on sweet potato pyralid moth, *Megastes grandalis,* Guen. Bulletin of Entomological Research. 16, 369-372.

CTCRI (Central Tuber Crops Research Institute). 1983. Entomology. Pages 124-150 *in* Two decades of research, 1963-83. Indian Council of Agricultural Research, Trivandrum, India.

Edward, W. H. 1937. Horn-worms which defoliate sweet potato vines. Journal of Jamaican Agricultural Society 41:515.

Faure, J. C. 1914. Sweet potato sphinx. Agricultural Journal Union of South Africa 7:515-519.

Hahn, S. K., and K. Leuschner. 1981. Resistance of sweet potato cultivars to African sweetpotato weevil. Crop Science 21:499-503.

Ho, T. H. 1970. Studies on some major pests of sweet potatoes and their control. Malaysian Agricultural Journal 47:437-452.

Jansson, Richard K., and Kandukuri V. Raman. 1992. Applications of new technologies to integrated pest management in sweetpotato. Pages 495-506 *in* Sweetpotato technology for the 21st century, edited by W.A. Hill, C.K. Bonsi and P.A. Loretan. Tuskegee University, Tuskegee, AL

Kemner, N. A. 1924. Der betatenkafer (*Cylas formicarius F.*) auf Java und den benachbarten Inseln Ostindiens. Zeitschrift fuer angewandte entomologie 10:398-435.

Lema, K. M., and S. K. Hahn. 1987. Integrated management of the sweetpotato weevils in Africa: An example of low input package. *In* Proceedings of 11th International Congress of Plant Protection, October 5-9, 1987, Manila, Philippines (In press).

Lowe, S. B., and L. A. Wilson. 1972. Preliminary evidence for the existence of differential susceptibility to *Megastes grandalis* (Guen.) infestation in West Indian sweet potato cultivars. Tropical Agriculture 49:361-362.

Messenger, A. P. 1954. Organization of plant quarantine in Okinawa. Journal of Economic Entomology 47:703-704.

Mullen, M. A. 1984. Incidence of sweetpotato weevil infestation on the yields of twelve sweet potato lines. Journal of Agricultural Entomology 1:227-230.

Parasram, S. 1969. Effects of *Megastes* incidence on yield of sweet potato. Page 102 *in* Annual Report of the Department of Crop Science, Section E; Faculty of Agriculture, University of West Indies, 1968-69, St. Augustine, Trinidad.

Sherman, M., and M. Tamashiro. 1954. The sweet potato weevils in Hawaii, their biology and control. Hawaii Agricultural Experiment Station Technical Bulletin No. 23, 36 pp.

Sutherland, J. A. 1986a. Damage by *Cylas formicarius* Fab. to sweet potato vines and tubers, and the effect of infestations on total yield in Papua New Guinea. Tropical Pest Management. 32, 316-323.

Sutherland, J . A. 1986b. A review of the biology and control of the sweetpotato weevil C*ylas formicarius* (Fab.). Tropical Pest Management 32:304-315.

Talekar, N. S. 1982a. Effects of sweetpotato weevil (Coleoptera: Curculionidae) infestation on sweet potato root yield. Journal of Economic Entomology 75, 1042-1044.

Talekar, N. S. 1982b. A search for sources of resistance to sweetpotato weevil. Pages 147-156 *in* Sweet potato. Proceedings, First International Symposium, edited by R. L. Villareal and T. D. Griggs. Asian Vegetable Research and Development Center, Shanhua, Taiwan.

Talekar, N. S. 1983. Infestation of a sweetpotato weevil (Coleoptera: Curculionidae) as influenced by pest management techniques. Journal of Economic Entomology 76:342-344.

Talekar, N. S. 1987a. Insect pests of sweet potato in the tropics. *In* Proceedings of 11th International Congress of Plant Protection, October 5-9, 1987, Manila, Philippines (In press).

Talekar, N. S. 1987b. Influence of cultural pest management techniques on the infestation of sweetpotato weevil. Insect Science and Its Application 8:809-814.

Talekar, N. S. 1987c . Resistance in sweet potato to sweetpotato weevil. Insect Science and Its Application 8:819-823.

Talekar, N. S. 1987d. Feasibility of the use of resistant cultivar in sweetpotato weevil control. Insect Science and Its Application 8:815-817.

Talekar, N. S., and K. W. Cheng. 1987. Nature of damage and sources of resistance to sweetpotato vine borer (Lepidoptera: Pyralidae) in sweet potato. Journal of Economic Entomology 80:788-791.

Talekar, N. S. 1988. How to control sweetpotato weevil: a practical IPM approach. International cooperator's guide. Asian Vegetable Research and Development Center, Shanhua, Taiwan, 6 pp.

Talekar, N. S., R. M. Lai, and K. W. Cheng. 1989. Integrated control of sweetpotato weevil at Penghu island. Plant Protection Bulletin (Taiwan) 31:185-191.

Tucker, R. W. E. 1937. The control of scarabee *(Euscepes batatae* Waterh.) in Barbados. Agricultural Journal 6:133-156.

Watson, J. R. 1944. *Herse cingulata* Fab. as an armyworm. Florida Entomologist 27:58.

West, S. A. 1977. Studies on the biology and ecology of the sweet potato stem borer *Megastes grandalis* Guen. in Trinidad. M. S. Thesis, University of West Indies, St. Augustine,

151

Trinidad, 85 pp.

Wilson, L. A., and S. B. Lowe. 1973. Development of supplementary tissues in intact and *Megastes*-infestated 'tuber stalk' of sweet potato *(Ipomoea batatas* L. Lam.). Journal of Horticultural Sciences 48:223-226.

Wolfe, G. W. 1991. Origin and dispersal of the pest species of *Cylas* with a key to the pest species group of the world. Pages 13-43 *in* Sweet potato pest management: A global perspective, edited by R. K. Janssen and K. V. Raman. Westview Press, Boulder CO, USA.

Yen, D. E. 1982. Sweet potato in historical perspective. Pages 17-30 *in* Sweet potato, edited by R. L. Villareal and T. D. Griggs. Proceedings, First International Symposium, Asian Vegetable Research and Development Center, Shanhua, Taiwan.

Sweetpotato Technology for the 21st Century. W.A. Hill, C.K. Bonsi and P.A. Loretan (Eds.) 1992.Tuskegee University, Tuskegee, AL

Jia Lian Sheng*, Qi Han Xue**, Da Peng Zhang***

Sweetpotato Breeding, Production and Utilization in China

INTRODUCTION

China has a total area of 9.6 million km^2 of which only 10 percent, i.e., 96.85 million ha, is cultivable. That equals half of the cultivated area of the U.S. However, China has the largest population in the world with 1.16 billion people (1990). At the present growth rate, China's population will reach 1.4 billion by the year 2000.

During the period 1969 to 1989, China's population increased by 46.95%, but total cereal production increased by 88.48% (Table 1). Now, China's food supply has reached a self-sufficient level that is about 370 kg per capita provided mainly by cereals supplemented with other crops such as legumes, potatoes and sweetpotato. According to the latest National Economic Development Plan, China's food production should reach a half billion tons by the year 2000.

Table 1. Population and Cereal Production in China from 1969-1989.

Year	Population (x 10^3)	Cereal Production (t x 10^3)
1969	760,255	193,910
1978	933,032	270,325
1980	956,848	283,277
1987	1,086,328	359,330
1989	1,117,173	365,472
Percentage increased (1969-1989)	46.95	88.48

Source: FAO Yearbook

Sweetpotato is one of the most important crops in China. It ranks fourth in terms of sown area after rice, wheat and maize. On a worldwide basis, China is the largest sweetpotato producer. In 1989, about 6.5 million hectares, 69.91% of the world's total area in sweetpotato production, were cropped in China to produce about 114 million tons, 85.56% of the world's total output. The average yield of sweetpotato in China in 1989 was 17,633 kg/ha, 22.38% above the world average (14,408 kg/ha).

*Xuzhou Sweet Potato Research Centre, Jiangsu Xuzhou 221121, China.
**Institute of Agrobiological Genetics and Physiology, Jiangsu Academy of Agricultural Sciences, Nanjing 210014, China.
***Sichuan Academy of Agricultural Sciences, Chengdu, China.

153

Table 2. Production data of the top 10 sweetpotato producing provinces in China (1986).

Provinces	Sown area (ha x 10³)	Yield (t/ha)	Total output (t x 10³)
Sichuan	1,229.50	15.53	19,100.00
Shandong	818.00	24.46	20,015.00
Henan	783.30	11.38	8,910.00
Anhui	658.20	21.06	13,860.00
Guangdong	579.50	11.96	6,930.00
Hebei	351.90	15.98	5,625.00
Jiangsu	275.10	24.17	6,650.00
Hunan	265.20	13.39	3,350.00
Guangxi	236.70	4.94	1,170.00
Fujian	216.80	15.25	3,305.00
China total	6,174.70	16.22	100,165.00

PRODUCTION OF SWEETPOTATO IN CHINA

Even though sweetpotato can be grown in most provinces in China, the main production area is concentrated in the middle and east of China, i.e., the Yellow River and Yangtze River basins and the southeast coastal area. Some important sweetpotato provinces such as Sichuan, Shandong, Henan, Anhui, Hebei, Jiangsu and Guangdong are involved in about 87.68% of the total land under sweetpotato cultivation, and they produce about 88.77% of the total sweetpotato production in China (Table 2).

The amount of land in sweetpotato in China changed regularly during the 1940s to the 1980s. Before the 1970s, it had an upward trend which peaked in 1971 with 12 million hectares. From then on, it came down steadily due to a rapid increase in cereal production. In 1989, only 6.5 million hectares were cropped with sweetpotato in China, a reduction of 85% compared with 1971.

The production of sweetpotato, however, has increased steadily from 51.5 million tons in the 1940s to 110.5 million tons in the 1980s with an average yield increasing from 8.90 t/ha in the 1940s to 17 t/ha in the 1980s (Table 3). The stable increase in sweetpotato production before the 1970's was mainly a result of increased planting area. After the 1970's, increased production resulted from higher yield per unit area. Recently, production has increased slightly, though land under sweet-

Table 3. Sweetpotato sown area, yield and total output in China in the last five decades.

Decades	Sown area (ha x 10³)	Yield (t/ha)	Total output (t x 10⁶)
1940's	581.1	8.90	51.50
1950's	721.8	10.65	76.59
1960's	948.7	9.60	90.95
1970's	813.0	13.35	105.63
1980's	675.0	17.00	110.50

Table 4. A comparison of sown area, yield, total output of rice, wheat, maize and sweetpotato in China in 1962 and 1989.

Crops	Sown area (ha x 10^3)		Yield (kg/ha)		Total output (t x 10^3)	
	1962	1989	1962	1989	1962	1989
Rice	30,094	32,400	2,784	5,537	83,768	179,403
Wheat	24,420	29,801	870	3,054	21,242	91,002
Maize	8,918	20,385	2,471	3,720	22,036	75,840
Sweetpotato	9,384	6,465	8,481	17,633	79,580	114,000

potato production has continued to decline. From 1962 to 1989, the production of rice, wheat and maize increased by 114, 328 and 244 percent, respectively, while sweetpotato only increased by 43.25 percent during the same period (Table 4). Nevertheless, sweetpotato, as the fourth most important crop, has played an historic and complementary role in keeping agricultural development in balance in China.

IMPORTANCE AND USE OF SWEETPOTATO IN CHINA

Sweetpotato has been cultivated in China for more than 400 years. It used to be considered a poor man's crop or a relief food against famine in the event of calamity when rice, wheat and other staple cereals were in short supply. Before the 1960s, about 60% of China's sweetpotato was used for direct human consumption particularly in the rural area.

Since the 1970s sweetpotato has not been cultivated as a staple food crop in the country. As more attention was paid to staples such as rice, wheat and maize, sweetpotato has become a neglected crop in most areas where productivity was formerly high. Now, sweetpotatoes are mainly used as feed, food processing, industrial processing or raw material for export. A small portion of sweetpotato is still used for supplemental food consumption mostly in hilly or marginal areas.

About 45% of China's sweetpotato output is now used for pig feed, the major source of meat for the Chinese people. Other uses include 32% for industrial purposes including raw material for export, 15% for human food and food processing, and 8% for seed storage and losses. In Sichuan, one of the richest and most populous provinces of China—more than 100 million people, about 60% of the sweetpotato produced is used as feed for the largest pork producing region in the country.

In order to meet the basic protein needs and to keep pace with the changing food requirements of the Chinese people, much more research is needed to improve feed use efficiency of sweetpotato for pigs. For this reason, sweetpotato has more potential than cereals due to its high productivity, stable yield, wide adaptability and lower input requirements.

During the last ten years, the rapid development of township enterprises has made it possible to increase the multi-usage of sweetpotato, particularly in post-

Table 5. Utilization of sweetpotato in Jiangsu, Anhui and Shandong provinces in the 1950's and the 1980's (percentage).

Usage	1950's	1980's
Food	50	12
Feed	30	30
Industry	10	45
Seed + losses	10	8
Export	0	5

harvest processing. A recent survey conducted by JAAS (Jiangsu Academy of Agricultural Sciences) and AAAS (Anhui Academy of Agricultural Sciences) showed that between the 1950's and the 1980's, sweetpotato consumption for human food decreased by 38% in Jiangsu, Anhui and Shandong, the three major sweetpotato provinces; seed storage plus losses decreased by 20%. Industrial use and export increased by 35% and 5%, respectively (Table 5).

For industrial processing, starch and dry chips of sweetpotato have been used as raw material in the manufacture of products such as deep processing starch, alcohol, liquid glucose, high fructose syrup, maltose, citric acid and monosodium glutamate. The demand for sweetpotato in industrial processes is increasing. The annual production of fermented alcohol had been only 0.3 million tons, but the domestic market required about 0.6 million tons in 1990 in China.

For food processing, fresh roots, dry flour or starch of sweetpotato can be used for noodles, fried chips, canned flakes and candied pulp production. Some attempts have been made to produce bread and biscuits using sweetpotato flour as a substitute for wheat flour. More than 30 food products using sweetpotato with a total of 0.8 million tons output were produced annually in the 1980's and 1.2 million tons in 1990 in China.

For feed processing, the main product is sweetpotato flour used by the compound feed industry. Besides the storage root, other parts like leaves, vines, pencil roots, even residues after starch processing can also be dehydrated and powdered and used as a supplement to cereal flour for compound feed manufacture in Anhui province. In 1984, more than 70 feed processing factories were built and produce 216,900 tons of compound feed using 26,000 tons of sweetpotato components. In 1990, about 0.9 million tons of compound feed with 0.1 million tons of sweetpotato components were produced. Use of sweetpotato in feed processing was increased by almost 362% from 1984 to 1990 in the province.

VARIETY AND NATIONAL BREEDING PROGRAM

Since 1950, more than 100 new varieties and superior parental clones have been developed. This contributed a lot to the development of sweetpotato breeding and production in China. The most successful example is 'Xushu-18,' a high-yielding variety with a high resistance to root rot developed by Xuzhou Sweet Potato Research Centre. It was released in 1976 and extended to an area of 1.67 million

Table 6. Characteristics and extension speed of variety 'Xushu-18.'

Characteristic	Years	Sown area (ha x 10³)
Spindle-shaped storage root, red skinned with	1979-1980	693.8
yellow-white flesh,	1981-1982	1,933.9
high productivity, wider adaptability,	1983-1984	3,004.0
high resistance to root rot, dry matter	1985-1986	3,105.4
27-28%, starch 20%, susceptible to black	1987-1988	2,971.3
rot and rot nematode		
Total		11,708.4

Source: Seeds Bureau of Chinese Agricultural Ministry.

hectares in 1988. During the period of 1979-1988, a total of 11.70 million hectares was cropped with this variety in China (Table 6). Afterward, four starch type varieties were released in the Sixth Five Year Plan (1980-1985), and 25 new varieties including 11 edible types, eight industrial types and six feed types were released in the Seventh Five Year Plan (1985-1990).

All the breeding objectives in the national research program are carried out under the leadership of the Chinese Agricultural Ministry and National Science and Technology Committee. Most of the breeding projects are carried out in agricultural research institutes and universities in more than 20 provinces with more than 100 breeders and scientists.

In the Seventh Five-Year Plan, breeding objectives were set up for three types of use. The breeding targets for each type are as follows:

For edible varieties, high nutritional value, suitable sweetness (5 mg β-carotene, 10 mg Vitamin C and 3% soluble sugar/100 g fresh tuber), good shape (spindle type) and an acceptable yield capacity should be considered.

For feed usage, new varieties should have vigorous vine regrowth after vine cutting as well as a high root yield with the total dry matter yield (vines and roots) 10% higher than that of 'Xushu-18,' the leading variety.

For industrial varieties, the aim is to produce varieties which have a total starch yield per unit area 10% higher than that of 'Xushu-18' (dry matter content of 27 to 28% and starch content of 20% in 'Xushu-18').

In the Eighth Five-Year Plan, development of multiple usage types has been the priority. New variety needs include high productivity, high starch content, and good nutritional value for food, feed and industrial uses.

MAJOR PROBLEMS AND STRATEGIES OF BREEDING

Bio-stresses have been the most important problems to be considered in sweetpotato breeding. So far, no one variety containing multi-resistance has been

157

selected. Even 'Xushu-18,' which has high productivity and good resistance to root rot is highly susceptible to black rot and root nematode. The reasons for this are lack of good resistant parental materials, effective breeding approaches and good selection methods.

Major sweetpotato diseases in China are black rot (*Ceratocystis fimbriata*), root rot (*Fusarium solani*), rot nematode (*Ditylenchus destructor*), and bacterial wilt (*Pseudomonas solanacearum*) which cause yield reduction in the range of 10 to 100% in different regions. Scab (*Sphaceloma batatas*) and fusarium wilt (*Fusarium oxysporum* var. *batatas*) are also important diseases in some sweetpotato areas. Soft rot (*Rhizopus nigricants*) and dry rot (*Fusarium* spp.) are the major pathogens that cause root damage during the storage period.

Virus disease is another important problem that should be considered in breeding but so far has not received attention. Sweetpotato feathery mottle virus and sweetpotato latent virus are the main virus types existing in the germplasm collection and production fields according to a primary investigation based upon ELISA tests.

The sweetpotato weevil (*Cylas formicarius*) is the important insect pest in Southern China causing yield loss in the range of 5-20 percent generally.

Abiological stresses such as drought, waterlogging, shade under intercropping, low soil fertility and early frost are also problems to be addressed by sweetpotato breeding programs.

Methodologies employed in sweetpotato breeding in China mainly depend on the traditional breeding system involving germplasm introduction, intervarietal hybridization and natural mutation selection. Almost all of the improved varieties released in the past were derived from this approach. For instance, a new food-type variety, 'Nanshu-88' with a productivity of 20% more than that of control ('Xushu-18') was released in 1985-1990 by Sichuan province and extended to more than 420 thousand hectares. Another example is 'Jishu-10' created by Shandong Province during the same period. It has high yield, high multi-resistance to black rot, rot nematode and root rot, and was used as a superior material in the breeding program.

Recently, attempts for exploring new approaches in sweetpotato breeding have been made with some good results. In the case of interspecific hybridization, Jiangsu Province delivered a few new breeding materials with good disease resistance and high starch content selected from BCl or BC2 offsprings of interspecific hybridization when the hexaploid wild species, *Ipomoea trifida*, was used as one of the parents.

For indirect utilization of wild species, the Japanese variety 'Minamiyutaka' containing 1/8 of *Ipomoea trifida* (6x) was used as one parent to cross with Chinese local varieties from which a few better varieties or materials were obtained such as 'Sushu-2.' 'Sushu-2' is a new variety that has a high starch content of 25.6-27.3%— 3.4-4.5% higher than that of 'Xushu-18'—and high resistance to root rot. This variety was released during the period of 1985-1990 and extended to more than 70 thousand hectares.

In the case of radiation selection, Shandong province produced a few superior intermediate materials with resistance to black rot by using fast neutrons in the dosage of 3.8 x 10 n/cm to irradiate epidermal tissue of hypocotyl of sweetpotato.

Selection efficiency has been increased obviously by this approach compared to the conventional breeding method.

Sweetpotato germplasm collection, characterization and preservation have been taken into consideration as an important part of sweetpotato breeding. So far, more than 1,090 varieties have been registered and mainly maintained in Xuzhou and Guangzhou institutes respectively with an *in vitro* duplex stored in the National Germplasm Bank (Beijing).

PERSPECTIVE ON SWEETPOTATO IN CHINA

Even though sweetpotato production in China has declined for several years, there will not be rapid development of the crop in the coming years for human food, because more attention will still be paid to the major cereals, which are essential for the basic food supply requirement under our continuously increasing population pressure. The increased demand for sweetpotato for feed and industrial uses, however, will greatly stimulate further development of this crop, particularly in terms of the yield increase.

It is obvious that conventional breeding based on enhancement of selective efficiency rather than expansion of the breeding scale should still be considered as the main approach for sweetpotato yield increase. Simultaneously, the breeding goal has to be altered from the single quantitative selection into intensive qualitative selection especially for multi-resistance and wide-adaptability purposes.

Compared to the conventional approach, biotechnology probably can bring a bright future to sweetpotato variety improvement. For instance, alien gene transfer systems either by somatic cell fusion or by genetic transformation seem to be promising approaches for sweetpotato protein content and disease resistance.

Besides breeding, post-harvest processing may also determine the fate of sweetpotato's development in China. More investment, better equipment and advanced technology are needed particularly in feed processing.

Chinese scientists hope to further strengthen and broaden international collaboration in all the above aspects with the Food and Agricultural Organization of the United Nations, the International Development Research Center, the International Potato Center, the International Institute of Tropical Agriculture and the Asian Vegetable Research and Development Center and other national and international institutions and agencies in the form of materials, information and experiences exchange.

Sweetpotato Technology for the 21st Century. W.A. Hill, C.K. Bonsi and P.A. Loretan (Eds.) 1992. Tuskegee University, Tuskegee, AL

Poster Presentations

EFFECT OF FLOW RATE ON HYDROPONICALLY-GROWN SWEETPOTATOES

E. R. Carlisle, D. G. Mortley, P. A. Loretan, C. K. Bonsi, W. A. Hill, C. E. Morris, A. A. Trotman

George Washington Carver Agricultural Experiment Station, Tuskegee University, Tuskegee, AL 36088 USA.

In a greenhouse study, 'Georgia Jet' sweetpotatoes were grown hydroponically using the Tuskegee nutrient film technique system. The objective was to determine the effect of nutrient solution flow rate on storage root yield and foliage production. Two flow rates were examined: low, .1 L min^{-1}, and high, 1.0 L min^{-1}. Four vine cuttings spaced at 25 cm in channels (122 cm by 15 cm by 15 cm) were used per treatment and grown for 120 days. The nutrient solution supplied was a modified half-Hoagland solution. Number and weight of storage roots and weight of foliage were not significantly different due to flow rate. Storage root weight tended to be highest for the .1 L min^{-1} flow rate.

An important aspect of growing plants in hydroponic systems is the timely supply of nutrients in solution. Therefore, flow rate can be expected to influence the availability of nutrients in the root zone. There is little published information on the effects of rate of nutrient solution flow on plants grown in hydroponic systems. In a previous study, a flow rate of 1.0 L min^{-1} per pot or higher resulted in excessive loss of plant nutrient solution (PNS) for wheat grown hydroponically in pots for 21 days (Edwards and Asher 1974). Acceptable yields (>2.0 kg/plant) of white potato were obtained with a flow rate of 2.0 L m^{-2} day^{-1} using a continuous nutrient film technique (NFT) over a 112-day growth period (Wheeler et al. 1990). Neither of these studies addressed the influence of flow rate in solution culture on yield.

To date, experiments performed on sweetpotato using the Tuskegee NFT system have used a flow rate of 1.0 L min^{-1} (Hill et al. 1989; Mortley et al. 1992). In this experiment, we conducted two greenhouse studies to evaluate two solution flow rates: (1) high, 1.0 L min^{-1} and (2) low, 0.1 L min^{-1}.

MATERIALS AND METHODS

Four sweetpotato (cv. 'Georgia Jet') vine cuttings of 18 cm length and spaced 25 cm apart were planted in channels (122 cm by 15.24 cm). The two treatment flow rates were .1 and 1.0 liters per minute. The experimental design was a completely randomized design with two replications. Plants were maintained with half-strength modified Hoagland's nutrient solution. Each channel was supplied with PNS from an 8-gallon reservoir for 14-day intervals when the solution was replaced with new PNS. Solution flow was achieved with a submersible pump in the reservoir. The

Table 1. Effect of nutrient solution flow rate on storage root and foliage production of sweetpotato grown for 120 days in a continuous flow nutrient film technique system.[1]

Flow Rate	Storage Roots			Foliage	
L min^{-1}	No.	Fresh Wt.	Dry Wt.	Fresh Wt.	Dry Wt.
1.01	3.0	564	96	546	55
0.11	2.6	685	123	528	56
LSD	NS	NS	NS	NS	NS

[1]Data are reported as number or g plant $^{-1}$.

required flow rate was achieved and maintained with a needle valve in the feedline. The parameters measured in this study were storage root count, fresh and dry weights and foliage fresh and dry weights after plants had been grown for 120 days using the Tuskegee NFT system.

RESULTS AND IMPLICATIONS

Plant growth, foliage and storage root production were not inhibited under the NFT system used in this study. Although there tended to be differences in the fresh and dry weights and number of sweetpotato storage roots, they were not significant at the 5% level when the solution flow rate was reduced by a factor of 10 (Table 1). A similar response was found for foliage production. These results indicate that, for a continuous flow system when nutrients are supplied in the concentration required for plant growth, solution flow rate may not limit growth when channels of 122 cm length are used. Also, in a recirculating, flowing culture system, solution flow rates of 1.0 L min^{-1} may be excessive, particularly when PNS in reservoirs is changed at 14-day intervals. But we cannot conclude from this study that solution flow rate does not influence the growth of sweetpotato grown in NFT because the effect of lower flow rates is not known. These results suggest that further studies on the effects of solution flow rates lower than 0.1 L min^{-1} on sweetpotato storage root and foliage production might be helpful.

LITERATURE CITED

Edwards, D. G,. and C. J. Asher. 1974. The significance of solution flow rate in flowing culture experiments. Plant Soil 41:161-175.

Hill, W.A., P.A. Loretan, C.K. Bonsi, C.E. Morris, J.Y. Lu, and C. Ogbuehi. 1989. Utilization of sweetpotatoes in Controlled Ecological Life Support Systems (CELSS). Adv. Space Res. 9(8):29-41.

Mortley, D.G., C.K. Bonsi, P.A. Loretan, C.E. Morris, W.A. Hill, and C.R. Ogbuehi. 1991. Evaluation of sweetpotato genotypes for adaptability to hydroponic systems. Crop Sci. 31:845-847.

Wheeler, R. M., C. L. Mackowiak, J. C. Sager, W. M. Knott, and C. R. Hinkle. 1990. Potato growth and yield using nutrient film technique (NFT). Am. Pot. J. 67:177-187.

Sweetpotato Technology for the 21st Century. W.A. Hill, C.K. Bonsi and P.A. Loretan (Eds.) 1992. Tuskegee University, Tuskegee, AL

EVALUATION OF SWEETPOTATO VARIETIES FROM THE ATLANTIC REGION OF COSTA RICA

Elizondo Solis Jorge
Instituto Technologico de Costa Rica, San Carlos, Santa Clara, Apartado 223, Costa Rica.

Eight varieties of sweetpotato (C-79 [Orlando]; C-23 'Wenholz' II]; C-25 ['Brasilera Blanca']; C-15 ['Salvador B-4096']; C-10 ['Puerto Rico 2']; C-80, C-81 and C-82 (from Taiwan), were evaluated for protein and starch levels, growth behavior and harvest evaluation. Variety C-82 presented the highest overall yields of 66.4 t/ha with the greatest production of grade A storage roots—4.4 to 8.3 cm (dia.), 7.5 to 23 cm (length) and individual weight of 250 to 500 g (45.2 t/ha). The highest percentage of starch was also found in the storage roots of C-82. The C-15 variety also realized high yields (58.1 t/ha) with a high yield of grade A storage roots (39.5 t/ha). Protein percentage reached its highest level in storage roots of C-79 (8.05%) and in leaves of C-80 (24.19%). For C-10, C-80 and C-82 the level of protein decreased 115 days after planting. For all other varieties protein levels decreased 85 to 100 days after planting. An inverse relation was found (r = -0.43) between the weight of storage roots and leaves.

The ecological conditions of the Atlantic region of Costa Rica is suitable for the cultivation of sweetpotato. However, experiments on the sweetpotato have been few, especially with reference to the evaluation of the varieties which appear promising. Montero (1974) evaluated 25 varieties of sweetpotato in Santa Clara, San Carlos. The highest yields of commercial storage roots were obtained with 'Wenholz II' - white color (C-23) with 40 t/ha, 'Wenholz II' - purple color (C-15) with 28 t/ha, and 'Puerto Rico No. 2' (C-10) with 25 t/ha.. The weight of the foliage varied from 75 to 115 t/ha in the highest yielding varieties (C-29, C-70, C-6, C-12, C-23). The protein in the foliage was 18 to 20% on a dry weight basis in 'Brasilian White' (C-25); C-10, C-12, C-23 and C-69. The starch level after six months was high (71 to 73%) in the varieties C-57, C-54, C-23, UCR-15 and C-25.

According to Armijo (1962), the Costa Rican consumer prefers the sweetpotato with purple skin color like the variety C-15. In previous studies in Alajuela, Garita this investigator obtained high yields of storage roots for the varieties C-11, C-8, C-15 and C-17. In spacing trials with C-15, C-10 and C-17, the greatest weight of storage roots and foliage (41 t/ha) were obtained with C-15. With C-10 the yield of storage roots and foliage was high (31 and 19 t/ha, respectively).

Of the 68 varieties evaluated in Parrita, in the south of Costa Rica, those that presented the greatest yield in terms of weight of storage roots were 'Wenholz II' (26 t/ha) and 'Puerto Rico No. 2' (22 t/ha) (Loria et al. 1965). The objective of this experiment was to evaluate the behavior of eight varieties of sweetpotato in the environmental conditions of Santa Clara, San Carlos based upon yield of storage roots and foliage, percentage of protein in the leaves and the storage roots and percentage of dry matter in the leaves.

MATERIALS AND METHODS

The experiment was established on the farm (ranch) of La Esmeralda in Santa Clara, San Carlos located at 10 degrees 30 minutes and 10 degrees 22 minutes of latitude North and 84 degrees 30 minutes and 84 degrees 34 minutes of longitude west at 172 masl. During the time of the experiment (five months), the average monthly temperature was 25.5°C and the precipitation 376.7 mm.

Sweetpotatoes were planted at .90 m between rows and .20 m between plants. The plants were fertilized with 41 kg/ha N, 78 kg/ha P_2O_5 and 41 kg/ha K_2O. Fertilizer was split applied 41 and 75 days after planting. The experimental design was a randomized complete block with four replications. The independent variables were the varieties of sweetpotato C-80, C-81, C-82, C-79, C-23, C-25, C-15 and C-10. The factors evaluated were: yield of grade A storage roots (diameter from 4.4 to 8.3 cm, weight of 250 to 500 g and length of 7.5 to 23 cm); grade B storage roots (diameter of 3.8 to 11.5 cm, weight of 100 to 1020 g and length from 7.5 to 28 cm); grade C storage roots (all of the storage roots with morphological defects and with a diameter and longitude less than 3.8 and 7.5 cm respectively; total yield of all storage roots; percentage of starch in the storage roots at harvest (A.O.A.C. procedure); percentage of dry matter in the leaves at the harvest; and percent of protein in the leaves at 15 day intervals.

RESULTS AND DISCUSSION

The highest yields of grade A storage roots were obtained with C-82 from Taiwan ('Tainung 9') (45.2 and 66.4 t/ha). High yields were also obtained for C-15 of Costa Rica ('Salvador B-4906') (39 to 58 t/ha). The yield of grade B storage roots was highest for C-25 of Argentina ('Brazilian White') (20 t/ha) and C-23 also from Argentina ('Wenholz II') 14 t/ha (Table 1). The variety that presented the lowest yield in weight of total storage roots was C-81 of Taiwan ('Tainung 57').

Table 1. Average yields of grades A, B, C and total storage roots for eight varieties of sweetpotato.

| Varieties | Yield (kg/ha) | | | |
	Grade A	Grade B	Grade C	Total
C-82	45,208 a	12,958 ab	7,222 bc	66,388 a
C-15	39,514 ab	13,542 ab	5,208 cd	58,111 a
C-23	25,486 bc	14,444 ab	3,889 d	43,888 abc
C-25	24,167 bc	20,069 a	9,656 ab	53,888 ab
C-80	22,500 bc	14,236 ab	11,042 a	48,055 abc
C-10	18,750 cd	7,708 b	4,306 cd	25,555 bc
C-81	3,056 d	1,042 c	764 e	4,861 d

Values with the same letters do not differ significantly (DMRT, P <.05).

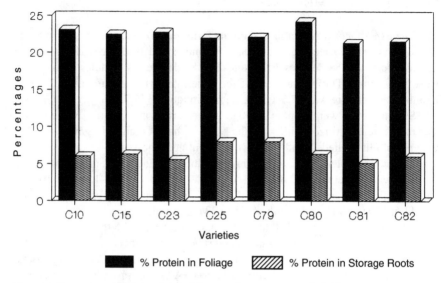

Figure 1. Percentage of total protein in foliage and storage roots of eight sweetpotato varieties at harvest.

Montero (1974) obtained the highest yield of storage roots with 'Wenholz II' white color (C-23) (40 t/ha) and 'Wenholz II' purple color (C-15) (28 t/ha) and 'Puerto Rico No. 2' (C-10) (25 t/ha). In this experiment C-15 and C-82 exceeded C-23 in total yield of storage roots produced. Variety C-79 ('Orlando') had the lowest total yield but the highest protein content in storage roots (8%) at harvest. McDowell et al. (1974) found that sweetpotato storage roots contained from 4 to 7% crude protein. With C-82 the percentage protein in the leaves was 21% and in the storage roots 6%, which was intermediate in comparison with the other varieties. Montero (1974) obtained percentages of protein in the leaves of up to 20% with C-25.

The variety C-80 from Costa Rica ('Pototoro') gave the highest percentage (24%) of protein in the leaves (Fig. 1). This variety also gave the highest percentage of dry matter in the foliage at harvest (19.7%), which makes it suitable for animal feed. Austin and Aung (1973) reported values of 17 to 30% dry matter in the leaves from 85 days until 100 days after planting. In some varieties like the C-23, C-79, C-81, C-25 and C-15, an increase in the protein content of leaves occurred between 100 and 115 days after planting and then protein content began to decrease. In C-10, C-80 and C-82, the maximum protein content in the leaves was found after 130 days of growth. These harvest periods for maximum nutritional advantage of protein content are indicative of foliage as animal feed without detriment to storage root yields (Fig. 2a and 2b).

The varieties that had the highest yields of storage roots had low foliage weights at harvest (r=0.43). For example, C-82 produced the highest storage root yield and a low weight of foliage at harvest. In this regard, a negative correlation between the

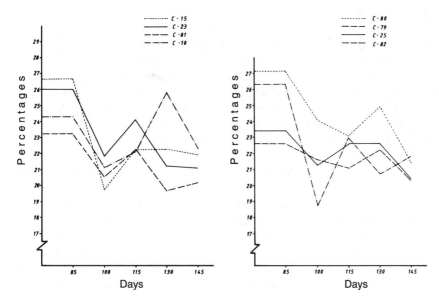

Figures 2a and 2b. Percentage of protein in the leaves during the cycle of cultivation in an evaluation of eight varieties of sweetpotato.

production of foliage and the yield of storage roots was observed as was previously reported by Austin et al. (1973).

The percentage of starch in the storage roots of C-82 was higher than for other varieties with a value of 31.6%; the lowest content of starch was obtained for C-23 (21.5%) (Table 2). In this experiment the variety 'Tainung 9' from Taiwan (C-82) surpassed in yield the local varieties and some South and North American introductions that had been evaluated in earlier experiments. Because of its high yield, relatively high protein and starch content, C-82 has good potential as an animal feed.

Table 2. Percentage of dry matter, starch and total protein in the leaves and storage roots of eight varieties of sweetpotato at harvest.

Varieties	Foliage		Storage Roots	
	% Protein	% Dry Matter	% Protein	% Starch
C-80	24.2 a	19.7 a	6.3 b	28.6 c
C-10	23.1 ab	15.9 b	6.0 c	23.6 e
C-23	22.8 ab	17.7 ab	5.6 d	21.5 g
C-15	22.5 ab	15.9 b	6.3 b	28.3 c
C-79	22.1 b	15.2 b	8.0 a	29.6 b
C-25	22.0 b	16.3 b	8.0 a	25.7 d
C-82	21.5 b	16.5 b	6.0 c	31.6 a
C-81	21.3 b	15.2 b	5.1 e	22.4 f

Values with the same letters within columns do not different significantly (DMRT, P < 0.05).

CONCLUSIONS

The varieties C-82 and C-15 produced the highest weight of grade A and total storage roots. An inverse relationship (r=0.43) was found between total storage roots and foliage yields in such a manner that the varieties most productive in total storage roots produced the least weight of green foliage at harvest. The variety C-80 produced the highest yield of grade C storage roots. The greatest yield of grade B storage roots was obtained for varieties C-25 and C-23 ('Wenholz II'). The variety C-82 produced the greatest percentage of starch in the storage roots and the least was obtained from the C-23.

The protein content in the storage roots was highest for C-79 and C-25 and lowest for C-81 and C-23. The crude protein content in the leaves was highest in C-80, C-10, C-23, and C-15 and lowest in C-81. Varieties such as C-80 and C-23 with a high content of total protein in the leaves should be considered as promising for their use as a supplemental animal feed. The variety C-82 ('Tainung 9') from Taiwan, in the environmental conditions of this experiment, surpassed the local varieties in yield. Moreover, because of its protein and starch content and weight of foliage at harvest, it is a variety which has great potential as an animal feed.

INDUCED RESISTANCE OF SWEETPOTATO AGAINST STEM ROT IN JAPAN

Tomoko Kawasaki, Yutaka Shimazaki
Saitama Prefecture Horticultural Experiment Station, Tsurugashima City, Ohta-ga-ya 25, Saitama Prefecture, Japan. (Translated by Barry Duell)

Farmers in Saitama Prefecture currently control sweetpotato stem rot by using agricultural chemicals. Even so, an average of 5% of sweetpotato plants are annually damaged by stem rot. It is becoming increasingly undesirable to use chemical soil disinfestants in areas of rapid urbanization near agricultural zones. The authors tested an alternative method of preventing stem rot; the successful induced resistance of sweetpotato with a weakened strain of *Fusarium*—a method reported by the Ibaraki Prefectural Experiment Station.

Six sweetpotato growing areas in Saitama were selected and three types of experimental fields prepared: (1) fields planted with sweetpotato cuttings treated with weakened *Fusarium* to induce resistance; (2) fields disinfested using the current practice and then planted with *Fusarium*-induced resistant sweetpotato plants; and (3) control fields disinfested using the current practice. Resistance of sweetpotato cuttings was induced by soaking them for 17 hours in a solution containing weakened *Fusarium* at a concentration of at least 1.7×10^5 microorganisms per mL.

To determine what factors contribute most to induced resistance, the cuttings were planted in fields with three different soil temperatures and three different levels

Sweetpotato Technology for the 21st Century. W.A. Hill, C.K. Bonsi and P.A. Loretan (Eds.) 1992. Tuskegee University, Tuskegee, AL

of soil moisture. To test the effectiveness of the induced resistance procedure, cuttings that were treated with weakened *Fusarium* were infected by soaking them in a solution containing active *Fusarium*. The cuttings were examined for signs of infection two weeks after planting. Data taken were the degree of *Fusarium* infection of plants and the yield of the sweetpotato at harvest. These observations were made:

(1) The nine strains of *Fusarium* gathered from sweetpotato growing areas in Saitama Prefecture proved to have a high degree of induced resistance. Of the six test areas, in only one area did induced resistance prove less effective than currently used techniques for controlling *Fusarium*.

(2) In the case of cuttings that had been infected with *Fusarium* as well as those treated with weakened *Fusarium*, it was found that as soil temperature rose or soil moisture content dropped, disease symptoms and plant mortality increased. It is likely that the method of production of weakened *Fusarium* and the length of time between inducing the resistance and planting, as well as other untested factors, could have an influence on the effect of induced resistance of the cuttings.

It is becoming increasingly difficult to use soil fumigants such as chloropicrin due to the danger they pose to residential areas rapidly encroaching into agricultural zones. In such districts, it is especially desirable to consider using biological techniques such as induced resistance to reduce crop damage. However, the above experiment suggests that field conditions have to be carefully considered in order to maximize the effects of induced resistance in sweetpotato.

SWEETPOTATO SCREENING AND SELECTION BETWEEN 1977 AND 1990 IN CAMEROON

Simon Ngale Lyonga, Sam Nzietchueng
University Centre, Dschang, B.P. 110, Dschang, Cameroon.

Cameroon produces annually 70,000 tons of sweetpotatoes with a 5.8% growth rate and a demand forecast of 175,000 tons per year up to 1992. However, the per capita calories consumption of 34 is lower than the African average of over 200. The main constraints of the crop are susceptibility to sweetpotato virus disease (SPVD) complex, weevil (*Cylas* spp.) attack, poor cultural practices, postharvest losses and the lack of improved planting material for growers. The Cameroon National Root Crops Improvement Program, in collaboration with the International Institute for Tropical Agriculture (IITA), has screened and selected cultivars against those constraints which are yield stable at different agro-ecological locations. Particularly adapted to most locations are cultivars '1112' and '1611' which, including 'TIB 1', have been multiplied, with the limited funds supplied by friendly donor agents, to plant 500 hectares of peasant farms. As in some other root crops, future research should face squarely post-harvest problems including marketing and new food and feed products.

INTRODUCTION

Sweetpotato (*Ipomoea batatas* L.) is one of the five major root and tuber crops cultivated in Cameroon and is a popular vegetable in many communities. It is produced on a peasant scale in most of the six ecological zones of the country with altitudes between 0 to 2000 meters above sea level (masl) and a rainfall range of 0.4 to 10 m per year. Most production occurs in the higher rainfall southern region of the country. It serves as a soil cover during the dry season.

Sweetpotato competes with cassava (*Manihot esculenta*) as a replacement for macabo (*Xanthosoma saqittifolium*) as a staple where the latter is threatened by root rot disease (*Pythium myriotylum*).

The storage root and, to a lesser extent, the leaves are used as a vegetable. It is a major staple in some African countries like Uganda, Rwanda, Tanzania where about 15 million people depend on it for a daily per capita calorie consumption of over 200. Cameroon consumption is generally lower averaging only 34 calories per capita (Compiled from FAO Food Balance Sheets, 1979-81 averages, *Time Magazine*, November 11, 1974).

Annual production figures range between 70,000 and 130,000 tons of roots (FAO 1980; Ministry of Agriculture, Department of Studies and Projects, 1984). The crop has an annual growth rate of 5.8% and an annual demand forecast of 175,000 tons for 1992 (VIth Five Year Plan, 1986-1991).

The problems encountered in the cultivation of sweetpotatoes are mainly diseases and pests. First among these are the sweetpotato virus disease complex (SPVD) and weevils (*Cylas Puncticollis* Boh.). Other problems include poor cultural methods, post-harvest losses and the need to develop new products so as to expand production. The color and shape of storage roots and gaseous effects in the stomach are other characteristics of the crop which must be improved in order to increase its acceptance with consumers.

In 1976, the Institute of Agronomic Research organized the Cameroon National Root Crops Improvement Program to address these problems. This was carried out in collaboration with the International Institute of Tropical Agriculture (IITA) and the Donor Agents of IDRC of Canada, AGCD of Belgium, IFS of Sweden, the Gatsby Foundation of Great Britain and USAID/ROTREP, University of Maryland - Eastern Shore, Florida A&M University and Alabama A&M University.

Sweetpotato families mainly from IITA have been screened and selected for tolerance to virus and weevils and adaptation to various climatic conditions. IITA screening and selection procedures were adopted and with their cooperation stable varieties have been obtained.

Table 1 shows seven cultivars that have been selected and are being multiplied for growers. The cultivars '1112', '1611' and 'TIbl' are adapted to all ecological zones, i.e., from 0 to above 2000 masl. The cultivars 'TIS 2498' and '1692' performed better in the high rainfall lowlands.

Many agronomic trials were carried out and consistent findings are presented below. Vine slips of 33 cm length produced higher yields than longer ones, while top

Table 1. Average yields (t/ha) of sweetpotato clones in different agro-ecological zones of Cameroon.

ZONES	I	II	III	IV	V	
Altitude (masl)	1000	500	700	1200	500	Mean
Rainfall (mm)	2000	2000	1500	1250	1000	
Vegetation	Savanna	Forest	Forest	Savanna	Savanna	
CLONES						
1611	27.8	29.0	22.1	23.4	19.9	24.4
1112	27.5	26.1	27.6	22.8	17.8	24.4
502	27.2	22.1	23.1	22.2	24.0	23.7
TIS 2544	24.5	23.2	18.0	24.0	18.4	21.6
1639	20.9	23.4	24.8	19.4	18.2	21.3
002	21.0	20.5	19.6	-	-	20.4
Tlb 1	25.7	22.0	18.5	21.1	13.5	20.2
1592	21.1	24.9	13.1	14.4	17.5	18.2
Tlb 2	23.2	17.8	17.2	13.9	-	18.0
TTS 2498	18.1	25.7	17.1	17.6	10.0	17.7
1602	18.5	20.3	18.2	11.8	14.6	16.7
1692	17.4	25.4	15.6	12.7	10.0	16.2
TIS 3017	13.2	21.8	14.1	-	13.5	15.7
1669	14.1	27.0	7.0	9.6	16.7	14.9
1035	18.2	19.4	10.2	9.5	-	14.3
LOCAL	9.4	16.3	7.0	7.7	11.5	10.4
MEAN	20.5	22.8	17.1	16.4	15.8	
C of C	12.8%	15.0%	8.5%	20.3%	17.5%	
S.D.	4.8	3.6	6.7	7.4	8.7	

and middle cuttings produced similarly good yields. Burying two-thirds of each slip 7 to 8 cm deep produced the best results. A planting density of 30,000 plants per hectare seemed the best for most conditions.

Competition with other crops for light, water and nutrients at full density of sweetpotato and half the recommended densities of other food crops depressed yields, particularly of sweetpotato. However, land equivalent ratio (LER) calculations indicated that the total yield per unit area of land was improved. Table 2 gives the yield depression of sweetpotato.

Table 2. Percentage yield reduction of sweetpotato clones intercropped with maize, cassava and soya.

Clone	Maize	Cassava	Soya	Mean
Tlb 1	59	67	20	49
Tlb 2	66	64	26	52
527034	68	46	37	50
23303	70	40	27	45
Mean	65	54	28	

Table 3. Effect of seed bed preparation on yields (t/ha) of sweetpotato at different locations.

| Seedbed | | Locations | | |
Preparation	Season	Ekona	Bertoua	Sanguere
Ridges	First	17.7	14.5	8.6
	Second	8.6	-	-
Flat	First	15.1	15.5	4.6
	Second	6.8	-	-

Preparation of a good, deep seed bed was important, but ridges did not seem to provide a yield advantage over planting on flat land. Ridges did, however, produce preferred storage root shape. The first season obviously produced higher storage root yields than the late season; this was directly related to rainfall (Table 3).

Fertilizer trials in many locations showed that a compounded mixture of 30N-$45P_2O_5$-$75K_2O$ (kg/ha) produced the best responses. Higher nitrogen and high phosphorus regimes depressed yields and sulphur additions did not increase yields.

On-farm research and the technology transfer process to farmers is being carried out by a Testing and Liaison Team (TLU)—an extension expert, a social scientist, an agricultural economist and an agronomist. This multidisciplinary approach seems to work well. The International Potato Center's (CIP) regional center in Cameroon is presently maintaining a germplasm collection of 153 sweetpotato cultivars.

The Cameroon National Root Crop Improvement Program (CNRCIP) has worked over the years to foster the cultivation of sweetpotato and other root crops in Cameroon. The collaboration between CNRCIP and the international institutes IITA and CIP in this effort has been exemplary.

The future focus should be on post-harvest technology which will lead to more sweetpotato food and feed products with a longer shelf life. This will help to expand production. Also, more research attention should turn toward the quality of the sweetpotato crop.

REFERENCES

CNRCIP 1977 - 1986 Synthesis Report.
CNRCIP 1987-88 Annual Report.
Kamajou, F. 1989. A Socio-Economic Evaluation of the CNRCIP of the Institute of Agronomic Research.
Ngeve, J.M. 1988. Evaluation of statistical models for determining yield stability among sweetpotato genotypes.
Sixth Five Year Economic Social and Cultural Development Plan, 1986-1991.
Tchaba, Jean-Michel. 1982. Contribution a l'etude de la de *Cylas puncticollis* Boh: Charoncon de la Patate Douce.

Sweetpotato Technology for the 21st Century. W.A. Hill, C.K. Bonsi and P.A. Loretan (Eds.) 1992. Tuskegee University, Tuskegee, AL

EFFECT OF CONSTANT pH VS. PERIODIC pH ADJUSTMENT OF NUTRIENT SOLUTION ON YIELD OF SWEETPOTATO USING NFT

E.R. Martinez, C.K. Bonsi, P.P. David, D.G. Mortley, W.A. Hill, P.A. Loretan, C.E. Morris

George Washington Carver Agricultural Experiment Station, Tuskegee University, Tuskegee, AL 36088.

The effects of constant pH vs periodic pH adjustment of nutrient solution on yield of sweetpotato grown hydroponically using a closed nutrient film technique system were evaluated in a greenhouse study. Vine cuttings from the cultivar 'Georgia Jet' were planted 25cm apart in 0.15 by 0.15 x by 1.2 m growth channels. A modified half Hoagland nutrient solution with a 1:2.4 N:K ratio was used. Solution pH levels of 4.5 and 6 were held constant throughout the growing period and were compared to a control in which the pH of the nutrient was allowed to fluctuate but was periodically adjusted to 6. There were significant increases in yield of storage roots when solution pH was periodically adjusted to 6 compared to treatments with a constant pH of 5 or 6. Storage root yields for periodic pH adjustment and constant pH 4 were not significantly different.

Plant responses may vary depending on nutrient solution composition used in hydroponic systems, and pH plays a major role in the availability of these mineral ions in solution culture. Sweetpotatoes have the ability to grow over a wide pH range. However, a slightly acid condition seems to be more favorable for higher yields of storage roots (Bouwkamp 1985.).

According to Hill et al. (1984) and Nikishanova (1977), sweetpotatoes rank high among root and tuber crops as a potential food source for Controlled Ecological Life Support Systems associated with manned space missions. Several studies have assessed the effects of environmental conditions such as light, photoperiod and spacing on hydroponically grown sweetpotatoes (Bonsi et al. 1992; Mortley 1991; Loretan 1989). However, the specific role of nutrient solution pH on the growth of sweetpotatoes has not been addressed.

The objective of this study was to evaluate the effects of nutrient solution pH on the growth and yield of sweetpotato storage roots grown with the nutrient film technique (NFT).

Materials and methods

Sweetpotato (*Ipomoea batatas* L. 'Georgia Jet') vine cuttings of 15 cm length were planted in a closed NFT system as described by Hill et al. (1989) and Morris et al. (1989).

Four vine cuttings were planted 25 cm apart in 0.15 by 0.15 by 1.2 m growth channels. Growing vines were trained by tying them to vertical strings suspended from one meter above each growing channel. A total of six growing channels were used in the first experiment and eight in the second. Each channel was supplied by a 30.4 liter volume reservoir which consisted of a modified half Hoagland nutrient solution with a 1:2.4 N:K ratio. The nutrient solution was changed at biweekly intervals and the reservoir topped with deionized water if the volume of nutrient solution was reduced to 8 liters or less prior to the biweekly interval.

The treatments were as follows: (1) constant pH of 4.0, (2) constant pH of 6.0 and (3) a fluctuating pH. In the latter treatment the pH of the nutrient solution was allowed to fluctuate but was periodically adjusted to a pH of 6.0 at biweekly nutrient solution changeouts or when the reservoir was topped with deionized water. After 120 days of growth, storage roots were weighed. The treatments consisted of two channels per treatment arranged in a complete randomized design with two replications. The experiment was repeated and the data pooled for statistical analysis.

Results

Storage root fresh and dry weights were higher when plants were grown in the nutrient solution where the pH was periodically adjusted to 6 or was maintained at 4 compared to those grown in the nutrient solution where the pH was held constantly at 6 (Table 1).

Conclusion

Results from this study showed that periodically adjusting the pH of nutrient solution to 6 as opposed to having solution pH held constant at 6 enhanced growth of sweetpotato grown hydroponically. Periodically adjusting the pH allowed for lowering of pH in the solution between solution changeouts. The pH range between 3.8-6.2 may have resulted in greater uptake of K^+ which has been shown to enhance accumulation of photosynthates into the storage roots of sweetpotatoes. This agrees with the work of Ho et al. (1984) who showed that sweetpotato storage root yields increased proportionally with an increase in K dosage. A pH of 4 was low enough to allow for greater uptake of K^+ and hence greater accumulation of photosynthetates into the storage roots.

Table 1. Effect of pH on fresh and dry weight of ('Georgia Jet') sweetpotato grown in NFT.

Treatment	Storage Roots			Foliage	
pH	Number	Fresh Wt.	Dry Wt.	Fresh Wt.	Dry Wt.
		(g/plant)		(g/plant)	
Constant (4)	3 a[z]	987 b	125 b	397 a	54 a
Constant (6)	2 a	123 a	25 a	349 a	53 a
Periodic (6)	5 a	904 b	158 b	475 a	66 a

[z]Means with the same letter within a column are not significantly different at the 5% probability level according to DMRT.

LITERATURE CITED

Bouwkamp, J.C. 1985. Production requirements. Pages 9-34 *in* Sweetpotato products: A natural resource for the tropics, edited by J.C. Bouwkamp. CRC Press, Inc., Boca Raton, FL.

Hill, W.A., P.A. Loretan, and C.K. Bonsi (eds.). 1984. The sweet potato for space missions. Tuskegee University, Tuskegee, AL.

Hill, W.A., P.A. Loretan, C.K. Bonsi, C.E. Morris, J.Y. Lu, and C. Ogbuehi (Eds). 1989. Utilization of sweetpotatoes in Controlled Ecological Life Support Systems (CELSS) Adv. Space Res. 9:29-41.

Ho, C.T., N.R. Su, C.N. Tang, and C.Y. Sheng. 1967. Studies on correlation of soil and plant potassium with response of sweetpotato to added potash in Chiayi prefecture. Soil and Fertilizers in Taiwan. 1967:32-37.

Morris, C.E., P.A. Loretan, C.K. Bonsi, and W.A. Hill. 1989. Movable root contact pressure plate assembly for hydroponic systems. U. S. Patent 860 490. Date issued: August 29, 1989.

Nikishanova, T. I. 1977. Plants for space explorations NASA-TM-75314. {Transl. from Privaler [USSR] 10:105-117[1977]).

EFFECTS OF RELATIVE HUMIDITY ON SWEETPOTATO GROWTH IN AN NFT SYSTEM

D.G. Mortley, C.K. Bonsi, P.A. Loretan, W.A. Hill, E. Carlisle, C.E. Morris

George Washington Carver Agricultural Experiment Station, Tuskegee University, Tuskegee, AL 36088.

Experiments were conducted in environmental growth chambers to study the response of sweetpotato to relative humidity (RH) level. Vine cuttings of 'TI-155' sweetpotato were planted in PVC-1 plastic growth channels (0.15 by 0.15 by 1.2m) using the nutrient film technique with a modified half Hoagland solution. Plants were exposed to constant RH levels of 50% or 85%. Temperature regimes of 28/22°C were maintained during the light/dark periods with an irradiance level of 600 μmol m^{-2}s^{-1} and a 14/10 hr photoperiod. Leaf photosynthesis and stomatal conductance measurements were taken 81 days after planting. Plants were harvested 120 days after planting and yield data were taken. High RH (85%) tended to increase the number of storage roots/plant, and significantly increased storage root fresh and dry weight. Foliage fresh and dry weights were higher in response to 50% RH. Leaf photosynthesis and stomatal conductance were higher for plants at 85% than at 50% RH. Uptake of N, P, and K was not influenced by RH levels, while uptake of Ca, Mg, Zn, and B tended to be higher at 50% vs 85% RH.

Research on growth response of food crops under controlled environmental conditions is currently being conducted by the U.S National Aeronautics and Space Administration (NASA) for long-termed manned space missions through its Controlled Ecological Life Support Systems (CELSS) program. Studies in progress (Hill et al. 1989) at Tuskegee University are evaluating hydroponic sweetpotato production using the nutrient film technique (NFT).

Studies on the effects of relative humidity (RH) on growth of root and tuber crops are few. Available literature is generally in agreement that the main effect of RH on plant growth is mediated through its influence on transpiration, which in turn affects translocation of mineral ions and leaf temperature (O'Leary and Knecht 1971). Wheeler and Tibbitts (1989) reported that three potato cultivars grown at high RH (85%) produced increased tuber yields compared to plants grown at low RH (50%), while leaf area was greater at the lower RH level.

Agricultural plants including lettuce (Tibbitts and Bottenburg 1976), wheat, sugar beets and kale (Ford and Thorne 1973) have all responded positively to increased RH. The purpose of this study was to evaluate the effects of two RH levels on sweetpotato growth and yield in NFT.

MATERIALS AND METHODS

Four 15 cm long vine cuttings of 'TI-155' sweetpotato were grown in 0.15 by 0.15 by 1.2 m Tuskegee University NFT channels (Morris et al. 1989) in controlled environment walk-in growth chambers (Conviron Model PGW 36). A randomized complete block design with two RH levels (50% and 85%) and three replicates was used. The chambers were supplied with a mixture of cool-white fluorescent (CWF) and incandescent (INC) lamps providing an irradiance level of 600 μmol m^{-2} s^{-1}. The photoperiod in the chambers was set for 14/10 h light/dark. Temperature was maintained at 28°/22°C during light/dark periods.

Each growth channel was supplied by a 30.4 liter volume reservoir using a modified half-Hoagland nutrient solution providing a 1:2.4 N:K ratio. The nutrient solution pH was maintained between 5.5 and 6.0 by the addition of either dilute NaOH or H_2SO_4. Temperature and electrical conductivity were monitored at regular intervals. Solutions were changed every two weeks and were topped with deionized water if the volume of nutrient solution fell to 8 liters or less prior to the 2-week changeout. The nutrient solution was continuously pumped from each reservoir to the high end of each channel by small magnetic drive pumps (Little Giant Model 2PO37). The channels were graded with a 1% downward slope toward each reservoir. A flow rate of 1 L min^{-1} was set using a bypass line back to the reservoir with a control value.

Plants were spaced 25 cm apart within channels and channels were spaced 25 cm apart. Each vine cutting was held in place by a flat-plate assembly (Morris et al. 1989) attached to the sides of the channel by a flexible black/white vinyl covering. Plants were trained by tying them to vertical strings dropping 1 m above each growing channel. Photosynthetic and stomatal conductance data were collected over

Table 1. Effects of relative humidity on growth responses of sweetpotatoes in NFT.

Treatment RH (%)	No.	Storage root Fresh Wt.	Dry Wt.	Foliage Fresh Wt.	Dry Wt.
			(g/plant)		
50	4.8	611.7	116.7	672.6	88.7
85	6.3	841.5	157.0	581.9	74.3
P>F	0.10	0.009	0.03	0.10	0.05

five consecutive days beginning 81 days after planting with the use of a Licor-6200 portable photosynthesis system.

Plants were harvested at 120 days after planting. All foliage was cut at the base of the plant, weighed fresh and dried for 48h at 70°C. A 25 g sample of one storage root from each plant was dried at 70°C for 48 h to determine storage root dry weight. All data were analyzed by the general linear models procedure.

RESULTS

Sweetpotato plants grown in NFT showed healthy leaf and stem development similar to plants grown in solid rooting medium in previous studies. Plants grown under 85% RH tended (P> 0.10) to produce higher numbers of storage roots/plant than plants grown under 50% RH (Table 1). At final harvest, storage roots that formed in NFT were normal for shape, size and color. Storage root fresh and dry weight/plant were 37% and 34% higher under 85% than 50% RH. There was a trend (P> 0.10) toward lower foliage fresh weight for plants grown under 85% RH and a significantly lower foliage dry weight when compared to plants grown at 50% RH (Table 1).

Leaves of plants grown under 50% RH exhibited higher leaf temperature than plants grown at 85% RH (Table 2). This was somewhat surprising since one would expect higher rates of transpiration and hence greater cooling of leaves at the lower humidity (Kinbacher 1962). However, stomatal conductance rates were higher at 85° RH than at 50% RH. The higher conductance may have offset the reduced vapor

Table 2. Effects of relative humidity on physiological responses of sweetpotatoes grown in NFT.

RH (%)	Leaf temp. (C)	P_n (μmol/m^{-2}/s^{-1})	Cond. (s/m^{-1})
50	33.2	3.5	0.37
85	31.9	9.3	1.65
Sig.[z]	**	*	*

[z]Significant at 0.05 (*), or 0.001 (**).

Table 3. Effects of relative humidity on whole-plant elemental concentration in sweetpotatoes grown in NFT.

RH	N	P	K	CA	MG	MN	ZN	B
50	1.72	0.38	2.51	1.34	0.40	68.8	12.7	71.2
85	.73	0.34	2.35	1.17	0.34	60.5	9.9	60.4
P>F	NS	NS	NS	0.10	0.01	NS	0.10	0.08

pressure deficit at the higher humidity thereby allowing more rapid cooling of the leaves. Leaf temperatures were obtained on the fourth leaf from the end of the vine at the top of the canopy during photosynthesis measurements and may have been affected by the proximity of the leaves to the lamps.

Single-leaf P_n measured at 81-85 days after planting was consistently higher for plants at 85% than at 50% RH. It should be noted that P_n was measured on exposed leaves at the top of the plant canopy, which may not have represented whole-plant P_n accurately (Elmore 1980). The fact that leaves on plants grown under 85% RH exhibited higher stomatal conductance than those grown at 50% RH suggests that stomata of plants grown under 50% RH showed a greater degree of partial closure than plants grown at 85% RH (Tibbitts and Bottenburg 1976), which in turn may explain the lower photosynthetic rates at 50% RH.

Relative humidity levels did not affect whole-plant concentration of N, P, or K (Table 3). However, there were trends (P> 0.10, 0.10, 0.08) toward higher Ca, Zn and B concentration and significantly higher Mg in plants grown under 50% RH compared to those plants at 85% RH. Higher Ca and Mg concentration have been reported for *Begonia* at low RH (Gislerod and Mortensen 1990), whereas Collier and Tibbitts (1984) reported lower Ca concentration in outer leaves of lettuce at high RH. Present results suggest that Ca, Mg, Zn, and B uptake and transport in the sweetpotato in NFT is less sensitive to increasing RH than lettuce, while N, P, K, and Mn uptake seemed not to be affected by these two RH levels.

SUMMARY AND CONCLUSIONS

It is clear from these results that increased RH under the conditions in this study did enhance sweetpotato storage root yield. Increased growth under high RH may result either from reduced stomatal resistance (higher conductance) and thus increased CO_2 uptake (Slavi 1973) or from increased cell enlargement which provides a large leaf area for light absorption (Hoffman et al. 1971).

That stomatal conductance was low under 50% RH probably indicates decreased CO_2 uptake and thus lower P_n rate. Judging from the higher foliage fresh and dry weight under low RH, it appeared that in response to low RH the plant shifted its allocation pattern of photosynthates to favor allocation to foliage over allocation to storage roots and vice versa under 85% RH. Whole-plant elemental uptake of Ca, Mg, Zn, and B at 50% RH vs 85% RH appeared to be less sensitive to increasing RH in NFT compared to other crops such as lettuce, while N, P, K, and Mn concentrations were similar under both RH levels.

REFERENCES

Collier, G.F., and T.W. Tibbitts. 1984. Effects of relative humidity and root temperature on calcium concentration and tipburn development in lettuce. J. Am. Soc. Hort. Sci. 109:128-131.

Elmore, C.D. 1980. The paradox of no correlation between leaf photosynthetic rates and crop yields. Pages 155-168 *in* Predicting photosynthesis for ecosystem models. vol . II, edited by J.D. Hesketh and J.W. Jones, CRC Press, Boca Raton, Fla.

Ford, M.A., and G.N. Thorne. 1974. Effects of atmospheric humidity on plant growth. Ann. Bot. 38:441-452.

Gislerod, H.R., and L.M. Mortensen. 1990. Relative humidity and nutrient concentration affect nutrient uptake and growth of *Begonia x hiemalis*. HortScience 25:524-526.

Hill, W.A., P.A. Loretan, C.K. Bonsi, C.E. Morris, J.Y. Lu, R.D. Pace, and C.R. Ogbuehi. 1989. Utilization of sweetpotatoes in controlled ecological life support systems (CELSS). Adv. Sp. Res. 9:29-41.

Hoffman, G.J., S.L. Rawlins, M.J. Garber, and E.M. Cullen. 1971. Water relations and growth of cotton as influenced by salinity and relative humidity. Agron. J. 63:822-826.

Kinbacher, E.J. 1962. Effect of relative humidity on the high temperature resistance of winter oats. Crop Sci. 2:437-440.

O'Leary, J.W., and G.W. Knecht. 1971. The effect of relative humidity on growth, yield, and water consumption of bean plants. J. Amer. Soc. Hort. Sci. 96:263-265.

Slavik, B. 1873. Transpiration resistance in leaves of maize grown in humid and dry air. Pages 267-269 *in* Plant response to climatic factors, edited by R.O. Slatyer, UNESCO, Place de Fontenay, Paris.

Tibbitts, T.W., and G. Bottenberg. 1976. Growth of lettuce under controlled humidity levels. J. Amer. Soc. Hort. Sci. 101:70-73.

Wheeler, R.M., T.W. Tibbitts, and A.H. Fitzpatrick. 1989. Potato growth in response to relative humidity. HortScience. 24:482-484.

Sweetpotato Technology for the 21st Century. W.A. Hill, C.K. Bonsi and P.A. Loretan (Eds.) 1992. Tuskegee University, Tuskegee, AL

SWEETPOTATO VARIETAL IMPROVEMENT IN INDIA FOR THE 21st CENTURY

G.G. Nayar, B. Vimala, P.G. Rajendran, C.S. Easwari Amma, M. Unnikrishnan

Central Tuber Crops Research Institute, Sreekariyam, Thiruvananthapuram, Kerala, India.

This report briefly describes the present status and projected goals for sweetpotato improvement in India.

The population of India is expected to reach 1,000 million in the 21st century and will require about 225 million tons of food grains. The present production of food grains in India is 175 million tons leaving a shortfall of about 50 million tons. In order to address this projected food shortage, the National Commission on Agriculture, Government of India has projected an increased role for root and tuber crops. Sweetpotato is the third most-produced root and tuber crop in India, following potato and cassava. Potato is grown in the temperate regions; cassava is grown in the southern states, and sweetpotato is grown throughout the country. The major sweetpotato producing states are Orissa, Bihar, Uttar Pradesh, Madhya Pradesh and Karnataka.

Sweetpotato root production in India is compared to selected Asian countries in Table 1. The yield per hectare of sweetpotato in India is 45 and 38% of yield per hectare in Japan and China. The production of sweetpotato in India was 1.66 million tons on 0.23 million ha (7.19 t/ha) in 1974 and decreased to 1.35 million tons on 0.17 million ha (7.94 t/ha) in 1989. The Government of India has developed a target of 10 million tons on 0.5 million hectares (20 t/ha) for the year 2,000 A.D.

In any meaningful crop improvement program, the accumulation of the maximum possible number of genetic variables in a crop is of prime importance. Institutions in India with sweetpotato germplasm are listed in Table 2 along with the number of accessions based on passport data available at the Central Tuber Crops Research Institute (CTCRI).

Table 1. Sweetpotato production in selected locations*.

	Production (tons x 10^6)	Area (ha x 10^6)	Productivity (t/ha)
India	1.3	0.17	7.94
China	114.0	6.47	17.63
Japan	1.3	0.06	21.11
Indonesia	2.1	0.23	9.10
World	133.2	9.25	14.41

*FAO Production Yearbook 1989.

Table 2. Passport data on sweetpotato germplasm at the Central Tuber Crops Research Institute.

Source	Donor	No. of Accessions
Indigenous	CTCRI	382
	University of Kerala	41
	NPBGR	30
	Agricultural College	34
	Others	41
Exotic	Known country of origin	180
	Unknown country of origin	68

The CTCRI collection has over 776 lines including 248 lines that are exotic in origin from Japan, Nigeria, Puerto Rico, the USA, Sudan, New Zealand, Kenya, China and Argentina. Apart from CTCRI, the Rajendra Agricultural University at Delhi (Bihar) and CTCRI Regional Center at Bhubaneswar (Orissa) each have over 400 accessions. These collections show high variability with regard to morphological and root characters. Clones are available in the collection with compact to highly spreading foliage, leaves of a simple to highly-lobed nature, roots with skin colors from dark pink to light cream and flesh colors from dark orange to white. Selected sweetpotato varieties (Magoon et al. 1986; Nayar et al. 1984) in the CTCRI collection are described in Table 3 on the following page.

In addition to conventional breeding methods, tissue culture techniques are being used for the production of disease-free planting material and germplasm conservation. Haploid breeding, embryo culture and somatic hybridization (Miyazaki and Kobayashi 1975) are being assessed for inducing genetic variation and selection.

REFERENCES

Food and Agriculture Organization of the United Nations. 1989. FAO Production Yearbook, Vol. 43. Rome.

Magoon, M.L., S.G. Nair, R. Krishnan, and R.C. Mandal. 1970. Three promising high yielding hybrids of sweetpotato. SABRAO Newsletter 2: 115-118.

Miyazaki, T., and M. Kobayashi. 1975. Tetraploid sweetpotato. Trop. Root and Tuber Crops Newsletter 8: 37-38.

Nair, R.B, B. Vimala, G. Nayar, and G. Padmaja. 1986. 'H-80/168' – A new high carotene short duration hybrid in sweetpotato. J Root Crops (India).

Nayar, G.G., P. Kamalam, and R.B. Nair. 1984. Two promising sweetpotato selections from early harvest. J. Root Crops (India) 10:79-80.

Table 3. Source and properties of select sweetpotato varieties in India.

Source	Name	Yield (t/ha)	Growth period	Shape	Skin color	Flesh color	Quality*	Weevil resistance
Hybrid	H-1 (*2)	20-25	120	fusiform	white	white	s,cw, lf	tolerant
hybrid	H-42 (*2)	20-25	120	fusiform	pink	yellow-white	s, lf	high tolerance
hybrid	H-268 (*2)	18-22	120	fusiform	red	light yellow	s, cw	tolerant
hybrid	Rajendra Sakarkand-5 (*3)	20-25	120	cylindrical	white	white	cw	tolerant
open pollination	Sree Nandini (*2)	20-25	105	fusiform	cream	white	cw, t	high tolerance
open pollination	Sree Vardini (*2)	20-25	105	rounded	pink	light orange	cw, t	high tolerance
open pollination	Co-3	—	120	—	red	dark orange	—	—
open pollination	Samrat (*4)	18-24	105	fusiform	pink	white	—	moderate
USA (Regal)	VL Sakarkand-6	18-22	120	elongated	purple	light yellow	cw, t	tolerant
indigenous	Co-1	18-22	120	—	pink	white	—	tolerant

*s-sweet; cw-cooks well; lf-low fiber; t-tasty
*2 released from Central Tuber Crops Research Institute
*3 released from the Agricultural University in Bihar
*4 released from the Agricultural University in Andhra Pradesh

ON-LINE SPECTROSCOPIC MONITORING OF PLANT NUTRIENTS IN HYDROPONIC SPACE APPLICATIONS USING PHOTODIODE ARRAY ABSORPTION AND EMISSION SPECTROMETRY

Kenneth J. Schlager, Bernard J. Beemster

Biotronics Technologies, Inc., 12020 W. Ripley Ave., Wauwatosa, WI 53226.

The need exists for on-line real-time monitoring of plant nutrients for space applications. Macro- and micro-level nutrients including nitrate, potassium, phosphate, iron, copper, magnesium and molybdenum are of major interest and are more often effectively controlled by on-line monitoring. In long-duration NASA space missions, food production systems in space will benefit from on-line monitoring of elements in order to manage crop yields and allow for control of the plant production system. An on-line fiber optic ultraviolet-visible photodiode array spectrometer provides a very effective instrument for absorbance and atomic emission measurements of metal and non-metal ion solutions for chemical concentration analysis. Problems created by interfering and overlapping spectra are solved through the use of statistical and pattern recognition methods of multicomponent chemical analysis.

THE NEED FOR ON-LINE MONITORING OF PLANT NUTRIENTS

Hydroponic plant production systems are critically dependent on the chemical composition of nutrient solutions for effective yields. Although innovative concepts in open-loop nutrient feeder and blender systems have been implemented in recent years, the need still exists for close loop control of hydroponic nutrient systems. Close loop control requires the use of an analytical instrument able to provide on-line, real-time measurements of nutrient chemical concentrations.

Although atomic absorption spectrometry and gas chromatography are the typical methods of analysis for most of the nutrient components, these methods are not practical for continuous on-line monitoring in multi-constituent media due to sample preparation requirements and apparatus that can handle only a limited number of samples. Another limitation is the need to change lamps if more than one metal ion is to be analyzed. Multiple instruments would be required for analysis of more than one nutrient. These methods are also impractical for remote automated analysis because of their need for a controlled operating environment and peripheral equipment for sample processing. The power requirements, optical stability, weight, envelope dimensions, special gasses required and operator skills needed are also factors that preclude use of conventional instruments for this application.

However, another form of optical spectrometry, ultraviolet absorption spectrometry, is ideally suited to the needs of on-line nutrient analysis in space. Traditionally, ultraviolet-visible absorption measurements such as colorimetry have required the use of chemical reagents specific to a particular analyte (nutrient component) to react with the analyte and produce a color change proportional to the concentration of the analyte. Recent advances in spectrometry now make it possible to determine chemical concentrations in liquids based on ultraviolet light measurements without the need for reagents of any kind. It is now possible to mathematically transform an ultraviolet light spectra into an estimation of the chemical composition of a particular solution using pattern recognition techniques. A number of plant nutrients such as nitrate, iron and copper produce strong spectra in the ultraviolet region. These spectra can be measured on-line and then mathematically transformed into estimates of nutrient concentrations. This paper will briefly review the principles that make this analysis possible.

DETECTION OF ABSORPTION SPECTRA

Absorption in the ultraviolet and visible region of the spectrum is a result of the changes in energy levels that occur in the bond structures and valence electrons of atoms when in contact with a source of ultraviolet-visible light. The energy changes occur in the outermost orbital, which consists of two high energy levels and three lower energy levels. Electrons will normally be found in the lowest energy level, but can become "excited" from absorption of a photon of electromagnetic energy from light in the proper frequency, causing the electron to temporarily occupy one of the higher energy levels (Rao 1967; Thompson 1974; Silverstein 1981). Many heavy metals have strong absorption spectra in the ultraviolet-visible region due to the formation of ion complexes and ligands in water. It is well known that many of the heavy metals classified as transition elements possess the characteristic of forming complexes that are highly colored, that is, they absorb light in the visible wavelength range which is one reason why they are often used in pigments and dyes (Hopp 1983).

The term "absorption" refers to the characteristic of allowing only some fraction of light at certain wavelengths to pass through an otherwise transparent substance (or be reflected off of a solid), the balance being "absorbed" by the substance. Thus, absorption is the inverse of transmittance, and solutions that are fully transmissive within a certain wavelength range will not absorb any light within that range. Conversely, solutions that fully absorb within a certain wavelength range will not permit any light within that range to be transmitted through the solution (Thompson 1974).

Chemical analysis using ultraviolet-visible absorption spectra relies upon the same basic principles used for color analysis, but with far more attention to relative absorption characteristics at many specific wavelengths over the entire ultraviolet and visible range. It is possible to analyze solutions qualitatively and quantitatively based on the pattern of absorption observed for the solution across this wide range of wavelengths, but special apparatus is required to detect the spectra and interpret the information. The absorption observed will be a function of all of the absorbing components within the solution, which complicates the problem of analysis.

APPARATUS REQUIRED FOR DETECTION OF ABSORPTION SPECTRA

The pattern of absorption (or transmittance) across a range of wavelengths defines an absorption spectrum for the substance being analyzed. If the substance is an element dissolved in a transparent solvent, such as pure water, the absorption spectrum that can be observed using the appropriate equipment defines the absorption spectra for that element (in that solvent).

The apparatus required to accomplish analytical tasks in absorption spectroscopy is well known to analytical chemists but may not be evident to others who do not regularly work in the analytical or research sciences. Basic elements of any system include a source of light in the wavelength range of interest, a transparent cell to hold the sample and permit the light to be transmitted through the sample for a specific distance, a detector to measure the amount of light that has been transmitted through the sample and convert this information into numbers, and finally a means to process and interpret the information detected from the sample. The instruments currently in use range from the simple to the sublime.

Simple absorption spectroscopy systems have a limited (or single) wavelength range, and very simple fixed computational capabilities built into the instrument. These systems recognize only one substance (or family of substances) and usually require that the samples be processed or chemically altered to yield an indicator color prior to analysis. Systems with a broader range of capabilities are designed to permit analysis of a greater amount of information by detecting absorption at several (or many) wavelengths. This is accomplished by either altering the wavelength at the light source and using a fixed detector, or using a broad band light source and then selecting wavelengths for detection after transmission through the sample. In either case, the instrument must mechanically step through a sequence of wavelengths in order to collect information from the entire range of interest. This makes the instrument slow, fragile, and mechanically complicated, none of which are qualities that are suitable for use in field or space environments for real time/on-line analysis of unaltered flowing samples.

TECHNOLOGY ADVANCES FOR ON-LINE ABSORPTION SPECTROMETRY

Several recent developments have made ultraviolet-visible absorption spectroscopy a feasible technology for use in space:

Fiber optics permit substantial distance between the analyzer and the substance to be analyzed. The remote analyzer can house a light source, detector, and electronic components. Fiber optic cables convey the source light to an OPTRODE, where the light is transmitted through the sample before being collected and returned to the detector through a companion cable. Optrodes may be immersed in a process tank or flow stream, then removed after the analysis has been performed, or may be permanently located at the sample point for continuous monitoring. These are two types of *in situ* analysis. Alternatively, a sample line may be connected to a flow through cell containing the optrode. This is ON-LINE analysis.

Photodiode array detectors permit a broad wavelength range to be simultaneously detected at discrete intervals. This eliminates the need to create intervals by altering wavelengths at the source or prior to detection. Instead, a broad source can be used and fully detected. An evaluation can be made of wavelengths which contain absorption features relevant for the analysis. Wavelengths and ranges which do not contain

183

information that contribute to the analysis can be ignored, even though the detection will include information from the entire range. If used to detect uv-vis absorption, the original excitation is from a xenon lamp with an output ranging from 200 nm to 800 nm. If used to detect atomic emission spectra, excitation is from an energy pulse (spark) within the liquid. For nutrient analysis, an array detector that segments the detection range into 1024 equal intervals and scans across this entire range is used.

Chemometrics may be the most meaningful advance in technology that makes on-line analysis possible. The more specific the sensor is to a particular chemical, the less sophisticated the model required to extract meaningful information. Sensors that detect information for multiple constituents in a complex chemical matrix must rely upon very capable analysis algorithms in order to extract information for a specific chemical constituent. Although one trend in analytical chemistry is toward sensors that are ion or chemical specific, a less publicized trend is toward general purpose analyzers that have very sophisticated data analysis capabilities available within the instrument. These chemometric techniques are used to compare unknowns with calibrated standards and data bases, to perform advanced forms of cluster analysis, and to extract features from unknowns that are used as information in statistical and mathematical models.

REFERENCES

Rao, C.N.R. 1967. Ultraviolet and visible spectroscopy chemical applications. Plenum Press, New York. Pages 1-12.

Schlager, Kenneth. 1990. Final Report. Fiber fluorometry (spectrometry) for on-line chemical analysis of nutrient solutions. NASA Kennedy Space Center, Contract Number NAS10-11656.

Silverstein, Robert. 1974. Spectrometric identification of organic compounds. John Wiley & Sons, New York. Pages 305-310.

Thompson, Clifton, 1974. Ultraviolet - visible absorption spectroscopy. Willard Grant Press, New York. Pages 17-45.

SWEETPOTATO CROPPING SYSTEMS AT PRODUCTION CENTER AREAS IN INDONESIA

J. Wargiono, E. Tuherkih, D. Pasaribu

Research Institute for Food Crops, Bogor, Indonesia.

An appraisal was done to collect information on cultural practice technologies available at the farmer level for various agro-ecological conditions in major sweetpotato growing areas of the country. The results of this survey revealed that farmers prefer this crop as their main reliable commercial crop because they can obtain high yields and profits with minimum inputs. Cultural practice technologies which are already available to farmers include land preparation, preparing planting material and cultivation. Cropping systems, fertilization practices and varieties used in each production center area need to be backed up by new recommended technologies. The sweetpotato is generally grown as an intercrop with maize on lowlands after rice is harvested. Studies on a sweetpotato-maize intercropping system indicated that planting the maize spaced at 25 to 30 cm in rows on the slopes of ridges in between two rows of sweetpotato gave the highest total gross returns. The yield of maize grain in this system ranged from 2.2 to 3.0 t/ha. The reduction of light interception due to the shading effect of maize ranged from 24 to 41 percent resulting in yield reductions of 31 to 70 percent compared to that of sweetpotato monoculture. Harvesting maize at the milking stage and sweetpotato planting at four weeks following maize planting shortened the shading duration. This resulted in a reduction of sweetpotato yield of less than 5 percent compared to monoculture and a land equivalent ratio of 2.0. The leaf area index and crop growth rate of sweetpotato were affected by both population of intercropped maize and altitude. Since sweetpotato and maize are important staple food crops, this intercropping system has good prospects for farmers with less than 0.5 hectare per household.

INTRODUCTION

Sweetpotato is used as staple food by Papua people and people who live in several small islands in the eastern part of Indonesia. During the last five years the annual growth of production and harvested area of this crop has slightly increased by 1.7 and 1.4 percent, respectively. During this time, the proportion of sweetpotato in the diet of most people has been constant. However, its use by industry has increased and the population has increased. In order to meet the increasing demand for sweetpotato, the rate of production must increase. Among the problems to be addressed is that 17 of the 21 production centers are located on Java Island—which is only about seven percent of the total area of Indonesia.

In the order of priority, development of other major food crops is higher and thus information on the agroecology of growing areas and the production technology for rice, maize and soybeans is more available compared with that of sweetpotato. Also, farmers assume that sweetpotato, a traditional crop, is easier to cultivate than other crops and, therefore, the adoption of new technology has been very slow.

THE PERFORMANCE OF SWEETPOTATO FARMING

Several surveys were conducted by interviews with farmers and by field observations in various production centers on Java island to identify and recognize the agroecology, cropping systems, available technologies and expected technology of sweetpotato.

In all production centers surveyed, sweetpotato was considered the most dependable and reliable source of income among the major food crops. Farmers' preference toward sweetpotato as their main commercial crop is supported by their experience that this crop gives the highest profit with minimum input. In addition, sweetpotato is a traditional crop and farmers believe they have sufficient skill and knowledge to cultivate and market the crop. Consequently, the adoption of new technology has been very slow.

Surveys of central markets in several cities indicated that the consumers prefer sweetpotatoes with the following characteristics: good taste and sweetness, high starch content, low fiber content, oval shape, weights of 250 to 350 g/storage root and white or yellow flesh. Varieties grown by farmers in major producing areas have all of these characteristics and all are improved varieties except for 'SQ-27,' a local variety. Changing from local to improved varieties will take time because traders and farmers must be convinced of the benefits. In order to shorten the time of the change process, the Bogor Research Institute for Food Crops (BORIF) has taken two approaches—varietal testing in various production centers and yield performance exhibitions for farmers and traders. It is expected that the adoption of improved varieties will be faster if these approaches can be carried out regularly and simultaneously (Bagyo 1991). Several varieties of sweetpotato which are widely planted by farmers are listed in Table 1.

Land preparation is similar in most production centers and usually done manually or using animal power for the first plowing. Some differences in size of ridge, distance of ridge and tools used are due to soil type and topography.

Table 1. Average yield of local varieties of sweetpotatoes.

Province	Elevation (masl)	Variety	Average yield (t/ha)
West Java	< 400	SQ-27 *	15
		Jitok	20
	< 400	Tumpluk	20
Central Java	< 400	PB	10
		Sembawa15	
	> 400	Bestak	25
East Java	< 400	Bestak	25
	> 400	Bestak	25

*Old recommended variety

Table 2. Fertilization of sweetpotato in several major growing provinces.

Province	Kind of fertilizer	Time of application (WAP)*	Rate (kg/ha)
West Java	Urea	0	0- 20 (N)
		4	15- 70 (N)
	AS	4	10- 30 (N)
	TSP	0	0- 25 (P_2O_5)
	KCl	4	0- 15 (K_2O)
Central and	Urea	0	0- 45 (N)
East Java		4	30- 60 (N)
		12	30- 45 (N)
	TSP	0	0- 45 (P_2O_5)
	KCl	4	0- 30 (K_2O)

*WAP= Weeks after planting

Seedlings are produced by making seedbeds of storage roots followed by cuttings. Generally, big, round and healthy roots are selected at harvest time for nursery stock. The cuttings from this nursery (the whole stems with green leaves) are planted in a multiplication nursery.

In general, crop cultivation is also similar. At 3 weeks after planting (WAP) both sides of the ridges are concurrently cut vertically to improve soil structure and prepared for band fertilizer placement. Soil from both ridge sides is returned a week later to cover the fertilizer on either side of the ridge. Creeping stems toward the slopes of the ridge are lifted once a month to cut unproductive roots.

Fertilization of sweetpotato is commonly practiced; however, the rate of fertilizer applied varies (Table 2) depending on the capital and the habit of the farmer.

The results of on-farm research (OFR) studies in major growing areas of West Java showed that maximum yield was achieved at rates of 60-75 kg N/ha, while the effect of K was inconsistent. However, K application was considered as needed to maintain the K availability in the soil (Wargiono 1990).

Growth duration of sweetpotato is affected by altitude. For areas with elevations less than 500 meters above sea level (masl) it takes 4 to 5 months to mature and 5 to 6 months are required for higher elevations. Harvesting time affects the yield of sweetpotato. In areas of 500 to 600 masl when harvest is done at 4 months after planting, the yield can decrease by 50 to 70 percent compared with harvest at 5 to 6 MAP. For low elevation areas, harvesting after 5 MAP can reduce storage root quality because of increased fiber content and damage by weevils (Wargiono 1990). As mentioned earlier, sweetpotato is an important source of income for farmers and harvesting time is frequently affected by prices of storage roots (Table 3). A good price can stimulate farmers to harvest and sell their crops early. This can decrease the price in the following month when the supply becomes greater than the demand. Although there is fluctuation in monthly prices and harvested area, the variation is relatively small and the monthly production is minimally affected.

In Indonesia rice is the main staple food followed by maize. Sweetpotato is a main source of cash income for farmers and is mainly grown after rice especially in

Table 3. Monthly harvested area and fresh root prices of sweetpotato in Indonesia (Saroso 1990).

Month	Sumatra		Java		Kalimantan		Sulawesi		East Indon.	
	1	2	1	2	1	2	1	2	1	2
January	2.6	7.4	9.1	5.4	0.6	6.9	1.4	7.0	1.4	6.7
February	2.7	2.8	8.5	5.7	0.6	7.9	1.6	8.4	1.4	6.9
March	1.7	6.4	7.7	6.2	0.6	7.7	2.0	8.3	3.5	7.0
April	2.9	6.6	8.1	6.1	0.5	8.7	2.2	7.2	3.7	6.9
May	2.7	7.3	7.6	5.9	0.6	7.7	2.3	6.9	4.2	8.5
June	3.3	7.1	7.7	5.3	0.5	8.9	2.1	6.5	4.0	7.7
July	3.1	7.1	8.8	6.1	0.6	10.8	2.2	5.8	3.5	7.6
August	3.5	7.2	9.7	5.8	0.7	10.1	2.8	6.4	7.3	12.5
September	3.3	7.2	10.1	5.9	1.1	11.4	2.5	6.7	8.6	10.6
October	2.8	7.9	9.0	5.7	0.8	13.2	2.0	7.8	7.1	9.6
November	2.7	7.6	8.4	6.1	0.9	11.2	1.6	7.8	5.6	9.3
December	3.4	9.7	8.1	5.6	1.2	9.2	1.5	8.4	3.4	6.8
r1	0.4223		- 0.0524		0.4729		0.5524		0.8795	
r2	0.2730		- 0.0088		0.7023		-0.5785		0.7460	

r1 = Correlation of root price with harvested area at the same month
r2 = Correlation of root price with the next month's harvested area
1 = Harvested area (000 ha); 2 = Average price/district market (US $/100 kg fresh root).

the lowland areas. In intercropping sweetpotato, maize is the main interplanted crop because it can substitute for rice as food or as a cash crop in urban areas. In general, the major cropping patterns involving sweetpotato are: rice-sweetpotato or rice-maize-sweetpotato. Planting time of sweetpotato is affected by type of land, irrigation zone, and farmer's habit. Figure 1 shows the general cropping pattern:

```
Oct  Nov  Dec  Jan  Feb  Mar  Apr  May  Jun  Jul  Aug  Sep  Oct  Nov  Dec

|- - - - Rice - - - - - |   | - - - - - Sweetpotato - - - - -|     (when rainfall distribution is normal)

|- - - - - - Sweetpotato- - - - - - - |  | - - - - Sweetpotato- - - - |  (when rainfall distribution is
                                                                           not sufficient to grow rice)
|Veg.| | - - - Rice - - - |   | - - - - - Sweetpotato - - - - - |   (Simple irrigated lowland)

| - - - Rice - - - | | - - Maize - - |            ( Rotated irrigated lowland)
                    | - - Sweetpotato- - |
|Maize|
  | - -Sweetpotato - - | | - - - - - - Rice - - - - - - |

   |- - - - Rice - - - - |  | - - - Sweetpotato - - - |   | - - - - Sweetpotato - - - - |(Lowland irrig.)

    | Veg. |  | - - - - - Rice - - - - - |  | - - - - - - - Sweetpotato + Maize - - - - - - -|
```

Figure 1. Cropping pattern of sweetpotato with maize after lowland rice at major production center areas in Indonesia.

188

INTERCROPPING SWEETPOTATO WITH MAIZE

In Indonesia, maize is used as processed flour or direct food in the form of grain or fresh maize. Therefore, it has a high priority in development. Intercropping of maize with other food crops can reduce the yield of each crop. The land equivalent ratio (LER) and total income, however, is high (Guritno 1990). Under intercropping, the decrease in yield of sweetpotato is due to the light interception by maize and competition for nutrients and water primarily during a low rainfall period (Moreno 1981). Therefore, the position of the sweetpotato and maize on the ridge and planting time for both crops are among the important factors minimizing competition under intercropping.

Table 4 shows that the population of maize and its planting position on the ridges of sweetpotato affected the yields of both crops and gross returns. Among seven treatments applied, maize put on the slope of the ridge, spaced at 160 cm by 30 cm and planted at the same time as sweetpotato gave the highest gross returns. The maize yield decreased by only 4 percent when compared to that of the monoculture. This system has good prospects and is in line with the food diversification program that is presently encouraged by the government.

A continuation of the study mentioned above was carried out at two sites in West Java (Bogor, 250 masl and Kuningan, 400 masl) by simultaneous planting of maize and sweetpotato. Maize was planted on the ridge slopes, spaced at 150 cm by 50 cm, two plants per hill. The sweetpotato grossed high returns although less than those of monoculture, and in addition, the yield of maize was reasonably high (3t/ha of dry grain). This pattern is practiced by farmers who use maize to substitute for rice as

Table 4. Effect of population and planting of intercropped maize on yield of sweetpotato and maize (Lampung 1986).

Treatment	LER	Fresh root (t/ha)	Dry grain (t/ha)	Gross return (US$/ha)
Sweetpotato monocrop	-	19.6	-	1254.4
Maize monocrop	-	-	2.2	255.3
Sweetpotato + Maize (80 x 30 cm at T)	1.51	9.2	2.4	855.2
Sweetpotato + Maize (160 x 30 cm at T)	1.49	16.4	1.5	1216.1
Sweetpotato + Maize (80 x 30 cm at S)	1.68	14.0	2.2	1146.6
Sweetpotato + Maize (160 x 30 cm at S)	1.42	18.5	1.1	1306.1
Sweetpotato + Maize (80 x 30 cm at F)	1.28	14.0	1.3	1040.3
Sweetpotato + Maize (160 x 30 cm at F)	1.20	17.7	0.7	1210.5

T = Top of sweetpotato ridges
S = Slope of sweetpotato ridges
F = Furrow of sweetpotato ridges
Local prices (US $/100 kg) : Fresh root of sweetpotato : 6.4
                             Dry grain of maize   : 11.1

staple food. One of the factors contributing to the decrease in the yield of sweetpotato is the shading effect created by the maize. The decrease in light intercepted ranged from 26 to 41 percent, causing yield reductions of 31 to 70 percent (Table 5). Decreased root yield has also been reported by other investigators when sweetpotato was intercropped with maize, sugar cane or coconut (Moreno 1983; Wan 1983; Zara 1983).

In areas where farmers do not substitute maize for rice, this type of intercropping combination cannot be developed and alternative patterns are needed. The justification for the alternative pattern is to select a crop of short duration with a reasonable economic value. Other alternatives are to harvest the maize crop at milking stage (about 70 days) to shorten the shading period during the rapid growing phase of the sweetpotato—4 to 12 WAP for low elevations and 6 to16 WAP for high elevations. Figure 2 shows that the decrease in leaf area of sweetpotato was parallel to the increase in maize population intercropped, while Figure 3 shows an interaction between CGR of sweetpotato and the population of maize intercropped.

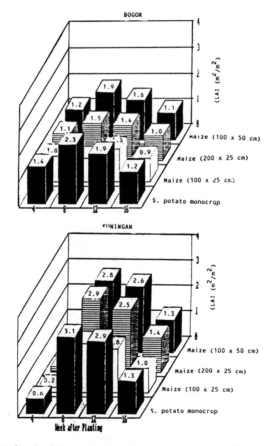

Figure 2. Effect of maize intercropped spacing on sweetpotato LAI, West Java, 1987.

Table 5. Effect of maize population intercropped population on light interception and yield of sweetpotato and maize in West Java, 1987.

Treatment	Light Interception (%)	Yield (t/ha)* Sweetpotato (fresh root)	Maize (dry grain)	Gross returns (US$/ha)
Sweetpotato	100	25.3	-	1718
Sweetpotato+ Maize (100x25 cm)	59	16.8	3.7	1008
Sweetpotato+ Maize (200x25 cm)	63	19.8	3.0	1292
Sweetpotato+ Maize (100x50 cm)	68	20.4	2.2	1387
Sweetpotato+ Maize (200x50 cm)	74	21.4	1.6	1425

*Average from two locations

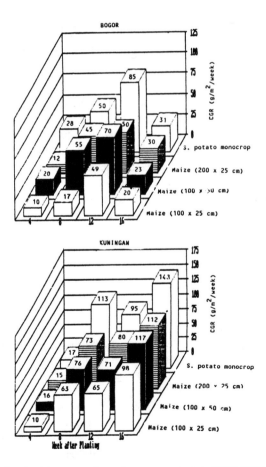

Figure 3. Effect of maize intercropped spacing on sweetpotato CGR, West Java, 1987.

Table 6. Effect of planting time of sweetpotato intercropped with maize on yield of sweetpotato and maize, West Java, 1989.

Planting time of sweetpotato (WAM)	Sweetpotato harvest index (%)	LER	Yield (USS/ha)			
			Sweet-potato	Maize	Total gross returns	Gross return/day
0	58.4	1.61	939.6ab	717.7a	1657.2bc	13.8a
1	56.3	1.75	988.2ab	809.6a	1797.9bc	14.2a
2	58.4	1.45	647.6a	792.5a	1440.1ab	10.8a
3	55.2	1.90	1033.7a	894.7a	1928.3bc	14.2a
4	59.5	2.04	1215.0b	891.4a	2106.4c	14.2a
Sweetpotato (m)	65.4	1.0	1316.0b	-	1316.4a	11.2a
Maize (m)	-	1.0	-	795.7a	795.7a	11.4a

WAM = Week after maize planted; m = monocrop. Means followed by the same letter(s) are not significantly different at 5% level of probability (DMRT).

The time of planting sweetpotato intercropped with maize was also evaluated at Cipanas, West Java (110 masl). The planting time of sweetpotato did not affect the yield of green cob maize harvested. However, the yield of sweetpotato and total gross returns were affected by planting time (Table 6).

The decrease in yield of sweetpotato due to the intercrop was significant when the sweetpotato was planted at 0 to 3 weeks after maize. Sweetpotato planted at 4 weeks following maize planting, when maize was harvested at the milking stage, gave the highest gross returns. This system is widely practiced by farmers where the green cob can be sold easily at a reasonable price. Though this system gave the highest total yield with an LER of 2.04 the intercrop duration was longer compared with other patterns tested. In terms of gross income per day, there were no significant differences among treatments. This pattern could be used as a check for evaluating other improved intercrop combinations.

Maize yields planted 2 weeks or longer following sweetpotato planting decreased linearly with time of planting. The maize could not compete with the vigorous sweetpotato growth (Table 7).

CONCLUSIONS

1. Farmers prefer sweetpotato as the main reliable commercial crop because they can obtain high yields and profits with minimum inputs.

2. Technologies available and already practiced by farmers are land preparation, preparing planting material and cultivation.

3. Cropping systems, fertilization practices and varieties used in each production area should be backed up by new recommended technologies.

4. Sweetpotato characteristics preferred by consumers are good taste, sweetness, high starch content, low fiber content, oval shape with a weight of 250 to 350 g/storage root and white or yellow flesh.

Table 7. Effect of planting time of maize on yield of sweetpotato and maize intercropped, West Java, 1989.

Planting time of maize (WAS)	Sweetpotato harvest index (%)	LER	Yield (US $/ha)		Total gross returns	Gross returns /day
			Sweetpotato	Maize		
0	6.0	1.85	1053.5 a	785.6 c	1839.0 b	15.4a
2	53.8	1.40	938.1 a	509.1 bc	1447.1 ab	11.9a
6	50.0	1.19	757.2 a	454.6abc	1211.8 ab	10.1a
8	50.9	1.23	1119.8 a	264.7 ab	1384.5 ab	11.6a
Sweetpotato(m)	65.7	1.0	1239.0 a	-	1239.0 ab	10.3a
Maize (m)	-	1.0	-	779.7 b	779.7 a	11.1a

WAS = Week after sweetpotato planted; m = monocrop. Means followed by the same letter(s) are not significantly different at 5% level of probability by DMRT.

5. Planting maize spaced in rows 25 to 30 cm on ridge slopes in between two rows of sweetpotato gave the highest total yield of intercropped grain maize (2.2 to3.0 t/ha) when compared with planting maize on top or in furrows of sweetpotato ridges.

6. The reduction of light interception due to shading effect of a maize intercrop ranged from 24 to 41 percent resulting in yield reduction of 31 to 70 percent compared to that of sweetpotato monoculture.

7. Leaf area index and crop growth rate of sweetpotato were affected by both elevation and population of intercropped maize. A shortening of the shading period by planting sweetpotato 4 weeks following maize planting and harvesting the maize at milking stage gave the highest gross returns as well as LER.

REFERENCES

Bagyo, A.S., A. Dimyati and K. Waluyo. 1995. Respon pedagang ubi jalar terhadap varietas 'SQ-2' dan 'BlS-183' di Yogyakarta Propince (Response sweet potato trades to varieties 'SQ-27' and 'BlS-183') Sem. Res. Inst. Food Crops, Bogor.

Guritno, B. 1989 Usaha peningkatan produksi ubikayu di lahan masam (Effort in increasing cassava production on acid soil) PT. Jawa Pes. Malang, Indonesia. 51 pp.

Hahn, S.K., and Y. Hozyo. 1983. Sweet potato and yam. Pages 319-339 *in* Proceedings, Symposium on potential productivity of field crops under different enviroments, Los Bannos.

Hozyo, Y., M. Megawati, and J.Wargiono. 1983. Plant production and potential productivity of sweet potato. Sem. Centr. Res. Inst. Food Crops, Bogor. 19 pp.

Moreno, H.A. 1983. Intercropping with sweet potato (*Ipomoea batatas*) in Central America. Pages 244-254 *in* Sweet potato, edited by R. L. Villareal and T.D. Griggs. Proceedings, 1st International Symposium, AVRDC, Taiwan.

Pusat Penelitian dan Pengembangan Tanaman Pangan. 1988. Data Penting Tanaman Pangan. Nasional Centr. Res. Inst. Food Crops, Bogor. 13 pp.

Saroso, S. 1990. Vademekun Palawija 2, jagung, ubikayu dan ubijalar. Dirjentan, SFCDP-

USAID, Jakarta. 93 pp.

Wan, H. 1983. Cropping system involving sweet potato in Taiwan. Pages 225-232 *in* Sweet potato, edited by R. L. Villareal and T.D. Griggs, Proceedings, 1st International Symposium, AVRDC, Taiwan.

Wargiono, J. 1980. Ubijalar dan cara bercocok tanamnya (Sweet potato and its cultural practices). Centr. Res. Inst. Food Crops, Bogor. 37 pp.

Wargiono, J., and E. Tuherkih. 1983. Umur panen dan waktu pemupukan ubijalar di lahan dataran tinggi (Maturity and time of fertilizer application of sweet potato at high elevation condition) Proc. Sem. Hasil Penelitian Tanaman Pangan. Centr. Res. Inst. Food Crops, Bogor, Vol. 1: 222-227.

Zara, D.L., S.E. Cuevas, and J.T. Carlos Jr. 1983. Performance of sweet potato varieties grown under coconuts. Pages 233-242 *in* Sweet potato, edited by R.L. Villareal and T.D. Griggs, Proceedings of the First International Symposium, AVRDC, Taiwan.

REDUCTION OF FUNGAL AND BACTERIAL CONTAMINANTS IN TISSUE CULTURES OF ROOT AND TUBER CROPS

S. Zok, J.T. Tambong, A. Sama, L. Nyochembeng, J.G. Wutoh*

Roots and Tubers Research Project (ROTREP), Institute of Agronomic Research, Ekona Centre. P.M.B 25, Buea, Cameroon; *University of Maryland, Eastern-Shore, Princess Anne, Maryland, 21853.

Attempts to mass propagate yam and cocoyam by the tissue culture method were seriously hindered by a very high rate of fungal and bacterial contamination ranging from 80% to 100%. This paper discusses results of Surface Sterilization Procedure studies to reduce contamination. For yam cultures, the development of the double Surface Sterilization Procedure [8% Calcium hypochlorite, $Ca(OCl)_2$ for 10 minutes followed by 6% $Ca(OCl)_2$ for 5 minutes, finally rinsing thoroughly in three changes of sterile, double distilled, deionized water] was found to have drastically reduced the contamination rate to an acceptable range of 8% to 10%. In the case of cocoyam rhizome buds, the use of the 10% calcium hypochlorite for 10 minutes gave similar acceptable rate of contamination. The results have implications for propagation of sweetpotato nodes in tissue culture.

Contamination of cultures is a serious limitation for the utilization of *in vitro* method for mass propagation (Dublin 1980; Merchant 1973; Siriwardana 1988; Withers 1985). Attempts to multiply yam nodal material by the tissue culture method at IITA Ibadan (Ng, personal communication) and yam and cocoyam rhizomes buds at the ROTREP laboratory (ROTREP, 2nd Annual Report 1988) were not successful due to severe culture contamination. A study of yam and cocoyam tissue culture indicated two sources of contaminants; a bacterial and a fungal source, present on the nodal segments of the vines and shoot tips of the cocoyam.

The objective of this study was to determine the effect of different disinfecting agents in reducing bacterial and fungal contaminants in the culture of yam nodes and cocoyam rhizome buds *in vitro.*

MATERIAL AND METHODS

Yams

Yam explants consisting of nodal sections 2 to 4 months old were collected from *Dioscorea rotundata* Poir (cv 'Bonakanda') plants in the greenhouse. They were washed with distilled water containing a few drops of a surfactant, Tween 80. After three minutes of soaking in 70% ethanol, they were rinsed with distilled water before undergoing the following treatments: *1: Double Surface Sterilization.* The explants were place in 8% aqueous calcium hypochlorite $Ca(OCl)_2$ solution for 10 minutes, rinsed once with sterile, double distilled, demineralized water and then soaked in 6% $Ca(OCl)_2$ solution for 5 minutes. This was followed by three thorough rinses with sterile, double distilled, demineralized water; and *2: Use of 5.25% NaOCl.* This treatment was used for comparison. Explants were soaked in 1:1 NaOCl-ethanol solution for seven minutes followed by three rinses in sterile water.

After the application of the treatments all the explants were cultured in a yam medium (Y1) composed of Murashige and Skoog mineral salts. The pH was adjusted to 5.8.

Cocoyam

Dormant buds were collected from a 24 month-old white cocoyam rhizome (*Xanthosoma sagittifolium*, cv 'Mamu').

Three sterilization solutions were used: Calcium hypochlorite, $Ca(OCl)_2$; sodium hypochlorite, NaOCl; and hydrogen peroxide H_2O_2; at two concentrations each as given below: A-6% calcium hypochlorite; B-10% calcium hypochlorite; C-15% sodium hypochlorite; D-50% sodium hypochlorite; E-10% hydrogen peroxide; F-15% hydrogen peroxide.

The explants were surface sterilized using these treatments for 15 minutes. One drop of a surfactant (Tween 80) was added during sterilization as a wetting agent. The sterilized explants were then rinsed 5 times with 0.1% L-ascorbic acid followed by rinsing with 3 changes of sterilized distilled water. The treated explants were then aseptically transferred into culture media comprised of B5 micro- and macronutrients including 3% sucrose without agar. All the yam and cocoyam cultures were kept

Table 1. Contamination of yam nodal explants observed with two treatments of sterilization, after 16 days.

Methods	No. explants cultured	No. explants contaminated	% contamination
Double Sterilization	118	10	8.47a*
NaOCl: Ethanol	117	45	38.46b

*Means within the column having a different letter are significantly different (Chi^2 test, P < .05).

in a controlled environmental chamber at (26-28°C, 15,000 lux, 16 hours light and 8 hours darkness). Data was collected weekly on the rate of contamination of the cultures.

RESULTS AND DISCUSSION

Results of the yam studies showed that the double sterilization procedure with only 8.47% contamination was more efficient in surface sterilizing yam nodal explants compared to the NaOCl (Table 1). Soaking the explants in 0.1% $Ca(OCl)_2$ solution after pretreating them with the double sterilization method further reduced the contamination to 2.5% compared to soaking in sterile water (10.2%).

Table 2 shows results of different surface sterilization treatments on cocoyam rhizome buds. The best results were obtained with 10% $Ca(OCl)_2$, 15% NaOCl, and 50% NaOCl treatment with only 5, 7, and 5% contamination respectively.

Only treatments with $Ca(OCl)_2$ gave good results on sprouting (data not presented). In all the other treatments, the percentage of sprouting was below 50% of the cultured explants. It has been reported (Murashige 1974) that, unlike the other chemicals, $Ca(OCl)_2$ does not penetrate the tissues of the explants and therefore does not inhibit sprouting.

Table 2. Percent contamination of *in vitro* yam cultures using different surface sterilization treatments, 10 days after culture.

Treatments	Number of explants alive	Number of explants contaminated	% contamination
6% $Ca(OCl)_2$	25	4	16
10% $Ca(OCl)_2$	20	1	5
15% NaOCl (control)	26	2	7
50% NaOCl	19	1	5
10% H_2O_2	33	16	48
15% H_2O_2	27	5	18

Results of these studies indicate that the double surface sterilization procedure using $Ca(OCl)_2$ is considered as a reliable means of eliminating the contaminants in yam nodal cultures. The efficiency of this method can be increased when topmost nodes on the vines are used and when these are dipped in 0.1% $Ca(OCl)_2$ solution prior to incubation. A disinfecting treatment with 10% $Ca(OCl)_2$ of the cocoyam rhizome buds was found to be very effective in reducing contaminants and in promoting sprouting.

These results suggest that double surface sterilization procedures should be evaluated for mass propagation of sweetpotato from nodal sections in tissue culture.

REFERENCES

Dublin, P., 1980. Induction de bourgeous neoformes et embryogenese somatique: deuz voies de multiplication vegetative *in vitro* des cafeiers cultives. Cafe - Cacao -The 24(2):121-130.

Merchant, D. J., 1973. Summary, *In* Contamination in tissue culture, Jorgen Fogh, 257-269.

Murashige, T., 1974. Plant propagation through tissue culture. Ann. Rev. Plant Physiol. 25: 135-166.

Roots and Tubers Research Project (ROTREP), 1988, 2nd Annual Report, 68 pp.

Siriwardana, S., 1988. Plant tissue culture methods. A laboratory manual. T.C.C.P. Colorada State University, 59 pp.

Withers, L. A., 1985. Minimum requirements for receiving and caintaining tissue culture propagation material FAO Plant Production Paper No. 60, 34 pp.

SECTION 3

DEVELOPMENTAL PHYSIOLOGY AND BIOCHEMISTRY

Sweetpotato Technology for the 21st Century. W.A. Hill, C.K. Bonsi and P.A. Loretan (Eds.) 1992. Tuskegee University, Tuskegee, AL

Stanley J. Kays

The Chemical Composition of the Sweetpotato

Why study the chemistry of the sweetpotato? At a very simplistic level, the sweetpotato is nothing more than an elegantly packaged collection of organic and inorganic chemicals. Everything of importance is determined by quantitative and qualitative differences in individual chemical components and their three-dimensional arrangement within the plant. When we make genetic crosses and select for new, improved lines, whether for insect or disease resistance, shape, color, flavor, yield, or any other trait, we are simply creating and assessing quantitative and qualitative changes in the plant's chemical components and their spacial arrangement. By better understanding the chemistry of the sweetpotato, the more readily we can alter the plant, enhancing the expression of traits deemed desirable. At present, we lack a thorough understanding of what compounds are found in the sweetpotato, the range of genetic diversity of these compounds, and the genes controlling their expression.

Breeding for insect resistance is a classical example of the importance of plant chemistry. Host plant selection decisions by insects are dominated at every stage by specific chemicals found on, in, or given off by the plant. Typically, plant breeders cross lines they either know or hope have some resistance to the insect in question and then allow the insect to make the selection decisions. Lines displaying lower preference, whether due to a lower level of chemical stimulants or a higher concentration of chemical deterrents, are selected and used as parents for further crosses. While the breeder may be unaware of what chemical differences are beneficial or detrimental and which have been selected, with the appropriate selection protocol and the right crosses, genetic improvements can be obtained. If, however, the breeder knows what the critical chemical components are and can readily measure them, a number of advantages may be realized. For example, this ability greatly enhances the accuracy of both parent line and progeny selection (Kays 1989), often two of the weakest links in a breeding program. For many traits, especially those that are difficult to accurately measure by conventional means, the sample population can be substantially increased. For traits such as insect resistance and flavor, an analytical approach allows separating breeding and initial selection cycles from the organism in question. For example, breeding for resistance to a specific insect pest can be carried out in geographical areas in which the insect is not present. Likewise, one could select for flavor traits at one location that are preferred

---

University of Georgia, Athens, GA 30602, USA.

by an indigenous population halfway around the world. While final selection decisions would be made using the target population, an analytical approach for initial selection can greatly facilitate the rate at which new, improved cultivars can be developed.

The following paper briefly critiques our basic understanding of the chemistry of the sweetpotato, focusing primarily on research from the past eight years. Included are chemical components that have been identified from the storage roots, vines, petioles, leaves, and fibrous roots and compounds that are synthesized by the plant in response to physical, chemical, or biological stresses. Chemicals excreted by invading organisms have been excluded as are compounds that are manufactured from existing components of the sweetpotato (e.g., cyclodextrans). The literature search covers Chemical Abstracts from January 1, 1982, through March 18, 1991, and reprints obtained using Current Contents. The review is divided into thirteen general topics of components: (1) carbohydrates; (2) proteins; (3) lipids; (4) organic acids; (5) pigments; (6) terpenes; (7) phenolics; (8) waxes; (9) volatiles; (10) vitamins; (11) minerals; (12) phytohormones; and (13) stress metabolites.

1. Carbohydrates

Carbohydrates are the most abundant constituent in the sweetpotato, making up 80-90% of the dry matter of the storage roots. They function as stored energy reserves, make up much of the structural framework of the plant, and impart the sweetness which is the dominant taste sensation in the cooked roots. Carbohydrates are normally separated into three general classes based upon the degree of polymerization: (1) monosaccharides, (2) oligosaccharides, and (3) polysaccharides. The oligosaccharides yield 2 to 6 monosaccharides upon hydrolysis. Examples in the sweetpotato are sucrose and maltose. Sugars make up approximately 4.5% of the dry weight. The polysaccharides are a much more diverse group which includes cellulose (~2% of total dwt), starch (~70%), pectic substances (~2.5%), hemicelluloses (3-4%), and other substances.

Quantitative and qualitative differences between the various carbohydrate components appear to partially account for differences in rheological properties between moist and dry fleshed lines (Sterling and Aldridge 1977). Both cultivar and field conditions at harvest can affect the carbohydrate composition of the roots (Jenkins and Anderson 1956; Schadel and Walter 1980; Sistrunk et al. 1954). During curing, the starch content declines, and there is an increase in sugars (Jenkins and Gieger 1957a; Picha 1987; Scott and Matthew 1957). Likewise, during storage there is a progressive hydrolysis of starch, with changes in the pool size of individual sugars varying among and between cultivars (Hammett and Barrentine 1961; Jenkins and Anderson 1956; Picha 1986b; Scott and Matthew 1957; Sistrunk 1971; Sistrunk et al. 1954). Pathogen invasion (Kato and Uritani 1976) and sprouting (Collins et al. 1990) also result in significant alterations in the root carbohydrate composition.

1.1. Monosaccharides and Oligosaccharides

The monosaccharides and oligosaccharides identified in cooked sweetpotato storage roots are sucrose, glucose, fructose, inositol, verbascose, stachyose, cellobiose, raffinose, maltose, and maltotriose (Son et al. 1991a; Truong Van Den et al. 1986) with the primary sugars in the raw roots being sucrose, glucose, and fructose (Kays and Horvat 1984; Martin 1986; Picha 1985b; 1986c; 1987; Tamate and Bradbury 1985). Maltose and maltotriose are formed during cooking due to the action of the amylase enzymes. During cooking, approximately 65 to 70% of the starch is hydrolyzed to maltose (Walter et al. 1975). The pool sizes of the other primary sugars, however, change little during baking (Horvat et al. 1991; Kays and Horvat 1984; Picha 1985b; 1987). After baking, some cultivars may contain up to 50% sugar on a dry weight basis (Kays and Horvat 1984). The higher the sugar concentration, up to a point, in the cooked product, the higher the sensory acceptance scores given by taste panels (Koehler and Kays 1991). It was possible, however, to have a too-sweet sweetpotato. In addition, maltose was the preferred sugar. This is important since the individual sugars vary widely in their contribution to the sensation of sweetness (e.g., sucrose = 1.00, fructose = 1.73, glucose = 0.74, and maltose = 0.33). As a consequence, expression of sweetness as sucrose equivalents can give a more meaningful estimate of the relative sweetness of a clone. Cooked staple-type sweetpotato lines often have sucrose equivalents of 1 to 3 while normal lines are commonly in the 30 to 45 range (Kays 1989).

Cultivars vary widely in the concentration of total sugars and specific sugars (Kays and Horvat 1984; Kanie et al. 1970). Changes in sugar concentration during storage are dependent upon the specific sugar, the cultivar, and the storage conditions. Many cultivars remain relatively high in sugar during storage, while others decline after several months (Jenkins and Gieger 1957a; 1957b; Picha 1987; Scott and Matthew 1957; Sistrunk et al. 1954). Significant alterations in root sugars also result from low temperature chilling injury (Picha 1987). Exposure to 7°C resulted in a significant increase in sucrose and total soluble sugars. Likewise, exposure of the roots to γ-irradiation causes an increase in sucrose accumulation (Ajlouni and Hamby 1988; Hayashi 1986).

1.2. Starch

Starch in the sweetpotato can be separated into two categories: transitory starch that is formed in the leaves during the day and then degraded, converted to sucrose, and translocated out during the night; and reserve starch that is synthesized and stored in the enlarged edible storage roots of the plant. The subsequent critique deals with the latter form.

Starch is a large molecular weight polysaccharide that is found as water-insoluble granules which are semi-crystalline in nature (for an excellent overview see Bank and Muir 1980). As starch begins to accumulate in the roots, there is an increase in the starch content per cell and the percentage of starch of the fresh and dry weight. A linear relationship has been found between root dry weight and starch content (Liu et al. 1985b). During accumulation, most starch is deposited in amyloplasts within the roots.

Starch content has been measured in a number of general studies (Candish et al. 1987; Cereda et al. 1985; Gu 1983; Madamba and San Pedro 1976b; Wang, 1987) and considerable work has been directed toward improving the techniques for measuring both starch (Chang and Tsai 1986; Uehara 1983; Walker et al. 1989) and amylose content in the sweetpotato (Huang and Wu 1985). Starch represents the primary carbohydrate found in the roots. It is found in two general forms - amylose, an α-1,4 linked, largely linear chain of glucose molecules (molecular weight ~106) and amylopectin, a branched molecule made up of a linear α-1,4 glucose chain which has α-1,6 branches at varying intervals. The latter is a substantially larger molecule than amylose (molecular weight ~108). The properties of amylose and amylopectin differ considerably. Amylose displays a crystalline structure that is unstable in aqueous solutions. The larger amylopectin molecule is amorphous and stable in aqueous solutions. As a consequence, the ratio of amylose to amylopectin exerts a pronounced influence over the properties of the starch in the roots. The ratio is genetically controlled and varies between lines. Considerable genetic diversity in starch chemistry (e.g., branching frequency, amylose to amylopectin ratio) is found in the sweetpotato germplasm, one of the many traits that has yet to be adequately explored in the crop.

Starch is synthesized from sucrose translocated from the leaves to the roots. Upon arrival, sucrose is hydrolyzed to glucose and fructose, with glucose subsequently being converted to a nucleotide sugar (e.g., ADP- or UDP-glucose). Subsequent polymerization is carried out by the enzyme starch synthase, which requires an existing α-(1,4)-glucan primer molecule of at least two glucose residues (e.g., $\geq$ maltose). ADP-glucose molecules are then sequentially added, building up the chain. The branch points are catalyzed by the Q enzyme [α-(1,4)-glucan 6-glycosyl transferase] which transfers one amylose subunit chain to a second. After reaching at least 30 glucose subunits, the starch molecule begins to develop a double helix configuration in which two chains interlock via hydrogen bonding. In amylopectin, the linear side chains may also exhibit a double helical structure with parallel chains. The role of phytohormones in regulating starch synthesis has not been established. In isolated root cells, however, gibberellic acid decreased the incorporation of UDP- and ADP-glucose into starch (Sasaki and Kainuma 1982). It is not clear, however, if this represents a natural role of the hormone or simply a pharmacological effect.

Starch granules are formed within the amyloplasts and display a range in sizes and shapes (Liu et al. 1985b). The granules enlarge by a symmetrical aggregation around a crystallized α-(1,4)-glucan primer with glucose subunits being added to the growing chain. Starch synthase bound to sweetpotato starch granules transfers ADP- or UDP-glucose into specific outer chains of amylopectin while nucleotide glucose is incorporated into short-chain outer amylose molecules by starch synthetase (Baba et al. 1987). Starch granules form in concentrically arranged rings or shells which are about 10.5Å wide. As the ring grows, the size of the amylose and amylopectin molecules and their ratio affects the properties of the granule. The starch content in sweetpotato roots varies with cultivar, location in the root, and stage of development (Boswell 1944), while cultivar and environmental factors affect granule structure. Sweetpotato granules vary in shape (spherical to irregular) and size (i.e. 1 to 30µm in diameter). This is approximately 1 to 1.5 times the size of maize granules (Sjistrom 1936). Therefore, starch in the sweetpotato represents a population of granules that vary in size and physicochemical properties.

The physicochemical properties of the starch strongly influence the potential uses and the characteristics of the roots when they are cooked. Important properties affecting the physicochemical characteristics of a starch include: (1) the amylose to amylopectin ratio; (2) the average length of the amylose chains; (3) the average length of the amylopectin branches in the molecule; and (4) the molecular size of the amylose and amylopectin molecules. In white potatoes, a high amylose concentration is associated with mealiness, while a high amylopectin content increases the pastiness of the product due to the increased tendency to hydrate (Unaru and Nylund 1957a; 1957b). Starch properties are analyzed using a number of spectral (Santha et al. 1990; Seog et al. 1987), microscopic (Bank and Muir 1980), chemical, and physical techniques (Boki et al. 1990). The following are properties of sweetpotato starches from a cross-section of cultivars grown in the Philippines: amylose content (29.4 to 32.2%); organic phosphorus content (9 to 22%); shape (non-aggregated granules of variable shape); size distribution (7 to 43µm); mean size (12.3 to 21.5µm); intrinsic viscosity (120 to 155 mL·g^{-1}); average and mean gelatinization temperatures (63.6 to 70.7°C and 57 to 72°C, respectively); and granule swelling (single stage)(Madamba et al. 1975). Gelatinization appeared to start at the hilum and progress to the granule periphery. It is believed to begin in the intermicellar areas of the granule where bonding is weakest. The gelatinization temperature is affected by a number of factors; for example, an increase in amylose content results in an increase in gelatinization temperature. Data by Lim et al. (1985) indicated a two-stage gelatinization process. This is indicative of two types of bonding forces which are relaxed at differing temperatures.

Starch granules also vary in their X-ray diffraction patterns, which gives an indication of the crystalline order. Three patterns are known. The A-pattern is largely associated with cereal starches, the B-pattern with potato starch, and the C-pattern in sweetpotato starch. The C-pattern of X-ray diffraction is a composite of A and B, and the subset Ca [typical of sweetpotato root starch (Hizukuri 1985; Nagashima et al. 1989; Shin and Ahn 1983; Takeda et al. 1986)] indicates the composite has a dominate A form. Differences in diffraction of the granules appears to be due to differences in the helical structure of the amylose (called A-amylose and B-amylose)(Wu and Sarko, 1987a; 1987b).

The amylose content has been measured in several laboratories and consistently falls in the 21 to 28% range (Kitada et al. 1988; Nagashima et al. 1989; Seog et al. 1987; Shin and Ahn 1983). Several lines have displayed higher levels (Madamba and San Pedro 1976b; Madamba et al. 1975). Although amylose is generally considered to be a straight chain molecule, it can display a limited amount of branching (Takeda et al. 1986). Lii et al. (1987) found an average number of 7.9 branches.

Techniques for commercial sweetpotato starch isolation and processing generally utilize the same general methods developed for other root and tuber crops (e.g., cassava)(Chiang and Pan 1986; Ishida et al. 1984; Roushdi et al. 1982; for a more detailed review see Sakamoto and Bouwkamp 1985). A number of starch-derived products and commercial uses for the starch have been explored (e.g., caramel and amylodextrin production, used in soups)(Baba and Kainuma 1987; Baba et al. 1987; Huang et al. 1983; Mihashi et al. 1987; Watanabe et al. 1982; 1983). Sweetpotato flour differs from starch in that essentially all of the cellular constituents are utilized in contrast to only the starch granules. The presence of non-starch polysaccharides, proteins, and other components alters the properties and potential uses of the material. Due to its high moisture content and distinct chemistry, flour production methods require additional steps than needed for wheat or other cereal flours (Chen and Chiang 1985) or an inferior product is produced (Martin 1984). A good quality flour can be made by washing the roots, cutting into strips, submerging in a 1.5% $Na_2S_2O_5$ solution for 30 min, rinsing 1 hr, oven drying at 50°C, and then grinding. As with starch, the properties of the flour vary with cultivar (Madamba and San Pedro 1976a). One primary use for sweetpotato flour has been to replace part of the wheat flour that is imported into tropical countries for use in raised breads. Acceptable products can be made with up to 30% sweetpotato flour (Chen and Chiang 1985).

1.3. Cellulose

Cellulose is a straight chain polysaccharide of glucose molecules linked *via* β-1,4 bonds. The chain length ranges from 1,000 up to 10,000 glucose subunits. Cellulose is a major component of the cell walls of the sweetpotato. In the storage roots, the concentration of cellulose is approximately 2 to 5% (Holloway et al. 1985; Sistrunk 1977). Cellulose is a very stable molecule, and during storage and sprouting it is not broken down and utilized as a carbon or energy source. Degradation of the molecule does occur with the invasion of pathogens that excrete cellulase.

1.4. Pectin

Pectins make up the dense gel-like noncellulosic component of the cell walls. They are found predominately in the middle lamella and function as a binding agent between neighboring cell walls. Pectins are comprised largely of α-(1-4) linked D-galacturonic acid subunits but many contain a number of other monosaccharides (e.g., arabian, galactan, rhamnose, xylose). Pectins are separated into three general fractions based upon their solubility: pectic acids, pectins, and protopectins. Each fraction represents a population of compounds rather than one distinct form.

The concentration of total pectin in cooked sweetpotatoes is approximately 2.5 to 3.0% (Holloway et al. 1985; Sistrunk 1977). Pectins in the sweetpotato do not undergo the substantial alterations during storage that occur with the softening of ripening fruit. There are, however, significant changes, and their importance in the textural properties of the roots has yet to be sufficiently established. Typically, total pectins increase during storage, while the HCl-soluble pectin component declines (Hamasaki and Yamaguti 1985). Large changes in the storage root pectin fraction occur mainly during processing and with invasion of some fungi that excrete their own polygalacturonase enzymes. Changes in the pectic components have been monitored to ascertain their relationship to subsequent firmness of the processed sweetpotatoes. The concentration of protopectin was found to decline during curing while the concentration of soluble pectins increased. During subsequent storage, however, the opposite was true. Baking and processing resulted in a decrease in total pectins (Ahmed and Scott 1958; Baumgardner and Smith 1963; Heinze and Appleman 1943). Baking causes a conversion of HCl-soluble pectins to smaller molecular weight pectins (Lee et al. 1985).

1.5. Hemicellulose

Hemicellulose represents a heterogenous group of polysaccharides that are in many ways similar to cellulose. They are comprised of glucose, galactose, mannose, xylose, and arabinose molecules linked in various combinations and degrees of branching. Hemicellulose comprises approximately 2 to 4% of the dry weight of the roots (Holloway et al. 1985; Ohtani and Misaki 1985; Sistrunk 1977).

1.6. Fiber

Fiber normally includes the soluble non-starch polysaccharides, pectin, hemicellulose, cellulose, and lignin (Holloway 1983; Lund 1982). Recent interest in fiber has been kindled by a possible negative relationship between dietary fiber intake and the incidence of a variety of noninfectious gastrointestinal diseases in humans (Burkitt et al. 1972). Fiber has also been shown to decrease blood cholesterol levels. The fiber content of sweetpotatoes has been determined in several studies (Holloway 1983; Holloway et al. 1985, Larbi and M'barek 1985; Lund 1982). The average dietary fiber content of Tongan sweetpotatoes was 14% on a dry weight basis (Holloway et al. 1985). In a separate study, the percentage of crude fiber was substantially lower, i.e., 0.58% (Larbi and M'barek 1985). Generally, sweetpotatoes are selected for low fiber content (Hammett et al. 1966; Jones et al. 1980). The fiber content in sweetpotato lines from a polycross nursery ranged from exceedingly low to such a high level that the roots were woody.

2. Proteins

Proteins represent an extremely important class of organic components in that they regulate metabolism, act as structural molecules and in sweetpotato storage roots, several represent storage forms of carbon and nitrogen. Proteins are composed of long chains of amino acids linked *via* peptide bonds. Shorter chains (i.e., < 100 amino acids) are commonly referred to as polypeptides while those of greater length are considered proteins.

2.1. Crude Protein and Non-protein Nitrogen

Sweetpotato crude protein, determined by multiplying the elemental nitrogen concentration times a conversion factor (6.25), is comprised of both protein (63 to 85% of the total) and non-protein nitrogen compounds. The non-protein nitrogen component ranges from 15 to 37% of the total crude protein content at harvest (Purcell and Walter 1980; Dichey et al. 1984) (for additional details see reviews by Walter and Purcell 1986; Walter et al. 1984; Woolfe 1991). The non-protein nitrogen is found primarily in amino acids (88%) and amides (Purcell and Walter 1980). The protein concentration in the storage roots ranges from 1.3 to >10% on a dry weight basis (Purcell et al. 1972; Li 1974; Goodbody 1984; Zanariah et al. 1986; Bradbury et al. 1984; Bhattacharya et al. 1989), averaging approximately 5% or on a fresh weight basis, 1.5%. When the nitrogen concentration alone is used as a measure of the protein content, the contribution of the non-protein nitrogen can give a somewhat inflated protein value. Leaf protein content is generally in the 3.5 to 12% of dry weight range (Lin and Ho 1986; Ghazi et al. 1989; Bhattacharya et al. 1989; Biswas et al. 1988).

The protein concentration in sweetpotato roots varies widely between individual lines, and mass selection has been shown to be an effective means of increasing the crude protein content (Li 1977). Within-cultivar variation and root-to-root variation between roots taken from a single plant is also high (Purcell et al. 1978b). The same cultivar grown under differing environmental conditions will often display significantly different levels of protein (Collins and Walter 1982; Bradbury et al. 1985). Likewise, cultural practices (Yeh et al. 1981), length of growing season (Purcell et al. 1976a), nitrogen fertilization rate (Purcell et al. 1982; Constantin et al. 1984; Yeh et al. 1981; Gonzales et al. 1977), and storage (Purcell et al. 1978a) can each have a pronounced effect on protein concentration within the storage roots.

The concentration of protein is not uniform throughout the storage roots but is generally higher at the proximal (stem) end (Purcell et al. 1976b). The cross-sectional distribution finds a significantly higher concentration in the outer cortex adjacent to the surface (Purcell et al. 1976b; Makki et al. 1986; Kimber 1976); subtending tissues, however, tend to be relatively uniform.

Sweetpotato protein can also be obtained from the material remaining after various storage root processing operations, e.g., starch isolation and alcohol production. During starch extraction, the residual liquid contains a significant quantity of protein (Horigome et al. 1972). Drying produced a product that was 8.7% crude protein. Although lower in methionine and lysine than egg protein, the composition is superior to that of soybean protein. Its efficiency ratio was 1.9 for weanling rats but was increased to 2.5 by supplementation with methionine and lysine. The biological value and true digestibility of the protein varied with extraction and drying methods but were generally in the 72 to 74% and 79 to 82% range, respectively.

A protein-rich product can be likewise obtained from the sweetpotato fermentation residue that remains after ethanol production (Wu and Bagby 1987). Filter cake and centrifuged solids had crude protein contents of 22 to 32% and 42 to 57%, respectively.

Flour produced from sweetpotato storage roots contains a small [2.5% fwt of flour (Madamba and San Pedro 1976a)] component of protein which has a protein efficiency ratio ranging from 2.2 to 1.3 depending upon the cultivar and dehydration method (Walter et al. 1983). The lysine content of the flour protein correlated well with protein efficiency ratio values.

2.2. Amino acids

The amino acid analysis of storage root protein has been published by a number of authors (Bradbury et al. 1984; 1985; Goodbody 1984; Walter et al. 1983; Meredith and Dull 1979). Analysis of the crude protein fraction after hydrolysis into component amino acids is presented in Table 1. The non-protein nitrogen portion was primarily asparagine (61%), aspartic acid (11%), glutamic acid (4%), serine (4%), and threonine (3%). The protein's nutritional quality is good, although the quantity is

Table 1. Amino acid composition of sweetpotato storage root crude protein from three analyses.

Amino Acid	Grams of Amino Acid per 100 gm Crude Protein		
	Meredith and Dull (1979)[1]	Purcell and Walter (1968)[2]	Walter et al. (1984)[2]
Essential			
threonine	4.1	4.5	5.3
valine	4.9	6.8	6.7
methionine	2.6	2.7	1.0
total sulfur	2.6	3.3	2.2
isoleucine	3.6	4.6	3.9
leucine	5.4	7.5	5.9
tyrosine	3.1	5.8	4.0
phenylalanine	4.3	7.3	5.9
lysine	4.0	6.6	3.8
tryptophan	—	0.4	—
Nonessential			
aspartic acid	28.3	20.2	22.4
serine	3.9	4.4	3.8
glutamic acid	8.0	7.4	11.0
proline	2.7	4.0	2.5
glycine	4.3	4.2	4.3
alanine	5.2	6.2	3.6
histidine	1.7	2.8	3.1
arginine	3.5	4.3	4.2

[1] Cultivar: Jasper
[2] Cultivar: Jewel

typically low. An adequate nitrogen balance can be maintained in humans, however, if sufficient amounts of sweetpotato are consumed (Adolph and Liu 1939). Isolated sweetpotato storage root protein has a protein efficiency ratio equal to that of casein (Walter and Catignani 1981). Factors causing quantitative and/or qualitative changes in protein or individual amino acids are of primary concern since they can significantly influence the nutritional value of the product. The most pronounced alterations result from the thermal degradation of the amino acid lysine which occurs during cooking. Cooking method has been shown to have a significant effect on nutritional quality of the protein (Purcell and Walter 1982), with baking resulting in less loss than canning in syrup or dehydration of flakes. Once processed to a puree, the protein component was found to remain stable over a 6-month period with proper storage (Creamer et al. 1983).

2.3. Storage Proteins

Storage proteins represent carbon- and nitrogen-containing compounds that are utilized during seed, tuber, and storage root sprouting and initial growth. In grains and legumes, seed storage proteins make up a major source of protein for humans and livestock. Common cereal grain storage proteins are gliadin (wheat), oryzin (rice), zein (corn), kafirin (sorghum), secalin (rye), hordein (barley), and avenin (oat). The storage roots of sweetpotato, likewise, contain the storage protein sporamin, first identified by Jones and Gersdoff in 1931 as ipomoein. Existing evidence suggests that sporamin and ipomoein are synonymous (Maeshima et al. 1985; Varon et al. 1989). The protein has an apparent molecular weight of 25,000 (Maeshima et al. 1985) and makes up 60 to 81% of the total soluble storage root protein. Sporamin mRNA does not appear to be expressed in leaves, petioles, or fibrous roots (Hattori et al. 1985.).

Two classes (A and B) of the storage protein are encoded by genes g*SPO-A1* and g*SPO-B1* which are members of two distinct subfamilies of a multigene family for the protein (Hattori and Nakamura 1988; Shigeki et al. 1986). The nucleotide sequences for both genes have been determined, as were 5' upstream transcriptional start sites and a TATA box sequence. Homology between the genes was assessed as were upstream sequences, several of which appeared to be highly conserved and may play a regulatory role. Neither gene contained introns.

Analysis of the multigene family coding for the storage protein indicated that intra-subfamily homologies (94 to 98%) were much higher than inter-subfamily homologies (82 to 84%) (Hattori et al. 1989). Large portions of the base substitutions in the coding region of the gene resulted in amino acid substitutions. Deletions appeared to have been generated by slipped mispairing during DNA replication (Murakami et al. 1986).

Sporamin is synthesized by membrane bound polyribosomes (Hattori et al. 1985) and the precursor is approximately 4000 daltons larger than the mature protein. The nucleotide sequence of its cDNA and the *in vitro* processing of the precursor (Hattori et al. 1987) indicate the presence of a signal peptide on the precursor which may function in controlling its movement from the endoplasmic reticulum to, and subsequent sequestering into, the vacuole (Hattori et al. 1988). The mechanism of sporamin synthesis and accumulation has been reviewed by Nakamura et al. 1988. Sporamin appears to be degraded into lower molecular weight peptides after extended storage, cutting, or fungal infection (Li and Oba 1985).

2.4. Enzymes

Enzymatic proteins are extremely important in that they regulate virtually all of the biochemical reactions taking place within the sweetpotato. Control is exerted over the rate of specific processes within the plant (e.g., terpene synthesis) largely through enzyme synthesis, activation, and degradation. This allows the plant/organ/cell to adjust to changes in its environment. Individual enzymes are classified based on their catalytic function (e.g., oxidoreductases, transferases, hydrolases, lyases, isomerases, ligases). Our existing understanding of the enzymes operative in the sweetpotato is highly variable, ranging from simply establishing the presence of the enzyme to ascertaining the amino acid sequence, active sites, and three-dimensional structure. β-amylase, for example, represents quantitatively the second most abundant protein in the storage roots (after sporamin), and it has long been used as a model to study enzyme function. Due to this variation in the amount of information available on each enzyme and the fact that each enzyme represents a separate story, only individual enzymes and their more recent references are listed in Table 2.

Table 2. Enzymes identified and partially characterized in the sweetpotato.

Enzyme	Reference
Acetyl CoA synthase	Takeuchi et al. 1977; 1980
Aldehyde dehydrogenase	Takeuchi et al. 1980
Alcohol dehydrogenase	Chang et al. 1983
Allantoate amidohydrolase	Osuji and Ory 1987
Allantoicase	Osuji and Ory 1987
Allantoinase	Osuji and Ory 1987
α- *Amylase*	Deobald et al. 1968, Deobald et al. 1969; Deobald et al. 1971; Diaz et al. 1989; Doehlert and Duke 1983; Hollo et al. 1982; Ikemiya and Deobald 1966; Kimura and Chiba 1983; Morrison 1990; Szyperski et al. 1986; Walter and Purcell 1973

β- *Amylase*

Ajlouni and Hamby 1988; Ann et al. 1989; 1990a; 1990b; Bank and Greenwood 1969; Baba and Kainama 1987; Balls et al. 1948; Chiang and Chen 1988; Colman and Matthews 1971; Diaz et al. 1989; Doehlert and Duke 1983; Gray et al. 1982; Hehre et al. 1986; Hollo et al. 1982; Kainuma and French 1970; Kanie et al. 1974; 1976; Hegde et al. 1979; Kim et al. 1985; Kimura and Chiba 1983; Lineback and Sayed 1971; McArdle 1983; Morrison 1990; Ohi and Miyagawa, 1982; Ohtani et al. 1987; Roy and Hedge 1985; Takeda et al. 1972; Takeda and Hizukuri 1981; Toda 1989

ATPase

Iwasaki et al. 1984; Iwasaki and Asahi 1983; 1985; Kimura et al. 1989; Kobayashi et al. 1986; 1987; Nakamura and Asahi 1990

Catalase

Esaka and Asahi 1979; 1982; Esaka et al. 1982; 1983a; 1983b; Yamaguchi et al. 1987

Catechol oxidase

Yuan and Yang 1982; 1985

Chlorogenate caffeoyl transferase

Villegas et al. 1987

Cinnamic acid 4-hydroxylase

Fujita and Asahi 1985a; Tanaka et al. 1974

UDPG: t-Cinnamate glycosyltransferase

Shimizu and Kojima 1982; 1984

p-Coumaroyl-D-glucose hydroxylase

Tanaka and Kojima 1991

Cytochrome C oxidase

Asahi et al. 1982; Esaka and Asahi 1979; Maeshima et al. 1980; 1981; 1987; 1989; Maeshima and Asahi 1981; Nakagawa et al. 1990

NADPH-Cytochrome C reductase

Fujita and Asahi 1985b

5-Dihydroquinate hydrolyase

Minamikawa et al. 1966

Farnesol dehydrogenase

Inoue et al. 1984b

Fumurase

Esaka and Asahi 1979

β-*Galactosidase*

Nashio 1984

Glyceraldehyde-3-phosphate decarboxylase

Haissig and Schipper 1975

Glucose-6-phosphate dehydrogenase	Haissig and Schipper 1975
β-Glucosidase	Nashio 1984
Glucose phosphate isomerase	Sasaki et al. 1972
3-Hydroxy-3-methylglutaryl-CoA reductase	Ito et al. 1979; 1982; Suzuki and Uritani 1975a; 1975b; 1976
Indoleacetic acid (IAA) oxidase	Chen 1988; Hancock 1984; Imbert and Wilson 1970; 1972a; 1972b; Sirju and Wilson 1974
Invertase, acid	Acock and Garner, 1987; Matsushita and Uritani 1975
Ipomeamarone 15-hydroxylase	Fujita and Asahi 1985a
Lactate dehydrogenase	Oba and Uritani 1982a
Lipoxygenase	Shingles et al. 1982
Malate dehydrogenase	Esaka and Asahi 1979; Haissig and Schipper 1975; Wedding et al. 1976
Malic enzyme	Wedding et al. 1976
Nitrate reductase	Sung 1981

Peptidase
    a. *aminopeptidase*   Lin and Chan 1990
    b. *carboxypeptidase*   Lin and Chan 1990
    c. *endopeptidase*   Lin and Chan 1990

Peroxidase	Chang et al. 1986; Floris et al. 1984; Gahagan et al. 1968, Gaither et al. 1973; Haard and Marshall 1976; Imaseki 1970; Kawashima and Uritani 1963; 1967; Kawashima 1965; Kanazawa et al. 1965; Kondo and Morita 1952; Loebenstein and Linsey 1961; Matsuno and Uritani 1972; Neves and Laurenco 1985; Shannon et al. 1971; Stahmann and Demorest 1973; Xue et al. 1988
Phosphatase, acid	Fujimoto et al. 1985; 1986; 1987; Kawabe et al. 1984
Polygalacturonase	Arinze and Smith 1982
Polyphenol oxidase	Arinze and Smith 1982; Arthur and McLemore 1956; Chung 1988; Eiger and

213

	Dawson 1949; Hyodo and Uritani 1965; Neves and Laurence 1985; Scott and Kattan 1957; Scott et al. 1944; Walter and Purcell 1980; Walter and Schadel 1982
o-diPhenol oxidase	Esaka and Asahi 1979, Hyodo and Uritani 1966
6-Phosphogluconate dehydrogenase	Haissig and Schipper 1975
Phosphoglucose isomerase	Ajlouni and Hamby 1988
L-Phenylalanine ammonia-lyase	Haard and Wasserman 1976; Minamikawa and Uritani 1965; Sato and Sankawa 1983; Sato et al. 1982; Tanaka and Uritani 1976; 1977b; 1977c; Tanaka et al. 1989
Pyruvate decarboxylase	Chang et al. 1982; 1983; Oba and Uritani 1975; 1982b; Takeuchi et al. 1980
RNAase	Sacher et al. 1982
RNA polymerase	Kahl et al. 1982
Shikimate - NADP oxidoreductase	Minamikawa et al. 1966
Starch phosphorylase	Chang et al. 1987; Chang and Su 1986a; 1986b; Pan et al. 1988
Starch synthase	Baba et al. 1987
Starch synthetase a. *ADPG-starch transglucosylase*	Downton and Hawker 1975; Murata and Akazawa 1968; 1969; Sasaki and Kainuma 1981
b. *UDPG-starch transglucosylase*	Murata and Akazwa 1969; Sasaki and Kainuma 1981
Succinate dehydrogenase	Hattori and Asahi 1982; Hattori et al. 1983; Maeshima et al. 1987
Sucrose synthase	Ajlouni and Hamby 1988; Hayashi et al. 1984; Murata 1971
Sucrose phosphate synthetase	Hayashi et al. 1984; Murata 1972
Tyrosine deaminase	Minamikawa and Uritani 1964
Urate oxidase	Esaka and Asahi 1979

2.5. Proteinase Inhibitors

Peptidases (also called proteinases) represent enzymes in plants, animals, and microorganisms that break down protein into their component amino acids. In intact cells, peptidases are essential for recycling amino acids, allowing them to be incorporated into new proteins. In animals, peptidases found in the digestive tract mediate the degradation of ingested proteins allowing absorption.

Sweetpotatoes and a number of other plants possess several polypeptides and proteins that are potent inhibitors of these protolytic enzymes (for a thorough overview see Ryan 1981). Proteinase inhibitors (commonly referred to as trypsin inhibitors) display a high level of specificity, binding very tightly to a number of protein degrading enzymes and in so doing eliminating the enzymes' ability to function. When plant proteinase inhibitors impede the degradation of proteins in the digestive tract, it significantly decreases the nutritive value of the food.

Most plant proteinase inhibitors inhibit serine endopeptidases and are composed of L-amino acids of which a high percentage are half-cystine residues (Ryan 1981). The presence of cystines allows frequent disulfide cross-linking, enhancing the stability of the molecule. Proteinases display a relatively high level of thermal stability but are degraded during normal cooking. Thus, proteinase inhibitors are of primary concern when the plant material is utilized in an uncooked state, a common situation with animal feeds.

The presence of proteinase inhibitors in sweetpotato was first reported in 1954 (Sohonie and Bhandarker). Concern over the presence of those inhibitors stemmed largely from the fact that raw sweetpotatoes are widely used as swine feed in parts of Asia. When sweetpotatoes are used as 25-30% or greater of the diet, growth is significantly retarded (Yeh, 1983). Proteinase inhibitors from sweetpotatoes appear to represent a population of proteins with varying properties (Suguria et al. 1973; Lin et al. 1983, Dickey and Collins 1984). The approximate molecular weights of two inhibitors were 23,000 and 24,000. They are stable over a pH range of 2 to 11 and are thermally stable at 70°C. Some sweetpotato proteinase inhibitors appear to retain their functional ability up to 100°C (Lin 1989b; Lin and Chen 1980).

Generally, the concentration of proteinase inhibitor decreases from the proximal (stem) end of the storage root to the distal end (Dichey and Collins 1984; Lin and Tsu 1987). In cross-section, the highest activity is in the cortical region adjacent to the surface (Dickey et al. 1984). Likewise, cultivar (Bouwkamp et al. 1985; Dickey and Collins 1984; Lin 1989; Lin and Chen 1980; Pan and Tsai 1987), planting time (Lin 1987; 1989a), rainfall (Lin 1989a), and season (Lin and Ho 1986) can affect the concentration. Sweetpotato leaves also contain proteinase inhibitors, the concentration of which appears to correlate with storage root levels (Lin and Ho 1986).

3. Lipids

Lipids represent a very broad group of compounds that have diverse roles in the sweetpotato. Lipids act as storage forms of carbon (particularly in the seeds), function as components of cellular membranes, and are cuticular waxes on the surface of the plant, as well as having other functions (e.g., pigments, sterols, vitamins). Biochemically, lipids are separated into neutral lipids, phospholipids, glycolipids, waxes, and terpenes (the latter two classes, waxes and terpenes, will be discussed separately). Neutral lipids, phospholipids, and glycolipids are comprised of a glycerol backbone and fatty acids (acyl groups) attached to 1 to 3 of the glycerol carbons. In the case of phospholipids and glycolipids, a component other than a fatty acid is attached to the third carbon.

The acyl or fatty acid groups are long chains which may be saturated or unsaturated to varying degrees (generally 1 to 3 double bonds). The length of the fatty acid chain in plants ranges from 4 to 26 carbons, most of which have an even number of carbons. Within this group, the fatty acids may be saturated or unsaturated. Although numerically most are saturated, unsaturated fatty acids are quantitatively the most abundant in the sweetpotato (Walter et al. 1971). Given this large number of fatty acids and three sites for attachment on the glycerol molecule, if all possible combinations occurred in nature, the number of individual species would be tremendous. Thus, when one describes the concentration of neutral lipids, it includes all of these various combinations, therefore a population of individual compounds. The general properties of the neutral fraction are further characterized by removing the individual fatty acids and quantifying them. Again, it only gives an idea of the general character of the family of neutral lipids.

Phospholipids and glycolipids are components of cellular membranes. Phospholipids are generally diacylglycerols (2 fatty acids) that yield inorganic phosphate upon hydrolysis and an additional group such as serine, ethanolamine, choline, glycerol, or inositol. The group is bonded to a phosphate on the number 3 carbon of glycerol. Phospholipids are important components of mitochondrial and cytoplasmic membranes. Glycolipids have a carbohydrate substitution (without phosphate) and are important components of the chloroplast membranes.

The lipid component of sweetpotato storage roots represents approximately 1.2 to 2.7% of the total fresh weight, varying somewhat with cultivar (Boggess et al. 1970; Walter et al. 1971). It is composed of neutral lipids, glycolipids, and phospholipids. Fatty acids, both free and comprising part of the lipid molecules, range from C_{14} to C_{20} (Walter et al. 1971; Osagie 1981; Sanchez et al. 1988) with hexadecanoic and octadecadienoic acids the most prevalent. Lipids and fatty acids that have been identified in sweetpotato roots are listed in Table 3. Changes in the root lipid fraction have been studied by several groups (Boggess et al. 1967; Boggess et al. 1970; Fontenot 1966; Tereshkovich and Newsom 1963; Walter et al. 1971). There are significant differences in total lipid and lipid fractions during storage (Boggess et al. 1970). Both total and various individual lipids are known to vary quantitatively between cultivars (Boggess et al. 1970), and total lipids and certain fatty acids may change with storage duration (Boggess et al. 1967).

A detailed analysis of the lipid component in sweetpotato leaves was made to assess differences in lipids between chilling sensitive and insensitive plants (Murata et al. 1982; Murata and Yamaya 1984). Leaf lipids were separated into seven major

Table 3. Lipid and fatty acid composition of sweetpotato storage roots (% of total by weight) (Walter et al. 1971).

Component	%	Component	%
Neutral lipids	42.1	phosphatidyl glyceride	1.2
triacylglycerol	26.9	phosphatidyl serine	1.1
steryl esters	6.1	phosphatidic acid	0.4
diglycerides	3.8	Fatty Acids	
hydrocarbons	2.8	tetradecanoic acid (14:0)	1.7
sterol (free)	2.5	tetradecenoic acid (14:1)	
glycolipids	30.8	pentadecanoic acid (15:0)	1.3
monogalactosyl diglyceride	13.6	hexadecanoic acid (16:0)	29.3
digalactosyl diglyceride	6.3	hexadecenoic acid (16:1)	2.0
cerebroside	4.7	heptadecanoic acid (17:0)	1.5
esterified steryl glucoside	35.0	octadecanoic acid (18:0)	6.8
steryl glucoside	0.6	nonadecanoic acid (19:0)	tr
Phospholipids	27.1	eicosanoic acid (20:0)	2.4
phosphatidyl ethanolamine	7.8	octadecenoic (18:1)	2.0
phosphatidyl choline	7.0	octadecadienoic (18:2)	44.7
phosphatidyl inositol	5.1	octadecatrienoic (18:3)	8.8
cardiolipid	1.6		

classes: phosphatidylglycerol; phosphatidylcholine; phosphatidylethanolamine; phosphatidylinositol; monogalactosyl diacylglycerol; digalactosyl diacylglycerol; and sulfoquinovosyl diacylglycerol. Upon hydrolysis the relative percent of individual fatty acids making up each class was determined (Table 4) (Murata and Yamaya 1984). The sulfoquinovosyl diacylglycerols (Murata and Hoshi 1984) and phosphatidylglycerols (Murata 1983) were sequentially hydrolyzed and the molar percentage of each fatty acid at carbon 1 and 2 on the glycerol backbone determined (Table 5). In the case of phosphatidylserine, a small but significant amount of long chain length fatty acids were identified [i.e., (20:0), (21:0), (22:0), (23:0), and (24:0)](Murata et al. 1984a).

Table 4. Fatty acid composition of sweetpotato leaf phospholipids and glycolipids (Murata and Yamaya 1984).

Lipid Class	Fatty acid composition (%)							
	16:0	16:1	16:1	18:0	18:1	18:2	18:3	18:4
Phosphatidylglycerol	44	32	0	4	8	5	5	0
Phosphatidylcholine	20	0	tr	8	3	33	36	tr
Phosphatidylethanolamine	23	0	tr	7	1	38	30	1
Phosphatidylinositol	46	0	1	3	1	18	31	0
Monogalactosyl diacylglycerol	3	0	1	1	1	4	73	0
Digalactosyl diacylglycerol	16	0	tr	4	3	4	73	0
Sulfoquinovosyl diacylglycerol	34	0	1	7	2	8	48	0

Table 5. Sweetpotato leaf sulfoquinovosyl diacylglycerol and phosphatidylglycerol fatty acid molecular species composition on carbon 1 and 2 of the glycerol molecule (Murata 1983; Murata and Hoshi 1984).

	Molecular Species % Composition									
Lipid Carbon 1	16:0	16:0	18:0	18:0	18:1	18:1	18:2	18:2	18:3	18:3
Carbon 2	16:0	16:1	16:0	16:1	16:0	16:1	16:0	16:1	16:0	16:1
Phosphatidyl-glycerols	26	39	3	3	7	8	4	4	2	4

Carbon 1	16:0	16:0	16:0	16:0	16:0	16:0	16:1	18:0	18:0	18:0	18.1	18.1	18.1	18:2	18:3
Carbon 2	16:0	16:3	18:0	18:1	18:2	18:3	18:1	18:1	18:2	18:3	18:1	18:2	18:3	18:3	18:3
Sulfoquinovosyl-diacylglycerols	3	0	0	1	4	51	0	0	0	5	0	1	2	0	25

Sweetpotato starch contains a lipid fraction which is thought to play a role in starch metabolism. As starch molecules are being assembled, there is simultaneous deposition of amylose and amylopectin in the granules. Since these two classes of starch differ in the presence (amylopectin) or absence (amylose) of branching, it has not been understood how the amylose chains keep from being modified to amylopectin by the branching enzyme. Starch phospholipids appear to protect the newly formed glucose chains by inhibiting the activity of the branching enzyme (Vieweg and de Fekete 1976). In addition, they appear to also inhibit the activity of starch degrading enzymes (α- and β-amylase) that are also present.

Fatty acids identified in the root starch component were dodecanoic (12:0), tetradecanoic (14:0), hexadecanoic (16:0), hexadecenoic (16:1), octadecanoic (18:0), octadecenoic (18:1), octadecadienoic (18:2), and jalapinolic, with hexadecanoic predominating (Fujimoto et al. 1971a). The ratio of hexadecanoic acid to total fatty acids varied with cultivar and geographical location. As the fatty acid component of the starch increased, the proportion of hexadecanoic increased and that of octadecenoic decreased (Fujimoto et al. 1971b). As the storage roots grew, the amylose and fatty acid content increased (Fujimoto et al. 1971c), and the hexadecanoic content decreased. The smaller the starch granules and the earlier the harvest, the higher the amylose and fatty acid content of the starch (Fujimoto et al. 1972a). When the roots are small, different sized starch granules had approximately the same amount of fatty acids but differed in the amount of amylose which was greater in small granules (Fujimoto et al. 1972b).

The lipid fraction in sweetpotato puree that is processed to produce precooked dehydrated flakes is critical in that degradation of the lipids results in off-flavors (Walter and Purcell 1974). Typically the flakes will smell rancid and have a strong hay-like odor (Alexandridis and Lopez 1979). This is largely caused by the oxidation of the unsaturated fatty acids present which are thought to be converted to hydroperoxides and subsequently to aldehydes. Critical factors affecting the rate and extent of degradative changes in lipids include: the amount of lipid present; the percentage of unsaturated fatty acids; the degree of unsaturation; the location of the lipid in the flake [i.e. surface vs bound (Walter et al. 1972)], and storage conditions [e.g., oxygen concentration (Walter and Purcell 1974), storage duration (Walter et al. 1978a), packaging material, and storage temperature]. Antioxidants have proven to be ineffective in controlling off-flavor development (Deobald and McLemore 1964), and, as a consequence, storage of flakes in packages with nitrogen atmospheres has proven to be the best alternative.

4. Organic Acids

A number of organic acids, in addition to functioning as intermediates in metabolism (e.g., tricarboxylic acid cycle), may also contribute to taste. In the sweetpotato, the most quantitatively prevalent organic acids are malic, quinic, succinic, and citric, with traces of oxalic and oxaloacetic (Bando et al. 1988; Chapman and Horvat 1989; Holloway et al. 1989; Picha 1986c). The concentration of each is known to vary with cultivar [e.g., 'Jewel'/'Tainung 57': malic (0.16/0.26); quinic (0.06/0.06); succinic (0.05/0.06); and citric (0.05/0.02) percent on a fresh weight basis (Chapman and Horvat 1989)]. Oxalic acid concentration in the roots, although low, was the highest of the root and tuber crops eaten in Nigeria (Faboya et al. 1983). The importance of organic acids in the overall taste sensation has yet to be established. When sweetpotatoes were used as a carbohydrate base for a red pepper paste (kochuzang) eaten in Korea, the succinic and fumaric acid concentrations were highest when compared with other carbohydrate bases tested (Lee et al. 1981).

Oxalates can be found as soluble salts of potassium, sodium, and ammonium, as oxalic acid, and as insoluble crystals of calcium oxalate. The latter form is of importance in some food products in that the crystals can create serious physical and chemical problems with ingestion. The structure of calcium oxalate crystals varies, ranging from needle-like raphides to small clusters of plates in various orientations called druse, the latter being the form found in sweetpotato roots (Schadel and Walter 1980) and leaves (Umemoto 1974). In roots, the druse are 10 to 50 μm in diameter and are found in parenchyma cells. In the leaves, the druse are much smaller (5 to 15 μm). The concentration of total oxalates and soluble and insoluble forms in sweetpotato roots varies with cultivar. Samples of roots collected in Fiji and the Solomon Islands displayed the following range in concentration of the three classes: total = 40 to 150 mg/100 g fwt; soluble = 23 to 52 mg/100 g fwt; and calcium oxalate = 25 to 38 mg/100 g fwt (Bradbury and Holloway 1988).

5. Pigments

Of the four primary classes of pigments, three are found in the sweetpotato—carotenoids, flavonoids, and chlorophylls. These pigments impart the characteristic colors found in the roots and leaves of the plant.

5.1. Chlorophyll

Chlorophyll, a magnesium-containing porphyrin, is formed from 4 pyrrole rings and a 20 carbon phytol tail. The two primary forms, 'a' and 'b', differ structurally only in the replacement of a methyl group on chlorophyll 'a' with an aldehyde. Like the carotenoids, the chlorophylls are hydrophobic and as a consequence, are only soluble in organic solvents. The chlorophylls are found in specialized plastids, the chloroplasts. Their primary function in the plant is to absorb light energy and convert it to chemical energy. In the sweetpotato, chlorophyll can be found in the leaves, stems, and roots, the latter after exposure to light (Data and Kays 1991).

The leaves of sweetpotatoes contain chlorophyll 'a' and 'b', and there are significant differences in concentrations between cultivars (Bhagsari 1981; Katayama and Shida 1961). For example, leaf chlorophyll 'a' and 'b' concentrations for 15 genotypes ranged from 5.3 to 7.8 mg/g dwt and from 2.4 to 3.8 mg/g dwt, respectively (Bhagsari 1981), while the total chlorophyll content ranged from 7.6 to 10.6 mg/g dwt (Bhagsari and Brown 1986).

5.2. Carotenes

Research on the pigments of the sweetpotato has focused upon the carotenoids which are made up of the carotenes and their oxygenated derivatives, the xanthophylls. The xanthophylls differ from the carotenes due to the presence of oxygen(s). For example, lutein, a common xanthophyll found in plants, is structurally the same as β-carotene, differing only in the presence of a hydroxyl group on carbon 3 of both end groups. Both the carotenes and xanthophylls are water insoluble and are found sequestered in chloroplasts and/or chromoplasts. Of the over 400 carotenoids that have been identified in the plant kingdom, β-carotene and its close derivatives predominate in sweetpotato storage roots, making up 86 to 90% of the carotenes present (Ezell et al. 1952; Purcell 1962; Purcell and Walter 1968b). The orange and yellow colors of the roots are due to the presence of these carotenes, and normally there are multiple forms of carotene present within the roots of a cultivar. The intensely pigmented North American cultivars have been selected for high levels of β-carotene; however, in some light fleshed lines, other carotenes may predominate.

Interest in the carotenes centers around their importance in human nutrition. The carotene molecule can be cleaved in the intestinal mucosa cells and subsequently converted to vitamin A if it contains at least one β end group. β-carotene, which has two β end groups, can be converted into two vitamin A molecules. In addition, several studies have implicated the ingestion of foods containing carotenes with a decrease in the incidence of certain cancers (Peto et al. 1981; Menkes et al. 1986). In the plant, carotenoids in the leaves function both in photosynthesis and in preventing the chlorophyll molecule from being photooxidized in the presence of light and oxygen. In flowers, carotenoids act as attractants; however, their presence in subterranean plant parts may largely represent selection by man rather than an essential biological role.

Measures of total carotene in the sweetpotato have been reported in a number of general compositional studies (recent reports include: Bureau and Bushway 1986; Pepping and Venicken 1988; Yamashita et al. 1986). The concentration of total carotenes ranges from 0.5 to 44.6 mg/100 g dwt (Speirs et al. 1953). Typically the predominate form is β-carotene (Ezell and Wilcox 1946; Purcell 1962), with cultivar being the primary source of variation (Constantin and Morris 1972; Cordner et al. 1959; Ezell and Wilcox 1946; 1948; 1952; MacLeod et al. 1935; Picha 1985a; Speirs et al. 1953).

Carotenoids that have been identified in raw and/or processed sweetpotato roots include *all-trans*-β-carotene, 15,15'-*cis*-β-carotene, 13-*cis*-ß-carotene, 9-*cis*-ß-carotene, neo-ß-carotene, neo-ß-carotene U, ß-carotene epioxide, ß-carotene furanoxide, tetrahydro-ß,ß-carotene, α-carotene, γ-carotene, ζ-carotene, hydroxy-ζcarotene, ß,ζ-carotene, neurosporene, phytoene, phytofluene, luteochrome, and several unspecified xanthophylls (Chandler and Schwartz 1988; De Almeida and Penteado 1988; De Almeida et al. 1986; 1988; Garlich et al. 1974; Khachik and Beecher 1987; Martin 1983; Picha 1987; Purcell 1962). The range of possible carotenoids that may be present and the occurrence of isomerization during processing has resulted in considerable attention being directed toward isolation techniques (Bushway 1985; 1986; Chandler and Schwartz 1987; Khachik and Beecher 1987; Schwartz and Patroni-Killam 1985).

Carotene concentration in processed orange fleshed types varies with the processing method utilized (Lee and Ammerman 1974). Likewise, the concentration in unprocessed roots may increase during curing and storage of some cultivars, while exhibiting no change in others (Ezell and Wilcox 1946; 1948; 1952; 1958; Ezell et al. 1952; 1956; MacLeod and Utley 1938; Miller and Covington 1942; Picha 1985a; Speirs et al. 1953). Other agronomic factors that have been shown to affect root carotene content are planting time (Anderson et al. 1945; Cummings et al. 1953; Kimbrough et al. 1946), harvest date (Ezell et al. 1952), year, and location (Speirs et al. 1953). However, fertilization rate had little effect (Speirs et al. 1953).

While carotene concentration tends to increase in stored roots, considerable loss commonly occurs during and after processing (for additional information see the section on vitamin A). These losses arise from thermally mediated isomerization (Chandler and Schwartz 1987; 1988; Schwartz and Catignani 1989; Van der Pol et al. 1988) and oxidation, the latter occurring largely in sweetpotato flakes. During the processing operation, the *all-trans* form of β-carotene is isomerized to less or inactive forms (e.g., 13-*cis*-β-carotene and 13-*cis*-β-carotene)(Lee and Ammerman 1974; Schwartz and Catignani 1989) lowering the provitamin A value of the product. For example, the following changes were found in provitamin A activity at each processing step: blanching (4 to 11.9% increase); lye peeling and pureeing (10.4% increase); steam injection (8.0% decrease); canning (19.7% decrease); dehydration (20.5% decrease); microwaving (22.7% decrease); and baking (31.4% decrease) (Chandler and Schwartz 1988).

Oxidation represents the primary means of decomposition of carotenes in precooked dehydrated flakes (Purcell and Walter 1968a; Walter and Purcell 1971;

1974; Walter et al. 1970). Autoxidation of carotenes located on or near the surface, where their access to free oxygen is greatest, was about 100 times greater than for carotene molecules bound within the flake.

The possibility of concentrating xanthophyll and protein from sweetpotato leaves to use as a supplement for animal feeds has been studied (Walter et al. 1978b). The dried protein concentrate contained 0.12 to 0.15% xanthophyll. Xanthophylls from the leaves and vines can be used as a supplement in poultry feed to increase the pigment content of the egg's yolk and the skin of broilers (Garlich et al. 1974).

5.3. Flavonoids

Flavonoids are a group of pigments that consist of two benzene rings joined by a 3-carbon link that forms a γ-pyrone ring through oxygen. The various classes of flavonoids (anthocyanidins, flavones, catechins, flavonols, flavanones, dihydroflavonols, and flavan-3,4-diols) differ only in the oxidation state of the 3-carbon link. Individual compounds within each class differ mainly in the number and position of hydroxy, methoxy, and other groups on the two benzene rings. This gives a tremendous variety of potential compounds, with colors ranging from yellows, oranges, reds, and blues to purple. Unlike the chlorophylls and carotenoids, flavonoids are water soluble and are found both in the cytosol and vacuole. Most are found as glycosides with one or more of their hydroxyl groups joined to a sugar. The sugar in turn may be esterified to an organic acid.

In sweetpotatoes, the flavonoids have been studied in a number of selections that display varying degrees of red to purple pigmentation. This interest has been due to the possible use of the isolated pigment as a food colorant. Betalains, another major class of pigments, also may be red to purple; however, their instability has prevented them from being used as a natural source of color for foods.

Sweetpotato roots of some cultivars contain anthocyanins giving colors ranging from red to purple (Cascon et al. 1984a; 1984b; Imbert et al. 1966). Those identified thus far are cyanidin and peonidin glucosides [i.e. cyanidin-3-sophoroside-5-glucoside, peonidin-3-sophoroside-5-glucoside and cyanidin-3-(α-D-glucopyranosyl-β-D-fructo-furanoside)-5-(α-D-xyloside) which are acylated with caffeic, ferurlic, or β-hydroxybenzoic acid (Imbert et al. 1966; Nozue et al. 1987; Tsukui et al. 1983)].

The use of cell suspension cultures as a means of producing anthocyanins has been explored (Nozue and Yasudo 1985; Nozue et al. 1987; 1988). In tissue culture cells, the pigment is sequestered in spherical organelles which may also represent the site of synthesis (Nozue and Yasudo 1985). Techniques for isolation of anthocyanins from root tissue for use as a food colorant have also been studied (Cascon et al. 1984a; 1984b). The drying process following isolation appears to be a major source of loss (Cascon et al. 1984b). The addition of several phenolic compounds [D-(+)-catechin, vanillin, and resorcin] has been shown to decrease discoloration of the pigment during heating (60°C)(Tsukui, 1989). In a model beverage, sweetpotato anthocyanins were the most stable of three anthocyanin sources tested (Bassa and Francis 1987).

Generally, the presence of anthocyanins in yellow and orange fleshed lines is considered undesirable since they cause an unpleasant coloration in the cooked roots. Therefore, considerable effort is exerted to remove lines expressing the genes for anthocyanin synthesis from breeding stock.

6. Terpenes

Terpenes of both lower [hemiterpenes (C_5), monoterpenes (C_{10}), and sesquiterpenes (C_{15})] and higher molecular weight are widely distributed in the plant kingdom. Of the terpenes, the sesquiterpene and triterpene groups have been the most closely studied in the sweetpotato due to their involvement as toxins and modulators of plant/insect interactions, respectively. Those formed in response to pathogen invasion and other forms of stress are discussed in the section on Stress Metabolites. Several monoterpenes have been identified in the volatile compounds emanating from the cooked roots (see Volatiles).

Triterpenoids are extensively distributed in the plant kingdom, both free and as glycosides. Many are found as triterpenoid sapogenins, of which the pentacyclic β-amyrin group predominates, usually as simple alcohols or acids. Triterpenes are known to be significant components in some plant-insect interactions. Existing evidence indicates predominately an anti-feedant and growth inhibitory role. In most plant species, triterpenes are found in very low concentrations; however, the concentration on the surface of sweetpotato leaves and storage roots is relatively high. Oleanolic and ursolic acids have been identified as major components on the surface of sweetpotato leaves and boehmerol and boehmeryl acetate on the surface of storage roots (Son et al. 1990). The latter, a pentacyclic triterpene which contains an acetate moiety, has been shown to act as an ovipositional stimulant for the sweetpotato weevil *Cylas formicarius elegantulus* Summers (Wilson et al. 1988; 1989). The concentration of boehmeryl acetate varies between cultivars (Son et al. 1990) and removal, using a surface wash with methylene chloride, inhibits egg laying by the female weevil (Wilson et al. 1988). Reapplication of the surface components reinstates the response.

7. Phenolics

Phenolics represent a wide range of compounds that have at least one aromatic ring and hydroxyl group. The diversity of phenolics is illustrated by the following examples: flavonoids, lignin, abscisic acid, coenzyme Q, and numerous end products of metabolism. Phenolics are generally separated into three classes based upon the number of phenol rings present: monocyclic; dicyclic; and polycyclic. As a group, their importance in sweetpotatoes centers around their role in discoloration reactions and in response to pathological and mechanical stress.

There is a marked increase in the synthesis of the polyphenols chlorogenic acid (3-O-caffenoylquinic acid) and isochlorogenic acid (dicaffenoylquinic acid)(Uritani 1953; Uritani and Muramatsu 1953) in response to mechanical damage and pathogen

(*Ceratocystis fimbriata*) invasion and in chlorogenic acid in response to low temperature (chilling) stress (Rhodes and Wooltorton 1978). The importance of these two compounds has resulted in considerable research being directed toward establishing the synthesis pathway (Kojima and Uritani 1972a; 1972b; 1973; Kojima and Kondo 1985; Moriguchi et al. 1988; Shimizu and Kojima 1984; Uritani 1953; Uritani and Miyano 1955; Uritani and Muramatu 1953; Villegas and Kojima 1986; Villegas et al. 1987). Moriguchi et al. (1988) have recently established the following sequence of intermediates: *trans*-cinnamic acid → *trans*-cinnamoyl-D- glucose → *p*-coumaroyl-D-glucose → chlorogenic acid → isochlorogenic acid.

When sweetpotato tissue was infected with a cross-section of pathogens (*Botrytis cinerea, Phoma exigua* var. *foveata, Fusarium solani* var. *coeruleum*) a lesion was formed. The lesion border could be separated into uninfected tissue and infected, rotting tissue. The total phenolic concentration was typically greater in and around limited lesions indicating a defense reaction by the tissue.

Discoloration of sweetpotatoes during lye peeling can be a serious problem affecting the appearance of the processed product (Scott et al. 1944). The degree of discoloration varies with cultivar (Scott and Kattan 1957) and the lye peeling protocol utilized (Walter and Giesbrecut 1982; Walter and Schadel 1982). The concentration of phenolics in the tissue was found to be directly proportional to the degree of darkening (Walter and Purcell 1980). Discoloration is thought to be mediated by the action of polyphenol oxidase on phenolics which are found, primarily as esters formed between quinic acid and *o*-dihydroxyphenol caffeic acid. Quantitatively the most important compounds are chlorogenic acid, neochlorogenic acid, and three isomers of isochlorogenic acid (Walter and Purcell 1980; Walter et al. 1979). Root phenolics are located in the: (1) periderm; (2) tissue 1 mm under the periderm; (3) latex of laticifers; (4) phloem; (5) cambium separating the secondary xylem and phloem; (6) anomalous secondary cambia of the central core; and (7) parenchyma cells (Schadel and Walter 1981). The skin and outer 5 mm of tissue contain nearly 80% of the total phenolics in the roots (Tanka and Uritani 1977a; Walter and Schadel 1981).

Considerable genetic diversity is found in the sweetpotato gene pool for the propensity to discolor (Jones 1972; Jones et al. 1969). Assessment of lines for discoloration involves a simple assay for polyphenol oxidase activity. The cut surface of the root is dipped in 0.25 M catechol for 10 minutes, and the level of discoloration is then subjectively scored using a 1 to 5 scale.

Lignin is an example of a polyphenol with a basic skeleton formula of $(C_6-C_3)_n$. It is a heterogenous group of molecules that are typically substantial in size. In the sweetpotato roots, the concentration of lignin is approximately 1.5%.

8. Waxes

Waxes, typically esters of large molecular weight fatty acids and a higher aliphatic alcohol, act as a protective coating on much of the above- and below-ground parts of the plant. A primary function of waxes is in the inhibition of water loss from the plant. Their presence significantly increases the surface diffusion resistance to water vapor. Differences in root surface wax concentration and composition between cultivars in relation to fresh weight loss during storage have not been assessed.

The concentration of long chain hydrocarbons on the surface of above-ground plant parts is quite low. The following compounds have been identified: pentacosane, hexacosane, heptacosane, octacosane, nanacosane, triacontane, hentriacontane, doctriacontane, tritriacontane, tetratriacontane, and pentatriacontane. Aerial waxes displayed predominately odd chain length alkanes, and these were typically larger than alkanes extracted from the surface of storage roots (Son et al. 1991b). Even numbered alkanes represented only about 9% of the total.

Waxes from the surface of the storage roots (ca. 65% of the chloroform extractable material) are comprised of hydrocarbons (9%), wax esters (1.2%), fatty alcohols (45%), fatty acids (18%), and an unidentified fraction (27%) (Espelie et al. 1980). Alkanes from the storage roots were almost exclusively odd chain lengths with C_{29} predominating [$C_{29} > C_{27} > C_{23}$] (Son et al. 1991b), the concentration of which varied somewhat between cultivars. Free and esterified fatty alcohols from root surface waxes were largely straight chain alcohols with an even number of carbon atoms (Espelie et al. 1980). The dominant component was a C_{30} esterified alcohol (72%), with C_{16} and C_{18} free alcohols making up 31 and 45%, respectively, of their fraction.

9. Volatile Compounds

In addition to carbon dioxide formed through normal dark and photorespiration, oxygen produced in photosynthetic reactions, and water vapor, the sweetpotato gives off a wide range of other volatile compounds. Typically volatile compounds have molecular weights of 222 and below; however, as the energy level of the molecules increases with temperature during cooking, larger molecular weight compounds become volatile. Sweetpotato volatiles come from two primary sources - those that represent natural products found within the plant or plant part and those that are formed in response to physical or biological stress. A number of non-stress volatiles emanate from both above- and below-ground parts of the plant. Recent interest in these secondary metabolic products has centered around their potential role as host plant locating clues used by insects feeding on the sweetpotato (Nottingham et al. 1989). Volatiles formed or intensified with cooking or other forms of processing likewise represent an extremely important group of compounds.

Humans exhibit distinct patterns in the foods that they choose to consume, and flavor is known to be a primary criterion in this selection. Flavor is comprised of a combination of both taste and odor. Taste is thought to be largely limited to four basic sensations - sweet, sour, salty, and bitter. In contrast to taste, humans have the potential to distinguish up to 10,000 distinct odors. Hence, the aromatic properties of foods provide an almost unlimited potential for diversity of flavor.

9.1. Volatiles From Cooked Sweetpotatoes

The importance of aroma in perception of quality and in food selection by consumers stimulated a series of studies in an attempt to identify the character impact compound or compounds responsible for the unique aroma of cooked sweetpotatoes. A relatively wide cross-section of volatile compounds has been identified from baked sweetpotatoes (Table 6)(Horvat et al. 1991; Kays and Horvat 1984; Nagahama et al. 1977; Purcell et al. 1980; Sun 1988; Tiu et al. 1985) and from fermented sweetpotato products and by-products (Ohta et al. 1990; Taira 1963a; 1963b). Chemically, these compounds include hydrocarbons, acids, alcohols, aldehydes, esters, furans, ketones, and nitrogen containing compounds.

Table 6. Volatile compounds emanating from cooked sweetpotatoes (Horvat et al. 1991; Kays and Horvat 1984; Nagahama et al. 1977; Purcell et al. 1980; Sun 1988; Taira 1963ab; Tiu et al. 1985).

Hydrocarbons	benzaldehyde
docosane	butyraldehyde
heptylbenzene	cinnamaldehyde
n-hexane	decanal
1-isopropyl-4-isopropenylbenzene	formaldehyde
limonene	phenylacetaldehyde
methylnaphthalene	propylaldehyde
octyl-benzene	Esters
pentene	methyl acetate
2-phenyl-2-methylbutane	Furans
n-propylbenzene	2-acetylfuran
sabinene	carboxaldehyde
sabinene hydrate	2-furancarboxaldehyde
toluene	2-furanmethanol
tricosane	2-hydroxymethyl-5-furan
trimethylbenzene	carboxaldehyde
xylene	5-methyl-2-furaldehyde
Acids	2-methyltetrahydrofuran-3-one
decanoic acid	Ketones
dodecanoic acid	acetone
hexadecanoic acid	2,3-butanedione
octadecanoic acid	2-furylmethylketone
octadecenoic acid	5-hydroxy-2-methyl-4H-pyran-4-one
octadecadienoic acid	β-ionone
tetradecanoic acid	ipomeamarone
Alcohols	2-octanone
benzyl alcohol	3-octen-2-one
geraniol	2,3-pentadione
heptadecanol	pentane-2-one
hexadecanol	2-pyrone
p-menth-2-en-7-ol	Nitrogen Containing Compounds
nerol	isobutyronitrite
α-terpinol	2-methyl-6-ethylpyridine
Aldehydes	nonanalpyridine
acetaldehyde	2,4,6-trimethylpyridine

To date, the compound(s) responsible for the characteristic aroma of the cooked sweetpotato have eluded identification. It has been established, however, that there is considerable diversity in the volatiles present and their relative concentrations between different sweetpotato cultivars (Horvat et al. 1991; Kays and Horvat 1984). This is especially evident when contrasting cultivars developed in different areas of the world. Preliminary work on establishing a quantitative technique for comparison of the volatiles between different selections (Sun 1988) and the potential for incorporation of it into breeding programs has been recently published (Kays 1989).

Recent work by Ohta et al. (1990) on the volatile components of kansho-shochu, a traditional alcoholic beverage made from sweetpotatoes and rice in Japan, is of considerable interest in that the authors attempted to ascertain the origin of the critical odor components. Several monoterpene glycosides appear to be hydrolyzed by glycosidic enzymes in the ground mash liberating geraniol and nerol. These represent the precursors of linalool and α–terpinol, neither of which were present in steamed sweetpotatoes, and are formed in response to the thermal treatment the mash receives. Citronellol, in contrast, appears to be formed from linalool and α-terpinol by the yeast added for fermentation. Previous terpene alcohols that had been identified from fermented sweetpotatoes are citronellol, α-terpineol, linalool, and geraniol (Taira 1963a; 1963b).

9.2. Volatiles from Sweetpotato Plants

Interest in non-stress volatiles developed from the realization that the sweetpotato weevil (*Cylas formicarius elegantulus*, Summers) could readily orient in the dark to sweetpotato storage roots or to sweetpotato leaves placed in their vicinity. The rate and consistency at which they could find the plant precluded random movement and chance discovery. Subsequently, in olfactometer experiments both male and female weevils were found to be attracted to volatiles given off from above-ground plant parts (Nottingham et al. 1989). In contrast, only the female weevils responded to volatiles given off by the storage roots, the site for egg laying by the female. Preliminary analysis of volatiles given off by the leaves indicated the presence of seven sesquiterpenes, five of which were tentatively identified using mass spectral data as: copaene; *trans*-caryophyllene; α-humulene; γ-cadinene; and γ–elemene (Nottingham et al. 1989).

10. Vitamins

Vitamins are organic compounds that are required in relatively small amounts for normal plant metabolism and growth. Typically we think of vitamins in regard to dietary requirements of humans; however, in plants vitamins perform, for the most part, the same biochemical functions. Most act in a catalytic capacity as coenzymes —organic compounds that participate in the function of an enzyme. They are commonly separated into two classes based on their solubility: the water soluble

Table 7. Vitamin content of raw sweetpotato roots and leaves (composite of data from Bradbury and Singh 1986a,b; Bureau and Bushway 1986; Caldwell 1972; Caldwell and Enoch 1972; Garcia et al. 1970; Guilarte 1985; Huq et al. 1983; Leung and Flores 1961; Leung et al. 1968, 1972; Pellett and Shadarevian 1970; Rao and Polachi 1972; Villareal et al. 1979; Visser and Burrows 1983; Watt and Merrill 1975).

Vitamin	Storage Roots	Leaves	Vitamin	Storage Roots	Leaves
	(Amount/100 g fwt)			(Amount/100 g fwt)	
Ascorbic acid	20-35mg	21-136mg	Pantothenic acid	0.8mg	—
Biotin	3.3µg	—	Pyridoxine	0.3mg	0.21mg
Carotene	70->11,000µg	3520-8820 IU	Riboflavin	0.3-0.5mg	0.3-0.4mg
Folic acid	50mg	88.4µg	Thiamine	0.04-0.12mg	0.3-0.12mg
Niacin	0.2-0.8mg	0.6-1.0mg	Vitamin E	0.75mg	—

vitamins (ascorbic acid, biotin, folic acid, nicotinic acid, pantothenic acid, pyridoxine, riboflavin, thiamine); and the lipid soluble vitamins (A, E, and K).

The concentration of ascorbic acid, biotin, provitamin A (carotene), folic acid, niacin, pantothenic acid, pyridoxine, riboflavin, thiamine, and vitamin E have been reported in a number of studies directed toward assessing the general vitamin content of the storage roots and leaves of sweetpotatoes (Leung and Flores 1961; Leung et al. 1968; 1972; Pellett and Shadarevian 1970; Watt and Merrill 1975; Collazos et al. 1974; Rao and Polachi 1972; Garcia et al. 1970; Bureau and Bushway 1986; Visser and Burrows 1983; Bradbury and Singh 1986a; 1986b; Caldwell 1972; Caldwell and Enoch 1972; Huq et al. 1983; Villareal et al. 1979). In addition, a number of reports in which only one or several vitamins were assessed have been published: ascorbic acid (Bradbury and Singh 1986a; Izumi et al. 1984; Kim et al. 1987; Kujira 1986; Matsuo et al. 1988; Visser 1984); biotin (Guilarte 1985); carotene-provitamin A (Ranganath and Dubash 1981; Singh and Bradbury 1988); folic acid (Huq et al. 1983; Keshinro 1983); niacin (Bradbury and Singh 1986b); riboflavin (Bradbury and Singh 1986b; Watada and Tran 1985; 1987); and thiamine (Bradbury and Singh 1986b). Sweetpotatoes are an excellent dietary source of provitamin A, a good source of ascorbic acid, pyridoxine, pantothenic acid, and folic acid and a moderate source of thiamine, riboflavin, and niacin (Table 7).

10.1. Vitamin A

Vitamin A is formed in the intestine of animals from plant derived carotenes. Carotenes, therefore, are precursors of vitamin A and are commonly referred to from a nutritional standpoint as provitamin A. Chemically, carotenes are terpenoids comprised of eight isoprene (5-carbon) subunits. Nearly all carotenes have 40 carbon atoms. Their nomenclature is based on the end groups, commonly a 9 carbon ionone ring structure, which are found at each end of a linear carbon chain. Various combinations of end groups (e.g., β, ε, ψ, γ, etc.) give a significant range in possible roots. Plant Cell Physiol. 15:1093-1098.

Kimber, A.J. 1975. Papua New Guinea Food Crops Conference Proceedings. Dept. Prim. Indust. K. Wilson, and R.M. Bourke (eds.), Port Moresby, New Guinea, p. 63.

Kimbrough, W.D., E.A. Fieger, and H. Lewis. 1946. Effect of date of planting and time of harvesting on the carotene content of sweetpotatoes of the Porto Rico Variety. Proc. Am. Soc. Hort. Sci. 47:400-402.

Kimura, A. and S. Chiba. 1983. Studies on anomeric forms of products of carbohydrases. Part II. Quantitative study of anomeric forms of maltose produced by α- and β-amylases. Agric. Bio. Chem. 47:1747-1753.

Kimura, T., K. Nakamura, H. Kajiura, H. Hattori, N. Nelson, and T. Asahi. 1989. Correspondence of minor subunits of plant mitochondrial FATPase to FATPase subunits of other organisms. J. Biol. Chem. 264:3183-3186.

Kitada, Y., M. Sasaki, Y. Yamazoe, and H. Nakazawa. 1988. Measurement of thermal behavior and amylose content of kudzu and sweet potato starches. Nippon Shokuhn Kogyo Gakkaishi 35:135-140.

Kobayashi, K., K. Nakamura, T. Asahi. 1987. CF_1ATPase α- and ϵ-subunit genes are separated in the sweet potato chloroplast genome. Nucleic Acids Res. 15:7177.

Kobayashi, K., I. Yukimoto, T. Sasaki, K. Nakamura, and T. Asahi. 1986. Putative amino-terminal presequence for β-subunit of plant mitochondrial FATPase deduced from the amino-terminal sequence of the mature subunit. FEBS Lett. 203:144-148.

Koehler, P. E. and S. J. Kays. 1991. Sweetpotato flavor: Quantitative and qualitative assessment of optimum sweetness. J. Food Qual. (in review).

Kojima, M. 1976. Possible involvement of furanoterpenoid phytoalexins in establishing host-parasite specificity between sweet potato and various strains of *Ceratocystis fimbriata*. Physiol. Plant Path. 8:97-111.

Kojima, M. 1982. Biochemical studies on high and low molecular weight substances which are involved in defence reactions of host plant. Nippon Nogei Kagaku Kaishi 56:675-683.

Kojima, M. and T. Kondo. 1985. An enzyme in sweet potato root which catalyzes conversion of chlorogenic acid, 3-O-caffeoylquinic acid, to isochlorogenic acid, 3,5-dicaffeoylquinic acid. Agric. Biol. Chem. 49:2467-2469.

Kojima, M., T. Minamikawa, H. Hyodo, and I. Uritani. 1969. Incorporation of some possible radioactive intermediates into chlorogenic acid in sliced sweet potato tissues. Plant Cell Physiol. 10:471-474.

Kojima, M. and I. Uritani. 1972a. Elucidation of the structure of a possible intermediate in chlorogenic acid biosynthesis in sweet potato root tissue. Plant Cell Physiol. 13:1075-1084.

Kojima, M. and I. Uritani. 1972b. Structure of possible intermediate of chlorogenic acid biosynthesis in sweet potato root tissue. Agr. Biol. Chem. 36:1643-1645.

Kojima, M. and I. Uritani. 1972c. Studies on chlorogenic acid biosynthesis in sweet potato root tissue using *trans*-cinnamic acid-2-^{14}C and quinic acid-G-[3]H[1]. Plant Cell Physiol. 13:311-319.

Kojima, M. and I. Uritani. 1973. Studies on chlorogenic acid biosynthesis in sweet potato root tissue in special reference to the isolation of a chlorogenic acid intermediate. Plant Physiol. 51:768-771.

Kojima, M. and R.J.A. Villegas. 1984. Detection of the enzyme in sweet potato root which catalyzes trans-esterification between 1-O-p-Coumaroyl-D-glucose and D-Quinic acid. Agric. Biol. Chem. 48:2397-2399.

Kondo, J. and Y. Morita. 1952. Studies on phytoperoxidase. Isolation and purification of sweet potato peroxidases and their absorption spectra. Bull. Res. Inst. Food Sci. Kyoto Univ. (10):33-45.

Kujira, Y. 1986. Effect of culture conditions on L-ascorbic acid content in sweet potato. Nippon Eiyo, Shokuryo Gakkaishi 39:234-237.

Lanier, J. J. and W. A. Sistrunk. 1979. Influence of cooking method on quality attributes and vitamin content of sweet potatoes. J. Food Sci. 44:374-376,380.

Larbi, A. and E. M'barek. 1985. Dietary fiber and phytic acid levels in the major food items consumed in Morocco. Nutr. Rep. Int. 31:469-476.

Lee, W.G. and G. R. Ammerman. 1974. Carotene stereoisomerization in sweet potatoes as affected by rotating and still retort canning processes. J. Food Sci. 39:1188-1190.

Lee, T.S., S.O. Park, M.W. Lee. 1981. Determination of organic acid of Kochuzang prepared from various starch sources. Hanguk Nonghwa Hakhoe Chi 24:120-125.

Lee, K.A., M.S. Shin, and S.Y. Ahn. 1985. Changes in pectic substances of sweet potato cultivars during baking. Han'guk Sikp'um Kwahakhoechi 17:421-425.

Leung, W.T. Wu, F. Busson, and C. Jardin. 1968. Food composition table for use in Africa. US Department of Health, Education and Welfare Public Health Service, Maryland and FAO Nutrition Division, Rome. 306 pp.

Leung, W.T. Wu, R.R. Butrum, and F.H. Chang. 1972. Part I. Proximate composition, mineral and vitamin contents of East Asian foods. Pages 1-187 in Food composition table for use in East Asia", US Department of Health, Education and Welfare and FAO of the UN, Bethesda, MD.

Leung, W.T. Wu and M. Flores. 1961. Food composition table for use in Latin America. Institute of nutrition of Central America and Panama, Guatemala/Interdepartmental Committee on nutrition for national defense, Bethesda, MD. 145 pp.

Li, H.S. and K. Oba. 1985. Major soluble proteins of sweet potato roots and changes in proteins after cutting, infection, or storage. Agric. Biol. Chem. 49:737-744.

Li, L. 1974. Variation in protein content and its relation to other characters in sweet potato. J. Agric. Assoc. China 88:17-22.

Li, L. 1977. J. Agric. Assoc. China. The inheritance of crude protein content and its correlation with root yield in sweet potatoes. 100:78-86.

Lii, C.Y., T.W. Chiou, and Y.L. Chu. 1987. The degree of branching in amylose from tuber and legume starches. Proc. Natl. Sci. Counc. Repub. China, Pt.A: Phys. Sci. Eng. 11:341-345.

Lim, S.Y., M.S. Shin, and S.Y. Ahn. 1985. Physicochemical properties and characteristics on lintnerization of sweet potato starches from three cultivars. Han'gu, Nonghwa Hakhoechi 28:156-161.

Lin, Y.H. 1987. Some factors affecting levels of trypsin inhibitor activity of sweet potato (Ipomoea batatas Lam.) roots. Bot. Bul. Acad. Sinica. 28:139-149.

Lin, Y.H. 1989a. Relationship between trypsin-inhibitor activity and water-soluble protein and cumulative rainfall in sweet potatoes. J. Amer. Soc. Hort. Sci. 114:814-818.

Lin, Y.H. 1989b. Trypsin inhibitors and proteases of sweet potatoes. Chung Yang Yen Chiu Yuan Chih Wu Yen Chiu So Chuan K'an 8:57-62.

Lin, Y.H. and H.Y. Chan. 1990. Purification and properties of endopeptidases of sprouts of sweet potato (Ipomoea batatas L. Lam. Cv. Tainong 64). Bot. Bull. Academia Sinica 31:19-27.

Lin, Y.H. and H.L. Chen. 1980. Level and heat stability of trypsin inhibitor activity among sweet potato (Ipomoea batatas Lam.) varieties. Bot. Bull. Acad. Sinica 21:1-13.

Lin, Y.H., J.F. Cheng, and H.Y. Fu. 1983. Partial purification and some properties of trypsin inhibitors of sweet potato (Ipomoea batatas Lam.) roots. Bot. Bull. Academia Sinica 24:103-113.

Lin, Y.H. and S.P. Ho. 1986. Soluble leaf protein of sweet potato cultivars. Bot. Bull. Academia Sinica 27:175-186.

Lin, Y.H. and B.S. Tsu. 1987. Some factors affecting levels of trypsin inhibitor activity of sweet potato (Ipomoea batatas Lam.) roots. Bot. Bull. Academia Sinica 28:139-149.

Lineback, D.R. and A.L. Sayed. 1971. Effect of dimethyl sulfoxide on amylase activity. Carbohyd. Res. 17:453-456.

Liu, G., F. Cheng, S. Gao, and M. Li. 1985a. Effect of arsenic in soil on plants - research on "arsenic-toxic field" in South China. Zhongguo Nongye Kexue (Beijing) 4:9-16.

Liu, S.Y., C.L. Liang, and L. Li. 1985b. Studies on the physicochemical properties of the tubers of new sweet potato lines. Chung-hua Nung Yeh Yen Chiu 34:21-32.

Loebenstein, G. and N. Linsey. 1961. Peroxidase activity in virus-infected sweet potatoes. Phytopath. 51:533-537.

Lopez, A., H.L. Williams, and F.W. Cooler. 1980. Essential elements in fresh and in canned sweet potatoes. J. Food Sci. 45:675-680.

Lund, E.D. and J.M. Smoot. 1982. Dietary fiber content of some tropical fruits and vegetables. J. Agric. Food Chem. 39:1123-1127.

MacLeod, F.L., M.R. Armstrong, M.E. Heap, and L.A. Tolbert. 1935. The vitamin A content of five varieties of sweet potatoes. J. Agr. Res. 50:181-187.

MacLeod, F.L. and E. Utley. 1938. Vitamin A values. Tenn. Agr. Exp. Sta. Ann. Rept. 51:64.

MacNair, V. 1956. Effects of storage and cooking on carotene and ascorbic acid content of some sweet potatoes grown in northwest Arkansas. Ark. Agr. Expt. Sta. Bull. 574.

Madamba, L.S.P., A.R. Bustrillos, and E.L. San Pedro. 1975. Sweet potato starch: Physicochemical properties of the whole starch. Philipp. Agric. 58(9-10):338-350.

Madamba, L.S.P. and E.L. San Pedro. 1976a. Chemical composition of sweet potato flour. Philipp. Agric. 59(9-10):350-355.

Madamba, L.S.P. and E.L. San Pedro. 1976b. Varietal differences in amylose content of sweet potato starch. Kimika 1:26-32.

Maeshima, M. and T. Asahi. 1981. Mechanism of increase in cytochrome c oxidase activity in sweet potato root tissue during aging of slices. J. Biochem. 90:391-397.

Maeshima, M., T. Asahi, and I. Uritani. 1980. Effect of temperature on the activity and stability of plant cytochrome c oxidase. Agri. Biol. Chem. 44:2351-2356.

Maeshima, M., T. Hattori, and T. Asahi. 1987. Purification of complexes II and IV from plant mitochondria. Methods Enzymol. 148:491-501.

Maeshima, M., T. Nakagawa, and T. Asahi. 1989. N-terminal amino acid sequence and processing site of sweet potato cytochrome c oxidase subunit II. Plant Cell Physiol. 30:1187-1188.

Maeshima, M., T. Saska, and T. Asahi. 1985. Characterization of major proteins in sweet potato tuberous roots. Phytochem. 24:1899-1902.

Makki, H.M., A.Y. Abdel-Rahman, M.K.M. Khalil, and M.S. Mohamed. 1986. Chemical composition of Egyptian sweet potatoes. Food Chem. 20:39-44.

Martin, F.W. 1983. The carotenoid pigments of white-fleshed sweet potatoes-reference to their potential value as sources of vitamin A activity. J. Agric. Univ. P.R. 67:494-500.

Martin, F.W. 1984. Techniques and problems in small scale production of flour from sweet potato. J. Agric. Univ. P.R. 68:423-432.

Martin, F.W. 1986. Sugars in staple type sweet potatoes as affected by cooking and storage. J. Agric. Univ. P.R. 70:121-126.

Martin, W. J., V. C. Hasling, and E. A. Catalano. 1976. Ipomeamarone content in diseased and nondiseased tissues of sweet potatoes infected with different pathogens. Phytopath. 66:678-679.

Martin, W. J., V. C. Hasling, E. A. Catalano, and H. P. Dupuy. 1978. Effect of sweet potato cultivars and pathogens Ceratocystis fimbriata, Sclerotium rolfsii, Diplodia tubericola on ipomeamarone content of diseased tissue. Phytopath. 68:863-865.

Matsuno, H. and I. Uritani. 1972. Physiological behaviour of peroxidase isozymes in sweet potato root tissue injured by cutting or with black rot. Plant Cell Physiol. 13:1091-1101.

Matsuo, M., K. Azuma, and S. Morimoto. 1986. Suppressive effect of seasonings on heat-degradation of ascorbic acid in potatoes and sweet potatoes. Nippon Eiyo, Shokuryo Gakkaishi 39:479-483.

Matsuo, T., S. Itoo, N. Murofushi, N. Takahashi, M. Kobayashi, and T. Chishiki. 1984. Identification of gibberellins in the seeds of sweet potato (Ipomoea batatas Lam.) and several other Convolvulaceae plants. Agric. Biol. Chem. 48:2935-2941.

Matsuo, T., H. Mitsuzone, R. Okada, and S. Itoo. 1988. Variations in the levels of major free cytokinins and free abscisic acid during tuber development of sweet potato. J. Plant Growth Regul. 7:249-258.

Matsuo, T., T. Yoneda, and S. Itoo. 1983. Identification of free cytokinins and the changes in endogenous levels during tuber development of sweet potato. Plant Cell Physiol. 24:1305-1312.

Matsuoka, K. 1988. The determination of vitamin C in Benihayato (sweet potato, Kyushu No. 87). Kumamoto Joshi Daigaku Gakujutsu Kiyo 40:113-119.

Matsushita, K. and I. Uritani. 1975. Effects of cycloheximide, actinomycin D and ethylene on the increase and subsequent decrease in acid invertase activity in wounded sweet potato. Plant Cell Physiol. 16:203-210.

McArdle, R.N. 1984. The use of endogenous amylase to produce fermentable saccharides in *Ipomoea batatas* (L.) Lam. and *Zea mays* (L.). Diss. Abstr. Int. B. 45:1418.

Meredith, F. and G. Dull. 1979. Amino acid levels in canned sweet potatoes and snap beans. Food Tech. 38:55-57.

Mihashi, M., S. Sakai, and T. Miyake. 1987. Manufacture of dehydrated foods. Jpn. Kokai Tokkyo Koho JP 62,126,939.

Miller, J.C. and H.M. Covington. 1942. Some factors affecting the carotene content of sweet potato. Proc. Amer. Soc. Hort Sci. 40:519-522.

Minamikawa, T., M. Kojima, and I. Uritani. 1966. Changes in activities of 5-dihydroquinate hydrolyase and shikimate-NADP oxidoreductase in sliced sweet potato roots. Plant Cell Physiol. 7:583-591.

Minamikawa, T. and I. Uritani. 1965. Phenylalanine ammonia-lyase in sliced sweet potato roots. J. Biochem. (Tokyo) 57:678-688.

Monro, J.A., W.D. Holloway, and J. Lee. 1986. Elemental analysis of fruit and vegetables from Tonga. J. Food Sci. 51:522-523.

Moriguchi, T., R.J.A. Villegas, T. Kondo, and M. Kojima. 1988. Isolation of 1-O-*trans*-p-coumaroyl-β-D-glucopyranose from sweet potato roots and examination of its role in chlorogenic acid biosynthesis. Plant Cell Physiol. 29:1221-1226.

Morrison, T.A. 1990. The activity of α- and β-amylase in staple-type and traditional sweet potato lines with varying starch hydrolysis potential. Diss. Abstr. Int. B 51:1571.

Murakami, Y. 1968. Gibberellin-like substances in roots of *Oryza sativa, Pharbitis nil*, and *Ipomoea batatas*, and the site of their synthesis in the plant. Bot. Mag. Tokyo 81:334-343.

Murakami, Y. 1970. A survey of gibberellins in shoots of angiosperms by rice seedling test. Bot. Mag. Tokyo 83:312-324.

Murakami, S., T. Hattori, and K. Nakamura. 1986. Structural differences in full-length cDNAs for two classes of sporamin, the major soluble protein of sweet potato tuberous roots. Plant Mol. Biol. 7:343-355.

Murata, N. 1983. Molecular species composition of phosphatidylglycerols from chilling-sensitive and chilling-resistant plants. Plant Cell Physiol. 24:81-86.

Murata, N. and H. Hoshi. 1984. Sulfoquinovosyl diacylglycerols in chilling-sensitive and chilling-resistant plants. Plant Cell Physiol. 25:1241-1245.

Murata, N., N. Sato, and N. Takahashi. 1984a. Phosphatidylserines from higher plants contain very-long-chain saturated fatty acids. Dev. Plant Biol. 9:153-156.

Murata, N., N. Sato, and N. Takahashi. 1984b. Very-long-chain saturated fatty acids in phosphatidylserine from higher plant tissues. Biochim. Biophys. Acta 795:147-150.

Murata, N., N. Sato, N. Takahashi, and Y. Hamazaki. 1982. Compositions and positional distributions of fatty acids in phospholipids from leaves of chilling-sensitive and chilling-resistant plants. Plant Cell Physiol. 23:1071-1079.

Murata, N. and J. Yamaya. 1984. Temperature-dependent phase behavior of phosphatidylglycerols from chilling-sensitive and chilling-resistant plants. Plant Physiol. 74:1016-1024.

Murata, T. 1971. Sucrose synthetase of sweet potato roots. II. A kinetic study. Agr. Biol. Chem. 35:1441-1448.

Murata, T. 1972. Sucrose phosphate synthetase from various plant origins. Agr. Biol. Chem. 36:187-1884.

Haard, N.F. and M. Marshall. 1976. Isoperoxidase changes in soluble and particulate fractions of sweet potato root resulting from cut injury, ethylene and black rot infection. Physiol. Plant Path. 8:195-205.

Haard, N.F. and B. Wasserman. 1976. Induction of phenylalanine ammonia lyase in sweet potato (*Ipomoea batatas*) root by light irradiation and black rot infection. Physiol. Plant Path. 8:207-213.

Haard, N.F. and P.D. Weiss. 1976. Influence of exogenous ethylene on ipomeamarone accumulation in black rot infected sweet potato roots. Phytochem. 15:261-262.

Haissig, B.E. and A.L. Schipper. 1975. Effect of oxidized nucleotide coenzymes and mercaptoethane on stabilization of plant dehydrogenase activity in crude extracts. Physiol. Plant 35:249-255.

Hamasaki, Y. and I. Yamaguti. 1985. Studies of sweet potatoes used for production of sweet potato distilled spirits. (4). Changes in composition during storage. Kagoshima-ken Kogyo Shikenjo Nenpo 31:81-85.

Hammett, H.L. 1974. Total carbohydrate and carotenoid content of sweet potatoes as affected by cultivar and area of production. HortScience 9:467-468.

Hammett, H.L. and B.F. Barrentine. 1961. Some effects of variety, curing, and baking upon the carbohydrate content of sweet potatoes. Proc. Amer. Soc. Hort. Sci. 78:421-426.

Hammett, H.L., T.P. Hernandez, and J.C. Mutler. 1966. Inheritance of fiber content in sweet potato (*Ipomoea batatas* (L.) Lam.) Proc. Amer. Soc. Hort. Sci. 88:486-490.

Hancock, K.W. 1984. A study of growth regulators, IAA-oxidase, and watering levels on storage root initiation in sweet potato (*Ipomoea batatas*). Diss. Abstr. Int. B 45:736-737.

Hashizume, T., S. Suye, T. Soeda, and T. Sugiyama. 1982a. Isolation and characterization of a new glucopyranosyl derivative of 6-(3-methyl-2-butenylamino) purine from sweet potato tubers. FEBS Lett. 144:25-28.

Hashizume, T., S. Suye, and T. Sugiyama. 1981. Occurrence and level of cis-zeatin riboside in sweet potato tubers. Nucleic Acids Symp. Ser. 10:131-134.

Hashizume, T., S. Suye, and T. Sugiyama. 1982b. Isolation and identification of cis-zeatin riboside from tubers of sweet potato. Agric. Biol. Chem. 46:663-665.

Hattori, T. and T. Asahi. 1982. The presence of two forms of succinate dehydrogenase in sweet potato root mitochondria. Plant Cell Physiol. 23:515-523.

Hattori, T. , S. Ichihara, and K. Nakamura. 1987. Processing of a plant vacuolar protein precursor in vitro. Eur. J. Biochem. 166:533-538.

Hattori, T., Y. Iwasaki, S. Sakajo, T. Asahi. 1983. Cell-free synthesis of succinate dehydrogenase and mitochondrial adenosine triphosphatase of sweet potato. Biochem. Biophys. Res. Commun. 113:235-240.

Hattori, T., K. Matsuoka, and K. Nakamura. 1988. Subcellular localization of the sweet potato tuberous root storage protein. Agric. Biol. Chem. 52:1057-1059.

Hattori, T., T. Nakagawa, M. Maeshima, K. Nakamura, and T. Asahi. 1985. Molecular cloning and nucleotide sequence of cDNA for sporamin, the major soluble protein of sweet potato tuberous roots. Plant Mol. Biol. 5:313-320.

Hattori, T. and K. Nakamura. 1988. Genes coding for the major tuberous root protein of sweet potato: Identification of putative regulatory sequence in the 5' upstream region. Plant Mol. Biol. 11:417-426.

Hattori, T., N. Yoshida, and K. Nakamura. 1989. Structural relationship among the members of a multigene family coding for the sweet potato tuberous root storage protein. Plant Mol. Biol. 13:563-572.

Hayase, F. and H. Kato. 1984. Antioxidative components of sweet potatoes. J. Nur. Sci. Vitaminol. 39:37-46.

Hayashi, T. 1986. Accumulation of sucrose in irradiated agricultural products. JARQ 18:295-301.

Hayashi, T., T. Sugimoto, and K. Kawashima. 1984. Effect of gamma-irradiation on the activities of sucrose synthase and sucrose phosphate synthase in potato tubers and sweet potato roots. Nippon Shokuhin Kogyo Gakkaishi Vol. 31:281-284.

Hegde, M.V., F. Roy, and P.N. Joshi. 1979. A new method of the preparation of β-amylase from sweet potato. Prep. Biochem. 9:71-84.

Heinze, P. H. and C. O. Appleman. 1943. A biochemical study of the curing processes in sweet potatoes. Plant Physiol. 18:548-555.

Hiura, M. 1943. Studies in storage and rot of sweet potato. Rept. Gifu Agri. Col. 50:1-5.

Hizukuri, S. 1985. Relationship between the distribution of the chain length of amylopectin and the crystalline structure of starch granules. Carbohydr. Res. 14:295-306.

Hollo, J., E. Laszlo, A. Hoschke, F. El Hawary, and B. Banky. 1982. Recent data on the active center of amylolytic enzymes. Starch 34:304-308.

Holloway, W.D. 1983. Composition of fruit, vegetable, and cereal dietary fiber. J. Sci. Food Agric. 34:1236-1240.

Holloway, W.D., M.E. Argall, W.T. Jealous, J.A. Lee, and J.H. Bradbury. 1989. Organic acids and calcium oxalate in tropical root crops. J. Agric. Food Chem. 37:337-341.

Holloway, W.D., J.A. Monro, J.C. Gurnsey, E.W. Pmare, and N.H. Stace. 1985. Dietary fiber and other constituents of some Tongan foods. J. Food Sci. 50:1756-1757.

Hong, Z., D. Wu, and W. Qi. 1985. Determination of copper, zinc, lead, and cadmium in grains by using atomic absorption spectrophotometry. Huanjing Kexue 6(5):70-72.

Horigome, T., N. Nakayama, and M. Ikeda. 1972. Nutritive value of sweet potato protein produced from the residual products of sweet potato starch industry. Nippon Chikusan Gakkahi-Ho 43:432-437.

Horvat, R. J., R. B. Arrendale, G. G. Dull, G.W. Chapman, Jr., and S. J. Kays. 1991. Volatile constituents and sugars of three diverse cultivars of sweetpotatoes [*Ipomoea batatas* (L.) Lam.]. J. Food Sci. 56:714-715, 742.

Huang, S.Y. and H.S. Wu. 1985. Redox potential used to measure amylose in starch. Hakko Kogaku Kaishi 63:31-37.

Huang, Y., S. Zhang, and R. Yang. 1983. Survey of communal industrial production of caramel by the ammonium process. Tiaowei Fushipin Keji 3:11-12.

Huq, R.S., J.A. Abalaka, and W.L. Stafford. 1983. Folate content of various Nigerian foods. J. Sci. Food Agric. 34:404-406.

Hyodo, H. and I. Uritani. 1965. Purification and properties of o-diphenol oxidases in sweet potato. J. Biochem. (Tokyo) 58:388-395.

Hyodo, H. and I. Uritani. 1966. A study on increase in o-diphenol oxidase activity during incubation of sliced sweet potato tissue. Plant Cell Physiol. 7:137-144.

Hyodo, H. and I. Uritani. 1984. Ethylene production in sweet potato root tissue infected by *Ceratocystis fimbriata*. Plant Cell Physiol. 25:1147-1152.

Ikemiya, M. and H.J. Deobald. 1966. New characteristic α-amylase in sweet potatoes. J. Agr. Food Chem. 14:237-241.

Imaseki, H. 1970. Induction of peroxidase activity by ethylene in sweet potato. Plant Physiol. 46:172-174.

Imaseki, H., T. Asahi, and I. Uritani. 1968a. Investigations on the possible inducers of metabolic changes in injured plant tissues. Pages 189-201 *in* Biochemical Regulation in Diseased Plants or Injury, edited by T. Hirai, J. Hidaka and I. Uritani. Phytopath. Soc. Japan, Tokyo.

Imaseki, H., T. Teranishi, and I. Uritani. 1968b. Production of ethylene by sweet potato roots infected by black rot fungus. Plant Cell Physiol. 9:769-781.

Imaseki, H., T. Teranishi, and I. Uritani. 1968e. Production of ethylene by sweet potato roots infected by black rot fungus. Plant Cell Physiol. 9:769-781.

Imaseki, H., M. Uchiyama, and I. Uritani. 1968c. Effect of ethylene on the inductive increase in metabolic activities in sliced sweet potato roots. Agric. Biol. Chem. 32:387-389.

Imaseki, H., I. Uritani, and M.A. Stahmann. 1968d. Production of ethylene by injured sweet potato tissue. Plant Cell Physiol. 9:757-768.

Imbert, M.P., C.E. Seaforth, and D.B. Williams. 1966. The anthocyanin pigments of the sweet potato *Ipomoea batatas* (L.) Lam. J. Am. Soc. Hort. Sci. 88:481-485.

Imbert, M.P. and L.A. Wilson. 1970. Stimulatory and inhibitory effects of scopoletin on IAA oxidase preparations from sweet potato. Phytochem. 9:1787-1794.

Imbert, M.P. and L.A. Wilson. 1972a. Effects of chlorogenic and caffeic acids on IAA oxidase preparations from sweet potato roots. Phytochem. 11:2671-2676.

Imbert, M.P. and L.A. Wilson. 1972b. IAA oxidase preparations from sweet potato roots. Phytochem. 11:29-36.

Inoue, H., K. Oba, M. Ando, and I. Uritani. 1984a. Enzymic reduction of dehydroipomeamarone to ipomeamarone in sweet potato root tissue infected by *Ceratocystis fimbriata*. Physiol. Plant Path. 25:1-8.

Inoue, H., H. Tsuji, and I. Uritani. 1984b. Characterization and activity change of farnesol dehydrogenase in black rot fungus-infected sweet potato. Agric. Biol. Chem. 48:733-738.

Inoue, H. and I. Uritani. 1980. Conversion of 4-Hydroxydehydromyoporone to other furano-terpenes in *Ceratocystis fimbriata*-infected sweet potato. Agric. Biol. Chem. 44:1935-1936.

Ishida, M., R. Haga, Y. Odawara, T. Yoji, S. Takahashi, and K. Ebara. 1984. Recovering subterranean stem starch and protein. Eur. Pat. Appl. EP 155, 557.

Ito, R., K. Oba, and I. Uritani. 1979. Mechanism for the induction of 3-hydroxy-3-methylglutaryl coenzyme A reductase in $HgCl_2$-treated sweet potato root tissue. Plant Cell Physiol. 20:867-874.

Ito, R., K. Oba, and I. Uritani. 1982. Some problems in the assay method of HMG-CoA reductase activity in sweet potato in the presence of other HMG-CoA utilizing enzymes. Agric. Biol. Chem. 46:2087-2091.

Iwasaki, Y. and T. Asahi. 1983. Purification and characterization of the soluble form of mitochondrial adenosine triphosphatase from sweet potato. Arch. Biochem. Biophys. 227:164-173.

Iwasaki, Y. and T. Asahi. 1985. Intracellular sites of the synthesis of sweet potato mitochondrial FATPase subunits. Plant Mol. Biol. 5:339-346.

Iwasaki, Y., M. Matsuoka, T. Asahi. 1984. Immunological comparisons among energy transducing adenosine triphosphatases from higher plants with respect to the structures of their subunits. FEBS Lett. 17:249-252.

Izumi, H., Y. Tatsumi, and T. Murata. 1984. Effect of storage temperature on changes of ascorbic acid content of cucumber, winter squash, sweet potato, and potato. Nippon Shokuhin Kogyo Gakkaishi 31:47-49.

Jenkins, W.F. and W.S. Anderson. 1956. Geographical location and storage affecting carbohydrates and canning quality in sweet potatoes. Proc. Amer. Soc. Hort. Sci. 68:407-411.

Jenkins, W.F. and M. Gieger. 1957a. Curing, baking time and temperatures affecting carbohydrates in sweet potatoes. Proc. Amer. Soc. Hort. Sci. 70:419-424.

Jenkins, W.F. and M. Gieger. 1957b. Quality in baked sweet potatoes affected by varieties and post-harvest treatments. Food Res. 22:32-36.

Jenkins, W.F. and E.L. Moore. 1954. The distribution of ascorbic acid and latex vessels in three tissue regions of sweet potatoes. Proc. Amer. Soc. Hort. Sci. 63:389-392.

Jenkins, W.F. and E.L. Moore. 1956. Carbohydrate and ascorbic acid in sweet potatoes as affected by time and sampling techniques. Proc. Amer. Soc. Hort. Sci. 67:490-492.

Jones, A. 1972. Mass selection for low oxidation in sweet potato. J. Amer. Soc. Hort. Sci. 97:714-718.

Jones, A, P.D. Dukes, M.G. Hamilton, R.A. Baumgardner. 1980. Selection of low fiber content in sweet potato. HortScience 15:797-798.

Jones, D.B. and C.E.F. Gersdorff. 1931. Ipomoein, a globulin from sweet potatoes, *Ipomoea batatas*. Isolation of a secondary protein derived from ipomoein by enzymic action. J. Biol. Chem. 93:119-126.

Jones, A., C.E. Steinbauer, and D.T. Pope. 1969. Quantitative inheritance of ten root traits in sweetpotatoes. J. Amer. Soc. Hort. Sci. 94:271-275.

Kahl, G., M. Furuta, K. Oba, and I. Uritani. 1982. Wounding-induced enhancement of the activity of chromatin-bound DNA-dependent RNA polymerases in sweet potato root. Agric. Biol. Chem. 46:2457-2463.

Kainuma, K. and D. French. 1970. Action of pancreatic α-amylase and sweet potato β-amylase on 6^2-and 6^3-α-glucosylmalto-oligosaccharides. North-Holland Pub. Co. 6:182-186.

Kanazawa, Y., T. Asahi, and I. Uritani. 1967. Changes in b-type heme content in relation to peroxidase biosynthesis in injured sweet potato roots. Plant Cell Physiol. 8:249-262.

Kanazawa, Y., H. Shichi, and I. Uritani. 1965. Biosynthesis of peroxidases in sliced or black rot-infected sweet potato slices. Agr. Biol. Chem. 29:840-847.

Kanie, M., T. Nagahama, and S. Fujimoto. 1974. Studies on some effects of the treatments with hot water on sweet potatoes. Bull. Fac. Agr. Kagoshima Univ. 24:155-164.

Kanie, M., T. Nagahama, and S. Fujimoto. 1976. Fractionation of tuber components by a membrane system of the sweet potato treated with "hot water": Movement of β-amylase. Nippon Nogei Kogaku Kaishi 50:163-168.

Kanie, M., T. Nagahama, S. Fujimoto, and S. Kijima. 1970. A screening test for high-sugar individuals and lines of sweet potato. Bull. Fac. Agr. Kagoshima Univ. 20.

Katayama, Y. and S. Shida. 1961. Studies on the variation in leaf pigment by means of paper chromatography. III. Leaf pigments and carbon assimilation in some strains of sweet potato. Mem. Fac. Agric. Univ. Miyasaki 3:11-16.

Kato, Y. and I. Uritani. 1972. Ethylene biosynthesis in diseased sweet potato root tissue with special reference to methionine system. Agri. Biol. Chem. 36:2601-2604.

Kato, C. and I. Uritani. 1976. Changes in carbohydrate content of sweet potato in response to cutting and infection by black rot fungus. Ann. Phytopath. Soc. Jpn. 42:181-186.

Kawabe, H., Y. Sugiura, M. Terauchi, and H. Tanaka. 1984. Manganese (III)-containing acid phosphatase. Properties of iron (III)-substituted enzyme and function of manganese (III) and iron (III) in plant and mammalian acid phosphatases. Biochem. Biophys. Acta 784:81-89.

Kawashima, K. and I. Uritani. 1963. Occurrence of peroxidase in sweet potato infected by the black rot. Agric. Biol. Chem. 27:409-417.

Kawashima. 1965. Some properties of peroxidase produced in sweet potato infected by the black rot fungus. Plant Cell Physiol. 6:247-265.

Kays, S.J. 1989. Strategies for selecting conventional and new flavor types of tropical root and tuber crops to increase consumer acceptance and use. Eighth Intern. Symp. Trop. Root Crops, p. 178-188, Bangkok, Thailand.

Kays, S.J. 1991. Postharvest physiology of perishable plant products. Van Nostrand Reinholt, N.Y. 532pp.

Kays, S.J. and R.J. Horvat. 1984. A comparison of the volatile constituents and sugars of representative Asian, Central American and North American sweet potatoes. Sixth Intern. Symp. Trop. Root Crops, pp. 577-586, Intern. Potato Center, Lima, Peru.

Keshinro, O.O. 1983. The free and total folate activity in some commonly available tropical foodstuffs. Food Chem. 11:87-93.

Khachik, F. and G.R. Beecher. 1987. Application of a c-45-d-carotene as an internal standard for the quantification of carotenoids in yellow/orange vegetables by liquid chromatography. J. Agric. Food Chem. 35:732-738.

Kim, J.P., Y.G. Ann, W.M. Shim. 1985. Purification of sweet potato β-amylase. Han'guk Saenghwa Hakhoechi 18:290-296.

Kim, S.R., R.H. Lane, M. Abdel-Ghany, K.R. Stitt. 1987. Influence of extractant on L-ascorbic acid recovery from selected foods and beverages. J. Food Qual. 10:1-7.

Kim, W.K., I. Oguni, and I. Uritani. 1974. Phytoalexin induction in sweet potato roots by amino acids. Agr. Biol. Chem. 38:2567-2568.

Kim, M.C., N.K. Sung, K.H. Shim, M.H. Lee, and I. Lee. 1981. The contents of heavy metal in fruits and vegetables collected from Jinju district, Korea. Korean J. Food Sci. Technol. 13:299-306.

Kim, W.K. and I. Uritani. 1974. Fungal extracts that induce phytoalexins in sweet potato

Mol. Biol. 7:343-355.

Shimizu, T. and M. Kojima. 1982. Detection and some properties of the enzyme in sweet potato root which catalyzes the formation of t-cinnamoyl-D-glucose. Agric. Biol. Chem. 46:2617-2619.

Shimizu, T. and M. Kojima. 1984. Partial purification and characterization of UDPG:t-cinnamate glucosyl transferase in the root of sweet potato, *Ipomoea batatas* Lam. J. Biochem. 95:205-212.

Shin, M.S. and S.Y. Ahn. 1983. Studies on physicochemical properties of starches from sweet potatoes of Korean cultivars. Hanguk Nonghwa Hakhoe Chi 26:137-142.

Shingles, R.M., G.P. Arron, and R.D. Hill. 1982. Alternative pathway respiration and lipoxygenase activity in aged potato slice mitochondria. Plant Physiol. 69:1435-1438.

Singh, U. and J.H. Bradbury. 1988. HPLC determination of vitamin A and vitamin D_2 in South Pacific root crops. J. Sci. Food Agric. 45:87-94.

Sirju, G. and L.A. Wilson. 1974. IAA oxidase preparations from fresh and aged *Ipomoea batatas* tuber discs. Phytochem. 13:111-117.

Sistrunk, W. A. 1971. Carbohydrate transformations, color and firmness of canned sweet potatoes as influenced by variety, storage, pH and treatment. J. Food Sci. 36:39-42.

Sistrunk, W. A. 1977. Relationship of storage, handling, and cooking method to color, hardcore tissue, and carbohydrate composition in sweet potatoes. J. Amer. Soc. Hort. Sci. 102:381-384.

Sistrunk, W. A., J. C. Miller, and L. G. Jones. 1954. Carbohydrate changes during storage and cooking of sweet potatoes. Food Technol. 8:223-226.

Siti, M.B.S., E.S. Tee, and Y.H. Chong. 1987. Lead content of some Malaysian foodstuffs. ASEAN Food J. 3:25-29.

Sjostrom, O.A. 1936. Microscopy of starches and their modifications. Ind. Eng. Chem. 28:63-74.

Sohonie, K. and A.P. Bhandarker. 1954. Trypsin inhibitors in Indian foodstuffs. I. Inhibitors in vegetables. J. Sci. Ind. Res. 13B:500-503.

Son, K.-C., R. F. Severson, R. F. Arrendale, and S. J. Kays. 1990. Isolation and characterization of pentacyclic triterpene ovipositional stimulant for the sweetpotato weevil from *Ipomoea batatas* (L.) Lam. J. Agric. Food Chem. 38:134-137.

Son, K.-C., R. F. Severson, and S. J. Kays. 1990. Surface chemical differences between sweetpotato lines with varying levels of resistance to the sweetpotato weevil, *Cylas formicarius elegantulus* (Summers). J. Amer. Soc. Hort. Sci. 115:696-699.

Son, K.-C., R. F. Severson, and S. J. Kays. 1993. Pre- and postharvest changes in the composition of hydrocarbons from the periderm of sweetpotato [*Ipomoea batatas* (L.) Lam.] storage roots. HortScience 27: (In press).

Speirs, M., A.H. Dempsey, J. Miller, W.J. Peterson, J.T. Wakeley, F.D. Cochran, R. Reder, H.B. Cordner, E.A. Fieger, M. Itollinger, W.J. James, H. Lewis, J.F. Eheart, M.S. Eheart, F.S. Andrews, R.W. Young, J.H. Mitchell, O.B. Garrison, and F.T. McLean. 1953. The effect of variety, curing, storage, and time of planting and harvesting on the carotene, ascorbic acid, and moisture content of sweet potatoes grown in six southern states. S. Coop. Ser. Bull. 30, 48pp.

Speirs, M., H.L. Cochran, W.J. Petterson, F.W. Sherwood, and J.G. Weaver. 1945. The effects of fertilizer treatments, curing, storage, and cooking on the carotene and ascorbic acid content of sweet potatoes. S. Coop Ser. Bull. 3, 31pp.

Stahmann, M.A., B.G. Clare, and W. Woodbury. 1966. Increased disease resistance and enzyme activity induced by ethylene and ethylene production by black rot infected sweet potato tissue. Plant Physiol. 41:1505-1512.

Stahmann, M.A. and D.M. Demorest. 1973. Changes in enzymes of host and pathogen with special reference to peroxidase interaction. Pages 405-420 *in* Fungal pathogenicity and the plant's response, edited by R. Byrde and C. Cutting, Academic Press, NY.

Sterling, C. and M.L. Aldridge. 1977. Mealiness and sogginess in sweet potato. Food Chem. 2:71-76.

Suge, H. 1979. Gibberellin relationships in a dwarf mutant of sweet potato. Japan. J. Genetics 54:35-42.

Sugiura, M., T. Ogiso, K. Takeuti, S. Tamura, and A. Ito. 1973. Studies on trypsin inhibitors in sweet potato. I. Purification and some properties. Biochem. Biophys. Acta. 328:404-417.

Sugiyama, T. and T. Hashizume. 1989. Cytokinins in developing tuberous roots of sweet potato. Agric. Biol. Chem. 53:49-52.

Sugiyama, T., Y. Nieda, Y. Irie, and T. Hashizume. 1988. Occurrence and levels of cytokinins in calluses of *Ipomoea* species. Shokubutsu Soshiki Baiyo 5:93-95.

Sugiyama, T., S. Suye, and T. Hashizume. 1983. Mass spectrometric-determination of cytokinins in young sweet potato plants using deuterium-labeled standards. Agric. Biol. Chem. 47:315-318.

Sun, J. B. 1988. Quantitative analysis of the volatile components of baked sweetpotatoes. MS Thesis, University of Georgia, 73pp.

Sung, F.J.M. 1981. The effect of leaf water status on stomatal activity, transpiration, and nitrate reductase of sweet potato. Agric. Water Manage. 4:465-470.

Suye, S., T. Sugiyama, and T. Hashizume. 1983. Mass spectrometric determination of ribosyl trans-zeatin from sweet potato tubers. Agric. Biol. Chem. 47:1665-1666.

Suzuki, H., K. Oba, and I. Uritani. 1975a. Improved synthesis of 3-1^{4}C-3-hydroxy-3-methylglutaryl coenzyme A. Agr. Biol. Chem. 39:1657-1676.

Suzuki, H., K. Oba, and I. Uritani. 1975b. The occurrence and some properties of 3-hydroxy-3-methylglutaryl coenzyme A reductase in sweet potato roots infected by *Ceratocystis fimbriata*. Physiol. Plant Path. 7:265-276.

Suzuki, H. and I. Uritani. 1976. Subcellular localization of 3-hydroxy-3-methylglutaryl coenzyme A reductase and other membrane-bound enzymes in sweet potato roots. Plant Cell Physiol. 17:691-700.

Sweeney, J.P. and A.C. Marsh. 1971. Effect of processing on provitamin A in vegetables. J. Am. Diet. Assoc. 59:238-245.

Szyperski, R.J., D.D. Hamann, and W.M. Walter, Jr. 1986. Controlled alpha amylase process for improved sweet potato puree. J. Food Sci. 51:360-363,367.

Taira, T. 1963a. By-products of alcoholic fermentation by gas chromatography. II. Unsaponifiable substance of sweet potato fusel oil boiled at a higher temperature than amyl alcohol. Nippon Nogei Kagaku Kaishi 37:49-52.

Taira, T. 1963b. By-products of alcoholic fermentation by gas chromatography. III. Occurrence of methylamylcarbinol and geraniol in cane molasses and sweet potato fusel oil. Nippon Nogei Kagaku Kaishi 37:630-631.

Takeda, Y. and S. Hizukuri. 1981. Re-examination of the action of sweet-potato beta-amylase on phosphorylated (1-4)-x-D-glucan. Carbohyd. Res. 89:174-178.

Takeda, Y., S. Hizukuri, and J. Shimada. 1972. Structural change of sweet potato β-amylase by sodium dodecyl sulfate. 46:367-371.

Takeda, Y., N. Tokunaga, C. Takeda, S. Hizukuri. 1986. Physicochemical properties of sweet potato starches. Starch 38:345-350.

Takeuchi, A., K. Oba, and I. Uritani. 1977. Change in acetyl CoA synthetase activity of sweet potato in response to infection by *Ceratocystis fimbriata* and injury. Agric. Biol. Chem. 41:1141-1145.

Takeuchi, A., I. Oguni, K. Oba, M. Kojima, and I. Uritani. 1978. Interactions between diseased sweet potato terpenoids and *Ceratocystis fimbriata*. Agric. Biol. Chem. 42:935-939.

Takeuchi, A., K.J. Scott, K. Oba, and I. Uritani. 1980. Possible role of the cytosol pathway of acetyl-CoA supply in terpene biosynthesis in sweet potato infected with *Ceratocystis fimbriata*. Plant Cell Physiol. 21:917-922.

Tamate, J. and J.H. Bradbury. 1985. Determination of sugars in tropical root crops using carbon-13 NMR spectroscopy: comparison with the HPLC method. J. Sci. Food Agric. 36:1291-1302.

Tanaka, Y., M. Kojima, and I. Uritani. 1974. Properties, development and cellular-localization of cinnamic acid 4-hydroxylase in cut-injured sweet potato. Plant Cell Physiol. 15:843-854.

Tanaka, Y., M. Matsuoka, N. Yamanoto, K. Ohashi, Y. Kano-Murakami, and Y. Ozeki. 1989. Structure and characterization of a cDNA clone for phenylalanine ammonia-lyase from cut-injured roots of sweet potato. Plant Physiol. 90:1403-1407.

Tanaka, Y. and I. Uritani. 1976. Immunochemical studies on fluctuation of phenylalanine ammonia-lyase activity in sweet potato in response to cut injury. J. Biochem. (Tokyo) 79:217-219.

Tanaka, Y. and I. Uritani. 1977a. Polarity of production of polyphenols and development of various enzyme activities in cut-injured sweet potato root tissue. Plant Physiol. 60:563-566.

Tanaka, Y. and I. Uritani. 1977b. Purification and properties of phenylalanine ammonia-lyase in cut-injured sweet potato. J. Biochem. 81:963-970.

Tanaka, Y. and I. Uritani. 1977c. Synthesis and turnover of phenylalanine ammonia-lyase in root tissue of sweet potato injured by cutting. Eur. J. Biochem. 73:255-260.

Tanaka, Y. and I. Uritani. 1979. Polar transport and content of indole-3-acetic acid in wounded sweet potato root tissues. Plant Cell Physiol. 20:1087-1096.

Tee, E.S. and Y.H. Chong. 1987. Lead content of some Malaysian foodstuffs. ASEAN Food J. 391:25-29.

Tereshkovich, G. and D.W. Newsom. 1963. Identification of some fatty acids in periderm tissue of the sweet potato. Proc. Assoc. Southern Agr. Workers 60:244.

Timbie, M. and N.F. Haard. 1977. Involvement of ethylene in the hardcore syndrome of sweet potato roots. 42:491-493.

Tiu, C. S., A. E. Purcell, and W. W. Collins. 1985. Contribution of some volatile compounds to sweet potato aroma. J. Agric. Food Chem. 33:223-226.

Toda, H. 1989. Sequence analysis of sweet potato β-amylase. Denpun Kagaku 36(2):87-101.

Truong Van Den, C.J. Beiermann, and J.A. Marlett. 1986. Simple sugars, oligosaccharides and starch concentrations in raw and cooked sweet potato. J. Agric. Food Chem. 34:421-425.

Tsukui, A. 1989. Stability of anthocyanin pigments of Philippine powdered purple yam - effect of inorganic salts, organic acids, sugars, phenols, L-ascorbic acid, and hydrogen peroxide. Nippon Kasei Gakkaish 40:15-22.

Tsukui, A., K. Kuwano, T. Mitamura. 1983. Anthocyanin pigment isolated from purple root of sweet potato. Kaseigaku Zasshi 34:153-159.

Uehara, S. 1983. Amylose-amylopectin ratio of soluble and insoluble fractions of sweet potato starch granules treated with urea. Nippon Nogei Kagaku Kaishi 57:529-533.

Umemoto, K. 1974. Morphological character of crystalline inorganic components present in plants: Calcium oxalate crystals in the leaves of sweet potato grown in natural light and in darkness. Chem. Pharm. Bull. 22:1968-1974.

Unarau, M.A. and R.E. Nylund. 1975a. The relation of physical properties and chemical composition to mealiness in the potato. I. Physical properties. Amer. Potato J. 34:245-253.

Unarau, M.A. and R.E. Nylund. 1975b. The relation of physical properties and chemical composition to mealiness in the potato. II. Chemical composition. Amer. Potato J. 34:303-311.

Uritani, I. 1953. Phytopathological chemistry of black-rotted sweet potato. Part 7. Isolation and identification of polyphenols from the injured sweet potato. Nippon Nougeikagaku Kaishi 27:165-168.

Uritani, I. and M. Miyano. 1955. Derivatives of caffeic acid in sweet potato attacked by black rot. Nature 175:812.

Uritani, I. and K. Muramutu. 1953. Phytopathological chemistry of black-rotted sweet potato. Part 4. Isolation and identification of polyphenols from the injured sweet potato. Nippon Nougeikagaku Kaishi 27:29-33.

Uritani, I., M. Uritani, and H. Yamada. 1960. Similar metablolic alterations induced in sweet potato by poisonous chemicals and by *Ceratostomella fimbriata*. Phytopath. 50:30-34.

Van der Pol, F., S.U. Purnomo, and H.A. Van Rosmalen. 1988. Trans-cis isomerization of carotenes and its effect on the vitamin A potency of some common Indonesian foods. Nutr.

Rep. Int. 37:785-793.

Varon, D. and W. Collins. 1989. Ipomoein is the major soluble protein of sweet potato storage roots. HortScience 24:829-830.

Venkateswara, R.K. and C.L. Mahajan. 1990. Fluoride content of some common South Indian foods and their contribution to fluorosis. J. Sci. Food Agric. 51:275-279.

Vieweg, G.H. and M.A.R. de Fekete. 1976. The effect of phospholipids on starch metabolism. Planta (Berl.) 129:155-159.

Villareal, R.L., S.C.S. Tsou, S.K. Lin, and S.C. Chiu. 1979. Use of sweet potato (*Ipomoea batatas*) leaf tips as vegetables II. Evaluation of yield and nutritive quality. Expl. Agric. 15:117-122.

Villegas, R.J.A., and M. Kojima. 1985. Sweet potato root enzyme which catalyzes the formation of chlorogenic acid from 1-O-caffeoyl-D-glucose and D-quinic acid. Agric. Biol. Chem. 49:263-265.

Villegas, R.J.A., and M. Kojima. 1986. Purification and characterization of hydroxycinnamoyl D-glucose: quinate hydroxycinnamoyl transferase in the root of sweet potato, *Ipomoea batatas* Lam. J. Bio. Chem. 26:8729-8733.

Villegas, R.J.A., T. Shimokawa, H. Okuyama, and M. Kojima. 1987. Purification and characterization of chlorogenic acid: Chlorogenate caffeoyl transferase in sweet potato root. Phytochem. 26:1577-1580.

Visser, F.R. 1984. Variations in the vitamin C content of some New Zealand grown fruit and vegetables. NZ J. Sci. 27:105-112.

Visser, F.R., and J.K. Burrows. 1983. Composition of New Zealand foods. 1. Characteristic fruits and vegetables. Science Information Publishing Centre, Wellington, NZ, p. 31-32.

Walker, C.E., L.B. Detfenbaugh, C.E. Lang, and C.W. Wrigley. 1989. Modified rapid method for measuring starch quality with the Australian Rapid Visco-Analyser. Veroeff Arbeitsgem. Getreideforson. 220:2-12.

Walter, W.M., Jr., and G.L. Catignani. 1981. Biological quality and composition of sweet potato protein fractions. J. Agric. Food Chem. 29:797-799.

Walter, W.M., Jr., G.L. Catignani, L.L. Yow, and D.H. Porter. 1983. Protein nutritional value of sweet potato flour. J. Agric. Food Chem. 31:947-749.

Walter, M. W., Jr., W. W. Collins, and A. E. Purcell. 1984. Sweet potato protein: A review. J. Agri. Food Chem. 32:695-699.

Walter, W. M., Jr. and F. G. Giesbrecht. 1982. Effect of lye peeling conditions on phenolic destruction, starch hydrolysis, and carotene loss in sweet potatoes. J. Food Sci. 47:810-812.

Walter, W. M., Jr., A. P. Hansen, and A. E. Purcell. 1971. Lipids of cured Centennial sweet potatoes. J. Food Sci. 36:795-797.

Walter, W.M., Jr., and A.E. Purcell. 1971. Characterization of a stable water-dispersible carotene fraction from dehydrated sweet potato flakes. J. Agr. Food Chem. 19:175-178.

Walter, W.M., Jr., and A.E. Purcell. 1973. α-amylase in sweet potatoes. A comparison between the amyloclastic and chromogenic starch methods of analysis. J. Food Sci. 38:548-549.

Walter, W.M., Jr. and A. E. Purcell. 1974. Lipid autoxidation in precooked dehydrated sweet potato flakes stored in air. J. Agric. Food Chem. 22:298-302.

Walter, W.M., Jr. and A. E. Purcell. 1980. Effect of substrate levels and polyphenol oxidase activity on darkening in sweet potato cultivars. J. Agric. Food Chem. 28:941-944.

Walter, W.M., Jr., A.E. Purcell, and W.Y. Cobb. 1970. Fragmentation of β-carotene in autoxidizing dehydrated sweet potato flakes. J. Agr. Food Chem. 18:881-885.

Walter, W.M., Jr., A.E. Purcell, and A.P. Hansen. 1972. Autoxidation of dehydrated sweet potato flakes. The effect of solvent extraction on flake stability. J. Agr. Food Chem. 20:1060-1062.

Walter, M.W., Jr., A.E. Purcell, and G.K. McCollum. 1978. Laboratory preparation of a protein-xanthophyll concentrate from sweet potato leaves. J. Agric. Food Chem. 26:1222-1226.

Walter, W. M., Jr., A. E. Purcell, and G. K. McCollum. 1979. Use of high-pressure liquid

Murata, T. and T. Akazawa. 1968. Enzymic mechanism of starch synthesis in sweet potato roots. I. Requirement of potassium ions for starch synthetase. Arch. Biochem. Biophys. 126:873-879.

Murata, T. and T. Akazawa. 1969. Enzymic mechanisms of starch synthesis in sweet potato roots. II. Enhancement of the starch synthetase activity by maltooligosaccharides. Arch. Biochem. Biophys. 130:604-609.

Nagahama, T., K. Inoue, Y. Nobori, S. Fujimoto, and M. Kanie. 1977. On some components in a steam distillate of sweet potato. Nippon Nogei Kagaku Kaishi 51:597-602.

Nagashima, N., M. Yamazaki, and A. Kawabata. 1989. Some physicochemical properties of starches from kudzu and sweet potato. Nippon Kasei Gakkaishi 40:683-690.

Nakagawa, T., M. Maeshima, K. Nakamura, and T. Asahi. 1990. Molecular cloning of a cDNA for the smallest nuclear-encoded subunit of sweet potato cytochrome c oxidase. Analysis with the cDNA of the structure and import into mitochondria of the subunit. Eur. J. Biochem. 191:557-561.

Nakamura, K. and T. Asahi. 1990. Cloning of a mitochondria-targeting signal sequence from sweet potato. Jpn. Kokai Tokkyo Koho JP 02 97, 390.

Nakamura, K., T. Hattori, and K. Matsuoka. 1988. Mechanism of protein accumulation and its control in the root of sweet potato. Kagaku to Seibutsu 26:391-398.

Nakatani, M. 1989. Application of enzyme immunoassay for determination of endogenous abscisic acid in sweet potato. Japan J. Crop Sci. 58:137-139.

Nakayama, S. and S. Amagase. 1963. An improved method for the purification of sweet potato β-amylase. J. Biochem. 54:375-377.

Neves, V.A. nd E.J. Lourenco. 1985. Extraction and the activity of the peroxidase and polyphenoloxidase of sweet potatoes (Ipomoea batatas Lam.). Rev. Cienc. Farm. 7:101-107.

Nishio, K. 1984. Activities of β-glucosidase and β-galactosidase in plants. Shokumotsu-hen 32:37-42.

Nottingham, S. F., K.-C. Son, R. F. Severson, R. F. Arrendale, and S. J. Kays. 1989. Attraction of adult sweetpotato weevils, Cylas formicarius elegantulus (Summers), (Coleoptera:Curculionidae), to sweetpotato leaf and root volatiles. J. Chem. Ecol. 15:895-903.

Nozue, M., J. Kawai, and K. Yoshitama. 1987. Selection of a high anthocyanin-producing cell line of sweet potato cell cultures and identification of pigments. J. Plant Physiol. 129:81-88.

Nozue, M., M. Kikuma, Y. Miyamoto, E. Fukuzaki, T. Matsumura, and Y. Hashimoto. 1988. Red anthocyanin pigment and its manufacture with callus culture of Ipomoea batatas. Jpn. Kokai Tokyo Koho JP 63,233,993.

Nozue, M. and H. Yasudo. 1985. Occurrence of anthocyanoplasts in cell suspension cultures of sweet potato. Plant Cell Rep. 4:252-255.

Oba, K., H. Shibata, and I. Uritani. 1970. The mechanism supplying acetyl-CoA for terpene biosynthesis in sweet potato with black rot; incorporation of acetate-2-^{14}C, pyruvate-3-^{14}C and citrate-2-^{14}C into ipomeamarone. Plant Cell Physiol. 11:507-510.

Oba, K., H. Tatematsu, K. Yamashita, and I. Uritani. 1976. Induction of furano-terpene production and formation of the enzyme system from mevalonate to isopentenyl pyrophosphate in sweet potato root tissue injured by Ceratocystis fimbriata and by toxic chemicals. Plant Physiol. 58:51-56.

Oba, K. and I. Uritani. 1975. Purification and characterization of pyruvate decarboxylase from sweet potato roots. J. Biochem. 77:1205-1213.

Oba, K. and I. Uritani. 1982a. L-Lactate dehydrogenase isozymes from sweet potato roots. Methods Enzymol. 89:345-351.

Oba, K. and I. Uritani. 1982b. Pyruvate decarboxylase from sweet potato roots. Methods Enzymol. 90:528-532.

Oba, K., R. Yu, and M. Fujita. 1982. Metabolic alterations in response to wounding and infection. Plant Infect. 157-173.

Oguni, I. and I. Uritani. 1971. Utilization of ethanol-2-^{14}C for the biogenesis of ipomeamarone by sweet potato root tissue infected with *Ceratocystis fimbriata*. Agric. Biol. Chem. 35:357-362.

Oguni, I, K. Oshima, H. Imaseki, and I. Uritani. 1969. Biochemical studies on the terpene metabolism in sweet potato root tissue with black rot. Effect of C_{10}- and C_{15}-terpenols on acetate-2-^{14}C incorporation into ipomeamarone. Agr. Biol. Chem. 33:50-62.

Ohi, A. and F. Miyagawa. 1982. Studies on yam (*Discorea japonica*) amylase. Sagami Joshi Daigaku Kiyo 46:59-62.

Ohta, T., R. Ikuta, M. Nakashima, Y. Morimitsu, T. Samuta, and H. Saiki. 1990. Characteristic flavor of *Kansho-shochu* (sweet potato spirit). Agric. Biol. Chem. 54:1353-1357.

Ohtani, T. and A. Misaki. 1985. An in vitro study of the effects of cell wall polysaccharides of potatoes on digestibilities of their starches. Nippon Eiyo, Shokuryo Gakkaishi 38:363-370.

Ohtani, T., T. Ohi, H. Horikita, M. Nakajima, H. Nabetani, and A. Watanabe. 1987. Recovery of β-amylase from sweet potato with a self-rejection type of dynamic membrane. Nippon Shokuhin Kogyo Gakkaishi 34:640-646.

Osagie, A. and F.I. Opute. 1981. Total lipid and fatty acid composition of tropical tubers. Niger. J. Nutr. Sci. 291:39-46.

Oshima, K and I. Uritani. 1968. Enzymatic synthesis of a β-hydroxy-β-methylglutaric acid-derivative by a cell-free system from sweet potato with black rot. J. Biochem. 63617-625.

Oshima-Oba, K. and I. Uritani. 1969. Enzymatic synthesis of isopentenyl pyrophosphate in sweet potato root tissue in response to infection by black rot fungus. Plant Cell Physiol. 10:827-843.

Oshima-Oba, K., I. Sugiura, and I. Uritani. 1969. The incorporation of leucine-U-^{14}C into ipomeamarone. Agr. Biol. Chem. 33:386-391.

Osuji, G.O. and R.L. Ory. 1987. Regulation of allantoin and allantoic acid degradation in the yam and sweet potato. J. Agric. Food Chem. 35:219-223.

Pace, R.D., C. Bonsi, B.R. Phills, and I.T. Forrester. 1987. Iron content and iron availability in sweet potato tips collected at different times during season. Nutr. Rep. Int. 35:1151-1156.

Pace, R.D., T.E. Sibiya, B.R. Phills, and G.G. Dull. 1985. Calcium, iron, and zinc content of Jewel sweet potato greens as affected by harvesting practices. J. Food Sci. 50:940-941.

Pan, C. and W.F. Tsai. 1987. The occurrence and varietal difference of trypsin inhibitor in sweet potatoes. Kuo Li Tai-wan Ta Hsueh Nung Hsueh Yuan Yen Chiu Pao Kao 27:1-7.

Pan, S.M., T.C. Chang, R.H. Juang, and J.C. Su. 1988. Starch phosphorylase inhibitor is β-amylase. Plant Physiol. 88:1154-1156.

Paterson, D.R., D.R. Earhart, and M.C. Fuqua. 1979. Effects of flooding level on storage root formation, ethylene production, and growth of sweet potato. HortScience 14:739-740.

Peckham, J.C., F.E. Mitchell, Jones, O.H., Jr., and B. Doupnik, Jr. 1972. Atypical interstitial pneumonia in cattle fed moldy sweet potatoes. Amer. Vet. Medical Assoc. 160:169-172.

Pellett, P.L. and S. Shadarevian. 1970. Food composition tables for use in the Middle East, 2nd Ed., American University of Beirut, Beirut. 116 pp.

Pepping, F. and C.M.J. Venicken. 1988. Retinol carotene content of foods consumed in East Africa determined by high performance liquid chromatography. J. Sci. Food Agric. 45:359-371.

Picha, D.H. 1985a. Crude protein, minerals and total carotenoids in sweet potatoes. J. Food Sci. 50:1768-1769.

Picha, D.H. 1985b. HPLC determination of sugars in raw and baked sweet potatoes. J. Food Sci. 50:1189-1190.

Picha, D.H. 1985c. Organic acid determination in sweet potatoes by HPLC. J. Agric. Food Chem. 33:743-745.

Picha, D.H. 1986a. Carbohydrate changes in sweet potatoes during curing and storage. J. Amer. Soc. Hort. Sci. 111:89-92.

Picha, D.H. 1986b. Influence of storage duration and temperature on sweet potato sugar content and chip color. J. Food Sci. 51:239-240.

Picha, D.H. 1986c. Sugar content of baked sweet potatoes from different cultivars and lengths of storage. J. Food Sci. 51:845-846.

Picha, D.H. 1987. Chilling injury, respiration, and sugar changes in sweet potatoes stored at low temperature. J. Amer. Soc. Hort. Sci. 112:497-502.

Purcell, A. E. 1962. Carotenoids of Goldrush sweet potato flakes. Food Technol. 16:99-102.

Purcell, A. E., D. W. Later, and M. L. Lee. 1980. Analysis of the volatile constituents of baked 'Jewel' sweet potatoes. J. Agric. Food Chem. 28:939-941.

Purcell, A. E., D. T. Pope, and W. M. Walter, Jr. 1976a. Effect of length of growing season on protein content of sweet potato cultivars. HortScience 11:31.

Purcell, A. E., H. E. Swaisgood, and D. T. Pope. 1972. Protein and amino acid content of sweetpotato cultivars. J. Amer. Soc. Hort. Sci. 97:30-33.

Purcell, A.E. and W.M. Walter, Jr. 1968a. Autoxidation of carotenes in dehydrated sweet potato flakes using ^{11}C-β-carotene. J. Agr. Food Chem. 16:650-653.

Purcell, A. E. and M. W. Walter, Jr. 1968b. Carotenoids of Centennial Variety sweet potato, *Ipomoea batatas*, L. J. Agric. Food Chem. 16:769-770.

Purcell, A. E. and W. M. Walter, Jr. 1980. Changes in composition of the nonprotein-nitrogen fraction of 'Jewel' sweet potatoes [*Ipomoea batatas* (Lam.)] during storage. J. Agric. Food Chem. 28:842-844.

Purcell, A. E. and W. M. Walter, Jr. 1982. Stability of amino acids during cooking and processing of sweet potatoes. J. Agric. Food Chem. 30:443-444.

Purcell, A. E., W. M. Walter, Jr., and F. G. Giesbrecht. 1976b. Distribution of protein within sweet potato roots (*Ipomoea batatas* L.) J. Agric. Food Chem. 24:64-66.

Purcell, A. E., W. M. Walter, Jr., and F. G. Giesbrecht. 1978a. Changes in dry matter, protein and non-protein nitrogen during storage of sweet potatoes. J. Amer. Soc. Hort. Sci. 103:190-192.

Purcell, A. E., W. M. Walter, Jr., and F. G. Giesbrecht. 1978b. Root, hill, and field variance in protein content of North Carolina sweet potatoes. J. Agric. Food Chem. 26:362-364.

Purcell, A. E., W. M. Walter, Jr., J. J. Nicholoides, W. W. Collins, and H. Chancy. 1982. Nitrogen, potassium, sulfur fertilization, and protein content of sweet potato roots. J. Amer. Soc. Hort. Sci. 107:425-427.

Rao, M.N. and W. Polacchi. 1972. Part II. Amino acid, fatty acid, certain B-vitamin and trace mineral content of some Asian foods. Pages 189-334 *in* Food composition table for use in East Asia, U.S. Department of Health, Education and Welfare and FAO of the UN, Bethesda, MD.

Rebelo da Rocha, Y and R. Shrimpton. 1984. Zinc levels in selected Amazonian foods. Cienc. Tecnol. Aliment. 4:68-78.

Rhodes, M.J.C. and L.S.C. Wooltorton. 1978. Changes in the activity of hydroxycinnamyl CoA:Quinate hydroxycinnamyl transferase and in the levels of chlorogenic acid in potatoes and sweet potatoes stored at various temperatures. Phytochem. 17:1225-1229.

Roushdi, M., M.A. Sarhan, A.A. Fahmy. 1982. Effect of chemical treatments and gamma rays on starch content of sweet potatoes and its properties. Starch 34:243-246.

Roy, F. and M.V. Hedge. 1985. Rapid procedure for purification of β-amylase from *Ipomoea batatas*. J. Chromatogr. 324:489-494.

Ryan, C.A. 1981. Proteinase inhibitors. Pages 351-370, *in* The Biochemistry of Plants vol. 6, "Proteins and Nucleic Acids", A. Marcus (ed.), Academic Press, NY.

Sacher, J.A., J. Tseng, R. Williams, and A. Cabello. 1982. Wound-induced RNase activity in sweet potato. Evidence for regulation at transcription. Plant Physiol. 69:1060-1065.

Sakai, S., H. Imaseki, and I. Uritani. 1970. Biosynthesis of ethylene in sweet potato root tissue. Plant Cell Physiol. 11:737-745.

Sakamoto, S. and J.C. Bouwkamp. 1985. Industrial products from sweet potatoes. Pages 219-23 *in* Sweet potato products: A natural resource for the tropics, edited by J.C. Bouwkamp, CRC Press, Boca Raton, FL.

Sanchez, M.A., M.H. Bertoni, and P. Cattaneo. 1988. Contents and fatty acid composition

255

of total lipids from edible bulbs and roots. An Asoc. Quim. Argent 76:227-235.

Sasaki, T. and K. Kainuma. 1981. Solubilization of starch synthetase bound to starch granules in sweet potato root tubers. Nippon Shokuhin Kogyo Gakkaishi 28:640-646.

Sasaki, T. and K. Kainuma. 1982. Regulation of starch synthesis and external polysaccharide synthesis by gibberellic acid in cultured sweet potato cell. Plant Tissue Cell Cult. 5:255-256.

Sasaki, T. and K. Kainuma. 1984. Control of starch and exocellular polysaccharide biosynthesis by gibberellic acid with cells of sweet potato cultured *in vitro*. Plant Cell Rep. 3:23-26.

Sasaki, T., K. Tadokoro, and S. Suzuki. 1972. The distribution of glucose phosphate isomerase isoenzymes in sweet potato and its tissue culture. Biochem. J. 129:789-791.

Sato, K., I. Uritani, and T. Saito. 1982. Properties of terpene-inducing factor extracted from adults of the sweet potato weevil, *Cylas formicarius Fabricius* (Coleoptera: Brenthidae). Appl. Entomol. Zool. 17:368-374.

Sato, T., F. Kiuchi, and U. Sankawa. 1982. Inhibition of phenylalanine ammonia-lyase by cinnamic acid derivatives and related compounds. Phytochem. 21:845-850.

Sato, T. and U. Sankawa. 1983. Inhibition of phenylalanine ammonia-lyase by flavonoids. Chem. Pharm. Bull. 31:149-155.

Scarlett-Kranz, J.M., B.S. Shane, K.E. McCracken, C.A. Bache, C.B. Littman, and D.J. Lisk. 1986. Survey of nitrate, cadmium and selenium in baby foods-health considerations. J. Food Saf. 8:35-45.

Schadel, W. E. and W. M. Walter, Jr. 1980. Calcium oxalate crystals in the roots of sweet potato. J. Amer. Soc. Hort. Sci. 105:851-854.

Schadel, W. E. and W. M. Walter, Jr. 1981. Localization of phenols and polyphenol oxidase in 'Jewel' sweet potatoes (*Ipomoea batatas* 'Jewel'). Can. J. Bot. 59:1961-1967.

Schmandke, H. and O. Olivarez Guerra. 1969. The carotene, L-ascorbic acid, dehydroascorbic acid and tocopherol content of Cuban vegetable products. Nahrung 13:523-530.

Schneider, J.A. and K. Nakanishi. 1983. A new class of sweet potato phytoalexins. J. Chem. Soc. Chem. Commun. 7:353-355.

Schwartz, S.J. and G.L. Catignani. 1989. Analysis of cis-beta-carotenes in food and colorant additives. Spec. Pub.-R. Soc. Chem. 72:80-82.

Schwartz, S.J. and M. Patroni-Killam. 1985. Detection of cis-trans carotene isomers by two dimensional thin-layer and high-performance liquid chromatography. J. Agric. Food Chem. 33:1160-1163.

Scott, L. E., C. O. Appleman, and W. Wilson. 1944. The discoloration of sweet potatoes during preparation for processing and the oxidase of the root. MD Agric. Exp. Sta. Bull. A33:11-26.

Scott, L. E. and J. C. Bouwkamp. 1974. Seasonal mineral accumulation by the sweet potato. HortScience 9:233-235.

Scott, L. E. and A. A. Kattan. 1957. Varietal differences in the catechol oxidase content of the sweet potato root. J. Amer. Soc. Hort. Sci. 69:436-442.

Scott, L. E. and W. A. Matthew. 1957. Carbohydrate changes in sweet potatoes during curing and storage. Proc. Amer. Soc. Hort. Sci. 70:407-418.

Seog, H.M., Y.K. Park, Y.J. Nam, D.H. Shin, J.P. Kim. 1987. Physicochemical properties of several sweet potato starches. Han'guk Nonghwa Hakhoechi 30:179-185.

Shannon, L.M., I. Uritani, and H. Imaseki. 1971. *De nova* synthesis of peroxidase isozymes in sweet potato. Plant Physiol. 47:493-498.

Sharfuddin, A.F.M. and V. Voican. 1984. Effect of plant density and NPK dose on the chemical composition of fresh and stored tubers of sweet potato. Indian J. Agric. Sci. 54:1094-1096.

Shen, Y. and J. Jiang. 1984. Fluoride in water, soil, foods, and fluoride stains on teeth. Zhonghua Yufangyixue Zazhi. 18:230.

Shigeki, M., T. Hattori, and K. Nakamura. 1986. Structural differences in full-length cDNAs for two classes of sporamin, the major soluble protein of sweet potato tuberous roots. Plant

Haard, N.F. and M. Marshall. 1976. Isoperoxidase changes in soluble and particulate fractions of sweet potato root resulting from cut injury, ethylene and black rot infection. Physiol. Plant Path. 8:195-205.

Haard, N.F. and B. Wasserman. 1976. Induction of phenylalanine ammonia lyase in sweet potato (*Ipomoea batatas*) root by light irradiation and black rot infection. Physiol. Plant Path. 8:207-213.

Haard, N.F. and P.D. Weiss. 1976. Influence of exogenous ethylene on ipomeamarone accumulation in black rot infected sweet potato roots. Phytochem. 15:261-262.

Haissig, B.E. and A.L. Schipper. 1975. Effect of oxidized nucleotide coenzymes and mercaptoethane on stabilization of plant dehydrogenase activity in crude extracts. Physiol. Plant 35:249-255.

Hamasaki, Y. and I. Yamaguti. 1985. Studies of sweet potatoes used for production of sweet potato distilled spirits. (4). Changes in composition during storage. Kagoshima-ken Kogyo Shikenjo Nenpo 31:81-85.

Hammett, H.L. 1974. Total carbohydrate and carotenoid content of sweet potatoes as affected by cultivar and area of production. HortScience 9:467-468.

Hammett, H.L. and B.F. Barrentine. 1961. Some effects of variety, curing, and baking upon the carbohydrate content of sweet potatoes. Proc. Amer. Soc. Hort. Sci. 78:421-426.

Hammett, H.L., T.P. Hernandez, and J.C. Mutler. 1966. Inheritance of fiber content in sweet potato (*Ipomoea batatas* (L.) Lam.) Proc. Amer. Soc. Hort. Sci. 88:486-490.

Hancock, K.W. 1984. A study of growth regulators, IAA-oxidase, and watering levels on storage root initiation in sweet potato (*Ipomoea batatas*). Diss. Abstr. Int. B 45:736-737.

Hashizume, T., S. Suye, T. Soeda, and T. Sugiyama. 1982a. Isolation and characterization of a new glucopyranosyl derivative of 6-(3-methyl-2-butenylamino) purine from sweet potato tubers. FEBS Lett. 144:25-28.

Hashizume, T., S. Suye, and T. Sugiyama. 1981. Occurrence and level of cis-zeatin riboside in sweet potato tubers. Nucleic Acids Symp. Ser. 10:131-134.

Hashizume, T., S. Suye, and T. Sugiyama. 1982b. Isolation and identification of cis-zeatin riboside from tubers of sweet potato. Agric. Biol. Chem. 46:663-665.

Hattori, T. and T. Asahi. 1982. The presence of two forms of succinate dehydrogenase in sweet potato root mitochondria. Plant Cell Physiol. 23:515-523.

Hattori, T. , S. Ichihara, and K. Nakamura. 1987. Processing of a plant vacuolar protein precursor in vitro. Eur. J. Biochem. 166:533-538.

Hattori, T., Y. Iwasaki, S. Sakajo, T. Asahi. 1983. Cell-free synthesis of succinate dehydrogenase and mitochondrial adenosine triphosphatase of sweet potato. Biochem. Biophys. Res. Commun. 113:235-240.

Hattori, T., K. Matsuoka, and K. Nakamura. 1988. Subcellular localization of the sweet potato tuberous root storage protein. Agric. Biol. Chem. 52:1057-1059.

Hattori, T., T. Nakagawa, M. Maeshima, K. Nakamura, and T. Asahi. 1985. Molecular cloning and nucleotide sequence of cDNA for sporamin, the major soluble protein of sweet potato tuberous roots. Plant Mol. Biol. 5:313-320.

Hattori, T. and K. Nakamura. 1988. Genes coding for the major tuberous root protein of sweet potato: Identification of putative regulatory sequence in the 5' upstream region. Plant Mol. Biol. 11:417-426.

Hattori, T., N. Yoshida, and K. Nakamura. 1989. Structural relationship among the members of a multigene family coding for the sweet potato tuberous root storage protein. Plant Mol. Biol. 13:563-572.

Hayase, F. and H. Kato. 1984. Antioxidative components of sweet potatoes. J. Nur. Sci. Vitaminol. 39:37-46.

Hayashi, T. 1986. Accumulation of sucrose in irradiated agricultural products. JARQ 18:295-301.

Hayashi, T., T. Sugimoto, and K. Kawashima. 1984. Effect of gamma-irradiation on the activities of sucrose synthase and sucrose phosphate synthase in potato tubers and sweet potato roots. Nippon Shokuhin Kogyo Gakkaishi Vol. 31:281-284.

Hegde, M.V., F. Roy, and P.N. Joshi. 1979. A new method of the preparation of β-amylase from sweet potato. Prep. Biochem. 9:71-84.

Heinze, P. H. and C. O. Appleman. 1943. A biochemical study of the curing processes in sweet potatoes. Plant Physiol. 18:548-555.

Hiura, M. 1943. Studies in storage and rot of sweet potato. Rept. Gifu Agri. Col. 50:1-5.

Hizukuri, S. 1985. Relationship between the distribution of the chain length of amylopectin and the crystalline structure of starch granules. Carbohydr. Res. 14:295-306.

Hollo, J., E. Laszlo, A. Hoschke, F. El Hawary, and B. Banky. 1982. Recent data on the active center of amylolytic enzymes. Starch 34:304-308.

Holloway, W.D. 1983. Composition of fruit, vegetable, and cereal dietary fiber. J. Sci. Food Agric. 34:1236-1240.

Holloway, W.D., M.E. Argall, W.T. Jealous, J.A. Lee, and J.H. Bradbury. 1989. Organic acids and calcium oxalate in tropical root crops. J. Agric. Food Chem. 37:337-341.

Holloway, W.D., J.A. Monro, J.C. Gurnsey, E.W. Pmare, and N.H. Stace. 1985. Dietary fiber and other constituents of some Tongan foods. J. Food Sci. 50:1756-1757.

Hong, Z., D. Wu, and W. Qi. 1985. Determination of copper, zinc, lead, and cadmium in grains by using atomic absorption spectrophotometry. Huanjing Kexue 6(5):70-72.

Horigome, T., N. Nakayama, and M. Ikeda. 1972. Nutritive value of sweet potato protein produced from the residual products of sweet potato starch industry. Nippon Chikusan Gakkahi-Ho 43:432-437.

Horvat, R. J., R. B. Arrendale, G. G. Dull, G.W. Chapman, Jr., and S. J. Kays. 1991. Volatile constituents and sugars of three diverse cultivars of sweetpotatoes [*Ipomoea batatas* (L.) Lam.]. J. Food Sci. 56:714-715, 742.

Huang, S.Y. and H.S. Wu. 1985. Redox potential used to measure amylose in starch. Hakko Kogaku Kaishi 63:31-37.

Huang, Y., S. Zhang, and R. Yang. 1983. Survey of communal industrial production of caramel by the ammonium process. Tiaowei Fushipin Keji 3:11-12.

Huq, R.S., J.A. Abalaka, and W.L. Stafford. 1983. Folate content of various Nigerian foods. J. Sci. Food Agric. 34:404-406.

Hyodo, H. and I. Uritani. 1965. Purification and properties of o-diphenol oxidases in sweet potato. J. Biochem. (Tokyo) 58:388-395.

Hyodo, H. and I. Uritani. 1966. A study on increase in o-diphenol oxidase activity during incubation of sliced sweet potato tissue. Plant Cell Physiol. 7:137-144.

Hyodo, H. and I. Uritani. 1984. Ethylene production in sweet potato root tissue infected by *Ceratocystis fimbriata*. Plant Cell Physiol. 25:1147-1152.

Ikemiya, M. and H.J. Deobald. 1966. New characteristic α-amylase in sweet potatoes. J. Agr. Food Chem. 14:237-241.

Imaseki, H. 1970. Induction of peroxidase activity by ethylene in sweet potato. Plant Physiol. 46:172-174.

Imaseki, H., T. Asahi, and I. Uritani. 1968a. Investigations on the possible inducers of metabolic changes in injured plant tissues. Pages 189-201 *in* Biochemical Regulation in Diseased Plants or Injury, edited by T. Hirai, J. Hidaka and I. Uritani. Phytopath. Soc. Japan, Tokyo.

Imaseki, H., T. Teranishi, and I. Uritani. 1968b. Production of ethylene by sweet potato roots infected by black rot fungus. Plant Cell Physiol. 9:769-781.

Imaseki, H., T. Teranishi, and I. Uritani. 1968e. Production of ethylene by sweet potato roots infected by black rot fungus. Plant Cell Physiol. 9:769-781.

Imaseki, H., M. Uchiyama, and I. Uritani. 1968c. Effect of ethylene on the inductive increase in metabolic activities in sliced sweet potato roots. Agric. Biol. Chem. 32:387-389.

Imaseki, H., I. Uritani, and M.A. Stahmann. 1968d. Production of ethylene by injured sweet potato tissue. Plant Cell Physiol. 9:757-768.

Imbert, M.P., C.E. Seaforth, and D.B. Williams. 1966. The anthocyanin pigments of the sweet potato *Ipomoea batatas* (L.) Lam. J. Am. Soc. Hort. Sci. 88:481-485.

Imbert, M.P. and L.A. Wilson. 1970. Stimulatory and inhibitory effects of scopoletin on IAA oxidase preparations from sweet potato. Phytochem. 9:1787-1794.

Imbert, M.P. and L.A. Wilson. 1972a. Effects of chlorogenic and caffeic acids on IAA oxidase preparations from sweet potato roots. Phytochem. 11:2671-2676.

Imbert, M.P. and L.A. Wilson. 1972b. IAA oxidase preparations from sweet potato roots. Phytochem. 11:29-36.

Inoue, H., K. Oba, M. Ando, and I. Uritani. 1984a. Enzymic reduction of dehydroipomeamarone to ipomeamarone in sweet potato root tissue infected by *Ceratocystis fimbriata*. Physiol. Plant Path. 25:1-8.

Inoue, H., H. Tsuji, and I. Uritani. 1984b. Characterization and activity change of farnesol dehydrogenase in black rot fungus-infected sweet potato. Agric. Biol. Chem. 48:733-738.

Inoue, H. and I. Uritani. 1980. Conversion of 4-Hydroxydehydromyoporone to other furano-terpenes in *Ceratocystis fimbriata*-infected sweet potato. Agric. Biol. Chem. 44:1935-1936.

Ishida, M., R. Haga, Y. Odawara, T. Yoji, S. Takahashi, and K. Ebara. 1984. Recovering subterranean stem starch and protein. Eur. Pat. Appl. EP 155, 557.

Ito, R., K. Oba, and I. Uritani. 1979. Mechanism for the induction of 3-hydroxy-3-methylglutaryl coenzyme A reductase in $HgCl_2$-treated sweet potato root tissue. Plant Cell Physiol. 20:867-874.

Ito, R., K. Oba, and I. Uritani. 1982. Some problems in the assay method of HMG-CoA reductase activity in sweet potato in the presence of other HMG-CoA utilizing enzymes. Agric. Biol. Chem. 46:2087-2091.

Iwasaki, Y. and T. Asahi. 1983. Purification and characterization of the soluble form of mitochondrial adenosine triphosphatase from sweet potato. Arch. Biochem. Biophys. 227:164-173.

Iwasaki, Y. and T. Asahi. 1985. Intracellular sites of the synthesis of sweet potato mitochondrial FATPase subunits. Plant Mol. Biol. 5:339-346.

Iwasaki, Y., M. Matsuoka, T. Asahi. 1984. Immunological comparisons among energy transducing adenosine triphosphatases from higher plants with respect to the structures of their subunits. FEBS Lett. 17:249-252.

Izumi, H., Y. Tatsumi, and T. Murata. 1984. Effect of storage temperature on changes of ascorbic acid content of cucumber, winter squash, sweet potato, and potato. Nippon Shokuhin Kogyo Gakkaishi 31:47-49.

Jenkins, W.F. and W.S. Anderson. 1956. Geographical location and storage affecting carbohydrates and canning quality in sweet potatoes. Proc. Amer. Soc. Hort. Sci. 68:407-411.

Jenkins, W.F. and M. Gieger. 1957a. Curing, baking time and temperatures affecting carbohydrates in sweet potatoes. Proc. Amer. Soc. Hort. Sci. 70:419-424.

Jenkins, W.F. and M. Gieger. 1957b. Quality in baked sweet potatoes affected by varieties and post-harvest treatments. Food Res. 22:32-36.

Jenkins, W.F. and E.L. Moore. 1954. The distribution of ascorbic acid and latex vessels in three tissue regions of sweet potatoes. Proc. Amer. Soc. Hort. Sci. 63:389-392.

Jenkins, W.F. and E.L. Moore. 1956. Carbohydrate and ascorbic acid in sweet potatoes as affected by time and sampling techniques. Proc. Amer. Soc. Hort. Sci. 67:490-492.

Jones, A. 1972. Mass selection for low oxidation in sweet potato. J. Amer. Soc. Hort. Sci. 97:714-718.

Jones, A, P.D. Dukes, M.G. Hamilton, R.A. Baumgardner. 1980. Selection of low fiber content in sweet potato. HortScience 15:797-798.

Jones, D.B. and C.E.F. Gersdorff. 1931. Ipomoein, a globulin from sweet potatoes, *Ipomoea batatas*. Isolation of a secondary protein derived from ipomoein by enzymic action. J. Biol. Chem. 93:119-126.

Jones, A., C.E. Steinbauer, and D.T. Pope. 1969. Quantitative inheritance of ten root traits in sweetpotatoes. J. Amer. Soc. Hort. Sci. 94:271-275.

Kahl, G., M. Furuta, K. Oba, and I. Uritani. 1982. Wounding-induced enhancement of the activity of chromatin-bound DNA-dependent RNA polymerases in sweet potato root. Agric. Biol. Chem. 46:2457-2463.

Kainuma, K. and D. French. 1970. Action of pancreatic α-amylase and sweet potato β-amylase on 6^2-and 6^3-α-glucosylmalto-oligosaccharides. North-Holland Pub. Co. 6:182-186.

Kanazawa, Y., T. Asahi, and I. Uritani. 1967. Changes in b-type heme content in relation to peroxidase biosynthesis in injured sweet potato roots. Plant Cell Physiol. 8:249-262.

Kanazawa, Y., H. Shichi, and I. Uritani. 1965. Biosynthesis of peroxidases in sliced or black rot-infected sweet potato slices. Agr. Biol. Chem. 29:840-847.

Kanie, M., T. Nagahama, and S. Fujimoto. 1974. Studies on some effects of the treatments with hot water on sweet potatoes. Bull. Fac. Agr. Kagoshima Univ. 24:155-164.

Kanie, M., T. Nagahama, and S. Fujimoto. 1976. Fractionation of tuber components by a membrane system of the sweet potato treated with "hot water": Movement of β-amylase. Nippon Nogei Kogaku Kaishi 50:163-168.

Kanie, M., T. Nagahama, S. Fujimoto, and S. Kijima. 1970. A screening test for high-sugar individuals and lines of sweet potato. Bull. Fac. Agr. Kagoshima Univ. 20.

Katayama, Y. and S. Shida. 1961. Studies on the variation in leaf pigment by means of paper chromatography. III. Leaf pigments and carbon assimilation in some strains of sweet potato. Mem. Fac. Agric. Univ. Miyasaki 3:11-16.

Kato, Y. and I. Uritani. 1972. Ethylene biosynthesis in diseased sweet potato root tissue with special reference to methionine system. Agri. Biol. Chem. 36:2601-2604.

Kato, C. and I. Uritani. 1976. Changes in carbohydrate content of sweet potato in response to cutting and infection by black rot fungus. Ann. Phytopath. Soc. Jpn. 42:181-186.

Kawabe, H., Y. Sugiura, M. Terauchi, and H. Tanaka. 1984. Manganese (III)-containing acid phosphatase. Properties of iron (III)-substituted enzyme and function of manganese (III) and iron (III) in plant and mammalian acid phosphatases. Biochem. Biophys. Acta 784:81-89.

Kawashima, K. and I. Uritani. 1963. Occurrence of peroxidase in sweet potato infected by the black rot. Agric. Biol. Chem. 27:409-417.

Kawashima. 1965. Some properties of peroxidase produced in sweet potato infected by the black rot fungus. Plant Cell Physiol. 6:247-265.

Kays, S.J. 1989. Strategies for selecting conventional and new flavor types of tropical root and tuber crops to increase consumer acceptance and use. Eighth Intern. Symp. Trop. Root Crops, p. 178-188, Bangkok, Thailand.

Kays, S.J. 1991. Postharvest physiology of perishable plant products. Van Nostrand Reinholt, N.Y. 532pp.

Kays, S.J. and R.J. Horvat. 1984. A comparison of the volatile constituents and sugars of representative Asian, Central American and North American sweet potatoes. Sixth Intern. Symp. Trop. Root Crops, pp. 577-586, Intern. Potato Center, Lima, Peru.

Keshinro, O.O. 1983. The free and total folate activity in some commonly available tropical foodstuffs. Food Chem. 11:87-93.

Khachik, F. and G.R. Beecher. 1987. Application of a c-45-d-carotene as an internal standard for the quantification of carotenoids in yellow/orange vegetables by liquid chromatography. J. Agric. Food Chem. 35:732-738.

Kim, J.P., Y.G. Ann, W.M. Shim. 1985. Purification of sweet potato β-amylase. Han'guk Saenghwa Hakhoechi 18:290-296.

Kim, S.R., R.H. Lane, M. Abdel-Ghany, K.R. Stitt. 1987. Influence of extractant on L-ascorbic acid recovery from selected foods and beverages. J. Food Qual. 10:1-7.

Kim, W.K., I. Oguni, and I. Uritani. 1974. Phytoalexin induction in sweet potato roots by amino acids. Agr. Biol. Chem. 38:2567-2568.

Kim, M.C., N.K. Sung, K.H. Shim, M.H. Lee, and I. Lee. 1981. The contents of heavy metal in fruits and vegetables collected from Jinju district, Korea. Korean J. Food Sci. Technol. 13:299-306.

Kim, W.K. and I. Uritani. 1974. Fungal extracts that induce phytoalexins in sweet potato roots. Plant Cell Physiol. 15:1093-1098.

Kimber, A.J. 1975. Papua New Guinea Food Crops Conference Proceedings. Dept. Prim. Indust. K. Wilson, and R.M. Bourke (eds.), Port Moresby, New Guinea, p. 63.

Kimbrough, W.D., E.A. Fieger, and H. Lewis. 1946. Effect of date of planting and time of harvesting on the carotene content of sweetpotatoes of the Porto Rico Variety. Proc. Am. Soc. Hort. Sci. 47:400-402.

Kimura, A. and S. Chiba. 1983. Studies on anomeric forms of products of carbohydrases. Part II. Quantitative study of anomeric forms of maltose produced by α- and β-amylases. Agric. Bio. Chem. 47:1747-1753.

Kimura, T., K. Nakamura, H. Kajiura, H. Hattori, N. Nelson, and T. Asahi. 1989. Correspondence of minor subunits of plant mitochondrial FATPase to FATPase subunits of other organisms. J. Biol. Chem. 264:3183-3186.

Kitada, Y., M. Sasaki, Y. Yamazoe, and H. Nakazawa. 1988. Measurement of thermal behavior and amylose content of kudzu and sweet potato starches. Nippon Shokuhn Kogyo Gakkaishi 35:135-140.

Kobayashi, K., K. Nakamura, T. Asahi. 1987. CF_1ATPase α- and ϵ-subunit genes are separated in the sweet potato chloroplast genome. Nucleic Acids Res. 15:7177.

Kobayashi, K., I. Yukimoto, T. Sasaki, K. Nakamura, and T. Asahi. 1986. Putative amino-terminal presequence for β-subunit of plant mitochondrial FATPase deduced from the amino-terminal sequence of the mature subunit. FEBS Lett. 203:144-148.

Koehler, P. E. and S. J. Kays. 1991. Sweetpotato flavor: Quantitative and qualitative assessment of optimum sweetness. J. Food Qual. (in review).

Kojima, M. 1976. Possible involvement of furanoterpenoid phytoalexins in establishing host-parasite specificity between sweet potato and various strains of *Ceratocystis fimbriata*. Physiol. Plant Path. 8:97-111.

Kojima, M. 1982. Biochemical studies on high and low molecular weight substances which are involved in defence reactions of host plant. Nippon Nogei Kagaku Kaishi 56:675-683.

Kojima, M. and T. Kondo. 1985. An enzyme in sweet potato root which catalyzes conversion of chlorogenic acid, 3-O-caffeoylquinic acid, to isochlorogenic acid, 3,5-dicaffeoylquinic acid. Agric. Biol. Chem. 49:2467-2469.

Kojima, M., T. Minamikawa, H. Hyodo, and I. Uritani. 1969. Incorporation of some possible radioactive intermediates into chlorogenic acid in sliced sweet potato tissues. Plant Cell Physiol. 10:471-474.

Kojima, M. and I. Uritani. 1972a. Elucidation of the structure of a possible intermediate in chlorogenic acid biosynthesis in sweet potato root tissue. Plant Cell Physiol. 13:1075-1084.

Kojima, M. and I. Uritani. 1972b. Structure of possible intermediate of chlorogenic acid biosynthesis in sweet potato root tissue. Agr. Biol. Chem. 36:1643-1645.

Kojima, M. and I. Uritani. 1972c. Studies on chlorogenic acid biosynthesis in sweet potato root tissue using *trans*-cinnamic acid-2-^{14}C and quinic acid-G-[3]H[1]. Plant Cell Physiol. 13:311-319.

Kojima, M. and I. Uritani. 1973. Studies on chlorogenic acid biosynthesis in sweet potato root tissue in special reference to the isolation of a chlorogenic acid intermediate. Plant Physiol. 51:768-771.

Kojima, M. and R.J.A. Villegas. 1984. Detection of the enzyme in sweet potato root which catalyzes trans-esterification between 1-O-p-Coumaroyl-D-glucose and D-Quinic acid. Agric. Biol. Chem. 48:2397-2399.

Kondo, J. and Y. Morita. 1952. Studies on phytoperoxidase. Isolation and purification of sweet potato peroxidases and their absorption spectra. Bull. Res. Inst. Food Sci. Kyoto Univ. (10):33-45.

Kujira, Y. 1986. Effect of culture conditions on L-ascorbic acid content in sweet potato. Nippon Eiyo, Shokuryo Gakkaishi 39:234-237.

Lanier, J. J. and W. A. Sistrunk. 1979. Influence of cooking method on quality attributes and vitamin content of sweet potatoes. J. Food Sci. 44:374-376,380.

Larbi, A. and E. M'barek. 1985. Dietary fiber and phytic acid levels in the major food items consumed in Morocco. Nutr. Rep. Int. 31:469-476.

Lee, W.G. and G. R. Ammerman. 1974. Carotene stereoisomerization in sweet potatoes as affected by rotating and still retort canning processes. J. Food Sci. 39:1188-1190.

Lee, T.S., S.O. Park, M.W. Lee. 1981. Determination of organic acid of Kochuzang prepared from various starch sources. Hanguk Nonghwa Hakhoe Chi 24:120-125.

Lee, K.A., M.S. Shin, and S.Y. Ahn. 1985. Changes in pectic substances of sweet potato cultivars during baking. Han'guk Sikp'um Kwahakhoechi 17:421-425.

Leung, W.T. Wu, F. Busson, and C. Jardin. 1968. Food composition table for use in Africa. US Department of Health, Education and Welfare Public Health Service, Maryland and FAO Nutrition Division, Rome. 306 pp.

Leung, W.T. Wu, R.R. Butrum, and F.H. Chang. 1972. Part I. Proximate composition, mineral and vitamin contents of East Asian foods. Pages 1-187 in Food composition table for use in East Asia", US Department of Health, Education and Welfare and FAO of the UN, Bethesda, MD.

Leung, W.T. Wu and M. Flores. 1961. Food composition table for use in Latin America. Institute of nutrition of Central America and Panama, Guatemala/Interdepartmental Committee on nutrition for national defense, Bethesda, MD. 145 pp.

Li, H.S. and K. Oba. 1985. Major soluble proteins of sweet potato roots and changes in proteins after cutting, infection, or storage. Agric. Biol. Chem. 49:737-744.

Li, L. 1974. Variation in protein content and its relation to other characters in sweet potato. J. Agric. Assoc. China 88:17-22.

Li, L. 1977. J. Agric. Assoc. China. The inheritance of crude protein content and its correlation with root yield in sweet potatoes. 100:78-86.

Lii, C.Y., T.W. Chiou, and Y.L. Chu. 1987. The degree of branching in amylose from tuber and legume starches. Proc. Natl. Sci. Counc. Repub. China, Pt.A: Phys. Sci. Eng. 11:341-345.

Lim, S.Y., M.S. Shin, and S.Y. Ahn. 1985. Physicochemical properties and characteristics on lintnerization of sweet potato starches from three cultivars. Han'gu, Nonghwa Hakhoechi 28:156-161.

Lin, Y.H. 1987. Some factors affecting levels of trypsin inhibitor activity of sweet potato (Ipomoea batatas Lam.) roots. Bot. Bul. Acad. Sinica. 28:139-149.

Lin, Y.H. 1989a. Relationship between trypsin-inhibitor activity and water-soluble protein and cumulative rainfall in sweet potatoes. J. Amer. Soc. Hort. Sci. 114:814-818.

Lin, Y.H. 1989b. Trypsin inhibitors and proteases of sweet potatoes. Chung Yang Yen Chiu Yuan Chih Wu Yen Chiu So Chuan K'an 8:57-62.

Lin, Y.H. and H.Y. Chan. 1990. Purification and properties of endopeptidases of sprouts of sweet potato (Ipomoea batatas L. Lam. Cv. Tainong 64). Bot. Bull. Academia Sinica 31:19-27.

Lin, Y.H. and H.L. Chen. 1980. Level and heat stability of trypsin inhibitor activity among sweet potato (Ipomoea batatas Lam.) varieties. Bot. Bull. Acad. Sinica 21:1-13.

Lin, Y.H., J.F. Cheng, and H.Y. Fu. 1983. Partial purification and some properties of trypsin inhibitors of sweet potato (Ipomoea batatas Lam.) roots. Bot. Bull. Academia Sinica 24:103-113.

Lin, Y.H. and S.P. Ho. 1986. Soluble leaf protein of sweet potato cultivars. Bot. Bull. Academia Sinica 27:175-186.

Lin, Y.H. and B.S. Tsu. 1987. Some factors affecting levels of trypsin inhibitor activity of sweet potato (Ipomoea batatas Lam.) roots. Bot. Bull. Academia Sinica 28:139-149.

Lineback, D.R. and A.L. Sayed. 1971. Effect of dimethyl sulfoxide on amylase activity. Carbohyd. Res. 17:453-456.

Liu, G., F. Cheng, S. Gao, and M. Li. 1985a. Effect of arsenic in soil on plants - research on "arsenic-toxic field" in South China. Zhongguo Nongye Kexue (Beijing) 4:9-16.

Liu, S.Y., C.L. Liang, and L. Li. 1985b. Studies on the physicochemical properties of the tubers of new sweet potato lines. Chung-hua Nung Yeh Yen Chiu 34:21-32.

Loebenstein, G. and N. Linsey. 1961. Peroxidase activity in virus-infected sweet potatoes. Phytopath. 51:533-537.

Lopez, A., H.L. Williams, and F.W. Cooler. 1980. Essential elements in fresh and in canned sweet potatoes. J. Food Sci. 45:675-680.

Lund, E.D. and J.M. Smoot. 1982. Dietary fiber content of some tropical fruits and vegetables. J. Agric. Food Chem. 39:1123-1127.

MacLeod, F.L., M.R. Armstrong, M.E. Heap, and L.A. Tolbert. 1935. The vitamin A content of five varieties of sweet potatoes. J. Agr. Res. 50:181-187.

MacLeod, F.L. and E. Utley. 1938. Vitamin A values. Tenn. Agr. Exp. Sta. Ann. Rept. 51:64.

MacNair, V. 1956. Effects of storage and cooking on carotene and ascorbic acid content of some sweet potatoes grown in northwest Arkansas. Ark. Agr. Expt. Sta. Bull. 574.

Madamba, L.S.P., A.R. Bustrillos, and E.L. San Pedro. 1975. Sweet potato starch: Physicochemical properties of the whole starch. Philipp. Agric. 58(9-10):338-350.

Madamba, L.S.P. and E.L. San Pedro. 1976a. Chemical composition of sweet potato flour. Philipp. Agric. 59(9-10):350-355.

Madamba, L.S.P. and E.L. San Pedro. 1976b. Varietal differences in amylose content of sweet potato starch. Kimika 1:26-32.

Maeshima, M. and T. Asahi. 1981. Mechanism of increase in cytochrome c oxidase activity in sweet potato root tissue during aging of slices. J. Biochem. 90:391-397.

Maeshima, M., T. Asahi, and I. Uritani. 1980. Effect of temperature on the activity and stability of plant cytochrome c oxidase. Agri. Biol. Chem. 44:2351-2356.

Maeshima, M., T. Hattori, and T. Asahi. 1987. Purification of complexes II and IV from plant mitochondria. Methods Enzymol. 148:491-501.

Maeshima, M., T. Nakagawa, and T. Asahi. 1989. N-terminal amino acid sequence and processing site of sweet potato cytochrome c oxidase subunit II. Plant Cell Physiol. 30:1187-1188.

Maeshima, M., T. Saska, and T. Asahi. 1985. Characterization of major proteins in sweet potato tuberous roots. Phytochem. 24:1899-1902.

Makki, H.M., A.Y. Abdel-Rahman, M.K.M. Khalil, and M.S. Mohamed. 1986. Chemical composition of Egyptian sweet potatoes. Food Chem. 20:39-44.

Martin, F.W. 1983. The carotenoid pigments of white-fleshed sweet potatoes-reference to their potential value as sources of vitamin A activity. J. Agric. Univ. P.R. 67:494-500.

Martin, F.W. 1984. Techniques and problems in small scale production of flour from sweet potato. J. Agric. Univ. P.R. 68:423-432.

Martin, F.W. 1986. Sugars in staple type sweet potatoes as affected by cooking and storage. J. Agric. Univ. P.R. 70:121-126.

Martin, W. J., V. C. Hasling, and E. A. Catalano. 1976. Ipomeamarone content in diseased and nondiseased tissues of sweet potatoes infected with different pathogens. Phytopath. 66:678-679.

Martin, W. J., V. C. Hasling, E. A. Catalano, and H. P. Dupuy. 1978. Effect of sweet potato cultivars and pathogens Ceratocystis fimbriata, Sclerotium rolfsii, Diplodia tubericola on ipomeamarone content of diseased tissue. Phytopath. 68:863-865.

Matsuno, H. and I. Uritani. 1972. Physiological behaviour of peroxidase isozymes in sweet potato root tissue injured by cutting or with black rot. Plant Cell Physiol. 13:1091-1101.

Matsuo, M., K. Azuma, and S. Morimoto. 1986. Suppressive effect of seasonings on heat-degradation of ascorbic acid in potatoes and sweet potatoes. Nippon Eiyo, Shokuryo Gakkaishi 39:479-483.

Matsuo, T., S. Itoo, N. Murofushi, N. Takahashi, M. Kobayashi, and T. Chishiki. 1984. Identification of gibberellins in the seeds of sweet potato (Ipomoea batatas Lam.) and several other Convolvulaceae plants. Agric. Biol. Chem. 48:2935-2941.

Matsuo, T., H. Mitsuzone, R. Okada, and S. Itoo. 1988. Variations in the levels of major free cytokinins and free abscisic acid during tuber development of sweet potato. J. Plant Growth Regul. 7:249-258.

Matsuo, T., T. Yoneda, and S. Itoo. 1983. Identification of free cytokinins and the changes in endogenous levels during tuber development of sweet potato. Plant Cell Physiol. 24:1305-1312.

Matsuoka, K. 1988. The determination of vitamin C in Benihayato (sweet potato, Kyushu No. 87). Kumamoto Joshi Daigaku Gakujutsu Kiyo 40:113-119.

Matsushita, K. and I. Uritani. 1975. Effects of cycloheximide, actinomycin D and ethylene on the increase and subsequent decrease in acid invertase activity in wounded sweet potato. Plant Cell Physiol. 16:203-210.

McArdle, R.N. 1984. The use of endogenous amylase to produce fermentable saccharides in *Ipomoea batatas* (L.) Lam. and *Zea mays* (L.). Diss. Abstr. Int. B. 45:1418.

Meredith, F. and G. Dull. 1979. Amino acid levels in canned sweet potatoes and snap beans. Food Tech. 38:55-57.

Mihashi, M., S. Sakai, and T. Miyake. 1987. Manufacture of dehydrated foods. Jpn. Kokai Tokkyo Koho JP 62,126,939.

Miller, J.C. and H.M. Covington. 1942. Some factors affecting the carotene content of sweet potato. Proc. Amer. Soc. Hort Sci. 40:519-522.

Minamikawa, T., M. Kojima, and I. Uritani. 1966. Changes in activities of 5-dihydroquinate hydrolyase and shikimate-NADP oxidoreductase in sliced sweet potato roots. Plant Cell Physiol. 7:583-591.

Minamikawa, T. and I. Uritani. 1965. Phenylalanine ammonia-lyase in sliced sweet potato roots. J. Biochem. (Tokyo) 57:678-688.

Monro, J.A., W.D. Holloway, and J. Lee. 1986. Elemental analysis of fruit and vegetables from Tonga. J. Food Sci. 51:522-523.

Moriguchi, T., R.J.A. Villegas, T. Kondo, and M. Kojima. 1988. Isolation of 1-O-*trans*-p-coumaroyl-β-D-glucopyranose from sweet potato roots and examination of its role in chlorogenic acid biosynthesis. Plant Cell Physiol. 29:1221-1226.

Morrison, T.A. 1990. The activity of α- and β-amylase in staple-type and traditional sweet potato lines with varying starch hydrolysis potential. Diss. Abstr. Int. B 51:1571.

Murakami, Y. 1968. Gibberellin-like substances in roots of *Oryza sativa, Pharbitis nil,* and *Ipomoea batatas,* and the site of their synthesis in the plant. Bot. Mag. Tokyo 81:334-343.

Murakami, Y. 1970. A survey of gibberellins in shoots of angiosperms by rice seedling test. Bot. Mag. Tokyo 83:312-324.

Murakami, S., T. Hattori, and K. Nakamura. 1986. Structural differences in full-length cDNAs for two classes of sporamin, the major soluble protein of sweet potato tuberous roots. Plant Mol. Biol. 7:343-355.

Murata, N. 1983. Molecular species composition of phosphatidylglycerols from chilling-sensitive and chilling-resistant plants. Plant Cell Physiol. 24:81-86.

Murata, N. and H. Hoshi. 1984. Sulfoquinovosyl diacylglycerols in chilling-sensitive and chilling-resistant plants. Plant Cell Physiol. 25:1241-1245.

Murata, N., N. Sato, and N. Takahashi. 1984a. Phosphatidylserines from higher plants contain very-long-chain saturated fatty acids. Dev. Plant Biol. 9:153-156.

Murata, N., N. Sato, and N. Takahashi. 1984b. Very-long-chain saturated fatty acids in phosphatidylserine from higher plant tissues. Biochim. Biophys. Acta 795:147-150.

Murata, N., N. Sato, N. Takahashi, and Y. Hamazaki. 1982. Compositions and positional distributions of fatty acids in phospholipids from leaves of chilling-sensitive and chilling-resistant plants. Plant Cell Physiol. 23:1071-1079.

Murata, N. and J. Yamaya. 1984. Temperature-dependent phase behavior of phosphatidylglycerols from chilling-sensitive and chilling-resistant plants. Plant Physiol. 74:1016-1024.

Murata, T. 1971. Sucrose synthetase of sweet potato roots. II. A kinetic study. Agr. Biol. Chem. 35:1441-1448.

Murata, T. 1972. Sucrose phosphate synthetase from various plant origins. Agr. Biol. Chem. 36:187-1884.

Murata, T. and T. Akazawa. 1968. Enzymic mechanism of starch synthesis in sweet potato roots. I. Requirement of potassium ions for starch synthetase. Arch. Biochem. Biophys. 126:873-879.

Murata, T. and T. Akazawa. 1969. Enzymic mechanisms of starch synthesis in sweet potato roots. II. Enhancement of the starch synthetase activity by maltooligosaccharides. Arch. Biochem. Biophys. 130:604-609.

Nagahama, T., K. Inoue, Y. Nobori, S. Fujimoto, and M. Kanie. 1977. On some components in a steam distillate of sweet potato. Nippon Nogei Kagaku Kaishi 51:597-602.

Nagashima, N., M. Yamazaki, and A. Kawabata. 1989. Some physicochemical properties of starches from kudzu and sweet potato. Nippon Kasei Gakkaishi 40:683-690.

Nakagawa, T., M. Maeshima, K. Nakamura, and T. Asahi. 1990. Molecular cloning of a cDNA for the smallest nuclear-encoded subunit of sweet potato cytochrome c oxidase. Analysis with the cDNA of the structure and import into mitochondria of the subunit. Eur. J. Biochem. 191:557-561.

Nakamura, K. and T. Asahi. 1990. Cloning of a mitochondria-targeting signal sequence from sweet potato. Jpn. Kokai Tokkyo Koho JP 02 97, 390.

Nakamura, K., T. Hattori, and K. Matsuoka. 1988. Mechanism of protein accumulation and its control in the root of sweet potato. Kagaku to Seibutsu 26:391-398.

Nakatani, M. 1989. Application of enzyme immunoassay for determination of endogenous abscisic acid in sweet potato. Japan J. Crop Sci. 58:137-139.

Nakayama, S. and S. Amagase. 1963. An improved method for the purification of sweet potato β-amylase. J. Biochem. 54:375-377.

Neves, V.A. nd E.J. Lourenco. 1985. Extraction and the activity of the peroxidase and polyphenoloxidase of sweet potatoes (*Ipomoea batatas* Lam.). Rev. Cienc. Farm. 7:101-107.

Nishio, K. 1984. Activities of β-glucosidase and β-galactosidase in plants. Shokumotsu-hen 32:37-42.

Nottingham, S. F., K.-C. Son, R. F. Severson, R. F. Arrendale, and S. J. Kays. 1989. Attraction of adult sweetpotato weevils, *Cylas formicarius elegantulus* (Summers), (Coleoptera:Curculionidae), to sweetpotato leaf and root volatiles. J. Chem. Ecol. 15:895-903.

Nozue, M., J. Kawai, and K. Yoshitama. 1987. Selection of a high anthocyanin-producing cell line of sweet potato cell cultures and identification of pigments. J. Plant Physiol. 129:81-88.

Nozue, M., M. Kikuma, Y. Miyamoto, E. Fukuzaki, T. Matsumura, and Y. Hashimoto. 1988. Red anthocyanin pigment and its manufacture with callus culture of *Ipomoea batatas*. Jpn. Kokai Tokyo Koho JP 63,233,993.

Nozue, M. and H. Yasudo. 1985. Occurrence of anthocyanoplasts in cell suspension cultures of sweet potato. Plant Cell Rep. 4:252-255.

Oba, K., H. Shibata, and I. Uritani. 1970. The mechanism supplying acetyl-CoA for terpene biosynthesis in sweet potato with black rot; incorporation of acetate-2-^{14}C, pyruvate-3-^{14}C and citrate-2-^{14}C into ipomeamarone. Plant Cell Physiol. 11:507-510.

Oba, K., H. Tatematsu, K. Yamashita, and I. Uritani. 1976. Induction of furano-terpene production and formation of the enzyme system from mevalonate to isopentenyl pyrophosphate in sweet potato root tissue injured by *Ceratocystis fimbriata* and by toxic chemicals. Plant Physiol. 58:51-56.

Oba, K. and I. Uritani. 1975. Purification and characterization of pyruvate decarboxylase from sweet potato roots. J. Biochem. 77:1205-1213.

Oba, K. and I. Uritani. 1982a. L-Lactate dehydrogenase isozymes from sweet potato roots. Methods Enzymol. 89:345-351.

Oba, K. and I. Uritani. 1982b. Pyruvate decarboxylase from sweet potato roots. Methods Enzymol. 90:528-532.

Oba, K., R. Yu, and M. Fujita. 1982. Metabolic alterations in response to wounding and infection. Plant Infect. 157-173.

Oguni, I. and I. Uritani. 1971. Utilization of ethanol-2-^{14}C for the biogenesis of ipomeamarone by sweet potato root tissue infected with *Ceratocystis fimbriata*. Agric. Biol. Chem. 35:357-362.

Oguni, I, K. Oshima, H. Imaseki, and I. Uritani. 1969. Biochemical studies on the terpene metabolism in sweet potato root tissue with black rot. Effect of C_{10}- and C_{15}-terpenols on acetate-2-^{14}C incorporation into ipomeamarone. Agr. Biol. Chem. 33:50-62.

Ohi, A. and F. Miyagawa. 1982. Studies on yam (*Discorea japonica*) amylase. Sagami Joshi Daigaku Kiyo 46:59-62.

Ohta, T., R. Ikuta, M. Nakashima, Y. Morimitsu, T. Samuta, and H. Saiki. 1990. Characteristic flavor of *Kansho-shochu* (sweet potato spirit). Agric. Biol. Chem. 54:1353-1357.

Ohtani, T. and A. Misaki. 1985. An in vitro study of the effects of cell wall polysaccharides of potatoes on digestibilities of their starches. Nippon Eiyo, Shokuryo Gakkaishi 38:363-370.

Ohtani, T., T. Ohi, H. Horikita, M. Nakajima, H. Nabetani, and A. Watanabe. 1987. Recovery of β-amylase from sweet potato with a self-rejection type of dynamic membrane. Nippon Shokuhin Kogyo Gakkaishi 34:640-646.

Osagie, A. and F.I. Opute. 1981. Total lipid and fatty acid composition of tropical tubers. Niger. J. Nutr. Sci. 291:39-46.

Oshima, K and I. Uritani. 1968. Enzymatic synthesis of a β-hydroxy-β-methylglutaric acid-derivative by a cell-free system from sweet potato with black rot. J. Biochem. 63617-625.

Oshima-Oba, K. and I. Uritani. 1969. Enzymatic synthesis of isopentenyl pyrophosphate in sweet potato root tissue in response to infection by black rot fungus. Plant Cell Physiol. 10:827-843.

Oshima-Oba, K., I. Sugiura, and I. Uritani. 1969. The incorporation of leucine-U-^{14}C into ipomeamarone. Agr. Biol. Chem. 33:386-391.

Osuji, G.O. and R.L. Ory. 1987. Regulation of allantoin and allantoic acid degradation in the yam and sweet potato. J. Agric. Food Chem. 35:219-223.

Pace, R.D., C. Bonsi, B.R. Phills, and I.T. Forrester. 1987. Iron content and iron availability in sweet potato tips collected at different times during season. Nutr. Rep. Int. 35:1151-1156.

Pace, R.D., T.E. Sibiya, B.R. Phills, and G.G. Dull. 1985. Calcium, iron, and zinc content of Jewel sweet potato greens as affected by harvesting practices. J. Food Sci. 50:940-941.

Pan, C. and W.F. Tsai. 1987. The occurrence and varietal difference of trypsin inhibitor in sweet potatoes. Kuo Li Tai-wan Ta Hsueh Nung Hsueh Yuan Yen Chiu Pao Kao 27:1-7.

Pan, S.M., T.C. Chang, R.H. Juang, and J.C. Su. 1988. Starch phosphorylase inhibitor is β-amylase. Plant Physiol. 88:1154-1156.

Paterson, D.R., D.R. Earhart, and M.C. Fuqua. 1979. Effects of flooding level on storage root formation, ethylene production, and growth of sweet potato. HortScience 14:739-740.

Peckham, J.C., F.E. Mitchell, Jones, O.H., Jr., and B. Doupnik, Jr. 1972. Atypical interstitial pneumonia in cattle fed moldy sweet potatoes. Amer. Vet. Medical Assoc. 160:169-172.

Pellett, P.L. and S. Shadarevian. 1970. Food composition tables for use in the Middle East, 2nd Ed., American University of Beirut, Beirut. 116 pp.

Pepping, F. and C.M.J. Venicken. 1988. Retinol carotene content of foods consumed in East Africa determined by high performance liquid chromatography. J. Sci. Food Agric. 45:359-371.

Picha, D.H. 1985a. Crude protein, minerals and total carotenoids in sweet potatoes. J. Food Sci. 50:1768-1769.

Picha, D.H. 1985b. HPLC determination of sugars in raw and baked sweet potatoes. J. Food Sci. 50:1189-1190.

Picha, D.H. 1985c. Organic acid determination in sweet potatoes by HPLC. J. Agric. Food Chem. 33:743-745.

Picha, D.H. 1986a. Carbohydrate changes in sweet potatoes during curing and storage. J. Amer. Soc. Hort. Sci. 111:89-92.

Picha, D.H. 1986b. Influence of storage duration and temperature on sweet potato sugar content and chip color. J. Food Sci. 51:239-240.

Picha, D.H. 1986c. Sugar content of baked sweet potatoes from different cultivars and lengths of storage. J. Food Sci. 51:845-846.

Picha, D.H. 1987. Chilling injury, respiration, and sugar changes in sweet potatoes stored at low temperature. J. Amer. Soc. Hort. Sci. 112:497-502.

Purcell, A. E. 1962. Carotenoids of Goldrush sweet potato flakes. Food Technol. 16:99-102.

Purcell, A. E., D. W. Later, and M. L. Lee. 1980. Analysis of the volatile constituents of baked 'Jewel' sweet potatoes. J. Agric. Food Chem. 28:939-941.

Purcell, A. E., D. T. Pope, and W. M. Walter, Jr. 1976a. Effect of length of growing season on protein content of sweet potato cultivars. HortScience 11:31.

Purcell, A. E., H. E. Swaisgood, and D. T. Pope. 1972. Protein and amino acid content of sweetpotato cultivars. J. Amer. Soc. Hort. Sci. 97:30-33.

Purcell, A.E. and W.M. Walter, Jr. 1968a. Autoxidation of carotenes in dehydrated sweet potato flakes using ^{11}C-β-carotene. J. Agr. Food Chem. 16:650-653.

Purcell, A. E. and M. W. Walter, Jr. 1968b. Carotenoids of Centennial Variety sweet potato, *Ipomoea batatas*, L. J. Agric. Food Chem. 16:769-770.

Purcell, A. E. and W. M. Walter, Jr. 1980. Changes in composition of the nonprotein-nitrogen fraction of 'Jewel' sweet potatoes [*Ipomoea batatas* (Lam.)] during storage. J. Agric. Food Chem. 28:842-844.

Purcell, A. E. and W. M. Walter, Jr. 1982. Stability of amino acids during cooking and processing of sweet potatoes. J. Agric. Food Chem. 30:443-444.

Purcell, A. E., W. M. Walter, Jr., and F. G. Giesbrecht. 1976b. Distribution of protein within sweet potato roots (*Ipomoea batatas* L.) J. Agric. Food Chem. 24:64-66.

Purcell, A. E., W. M. Walter, Jr., and F. G. Giesbrecht. 1978a. Changes in dry matter, protein and non-protein nitrogen during storage of sweet potatoes. J. Amer. Soc. Hort. Sci. 103:190-192.

Purcell, A. E., W. M. Walter, Jr., and F. G. Giesbrecht. 1978b. Root, hill, and field variance in protein content of North Carolina sweet potatoes. J. Agric. Food Chem. 26:362-364.

Purcell, A. E., W. M. Walter, Jr., J. J. Nicholoides, W. W. Collins, and H. Chancy. 1982. Nitrogen, potassium, sulfur fertilization, and protein content of sweet potato roots. J. Amer. Soc. Hort. Sci. 107:425-427.

Rao, M.N. and W. Polacchi. 1972. Part II. Amino acid, fatty acid, certain B-vitamin and trace mineral content of some Asian foods. Pages 189-334 *in* Food composition table for use in East Asia, U.S. Department of Health, Education and Welfare and FAO of the UN, Bethesda, MD.

Rebelo da Rocha, Y and R. Shrimpton. 1984. Zinc levels in selected Amazonian foods. Cienc. Tecnol. Aliment. 4:68-78.

Rhodes, M.J.C. and L.S.C. Wooltorton. 1978. Changes in the activity of hydroxycinnamyl CoA:Quinate hydroxycinnamyl transferase and in the levels of chlorogenic acid in potatoes and sweet potatoes stored at various temperatures. Phytochem. 17:1225-1229.

Roushdi, M., M.A. Sarhan, A.A. Fahmy. 1982. Effect of chemical treatments and gamma rays on starch content of sweet potatoes and its properties. Starch 34:243-246.

Roy, F. and M.V. Hedge. 1985. Rapid procedure for purification of β-amylase from *Ipomoea batatas*. J. Chromatogr. 324:489-494.

Ryan, C.A. 1981. Proteinase inhibitors. Pages 351-370, *in* The Biochemistry of Plants vol. 6, "Proteins and Nucleic Acids", A. Marcus (ed.), Academic Press, NY.

Sacher, J.A., J. Tseng, R. Williams, and A. Cabello. 1982. Wound-induced RNase activity in sweet potato. Evidence for regulation at transcription. Plant Physiol. 69:1060-1065.

Sakai, S., H. Imaseki, and I. Uritani. 1970. Biosynthesis of ethylene in sweet potato root tissue. Plant Cell Physiol. 11:737-745.

Sakamoto, S. and J.C. Bouwkamp. 1985. Industrial products from sweet potatoes. Pages 219-23 *in* Sweet potato products: A natural resource for the tropics, edited by J.C. Bouwkamp, CRC Press, Boca Raton, FL.

Sanchez, M.A., M.H. Bertoni, and P. Cattaneo. 1988. Contents and fatty acid composition of total lipids from edible bulbs and roots. An Asoc. Quim. Argent 76:227-235.

Sasaki, T. and K. Kainuma. 1981. Solubilization of starch synthetase bound to starch granules in sweet potato root tubers. Nippon Shokuhin Kogyo Gakkaishi 28:640-646.

Sasaki, T. and K. Kainuma. 1982. Regulation of starch synthesis and external polysaccharide synthesis by gibberellic acid in cultured sweet potato cell. Plant Tissue Cell Cult. 5:255-256.

Sasaki, T. and K. Kainuma. 1984. Control of starch and exocellular polysaccharide biosynthesis by gibberellic acid with cells of sweet potato cultured *in vitro*. Plant Cell Rep. 3:23-26.

Sasaki, T., K. Tadokoro, and S. Suzuki. 1972. The distribution of glucose phosphate isomerase isoenzymes in sweet potato and its tissue culture. Biochem. J. 129:789-791.

Sato, K., I. Uritani, and T. Saito. 1982. Properties of terpene-inducing factor extracted from adults of the sweet potato weevil, *Cylas formicarius Fabricius* (Coleoptera: Brenthidae). Appl. Entomol. Zool. 17:368-374.

Sato, T., F. Kiuchi, and U. Sankawa. 1982. Inhibition of phenylalanine ammonia-lyase by cinnamic acid derivatives and related compounds. Phytochem. 21:845-850.

Sato, T. and U. Sankawa. 1983. Inhibition of phenylalanine ammonia-lyase by flavonoids. Chem. Pharm. Bull. 31:149-155.

Scarlett-Kranz, J.M., B.S. Shane, K.E. McCracken, C.A. Bache, C.B. Littman, and D.J. Lisk. 1986. Survey of nitrate, cadmium and selenium in baby foods-health considerations. J. Food Saf. 8:35-45.

Schadel, W. E. and W. M. Walter, Jr. 1980. Calcium oxalate crystals in the roots of sweet potato. J. Amer. Soc. Hort. Sci. 105:851-854.

Schadel, W. E. and W. M. Walter, Jr. 1981. Localization of phenols and polyphenol oxidase in 'Jewel' sweet potatoes (*Ipomoea batatas* 'Jewel'). Can. J. Bot. 59:1961-1967.

Schmandke, H. and O. Olivarez Guerra. 1969. The carotene, L-ascorbic acid, dehydroascorbic acid and tocopherol content of Cuban vegetable products. Nahrung 13:523-530.

Schneider, J.A. and K. Nakanishi. 1983. A new class of sweet potato phytoalexins. J. Chem. Soc. Chem. Commun. 7:353-355.

Schwartz, S.J. and G.L. Catignani. 1989. Analysis of cis-beta-carotenes in food and colorant additives. Spec. Pub.-R. Soc. Chem. 72:80-82.

Schwartz, S.J. and M. Patroni-Killam. 1985. Detection of cis-trans carotene isomers by two dimensional thin-layer and high-performance liquid chromatography. J. Agric. Food Chem. 33:1160-1163.

Scott, L. E., C. O. Appleman, and W. Wilson. 1944. The discoloration of sweet potatoes during preparation for processing and the oxidase of the root. MD Agric. Exp. Sta. Bull. A33:11-26.

Scott, L. E. and J. C. Bouwkamp. 1974. Seasonal mineral accumulation by the sweet potato. HortScience 9:233-235.

Scott, L. E. and A. A. Kattan. 1957. Varietal differences in the catechol oxidase content of the sweet potato root. J. Amer. Soc. Hort. Sci. 69:436-442.

Scott, L. E. and W. A. Matthew. 1957. Carbohydrate changes in sweet potatoes during curing and storage. Proc. Amer. Soc. Hort. Sci. 70:407-418.

Seog, H.M., Y.K. Park, Y.J. Nam, D.H. Shin, J.P. Kim. 1987. Physicochemical properties of several sweet potato starches. Han'guk Nonghwa Hakhoechi 30:179-185.

Shannon, L.M., I. Uritani, and H. Imaseki. 1971. *De nova* synthesis of peroxidase isozymes in sweet potato. Plant Physiol. 47:493-498.

Sharfuddin, A.F.M. and V. Voican. 1984. Effect of plant density and NPK dose on the chemical composition of fresh and stored tubers of sweet potato. Indian J. Agric. Sci. 54:1094-1096.

Shen, Y. and J. Jiang. 1984. Fluoride in water, soil, foods, and fluoride stains on teeth. Zhonghua Yufangyixue Zazhi. 18:230.

Shigeki, M., T. Hattori, and K. Nakamura. 1986. Structural differences in full-length cDNAs for two classes of sporamin, the major soluble protein of sweet potato tuberous roots. Plant

Mol. Biol. 7:343-355.

Shimizu, T. and M. Kojima. 1982. Detection and some properties of the enzyme in sweet potato root which catalyzes the formation of t-cinnamoyl-D-glucose. Agric. Biol. Chem. 46:2617-2619.

Shimizu, T. and M. Kojima. 1984. Partial purification and characterization of UDPG:t-cinnamate glucosyl transferase in the root of sweet potato, *Ipomoea batatas* Lam. J. Biochem. 95:205-212.

Shin, M.S. and S.Y. Ahn. 1983. Studies on physicochemical properties of starches from sweet potatoes of Korean cultivars. Hanguk Nonghwa Hakhoe Chi 26:137-142.

Shingles, R.M., G.P. Arron, and R.D. Hill. 1982. Alternative pathway respiration and lipoxygenase activity in aged potato slice mitochondria. Plant Physiol. 69:1435-1438.

Singh, U. and J.H. Bradbury. 1988. HPLC determination of vitamin A and vitamin D_2 in South Pacific root crops. J. Sci. Food Agric. 45:87-94.

Sirju, G. and L.A. Wilson. 1974. IAA oxidase preparations from fresh and aged *Ipomoea batatas* tuber discs. Phytochem. 13:111-117.

Sistrunk, W. A. 1971. Carbohydrate transformations, color and firmness of canned sweet potatoes as influenced by variety, storage, pH and treatment. J. Food Sci. 36:39-42.

Sistrunk, W. A. 1977. Relationship of storage, handling, and cooking method to color, hardcore tissue, and carbohydrate composition in sweet potatoes. J. Amer. Soc. Hort. Sci. 102:381-384.

Sistrunk, W. A., J. C. Miller, and L. G. Jones. 1954. Carbohydrate changes during storage and cooking of sweet potatoes. Food Technol. 8:223-226.

Siti, M.B.S., E.S. Tee, and Y.H. Chong. 1987. Lead content of some Malaysian foodstuffs. ASEAN Food J. 3:25-29.

Sjostrom, O.A. 1936. Microscopy of starches and their modifications. Ind. Eng. Chem. 28:63-74.

Sohonie, K. and A.P. Bhandarker. 1954. Trypsin inhibitors in Indian foodstuffs. I. Inhibitors in vegetables. J. Sci. Ind. Res. 13B:500-503.

Son, K.-C., R. F. Severson, R. F. Arrendale, and S. J. Kays. 1990. Isolation and character-ization of pentacyclic triterpene ovipositional stimulant for the sweetpotato weevil from *Ipomoea batatas* (L.) Lam. J. Agric. Food Chem. 38:134-137.

Son, K.-C., R. F. Severson, and S. J. Kays. 1990. Surface chemical differences between sweetpotato lines with varying levels of resistance to the sweetpotato weevil, *Cylas formicarius elegantulus* (Summers). J. Amer. Soc. Hort. Sci. 115:696-699.

Son, K.-C., R. F. Severson, and S. J. Kays. 1993. Pre- and postharvest changes in the composition of hydrocarbons from the periderm of sweetpotato [*Ipomoea batatas* (L.) Lam.] storage roots. HortScience 27: (In press).

Speirs, M., A.H. Dempsey, J. Miller, W.J. Peterson, J.T. Wakeley, F.D. Cochran, R. Reder, H.B. Cordner, E.A. Fieger, M. Itollinger, W.J. James, H. Lewis, J.F. Eheart, M.S. Eheart, F.S. Andrews, R.W. Young, J.H. Mitchell, O.B. Garrison, and F.T. McLean. 1953. The effect of variety, curing, storage, and time of planting and harvesting on the carotene, ascorbic acid, and moisture content of sweet potatoes grown in six southern states. S. Coop. Ser. Bull. 30, 48pp.

Speirs, M., H.L. Cochran, W.J. Petterson, F.W. Sherwood, and J.G. Weaver. 1945. The effects of fertilizer treatments, curing, storage, and cooking on the carotene and ascorbic acid content of sweet potatoes. S. Coop Ser. Bull. 3, 31pp.

Stahmann, M.A., B.G. Clare, and W. Woodbury. 1966. Increased disease resistance and enzyme activity induced by ethylene and ethylene production by black rot infected sweet potato tissue. Plant Physiol. 41:1505-1512.

Stahmann, M.A. and D.M. Demorest. 1973. Changes in enzymes of host and pathogen with special reference to peroxidase interaction. Pages 405-420 *in* Fungal pathogenicity and the plant's response, edited by R. Byrde and C. Cutting, Academic Press, NY.

Sterling, C. and M.L. Aldridge. 1977. Mealiness and sogginess in sweet potato. Food Chem. 2:71-76.

257

Suge, H. 1979. Gibberellin relationships in a dwarf mutant of sweet potato. Japan. J. Genetics 54:35-42.

Sugiura, M., T. Ogiso, K. Takeuti, S. Tamura, and A. Ito. 1973. Studies on trypsin inhibitors in sweet potato. I. Purification and some properties. Biochem. Biophys. Acta. 328:404-417.

Sugiyama, T. and T. Hashizume. 1989. Cytokinins in developing tuberous roots of sweet potato. Agric. Biol. Chem. 53:49-52.

Sugiyama, T., Y. Nieda, Y. Irie, and T. Hashizume. 1988. Occurrence and levels of cytokinins in calluses of *Ipomoea* species. Shokubutsu Soshiki Baiyo 5:93-95.

Sugiyama, T., S. Suye, and T. Hashizume. 1983. Mass spectrometric-determination of cytokinins in young sweet potato plants using deuterium-labeled standards. Agric. Biol. Chem. 47:315-318.

Sun, J. B. 1988. Quantitative analysis of the volatile components of baked sweetpotatoes. MS Thesis, University of Georgia, 73pp.

Sung, F.J.M. 1981. The effect of leaf water status on stomatal activity, transpiration, and nitrate reductase of sweet potato. Agric. Water Manage. 4:465-470.

Suye, S., T. Sugiyama, and T. Hashizume. 1983. Mass spectrometric determination of ribosyl trans-zeatin from sweet potato tubers. Agric. Biol. Chem. 47:1665-1666.

Suzuki, H., K. Oba, and I. Uritani. 1975a. Improved synthesis of 3-1^{4}C-3-hydroxy-3-methylglutaryl coenzyme A. Agr. Biol. Chem. 39:1657-1676.

Suzuki, H., K. Oba, and I. Uritani. 1975b. The occurrence and some properties of 3-hydroxy-3-methylglutaryl coenzyme A reductase in sweet potato roots infected by *Ceratocystis fimbriata*. Physiol. Plant Path. 7:265-276.

Suzuki, H. and I. Uritani. 1976. Subcellular localization of 3-hydroxy-3-methylglutaryl coenzyme A reductase and other membrane-bound enzymes in sweet potato roots. Plant Cell Physiol. 17:691-700.

Sweeney, J.P. and A.C. Marsh. 1971. Effect of processing on provitamin A in vegetables. J. Am. Diet. Assoc. 59:238-245.

Szyperski, R.J., D.D. Hamann, and W.M. Walter, Jr. 1986. Controlled alpha amylase process for improved sweet potato puree. J. Food Sci. 51:360-363,367.

Taira, T. 1963a. By-products of alcoholic fermentation by gas chromatography. II. Unsaponifiable substance of sweet potato fusel oil boiled at a higher temperature than amyl alcohol. Nippon Nogei Kagaku Kaishi 37:49-52.

Taira, T. 1963b. By-products of alcoholic fermentation by gas chromatography. III. Occurrence of methylamylcarbinol and geraniol in cane molasses and sweet potato fusel oil. Nippon Nogei Kagaku Kaishi 37:630-631.

Takeda, Y. and S. Hizukuri. 1981. Re-examination of the action of sweet-potato beta-amylase on phosphorylated (1-4)-x-D-glucan. Carbohyd. Res. 89:174-178.

Takeda, Y., S. Hizukuri, and J. Shimada. 1972. Structural change of sweet potato β-amylase by sodium dodecyl sulfate. 46:367-371.

Takeda, Y., N. Tokunaga, C. Takeda, S. Hizukuri. 1986. Physicochemical properties of sweet potato starches. Starch 38:345-350.

Takeuchi, A., K. Oba, and I. Uritani. 1977. Change in acetyl CoA synthetase activity of sweet potato in response to infection by *Ceratocystis fimbriata* and injury. Agric. Biol. Chem. 41:1141-1145.

Takeuchi, A., I. Oguni, K. Oba, M. Kojima, and I. Uritani. 1978. Interactions between diseased sweet potato terpenoids and *Ceratocystis fimbriata*. Agric. Biol. Chem. 42:935-939.

Takeuchi, A., K.J. Scott, K. Oba, and I. Uritani. 1980. Possible role of the cytosol pathway of acetyl-CoA supply in terpene biosynthesis in sweet potato infected with *Ceratocystis fimbriata*. Plant Cell Physiol. 21:917-922.

Tamate, J. and J.H. Bradbury. 1985. Determination of sugars in tropical root crops using carbon-13 NMR spectroscopy: comparison with the HPLC method. J. Sci. Food Agric. 36:1291-1302.

Tanaka, Y., M. Kojima, and I. Uritani. 1974. Properties, development and cellular-localization of cinnamic acid 4-hydroxylase in cut-injured sweet potato. Plant Cell Physiol. 15:843-854.

Tanaka, Y., M. Matsuoka, N. Yamanoto, K. Ohashi, Y. Kano-Murakami, and Y. Ozeki. 1989. Structure and characterization of a cDNA clone for phenylalanine ammonia-lyase from cut-injured roots of sweet potato. Plant Physiol. 90:1403-1407.

Tanaka, Y. and I. Uritani. 1976. Immunochemical studies on fluctuation of phenylalanine ammonia-lyase activity in sweet potato in response to cut injury. J. Biochem. (Tokyo) 79:217-219.

Tanaka, Y. and I. Uritani. 1977a. Polarity of production of polyphenols and development of various enzyme activities in cut-injured sweet potato root tissue. Plant Physiol. 60:563-566.

Tanaka, Y. and I. Uritani. 1977b. Purification and properties of phenylalanine ammonia-lyase in cut-injured sweet potato. J. Biochem. 81:963-970.

Tanaka, Y. and I. Uritani. 1977c. Synthesis and turnover of phenylalanine ammonia-lyase in root tissue of sweet potato injured by cutting. Eur. J. Biochem. 73:255-260.

Tanaka, Y. and I. Uritani. 1979. Polar transport and content of indole-3-acetic acid in wounded sweet potato root tissues. Plant Cell Physiol. 20:1087-1096.

Tee, E.S. and Y.H. Chong. 1987. Lead content of some Malaysian foodstuffs. ASEAN Food J. 391:25-29.

Tereshkovich, G. and D.W. Newsom. 1963. Identification of some fatty acids in periderm tissue of the sweet potato. Proc. Assoc. Southern Agr. Workers 60:244.

Timbie, M. and N.F. Haard. 1977. Involvement of ethylene in the hardcore syndrome of sweet potato roots. 42:491-493.

Tiu, C. S., A. E. Purcell, and W. W. Collins. 1985. Contribution of some volatile compounds to sweet potato aroma. J. Agric. Food Chem. 33:223-226.

Toda, H. 1989. Sequence analysis of sweet potato β-amylase. Denpun Kagaku 36(2):87-101.

Truong Van Den, C.J. Beiermann, and J.A. Marlett. 1986. Simple sugars, oligosaccharides and starch concentrations in raw and cooked sweet potato. J. Agric. Food Chem. 34:421-425.

Tsukui, A. 1989. Stability of anthocyanin pigments of Philippine powdered purple yam - effect of inorganic salts, organic acids, sugars, phenols, L-ascorbic acid, and hydrogen peroxide. Nippon Kasei Gakkaish 40:15-22.

Tsukui, A., K. Kuwano, T. Mitamura. 1983. Anthocyanin pigment isolated from purple root of sweet potato. Kaseigaku Zasshi 34:153-159.

Uehara, S. 1983. Amylose-amylopectin ratio of soluble and insoluble fractions of sweet potato starch granules treated with urea. Nippon Nogei Kagaku Kaishi 57:529-533.

Umemoto, K. 1974. Morphological character of crystalline inorganic components present in plants: Calcium oxalate crystals in the leaves of sweet potato grown in natural light and in darkness. Chem. Pharm. Bull. 22:1968-1974.

Unarau, M.A. and R.E. Nylund. 1975a. The relation of physical properties and chemical composition to mealiness in the potato. I. Physical properties. Amer. Potato J. 34:245-253.

Unarau, M.A. and R.E. Nylund. 1975b. The relation of physical properties and chemical composition to mealiness in the potato. II. Chemical composition. Amer. Potato J. 34:303-311.

Uritani, I. 1953. Phytopathological chemistry of black-rotted sweet potato. Part 7. Isolation and identification of polyphenols from the injured sweet potato. Nippon Nougeikagaku Kaishi 27:165-168.

Uritani, I. and M. Miyano. 1955. Derivatives of caffeic acid in sweet potato attacked by black rot. Nature 175:812.

Uritani, I. and K. Muramutu. 1953. Phytopathological chemistry of black-rotted sweet potato. Part 4. Isolation and identification of polyphenols from the injured sweet potato. Nippon Nougeikagaku Kaishi 27:29-33.

Uritani, I., M. Uritani, and H. Yamada. 1960. Similar metablolic alterations induced in sweet potato by poisonous chemicals and by Ceratostomella fimbriata. Phytopath. 50:30-34.

Van der Pol, F., S.U. Purnomo, and H.A. Van Rosmalen. 1988. Trans-cis isomerization of carotenes and its effect on the vitamin A potency of some common Indonesian foods. Nutr.

Rep. Int. 37:785-793.

Varon, D. and W. Collins. 1989. Ipomoein is the major soluble protein of sweet potato storage roots. HortScience 24:829-830.

Venkateswara, R.K. and C.L. Mahajan. 1990. Fluoride content of some common South Indian foods and their contribution to fluorosis. J. Sci. Food Agric. 51:275-279.

Vieweg, G.H. and M.A.R. de Fekete. 1976. The effect of phospholipids on starch metabolism. Planta (Berl.) 129:155-159.

Villareal, R.L., S.C.S. Tsou, S.K. Lin, and S.C. Chiu. 1979. Use of sweet potato (*Ipomoea batatas*) leaf tips as vegetables II. Evaluation of yield and nutritive quality. Expl. Agric. 15:117-122.

Villegas, R.J.A., and M. Kojima. 1985. Sweet potato root enzyme which catalyzes the formation of chlorogenic acid from 1-O-caffeoyl-D-glucose and D-quinic acid. Agric. Biol. Chem. 49:263-265.

Villegas, R.J.A., and M. Kojima. 1986. Purification and characterization of hydroxycinnamoyl D-glucose: quinate hydroxycinnamoyl transferase in the root of sweet potato, *Ipomoea batatas* Lam. J. Bio. Chem. 26:8729-8733.

Villegas, R.J.A., T. Shimokawa, H. Okuyama, and M. Kojima. 1987. Purification and characterization of chlorogenic acid: Chlorogenate caffeoyl transferase in sweet potato root. Phytochem. 26:1577-1580.

Visser, F.R. 1984. Variations in the vitamin C content of some New Zealand grown fruit and vegetables. NZ J. Sci. 27:105-112.

Visser, F.R., and J.K. Burrows. 1983. Composition of New Zealand foods. 1. Characteristic fruits and vegetables. Science Information Publishing Centre, Wellington, NZ, p. 31-32.

Walker, C.E., L.B. Detfenbaugh, C.E. Lang, and C.W. Wrigley. 1989. Modified rapid method for measuring starch quality with the Australian Rapid Visco-Analyser. Veroeff Arbeitsgem. Getreideforson. 220:2-12.

Walter, W.M., Jr., and G.L. Catignani. 1981. Biological quality and composition of sweet potato protein fractions. J. Agric. Food Chem. 29:797-799.

Walter, W.M., Jr., G.L. Catignani, L.L. Yow, and D.H. Porter. 1983. Protein nutritional value of sweet potato flour. J. Agric. Food Chem. 31:947-749.

Walter, M. W., Jr., W. W. Collins, and A. E. Purcell. 1984. Sweet potato protein: A review. J. Agri. Food Chem. 32:695-699.

Walter, W. M., Jr. and F. G. Giesbrecht. 1982. Effect of lye peeling conditions on phenolic destruction, starch hydrolysis, and carotene loss in sweet potatoes. J. Food Sci. 47:810-812.

Walter, W. M., Jr., A. P. Hansen, and A. E. Purcell. 1971. Lipids of cured Centennial sweet potatoes. J. Food Sci. 36:795-797.

Walter, W.M., Jr., and A.E. Purcell. 1971. Characterization of a stable water-dispersible carotene fraction from dehydrated sweet potato flakes. J. Agr. Food Chem. 19:175-178.

Walter, W.M., Jr., and A.E. Purcell. 1973. α-amylase in sweet potatoes. A comparison between the amyloclastic and chromogenic starch methods of analysis. J. Food Sci. 38:548-549.

Walter, W.M., Jr. and A. E. Purcell. 1974. Lipid autoxidation in precooked dehydrated sweet potato flakes stored in air. J. Agric. Food Chem. 22:298-302.

Walter, W.M., Jr. and A. E. Purcell. 1980. Effect of substrate levels and polyphenol oxidase activity on darkening in sweet potato cultivars. J. Agric. Food Chem. 28:941-944.

Walter, W.M., Jr., A.E. Purcell, and W.Y. Cobb. 1970. Fragmentation of β-carotene in autoxidizing dehydrated sweet potato flakes. J. Agr. Food Chem. 18:881-885.

Walter, W.M., Jr., A.E. Purcell, and A.P. Hansen. 1972. Autoxidation of dehydrated sweet potato flakes. The effect of solvent extraction on flake stability. J. Agr. Food Chem. 20:1060-1062.

Walter, M.W., Jr., A.E. Purcell, and G.K. McCollum. 1978. Laboratory preparation of a protein-xanthophyll concentrate from sweet potato leaves. J. Agric. Food Chem. 26:1222-1226.

Walter, W. M., Jr., A. E. Purcell, and G. K. McCollum. 1979. Use of high-pressure liquid chromatography for analysis of sweet potato phenolics. J. Agric. Food Chem. 27:938-941.

Walter, W. M., A. E. Purcell, and A. M. Nelson. 1975. Effect of amylolytic enzymes on "moistness" and carbohydrate changes of baked sweet potato cultivars. J. Food Sci. 40:793-796.

Walter, W. M., Jr., and W. E. Schadel. 1981. Distribution of phenols in 'Jewel' sweet potato [*Ipomoea batatas* (L.) Lam.] roots. J. Agric. Food Chem. 29:904-906.

Walter, W. M., Jr,. and W. E. Schadel. 1982. Effect of lye peeling conditions on sweet potato tissue. J. Food Sci. 47:813-817.

Wang, H., and C.T. Lin. 1969. The determination of the carotene content of sweet potato parental varieties and their offspring. J. Agric. Assoc. China 65:1-5.

Wang, W. 1987. Study on standardization of the assay method for crude starch in cereals and root crops. Hunan Shifan Daxue Ziran Kexue Xuebao 10(2):47-53.

Watada, A.E., and T.T. Tran. 1985. A sensitive high-performance liquid chromatography method for analyzing riboflavin in fresh fruits and vegetables. J. Liq. Chromatogr. 8:651-652.

Watada, A.E., and T.T. Tran. 1987. Vitamins C, B_1, and B_2 contents of stored fruits and vegetables as determined by high performance liquid chromatography. J. Am. Soc. Hort. Sci. 112:794-797.

Watanabe, T., Y. Akiyama, A. Matsumoto, and K. Matsuda. 1983. Structural features of N geli amylodextrins from waxy-maize, sweet potato, and potato starches. Presence of a linear polysaccharide in the purified Fraction II from sweet-potato and potato amylodextrins. Carbohydr. Res. 112:171-177.

Watanabe, T., Y. Akiyama, H. Takahashi, T. Adachi, A. Matsumoto, and K. Matsuda. 1982. Structural features and properties of N geli amylodextrin from waxy maize, sweet potato, and potato starches. Carbohydr. Res. 109:221-222.

Watt, B.K., and A.L. Merrill. 1975. Composition of foods: raw, processed, prepared. Agriculture Handbook No. 8, US Department of Agriculture, Washington, DC, 190p.

Wedding, R.T., M.K. Black, and D. Pap. 1976. Malate dehydrogenase and NAD malic enzyme in the oxidation of malate by sweet potato mitochondria. Plant Physiol. 58:740-743.

Wilson, B.J. 1973. Toxicity of mold-damaged sweet potatoes. Nutr. Rev. 31:73-78.

Wilson, B.J. 1979. Naturally occurring toxicants of foods. Nutr. Rev. 37:305-312.

Wilson, B.J. and L.T. Burka. 1979. Toxicity of novel sesquiterpenoids from the stressed sweet potato (*Ipomoea batatas*). Food Cosmet. Toxicol. 17:353-355.

Wilson, B.J., D.T.C. Yang, and M.R. Boyd. 1970. Toxicity of mould damaged sweet potatoes. Nature 227:521-522.

Wilson, D.D., K.-C. Son, S. F. Nottingham, R. F. Severson, and S. J. Kays. 1989. The role of a pentacyclic triterpene in the oviposition of the sweetpotato weevil, *Cylas formicarius elegantulus* (Summers). J. Econ. Ento. 51:71-75.

Wilson, D. D., R. F. Severson, K.-C. Son, and S. J. Kays. 1988. Oviposition stimulant in sweetpotato periderm for the sweetpotato weevil, *Cylas formicarius elegantulus*. Envir. Ento. 17:691-693.

Wood, T., and A. Huang. 1975. The detection and quantitative determination of ipomeamarone in damaged sweet potatoes (*Ipomoea batatas*). J. Agric. Food 23:239-241.

Woolfe, J.A. 1991. The Sweet Potato in the Human Diet. Cambridge University Press, Cambridge, England.

Wu, Y.V. and M.O. Bagby. 1987. Recovery of protein-rich byproducts from sweet potato stillag,e following alcohol distillation. J. Agric. Food Chem. 35:321-325.

Wu, H.-C.H., and A. Sarko. 1978a. The double-helical molecular structure of crystalline B-amylose. Carbohydr. Res. 61:7-25.

Wu, H.-C.H., and A. Sarko. 1978b. The double-helical molecular structure of crystalline A-amylose. Carbohydr. Res. 61:27-40.

Xue, Q., S. Shi, A. Liu, and Q. Yi. 1988. Analysis of peroxidase isoenzyme of *Ipomoea* species. Yichuan Xuebao 15:247-253.

Yamaguchi, J., M. Nishimura, and T. Akazawa. 1987. Distribution of 59- and 55-kDa catalase in dark and light-grown pumpkin and various other plant tissues. Plant Cell Physiol. 28:219-226.

Yamashita, M., N. Kadota, Y. Asano, and N. Yamazaki. 1986. Carotene from sweet potato for food coloring. Jpn. Kokai Tokkyo Koho JP 61,291,563

Yang, D. T. C., B. J. Wilson, and T. M. Harris. 1971. The structure of ipomeamaronol: A new toxic furanosesquiterpene from moldy sweet potatoes. Phytochem. 10:1653-1654.

Yao, G., Y. Li, X. Chang, and J. Lu. 1983. Vitamin C content in vegetables and fruits in Shenyang [China] market during four seasons. Yingyang Xuebao 5:373-379.

Yasuda, K. and M. Kojima. 1986. The role of stress metabolites in established host-parasite specificity between sweet potato and *Ceratocystis fimbriata*, black rot fungus. Agric. Biol. Chem. 50:1836-1846.

Yeh, T.P. 1983. Utilization of sweet potatoes for animal feed and industrial uses: potential and problems. Pages 385-392 *in* Sweet potato, edited by R.L. Villareal and T.D. Griggs, Proceedings of the First International Symposium, AVRDC, Shanhua, Tainan, Taiwan.

Yeh, T.P., Y.T. Chen, and C.C. Sun. 1981. The effects of fertilizer application on the nutrient composition of high protein cultivars of sweet potatoes on protein and lysine production. J. Agric. Assoc. China. 113:33-40.

Yuan Z. and L. Yang. 1982. Determination of the activity of catechol oxidase. Shipin Kexue 34:28-31.

Yuan, Z. and L. Yang. 1985. Enzymic characteristics of catechol oxidase. Zhongguo Niangzao (1):22-28, 48.

Zanariah, J., A. Rehan, R.O. Noor. 1986. Protein and amino acid compositions of Malaysian vegetables. MARDI Res. Bull. 14:140-147.

Sweetpotato Technology for the 21st Century. W.A. Hill, C.K. Bonsi and P.A. Loretan (Eds.) 1992. Tuskegee University, Tuskegee, AL

Joseph K. Peterson, Howard F. Harrison, Jr.

Chemical Factors Involved in Sweetpotato Pest Resistance and Allelopathy

The following is a review of research on the chemical basis for pest resistance and allelopathy in the sweetpotato. Sweetpotatoes, in particular recently developed cultivars, exhibit a remarkable resistance against microbial infections, nematodes and most common soil insects. In addition, a strong allelopathic defense against the proliferation of various weeds has been reported. A large number of secondary compounds, either induced or constitutive, has been isolated from the sweetpotato. The compounds belong to a limited number of classes, such as furanosesquiterpenoids, polyphenols, glycosides and proteinaceous protease inhibitors. Biological activity has been shown for many individual compounds; however, their roles—in particular quantitative aspects—have not been reported. Multiple functions, with respect to resistance, are indicated for several compound classes. Large quantitative differences between clones in concentrations of various compounds with biological activity suggest the presence of genetic diversity awaiting study by breeders and geneticists. The unique occurrence of some metabolites in the genus *Ipomoea* may be of interest in the fields of gene transfer and agro-chemistry.

INTRODUCTION

Ipomoea comprises the largest genus in the family Convolvulaceae and is represented by over 500 species throughout the tropics (Willis 1973). The genus contains a plethora of secondary chemical compounds (Anaya et al. 1990), produced either constitutively or upon induction by external agents (phytoalexins or stress metabolites). *Ipomoea* and related genera are characterized by an abundance of primitive chemical features, as evidenced by the presence of proanthocyanins and flavonols (Nair et al. 1986). Although commercial cultivars of sweetpotato (*Ipomoea batatas* Lam.) may have lost, through genetic manipulation, a considerable amount of their capacity for secondary metabolism, the presence of diversified chemical defense systems is evident. Recently released cultivars show a remarkable resistance to various soil insects, nematodes, fungi and bacteria (Hamilton et al. 1985; Jones et al. 1983, 1984; Schalk et al. 1986) as well as strong allelopathic properties (Harrison and Peterson 1986). The present discussion deals with published literature and work in progress concerning chemical evidence for pest resistance and allelopathy in sweetpotato. Both constitutive and stress-induced chemical factors are discussed.

U. S. Department of Agriculture, Agricultural Research Service, Vegetable Laboratory, 2875 Savannah Highway, Charleston, SC 29414 USA.

263

Phytoalexins

Phytoalexins have been defined as antimicrobial compounds of low molecular weight that are both synthesized and accumulated in plants after exposure to microorganisms (Paxton 1981). Recent information on induction processes suggests a definition of phytoalexins that excludes the origin of the elicitors (induction factors). It was shown that constitutive elicitors may be present in the phytoalexin producing plant itself and released after cell damage (Hargreaves and Bailey 1978; Bailey 1982). Other biotic factors such as components derived from macerated insect larvae can induce phytoalexin production (Uritani et al. 1975). Finally, abiotic factors such as heavy metals, detergents and UV light may serve as elicitors (Tomiyama and Fukuya 1975; Hargreaves 1979; 1981). A review on phytoalexins and their elicitors was presented by Darvill and Albersheim (1984).

Hansen (1928) described cattle poisoning caused by moldy sweetpotatoes. Symptoms of this usually fatal poisoning were congestion of the lungs with a white frothy exudate and the cause of death was listed as asphyxiation. Following this early report a number of cases appeared in the Japanese and U.S. literature. Monlux et al. (1953) gave a detailed description of symptoms and post-mortem clinical observations, ascribing the cause to sweetpotato infection by *Sclerotium bataticola*. Prior to this report, the first phytoalexin found in the plant kingdom had been isolated from sweetpotato by a Japanese investigator in 1943. The chemical structure of the compound—a furanoterpenoid called ipomeamarone [cis-5-(3-furyl)tetrahydro-2-methyl-2 (4-methyl-2-oxopentyl) furan]—was elucidated in 1952 (Schneider et al. 1984). Ipomeamarone and the closely related compound ipomeamaronol were shown to be major hepatotoxic agents. Various bacterial and fungal isolates from sweetpotato were not toxigenic themselves but induced production of toxic furanosesquiterpenoids. The compounds were present even in sweetpotatoes with minor blemishes, and baking or boiling did not remove them (Wilson et al. 1970). Wilson et al. (1971) identified 15 additional furanoterpenoids, including a lung edema factor, 4-ipomeanol. Boyd et al. (1973) showed that the lung edema factor consisted of four closely related compounds, 4-ipomeanol, the isomeric 1-ipomeanol, the diketone ipomeanine, and the diol 1,4-ipomeanol.

A biogenetic scheme of sweetpotato stress metabolites, including structures and nomenclature of around 30 compounds, was presented by Schneider et al. (1984). Ipomeamarone is the most abundant metabolite, the others are related as biosynthetic precursors or further conversion products; however, most showed antifungal properties. For ipomeamarone, antimicrobial, fungistatic and anthelminthic properties were established (Uritani and Akazawa 1954; Wilson 1973).

A considerable amount of research was directed toward elucidation of the induction processes. Hyodo et al. (1969) used strains of *Ceratocystis fimbriata* derived from sweetpotato, coffee and prune to inoculate a resistant and a non-resistant variety of sweetpotato. The prune and coffee isolates caused surface browning, and hyphal penetration was limited to a few surface cell layers in the two sweetpotato varieties. The sweetpotato isolate caused continuous infection in the susceptible variety; the resistant variety exhibited similar symptoms; however, fungal penetration was much slower. Cell-free fungal extracts of mycelia and conidia of a sweetpotato strain or a coffee strain induced terpene formation (Kim and Uritani 1974). The inducer had a low molecular weight, was heat stable and had no ionic properties. The fungi did not release the inducer into the culture media, unless a great deal of lysis had occurred. No differences in furanoterpenoid production was observed when sweetpotato tissue was treated with cell-free extracts of a compatible strain (sweetpotato strain), an incompatible strain (coffee strain), or with $HgCl_2$.

In all cases a substantial amount of ethylene production was observed, indicating cell injury. On the basis of these and additional observations it was concluded that each fungal strain has host specificity in relation to the induction of phytoalexin production, fungal penetration of host cells (Hyodo et al. 1969), and agglutination of spores by host extracts (Kojima and Uritani 1974). There is no specificity in induction by extracts of compatible or incompatible strains (Kim and Uritani 1974), or abiotic factors such as $HgCl_2$ or certain amino acids (Kim et al. 1974). Furanoterpenoid production was also induced by larval components of sweetpotato weevils (*Cylas formicarius* and *Euscepes postfasciatus*); in this case a high molecular weight compound, probably proteinaceous, was implicated (Uritani et al. 1975). Formation of ipomeamarone was also induced by feeding damage of the weevil (*C. formicarius*; Akazawa et al. 1960).

Induced resistance was obtained in a susceptible sweetpotato variety after inoculation with a non-pathogenic isolate of *C. fimbriata* and subsequently challenged with a pathogenic isolate (Weber and Stahmann 1964). The induced immunity was limited to a thin layer adjacent to the infected area. Only non-pathogenic isolates of *C. fimbriata*—for example, from almond, prune, cacao and oak—induced immunity, whereas isolates of other *Ceratocystis* species did not (Weber and Stahmann 1966). Induction of immunity paralleled increased activity of various enzymes, in particular peroxidase and polyphenoloxidase (Weber et al. 1967).

Resistance to black rot was also detected in susceptible sweetpotato roots incubated above infected ones; unidentified volatile products were implicated as causative agents (Clare et al. 1966).

Based on this information, it would appear that terpene chemistry plays a significant role in sweetpotato defenses against microbial infections. Since formation was also induced by sweetpotato weevil feeding damage, a more general defense role is implied. The ability of ipomeamarone to uncouple oxidative phosphorylation further supports this contention (Uritani and Akazawa 1954). Additional study is needed to relate induction and synthesis of triterpenoids and their quantitative contribution to defense systems in the sweetpotato.

Phenolic Stress Metabolites

Production of several phenolic compounds parallels the formation of triterpenoids in fungus infected sweetpotatoes (Akazawa and Wada 1961) but are also produced in sound sliced tissue. Rudkin and Nelson (1947) identified chlorogenic acid in sweetpotato roots and found several closely related compounds which produced caffeic acid upon alkaline hydrolysis. Accumulation of similar compounds occurred in tissue attacked by black rot (Uritani and Miyano 1955). These compounds, which are widely distributed in the plant kingdom, were also found in considerable quantities as constituents of sweetpotato peelings (Sondheimer 1958), primarily concentrated in the periderm (Hayase and Kato 1984). Chlorogenic acids accumulate in cells adjacent to mechanically damaged tissue and were suggested to be source materials for suberization leading to wound healing (McClure 1960). Large quantitative differences in the contents of chlorogenic acids were found between cultivars. Walter et al. (1979) found that 80% of the total phenolics in peeled sweetpotatoes consisted of isochlorogenic acid and the total phenolic content ranged from 14 to 51 mg per 100g fresh weight. The significance of phenolics production was indicated by Gapasin et al. (1988) who reported that sweetpotatoes resistant to nematodes accumulated larger amounts of phenolics than non-resistant sweetpotatoes. This function was shown in other crops (Farkas and Kiraly 1962; Hung and Rohde 1973). Chlorogenic acids impart a certain degree of resistance to fungal attack (Uritani 1967); however, very little study has been devoted to this subject in sweetpotato. Antibacterial and fungistatic properties of chlorogenic acids have been shown in potatoes (Kuc et al. 1956; Patil et al. 1964).

Concurrent with the accumulation of chlorogenic acids, several other phenolic compounds are produced when sweetpotatoes are infected by fungi. These stress metabolites include the coumarin derivatives umbelliferone, scopoletin, esculetin, scopolin (scopoletin-7-glucoside) and skimmin (umbelliferone-7-glucoside) (Uritani 1967; Uritani et al. 1975). Scopoletin and umbelliferone were also isolated from tissue injured by the sweetpotato weevil (Akazawa et al. 1960) and from tissue infected with nematodes (Gapasin et al. 1988). Although these compounds were implicated as part of a defense system, no quantitative data exist on the production of these substances, their individual roles in sweetpotatoes or their dose-response and structure-activity relationships.

Proteinase Inhibitors

The occurrence of proteinaceous proteinase inhibitors in sweetpotatoes was first reported by Sohonnie and Bhandarkar (1954). Sugiura et al. (1973) isolated three different proteins from Japanese cultivars which were strong inhibitors of trypsin, weak inhibitors of plasmin and kallikrein; no inhibitory activity was found toward pepsin and chymotrypsin. Seven different trypsin inhibitors were found in American cultivars; considerable quantitative but not qualitative differences were found (Dickey and Collins 1984). High levels of these inhibitors are unwanted when raw sweetpotatoes serve as a main dietary component for animals. Little problem with human consumption is anticipated since these proteins are heat deactivated; this property is cultivar-dependent (Dickey et al. 1984; Lin and Ho 1986). Trypsin inhibitors can play a major role in insect defense (Gatehouse and Boulter 1983);

however, scant information is available relating sweetpotato proteinase inhibitor composition and concentration to insect resistance.

Allelopathy

Sweetpotato and congeneric species have long been recognized as effective suppressants of weed growth (Taylorson 1967; Anaya et al. 1990). In the sugar fields of the state of Morelos, Mexico, *Ipomoea tricolor* Cav. is grown as a cover crop. The plants suppress all weeds in two to three months, after which they are incorporated into the soil as green manure (Anaya 1989). Anaya et al. (1990) partially identified an esterified glycoside of jalapinolic acid (11-hydroxy-hexadecanoic acid) as the major active component in *I. tricolor*.

Sweetpotato is effectively used as a natural suppressant of weeds in traditional polycropping systems (Caamal and del Amo 1987; Villamayor and Perez 1983) resulting in considerable increases in total yields.

Growth of yellow nutsedge (*Cyperus esculentus*) and alfalfa (*Medicago sativa*) was significantly reduced when these species were grown in soil obtained from sweetpotato fields or grown in potting soil into which sweetpotato plants were incorporated. In the latter case, allelopathic activity could be shown for 12 weeks when the soil was incubated at 25°C (Harrison and Peterson 1986). Decaying sweetpotato plant residues incorporated into the soil also inhibited growth of sweetpotato vine cuttings and cowpea (*Vigna unguiculata* L. [Welp]) plants, and nodulation in cowpea was negligible (Walker and Jenkins 1986). High applications of decaying plants caused impairments of Ca, Mg and S uptake (Walker et al. 1989).

Allelopathic activity differs greatly between clones (Harrison and Peterson 1986); the cultivar 'Regal' is especially potent. Bioassays of 'Regal' periderm extracts revealed that the more polar solvents contained most activity. Aqueous methanol extracts strongly inhibited seed germination of velvetleaf (*Abutilon theophrasti*), proso-millet (*Panicum milliaceum*), black nightshade (*Solanum nigrum*), goosegrass (*Eleusine indica*) and sweetpotato; tall morninglory (*Ipomoea purpurea*) and eclipta (*Eclipta alba*) were intermediate in sensitivity, whereas coffee senna (*Cassia occidentalis*) and redroot pigweed (*Amaranthus retroflexus*) were hardly affected (Peterson and Harrison 1991a). Subsequently, a substance or substance group was isolated from the periderm tissue which accounted for much of the inhibition of seed germination. The concentrations at which 50% inhibition occurred (I_{50}) were 0.16, 0.013 and 0.011 mg/mL for redroot pigweed, velvetleaf and proso-millet respectively. Tall morninglory was not affected at any concentration tested (Peterson and Harrison 1991b). This same fraction inhibited growth of yellow nutsedge roots severely; the I_{50} value was 11 ppm (Harrison and Peterson 1991).

Current Investigations in Pest Resistance

The banded cucumber beetle (*Diabrotica balteata* Le Conte) can cause significant losses of sweetpotatoes in the southern USA (Rolston 1977). Feeding experiments with the resistant variety 'Regal' indicated that a constitutive factor, primarily concentrated in the periderm, inhibited growth of second and third instar larvae (Schalk et al. 1986). Chromatographic efforts provided an isolate which accounted for much of the inhibitory activity (Peterson and Schalk 1990). Subsequently, it was shown that this substance was the same as the one causing allelopathic response. Recent work indicates that the isolate consists of several closely-related glycosidic compounds, the identification of which is currently underway.

Constitutive factors in the sweetpotato cultivar 'Regal' interfere with egg-hatching of nematodes (*Meloidogyne incognita* Chitwood). Hexane and ethylacetate extracts were mildly inhibitory; however, methanol and 50% aqueous methanol extracts caused almost total inhibition of hatching at concentrations of 0.2 g dry weight equivalent (extract obtained from 0.2 g periderm tissue) per mL of incubation water. Again, the polar extracts are most inhibitory, indicating the possibility of related chemicals being responsible for resistance to various pests (not published).

Chromatographic separations of various periderm extracts revealed the presence of a large number of compounds, most with phenolic properties, of which the identities or functions are unknown at the present.

CONCLUSIONS

Sweetpotatoes contain a large number of secondary metabolites, found either as constitutive components or produced upon elicitation by various biotic or abiotic agents. Prominent among the phytoalexins are the furanoterpenoids which afford resistance to certain microorganisms and may exhibit other biological functions. Other stress metabolites such as the coumarin derivatives have been implicated in defensive roles against microbial and nematode infections as well as attack by insects. The chlorogenic acids are present in healthy tissue at various levels, depending on clonal type, and accumulate rapidly in tissues subjected to cellular damage. Antibacterial, fungistatic and nematicidal properties have been demonstrated.

A number of compounds, many of which are phenolic in character, are present as constitutive factors. Their identities and functions are largely unknown. Various crude extracts are allelopathic, interfere with nematode egg-hatching, and inhibit development of insect larvae.

Finally, several proteinase inhibitors—present at varying levels—are thought to provide a degree of protection against certain phytophagous insects.

This overview of secondary metabolites in sweetpotatoes, although limited in scope, allows some observations:

(1) Although sweetpotato is the sixth most important food crop in the world, only a limited amount of research has been devoted to this crop. The diversity and complexity of chemical defense systems in sweetpotato are little understood and sufficiently unique as to represent an excellent model system for study. The identities and functions of the wealth of biologically active compounds within the study remains to be elucidated.

(2) Levels of a number of stress metabolites and constitutive secondary metabolites vary widely within the sweetpotato genepool. A better understanding of these biologically active compounds would allow breeders and geneticists to significantly enhance the rate at which pest resistance can be incorporated into new lines.

(3) The availability of several clones with resistance to specific microbial, fungal, nematode and insect problems provides the basis for development of a model for research of chemical resistance systems.

(4) Development of efficient chemical analytical protocols will assist in directed and accelerated breeding for specific parameters.

(5) The unique occurrence of some metabolites in sweetpotato, or the genus *Ipomoea* in general, may be of interest in the fields of recombinant DNA and agrochemistry.

REFERENCES

Akazawa, T., I. Uritani, and H. Kubota. 1960. Isolation of ipomeamarone and two coumarin derivatives from sweetpotato roots injured by the weevil, C*ylas formicarius elegantulus*. Arch. Biochem. Biophys. 88:150-156.

Akazawa, T. and K. Wada. 1961. Analytical study of ipomeamarone and chlorogenic acid alterations in sweetpotato roots infected by *Ceratocystis fimbriata*. Plant Physiol. 36:139-144.

Anaya, A.L., M.R. Calera, R. Mata, and R. Pereda-Miranda. 1990. Allelopathic potential of compounds isolated from *Ipomoea tricolor* Cav. Convolvulaceae. J. Chem. Ecol. 16:2145-2152.

Anaya, A. L. 1989. Recent advances in allelopathy research in Mexico. Pages 167-192 *in* Phytochemical ecology: allelochemicals, mycotoxins and insect pheromones and allomones, edited by C. H. Chou and G. R. Waller, Inst. Botany. Academia Sinica Monograph Series No. 9, Taipei, R.O.C.

Bailey, J. A. 1982. Mechanisms of phytoalexin accumulation. Pages 289-318 *in* Phytoalexins, edited by J.A. Bailey and J. W. Mansfield. Halsted, Wiley, New York.

Boyd, M. R., L. T. Burka, T. M. Harris, and B. J. Wilson. 1973. Lung-toxic furanoterpenoids produced by sweet potatoes (*Ipomoea batatas*) following microbial infection. Biochim. Biophys. Acta, 337:184-195.

Caamal, J. A., and S. del Amo. 1987. La milpa multiple como punto de partida del manejo de la sucesion secundaria. Turrialba 37:195-209.

Clare, B., D. J. Weber, and M. A. Stahmann. 1966. Peroxidase and resistance to *Ceratocystis* in sweetpotato increased by volatile materials. Science 153:62-63.

Darvill, A. G., and P. Albersheim. 1984. Phytoalexins and their elicitors—a defense against microbial infection in plants. Ann. Rev. Plant Physiol. 35:243-275.

Dickey, L. F., and W. W. Collins. 1984. Cultivar differences in trypsin inhibitors in sweetpotato roots. J. Am. Soc. Hort. Sci. 109:750-754.

Dickey, L. F., W. W. Collins, C. T. Young, and W. M. Walter. 1984. Root protein quantity and quality in a seedling population of sweetpotatoes. HortScience 19:684-692.

Farkas, G.L., and Z. Kiraly. 1962. Role of phenolic compounds in the physiology of plant disease and disease resistance. Phytopathol. Z. 44:105-150.

Gapasin, R.M., R.B. Valdez, and E.M.T. Mendoza. 1988. Phenolics involvement in sweetpotato resistance to *Meloidogyne incognita* and *M. javanica*. Ann. Tropical Res. 10:63-73.

Gatehouse, A.M.R., and D. Boulter. 1983. Assessment of the antimetabolic effects of trypsin inhibitors from cowpea (*Vigna unguiculata*) and other legumes on development of the

Bruchid beetle *Callosobruchus maculatus*. J. Sci. Food Agric. 34:345-350.

Hansen, A. A. 1928. Potato poisoning. North Am. Veterinarian 9:31-34.

Hamilton, M.G., P.D. Dukes, A. Jones, and J.M. Schalk. 1985. 'HiDry' sweetpotato. HortScience 20:954-955.

Hargreaves, J.A. 1979. Investigation into the mechanism of mercuric chloride stimulated phytoalexin accumulations in *Phaseolus vulgaris* and *Pisum sativum*. Physiol. Plant Pathol. 15:279-287.

Hargreaves, J.A. 1981. Accumulation of phytoalexins in cotyledons of french bean (*Phaseolus vulgaris* L.) following treatment with triton (T-octylphenol polyethoxyethanol surfactants). New Phytol. 87:733-741.

Hargreaves, J. A., and J.A. Bailey. 1978. Phytoalexin production by hypocotyls of *Phaseolus vulgaris* in response to constitutive metabolites released by damaged bean cells. Physiol. Plant Pathol. 13:89-100.

Harrison, H. F., Jr., and J. K. Peterson. 1986. Allelopathic effects of sweetpotatoes (*Ipomoea batatas*) on yellow nutsedge (*Cyperus esculentus*) and alfalfa (*Medicago sativa*). Weed Science 34:623-627.

Harrison, H.F., Jr., and J.K. Peterson. 1993. Isolation of a yellow nutsedge (*Cyperus esculentus*) root growth inhibitor from sweetpotato (*Ipomoea batatas*). (In press).

Hayase, F., and H. Kato. 1984. Antioxidative components of sweetpotatoes. J. Nutr. Sci. Vitaminol. 30:37-46.

Hung, C-L., and R. A. Rohde. 1973. Phenol accumulation related to resistance in tomato infection by root-knot and lesion nematodes. J. Nematol. 5:253-258.

Hyodo, H., I. Uritani, and S. Akai. 1969. Production of furanoterpenoids and other compounds in sweet potato tissue in response to infection by various isolates of *Ceratocystis fimbriata*. Phytopath. Z. 65:332-340.

Jones, A., P. D. Dukes, J. M. Schalk, M. G. Hamilton, M. A. Mullen, R. A. Baumgardner, D. R. Paterson, and T. E. Boswell. 1983. 'Resisto' sweetpotato. HortScience 18:251-252.

Jones, A., P. D. Dukes, J. M. Schalk, M. G. Hamilton, M. A. Mullen, R. A. Baumgardner, D. R. Paterson, and T. E. Boswell. 1984. 'Regal' sweetpotato. HortScience 20:781-782.

Kim, W. K., and I. Uritani. 1974. Fungal extracts that induce phytoalexins in sweet potato roots. Plant Cell Physiol. 15:1093-1098.

Kim, W. K., I. Oguni, and I. Uritani. 1974. Phytoalexin induction in sweetpotato by amino acids. Agric. Biol. Chem. 38:2567-2568.

Kojima, M., and I. Uritani. 1974. Possible involvement of spore agglutination factors of host plants in manifestation of host specificity by various strains of black-rot fungus, *Ceratocystis fimbriata*. Plant Cell Physiol. 15:733-737.

Kuc, J., R. E. Henze, A. J. Ullstrup, and F. W. Quackenbush. 1956. Chlorogenic and caffeic acids produced by potatoes in response to inoculation with *Helmintosporium carbonium*. J. Am. Chem. Soc. 78:3123-3125.

Lin, Y.-H., and S.-P. Ho. 1986. Soluble leaf proteins of sweetpotato. Bot. Bull. Acad. Sinica, 27:175-186.

McClure, T. T. 1960. Chlorogenic acid accumulation and wound healing in sweetpotato roots. Am. J. Bot. 47:277-280.

Monlux, W., J. Fitte, G. Kendrick, and H. Dubuisson, 1953. Progressive pulmonary adenomatosis in cattle. Southwestern Veterinarian 6:267-269.

Nair, G. G., M. Daniel, and S. D. Sabnis. 1986. Chemosystematics of *Ipomoea* Linn. and some related taxa. Current Science 55:961-965.

Patil, S. S., R. L. Powelson, and R. R. Young. 1964. Relation of chlorogenic acid and free phenols in potato roots to infection by *Verticillium albo-atrum*. Phytopathology 54:531-535.

Paxton, J. D. 1981. Phytoalexins-a working redefinition. Phytopathol. Z. 101:106-109.

Peterson, J. K., and H. F. Harrison. 1991a. Differential inhibition of seed germination by sweetpotato (*Ipomoea batatas*) root periderm extracts. Weed Science 39:119-123.

Peterson, J. K., and H. F. Harrison. 1991b. Isolation of substance from sweetpotato (*Ipomoea batatas*) periderm tissue that inhibits seed germination. J. Chem. Ecol. 17:943-951.

Peterson, J. K., and J. M. Schalk. 1990. Resistance factors against *Diabrotica balteata* Le Conte in the periderm of sweetpotato [*Ipomoea batatas* L. (Lam.)]. IOBC/WPRS/Eucarpia. Bulletin XIII (6):136-139.

Rolston, L. H. 1977. Cooperative Research Program submitted to the USDA-ARS. Control of the soil insect complex attacking sweetpotato by insecticidal and cultural methods with emphasis on host plant resistance. LSU, Baton Rouge, LA.

Rudkin, G. O., and J. M. Nelson. 1947. Chlorogenic acid and respiration in sweetpotatoes. J. Am. Chem. Soc. 69:1470-1475.

Schalk, J. M., A. Jones, and P. D. Dukes. 1986. Factors associated with resistance in recently developed sweetpotato cultivars and germplasm to the banded cucumber beetle, *Diabrotica balteata* Le Conte. J. Agric. Entomol. 3:329-334.

Schneider, J. A., J. Lee, Y. Naya, K. Nakanishi, K. Oba, and I. Uritani. 1984. The fate of the phytoalexin ipomeamarone: Furanoterpenes and butenolides from *Ceratocystes fimbriata* -infected sweetpotato tissue. Phytochemistry 23:759-764.

Sohonnie, K., and A. P. Bhandarkar. 1954. Tryspin inhibitors in Indian foodstuffs: I. Inhibitors in vegetables. J. Sci. Ind. Res. 13B: 500-503.

Sondheimer, E. 1958. On the distribution of caffeic acid and the chlorogenic acid isomers in plants. Arch. Bioch. Biophys. 74:131-138.

Sugiura, M., T. Ogiso, K. Takeuti, S. Tamura, and A. Ito. 1973. Studies of trypsin inhibitors in sweetpotato. I. Purification and some properties. Biochim. Biophys. Acta 328:407-417.

Taylorson, R. B. 1967. Some properties of a growth inhibitor in *Ipomoea*. Proc. So. Weed Sci. Soc. 19:370 (abstract).

Tomiyama, K,. and M. Fukaya. 1975. Accumulation of rishitin in dead potato-tuber tissue following treatment with $HgCl_2$. Ann. Phytopathol. Soc. Japan 41:418-420.

Uritani, I. 1967. Abnormal substances produced in fungus contaminated foodstuffs. J. Ass. Off. Anal. Chem. 50:105-114.

Uritani, I., and T. Akazawa. 1954. Antibiotic effect on *Ceratostomella fimbriata* of Ipomeamarone, an abnormal metabolite in black rot of sweetpotato. Science 121:216-217.

Uritani, I., and M. Myano. 1955. Derivatives of caffeic acid in sweetpotato attacked by black rot. Nature 175:812.

Uritani, I., H. Saito, H. Honda, and W. K. Kim. 1975. Induction of furanoterpenoids in sweetpotato roots by the larval components of sweetpotato weevils. Agric. Biol. Chem. 39:1857-1862.

Villamayor, F. G., Jr., and R. D. Perez. 1983. Sweetpotato as a weed control agent for cassava. The Radix 5:10-11.

Walker, D. W., T. J. Hubbell, and J. E. Sedberry. 1989. Influence of decaying sweetpotato crop residues on nutrient uptake of sweetpotato plants. Agric. Ecosyst. Environ. 26:45-52.

Walker, D. W., and D. D. Jenkins. 1986. Influence of sweetpotato plant residues on growth of sweetpotato vine cuttings and cowpea plants. Hort. Sci. 21:426-428.

Walter, W. M. Jr., A. E. Purcell, and G. K. Mc Collum. 1979. Use of high-pressure liquid chromatography for analysis of sweetpotato phenolics. J. Agric. Food Chem. 27:938-941.

Weber, D. J., B. Clare, and M. A. Stahmann. 1967. Enzymic changes associated with induced and natural resistance of sweetpotato to *Ceratocystis fimbriata*. Phytopathology 57:421-424.

Weber, D. J., and M. A. Stahmann. 1964. *Ceratocystis* infection in sweetpotato: Its effect on proteins, isozymes, and acquired immunity. Science 146:929-931.

Weber, D. J., and M. A. Stahmann. 1966. Induced immunity to *Ceratocystis* infection in sweetpotato root tissue. Phytopathology 56:1066-1070.

Willis, J. C. 1973. A dictionary of flowering plants and ferns, edited by H. K. Airy Shaw. Cambridge University Press. 594 pp.

Wilson, B. J. 1973. Toxicity of mold damaged sweetpotatoes. Nutrition Reviews 31:73-78.

271

Wilson, B. J., M. R. Boyd, T. M. Harris, and D.T.C. Yang. 1971. A lung edema factor from mouldy sweet potatoes (*Ipomoea batatas*). Nature 231:52-53.

Wilson, B. J., D.T.C. Yang and M. R. Boyd. 1970. Toxicity of mould damaged sweet potatoes (*Ipomoea batatas*). Nature 227:521-522.

R. H. Brown

Photosynthesis and Plant Productivity in Sweetpotato

The physiology of photosynthesis and productivity of sweetpotato are poorly understood. Leaf photosynthesis appears to be similar to that of other C_3 species although early studies showed low rates and saturation of photosynthesis at irradiances of about one-third of full sunlight. Sweetpotato canopies are characterized by nearly horizontal leaves and prostrate, trailing vines, which may result in poor illumination of leaves at high leaf area indexes and low canopy photosynthesis. A few data indicate that some cultivars may have more vertically oriented leaves and canopy photosynthesis may be quite high. However, respiration of vegetative portions of the plant may represent a relatively high energy cost in some cultivars. The partitioning of dry matter or harvest index appears to be one of the most important yield determinants among current cultivars. Higher yielding cultivars appear to partition more dry matter to storage roots, although high yields may be obtained even with low harvest index, by a prolonged bulking period in climates with long growing seasons. Much research needs to be done on photosynthesis and respiration of leaves and plant stands to better understand the potential for improvement. Partitioning of dry matter also needs further study to determine the optimum balance between vine and storage root production.

INTRODUCTION

Research on photosynthetic potential of sweetpotato has been limited. The data available in the literature do, however, give some indications of the limitations and potential for improvement of productivity.

The potential for storage of photosynthetic products in roots of sweetpotato has a profound effect on photosynthetic capacity of leaves. The interaction between source and sink has received considerable research attention, but since it is covered in another chapter (Kuo and Chen 1992), this subject will be referred to only indirectly in this one. Photosynthesis and yield potential will be dealt with in three broad aspects: (a) photosynthetic characteristics of individual leaves; (b) plant canopy structure and its relationship to photosynthesis; and (c) partitioning of dry matter.

PHOTOSYNTHESIS OF LEAVES

Early studies showed that sweetpotato leaves had low apparent photosynthesis (AP) with maximum rates at 20 to 25 mg CO_2 dm^{-2} hr^{-1} (Tsuno and Fujise 1965).

Department of Agronomy, University of Georgia, Athens, Georgia 30602, USA.

However, more recent investigations show maximum rates to be 1.5 to 2.0 fold higher (Bhagsari 1981; Bhagsari and Harmon 1982; Hozyo 1982). The higher rates reported recently may have been due to improved techniques for measurements or improved plant culture and sink strength. Bhagsari (1981) reported average AP of 15 cultivars to be nearly 50% higher for field-grown than greenhouse-grown plants. This was related to greater specific leaf dry weight of field-grown leaves and probably to greater bulking of roots and faster growth rates in the field.

There has been very little study of environmental effects on photosynthesis in sweetpotato. Tsuno and Fujise (1965) found that leaf photosynthesis responded to irradiance only up to about 1/3 of full sunlight (40 klux) (Fig.1). The leaves used were low in photosynthetic capacity reaching only about 8 to 10 mg CO_2 dm $^{-2}$ hr^{-1} (Tsuno and Fujise 1965). Vines et al. (1983) indicated that light saturation of AP for sweetpotato was approximately 750 μmol quanta m^{-2} s^{-1} (approximately 1/3 of full sunlight). It is likely that photosynthesis responds to somewhat higher irradiances when AP rates are in the range of 30 to 35 mg dm^{-2} hr^{-1} as reported recently (Bhagsari and Harmon 1982; Hozyo 1982).

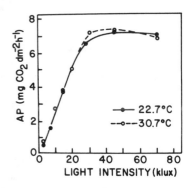

Figure 1. Response of apparent photosynthesis (AP) of sweetpotato leaves to light intensity (Redrawn from Tsuno and Fujise 1965).

Very little is known about the response of photosynthesis to leaf temperature in sweetpotato. Tsuno and Fujise (1965) found very little response to temperature in the range of about 23 to 30°C (Fig.1). Tsuno (1975) also showed little response from about 30 to 40°C in early stages of plant growth, but later there was a sharp decrease above 30°C. A lack of temperature response in the range of 20 to 40°C is very unusual in a C_3 species like sweetpotato and further research is needed to describe the temperature response of photosynthesis in this species. The high AP rates recorded by Bhagsari and Harmon (1982) and Hozyo (1982) were measured at 30 and 25°C, respectively, and it is likely that optimum AP occurs near 30°C.

Maximum AP rates of most crop species are obtained in young, fully expanded leaves, and photosynthetic capacity declines with age. In sweetpotato canopies the decline is likely to be influenced by shade from other leaves, development of sinks (roots) and environmental factors. Hozyo (1982) reported only a slow decline with age from about 40 mg CO_2 dm^{-2} h^{-1} on 7 July to just over 20 mg dm^{-2} h^{-1} on 1 October. Bhagsari (1988) reported a decrease from about 25 mg dm^{-2} h^{-1} in 20 day-old leaves to about 5 mg dm^{-2} h^{-1} at 40 days and a slight further decrease at 60 days.

Size of individual leaves of sweetpotato have been shown to increase with age of plants (Somda and Kays 1990) and to vary among cultivars (Bhagsari and Brown 1986). The variation in leaf size among cultivars was consistently and negatively related to AP. Correlation coefficients ranged from -0.22 to -0.77 in nine experiments (Table 1). This decrease in AP per unit area in larger leaves may be important in

Table 1. Relationships between leaf size and apparent photosynthesis (AP) in sweetpotato cultivars (from Bhagsari and Brown 1986).

Experiment No.	Range of Leaf area	Leaf area vs. AP[a]			
		Intercept(a)	Slope(b)	r	n
7	48-92	15.1	2.5	-0.22	17
8	50-143	17.5	4.4	-0.51*[b]	19
9	76-172	18.7	2.5	-0.29	20
10	69-188	25.4	3.8	-0.63**	16
11	89-215	26.3	5.7	-0.63**	16
12	100-208	23.7	4.4	-0.81***	16
13	71-181	25.0	5.0	-0.71**	15
14	94-192	29.0	6.9	-0.75**	15
15	62-186	25.0	5.0	-0.77**	15

[a]Coefficients for the linear regression AP = a-b (leaf area), AP in μmol CO_2 m^{-2} s^{-1} and leaf area in dm^2.

r = correlation coefficient and n = number of cultivars.

[b]*, **, *** indicate significance at the 0.05, 0.01, and 0.001 levels of probability, respectively.

comparing cultivars (Bhagsari and Brown 1986) and may mean that cultivars with small leaves have an advantage in the field. Tsunoda (1959) noted that cultivars suitable for "heavy manuring" (i.e., highly productive) tended to have smaller leaves.

The variation of leaf AP among cultivars is considerable (Bhagsari 1981; Bhagsari and Ashley 1990; Bhagsari and Harmon 1982). However, apparently because of environmental interactions, the ranking of cultivars is not consistent among years and dates within years and AP is not correlated with yield (Bhagsari and Harmon 1982). However, one selection (75-96-1) tested in five sets of measurements over three years was consistently higher (avg. 23%) than the mean of 15 cultivars (Bhagsari and Ashley 1990; Bhagsari and Harmon 1982). Final plant weights of this selection were the highest of 15 cultivars in two of three years and was third highest in the other year. Variation in AP among the cultivars was not consistently related to specific leaf weight, leaf N concentration or chlorophyll content.

CANOPY CHARACTERISTICS AND PHOTOSYNTHESIS

The extent of coverage of the soil by leaves is the major determinant of canopy photosynthesis and growth rate. The extent of coverage is expressed as leaf area index (LAI) and the maximum LAI has been found to vary in sweetpotato from about 2 to 10 (Bhagsari and Ashley 1990; Bourke 1984; Chapman and Cowling 1965; Enyi 1977). Although most cultivars have leaves that are oriented nearly horizontally (Kays 1985), it has been determined recently that some cultivars have leaves with mean angles 40 to 50 degrees from horizontal (S. Kays 1991, University of Georgia, unpublished data). Using an extinction coefficient of 1.0, which is characteristic of horizontal leaves, it can be calculated using the following equation that an LAI of 3.0 is needed to intercept 95% of the photosynthetically active radiation (PAR).

$$\frac{I}{Io} = e^{-K\,LAI}$$

Io = Irradiance at top of canopy; I = Irradiance beneath canopy; K = Extinction coefficient.

Thus, light interception should be nearly complete in most sweetpotato crops at LAIs of 3 to 4. Data are not available, however, on light interception and the efficiency of interception is uncertain. In an early experiment, Tsuno and Fujise (1965) indicated only about 75 or 80% of solar radiation was intercepted at an LAI of 3.0, but this measurement apparently included the infrared component of solar radiation which penetrates much more readily than PAR. It is apparent that much work needs to be done on characterizing the light intercepting capacity of sweetpotato canopies.

It is important for early growth of sweetpotato that LAI increase as rapidly as possible, and there appears to be substantial differences in the rates of early leaf area expansion. Bourke (1984) found that at 7 weeks after planting one cultivar had attained an LAI of about 3.2 whereas another had a value of only about 1.0. Likewise, Bhagsari and Ashley (1990) observed a range from 0.74 to 1.97 in LAI of 15 cultivars at 35 days after planting. Substantial cultivar differences in LAI may also occur later in the season, especially between indeterminate and determinate types (Huett and O'Neill 1976).

The optimum LAI for crop growth rate (CGR) has been reported to be between 3 and 4. In an experiment that involved soil fertility, plant spacing and early and late planting, Tsuno and Fujise (1965) showed that LAI was optimum between 3 and 4 and that, beyond an LAI of 4, CGR decreased substantially. Agata and Takeda (1982a) reported similar results with optimum LAI estimated at 4.0. This is in contrast to the results with other crops which show little or no decline in CGR above the optimum LAI (Hay and Walker 1989). There are no reports of optimum LAI for canopy photosynthesis of sweetpotato. Agata and Takeda (1982b) indicated linear increases in canopy photosynthesis up to LAI = 6, but it is unlikely that the optimum LAI for photosynthesis is much greater than that estimated for CGR.

When the leaf canopy is established, crop growth and yield may depend on the photosynthetic capacity of the canopy and the respiratory load of the various plant parts. Sweetpotato appears to be fairly typical of C_3 crop species in CGR and canopy photosynthesis. Maximum CGR of 20 to 25 g dry matter $m^{-2}\,d^{-1}$ (Agata and Takeda 1982a; Enyi 1977; Huett and O'Neill 1976) appear to be similar to other C_3 species (Hay and Walker 1989). The maximum canopy photosynthesis rates reported for sweetpotato range from 4.2 to 6.5 g CO_2 $m^{-2}\,h^{-1}$ (Tsuno and Fujise 1965; Agata and Takeda 1982; Bhagsari and Ashley 1990). The substantially higher value (6.5 g CO_2 $m^{-2}\,h^{-1}$) from Agata and Takeda (1982b) was estimated from a figure showing gross photosynthesis in g DW $m^{-2}\,h^{-1}$. The value was converted to AP by subtracting dark respiration and converting dry weight to CO_2 using a factor reported in the paper. The maximum canopy photosynthesis values reported by Agata and Takeda (1982b) and Bhagsari and Ashley (1990) are similar to maximum values for other C_3 crops (Brown et al. 1972; Fischer 1983; Larson et al. 1981). Over the period of maximum CGR, Agata and Takeda (1982b) reported daily net canopy photosynthesis of $34 g CO_2$ $m^{-2} d^{-1}$ (converted using dry weight / $0.61 = CO_2$). This daily rate compares to a net photosynthesis of 39.2 g CO_2 $m^{-2} d^{-1}$ for alfalfa (Brown et al. 1972) and 24.0 g $m^{-2} d^{-1}$ for barley (Biscoe et al. 1975).

The response of canopy photosynthesis to irradiance appears to be quite different than individual leaves. At low LAI, canopy photosynthesis saturates at low irradiance but, when LAI is high, canopy photosynthesis increases with irradiance up to full sunlight (Figure 2; see also Agata and Takeda 1982b; Tsuno and Fujise 1965). Since the leaves of sweetpotato are large and horizontally displayed (Kays 1985) it is surprising that canopy photosynthesis increases up to full sunlight. Tanaka et al. (1969) have shown that more horizontal display of rice leaves caused light saturation of canopy photosynthesis, whereas with more erect leaves increases up to full sunlight were obtained. The influence of leaf angle and plant structure needs further examination in sweetpotato. If selection can occur for more select leaves, higher canopy photosynthesis and yields may be obtained. More erect plants with a "gathering" type leaf arrangement may be beneficial (Tsunoda 1959). Chapman and Cowling (1965) showed in a preliminary experiment that making sweetpotato plants erect by supporting vines on wire mesh greatly increased yields.

The capacity to fix CO_2 is critical to high yield, but respiratory processes also play a role in yield determination. Respiration in sweetpotato is not well described, but it apparently accounts for a large percentage of CO_2 fixed. In the only fairly complete study of CO_2 balance in sweetpotato in the field, Agata and Takeda (1982b) estimated that respiration accounted for about 30 to 60% of gross canopy photosynthesis. This was similar to the estimates for a barley crop (Biscoe et al. 1975). Tsuno and Fujise (1965) reported that night-time respiration of potted plants was about 20 to 25% of day-time photosynthesis. The respiratory contribution was not equal among plant parts, however. On a weight basis, maximum respiration rates for

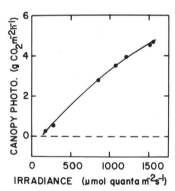

Figure 2. Canopy photosynthesis of 'Centennial' sweetpotato as a function of irradiance. Plotted from a diurnal trend of canopy photosynthesis and irradiance. (Bhagsari and Ashley 1990).

feeder roots, leaves, and petioles + stolons were 2.4, 2.7, and 1.6 times greater than for storage roots (Agata and Takeda 1982b). These data imply that the respiration cost of maintaining the vegetative portions of the plant are much greater than for storage roots and that excessive vine growth may decrease yield potential, in part because of the respiratory cost.

PLANT GROWTH AND DRY MATTER PARTITIONING

The relationship between vine and storage root growth appears to be a primary one in sweetpotato yield. Several researchers have emphasized the partitioning of dry matter to storage roots or increase in harvest index (HI) as a determinant of root yield. (Bhagsari and Harmon 1982; Bourke 1984; Enyi 1977; Huett 1976). A very close relationship of HI to storage root yield was evident in the work of Huett (1976) although he did not report the correlation coefficient (Fig. 3). Others have reported correlation coefficients ranging from 0.59 to 0.89 (Bhagsari and Ashley 1990; Bhagsari and Harmon 1982).

Although HI is normally determined at the end of the season, partitioning to storage roots may begin at different stages and occur at different rates in various cultivars. One way of looking at partitioning is to plot storage root weight against total weight at various times during the growing season as in Figure 4. These data from Huett and O'Neill (1976) show that partitioning to storage roots was greater for 'Nemagold' than 'White Maltese' and that 'Nemagold' consistently partitioned more than 0.5 of its dry weight to storage roots during bulking, whereas 'White Maltese' partitioned only 0.16 (early) and 0.37 (late) in the bulking period. The HI was obviously greater for 'Nemagold' (0.54) than for 'White Maltese' (0.27). Storage root yield of 'White Maltese' was 89% of that for 'Nemagold,' because bulking continued in the former until 39 weeks after planting, but ended in 'Nemagold' at 24 weeks. Leaf area index peaked at about 3.5 ten weeks after planting in 'Nemagold,' but continued to increase to a value of about 8 at 36 weeks in 'White Maltese.'

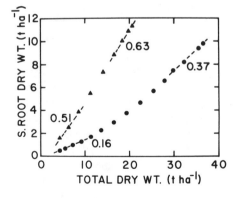

Figure 4. Relationships between total dry weight and storage root dry weight of 'Nemagold' (triangles) and 'White Maltese' (circles) sweetpotato cultivars. The slopes of the curves represent partitioning coefficients. The numbers associated with the broken lines are slopes calculated from the points connected by the lines. Points on the curves were calculated from Huett and O'Neill (1976) using their equations.

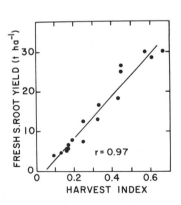

Figure 3. Relationship between harvest index and storage root yield of 16 cultivars of sweetpotato (From Huett 1976).

Analysis of yield differences among cultivars is not always as clear-cut as the example just cited. In an analysis of yield in seven cultivars, Enyi (1977) found that ranking of storage root yields was the same in two years (r= 0.99 for yields in 1974 vs 1975). The cultivar ranking for bulking rate was also similar (r = 0.92). On the other hand, HI and CGR ranking were not consistent (r = 0.43 and 0.25, respectively). Differences in yield responses for two of the cultivars in 1974 and 1975 are shown in Figure 5. In 1974, 'Laloki No. 1' and 'Naveto' partitioned dry matter to storage roots in a similar way. However, both total yield and root yield were much lower for 'Naveto' than 'Laloki No. 1.' In 1975, while total yields were similar for the two cultivars, root yields in 1975 were quite different (as in 1974). The difference in root yields were due to differences in partitioning throughout the bulking period. Harvest index was greater for 'Laloki No. 1' in both years, but the difference was greater in 1975. For both cultivars the partitioning coefficient was smaller in 1975 and vegetative growth continued longer into the season as indicated by LAI in Figure 6. The prolonged vegetative growth and lower dry weight partitioning may have been due to higher rainfall in 1975 (Enyi 1977). These data show that similar root yield rankings among cultivars may be obtained in two years when yield determining factors are quite different.

These data also emphasize that high storage root yield may be determined both by increased total production and/or increased partitioning of dry matter to roots. The principles highlighted in this paper indicate that yield potential in sweetpotato may be raised by increasing leaf photosynthetic capacity, better display of leaves to increase canopy photosynthesis, increased partitioning of dry matter to storage roots, and a prolonged bulking period. Much more research is needed on the interaction of these yield determining factors.

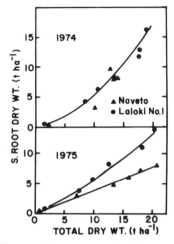

Figure 5. The relationship between total dry weight and storage root dry weight of two sweetpotato cultivars harvested at intervals during the bulking period during 1974 and 1975. The slope of the lines represent the dry matter partitioning to storage roots. Weights were estimated from Figures 1 and 2 of Enyi (1977).

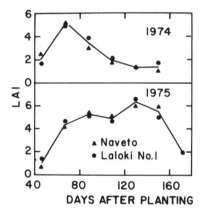

Figure 6. Leaf area index for two cultivars of sweetpotato during the growing seasons of 1974 and 1975. Redrawn from Enyi (1977).

REFERENCES

Agata, W. and T. Takeda. 1982a. Studies on matter production in sweet potato plants 1. The characteristics of dry matter and yield production under field conditions. Journal Faculty Agriculture, Kyushu University. 27:65-73.

Agata, W. and T. Takeda. 1982b. Studies on matter production in sweet potato plants 2. Changes of gross and net photosynthesis, dark respiration and solar energy utilization with growth under field conditions. Journal Faculty Agriculture, Kyushu University. 27:75-82.

Bhagsari, A.S. 1981. Relation of photosynthetic rates to yield in sweet potato genotypes. Hort Science 16:779-780.

Bhagsari, A.S. 1988. Photosynthesis and stomatal conductance of selected root crops as related to leaf age. Crop Science 28:902-906.

Bhagsari, A.S. and D.A. Ashley. 1990. Relationship of photosynthesis and harvest index to sweet potato yield. Journal American Society Horticultural Science 115:288-293.

Bhagsari, A.S. and R.H. Brown. 1986. Leaf photosynthesis and its correlation with leaf area. Crop Science 26: 127-132.

Bhagsari, A.S. and S.A. Harmon. 1982. Photosynthesis and photosynthate partitioning in sweet potato genotypes. Journal American Society Horticultural Science. 107:506-510.

Biscoe, P.V. R.K. Scott and J.L. Monteith. 1975. Barley and its environment III. Carbon budget of the stand. Journal Applied Ecology 12:269-293.

Bourke, R.M. 1984. Growth analysis of four sweet potato (*Ipomoea batatas*) cultivars in Papua New Guinea. Tropical Agriculture, Trinidad. 61:177-181.

Brown, R.H., R.B. Pearce, D.D. Wolf, and R.E. Blaser. 1972. Energy accumulation and utilization. Pages 143-166 *in* Alfalfa science and technology, edited by C.H. Hanson. American Society of Agronomy, Madison, Wisconsin.

Chapman, T. and D.J. Cowling. 1965. A preliminary investigation into the effects of leaf distribution on the yields of sweet potato (*Ipomoea batatas*). Tropical Agriculture, Trinidad. 42:199-203.

Enyi, B.A.C. 1977. Analysis of growth and tuber yield in sweet potato (*Ipomoea batatas*) cultivars. Journal Agricultural Science, (Cambridge) 88:421-430.

Fischer, R.H. 1983. Wheat. Pages 129-154 *in* Proceedings, Potential productivity of field crops under different environments. IRRI, 22-26 September, 1980, Los Banos, Laguna, Philipines.

Hay, R.K.M. and A.J. Walker. 1989. An introduction to the physiology of crop yield. Longman Scientific and Technical, Essex, England. 292 pp.

Hozyo, Y. 1982. Photosynthetic activity and carbon dioxide diffusion resistance as factors in plant production in sweet potato plants. Pages 129-133 *in* Sweet potato, edited by R.L Villareal and T.D. Griggs, Proceedings, First International Symposium, AVRDC, Taiwan, ROC.

Huett, D.O. 1976. Evaluation of yield, variability and quality of sweet potato cultivars in subtropical Australia. Experimental Agriculture 12:9-16.

Huett, D.O. and G.H. O'Neill. 1976. Growth and development of short and long season sweet potatoes in sub-tropical Australia. Experimental Agriculture 12:385-394.

Kays, S.J. 1985. The physiology of yield in the sweet potato. Pages 80-132 *in* Sweet potato products: A natural resource for the tropics, edited by J.C. Bouwkamp. CRC Press, Boca Raton, Florida.

Kuo, George, and Huei-Mei Chen. 1992. Source-sink Relationships of Sweetpotatoes. Pages 282-295 *in* Sweetpotato technology for the 21st century, edited by W.A. Hill, C.K. Bonsi and P.A. Loretan. Tuskegee, University, Tuskegee, Alabama.

Larson, E.M., J.D. Hesketh, J.T. Wooley, and D.B. Peters. 1981. Seasonal variations in apparent photosynthesis among plant stands of different soybean cultivars. Photosynthesis Research 2:3-20.

Somda, Z.C. and S. J. Kays. 1988. Sweet potato canopy morphology: leaf distribution. Journal American Society Horticultural Science. 115:39-45.

Tanaka, T., S. Matsushima, S. Kojyo, and H. Nitta. 1969. Analysis of yield determining process and its application to yield-prediction and culture improvement of lowland rice XC. On the relation between the plant type of rice plant community and the light curve of carbon assimilation. Proceedings, Crop Science Society Japan. 38:287-293.

Tsuno, Y. 1975. The influence of transpiration upon the photosynthesis in several crop plants. Proceedings, Crop Science Society Japan. 44:44-53.

Tsuno, Y. and K. Fujise. 1965. Studies on the dry matter production of sweet potato. Bulletin, National Insitute of Agricultural Sciences (Japan). Series D. No. 13. 136 pp.

Tsunoda, S. 1959. A developmental analysis of yielding ability in varieties of field crops. II. The assimilation-system of plants as affected by the form, direction and arrangement of single leaves. Japanese Journal Breeding 9:237-244.

Vines, H.M., Z-P. Tu, A.M. Armitage, S-S. Chen, and C.C. Black, Jr. 1983. Environmental responses of the post-lower illumination CO_2 burst as related to leaf photorespiration. Plant Physiology 73:25-30.

Sweetpotato Technology for the 21st Century. W.A. Hill, C.K. Bonsi and P.A. Loretan (Eds.) 1992. Tuskegee University, Tuskegee, AL

George Kuo and Huei-Mei Chen

Source-Sink Relationships of Sweetpotatoes

The nature of the source-sink relationship has been widely investigated in sweetpotato with the intent that acquired information would lead to an understanding of yield-forming processes so as to overcome limiting factors. There are marked differences in sink strength and source potential of sweetpotato clones. Both source potential and sink strength are important in determining the yield of sweetpotato. However, the evidence indicates that sink strength more than source potential affects photosynthesis and translocation, and that the sink thereby regulates dry matter production and yield formation in storage roots. Furthermore, since the source in sweetpotato is a more complex component than the sink, it seems probable that yield improvement, through genetic means or management practices, can be achieved more easily by improving the sink strength. Once the sink strength reaches its limit set by source potential, further progress requires both increased source potential and sink strength in a more or less coordinated manner.

The sweetpotato [*Ipomoea batatas* (L.) Lam.] is an important food crop in the tropics. It is grown mostly for its edible storage roots, and its yield formation depends upon a number of morphological and physiological characteristics. The yield of sweetpotato is a function of plant number/unit land area x storage root number/plant x average storage root weight. Storage root number and average storage root weight are determined in sequence by various physiological events. Changes in one yield component as a result of environment will often lead to subsequent adjustments by the plant in yield components. With the initiation of storage roots, their potential maximum number is determined first; next cell division and expansion determines the size of the storage roots; finally, the synthesis of starch granules determines the density of starch in the cells (Hahn and Hozyo 1984). Yield potential of storage roots essentially depends on the potential production of total dry matter, and the proportion of dry matter diverted to storage roots. The leaves are considered as the source for dry matter production through photosynthesis, and the storage roots as the sink for dry matter deposition. In this paper, a discussion will be made of improving sweetpotato through an understanding of the source-sink relationship in sweetpotato by: (1) defining the total dry matter production in the plant, (2) investigating dry matter partitioning as it relates to yield formation, and (3) characterizing genetic diversity in dry matter production and partitioning. Analysis of these characteristics as related to source-sink relationship could be useful in identifying the principal limiting factors of yield.

Asian Vegetable Research and Development Center, P.O. Box 42, Shanhua, Tainan 74199, Taiwan

SOURCE POTENTIAL

The maximization of total dry matter production depends on available solar radiation, photosynthetic capacity of the crop and duration of that capacity. Increasing radiation or photosynthetic activities and maintaining them for a longer period should also lead to increased dry matter production. Clonal differences in net photosynthesis of sweetpotato leaves have been observed; maximum net photosynthetic rates for mature leaves varied from 12.0 to 38.1 mg CO_2 dm^2 h^{-1} (Bhagsari 1981; Bhagsari and Harmon 1982; Fujise and Tsuno 1962; Tsuno and Fujise 1964b). Photosynthetic activity and CO_2 diffusion conductance of leaves were directly related to total dry matter production (Bhagsari and Harmon 1982; Hahn and Hozyo 1983), and photosynthetic CO_2 balance was also directly related to crop growth rate measured in the field (Agata and Takeda 1982b). Differences in photosynthetic activities were also modulated by external environmental factors (Bhagsari and Harmon 1982) such as excess soil moisture, high temperature and heavy soil (AVRDC 1988; Martin et al. 1988) and internal plant factors (Kays 1985) such as leaf nitrogen, chlorophyll content and stomatal density (Bhagsari 1981, Tsuno and Fujise 1965a). However, genotypic differences in dry matter production and photosynthetic activities and their associated physiological processes and morphological features often were not correlated with storage root yield (Bhagsari 1981; Bhagsari and Harmon 1982; Sadik 1972). The absence of strong correlations between total dry matter production and final storage root yield indicates that physiological and biochemical processes not related to source potential also affect final yield. Bhagsari and Brown (1988) suggested that the negative correlation between leaf area and photosynthetic rate could be one of the causes for the absence of a relationship between photosynthetic rate and yield. Sweetpotato produces new leaves until harvest. They provide enough dry matter production so that competition between new leaves and developing storage roots is minimized. Lemon et al. (1971) estimated that only about 7% of the visible radiation available for photosynthesis was converted to dry matter production. Based on calculations for an ideal leaf area index (LAI) of 3 to 4 with respect to early ground cover by the crop canopy (Loomis and Williams 1963), the net potential dry matter production by a crop receiving 450 cal/cm^2 d^{-1} during a 150-day growing period was estimated to be 36 t/ha^{-1} (Table 1).

Table 1. Estimation of potential yield by a sweetpotato crop surface receiving 450 cal cm^{-2} d^{-1} during 150-day growing period.

1.	Visible radiation, 400-700 nm (45% total)	202	cal cm^{-2}
2.	Less 20% albedo loss & inactive absorption	162	cal cm^{-2}
3.	[CH_2O] produced (1 μmole CO_2/1.16 cal)	140	μmole cm^{-2}
4.	Less 40% respiration loss	84	μmole cm^{-2}
5.	Daily net [CH_2O] production (30 g $mole^{-1}$)	25	g m^{-2}
6.	Net [CH_2O] production in 150 days	3.75	kg m^{-2}
7.	Net [CH_2O] of economic part (45% HI)	1.69	kg m^{-2}
8.	DM of economic part (75% efficiency)	1.27	kg m^{-2}
9.	Potential storage root yield (65% moisture)	36.3	t ha^{-1}

SINK STRENGTH

The realization of storage root yield relies on the amount of dry matter available for storage root growth, the rate of translocation and amount of assimilates translocated, and the ability of the roots to store the assimilate. The ability of the sink, i.e., the number and size of storage roots, to accept assimilates usually is considered a major factor leading to storage root yield. Storage roots of sweetpotato are derived from adventitious roots that arise from the nodes of the below-ground portion of the stem, and their initiation is the result of high primary cambial activity (Wilson 1982). On the other hand, the bulking of storage roots—during which starch accumulates— is the result of cell division of the anomalous cambia. Anomalous cambia originate in the parenchyma of the central portion of the axis, frequently occurring as cylinders which surround groups of xylem elements, and may increase in width until a region of considerable size is formed (Kokubun 1973). It was suggested that the translocation of assimilates to the storage roots was directly related to the development of anomalous cambia and the diffusion of assimilates from there into the storage parenchyma of the stele (Kato et al. 1972).

Plant growth regulators are responsible for the morphogenesis and growth of storage roots (Wilson 1982). Auxins are known to increase the number of storage roots (Jiménez and Garner 1983), and cytokinins are related to development and bulking of the storage roots (Matsuo et al. 1983; McDavid and Alamu 1980). Both auxins and cytokinins in total amount increased with advancing storage root development, and storage roots contained higher amounts of both cytokinins and auxins than did the fibrous roots (AVRDC 1990a). Cytokinins may be responsible for cell division and enlargement of the primary and secondary vascular cambia and subsequently of the large parenchymatous cells in storage roots, whereas auxins may be responsible for the initiation of secondary cambia.

In relation to cambial activity, potassium is also needed (AVRDC 1990a; Reshid and Waithaka 1988; Tsuno and Fujise 1965b). Potassium also probably affects the activity of the starch synthetase (Murata and Akazawa 1969). It is just as important to identify the critical period as it is to determine the critical level of the growth regulators to control the metabolic activities in storage roots.

LIMITING PROCESSES – SOURCE POTENTIAL OR SINK STRENGTH?

Yield of storage roots is controlled not only by the source potential but also by the sink strength. Whether the source or the sink is limiting the yield is difficult to determine. The evidence which suggests that source potential or sink strength may be limiting should therefore be considered.

Effects of sink strength

To discern whether source or sink limits yield in sweetpotato, reciprocal grafts of a set of clones in all possible combinations have been extensively employed

(AVRDC 1988 and 1990a; Hozyo 1977; Hozyo and Kato 1973 and 1976a and b; Hozyo and Park 1971; Kato and Hozyo 1974 and 1978; Li and Kao 1985b; Nakatani et al. 1988a and b). Growth rates of storage roots and relations between photosynthetic activity and yield of storage root were studied separately on the basis of differences in storage root development, photosynthetic activity, and dry matter partition. In general, grafts with a strong sink strength showed greater storage root yield than those with weak sink strength irrespective of source potential (Fig. 1). Reciprocally grafted plants with small source/strong sink or large source/weak sink produced intermediate levels of total dry matter (Fig. 2), and storage root yield (Fig. 1) in between self-grafted clones. The reciprocal treatment also showed that the ability of the clones to develop storage roots early or late was determined by their sinks, not by their sources (Hozyo et al. 1971). Therefore, a graft with a strong sink appeared to have greater response of sink to source than a graft with a weak sink; correspondingly, a graft with a large source appeared to have a greater response of source to sink (Hahn 1977).

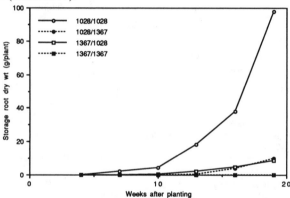

Figure 1. Storage root dry weight of self and reciprocally grafted (scion/stock) plants of two sweetpotato clones, CN 1028-15 and CN 1367-2, at different growth stages.

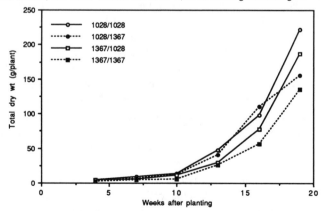

Figure 2. Total dry matter production of self and reciprocally grafted (scion/stock) plants of two sweetpotato clones, CN 1028-15 and CN 1367-2, at different growth stages.

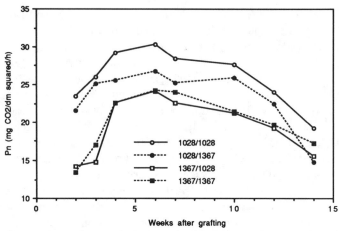

Figure 3. Changes in net photosynthetic rates of self and reciprocally grafted (scion/stock) leaf cuttings of two sweetpotato clones, CN 1028-15 and CN 1367-2, during the growth period of 2 to 14 weeks of growth.

Chemical analyses revealed that grafts of leaf-cuttings with large sources maintained high levels of soluble sugars in the leaf throughout the growing period, but high levels of starch only in the early growth stages (AVRDC 1990a). Since leaf photosynthetic rate was correlated with diffusive conductance for CO_2, the strong sink or the rapid bulking of a storage root elicited the highest net photosynthetic rate (Fig. 3) as well as leaf conductance (AVRDC 1988; Hozyo and Kato 1976; Kato and Hozyo 1978; Nakatani et al. 1988a). The sink effect on canopy photosynthesis was also considered large (Agata and Takeda 1982b). Grafts with a strong sink also brought about high diffusion conductance by reducing mesophyll resistance instead of stomatal resistance in the leaf (Nakatani 1988b). Since starch is an end-product of the photosynthetic process, the change in photosynthesis of leaf appears to be related to ribulose biphosphate carboxylase activity and relies on the sink strength through the control of leaf starch content.

Grafts with a strong sink accumulated a large amount of soluble sugars in developing storage roots and fibrous roots (AVRDC 1990a). But soluble sugars in fibrous roots declined at later growth stages, probably because developing storage roots had preferential ability to import soluble sugars for starch synthesis in storage roots resulting in a lower supply for fibrous roots. In contrast, grafts with a weak sink attracted less soluble sugars in developing storage roots but a sizeable amount of starch deposition elsewhere than in storage roots (AVRDC 1990a). In these grafts, the assimilates were apparently not imported to the developing storage root but diverted to other plant parts. Furthermore, the leaf of grafts with a weak sink accumulated more starch than those with a strong sink at later growth stages, which suggests that the starch synthesized in the leaf was not mobilized out from the leaf. Subsequently, this might be responsible for lowering photosynthetic activity in the leaf because of feedback inhibition on the photosynthetic process (Nakatani et al.

Table 2. Number of anomalous cambium per cross section of storage root as changed with age.

Grafting combination (scion/stock)	Weeks after grafting			
	2	3	6	12
CN1028/CN1028	0	32 a[1]	124 a	128 a
CN1028/CN1367	2	2 b	51 c	92 b
CN1367/CN1028	0	34 a	76 b	96 b
CN1367/CN1367	0	5 b	25 d	60 c

[1]Mean separation within columns by Duncan's multiple range test at $P = 0.05$.

1988a; Tsuno and Fujise 1965a). Apparently this lowers total dry matter production (AVRDC 1990b; Bhagsari and Harmon 1982; Nakatani et al. 1988a). The effect of feedback inhibition on photosynthesis, therefore, could be an important factor in governing dry matter production. Environmental or internal commands, therefore, could exert an adverse effect on photosynthesis through limiting rates of translocation (Gifford et al. 1984).

Grafts with a large source or a weak sink increased specific leaf weight (SLW), whereas grafts with strong sinks decreased SLW (AVRDC 1990a). The increase in SLW represented an increase in palisade thickness and may indicate the immobilization of material from the leaves. Under this situation, the leaf apparently changed from a source organ to a sink organ.

Anatomical observations of leaves with a weak sink also revealed that a large amount of starch granules were deposited in the ground tissue parenchyma and xylem and phloem parenchyma in the midrib. Developing storage roots of grafts with a strong sink, on the other hand, had greater anomalous cambium number (Table 2) and large parenchyma cells (Table 3), with a large amount of starch granules accumulated within or around these cells. These observations confirm previous contentions that the weak sink strength causes a build-up of starch in leaves and the entire translocation pathway, whereas the bulking of storage roots relies on the differentiation of anomalous cambium.

Table 3. Average cell size (x 10^{-3} mm^2) of storage root parenchyma cells at 6 and 12 weeks after grafting.

Grafting combination (scion/stock)	Weeks after grafting	
	6	12
CN1028/CN1028	4.59±1.03 [1]	8.03±1.05
CN1028/CN1367	3.26±0.39	5.47±0.63
CN1367/CN1028	4.25±0.58	6.32±0.76
CN1367/CN1367	2.86±0.78	5.88±0.86

[1]Each value is the mean of 23 determinations ± SD.

Partitioning

The rate at which assimilates move out from the leaf appears to be more important for storage root development than for an increase in leaf area (Austin and Aung 1973). Thus, partitioning of dry matter plays a deciding role in the determination of final storage root yield (Bouwkamp 1983; Pardales and Belmonte 1989). High yielding cultivars tended to have a strong ability to accommodate more assimilates in the storage root (Bhagsari and Harmon 1982). Storage root yield would be greatest in clones where vegetative growth is not too great, i.e., limited leaf growth at the bulking period was related to high yield (Bouwkamp 1983)—most likely due to re-mobilization of assimilates from leaves to developing roots. It is, therefore, possible that the primary factor affecting such partitioning is translocation efficiency. The phloem transport may play an important role in loading, transport and unloading of assimilates (Kays 1985). But it is suggested that the translocation speed and rate-limiting processes within the sinks during development rather than the amount of phloem tissue is contributing to the inherent difference in the translocation efficiency (De Calderon et al. 1983; Kato and Hozyo 1976, 1978; Kays et al. 1982, 1987).

Harvest index (HI) gives an indication of the relative distribution of assimilates between the storage root and the remainder of the plant. Clonal variation in HI, ranging from 5 to 75% in sweetpotato (AVRDC 1990b; Bhagsari and Harmon 1982; Bouwkamp 1983; Huett 1976; Li and Kao 1985a), is also influenced by plant nutrition and other cultural and environmental factors (Kays 1985). High-yielding clones generally had a higher harvest index than low-yielding clones (AVRDC 1990b; Huett 1976; Li and Kao 1985a; Lowe and Wilson 1974); high harvest indices indicate that these clones have high efficiency in storage root formation relative to their biological yield. Harvest indices of grafts with strong sinks were also higher than those with weak sinks (AVRDC 1988). On the contrary, grafts with a strong sink but a small source maintained a higher harvest index but lower storage root yield than grafts with a weak sink but a large source. This is likely due to low dry matter production because of the small source. Therefore, even though the harvest index appears more important than total dry matter production, a large source is still needed to couple with a strong sink to express its potential.

Assimilate supply

Studies indicated that the principal factors limiting yield are insufficient dry matter production before storage root initiation and during the period of storage root bulking. Canopy photosynthesis is closely correlated to the solar radiation received by the plants (Agata and Takeda 1982b), and high total solar radiation received during the bulking period is known to be related to high yield (Agata and Takeda 1982a). Furthermore, more than 50% of assimilates accumulated during the bulking period were translocated to the developing root (Bhagsari and Harmon 1982). Therefore, during the storage root bulking period, a high level of solar radiation, and an increasing efficiency of mobilization of current assimilates to the developing storage root are essential for high storage root yield. Thus, the assimilate supply from source leaves can limit sink yield (Gifford et al. 1984); the larger the supply of assimilates from the leaves to the developing roots, the greater the root number and average root weight.

Negative correlations among yield components are frequently observed in cereals and legumes (Evans 1975). Such negative correlations between yield components are often interpreted as indicating that yield is limited by the supply of assimilates. However, no such negative correlations were observed in sweetpotatoes (Bouwkamp and Hassam 1988). Thus, the supply of assimilates is not likely to be limited for sweetpotatoes.

If photosynthesis limited storage root yield, we might expect higher yielding clones to display higher photosynthetic rates. This proviso is important because photosynthetic rate may parallel yield but, as discussed above, there is little evidence of any positive relation between them or any instance where selection for a greater rate of photosynthesis has led to an increase in yield.

An increase in the concentration of carbon dioxide during the entire growing period may increase the total dry matter production and partitioning of biomass into storage roots. Bhattacharya et al. (1985) found a positive response of storage root bulking to CO_2 enrichment; the bulking storage roots translocated proportionately more assimilates than the shoots under CO_2 enrichment conditions. Results suggest that increase in source potential via CO_2 enrichment can lead to quite a substantial increase in storage root yield, i.e., that the source potential could be limiting, but this enhanced source potential is also able to modulate sink strength to increase the bulking of storage roots.

Source-sink conclusion

The evidence described above indicates that the genotypic ability to partition assimilates to the storage roots is important in determining yield potential, and the demand for assimilates by storage roots can have a pronounced feedback effect on the source potential. This implies that the sink strength is more important than the potential source in determining storage root yield. The precise mechanisms which regulate the sink strength to import assimilates into storage roots are still uncertain. The source potential and the sink strength may appear to be in balance although the sink strength may actually be limiting. Increasing assimilates without increasing the storage sink would not increase the yield, whereas increased storage sink without increased assimilate would merely result in storage roots that fail to enlarge. Therefore, both source potential and sink strength can be rate limiting in storage root formation. There must still be a balance between source potential and sink strength to increase yield potential.

IMPROVEMENT OF SOURCE POTENTIAL AND SINK STRENGTH

Despite marked differences in source potential and sink strength in sweetpotato clones (Li and Kao 1985a), it is only recently that the clonal improvement of sweetpotato has taken account of the relative importance of each. Hahn and Hozyo (1984) suggested making crosses which favor the combination of a large source and a strong sink to further increase yield. However, whether or not a cross between large source clones and strong sink clones will produce progenies with large source and strong sink still needs to be investigated.

It is apparent that there are clonal differences in total dry matter production (Pardales and Belmonte 1989; Tsuno 1971; Tsuno and Fujise 1963). It may be expected that the improvement of a large source will lead to high dry matter production and possibly result in high storage root yield. Despite the existence of variations in photosynthetic efficiency and net assimilation rate (Hahn and Hozyo 1984; Sadik 1973), there were no consistent correlations between these source parameters and total dry matter production. Thus, the screening for source potential appears complicated and difficult. Instead, the grafting method was employed for the screening of source potential (Hahn 1982); however, no attempt was made to relate high source potential with high dry matter production. There appears therefore to be little opportunity for enhancing storage root yield through increases of source potential alone. On the other hand, one approach which may be rewarding would be to evaluate total dry matter production at the final stage. Since the final dry matter production would be the integration of source activity, it could be a better indicator of source potential throughout the entire growing period.

As we have observed from the aforementioned evidence, the sink strength influences storage root yield more than the source potential. It seems probable, therefore, that sweetpotato yield improvement can be achieved more easily by selecting for the strong sink strength alone. Strong sink strength will, to a certain extent, lead to improvement of source and translocation efficiencies as well. Yield and sink strength will tend to increase in parallel until they reach their limits set by source potential. Once this limit has been reached, further progress will require that both sink strength and source potential be enhanced in a more or less coordinated manner. Under this condition, it would be much more effective to select for both traits at the same time.

It is much easier to identify, evaluate and select for sink strength than for source potential. The grafting method is often used in the screening for yield potential (Yoshida et al. 1987) and relative sink strength (Hahn 1977; Hahn and Hozyo 1984; Li and Kao 1985b). However, storage root number and average storage root weight are the most common parameters used by plant breeders to measure sink strength. The number of vascular bundles of developing storage roots has also been suggested as an indicator that differentiates the ability of clones to accumulate dry matter in storage roots (Lu et al. 1981 and 1983). As sink strength for assimilates are genetically determined, further improvement in yield can be achieved by genetic engineering if the genetic determinants are well defined.

The number, size, and potential growth rate of storage roots are undoubtedly important determinants of sink strength, but whether the latter depends on the translocation efficiency, enzymatic conversion or storage processes, with or without the aid of growth regulating hormones produced by the sink, is not clear. One approach to the assessment of translocation efficiency uses harvest index (HI)(Li 1986; Tsuno and Fujise 1964a). Specific leaf weight may also serve as a parameter for assessing sink strength.

Part of the complication in the evaluation of source potential and sink strength is the generally large and laborious sample size required to adequately assess any one of the parameters in field-grown plants. However, the leaf-cutting method (Spence 1971) has been used to measure source potential and sink strength because it requires less material and time (AVRDC 1988; Kato et al. 1972; Nakatani et al. 1988a and 1988b). The leaf-cutting method uses correlations between single plant systems and field-grown plants for such parameters as clonal differences in source potential, specific leaf weight, total dry matter production (Fig. 4), sink strength, storage root yield (Fig. 5), harvest index (Fig. 6), and starch accumulation processes (AVRDC 1990a and b). The reciprocal grafting of leaf cuttings has been employed for the study

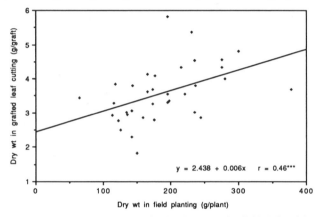

Figure 4. Relationship of total dry matter production between the field trial and the self-grafted leaf-cutting test of 35 sweetpotato clones.

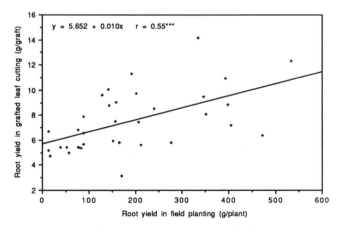

Figure 5. Relationship of storage root dry weight between the field trial and the self-grafted leaf-cutting test of 35 sweetpotato clones.

291

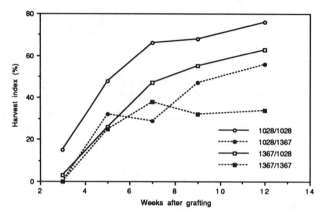

Figure 6. Changes in harvest index of self and reciprocally grafted (scion/stock) leaf cuttings of two sweetpotato clones, CN 1028-15 and CN 1367-2, during the growth period of 2 to 14 weeks of growth.

of translocation of assimilates (Spence and Humphries 1972) and the evaluation of yield potential and relative importance of source potential and sink strength (Nakatani et al. 1988a).

In summary, the best opportunities for sweetpotato improvement seem to be afforded total dry matter production and harvest index. It is also easier to evaluate total dry matter production and harvest index than individual physiological characteristics related to these parameters. Selection for strong sink strength, to a large extent, will lead to an improvement of the harvest index. The leaf-cutting method seems to be useful for estimation of both total dry matter production and harvest index.

REFERENCES

AVRDC. 1988. 1986 Progress Report. Asian Vegetable Research and Development Center. Shanhua, Tainan, Taiwan.

AVRDC. 1990a. 1987 Progress Report. Asian Vegetable Research and Development Center. Shanhua, Tainan, Taiwan.

AVRDC. 1990b. 1989 Progress Report. Asian Vegetable Research and Development Center. Shanhua, Tainan, Taiwan.

Agata, W. and T. Takeda. 1982a. Studies on matter production in sweet potato plants. 1. The characteristics of dry matter and yield production under field conditions. Journal of Faculty of Agriculture, Kyushu University 27(1•2):65-73.

Agata, W. and T. Takeda. 1982b. Studies on matter production in sweet potato plants. 2. Changes of gross and net photosyntheses, dark respiration and solar energy utilization with growth under field conditions. Journal of Faculty of Agriculture, Kyushu University 27(1•2):75-82.

Austin, M.E. and L.H. Aung. 1973. Patterns of dry matter distribution during development of sweet potato (*Ipomoea batatas*). Journal of Horticultural Science 48(1):11-17.

Bhagsari, A.S. 1981. Relation of photosynthetic rates to yield in sweet potato genotypes. HortScience 16(6):779-780.

Bhagsari, A.S. and R.H. Brown. 1986. Leaf photosynthesis and its correlation with leaf area.

Crop Science 26(1):127-132.

Bhagsari, A.S. and S.A. Harmon. 1982. Photosynthesis and photosynthate partitioning in sweet potato genotypes. Journal of the American Society for Horticultural Science 107(3):506-510.

Bhattacharya, N.C., P.K. Biswas, S. Bhattacharya, N. Sionit and B.R. Strain. 1985. Growth and yield response of sweet potato to atmospheric CO_2 enrichment. Crop Science 25(6):975-981.

Bouwkamp, J.C. 1983. Growth and partitioning in sweet potatoes. Annals of Tropical Research 5(2):53-60.

Bouwkamp, J.C. and M.N.M. Hassam. 1988. Source-sink relationships in sweet potato. Journal of the American Society for Horticultural Science 113(4):627-629.

De Calderon, C., M. Acock and J.O.J. Garner. 1983. Phloem development in sweet potato cultivars. HortScience 18(3):335-336.

Evans, L.T. 1975. Crop physiology; some case histories. Cambridge University Press, London, U.K. 374 pp.

Fujise, K. and Y. Tsuno. 1962. Studies on the dry matter production of sweet potato. I. Photosynthesis in the sweet potato with special reference to measuring of intact leaves under natural conditions. Proceedings of the Crop Science Society of Japan 31(2):145-149.

Gifford, R.M., J.H. Thorne, W.D. Hitz and R.T. Giaquinta. 1984. Crop productivity and photoassimilate partitioning. Science 225(4464):801-808.

Hahn, S.K. 1977. A quantitative approach to source potentials and sink capacities among reciprocal grafts of sweet potato varieties. Crop Science 17(4): 559-562.

Hahn, S.K. 1982. Screening sweet potato for source potentials. Euphytica 31(1):13-18.

Hahn, S.K. and Y. Hozyo. 1983. Sweet potato and yam. Pages 319-340 in Potential productivity of field crops under different environments. International Rice Research Institute, Los Baños, Laguna, the Philippines

Hahn, S.K. and Y. Hozyo. 1984. Sweet potato. Pages 551-567 in The physiology of tropical field crops, edited by P.R. Goldsworthy and N.M. Fisher. John Wiley & Sons, Chichester, U.K.

Hozyo, Y. 1977. The influences of source and sink on plant production of Ipomoea grafts. Japan Agricultural Research Quarterly 11(2):77-83.

Hozyo, Y. and C.Y. Park. 1971. Plant production in grafting plants between wild type and improved variety in Ipomoea. Bulletin of the National Institute of Agricultural Sciences (Japan) D(22):145-164.

Hozyo, Y. and S. Kato. 1973. The plant production of wild type plants in Ipomoea trifida (H. N. B.) Don. Bulletin of National Institute of Agricultural Sciences (Japan) D(24):35-60.

Hozyo, Y. and S. Kato. 1976a. The interrelationship between source and sink of the grafts of wild type and improved variety of Ipomoea. Proceedings of the Crop Science Society of Japan 45(1):117-123.

Hozyo, Y. and S. Kato. 1976b. Thickening growth inhibition and re-thickening growth of tuberous roots of sweet potato plants (Ipomoea batatas Poiret). Proceedings of the Crop Science Society of Japan 45(1):131-138.

Hozyo, Y., T. Murata and T. Yoshida. 1971. The development of tuberous roots in grafting sweet potato plants, Ipomoea batatas Lam. Bulletin of the National Institute of Agricultural Sciences (Japan) D(22):165-191.

Huett, D.O. 1976. Evaluation of yield, variability and quality of sweet potato cultivars in subtropical Australia. Experimental Agriculture. 12(1):9-16.

Jiménez, J.I. and J.O. Garner, Jr. 1983. Efecto de reguladores de crecimiento sobre la iniciación y desarrollo de aríces de almacenamiento, en hojas enraizadas de batata (Ipomoea batatas Lam.). FYTON 43(1):117-124.

Kato, S. and Y. Hozyo. 1974. Translocation of ^{14}C-photosynthates in several growth stages of the grafts between improved variety and wild type plants in Ipomoea. Bulletin of the

National Institute of Agricultural Sciences D(25):31-58.

Kato, S,. and Y. Hozyo. 1976. The interrelationship between translocation of ^{14}C-photosynthate and $^{14}CO_2$ exposed leaf position on the grafts of *Ipomoea*. Proceedings of the Crop Science Society of Japan 45(2):351-356.

Kato, S., and Y. Hozyo. 1978. The speed and coefficient of ^{14}C-photosynthates translocation in the stem of grafts between improved variety and wild type plant in *Ipomoea*. Bulletin of the National Institute of Agricultural Sciences D(29): 113-131.

Kato, S., H. Kobayashi, and Y. Hozyo. 1972. Translocation of ^{14}C-photosynthates in isolated sweet potato leaves, *Ipomoea batatas* Poiret. Proceedings of Crop Science Society of Japan 41(2):147-154.

Kays, S.J. 1985. The physiology of yield in the sweet potato. Pages 79-133 *in* Sweet potato products: a natural resource for the tropics, edited by J.C. Bouwkamp. CRC Press, Boca Raton, Florida, USA.

Kays, S.J., C.E. Magnuson, and Y. Fares. 1982. Assimilation patterns of carbon in developing sweet potatoes using ^{11}C and ^{14}C. Pages 95-118 *in* Sweet potato, edited by R.L. Villareal and T.D. Griggs. Asian Vegetable Research and Development Center, Shanhua, Tainan, Taiwan.

Kays, S.J., J.D. Goeschl, C.E. Magnuson, and Y. Fares. 1987. Diurnal changes in fixation, transport, and allocation of carbon in the sweet potato using ^{11}C tracer. Journal of the American Society for Horticultural Science 112(3):545-554.

Kokubun, T. 1973. Thremmatological studies on the relationship between the structure of tuberous root and its starch accumulating function in sweet potato varieties. Bulletin of the Faculty of Agriculture, Kagoshima University 23:1-126.

Lemon, E., D.W. Stewart, and R.W. Shawcroft. 1971. The sun's work in a cornfield. Science 174(4007):371-378.

Li, L. 1986. Variation in harvest index and its implication in breeding of sweet potatoes (*Ipomoea batatas* (L.) Lam.). Journal of Agricultural Association of China 136:25-36.

Li, L,. and C.H. Kao. 1985a. Dry matter production and partition of six sweet potato (*Ipomoea batatas* (L.) Lam.) cultivars. Journal of Agriculture Association of China 131:10-23.

Li, L., and C.H. Kao. 1985b. Investigation of source-sink relationship in sweet potato by reciprocal grafts. Botanical Bulletin of Academia Sinica 26:31-38.

Loomis, R.S., and W.A. Williams. 1963. Maximum crop productivity: an estimate. Crop Science 3(1):67-72.

Lowe, S.B., and L.A. Wilson. 1974. Comparative analysis of tuber development in six sweet potato (*Ipomoea batatas* (L.) Lam) cultivars. 1. Tuber initiation, tuber growth and partition of assimilates. Annals of Botany 38(155):307-317.

Lu, S.Y., W.J. Li, Q.H. Feng, X.R. Zheng, and C.G. Wu. 1983. The correlation between the numbers of the sieve tube bundles of the xylem tissue on per unit area and starch content at the harvest time in sweet potato (*Ipomoea batatas* Lam.). Acta Agriculturae Universitatis Pekinensis 9(3):1-6.

Lu, S.Y., X.R. Zheng, W.J. Li, and C.G. Wu. 1981. Morphology during the process of tuber formation and to research a method of early appraisal of the high starch breeding of sweet potato. Acta Agriculturae Universitatis Pekinensis 7(3):13-20.

Martin, F.W., N.A. Flores, and S.G. Carmer. 1988. Identification of a key environment for determination of yield stability in sweet potato. Tropical Agriculture (Trinidad) 65(4):313-316.

Matsuo, T., T. Yoneda, and S. Itoo. 1983. Identification of free cytokinins and the changes in endogenous levels during tuber development of sweet potato (*Ipomoea batatas* Lam.). Plant and Cell Physiology 24(7):1305-1312.

McDavid, C.R., and S. Alamu. 1980. The effect of growth regulators on tuber initiation and growth in rooted leaves of two sweet potato cultivars. Annals of Botany 45(3):363-364.

Murata, T., and T. Akazawa. 1969. Enzymic mechanism of starch synthesis in sweet potato roots. II. Enhancement of the starch synthetase activity by malto-oligosaccharides.

Archives of Biochemistry and Biophysics 130(-2):604-609.

Nakatani, M., A. Oyanagi, and Y. Watanabe. 1988a. Tuber sink potential in sweet potato (*Ipomoea batatas* Lam.). I. Development of tuber sink potential influencing the source activity. Japanese Journal of Crop Science 57(3):535-543.

Nakatani, M., M. Komeichi, and Y. Watanabe. 1988b. Tuber sink potential in sweet potato (*Ipomoea batatas* Lam.). II. Estimation of tuber sink potential of cultivars using single leaf grafts. Japanese Journal of Crop Science 57(3):544-552.

Pardales, J.R.J., and D.V.J. Belmonte. 1989. Comparative patterns of dry matter production in bushy and spreading sweet potato cultivars. Experimental Agriculture 25(2):243-247.

Reshid, K., and K. Waithaka. 1988. The relationship between N, P and K concentrations in sweet potato vines and dry matter accumulation in vines and tuberous roots as influenced by P fertilization. Acta Horticulturae 218:213-220.

Sadik, S. 1973. Screening sweet potato for low CO_2 compensation point. Proceedings, the Third International Symposium Tropical Root Crops. IITA, Ibadan, Nigeria.

Spence, J.A. 1971. Cultivation of detached sweet potato (*Ipomoea batatas* (L.) Lam.) leaves with tuberous roots for photosynthetic studies. Photosynthetica 5(4):424-425.

Spence, J.A., and E.C. Humphries. 1972. Effect of moisture supply, root temperature, and growth regulators on photosynthesis of isolated rooted leaves of sweet potato (*Ipomoea batatas*). Annals of Botany 36(144):115-121.

Tsuno, Y. 1971. Dry matter production of sweet potatoes and yield increasing technics. Fertilité 38:3-21.

Tsuno, Y., and K. Fujise. 1963. Studies on the dry matter production of the sweet potato. II. Aspect of dry matter production on the field. Proceedings of the Crop Science Society of Japan 31(3):285-288.

Tsuno, T., and K. Fujise. 1964a. Studies on the dry matter production of sweet potato. V. The differences in distribution ratio of dry matter produced among some varieties. Proceedings of the Crop Science Society of Japan 32(4):306-310.

Tsuno, Y,. and K. Fujise. 1964b. Studies on the dry matter production of sweet potato. VI. Varietal differences of respiration and respiration:photosynthesis ratio. Proceedings of the Crop Science Society of Japan 32(4):311-314.

Tsuno, Y., and K. Fujise. 1965a. Studies on the dry matter production of the sweet potato. VIII. The internal factors influence on photosynthetic activity of sweet potato leaf. Proceedings of the Crop Science Society of Japan 33(3):230-235.

Tsuno, Y., and K. Fujise. 1965b. Studies on the dry matter production of sweet potato. IX. The effect of potassium on the dry matter production of sweet potato. Proceedings of the Crop Science Society of Japan 33(3):236-241.

Wilson, L.A. 1982. Tuberization in sweet potato (*Ipomoea batatas* (L) Lam.). Pages 79-94 *in* Sweet potato, edited by R.L. Villareal and T.D. Griggs. Asian Vegetable Research and Development Center, Shanhua, Tainan, Taiwan.

Yoshida, T., M. Marumine, S. Sakamoto, and H. Kukimura. 1987. Selection for high yield sweet potato by individual leaf culture. Ministry of Agriculture, Forestry and Fisheries (Japan) Bulletin of Green Energy Program Group-II No. 14:84-89.

Sweetpotato Technology for the 21st Century. W.A. Hill, C.K. Bonsi and P.A. Loretan (Eds.) 1992. Tuskegee University, Tuskegee, AL

Lawrence A. Wilson, Lynda D. Wickham

New Perspectives on Tuberization in Sweetpotato*

Earlier definitions of tubers and tuberization are briefly reviewed and rethinking of the definition of the tuber with respect to what are commonly termed tropical carbohydrate root and tuber crops is pursued. A common nomenclature of tuber is proposed on the basis of the argument that genesis of tuberous organs is an inherent characteristic of the main and lateral axial organs of seven genera and nine species referenced in the paper. Moreover, such genesis is expressed with uniquely common manifestations, despite considerable diversity in the origin of the tuberous organs. Accordingly, tuberization is defined as the sum total of all the processes which lead to formation of mature root and stem tubers. The argument is supported by references to phylogenetic and ontogenetic interrelationships between a range of the presumptive yield organs of diverse origins as well as to trans-organ genesis of tuberous growth in six of the genera cited.

The sweetpotato tuber was defined by Wilson (1970) as the localized subapical, lateral "swelling" that developed on certain root types of the sweetpotato root system. This definition of the tuber was subsequently presented in many communications in the international literature, e.g., Wilson and Lowe (1973a,b); Wilson (1977), Wilson (1982), Lowe and Wilson (1974a,b), Roberts-Nkrumah, Wilson and Ferguson (1986). Later, Wilson (1982) defined root "tuberization" in sweetpotato as the sum total of all the processes leading to the formation of mature "tubers." These processes were described as
    –initiation of the tuber-bearing organ (TBO)(thick root)
    –tuber initiation on this organ
    –tuber growth and development to maturity.

In turn, tuber growth was defined in terms of the increase in tuber size, mediated through increases in cell number and cell size and in tuber weight, mediated through accumulation of assimilate in tuber cells. Alternatively, tuber development was defined to include the morphogenetic changes of:
    –tuber initiation and early tuber growth
    –formation of alternative root types, e.g., "pencil" and "string" roots
    –tuber "stalk" development

The University of the West Indies, Faculty of Agriculture, St. Augustine, Republic of Trinidad and Tobago.
*A response to this article by Kays et al. can be found on page 307. The response is followed by a rejoinder from the authors on page 314.

–development of buds
–development of lateral, tuber roots.

In other words, all the processes concerned either with the formation of tubers or with the "frustration" of tuber formation, e.g., "string" and "pencil" roots genesis, were included in the broad definition of tuber development in the sweetpotato root system. Also, the sum total of the processes (designated quantitative morphogenesis by Wilson and Lowe 1973b) was explicitly included in the process of tuberization because those processes which did not result in tuber formation were judged to lead to the precise definition of tuber number, through "frustration" of the process of tuberization in certain tuberous roots. Such "frustration" of tuberization occurred at an early stage in the crop growth cycle (Lowe and Wilson 1974a,b).

Subsequently, Wilson (1990) described the diversity of tuberous yield organ genesis in

–Sweetpotato and cassava (*Manihot esculenta*) roots;
–*Solanum* potato stolons and yam (*Dioscorea* spp) hypocotyls/
primary modal complexes; and
–*Colocasia* aroid main stems and *Xanthosoma* and *Colocasia* aroid
lateral stems.

The authors also recognized the classical botanical definitions of the tuberous organs involved as roots, tubers and corms/cormels, respectively. However, although such botanical definitions were acknowledged to be of undoubted taxonomic value, they were thought to "obscure the similar morphology and anatomy as well as the common physiology and ontogeny of these organs, which should be adumbrated by definitions" (Wilson 1990).

Accordingly, by analogy with fruits (Coombe 1976), a common definition of the organs described as tuber was espoused on the basis of commonalities in the processes of:

–generation of tuberous tissues in stelar parenchyma to create a
powerful SINK for assimilate early in the crop growth cycle; compared with cereals and legumes;
–function of these tissues in cell division, cell expansion and accumulation of water, inorganic ions (mainly potassium) and sucrose;
–storage of polysaccharide carbohydrate mainly as starch;
–dormancy and renewed growth in mature tubers
as well as in the capacity for
–dormancy and regrowth after perennation of mature tubers (albeit at
varying levels).

In the course of detailing evidence for commonalities in the generation of tuberous tissues, concepts of the presumptive yield organ (PYO) and trans-organ genesis (TOG) of tuberous yield organs (TYO) were formulated with reference to findings on phylogeny and ontogeny of these organs in the six tuberous species listed above.

In this paper, new perspectives on tuberization in sweetpotato are outlined in view of the new concepts of the PYO and TOG as well as of the common definition of TYO's in the six species (including sweetpotato) as tubers. The paper is presented under the following headings:

1. The concept of the presumptive yield organ in sweetpotato.
2. Trans-organ genesis of tuberous tissues.
3. Common definition of tuberous yield organs as tubers.
4. New perspectives on sweetpotato tuberization.

THE CONCEPT OF A PRESUMPTIVE YIELD ORGAN IN SWEETPOTATO

Tuber Bearing Organs of Sweetpotato

Wilson (1970) and Wilson and Lowe (1973a) defined thick, pentarch/hexarch, positively geotropic, adventitious roots of nodal origin on sweetpotato stem cuttings as tuber bearing organs (TBO) on the grounds of their capacity to initiate tuberous growth. Thin, tetrarch roots of internodal origin, lateral roots and tuber roots did not normally show such capacity for tuberous growth. However, tuberization was frustrated in certain TBOs to give rise to "string" roots and "pencil" roots and an apparently genetically defined number of tubers by 12 weeks after planting (Wilson and Lowe 1973b, Lowe and Wilson 1974a). Analysis of these processes of tuberization led to the concept of quantitative morphogenesis (Wilson and Lowe 1973b) as well as definition of the potential tuberization index (i.e., the total number of TBOs) and the percentage tuberization index (tuber number as a percentage of total TBO number) (Lowe and Wilson 1974a,b). Such definition of TBOs was derived from their distinctive characteristics—compared with other roots in the sweetpotato root system—and their analogy with the specialized stolons of *Solanum* potato, e.g., in the capacity for alternative shoot growth (Wilson 1973).

Presumptive Yield Organs in Tuberous Species

Alternatively, the concept of a PYO was proposed by Wilson (1990) after consideration of evidence of:

1. the diversity of organs which give rise to tuberous growth, e.g.,
   –compressed main and lateral shoots in the aroids;
   –the primary nodal complex in yams;
   –the stolon in *Solanum* potato; and
   –the adventitious root in sweetpotato and cassava stem cuttings.

Such diversity was interpreted to support the view that tuberization was the characteristic of the entire main and lateral axes of the plant body rather than of a specific organ.

2. the comparative phylogeny of certain of these organs, e.g.,
   –the rhizomes which replace corms in certain varieties of taro
   (*Colocasia esculenta*) (Ghani 1979);
   –the ancestral rhizome of the yams which evolved into the
   "yam head" or primary nodal complex (Ferguson 1973); and
   –the diageotropic stolons of *Solanum andigena* (Booth 1963)
   which can be induced to develop on any bud on stem cuttings.

The phylogenetic evidence indicated the common origin of tuberous growth in the stoloniferous organs of diverse species.

3. the recapitulation of phylogeny in the ontogeny of tuberous growth,
   e.g.,
   –in the suppression of tuberous growth and the alternative
   induction of stoloniferous growth in taro by gibberellic acid 3
   treatment (Alamu and McDavid1978).

In other words, the PYO was characterized by:
   –diversity in morphological origin in main, lateral and specialized stems as well as in specialized and normal roots; and
   –recognized phylogenetic origins in stolons in *Solanum* potato,
   aroids and yams and by demonstrated capacity for ontogenetic
   recapitulation of such phylogeny, e.g., in *Colocasia* aroids.

The sum total of this evidence supports the concept of organs which:
   –performed functions other than the initiation of tuberous
   growth earlier in their phylogeny;
   –developed the capacity for such growth by specialization,
   perhaps to meet certain environmental conditions; but
   –had the capacity to revert to their ancestral characteristics in
   response both to environmental and genetic stimuli, e.g., in the
   Colocasia aroids.

The organs were, therefore, judged to be PYOs in which the yield organ or tuber was initiated and developed only in certain species, under certain ontogenetic conditions of internal hormonal, mineral nutrient and carbohydrate metabolisms (Wilson 1977, 1982) and under environmental conditions conducive to tuberization.

The Presumptive Yield Organ in Sweetpotato

The question now arises as to whether the concept of the TBO of sweetpotato (Wilson 1970) is in accord with that of the PYO as described above for tuberous species. Although evidence of inter-species diversity does not apply in the single sweetpotato *Ipomoea batatas* species, it is interesting to note that wide variation in tuber length and tuber "stalk" length among sweetpotato varieties suggests variation in the capacity for tuber initiation along the length of the TBO. Also there are other non-tuberous (e.g., *I. gracilis, I. pes-caprae*) as well as tuberous (e.g., *I. costata, I. graminea*) *Ipomoea* species (Yen 1982). Existence of these species suggests a diversity in the evolution of tuberous growth in the roots of *Ipomoea* species, which is at least analogous to that in the stolons of the three species discussed earlier.

Evidence from phylogeny comes from the species *I. trifida*, thought by Nishiyama (1971) to be the direct progenitor of sweetpotato. *I. trifida* shows incipient tuberous thickening reminiscent of sweetpotato pencil roots. Moreover, a synthetic hexaploid *I. trifida* population produced viable seed when crossed with sweetpotato (CIP 1990). Also, at the physiological level, reciprocal grafts of sweetpotato rootstocks on *I. trifida* scions led to increased photosynthesis in the *I. trifida* leaves (Hozyo and Park 1971). This evidence is interpreted to mean that the ancestral tuberous root of *I. trifida* could have been the progenitor of the sweetpotato tuber and that subsequent evolution of the process of tuberization led to increased productivity, domestication and widespread distribution of the *I. batatas* species as sweetpotato in Andean South America at least 10,000 years ago (Ugent and Peterson 1988).

The suppression of sweetpotato tuberization by environmental conditions of waterlogged soils with low soil oxygen content (Togari 1950) and high nitrate-N supply (Wilson 1973b) as well as by long days and exogenous treatment with gibberellic acid 3 (McDavid and Alamu 1980) to result in string and pencil root formation *sensu* Wilson (1970) completes the analogy of sweetpotato tuberous roots with PYOs in other species.

Therefore, on the basis of evidence of phylogeny and ontogenetic reversal of normal tuber development, the TBO in sweetpotato is here designated as a presumptive yield organ, i.e., an organ with developmental flexibility either to generate a tuberous yield organ or tuber or to revert to alternative ancestral tuberous growth in "string" roots and "pencil" roots. Evidence is also adduced to suggest that increased photosynthetic productivity resulted from the evolution of tuberous growth in sweetpotato and that such productivity may have resulted in the early, widespread distribution of sweetpotato and other *Ipomoea* species.

TRANS-ORGAN GENESIS OF TUBEROUS TISSUES

TOG in Tuberous Species

Wilson (1990) defined the generation of tuberous growth in alternative organs to the one in which tuberization normally occurred as trans-organ genesis of tuberous growth. This phenomenon was first noted by Onwueme (1978) in sub-terranean, cassava stem tissue produced from stem cuttings, planted in the inverted position. Later, Sirju-Charran and Wickham (1988) described a similar phenomenon in sweetpotato stems. However, Wilson (1990) proposed that evidence of naturally occurring TOG of tuberous growth could also be found in certain tuberous species and cited:

–the cormels versus the corms of the aroids; and
–the aerial bulbils versus the underground tubers in yams (Burkill 1960; Wickham et al. 1982).

Further examples are here cited including:

–adventitious versus lateral tuber roots of cassava (Wickham and Wilson 1987);
–daughter tubers produced by gemmation or chain tuberization on immature *Solanum* potato tubers versus normal stolon-borne tubers (Burton 1963) ; and
–second tubers produced on stored yams after extended GA$_3$-promoted dormancy (Wickham et al. 1984) versus normal primary nodal complex-borne tubers.

Accordingly, it was concluded that tuberization was an inherent characteristic of both the main and lateral axial organs of certain species, that normal location of tubers in a certain organ might be a consequence of the environment in which the species originated and that such location could result from control mechanisms for gene expression rather than in the fundamental nature of the genes encoded for tuberization.

TOG in Sweetpotato

In studies on methodology for using small tuber sets in sweetpotato cultivation, Akita et al. (1962) showed that, during sprouting of partially buried mother tubers, tuberization was inhibited in the light-exposed proximal end and promoted in the subterranean, distal end of the mother tubers. Moreover, daughter tuber genesis was promoted in subterranean tuberous roots, produced from the distal end of partially exposed mother tubers and lignification stimulated in the stelar, storage parenchyma of the light-exposed proximal end of the mother tubers. Sirju-Charran and Wickham (1988) repeated these experiments and confirmed the original findings of Akita et al. (1962).

In further experimentation with partially buried, inverted, subterranean planting of "mother" tubers, Sirju-Charran and Wickham (1988) found that tuberization occurred in the etiolated, subterranean, portion of the sprouting stem. Such tuberization was located after negative geotropic curvature but before the emergence of the etiolated stem from the soil to form a chlorophyllous shoot. At the anatomical level, the generation and distribution of cells and tissues in the tuberized stems were found to be similar to those proceses in the tuberization in sweetpotato tuberous roots (Wilson and Lowe 1973). Specifically, generation of stelar, storage parenchyma from both the primary cambium and anomalous secondary and tertiary meristematic strips was the characteristic feature of both the normal and stem-based processes of tuberization.

The authors concluded that: "the development of storage sink sites in sweetpotato was not solely under genetic control but rather seems to be influenced by: (1) several environmental factors with light playing a major role; (2) physiological factors, which are in turn influenced by the environment and the stage of maturation of the plant and (3) anatomical factors, with the occurrence of lignification being a major limitation." These conclusions supported those of Wilson (1982).

Later, Dabydeen and Sirju-Charran (1990) described tuberization in the radicular root of yam bean (*Pachyrizhus erosus*) as similar to that in sweetpotato and concluded that light, endogenous hormone levels and enzymes concerned with lignin biosynthesis and starch accumulation were of greater significance in the process than anatomical features of the tuberizing organ, e.g., archy and centripetal development of the primary xylem elements. This interpretation questioned the validity of the inclusion of the primary development of the TBO *sensu* Wilson (1970, 1982) and/or the PYO *sensu* Wilson (1990) in the definition of tuberization. The case for inclusion of primary development in the definition is next made.

RETHINKING THE DEFINITION OF THE SWEETPOTATO TUBER

The major issue in the redefinition of the tuber is clear identification of the process of tuber initiation either in primary or in secondary tissues. However, wherever it occurs, the following processes are associated with tuberization:

1. Generation of stelar storage parenchyma through:

    –suppression of cell elongation;
    –suppression of lignin biosynthesis;
    –promotion of lateral cell expansion; and
    –promotion of plastid genesis for starch storage.

2. Generation of meristematicity in primary stelar cells, e.g., pith and cambium cells, as well as genesis of anomalous secondary and tertiary cambial strips.

3. Accumulation of water, sugars and K+ ions and storage of polysaccharides, mostly starch.

The change in polarity of cell expansion leading either to further cell meristematicity or to the formation of stelar storage parenchyma from primary pith tissues or from secondary or tertiary tissues derived from the primary cambium or anomalous cambial strips is here interpreted to be the primary event of tuber initiation.

Such a change in the polarity of cell expansion, as evidenced by the qualitative formation of parenchyma cells, rather than xylem elements first occurs in the primary pith cells of pentarch or hexarch tuberous roots (Wilson and Lowe 1973a). Pith cells also occur in etiolated stems produced from inverted, partially buried mother tubers

(Sirju-Charran and Wickham 1988) in sweetpotato. The same phenomenon was also recorded in the radicular root of the yam bean by Dabydeen and Sirju-Charran (1990).

However, only in *Solanum* potato tubers, has the three-fold quantitative increase in the lateral expansion of pith cells been definitely shown to be the first contributant to the lateral swelling of the stoloniferous PYO (Booth 1963), recognized as the tuber. There is no doubt, however, that the generation of secondary, tertiary and indeed quarternary storage stelar parenchymatous cells from cambia and cambial strips is the characteristic feature of developing sweetpotato tubers.

These processes are resumed in the subterranean portion of mature tubers, when they are planted either in an inverted or upright position (Sirju-Charran and Wickham 1988). It is suppressed by light and naturally frustrated in "string" and "pencil" root genesis during the quantitative morphogenesis of the sweetpotato root system (Wilson and Lowe 1973b).

Moreover, there is no doubt that such quantitative morphogenesis leading to characteristic tuber number and tuber shapes in different sweetpotato varieties is under genetic control.

Therefore, it is concluded on the basis of both qualitative and quantitative evidence that the change in polarity of cell expansion leading to generation of stelar storage parenchyma is not only the primary event in tuber initiation but also a characteristic feature of sweetpotato tuber growth and development. Since the change in the polarity of cell expansion occurs in primary pith cells only in certain tuberous roots of the sweetpotato root system, these roots, which are normally hexarch or pentarch, are the potential tuber bearing organs of the species. Such roots were designated PYOs by Wilson (1990) because of their capacity for alternative non-tuber development. It is most interesting to note that Burton (1963) considered that *Solanum* potato tuber dormancy should be regarded as dating from the time when stolon elongation ceased and lateral growth commenced.

Taken together, the evidence of TOG of tuberous growth on stems versus roots in sweetpotato and the mediation of tuber initiation through the change in polarity of cell expansion is interpreted to mean that:

1.   The process of tuberization may be under separate control from that of its location in a specific organ;
2.   Powerful internal stimuli for alternative location of tuberization are generated when planting sets are inverted and partially exposed to light;
3.   These stimuli may well derive from previously formed tubers, (especially in sweetpotato) through, for example, a process of hormonal control influenced by a genetic message;
4.   The essential characteristic of tuberous organs is the change in polarity of stelar cells resulting in the generation of storage parenchyma, which constitute a powerful sink for assimilate early in the crop growth cycle; and
5.   This latter process occurs both in the primary and secondary tissues of the PYO and predisposes the PYO to becoming a tuber bearing organ.

NEW PERSPECTIVES ON TUBERIZATION

The new perspectives on tuberization envisaged derive from five concepts on the process discussed in this paper as follows:

1.   The concept of a common definition of organs previously defined on the basis of taxonomic criteria as corms, cormels, tubers and roots as *tubers*.
2.   The concept of the capacity for tuberization as being the property of the main and axial organs of the entire plant body on the basis of evidence of TOG of tuberous growth.
3.   The concept of the PYO as the phylogenetic and ontogenetic predecessor of the tuber, on which tuber initiation normally occurs during the early development of the PYO.
4.   The concept that, although tuber initiation, growth and development may be greatly influenced by physiological and environmental conditions, both the capacity to respond to these conditions and the quantitative morphogenesis of PYO's which lead to definition of tuber number and tuber shape are under genetic control.
5.   The acceptance of the change in polarity in immature stelar parenchyma cells leading to the generation of the storage parenchymatous tissue, characteristic of all *tubers*, as the common characteristic of the process of *tuberization*.

The expected outcomes of this new perspective is the possibility for adopting a common approach to crop improvement in tuberous species similar to that adopted for cereal grain, legume grain and soft fruit species. This approach resulted in major innovations for crop improvement, e.g.,

–high density planting of short stemmed, early maturing, non-competitive, efficient high yielding varieties of wheat, rice and maize and to a lesser extent soyabean, cowpea and pigeon pea;
–high density planting of dwarf varieties of temperate fruit, e.g., peaches, apples;
–improvement of the shelf life of tomatoes using "antisense" biotechnology of an enzyme polygalacturonase, leading to similar approaches with other fruit.

Adoption of such a common approach to the improvement of tuberous crop species will lead to revision of the research agenda for improvement of tropical tuber crops. Such an agenda might focus on the use of biotechnology approaches to make use of the wide genetic variability of these crops for:

–Environmental adaptation and environmental stress resistance ranging from wetlands in *Colocasia* to near desert conditions in *Manihot*;
–Resistance to pests and diseases;
–Yield improvement based on the common characteristic of generation of stelar

storage parenchyma;
–Increased tuber shelf life based on the definition of dormancy as a developmental process commencing at tuber initiation;
–Species specific improvements, e.g.,
  –non-sweet sweetpotato
  –heat and stress tolerant *Solanum* potato.

It is expected that these and many other aspects of the improvement of tuberous species will be more easily realized by the adoption of a common approach in such a new agenda for research and development of tropical tuberous species. Sweetpotato research must play a major role in the formulation of this new agenda because of the relatively advanced stage of development of knowledge of this species.

REFERENCES

Akita, S., F. Yamamoto, M. Ono, M. Kushara, and S. Ikemoto. 1962. Studies on the small tuber sett method in sweet potato cultivation. Bulletin of the Chugoku Agricultural Experiment Station 8:75-128.

Alamu, S., and C.R. McDavid.1978. Promotion of flowering in edible aroids by gibberellic acid. Tropical Agriculture 55:81-86.

Booth, A. 1963. The role of growth substances in the development of stolons. *In* Growth of the potato, edited by J.D. Ivins and F.L. Milthorpe. Butterworths, London.

Burkill, I.H. 1960. The organography and the evolution of the Dioscoreaceae, the family of yams. Journal Linnaeaus Society (Botany) 56:319-412.

Burton, W.G. 1963. Concepts and mechanism of dormancy. Pages 17-41 *in* Growth of the Potato, edited by J.D. Ivins and F.L.Milthorpe. Butterworths, London.

CIP (International Potato Centre) 1990. Sweet Potato Germplasm Enhancement 1990. Annual report: Worldwide Potato and Sweet Potato Improvement.

Coombe, B.G. 1976. The development of fleshy fruits. Annual Review of Plant Physiology 27:508-527.

Dabydeen, S., and G. Sirju-Charran. 1990. The developmental anatomy of the root system in yam bean, *Pachyrhizus erosus*. Urban. Annals of Botany 66:313-320.

Ferguson, T.U. 1973. Tuber development in yams: physiological and agronomic implications. Proceedings, 3rd Symposium of the International Society for Tropical Root Crops, Ibadan, Nigeria. Dec. 2-9, 1973. 3: 72-77.

Ghani, F.D. 1979. The status of Keladi China. *Colocasia esculenta* (L.) Schott cultivation in Peninsula Malaysia. International Foundation for Science (Stockholm). Provincial Report. No. 5. pp. 35-54.

Hozyo, Y., and C.Y. Park. 1971. Plant production in grafting plants between wild type and improved variety in *Ipomoea*. Bulletin of the National Institute of Agricultural Science Series D. No. 12.

Lowe, S.B., and L.A. Wilson. 1974a. Comparative analysis of tuber development in six sweet potato (*Ipomoea batatas* L. Lam.) cultivars. i. Tuber initiation, tuber growth and partition of assimilate. Annals of Botany, (London) 38: 307-317.

Lowe, S.B., and L.A. Wilson. 1974b. Comparative analysis of tuber development in six sweet potato (*Ipomoea batatas* L. Lam.) cultivars. ii. Interrelationships between tuber shape and yield. Annals of Botany, (London) 38:319-326.

McDavid, C.R., and S. Alamu. 1980. The effects of daylength on the growth and development of whole plants and rooted leaves of sweet potato. Tropical Agriculture, Trinidad. 57(2):113-119.

Nishiyama, I. 1971. Evolution and domestication of sweet potato. Botany Magazine, Tokyo 84:377-387.

Onwueme, I.C. 1978. The tropical tuber crops. Yams, cassava, sweet potato and cocoyams. John Wiley & Sons. New York.

Roberts-Nkrumah, L.B., L.A. Wilson, and T.U. Ferguson. 1986. Responses of four sweet potato cultivars to levels of shade: 2. Tuberization. Tropical Agriculture, Trinidad. 63(4):265-270.

Sirju-Charran, G., and L.D. Wickham. 1988. The development of alternative storage sink sites in sweet potato. *Ipomoea batatas*. Annals of Botany (London) 61:99-102.

Ugent, D. and L.W. Peterson. 1988. Archaeological remains of potato and sweet potato in Peru. CIP (International Potato Centre). Circular 16(3): September 1988.

Wickham, L.D., L.A. Wilson, and H.C. Passam (1982). Origin, development and germination of bulbils of two *Dioscorea* species. Annals of Botany (London) 50:621-627.

Wickham, L.D., H.C. Passam, and L.A. Wilson. 1984. Dormancy responses to post-harvest application of growth regulators in *Dioscorea* species. 2. Dormancy response in ware tubers of *D. alata* and *D. esculenta*. Journal of Agricultural Sciences Cambridge 102:433-436.

Wickham, L.D., and L.A. Wilson. 1987. Quality changes during long term storage of cassava roots in moist media. Tropical Science 25:79-86.

Wilson, L.A. 1970. The process of tuberization in sweet potato (*Ipomoea batatas* L. Lam) Proceedings, 2nd International Symposium on Tropical Root Crops, Hawaii 2:24-26.

Wilson, L.A. 1973. Stimulation of adventitious bud production in detached sweet potato leaves by high levels of nitrogen supply. Euphytica 22:324-326.

Wilson, L.A. 1977. Root Crops. Pages 187-236 *in* Ecophysiology of tropical crops, edited by P. De T. Alvin and T.T. Kozlowski, Academic Press. New York.

Wilson, L.A. 1982. Tuberization in sweet potato (*Ipomoea batatas* L. Lam). Pages 79-94 *in* Sweet potato, edited by R.L. Villareal and T.D. Griggs. Proceedings, First International Symposium on Sweet Potato, AVRDC, Taiwan. March, 1981.

Wilson, L.A., and S.B. Lowe. 1973a. Anatomy of the root system in West Indian sweet potato (*Ipomoea batatas* L. Lam) cultivars. Annals of Botany 37: 633-643.

Wilson, L.A., and S.B. Lowe. 1973b. Quantitative morphogenesis of root types in the sweet potato (*Ipomoea batatas* (L.) Lam) root system during early growth from stem cuttings. Tropical Agriculture, Trinidad 54(4):343-345.

Wilson, L.A. 1990. New perspectives on tuberization in sweet potato. Prepared for the occasion of the joint award of the first Third World Network of Scientific Organizations (TWNSO) Prize in Agriculture to the author. November 1990. Caracas, Venezuela.

Yen, D.E. 1982. Sweet potato in historical perspective. Pages 2-30 *in* Sweet potato, edited by R.L. Villareal and T.D. Griggs, Proceedings, First International Symposium, Asian Vegetable Research and Development Centre, Taiwan.

A Response: The Sweetpotato Storage Organ Is A Root, Not A Tuber*

S. J. Kays, W. W. Collins, J. C. Bouwkamp

"The propagation of error, by endless transfer from textbook to textbook, is a troubling and amusing story in its own right—a source of inherited defect almost more stubborn than inborn errors of genetics" (S.J. Gould, *The Flamingo's Smile* 1985).

The following is in response to the previous paper's proposal (Wilson and Wickham 1992) to change the classical botanical definition of "tuber" to a very general agronomic term for storage organs. While there are both positive and negative arguments for a generalized terminology, there are, we believe, overwhelming problems with the proposed terminology which will further confuse, rather than clarify, the existing situation. We have, therefore, critiqued both the history of the use of the terms and arguments against such a change.

Botanical Definitions and Origins

Tuber is defined as an underground structure consisting of a solid thickened portion or outgrowth of a stem or rhizome, of a more or less rounded form, and bearing "eyes" or buds from which new plants may arise (Simpson and Weiner 1989). Tuber is derived from the Latin word *tuber*, a lump or swelling. It was first used in the English language in 1668 by Wilkins in his work "An Essay Towards a Real Character, and a Philosophical Language".

A **root** is the descending axis of a plant, tree, or shoot, developed from the radicle and serving to attach the plant to and convey nourishment from the soil, with or without subsidiary rootlets or fibers (Simpson and Wilkins 1989). In the English language, "root" predates "tuber" by 518 years, being first used in 1150 (Napier 1906). It is evident that the definition encompasses the entire root system, which is comprised of subclasses of roots displaying various characteristics, properties, and functions (e.g., fibrous roots, root hairs, tuberous roots).

A **tuberous root** is a true root (usually one of a cluster) thickened so as to resemble a tuber, but bearing no buds (Simpson and Weiner 1989). This term was also first used in the English language in 1668 by Wilkins. The problem arises when tuberous root (i.e., a root that resembles a tuber) is corrupted to "root tuber", now indicating a tuber that is a root, which is incorrect. One can readily see how this subtle difference in wording, but pronounced difference in meaning, can greatly exacerbate the confusion, a situation intensified if English is not an author's first language.

Tuberation is the formation or production of a tuber or tubers (Simpson and Weiner 1989) and **tuberization** is the process by which this occurs. Tuberation was

The University of Georgia, Athens, GA, North Carolina State University, Raleigh, NC and The University of Maryland College Park, respectively.
* See footnote on page 296.

first used in 1727 (Bailey 1727). One of the arguments for altering in some manner the existing terminology is that there is not a general term for the collective processes of induction, initiation, and development for storage organs that are roots, corms, rhizomes, and bulbs comparable to tuberization for tubers.

It is likewise important to note that words such as root and tuber have meanings other than those related to botany. For example, tuber and tuberation have medical and other meanings; root has an even greater diversity. Root is a mathematical term and, on the other end of the spectrum, a form of coarse Australian slang (Chamberlain 1973). It is evident, however, that there are well defined botanical meanings for both root and tuber. These have been used correctly, for the most part, by plant scientists over the past 300 years. While it is evident that the sweetpotato storage root is often incorrectly called a tuber, especially by scientists translating from Japanese or Chinese to English, translation errors, even when persistent, can hardly be construed a mandate. To change the meaning of the term tuber, therefore, would make the literally hundreds of thousands of times the word(s) were correctly used in the past now incorrect. It is hard to envision how this would serve to clarify the issue.

Is There a Mandate for the Proposed Change in the Terminology?

It is proposed in the preceding paper (Wilson and Wickham 1992) that tuber is used by many authors for the storage organ of the sweetpotato, i.e., there is a popular mandate for this change. While it is evident that the sweetpotato storage root is often incorrectly called a tuber, especially by scientists translating from Japanese or Chinese to English, translation errors, even when persistent, can hardly be construed a mandate. In support of the idea that there is widespread use of the term tuber for the sweetpotato storage root, the author lists his own redefinition of the term published in a non-refereed journal and several of his own papers. This can hardly be construed as a popular mandate for the change. Likewise, it is essential that a sweeping change in botanical meaning must be scrutinized with diligence through the peer-review process.

An Examination of the Proposed Definition of Tuber

Contrary to the opinion of Wilson and Wickham (1992), the botanical definitions for root and tuber do not "obscure the similar morphology and anatomy as well as the common physiology and ontogeny of these organs" .... but rather serve to distinguish the dissimilarities in morphology, anatomy, physiology, and ontogeny. These dissimilarities comprise in part a foundation for our arguments against the proposed terminology.

The following address the various parts of the proposed new definition of "tuber"[1] by Wilson and Wickham and the inherent weaknesses of each.

---

[1]Quotes are used to distinguish Wilson and Wickham's (1991) proposed new term "tuber" from the classical botanical tuber. Italics are used for the proposed new definition.

(a) "- *generation of tuberous tissues in stelar parenchyma to create a powerful sink early in the crop growth cycle...;*"

One of the initial problems with this portion of the definition is that it is quite impossible to accurately define a term (i.e., "tuber") with that term or in this case a word derived from it (i.e., tuberous). Therefore, for the sake of accuracy and clarity, we have substituted "storage" for "tuberous." A wide range of storage tissues are known to arise from stelar parenchyma. For example, with the proposed definition, enlarged stems of kohlrabi (*Brassica oleracea*, L. Gongylodes group) and tsatsai (*Brassica juncea* var. *tsatsai*, Makino) would be included as "tubers," although it is doubtful that it was the intent of Wilson and Wickham (1992) to include them. An additional problem is that the distinction of "early in the crop growth cycle" can be made for nearly all plants forming vegetative rather than reproductive storage organs. Finally, this portion of the definition does not actually describe roots and tubers, but rather an evolutionary strategy for survival and reproduction.

(b) "- *function of these tissues .... to accumulate water, inorganic ions (mainly potassium) and sucrose;*"

Nearly all starch-containing storage organs, including many fruits, meet this portion of the definition. The statement also opens a series of quantitative considerations. How much water/potassium/sucrose must be accumulated to warrant the distinction as a "tuber?"

(c) "- *storage of polysaccharide carbohydrate mainly as starch;*"

As with part b) of the definition, many storage organs that contain starch [e.g., banana (*Musa* spp.), apple (*Malus sylvestris*, Mill.), and pear (*Pyrus communis*, L.) are fruits but not tubers. When does an organ contain sufficient starch to become a "tuber"? Is the Jerusalem artichoke (*Helianthus tuberosus*, L.) which stores the fructosan inulin[2] rather than starch and is botanically a true tuber now not a "tuber?"

(d) "- *dormancy and renewed growth in mature tubers...*"

Again avoiding the defining of "tuber" with the term "tuber," and for clarity substituting instead "storage organ," we are left with several well defined physiological terms: "dormancy" and "mature." Dormancy appears to be a consistent feature of true tubers but only an occasional feature of roots in general and storage roots in particular. In the case of sweetpotatoes, storage roots usually do not produce sprouts as long as they are attached to the plant. Once they are detached, however, sprouts may be produced within a few weeks. We have also observed genotypes in our breeding programs in which sprouts are produced on storage roots while they are attached to the plant. Thus, the requirement for dormancy in the definition of "tuber" would seem to exclude sweetpotato storage roots.

---

[2]A non-starch polysaccharide comprised of a linear chain of fructose molecules.

Maturity, as a physiological term, refers to a state in which a plant or plant organ continues to function but no longer enlarges. There are many examples of such organs including leaves, fruits, bulbs, and tubers. Sweetpotato storage roots do not mature, but rather continue to enlarge as long as environmental and physiological conditions are favorable. This is probably true of storage roots in general. The requirement for maturation as a condition for renewed growth would appear to exclude sweetpotatoes and perhaps cassava and taro from being defined as "tubers."

(e) "- *dormancy and regrowth after perennation of mature* ('storage organs')[3] *tubers (albeit at varying levels)."*

This portion of the definition seems to recapitulate (d) and appears to further adumbrate the definition.

Taken together, the various features of the proposed definition of "tuber" are either so broad as to include many types of storage organs not intended to be included or so narrow as to exclude some of the storage organs which were intended to be included.

Is the Sweetpotato a Root or Tuber?

Although published in 1924, the work by Artschwager remains perhaps the most definitive treatment of the anatomy of the sweetpotato (Artschwager 1924), and analysis of the anatomy of the storage root of the sweetpotato leaves little question that it is a root. When contrasted with the anatomy of a tuber such as the potato (*Solanum tuberosum*, L.)(Artschwager 1918), pronounced anatomical differences are readily apparent. While there are some obvious similarities between storage roots and tubers (e.g., large numbers of parenchyma cells containing starch), there are likewise similarities with virtually every other plant organ. These similarities are not sufficient grounds to group storage roots and tubers into a common anatomical class any more than tubers and fruits.

Storage roots represent part of the water and nutrient conducting system, with the root system continuing beyond the organ and lateral roots from its periphery. This is clearly illustrated in the detailed drawing of the root system of the sweetpotato published by Weaver and Bruner (1927). The stolon of the potato typically terminates in the tuber which, as a modified stem, does not represent part of the primary water and nutrient acquisition and transport system. Sweetpotato storage roots display proximal dominance, sprouting at the stem end, while in potato tubers this is reversed (i.e., sprouts form at the most distal part of the organ). Sprouts arise in potato tubers from meristem areas (nodes), while on sweetpotato storage roots they arise adventitiously from the cambial area. The sweetpotato, unlike the potato tuber, does not appear to have a genetically controlled size limitation. The storage root, under appropriate conditions, will continue to grow indefinitely, with final size often

---

[3]Authors' insertion in lieu of "tubers".

being limited only by environmental conditions and/or increasing oxygen diffusion resistance with root size and the onset of anaerobic conditions causing the root to begin to rot. [Oxygen diffusion resistance increases because the volume of three-dimensional organs with sides of more or less equal dimensions increases by length to the third power while surface area increases only by length to the second power. As a consequence, with increasing size there is proportionally less surface area for oxygen to diffuse through and proportionally more interior cells requiring oxygen (Kays 1991)]. From the work of Artschwager and others, there is simply no question that anatomically, physiologically, and functionally the sweetpotato storage organ is a root.

An argument presented in favor of altering the terminology is that it is possible via pharmacological treatments or relatively unnatural forms of physical perturbment to cause non-root tissue of the sweetpotato to store starch (see Sirju-Charran and Wickham 1988). Being able to artificially create an alternative storage site, however, does not change the nature or anatomy of the storage organ that forms under normal conditions. The ability to induce other cells to mimic a storage organ is not surprising. Essentially all of the nucleated cells within a sweetpotato clone contain identical genetic information in the form of DNA. DNA is differentially expressed in the various cells within the plant, causing some to develop into and function as flowers while others become storage roots or other organs. It is possible through various artificial means to turn on certain genes in cells in which they are normally not expressed. For example, the mRNA for the sweetpotato storage protein sporamin is not normally expressed in the leaves, petioles or fibrous roots (Hattori et al. 1985). Under the appropriate pharmacological conditions (i.e., high sucrose), however, it is possible to induce the expression of the gene in non-storage root tissue (Nakamura 1991). Does this make a petiole or stem a storage root?

In that there is tremendous genetic diversity in the germplasm of the sweetpotato, it may be possible, if one searches thoroughly enough, to find a sweetpotato mutant line that has true tubers as the storage organ. Likewise, it will eventually be possible through the use of recombinant DNA to transfer the genes for tuber formation from the potato or other tuber bearing species to the sweetpotato, giving tuber-forming transgenic plants. In neither case will it alter the fact that the storage organ of the sweetpotato grown in commerce is a root. An exception simply does not make the rule.

Why Be Accurate?

Originally Latin was the universal language of botany and many of the earliest publications were in that language. Selection of Latin was not just a chance decision. Rather, with over a thousand languages and an even greater number of dialects in the world, it was essential that a reader in each language could understand precisely the meaning of a word or statement. While Latin has been largely superseded by English, the need for precision in our description of objects, processes, and events remains as important today as it was in the time of Linneaus. Accuracy and precision in terminology give the reader whose first language is not English a reasonable chance to determine the meaning of a particular word or phrase. As a consequence, precision and accuracy in terminology are not simply desirable, they are cornerstones of science. The correct terminology makes an idea clear to the reader rather than ambiguous.

Problems with the Existing Terminology

The term tuberous root, though based on botanical tradition, has given rise to considerable confusion due to incorrect usage. At the time of its origin, the term tuberous root (i.e., a root resembling a tuber) was accurate as far as the understanding of the day permitted. Modern science with a far better understanding of anatomy, physiology, and ontogeny should not be expected, however, to rely on definitions based on gross morphology alone. The confusion caused by the use and misuse of tuberous root is extensive. As mentioned previously, tuberous root reversed to root tuber changes the meaning. Likewise, should tuberous be applied to other storage organs? Does the terminology tuberous rhizome (lotus), tuberous bulb (lily), tuberous corm (gladiolus), tuberous tap root (carrot), tuberous root and hypocotyl (radish), tuberous fruit (peanut), and tuberous tuber (potato) clarify the situation?

Wilson and Wickham (1992) propose the use of "tuber" as a very general horticultural/agronomic term for a broad but not clearly defined class of carbohydrate (mainly starch) storage organs. Hence, "tuber" would now have both an applied meaning and a botanical meaning. It is not clear though how one would differentiate which use an author intended. The argument in support of this dual meaning for a single word is that a similar situation occurs with fruit (i.e., a botanical meaning and a horticultural meaning). Is the reproductive organ of a tomato (1) botanically a fruit, horticulturally not a fruit, (2) horticulturally a vegetable, and (3) both a botanical fruit and a vegetable. It is hard to fathom how such a system applied to roots, tubers, corms, rhizomes, and bulbs would enhance clarity and decrease confusion.

Conclusions

The primary problems with Wilson and Wickham's proposal to change the existing terminology are two-fold: (1) the redefinition of the word tuber which has a well defined meaning, and (2) the dual use, applied and botanical, of the same word without a clear distinction of which one is being utilized by an author. Problems with this approach range from making all previous use of the word over the past 323 years incorrect, to greatly increasing the reader's confusion as to what the author is referring. A more practical approach would be to retain the current botanical terms for tuber, corm, and bulb, which are by definition storage organs, and describe enlarged roots and rhizomes which act as storage organs as storage roots and storage rhizomes. This would distinguish them from other non-storage roots and rhizomes.

While similarities can be found among a diverse range of organs in the plant kingdom, it is the dissimilarities that are crucial when establishing groupings. The distinct differences in anatomy, physiology, and ontology of belowground asexual reproductive organs far outweigh their similarities. The confusion caused by the incorrect use of the term tuber for the storage organ of the sweetpotato dramatically underscores the introductory statement in this paper by Gould. Propagation of error is never justified and propagation of error by choice should be judiciously avoided, especially in science.

REFERENCES

Artschwager, E. 1918. Anatomy of the potato plant, with special reference to the ontogeny of the vascular system. J. Agr. Res. 14:221-252.

Artschwager, E. 1924. On the anatomy of the sweet potato root, with notes on the internal breakdown. J. Agr. Res. 27:157-166.

Bailey, N. 1721. An universal etymological English dictionary. London, unnumbered pages, 1 vol.

Chamberlain, R. 1973. The Stuart affair. Hale, London, 312 pp.

Gould, S.J. 1985. The flamingo's smile: reflections in natural history. W.W. Norton & Co., New York, 473 pp.

Hattori, T., T. Nakagawa, M. Maeshima, K. Nakamura, and T. Asahi. 1985. Molecular cloning and nucleotide sequence of cDNA for sporamin, the major soluble protein of sweet potato tuberous roots. Plant Mol. Biol. 5:313-320.

Kays, S.J. 1991. Postharvest physiology of perishable plant products. Van Nostrand Reinhold, New York, 532 pp.

Nakamura, K. 1992. Regulation of expression of genes coding for sporamin and β-amylase of the sweetpotato. Pages 20-26 in Sweetpotato technology for the 21st century, edited by W.A. Hill, C.K. Bonsi and P.A. Loretan, Tuskegee University, Tuskegee, AL.

Napier, A.S. 1906. Contributions to Old English lexicography. Pages 265-358 in Transactions of the Philological Soc., vol. 10, K. Paul, Trench, Truber, London.

Simpson, J.A., and E.S.C. Weiner. 1989. The Oxford English Dictionary. Clarendon Press, Oxford, 20 vols.

Surju-Charran, G., and L.D. Wickman. 1988. The development of alternative storage sink sites in sweet potato, Ipomoea batatas. Ann. Bot. 61:99-102.

Weaver, J.E., and W.E. Bruner. 1927. Root development of vegetable crops. McGraw-Hill, New York, 351 pp.

Wilkins, J., bp of Chester. 1668. An essay towards a real character, and a philosophical language. printed by J.M. for S. Gellibrand and John Martin, London, 157 pp.

Wilson, L.A., and L.D. Wickham. 1992. New perspectives on tuberization in sweetpotatoes. Pages 296-306 in Sweetpotato technology for the 21st century, edited by W.A. Hill, C.K. Bonsi, and P.A. Loretan, Tuskegee University, Tuskegee, AL.

A Rejoinder: Further Perspective on Tuberization*

L. A. Wilson and L. D. Wickham

This is a rejoinder by the authors to the previous paper by Kays et al. (1992) entitled: "Is the Sweetpotato Storage Organ a Root or a Tuber?"

The new perspective on tuberization (Wilson and Wickham 1992) highlighted the particularities of the case of sweetpotato in order to clarify the more general problem of the definition of the term "tuber." Therefore, the paper sought evidence across the plant kingdom from some seven genera and nine species. The authors would restate the conceptualization of science of Kays et al. (1992) to say that "modern science, with far better understanding of the (comparative) anatomy, physiology, ontogeny (and phylogeny in several species) should not be expected to rely on (classical) definitions based on gross morphology alone."

This expectation is equally valid for classical definitions of the noun "tuber" as it is for the adjective "tuberous" *sensu* Simpson and Weiner (1989). Moreover, the expectation is not based on inaccurate translations of the sweetpotato tuber from Chinese or Japanese into English, but rather, on additional information and new interpretations based in modern science.

Accordingly, the new perspective equally accepts the origin of sweetpotato and cassava tubers in roots as it accepts the origin of potato and yam tubers in stems, rhizomes and hypocotyls. However, it does contend that these tuber bearing organs (TBO) must be considered as quite different organs from the tubers which they generate. It also notes that the perennial habit of sweetpotato and cassava species confers characteristics on the tuberization process which are not observable in the annual, monocarpic potato species. The thrust of the new perspective is that the functional evolution of subterranean storage organs of diverse morphological origins so modified their anatomy, morphology, ontogeny, physiology, genetics and phylogeny as to result in organs with greater similarities at every level, than the differences which might be expected from their diverse morphological origins. Therefore, this rejoinder will simply state the similarities and explicable differences between classical tubers and roots, and here the terms "tuber" and "tuberous" are used in their "new perspective" sense to include both classical roots and tubers.

SIMILARITIES BETWEEN CLASSICAL ROOTS AND TUBERS

The similarities between classical roots and tubers are listed under headings of:
> Gross morphology
> Anatomy
> Physiology/ontogeny
> Genetics

---

*See footnotes on pages 296 and 307.

Gross Morphology

(1) Both classical roots and classical tubers originate as subterminal lateral pro-tuberances in what Wilson and Wickham (1992) defined as a tuber bearing organ.

(2) Whether stem, rhizome or root, the TBO becomes specialized during ontogeny to perform the function of translocation of assimilates to the tuber.

(3) Tubers are subterranean organs with lateral growth which make their diameters several multiples of that of their TBOs.

(4) Buds are developed on all tubers except cassava tubers in which the function of storage in the tuber is separated from that of perennation in the stem. A reason for this separation is suggested later.

Anatomy

(5) In tubers, storage tissue is always developed from a cambium and is stelar in origin.

(6) Storage tissue in tubers consists of polysaccharide (mainly starch) storing cells, including inulin in Jerusalem artichoke tubers.

(7) Storage tissue in tubers includes meristematic cells and strips as well as the capacity for resumed meristematicity in storage parenchyma.

Physiology/Ontogeny

(8) Storage tissue has the capacity for rapid accumulation of water, inorganic ions (mainly potassium) and sucrose to constitute a major sink early in ontogeny.

(9) Sucrose is stored in storage tissues of many tubers as polysaccharide carbohy-drate, mainly and usually starch.

(10) Maturity usually coincides with the termination of the growing season in tubers both of annual, monocarpic, e.g., potato, yams and perennial, polycarpic, e.g., sweetpotato.

(11) All tubers show capacity for regrowth after widely different periods of dormancy either through buds, roots or tuberous growth. Such wide differences in dormancy also occur in seeds.

(12) Alternative expression of tuberization in certain species can be manipulated during ontogeny by physical treatments, e.g, inverting planting material in cassava

and sweetpotato and exposure to light in sweetpotato mother tubers. This phenomenon was designated trans-organ genesis (TOG) of tuberous organs by Wilson and Wickham (1991). Reversion to TBO or rhizome can also be induced in taro by growth regulator treatment.

Genetics and Phylogeny

(13) TOG is considered to be prime evidence that the definition of the tuber is independent of its origin in a particular TBO and that ontogeny can be made to recapitulate phylogeny in certain instances of tuberization.

(14) The capacity for improvement of all aspects of tuberization in all species by genetic manipulation, including length of dormancy period, attests to the genetic control of the process, albeit by a complex system of genes.

EXPLICABLE DIFFERENCES BETWEEN CLASSICAL ROOTS AND TUBERS

The differences between classical roots and tubers raised by Kays et al. (1992) are all expected and explicable. They are based on at least three factors as follows:

—Annual versus perennial habits of tuberous species;
—The nature of the TBO on which the tuber is generated; and
—The diversity of secondary metabolism within and between species.

Annual versus Perennial Habits

(1) The annual habits of the potato and yam species account for the fact that their tubers seem to have a genetically controlled size limitation. It is contended that this limitation originates in the inability of the annual, monocarpic plant to continue growth even in favorable environmental conditions, due to internal changes involving senescence-inducing substances (Leopold 1975; Nooden and Leopold 1978).

(2) Alternatively, the perennial habits of the sweetpotato and cassava species allow the plant and hence the tuber to continue growing into second and third seasons, beyond seasonal maturity, if favorable environmental conditions prevail.

(3) It is also here proposed that the extreme perennial habit of the cassava, based mainly in the stem, has led to the transfer of the effective organ of regrowth (the bud) to the cassava stem (planting material which is also a substantial storage site.) The cassava tuber, nevertheless, retains capacity for tuberous and root regrowth.

The Nature of the TBO

(4) Species with multinode stem-based TBOs show axillary buds, e.g., in potato tubers and taro corms, whereas those with root-based TBOs show adventitious buds or no buds as in the case of sweetpotato and cassava, respectively.

However, in single-node stem-(rhizome) based yam tubers, as in the sweet-potato tuber, buds are also adventitious.

(5) The tubers derived from root-based TBOs, e.g., sweetpotato, show proximal end sprouting, but classical corms from stem-based TBOs also show proximal end sprouting dominance. Alternatively, potato tubers with stem-based TBOs show distal-end sprouting.

(6) Functional roots including "tuber roots" and "terminal end roots" exist in the sweetpotato with a root-based TBO, but functional "tuber roots" also occur in the yam tuber with a stem-based TBO.

It is contended that differences originating in the nature of the organ on which the tuber arises are neither consistent within TBO groups, nor are they important in the definition of the tuber.

Diversity In Metabolism

The secondary metabolism of plant tissues is very diverse and subject to environmental manipulation. This diversity explains equally the synthesis of starch in sweetpotato and potato tubers and inulin in Jerusalem artichoke tubers as well as the transfer of capacity for sporamin synthesis in sweetpotato tubers to the non-storage tissue under conditions of high sucrose content.

These phenomena only support our caution in designating polysaccharide stored in tubers as quantitatively and qualitatively "mainly starch" as well as our proposal that trans-organ genesis of tuberous organs and, as demonstrated by Nakamura (1992), of secondary metabolism attest to the capability of tubers for initiation on any organ, along the axes of the plant body either in ontogeny or in phylogeny.

REFERENCES

Kays, S.J., W.W. Collins, and J.C. Bouwkamp. 1992. Is the sweetpotato storage organ a root or tuber? Pages 307-313 *in* Sweetpotato technology for the 21st century, edited by W.A. Hill, C.K. Bonsi and P.A. Loretan. Tuskegee University, Tuskegee, Alabama.

Leopold, A.C. 1975. Ageing, senescence and turnover in plants. Bioscience 25: 659.

Nakamura, K. 1992. Regulation of expression of genes coding for sporamin and β-amylase of the sweetpotato. Pages 20-26 *in* Sweetpotato technology for the 21st century, edited by W.A. Hill, C.K. Bonsi and P.A. Loretan. Tuskegee University, Tuskegee, Alabama.

Nooden, L.D., and A.C. Leopold. 1978. Phytohormone and the regulation of senescence and abscission, *In* Phytohormones and regulated compounds. 11th ed. Letham, Goodwin and Higgins. Elsevier, Amsterdam.

Simpson, J.A., and E.S.C. Weiner. 1989. The Oxford English Dictionary. Clarendon Press, Oxford. 20 vols.

Wilson, L.A., and L.D. Wickham. 1992. New perspectives on tuberization in sweetpotatoes. Pages 296-306 *in* Sweetpotato technology for the 21st century, edited by W.A. Hill, C.K. Bonsi and P.A. Loretan. Tuskegee University, Tuskegee, Alabama.

James O. Garner, Jr., Chana Phromtong, Lavetta Newell,
Floyd M. Woods*, Juan L. Silva

Chilling and Drought Stress Tolerance in Selected Sweetpotato Genotypes

Selected sweetpotato (*Ipomoea batatas* L.) genotypes were screened for tolerance to two environmental stresses, drought and chilling temperatures. Differences among genotypes were investigated to determine the mechanism involved in tolerance to these stresses. Membrane lipid fatty acid composition did not show consistent differences that would support chilling tolerance. Methods used in chilling tolerance screening experiments included chlorophyll fluorescence and electrolyte leakage. Drought tolerance was detected by the leaf moisture loss method and chlorophyll fluorescence.

The growth of plants indigenous to tropical and subtropical lowland climates is generally adversely affected by temperatures below 12°C. Although chilling injury has been investigated with respect to the exposure of storage roots of sweetpotato (*Ipomoea batatas* L.) to below optimal temperatures, very little work has been conducted on the sweetpotato plant. Environmental variables, including temperature and rainfall, were reported to affect carbohydrate and carotenoid content of sweetpotatoes (Hammett 1974). Thompson (1931) stated that the sweetpotato should have four months of growth with nights as well as days being warm for a considerable portion of the time. Early planting in order to establish a long growing season often exposes sweetpotato plants to cool temperatures. Therefore, cultivar adaptation to cool temperatures could extend the growing season or allow production where cooler conditions prevail.

The fluorescence excitation spectrum of higher plants and algae is considered a useful diagnostic tool in estimating damage sustained by the photosynthetic processes of plants (Smillie 1979). Fluorescence excitation spectra are indicators of the relative efficiency of transfer of photochemical light energy from the accessory pigments to the reaction centers within a Photosystem II. Smillie (1979) considers the chloroplast and associated membrane systems as useful experimental tools for investigating the diverse responses of plant species to chilling stress, their growth, survival and genetic adaptations. Melcarek and Brown (1977) investigated the effects of a progressive decrease in temperature on the steady state chlorophyll fluorescence (CF) of chilling susceptible and resistant plants. CF induction transients typically increased in these plants as temperature decreased. In contrast, in sweet-potato foliage, low temperature exposure typically reduced CF activity (Woods et al. 1991a).

Mississippi State University, Mississippi State, MS 39762 and *Department of Horticulture, Auburn University, Auburn, Alabama 36849.

Daines et al. (1976) reported that hardcore, a response to chilling in storage roots, was related to modification of pectic substances in root tissue. Yamaki and Uritani (1972) found that differences between a chilling tolerant white sweetpotato and an orange-flesh cultivar were related to phosphatidylethanolamine content which decreased in the orange-fleshed storage root when chilled. Phosphatidylethanolamine was the major lipid component of the mitochondria membrane of both cultivars. Differences in severity of chilling injury have been reported for orange-flesh genotypes but the mechanism for these differences has not been given (Hammett et al. 1978).

Production of sweetpotatoes in semi-arid regions has not been feasible because of the intolerance of sweetpotato to a limited water supply (Yen 1982). Jones (1961) found that, if a crop was irrigated when the soil moisture level dropped to 20% of the total available moisture, it produced yields equivalent to an irrigated crop. Other researchers (Allison et al. 1981) have reported that there may be differences among cultivars in their tolerance to drought. Rapid and accurate selection of breeding lines which possess genetic adaptation to drought stress is of prime importance to plant breeders. Two commonly employed physiological methods of assessing cellular membrane damage and thus drought stress are measurements of leaf electrolyte leakage (EC) and leaf water content (LWC)(Vasquez-Tello et al. 1990; Walker and Miller 1986). Analyzing detached leaves for water loss offers the possibility of identifying genotypes possessing drought adaptation traits. When the detached leaf method was used to screen 15 sweetpotato genotypes for tolerance to water stress, differences in percent moisture loss were found (Newell 1991). This method has shown more promise than other techniques because it is considered rapid and has low technological requirements. Walker and Miller (1986), in their study on cuticular water loss in cowpea genotypes, found that specific drought resistant and susceptible genotypes of cowpea consistently expressed differences in LWC 48 hours after detachment with the resistant genotypes having higher LWC. They noted that in cowpea intraspecific variability for the trait appears to exist which might be related to drought adaptation. They also hold that measuring the water retention capacity of detached leaves was a drought-screening technique superior to measuring leaf diffusive resistance or leaf temperature. Experiments have also indicated that the induction of water stress in living plants is not a necessity in screening for drought adaptation using this method (Walker and Miller 1986).

The objectives of this study were to determine whether genotypic differences among sweetpotato foliage and storage roots are similar in response to tolerance to chilling injury and drought resistance.

MATERIALS AND METHODS

Plants used in these experiments were produced from 10 to 12 cm cuttings transplanted to 3.8 liter plastic pots containing a peat-lite medium consisting of 2 peat:1 perlite:1 vermiculite (v/v/v). Added nutrients were 4.56 kg dolomitic lime, 1.82 kg 0N-9P-0K, 1.42 kg calcium nitrate and 0.17 kg fritted trace elements per

Table 1. Percent electrolyte leakage and chlorophyll fluorescence ratio following 12 hours exposure time at 5°C.

Genotype	Temp	EC(%)^z	CF^y
'MS26-1'	25	3.96 c	0.39 b
	5	8.22 b	0.33 c
'MS23-1'	25	3.83 c	0.52 a
	5	39.95 a	0.25 d

^{z}EC is percent of total electrolyte leakage. Total leakage was determined after boiling tissue for five min.
^{y}CF is the ratio of variable fluorescence to maximum fluorescence.
Means separation within columns by LSD test; means within column followed by same letter are not significantly different (P = 0.05).

cubic meter. The cuttings were placed in a glasshouse under intermittent mist for 5 days and subsequently transferred to an adjacent glasshouse for an additional 5 days under ambient conditions before treatments were imposed. Ten-day-old cuttings were placed in constant temperature rooms maintained at 25°C or 5°C, 85% RH and 12 h light (Woods et al. 1991b).

Proximal expanding leaves were detached from the 10-day old plants in the laboratory, weighed and placed on benches at room temperature (21°C). Percent fresh weight loss was calculated after 24 and 48 hours. Chlorophyll fluorescence (Papageorgiou 1975) and leaf electrolyte leakage (Paull 1981) methods were used to investigate chilling tolerance as described by Woods et al. (1991b) while CF and the detached leaf water loss (Walker and Miller 1986) methods were used to evaluate drought tolerance. Procedures as outlined by Whitaker (1986) were used to determine fatty acid composition of chloroplast lipids of leaf tissues and storage roots. Total fatty acid composition of chilled storage roots was determined every 10 days from the start of storage through 40 days.

Table 2. Effect of temperature on the palmitoleic acid content in phosphatidylcholine of chloroplast polar lipids for two genotypes.

Genotype	Temperature (°C)	Palmitoleic Acid (%)
'MS26-1'	25	0.008 c
	5	0.031 bc
'MS23-1'	25	0.055 b
	5	0.435 a

Mean separation in columns by LSD test; means within column followed by same letter are not statistically different (P = 0.05).
Values are expressed as the percent of total fatty acids.

RESULTS AND DISCUSSION

Results shown in Table 1 agreed with previous screening experiments (Woods et al. 1991b) that indicated that genotype 'MS26-1' was more chilling tolerant than genotype 'MS23-1.' Differences in EC and CF were detected after 12 hours of exposure to chilling temperature. At 5°C the chilling tolerant genotype 'MS26-1' showed a lower EC and higher CF than did genotype 'MS23-1.' Increased EC in a genotype suggested that chilling may have damaged the associated chloroplast membrane system. Changes in CF indicated an alteration in the light trapping and utilization property of the chloroplast.

Changes in chloroplast lipid fatty acid composition was investigated to determine if an alteration in composition and, therefore, a chloroplast membrane phase change was involved when chilling occurred. Of the fatty acids surveyed only phosphatidylcholine showed significant changes in fatty acid content (Table 2). The genotypic difference found was in the percentage of palmitoleic acid in phosphatidylcholine (PC). This unsaturated fatty acid was highest in the genotype less tolerant to chilling. Genotypic differences, not affected by temperature, are presented in Table 3. The chilling tolerant genotype, 'MS26-1,' had higher percentages of stearic acid for PC and palmitic acid in phosphatidylglycerol (PG). Genotype 'MS23-1' had a higher percentage of linoleic acid and linolenic acid in both PG and phosphatidylinositol (PI). These findings are not in agreement with the prevailing theory that higher unsaturated fatty acids of membranes enhance chilling tolerance.

Chilling injury expressed as hardcore also showed genotypic differences. 'Beauregard' did not increase in hard tissue until 30 days' chilling duration (Table 4). The only fatty acid that could account for the tolerance of 'Beauregard' was

Table 3. Effect of chilling on the fatty acid compositions of two genotypes for the lipid classes phosphatidylcholine (PC), phosphatidylglycerol (PG), and phosphatidylinositol (PI) obtained from crude chloroplast preparations.

Lipid Class	Fatty Acid	Fatty Acid (%) Genotype	
		'MS26-1'	'MS23-1'
PC	Stearic	0.195a	0.083b
PG	Palmitic	0.709a	0.412b
	Linoleic	0.143b	0.419a
	Linolenic	0.000b	0.102a
PI	Linolenic	0.095b	0.410a

Values are means of four replications.
Mean separation in rows by LSD test; mean in row followed by same letter is not significantly different (P = 0.05).
Values are expressed as the percent of total fatty acids within an individual phospholipid class.

Table 4. Effect of cultivars and 2°C chilling storage times on percentage of hardcore of sweetpotato storage roots.

Storage time (days)	Hardcore (%)		
	Cultivars		
	'Beauregard'	'Centennial'	'Jewel'
0	$0.00c^z$	0.00d	0.00d
10	0.00c	10.29c	9.35c
20	1.32c	35.11ab	24.90b
30	26.60b	27.52b	29.29ab
40	36.71a	37.31a	33.14a

Values are means of three replications.
[z]Mean separation in columns by LSD test; means within columns not followed by the same letter are statistically different (P = 0.05).

linolenic acid (Table 5). The percentage of linoleic acid of the total lipids in the storage roots was high (59%) and remained high for up to 30 days of chilling. The reduction in linoleic acid in 'Beauregard' preceded hardcore development and was therefore implicated in hardcore development.

Two cultivars ('Travis' and 'Vardaman') were evaluated for water stress using the detached leaf method (Table 6). 'Vardaman' was determined to be capable of maintaining its cellular integrity during water stress due to its smaller loss in water content (transpired less), and therefore it was classified as drought tolerant. 'Travis' and 'Vardaman' were also evaluated for tolerance to water stress by examining CF transients. Variable fluorescence (Fv) of dark-adapted, detached leaves from 'Vardaman' did not decrease over a 48 hour period (Table 7) while a decrease in Fv for 'Travis' was detected in 36 hours. If the moisture loss from detached leaves is an indicator of tolerance to water stress—as reported for other crops, than the Fv value may also be used to discriminate among genotypes for tolerance.

Table 5. Percent linoleic acid of total lipids extracted from three sweetpotato cultivars stored 40 days at 5°C.

Days	Linoleic acid (%)		
	'Beauregard'	'Centennial'	'Jewel'
0	$59.6a^y A^z$	48.0 b B	51.3 aB
10	59.1a A	44.3 b C	51.3 aB
20	58.0ab A	46.3 b B	51.6 aB
30	55.0ab A	45.0 b C	51.0 aA
40	53.3b	56.0 a A	53.0 A

Values are means of four replications.
[yz]Mean separation within columns and rows by LSD test; means followed by same letter are not significantly different (P = 0.05).

Table 6. Percent moisture and dry weight loss of detached leaves and leaf punches of two greenhouse-grown sweetpotato genotypes 10 days after transplanting.

Genotype	% Moisture Loss	
	Leaves	Punches
'Travis'	69.48 a	66.17 a
'Vardaman'	50.10 b	47.31 b

Values are means of four replications.
Mean separation in columns by LSD test; means followed by the same letter are not significantly different (P = 0.05).

CONCLUSIONS

EC and CF were shown to be useful in detecting differences in tolerance of sweetpotato genotypes to chilling. Increased EC suggested that injury to the cell membrane was one possible response in sweetpotato plants to chilling. Reduced Fv indicated injury to the chloroplast; however, no significant changes were found in fatty acid composition of chloroplast lipids. Leaf dehydration associated with chilling injury may have been responsible for reduced Fv, but leaf dehydration was not monitored in these experiments. A higher percentage composition of linoleic acid in storage roots tolerant to chilling was implicated in reduced hardcore in 'Beauregard.' These methods may be useful in detecting leaf physiological responses associated with drought tolerance. However, additional research is needed to relate these findings to other plant factors imparting tolerance to drought stress.

Table 7. Variable fluorescence (Fv) and variable fluorescent quenching (FQ) of detached leaves of two greenhouse-grown sweetpotato genotypes.

Water Stress Duration	Cultivars			
	'Vardaman'		'Travis'	
(hours)	FQ	Fv	FQ	Fv
12	0.55 ab	0.59 a	0.59 a	0.74 ab
34	0.67 a	0.72 a	0.49 a	0.79 a
36	0.44 b	0.69 a	0.22 b	0.62 b
48	0.19 c	0.60 a	0.31 b	0.43 c

Values are means of four replications.
Mean separation in columns by LSD test; means followed by same letter are not significantly different (P = 0.05).

REFERENCES

Allison, M.L., G.R. Ammerman, J.O. Garner, H.L. Hammett, C. Singletary, F.T. Withers, and H.D. Palmertree. 1981. Vardaman, a new early maturing sweet potato variety for Mississippi. Information Sheet 1305 Miss. Agricultural and Forestry Experiment Station.

Daines, R.H., D.F. Hammond, N.F. Haard, and M.J. Ceponis. 1976. Hardcore development in sweet potatoes: a response to chilling and its remission as influenced by cultivar, curing temperatures, and time and duration of chilling. Phytopathology 66:582-587.

Hammett, H.L. 1974. Total carbohydrate and carotenoid content of sweet potatoes affected by cultivar and area of production. HortScience 9:467-468.

Hammett, H.L., R.C. Albritton, and F.T. Withers. 1978. Hardcore in some sweet potato cultivars and lines. J. Amer. Soc. Hort. Sci. 103:239-241.

Jones, S.T. 1961. Effect of irrigation at different levels of soil moisture on yield and evapotranspiration rate of sweet potatoes. J. Amer. Soc. Hort. Sci. Proc. 77:458-462.

Melcarek, P.K., and G.N. Brown. 1977. The effects of chilling stress on the chlorophyll fluorescence of leaves. Plant and Cell Physiol. 18:1099-1107.

Newell, L.L. 1991. Screening sweet potato genotypes (*Ipomoea batatas* L. Lam) for drought tolerance. MS Thesis. Mississippi State University, Miss. State, MS.

Papageorgiou, G. 1975. Chlorophyll fluorescence: an intrinsic probe of photosynthesis. *In* Govindjec, ed. Bioenergetics of photosynthesis. Academic Press, New York, pp. 319-371.

Paull, R.E. 1981. Temperature-induced leakage from chilling sensitive and chilling resistant plants. Plant Physiol. 68:149-153.

Smillie, R.M. 1979. The useful chloroplast: a new approach for investigating chilling stress in plants. Pages 187-202 *in* Low temperature stress in crop plants, edited by J.M. Lyons, D. Graham, J.K. Raison. Academic Press, New York.

Thompson, H.C. 1931. Vegetable crops. McGraw-Hill Book Company, New York. 560 pp.

Vasquez-Telleo, A., Y. Zuily-Fodil, A.T. Pham Thi, and J.B. Viera de Silva. 1990. Electrolyte and Pi leakages and soluble sugar content as physiological tests for screening resistance to water stress in *phaseolus* and *vigna* species. Journal of Experimental Botany 41(228): 827-832.

Walker, D.W., and C. Miller, Jr. 1986. Rate of water loss from detached leaves of drought resistant and susceptible genotypes of cowpea. HortScience 21:131-132.

Whitaker, B.D. 1986. Fatty-acid composition of polar lipids in fruit and leaf chloroplasts of "16:3" - and "18:3" - plant species. Planta 169:313-319.

Woods, F.M., J.O. Garner, Jr., Juan L. Silva, and Chana Phromtong. 1991a. Estimation of chilling sensitivity in leaves of sweet potato by chlorophyll fluorescence and electrolyte leakage. OYTON 52(1): 33-37.

Woods, F.M., J.O. Garner Jr., and J.L. Silva. 1991b. Chilling Tolerance in sweet potatoes. OYTON 52(1):39-41.

Yamaki, S., and I. Uritani. 1972. The mechanism of chilling injury in sweet potato VI. Changes of lipid components in the mitochondrial membrane during chilling storage. Plant and Cell Physiol. 13:67-79.

Yen, D.E. 1982. Sweet potato in historical perspective. Pages 2-30 *in* Sweet potato, edited by R.L. Villareal and T.D. Griggs. Proceedings of the 1st International Symposium, AVRDC, Taiwan.

Poster Presentations

STARCH AND SUCROSE SYNTHESES IN SWEETPOTATO PHYTOMODELS

A. M. Almazan, S. Adeyeye, X. Zhou, W. A. Hill, C. K. Bonsi, J. Y. Lu, P. A. Loretan

George Washington Carver Agricultural Experiment Station, Tuskegee University, Tuskegee, AL 36088.

Sweetpotato phytomodels were used to determine how sucrose and starch biosynthetic enzymes, and sugar concentrations contribute to the control of storage root development. Single leaves of cultivar 'TI-155' were planted in potted sand and irrigated with modified half-Hoagland solution three times per week and with water the rest of the week. Fresh weight per plant, protein content, starch phosphorylase, sucrose and starch synthase, ADPglucose and UDPglucose pyrophosphorylase activities, and sucrose, glucose and fructose concentrations were determined in the leaves, petioles, fibrous, string and storage roots once or twice per week from 14 to 70 days after planting (DAP). Fresh weights per plant of the different parts increased as the phytomodel grew; that of the storage roots increased rapidly at ca. 40 DAP. The different enzyme activities were generally high, especially in the storage roots, at this time. Sucrose concentration was highest in all plant parts. Except for sucrose content in the storage and string roots, and fructose levels in the leaf and petiole, the sugars continuously decreased with time. The possible role of the enzymes and sugar concentrations in sucrose and starch syntheses in the phytomodels is discussed.

Few investigations have been reported on sweetpotato sucrose and starch biosynthetic enzymes. Based on kinetic studies, Murata (1971) postulated that sucrose synthase (E. C. 2.4.1.13) is involved in the breakdown of sucrose rather than in its synthesis in the sweetpotato root tissues. Starch is synthesized mainly from ADPglucose by starch synthethase (E. C. 2.4.1.21) in both leaves (Murata and Akazawa 1964) and storage roots (Murata and Akazawa 1968). ADPG pyrophosphorylase (E. C. 2.2.2.27) activity was positively correlated with starch content in the storage root (Nakatani et al.1990). In these studies enzyme activity was determined at only one stage of growth in leaves or storage roots.

In this study, the activities of the above enzymes and those of starch phosphorylase (E. C. 2.4.1.1) and UDPG pyrophosphorylase (E. C. 2.7.7.9) in the leaves, storage roots, petiole/stem, fibrous and string roots of sweetpotato rooted leaves were monitored at different growth periods to determine how these enzymes contribute to the control of storage root formation. Changes in sucrose, glucose and fructose concentrations were also followed.

Rooted leaves were chosen because of their simplicity and uniformity as plant models. These had been used for studies on carbohydrate metabolism (Wilson 1969), photosynthesis (Spence and Humphries 1972), storage root initiation and growth

(McDavid and Alamu 1980), and storage root sink potential (Nakatani et al. 1990; Asian Vegetable Research and Development Center 1987).

MATERIALS AND METHODS

Plant materials

Sweetpotato (*Ipomoea batatas* (L) Lam.) cultivar 'TI-155' leaves with approximately 5 cm petioles were planted in potted sand (4/pot) in the greenhouse. The bench containing the pots was enclosed with translucent polyethylene sheets to maintain high humidity; the plants were watered once daily with deionized water. After two weeks, the plastic sheets were removed; modified half-Hoagland solution (Loretan et al. 1989; Hoagland and Arnon 1938) was used to irrigate three times per week instead of water. A minimum of twelve plants was harvested once or twice per week from 14 to 70 days after planting (DAP). Fresh weights of the leaves, petioles, fibrous, string and storage roots were obtained after each harvest.

Enzyme extraction and assay

The enzymes were extracted from the leaves, petioles, fibrous, string and storage roots separately at 0 to 4°C by homogenizing the tissue in 0.1M tris-acetate buffer pH 8.5 with 20 mM EDTA, 11mM diethyldithiocarbamic acid (DIECA), 15 mM cysteineHCl and 6% Carbowax 4000 (1 g/2 mL)(Hawker et al. 1979). The homogenate was centrifuged at 30,000 g for 30 min, and the supernatant was used directly for enzyme assays.

Protein in 10 µL extract was measured with the Folin phenol reagent (Lowry et al. 1951). Except for the starch phosphorylase assay, a 20-µl aliquot was used to determine enzyme activities. Three to 6 replicates per assay were made. Synthesis of sucrose by sucrose synthase was monitored according to the procedure of Murata (1971). ADPG formed from uniformly labeled [^{14}C] glucose-1-P by ADPG pyrophosphorylase (Shen and Preiss 1964), and UDPG formed from the same substrate by UDPG pyrophosphorylase (Gustafson and Gander 1972) were detected by a scintillation counter. Starch was hydrolyzed into glucose-1-P by starch phosphorylase (Kodenchery and Nair 1972); glu-1-P analyzed by the procedure of McCready and Hassid (1957) and colorimetrically measured at 730 nm. Incorporation of [^{14}C]-glucose into amylopectin by starch synthase was measured according to a modified method of Hawker et al. (1972) and Ozbun et al. (1971). The anion exchange resin was removed by centrifugation.

Sugar extraction and determination

Sugars were extracted by homogenizing the fresh plant tissues in 80% ethanol (5 to 10 g/50 mL) for 1 to 2 min using a blender at high speed (Picha 1985). The resulting slurry was immediately boiled for 15 min, cooled and filtered. The residue was washed with more 80% ethanol until the total filtrate was ca. 100 mL. The filtrate was decolorized with neutralized activated charcoal (2 to 5 g), filtered and concentrated to 10 mL, evaporating ethanol in the process. The colorless solution was filtered through a 0.45 m filter membrane before injection into the Bio-Rad HPLC system with a refractive index monitor. Sucrose, glucose and fructose were eluted through a Bio-Rad fast carbohydrate analysis column with HPLC grade water at a flow rate of 0.4 mL/min and at a temperature of 80°C in 15 min. The percent recovery of each sugar was determined by adding known amounts into another set of the plant materials during homogenization and was used to correct the concentrations. Two or four replicates were made depending on the availability of plant materials.

RESULTS AND DISCUSSION

Fresh weight and protein content

Harvest of the phytomodels commenced at 14 DAP. At this time, there were some short fibrous roots and/or calli at the petiole ends. The quantity of fibrous roots became sufficient for enzyme extraction at 21 DAP; storage roots were observed during the 4th week and string roots at the 6th week. Storage roots were at least 5 mm in diameter while the string roots were smaller, usually slightly more swollen than the fibrous roots and colored pink.

The fresh weights per plant (Fig. 1) of the leaves and petioles increased slightly; those of the string roots remained almost constant; those of the fibrous roots increased fast early (ca. 30 DAP) and approached a maximum at ca. 50 DAP; the storage roots increased slowly initially, then rapidly after 40 DAP reaching a maximum of 12.70 g at 70 DAP. During the last harvest, some of the petioles were cracked, the leaves had started to senesce and occasional sprouting either at the base of the petiole or on the storage root was observed. Due to the limited amount of plant materials, percent dry matter was not obtained. Thus, the data cannot be compared with published results expressed on a dry weight basis (McDavid and Alamu 1980).

Protein content of leaves was highest throughout the growth period. Although slight increases in the fibrous and storage roots were observed after 30 DAP, there was a decline in protein content in the petiole, fibrous, string and storage roots with time. Apparently, total extracted protein per gram fresh weight decreased as the plant matured.

Enzyme Activities

ADPG pyrophosphorylase and starch synthase activities (Fig. 1) were generally highest in the storage roots; they increased rapidly a few days before a similar trend was observed in the fresh weight per plant of the storage roots. Although protein concentration was high, the activities of both enzymes were essentially constant and low in the leaves. Starch synthase activity in the petiole was constant. ADPG pyrophosphorylase activity in the same plant part was high before storage roots were

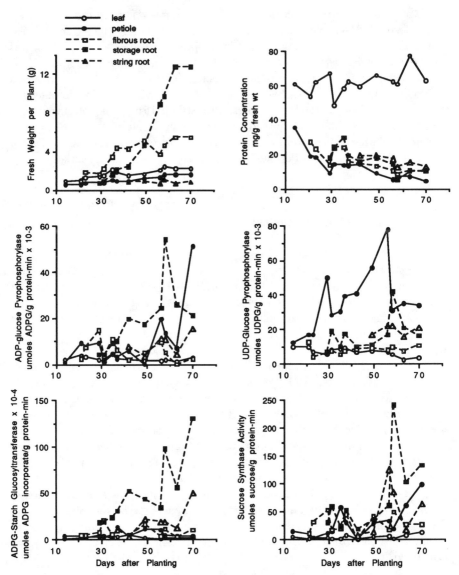

Figure 1. Changes in fresh weight, protein concentration and activities of ADPG and UDPG pyrophosphorylase, and sucrose and starch synthase in the different plant parts of the sweetpotato phytomodel during maturation. Each value is the mean of 3-6 replicates.

obtained (ca. 28 DAP), decreased after 30 DAP, then increased after 50 DAP. The petiole ends that were covered by sand were orange and probably contained more starch than the rest of the petiole which was green. In the fibrous roots, starch synthase activity was comparable to those of leaves and petioles; ADPG formation, however, was higher initially. Both enzymes were more active in the string roots than in the fibrous roots after 40 DAP. Sucrose synthase activity was also generally highest in the storage roots. An apparent decline in the activity of this enzyme in the petiole, fibrous and storage roots occurred after 40 DAP; this decline was followed by a small increase in activity. Activity in the petiole was maximum at ca. 60 DAP; activity in the leaf was constant and low. In contrast, sucrose cleavage activity in potato (*Solanum tuberosum*) was about twice that of the synthetic activity, and both cleavage and synthetic activities decreased as plants matured (Pressey 1969). UDPG pyrophosphorylase activities in the different plant plant parts were higher than those of ADPG pyrophosphorylase. A similar ratio of the pyrophosphorylase activities in the developing potato (*Solanum tuberosum*) storage root was also obtained by Hawker et al. (1979). UDGP pyrophosphorylase activity was highest in the petiole; then decreased to levels comparable to those of the string and storage roots at ca. 60 DAP. In the storage roots, it was similar to that of string roots after 55 DAP but higher than that of fibrous roots throughout the growth period. It decreased in the leaves as the plant matured.

Difficulty in the starch phosphorylase assay was encountered because the activity was not consistently detected. A competitive inhibitor of the enzyme in sweetpotato had been isolated and identified as beta-amylase (Chang and Su 1986; Pan et al. 1988). This degradative enzyme was probably present in the enzyme extracts and caused phosphorylase inhibition.

Sugar concentrations

Sucrose content was higher than fructose or glucose in all plant parts (Figure 2) and decreased with time especially in the fibrous roots. In the storage roots, it remained high after 40 DAP. Fructose content was lowest among the three sugars except at ca. 40 DAP in the leaf and petiole. A slight decline in fructose content was also observed as the phytomodel matured. Glucose content was initially highest in the petiole; it decreased with time in the petiole, fibrous and string roots. In the leaf and storage roots, it increased before 40 DAP and then decreased about 5 days later. The increases in glucose and fructose contents in some parts at around 40 DAP coincided with the beginning of a rapid increase in fresh weight of the storage root and a decrease in the synthetic activity of sucrose synthase. These sugar increases cannot be attributed to invertase activity because the plant materials were stored in the cold for a maximum of 30 h only. Higher invertase activity and sugar concentrations were obtained in potato only after at least 1 wk storage at 18°C (Pressey and Shaw 1966).

Although protein concentration in the phytomodel leaves was always high, ADPG and UDPG pyrophosphorylase and sucrose and starch synthase activities were constantly low even during increased starch deposition in the storage roots. Leaf protein increased only very slightly towards the end of the growth period. Leaf sucrose content decreased with maturation. These results suggest that even in the phytomodels, the main function of the leaves is photosynthesis and the photosynthate sucrose is transported to the other parts of the plant continuously.

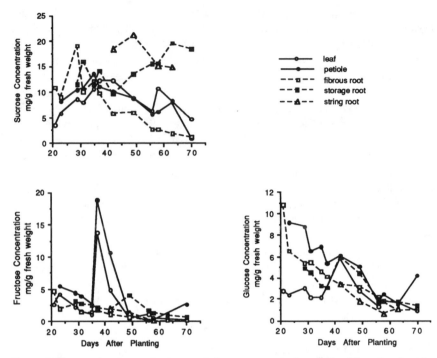

Figure 2. Changes in sucrose, fructose and glucose concentrations in the different parts of the sweetpotato phytomodels during maturation. Each point is a mean of 2 to 4 replicates.

In petioles, starch synthase activity was also constantly low and similar to that in the leaves; ADPG pyrophosphorylase activity was only slightly higher in petioles than in the leaves. However, UDPG pyrophosphorylase activity was highest in this plant part. Sucrose synthase activity in petioles was comparable to that in the storage roots before ca. 40 DAP, then remained higher than in the fibrous root but lower than in the string and storage roots. Apparently, starch synthesis in the petiole was more or less constant but formation of UDPG was high. The substrate for UDPG pyrophosphorylase (glu-1-P) was probably produced through cleavage of sucrose since fructose concentration was high when the synthetic activity of sucrose synthase was low. Fructose concentration then decreased to the original level through sucrose synthesis and/or conversion to glucose. UDPG probably acts as a reserve pool for sucrose in the phytomodel petiole before sucrose is ultimately transported to the storage root for starch formation.

ADPG pyrophosphorylase and starch synthesis activities in the fibrous roots remained low with slightly higher values than those for the leaves and petiole. UDPG pyrophosphorylase activity was also low in fibrous roots. The sucrose synthase level decreased when fresh weight per plant started increasing at a faster rate (ca. 30 DAP). The decrease in sucrose content with maturation was fastest in the fibrous roots. The results suggest that sucrose and starch synthesis in these roots were minimal.

Both string and storage roots originate from thick adventitious roots in the sweetpotato (Wilson 1982). Although differences in morphology of the two roots had been observed (Wilson and Lowe 1973), factors that control the initiation and development to maturity of the storage roots are still unknown. Information on the biochemical changes immediately prior, during and after initiation could lead to the identification of these factors. Storage roots were initially observed at ca. 28 DAP. Thus, initiation of storage root formation from the thick roots started before this period. The only notable change in the phytomodel at this time was the rapid increase in UDPG content in the petiole. If UDPG serves as a storage pool for sucrose in this plant part, this implies that there was an increase in the amount of sucrose available for transport to the storage roots before the fresh weight per plant of the storage roots increased at a fast rate (prior to 40 DAP). Both ADPG pyrophosphorylase and starch synthase activities were highest at this time also. Thus, the starch biosynthetic rate increased before rapid bulking of the storage root was observed. At the time ADPG synthesis in the storage root decreased (ca. 60 DAP), UDPG synthesis in the petiole also decreased. UDPG pyrophosphorylase activity in the storage root decreased slightly after 40 DAP, then increased at 60 DAP. Sucrose synthase activity increased also after 40 DAP, attaining a maximum value at 60 DAP. Sucrose concentration remained high and increased at about the same time as the increase in sucrose synthase activity. At ca. 60 DAP, starch formation rate in the storage root had probably slowed, thus more glucose was being incorporated into sucrose.

The ADPG pyrophosphorylase and starch synthase activities were higher in the string roots than in the fibrous roots but were much lower than those in the storage roots. UDPG synthesis was comparable to that of the storage root during the same period. The maximum sucrose synthase activity and its immediate rapid decrease were observed earlier than 60 DAP. A corresponding decrease in sucrose concentration was noted much earlier (after 50 DAP). It appears that there was less starch synthesis, and the reversal in the late high sucrose synthesis occurred earlier in the string roots than in the storage roots.

ACKNOWLEDGMENT

This study was supported by the U. S. Agency for International Development, Grant #DAN-5053-G-55-9063-00.

REFERENCES

Asian Vegetable Research and Development Center. 1988 . Starch synthesis of leaf cutting. Progress report summaries,1987, Shanhua, Taiwan: AVRDC, 36.

Chang, T.-C., and J.-C. Su. 1986. Starch phosphorylase inhibitor from sweet potato. Plant Physiol. 80:534-538.

Gustafson, G.L,. and J.E. Gander. 1972. Uridine diphosphate glucose pyrophosphorylase from *Sorghum vulgare*. Purification and kinetic properties. J. Biol. Chem. 247:1387-1397.

Hawker, J.S., H. Marschner, and A. Krauss. 1979. Starch synthesis in developing potato tubers. Physiologia Plantarum. 46:25-30.

Hawker, J. S., J. L. Ozbun, and J. Preiss. 1972. Unprimed starch synthesis by soluble ADPglucose-starch glucosyltransferase from potato tubers. Phytochem. 11:1287-1293.

Hoagland, D.R., and D. I. Arnon. 1938. The water-culture method for growing plants without soil. Revised Circular 347, Berkeley: Calif. Agric. Expt. Station, Univ. of Calif.

Kodenchery, U. K., and M. P. Nair. 1972. Metabolic changes induced by sprout inhibiting dose of gamma irradiation in potatoes. J. Agr. Food Chem. 20:282-285.

Loretan, P. A., C. K. Bonsi, W. A. Hill, C. R. Ogbuehi, D. G. Mortley, J. Y. Lu, C. E. Morris, and R. D. Pace. 1989. Sweet potato growth parameters, yield components and nutritive value for CELSS applications. SAE Transactions. J. Aeroscope. 98(1):1090-1094.

Lowry, O. H., N. J. Rosebrough, A. L. Farr, and R. J. Randall. 1951. Protein measurement with the Folin phenol reagent. J. Biol. Chem. 193:265-275.

McCready, R. M., and W. Z. Hassid. 1957. Preparation of alpha-D-glucose-1-phosphate by means of potato phosphorylase. Methods Enzymol. 3:137-143.

McDavid, C. R., and S. Alamu. 1980. The Effect of growth regulators on tuber initiation and growth in rooted leaves of two sweet potato cultivars. Ann. Bot. 45:363-364.

Murata, T. 1971. Sucrose synthetase of sweet potato roots. Part II. A kinetic study. Agric. Biol. Chem. 35:1441-1448.

Murata, T., and T. Akazawa. 1968. Enzymic mechanism of starch synthesis in sweet potato roots. I. Requirement of potassium ions for starch synthetase. Arch. Biochem. Biophys. 126:873-879.

Murata, T., and T. Akazawa. 1964. The role of adenosine diphosphate glucose in leaf starch formation. Biochem. Biophys. Res. Commun. 16:6-11.

Nakatani, M., M. Komeichi, and Y. Watanabe. 1990. Role of hormonal and enzymatic activities to sink potential of storage root in sweet potato. Pages 507-515 in Proceedings of the 8th Symposium of the International Soc. for Tropical Root Crops, edited by R. Howeler, Bangkok, Thailand, Oct 30-Nov 5, 1988.

Ozbun, J. L., J. S. Hawker, and J. Preiss. 1971. Multiple forms of alpha-1,4 glucan synthetase from spinach leaves. Biochem. Biophys. Res. Commun. 43:631-636.

Pan, S.-M., T.-C. Chang, R.-H. Juang, and J.-C Su. 1988. Starch phosphorylase inhibitor is beta-amylase. Plant Physiol. 88:1154-1156.

Picha, D. H. 1985. HPLC determination of sugars in raw and baked sweet potatoes. J. Food Sci. 50:1189-1190,1210.

Pressey, R. 1969. Potato sucrose synthethase: Purification, properties and changes in activity associated with maturation. Plant Physiol. 44:759-764.

Pressey, R., and R. Shaw. 1966. Effect of temperature on invertase, invertase inhibitor and sugars in potato tubers. Plant Physiol. 41:1657-1661.

Shen, L., and J. Preiss. 1964. The activation and inhibition of bacterial adenosine-diphosphoglucose pyrophosphorylase. Biochem. Biophys. Res. Commun. 17:424-429.

Spence, J. A., and E. C. Humphries. 1972. Effect of moisture supply, root temperature and growth regulators on photosynthesis of isolated rooted leaves of sweet potato (Ipomoea batatas). Ann. Bot. 36:115-121.

Wilson, L. A. 1969. The use of rooted leaves and grafted plants for the study of carbohydrate metabolism in sweet potato. Pages 46-57 in Proceedings, 1st International Symposium on Tropical Root Crops, Trinidad, 1967, Vol. 2.

Wilson, L. A. 1982. Tuberization in sweet potato (Ipomoea batatas (L) Lam). Pages 79-94 in Sweet potato, edited by R. L. Villareal and T. D. Griggs, Proceedings, 1st International Symp. Shanhua, Taiwan: AVRDC.

Wilson, L. A., and S. B. Lowe. 1973. The anatomy of the root system in West Indian sweet potato (Ipomoea batatas (L.) Lam.) cultivars. Ann. Bot. 37:633-643.

GROWTH AND YIELD OF SWEETPOTATO UNDER DIFFERENT CARBON DIOXIDE CONCENTRATIONS

N. C. Bhattacharya*, P. P. Ghosh, D. R. Hileman, M. Alemayehu, G. Huluka, P. K. Biswas

George Washington Carver Agricultural Experiment Station, Tuskegee University, Tuskegee, AL 36088; *Present address: USDA-ARS, Western Cotton Research Laboratory, 4135 E. Broadway, Phoenix, AZ 85040, USA.

INTRODUCTION

The level of atmospheric CO_2 is increasing annually and forecasts suggest that the present CO_2 concentration will be doubled by the middle of the next century (Clark et al. 1982). High levels of CO_2 concentration will likely increase net CO_2 fixation leading to increased plant dry weight at least in C_3 plants (Kramer 1981). Increased CO_2 may reduce stomatal aperture, thus reducing transpiration, and therefore increasing water use efficiency. However, more extensive data are required for modeling and accurately predicting future crop yields in response to the increasing atmospheric CO_2.

The primary objective of this study was to evaluate the biomass growth responses of sweetpotato to different levels of CO_2. Data obtained should also lead to a better understanding of source-sink relationships in sweetpotato.

MATERIALS AND METHODS

Sweetpotato (*Ipomoea batatas* L., 'Georgia Jet') plants that were 20 to 25 cm long with 4 to 5 leaves were planted (May 17, 1985) in two different size (30 x 25 x 28 cm and 15 x 10 x 15 cm) plastic pots containing Norfolk sandy loam soil. The pots were divided into four groups of 24 pots each. One group was placed in the open field. The other three groups were placed in three open-top chambers in the field.

The open-top chambers (Heagle et al. 1973; Rogers et al. 1983) were cylindrical aluminum frames covered with clear PVC plastic. A fan delivered ambient air into the chamber, and CO_2 was injected into the fan housing. A 45° cone of a frustum was placed over the top of the chambers (Rogers et al. 1984) to help achieve more uniform CO_2 levels. The actual season-long daytime mean CO_2 levels recorded for the treatments were 361 (open field), 364 (ambient chamber), 514 and 666 μmol mol^{-1}, respectively.

The plants were fertilized at the time of planting with ammonium nitrate and a mixture of muriate of potash and superphosphate at a rate of 0.94 and 1.35 g per pot, respectively. An additional 0.47 g of ammonium nitrate per pot was applied 55 days after planting. As a supplement to natural rainfall, plants were watered by hand to the drip point whenever soil tensiometer readings reached -30 to -35 centibars. The plants were rotated within the chambers periodically to overcome position effects.

Eight plants from each treatment were harvested at 30, 45, and 90 days after planting. The small pots were harvested at 30 and 45 days; the large pots were harvested at 90 days. Leaf area was determined using a LI-COR LI-3100 area meter. Dry weights of leaves and runners were determined after drying for 48 hours at 70°C. The leaf area and dry weight of abscised leaves (collected on alternate days) were included. The data were analyzed by analysis of variance.

RESULTS AND DISCUSSION

After 30 days of growth, the dry weight of leaves was higher in plants grown at 666 μmol mol^{-1} than in plants grown at 514 μmol mol^{-1} (Table 1). After 45 days of growth, the dry weight of leaves was highest in plants grown at 666 μmol mol^{-1}, but there were no significant differences among the groups of plants grown in open-top chambers (Table 1). There were no differences in stem dry weight at either 30 or 45 days.

At the final harvest (day 90), the dry weights of both leaves and stems were significantly greater at both elevated CO_2 concentrations than in the control chamber (Table 1). There were no significant differences in the number of leaves produced or in total leaf area at any harvest date (data not shown). These results indicate that the increase in leaf production with increasing CO_2 was due to an increase in specific leaf weight (weight/area).

There were no significant differences in root weight or in root/shoot ratio at any harvest date. However, the final harvest showed a small, non-significant increase in root weight with an increase in the CO_2 concentration (Table 1). In a different experiment done in the same year with sweetpotatoes grown in the field rather than in pots in the open-top chambers, there were significant increases in storage root weight at elevated CO_2 concentrations (Biswas et al. 1986).

There were no significant differences between plants placed in the open field and plants placed in the ambient CO_2 open-top chamber at any harvest date, except for a difference in the root/shoot ratio at 30 days (Table 1). Thus, the effect of the chamber appears to have been minimal. However, the environmental conditions inside and outside the chamber were clearly different. The plants inside the chamber were exposed to lower light levels, slightly warmer temperatures and different wind conditions. It is possible that some of these differences had offsetting effects on the growth of the plants.

Elevated levels of CO_2 lead to increased rates of photosynthesis in most C_3 plants (Cure and Acock 1986) including sweetpotatoes (Biswas et al. 1986). In field-grown sweetpotatoes, the storage roots provide a sink for the extra photosynthates produced under CO_2 enrichment (Biswas et al. 1986). The increase in specific leaf weight at elevated CO_2 was smaller in field-grown plants (18%) (Biswas et al. 1986) than in the pot-grown plants (43%). Thus in pot-grown plants, the export of photosynthates from the leaves may have been limited by restrictions on root growth imposed by the pots. Thus, the smaller increase in root yield at elevated CO_2 observed in these pot-grown sweetpotatoes could be due to the pot limitations.

Table 1. Effects of different CO_2 concentrations on dry weights of shoots, storage roots, root/shoot ratio and fresh weight of sweetpotato storage roots harvested at 30, 45 and 90 days after planting.

CO_2 (µmol mol^{-1})	Fresh Weight (g) Storage Roots	Dry Weight (g) Leaf	Stem	Storage Roots	Root/Shoot Ratio
Day 30					
361*	--	3.3b+	0.9a	5.7a	1.4a
364	--	3.6ab	1.1a	4.5a	1.0b
514	--	2.9b	0.8a	4.4a	1.2a
666	--	4.6a	1.2a	5.5a	1.0b
Day 45					
361	--	4.8b	4.5a	19.7a	2.1ab
364	--	6.9ab	4.1a	21.1a	1.9ab
514	--	6.6ab	4.1a	24.0a	2.2a
666	--	8.2a	4.9a	24.0a	2.0ab
Day 90					
361	328.9a	11.9b	8.3b	60.3b	3.0a
364	364.9a	10.7b	7.5b	68.9ab	3.9a
514	388.2a	15.1a	11.0a	79.5a	3.2a
666	395.9a	15.0a	11.0a	78.2ab	3.0a

+Mean values in each column at each harvest date followed by the same letter are not significantly different at the 0.05 level, according to Duncan's Multiple Range Test.
* Open field plot. Other three CO_2 concentrations are from open-top chambers.

REFERENCES

Biswas, P.K., D.R. Hileman, N.C. Bhattachayra, P.P. Ghosh, S. Bhattachayra, J.H. Johnson, and N.T. Mbikayi. 1986. Response of vegetation to carbon dioxide: Growth, yield and plant water relationships in sweet potatoes in response to carbon dioxide enrichment. Report 030, U.S. Department of Energy, Carbon Dioxide Research Division, Office of Energy Research, Washington DC, 95 pp.

Clark, W.C., K.H. Cook, G. Moorland, A.K. Weinberg, R.M. Rotty, R.P. Bell, L.J. Cooper, and C.L. Cooper. 1982. The carbon dioxide question: a perspective for 1982. Pages 3-43 in Carbon dioxide review, edited by W.C. Clark, Clarendon Press, Oxford.

Cure, J.D., and B. Acock. 1986. Crop responses to carbon dioxide doubling: a literature survey. Agric. For Meterol. 38:127-145.

Heagle, A.S., D.E. Body, and W.W. Heck. 1973. An open top field chamber to assess the impact of air pollution on plants. J. Environ. Qual. 2:365-368.

Kramer, P.J. 1981. Carbon dioxide concentration, photosynthesis, and dry matter production. Bioscience 31:29-33.

Rogers, H.H., W.W. Heck, and A.S. Heagle. 1983. A field technique for the study of plant responses to elevated carbon dioxide concentrations. J. Air Pollut. Control Assoc. 33:42-44.

Rogers, H.H., J.D. Cure, J.F. Thomas, and J.M. Smith. 1984. Influence of elevated CO_2 on growth of soybean plants. Crop Sci. 24:361-366.

EFFECT OF CO_2 IN THE ROOT ZONE ON THE GROWTH OF SWEETPOTATO

Yoshiaki Kitaya
Faculty of Horticulture, Chiba University, 648, Matsudo, Chiba, 271, Japan.
Makoto Kiyota, Tsutomu Uewada, Kazutoshi Yabuki
College of Agriculture, University of Osaka Prefecture, 4-804, Mozu-ume, Sakai, Osaka, Japan.

The photosynthetic rates of sweetpotatoes grown with different CO_2 concentrations in the root zone were investigated for six weeks. Pre-treatment photosynthetic rates were determined using fresh air that contained 0.03% CO_2. When treated with 1% CO_2, the photosynthetic rate decreased by 20% after four days. A 2% CO_2 treatment resulted in a rapid decrease in photosynthetic rate after two days; the reduced rate was maintained over the remainder of the six-week period. In a second experiment, atmospheric air saturated with water vapor was forced into soil in ridges using an air compressor in order to decrease the CO_2 concentration in the rhizosphere of sweet-potato roots. The mean CO_2 concentrations were 0.6% for the non-aerated control and 0.26% and 0.2%, respectively, when the ridges were aerated with air flow rates of 1.25 and 2.5 L min^{-1}m^{-1}. The dry weight of the storage roots for these same rates were 19 and 26% higher, respectively, than for the non-aerated control.

INTRODUCTION

Soil aeration is important in promoting plant growth. For many plants a decrease in the O_2 concentration in the soil inhibits plant growth. The O_2 concentration in the cultivated soil is generally 18 to 21% and seldom approaches the critical value below which plant growth is inhibited. The CO_2 concentration in the soil, however, may more readily influence plant growth, because it can increase to 1 to 2% (e.g., Yabuki 1956), which is more than 30 times higher than the level in the atmosphere. Kitaya et al. (1984) found that growth suppression of cucumber plants occurred with 0.5 to 2% CO_2 in the rhizosphere.

In this study, the photosynthetic rates of sweetpotatoes under different CO_2 concentrations in the soil were studied in order to investigate growth suppression of sweetpotatoes due to excess CO_2 in the soil. The soil was then aerated with atmospheric air to decrease the CO_2 concentration in the soil, and the effect of the forced aeration on the growth and yield of sweetpotatoes was investigated.

MATERIALS AND METHODS

Sweetpotato (*Ipomoea batatas* L., cv. Kokei No.14) was used in the study. The plants were propagated by cuttings.

The effect of CO_2 in the root zone on photosynthesis

Plants were grown by the single node cutting culture (Yabuki and Uewada 1978) and planted in the system shown in Fig. 1. Six cuttings were planted in each of three plastic boxes (45 cm by 30 cm by 18 cm) with vermiculite as the rooting medium.

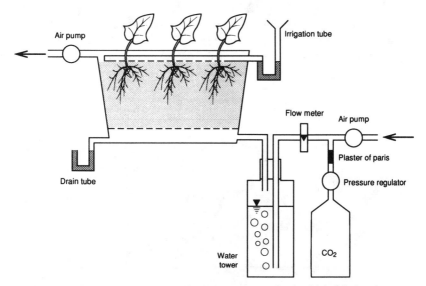

Figure 1. Plant culture system with root zone aerated using high CO_2 level.

The boxes were placed in a natural light growth chamber where the air temperature was maintained at 20°C and the relative humidity at 75%. Fresh air containing 21% O_2 and 0.03% CO_2 was pumped through the vermiculite in all of the boxes beginning 6 days after planting. Air containing 1 or 2% CO_2 was forced into two of the boxes 16 days after planting. The third box continued being aerated with fresh air and served as a control. The high CO_2 level air was prepared by mixing atmospheric air and pure CO_2 gas. The air was humidified using a water tower and flowed at a rate of 1 L min^{-1} into the boxes. The soil surface was covered with silver colored polyethylene film. Air from the soil surface, containing high levels of CO_2, was exhausted to the outside to prevent CO_2 leakage into the chamber.

Three plants whose leaf area were almost similar were chosen for measurement of the photosynthetic rate for each treatment and the control. The photosynthetic rate of the same leaf of each plant was observed for six weeks using the open assimilation chamber method with a differential infrared CO_2 gas analyzer (Holiba LAI-2). The air temperature in the assimilation chamber was 20°C and the photosynthetic photon flux density was 300 µmol m^{-2}s^{-1}.

The effect on sweetpotato growth of aeration of the root zone

In a second experiment sweetpotatoes were planted on ridges outdoors in alluvial soil. The length, width and height of each ridge was 10 m, 50 cm and 20 cm, respectively. The ridges were spaced 50 cm apart and cuttings within the ridge had the same spacing. A porous plastic pipe (diameter 1.3 cm) was buried at 20 cm depth in the center of each ridge, and fresh air was forced through the pipe into the soil to decrease the CO_2 concentration in the soil. The air was humidified with a water tower before being pumped through the soil.

Air flow rates were 1.25 or 2.5 L min^{-1}m^{-1} using two ridges per treatment with two non-aerated ridges as controls. The soil CO_2 concentration was collected with soil air sampling tubes (shown in Fig. 2) placed at depths of 1, 5, 10, 15 and 20 cm from the surface at the center of the ridge. The CO_2 and O_2 in the air were analyzed

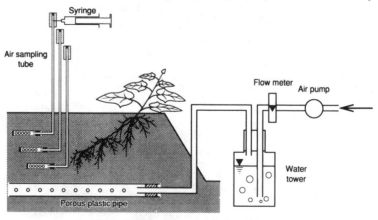

Figure 2. Forced aeration in the ridge.

by gas chromatography (Hitachi, Model 633). Sweetpotatoes were grown using the different flow rates for 69 days from August 4 to October 12.

In addition, in order to observe the long-term effects of aeration on sweetpotato growth, sweetpotatoes were also grown in ridges for 111 days (June 4 to September 23). This study examined sweetpotato growth using both dry and wetted ridges with an aeration rate in both of 1 L min^{-1}m^{-1}. For the dry ridges, the surface was relatively dry and the pF value at a depth of 10 cm was 2.8 (62 kPa). Fifteen millimeters of water decreased the pF value of the wetted ridges to 1.8 (6.1 kPa). Air samples for this study were collected at 5, 10 and 15 cm from the surface of the ridge on four different days after planting (DAP)—30, 52, 61 and 68.

RESULTS

The effect of CO$_2$ in the root zone on photosynthesis

Figure 3 shows the changes in the photosynthetic rates of sweetpotatoes when different CO$_2$ concentrations were forced into their rooting medium, vermiculite. The photosynthetic rate of sweetpotatoes grown in vermiculite which was aerated with fresh air remained almost constant during the 45-day period. The photosynthetic rate when the root zone was flooded with 1% CO$_2$ decreased by 20% four days after starting the treatment. When 2% CO$_2$ was used, the photosynthetic rate decreased similarly after two days. After six weeks, the photosynthetic rates for both treatments decreased to 70% of what the rates were at the start of the treatments.

The mean values of the photosynthetic rates over the six week period were 27, 22 and 20 mg CO$_2$ dm^{-2} h^{-1}, respectively, for the control, 1% CO$_2$ and 2% CO$_2$. During the six week growing period, the accumulated photosynthetic (CO$_2$) uptake for both treatments were about 80% of the control rate.

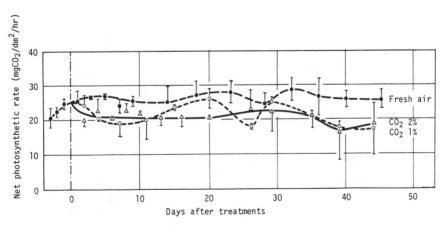

Figure 3. Effect of CO$_2$ concentration in the root zone on the photosynthetic rate of sweetpotato. Each plot indicates the average of three plants and the vertical bar indicates the standard deviation.

The effect on sweetpotato growth with aeration of the root zone

The CO_2 concentration on sweetpotato growth measured in soil at different depths from the center of a ridge on four different days after planting are shown in Figure 4 for three different aeration treatments. In the control ridge, which had no aeration, the CO_2 concentration tended to increase as the distance from the soil surface increased but varied depending on when the measurement was made. In the

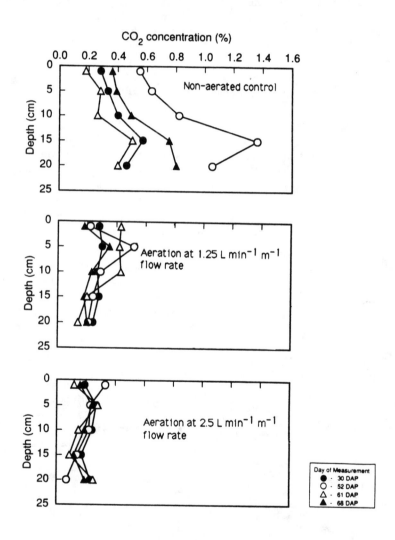

Figure 4. Profiles of CO_2 concentration in soil aerated with different air flow rates. Different symbols indicate the measurements on different days.

Table 1. Growth of sweetpotato after 69 days with the root zone aerated at different air flow rates.

Air Flow	Foliage	Fresh Wt. Storage Roots	Total	Dry Wt. Storage Roots
(L min^{-1}m^{-1})	----------------	(g·plant^{-1}) ----------------		(g·plant^{-1})
Non-aerated control	564	243	807	67.1
1.25	617	297	914	80.8
2.50	752	305	1057	84.7
LSD (p=0.05)	99	44	106	11.6

ridge aerated with atmospheric air at the rate of 1.25 L min^{-1}, the concentration at the depth of 5 to 10 cm was higher than that at the depth of 15 to 20 cm and seemed to be independent of time of measurement. In the ridge aerated at 2.5 L min^{-1}, the CO$_2$ concentration was almost uniform with depth and again independent of when the CO$_2$ level was measured. At the depth of 15 cm, the CO$_2$ concentrations of the control, 1.25 L min^{-1} and 2.5 L min^{-1} treatments ranged from 0.5 to 1.4%, 0.2 to 0.3% and 0.1 to 0.2%, respectively. The CO$_2$ concentrations decreased as the rate of aeration increased. Growth characteristics of sweetpotatoes treated with different root zone aeration rates are shown in Table 1. The dry weight of storage roots at the aeration rates of 1.25 and 2.5 liter min^{-1} were 19 and 26% higher, respectively, than the control. The foliage fresh weight at the air flow rate of 2.5 L min^{-1} was also higher by 26% than the control. The results indicate that the growth of sweetpotatoes was promoted when the CO$_2$ in the root zone was reduced by aeration.

For the long term study of the same effect on dry and wetted soil when a constant aeration rate was used and compared to a non-aerated control, a profile of the CO$_2$ concentration within each ridge was obtained. As shown in Figure 5, the profiles changed more dramatically and the magnitude of the CO$_2$ concentrations were higher when the soil was wetted than when it was dry. When the soil surface was relatively dry, the CO$_2$ concentration was 0.2% at the 5 cm depth and 0.7% at the 15 cm depth in the center of the non-aerated control ridge (Fig. 5, a-2); the CO$_2$ concentration generally increased with depth. In the aerated ridge, the CO$_2$ concentration was almost uniformly 0.2 to 0.3% even at the 15 cm depth (Fig. 5, a-1).

Fig 5. (b-1) and (b-2) show the CO$_2$ concentrations when the soil was wetted. Comparing these profiles to those for the dry ridges, the CO$_2$ concentration in the ridges increased in response to the rainfall. Comparison of only wetted ridges, however, also shows that aeration greatly affects CO$_2$ concentration, e.g., at the center of the ridge at a depth of 15 cm, the CO$_2$ concentration was reduced from 1.2 for the non-aerated control (Fig. 5, b-1) to 0.4 for the aerated ridge. Thus, aeration appeared to have even a greater influence when the ridge was wet.

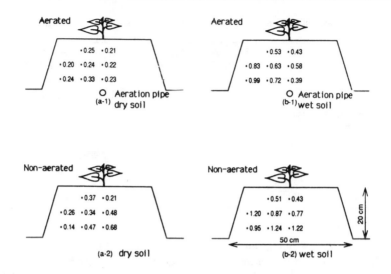

Figure 5. Distribution of CO_2 concentrations in dry (a-1 and a-2) and wet (b-1 and b-2) ridges with and without forced aeration, respectively. Right column of readings were taken at the center of the ridge. Rows of readings correspond to depths of 5, 10 and 15 cm from the ridge surface.

Table 2 shows the effect of aeration on growth characteristics of sweetpotato grown for the longer period of 111 days. With aeration, the dry weights of the foliage and the storage roots were higher by 28 and 18%, respectively, than the control. Thus when the soil was aerated at the rate of 1 L min^{-1} the yield of storage roots was about 1.2 times higher than without aeration.

DISCUSSION

For all treatments in this study the O_2 concentration in the soil was always 19 to 21% and the soil water content and soil temperatures were similar. Thus, the suppression of photosynthesis and growth of sweetpotatoes was probably not caused by the high level of CO_2 in the root zone. Such growth suppression might be due to the inhibition by CO_2 of water and nutrient absorption in the roots (Chang et al.

Table 2. Effect of soil aeration on yield of sweetpotato grown for 111 days.

Treat-ment	Fresh Wt.		Dry Wt.		Leaf Number	Leaf Area
	Foliage	Storage Root	Foliage	Storage Root		
	(g·plant^{-1})		(g·plant^{-1})		(plant^{-1})	(cm^2·plant^{-1})
Non-aerated	1014	794	115.4	238.5	176	12,980
Aerated	1210	926	147.6	281.7	187	13,970
LSD (p=0.05)	220	127	24.2	36.6	39	2,910

1945). The CO_2 level in the air adhering to the root surface is expected to be higher than the average CO_2 level in the root zone since it takes some time for CO_2, released from the root, to move through the root zone even in well cultivated soil. Therefore, the effect of aeration in the root zone may be not only to reduce CO_2 in that zone but also at the root surface. Thus, storage root formation may be promoted due to water and nutrient uptake at the root surface.

REFERENCES

Chang, H.T,. and W.E. Loomis. 1945. Effect of carbon dioxide on absorption of water and nutrients by roots. Plant Physiol. 20:221-232.

Kitaya, Y., K. Yabuki, and M. Kiyota. 1984. Studies on the control of gaseous environment in the rhizosphere. (2) Effect of carbon dioxide in the rhizosphere on growth of cucumber. Japan. J. Agr. Met. 40:119-124.

Yabuki, K. 1965. The carbon dioxide concentration of soil air in ridge. Japan. J. Agr. Met. 21:113-114.

Yabuki, K., and T. Uewada. 1978. High efficient starch production with single leaf and node cutting culture of sweetpotato. Acta Hort. 87:157-164.

SIMULATION MODELS FOR CROP GROWTH: THE IBSNAT APPROACH

Upendra Singh
International Fertilizer Development Center (IFDC), Muscle Shoals, Alabama
Joe T. Ritchie
Michigan State University, East Lansing, Michigan
Gordon Y. Tsuji
IBSNAT Project, University of Hawaii, Honolulu, Hawaii

Computer models that simulate the interactive effects of soil, weather, plants, and management factors on the growth and yield of crops are becoming a common tool in agricultural research and teaching. Their range of applications is extending now to agricultural planning, technology transfer, policymaking, and on-farm management. The complexity of agricultural systems, the lack of sufficient testing of the crop models, the difficulty of providing inputs to the models and operating them, and the failure to include many factors that may affect crops in the field had delayed the use of simulation modeling in agriculture. The International Benchmark Sites Network for Agrotechnology Transfer (IBSNAT) approach, characterized by a minimum data set requirement, standardized input and output to the crop models, similarity in

343

structure and level of detail of crop models, and the availability of user guides, has led to much wider acceptability, testing, and applications of the simulation models at field level. In the IBSNAT Project, scientists from several institutions have been developing and testing the models of wheat, maize, sorghum, rice, barley, pearl-millet, soybean, peanut, bean, potato, and aroids (taro and tanier). A brief review of IBSNAT crop models, their validation worldwide, and applications will be presented.

THE IBSNAT APPROACH

The purpose of the IBSNAT Project, a program of the United States Agency of International Development (USAID), implemented at the University of Hawaii, is to assemble and distribute a decision support software that enables its users to match biological requirements of crops to the physical characteristics of land so that the objectives specified by the user may be obtained.

The decision support software—Decision Support System for Agrotechnology Transfer (DSSAT)—is a microcomputer software designed to provide users with easy access to soil, weather, crop, and experimental data as well as simulation models to simulate outcomes of alternative management strategies. Simulation models have exacting data requirements. In the developing world, a crop model's usefulness will be limited by data availability. The development of crop models, particularly for root crops and other tropical crops, is limited by inadequate soil, crop, weather, and management data from widely contrasting environments.

Nix (1980) stated two ways of generating a minimum data set (MDS) for crop modeling: (1) the passive approach, which is least likely to disturb the traditional agricultural research strategies, and (2) the active approach, which involves radical revision of current strategies and aims at generating specified minimum data sets in the shortest possible time with the most economical use of land and labor resources.

Minimum data sets

A minimum data set of weather, soil management, and crop response data as identified by IBSNAT (1986) is essential for model development and for effective interpretation and comparison of field experiments. The MDS is an attempt to reduce the number of variables that have to be collected and yet be able to properly validate the crop model. The MDS contains data that are normally or readily available; however, there are some exceptions for the developing countries, for example, requiring solar radiation as one of the inputs.

The main elements of an MDS as indicated in Table 1 depend on the number of limiting factors that models take into account. At the simplest level, i.e., potential productivity, soil- and water-related inputs are not needed. The current version of IBSNAT models can simulate crop growth and yield under water and/or nitrogen limiting conditions. Future versions will include phosphorus dynamics as well (Singh and Godwin 1989).

Even at the simplest levels of MDS requirement, cultivar-specific genetic coefficients are the most difficult to obtain. Some IBSNAT crop models,

Table 1. Input and validation data requirements at three production levels.*

(a) Potential Productivity

Input	Daily weather	-	solar radiation (MJ m^{-2})
		-	maximum and minimum temperature (°C)
	Cultivar	-	variety name
	Site	-	latitude
	Management	-	beginning date
		-	sowing date
		-	plant population
		-	seeding depth
Validation	Development	-	emergence, anthesis, and maturity dates
	Growth	-	LAI, biomass, grain, leaf and stemweights with time
		-	final grain yield and biomass

(b) Productivity under Water Limiting Conditions

Input	Daily weather	-	rainfall (mm)
	Management	-	irrigation amounts and schedules
	Site	-	soil albedo, runoff curve number, drainage rate, stage 1 evaporation
	Soil (layer)	-	depth of each layer
		-	lower limit of plant-extractable water and drained upper limit
		-	saturated soil water content, bulk density, initial soil water content
Validation	Water Balance	-	soil water content with time

(c) Productivity under Water- and Nitrogen-limiting Conditions

Input	Management	-	residue type, amount, and depth of incorporation
		-	N fertilizer schedules, source, amount, depth and method of incorporation
	Soil	-	initial soil NO_3^- and NH_4^+ content
		-	initial soil pH and organic C (%)
Validation	Nitrogen	-	soil NO_3^- and NH_4^+ content with time
	Growth	-	grain and straw N uptake with time
		-	final N uptake for grain and straw.

---

*These data requirements are additive, i.e., to run the model at level (b), inputs for both (a) and (b) are required. Similarly, to run the model at level (c), inputs (a), (b) and (c) are required, and validation at any of the levels can be performed.

for example, the CERES models, have user options to estimate genetic coefficients from experimental data (Ritchie et al. 1991a; Godwin et al. 1990a). IBSNAT is developing a stand- alone, rule-based, intelligent genetic coefficient estimator which uses field observations. The estimation combines knowledge about crops, growth analysis data, and mathematical optimization to arrive at a set of genetic coefficients that match growth and development in the field (Hunt et al. 1990). Effort is under way to assemble a library of genetic coefficients for existing varieties from a network of ongoing experiments.

Table 2. IBSNAT crop growth models.

CERES-Maize	-	Ritchie et al. (1991a); Jones and Kiniry (1986).
CERES-Wheat	-	Godwin et al. (1990a); Ritchie at al. (1991b).
CERES-Rice	-	Singh et al. (1991a); Godwin et al. (1990b).
CERES-Barley	-	Ritchie et al. (1989).
CERES-Pearl Millet	-	Ritchie and Alagarswamy (1989).
CERES-Sorghum	-	Ritchie and Alagarswamy (1989); Singh et al. (1991b).
CERES-CEREAL (Generic)	-	Singh et al. (1989).
BEANGRO (Drybean)	-	Hoogenboom et al. (1989).
SOYGRO (Soybean)	-	Jones at al. (1989); Wilkerson et al. (1983).
PNUTGRO (Peanut)	-	Boote et al. (1989).
SUBSTOR - Potato	-	Hodges et al. (1989).
SUBSTOR - Aroids	-	Singh et al. (under development)

Networking knowledge

Systems-based research is multi- and interdisciplinary team work. The IBSNAT approach involves networking, collaboration, and cooperation. Development of appropriate simulation models and the testing of models developed in temperate regions are limited by inadequate data from widely differing environments of the tropics and a lack of genetic coefficients for local varieties. The IBSNAT network in the tropics is beginning to remedy the problem. Networking makes research more cost-effective, reduces duplication of effort, and disseminates research information.

Existing crop models for maize, wheat, soybean, and rice have been extensively tested in this network. Development of root crop models such as for potato, sweetpotato and the aroids, is now possible given the expertise available in the network and the sharing of data by collaborators and cooperators.

OVERVIEW OF IBSNAT CROP GROWTH MODELS

Table 2 lists the crop growth models developed under the auspices of the IBSNAT Project. The IBSNAT crop growth models are a combination of mathematical equations and logic used to conceptually represent a simplified crop production system. These models are primarily designed to solve problems; however, they could be used to better understand the processes involved in crop production. The models are user-oriented: they operate for the most part with readily available data (MDS); they are documented and made available to others; they are user-friendly and have been tested over a wide range of environments (Figure 1).

The crop models have been built at different levels of complexity. The IBSNAT models fit into one of the following production levels, where each new level is marked by an additional factor limiting plant growth: (a) temperature, light, and variety; (b) water availability; (c) nitrogen; and (d) phosphorus.

COUNTRIES WHERE THE IBSNAT MODELS HAVE BEEN TESTED

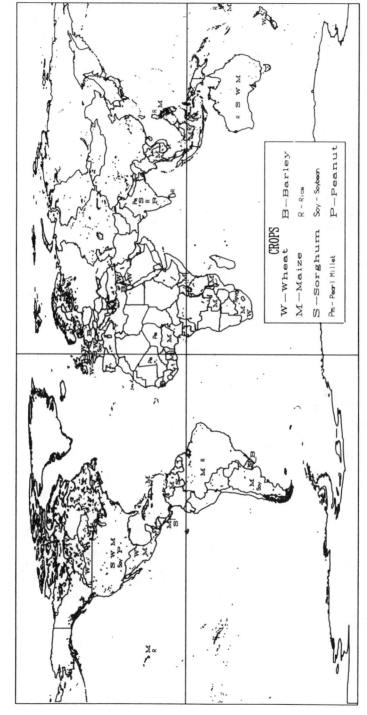

Figure 1. Countries where the IBSNAT crop models have been validated.

The SOYGRO and PNUTGRO models operate at level (b) while CERES and SUBSTOR models operate at level (c). Future versions of the models will be able to run at level (d). Also, in the future, overlaid on all these levels will be the interactive effect of plant diseases, pests, and competition.

Model Description

The model description is illustrated by the CERES model (Figures 2a and 2b); however, GRO models and SUBSTOR models have similar structures for calculating growth and development. The growth of the crop is simulated with a daily time step from sowing to maturity on the basis of physiological processes as determined by the crop's response to soil and atmospheric conditions. A detailed description of the individual crop models can be

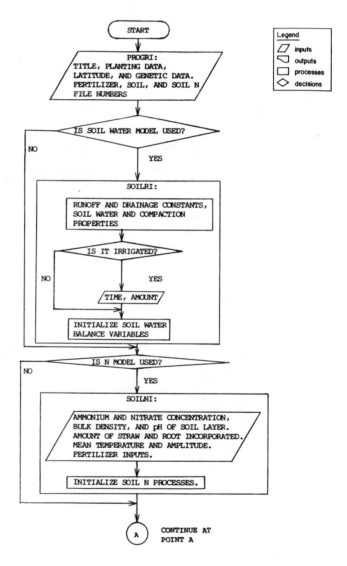

Figure 2a. Flow diagram of the IBSNAT/CERES Maize model (Reproduced from Singh (1985).

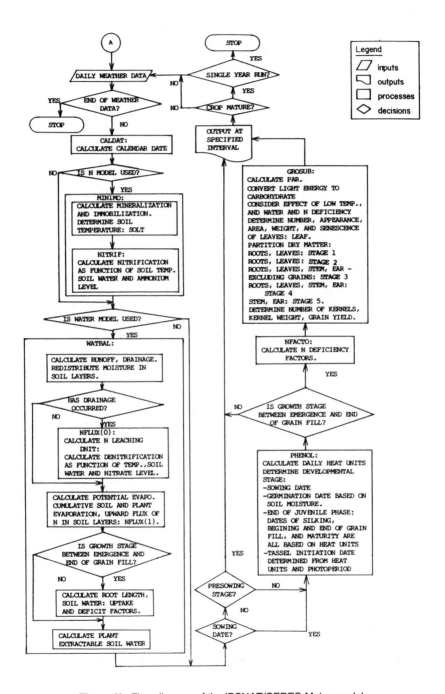

Figure 2b. Flow diagram of the IBSNAT/CERES-Maize model.

Table 3. Growth stages of crops as defined in CERES Models.

Stage[a]	Duration	Output	Growth
7	Fallow	Water, N,P	
8	Sowing to Germination	Germination day, water, N,P	
9	Germination to Emergence	Emergence day, water, N,P	Root
1	Emergence to End of Juvenile or Terminal Spikelet Initiation	All[b]	Root, leaf
2	End of Juvenile to Floral Initiation, or Terminal Spikelet to End Leaf Growth	All	Root, leaf, stem
3	Floral Induction to End of Leaf Growth/Anthesis (Flowering) or End of Leaf	All	Root, leaf, panicle (ear)
4	Anthesis to End of Panicle Growth/Beginning of Grain Filling or End of Pre-Anthesis Ear Growth to Grain Filling	All	Root, stem panicle
5	Grain Filling	All grain	Root, stem,
6	End of Grain Fill to Physiological Maturity	Water, N (tiller growth)	Tiller grain (only)

[a] Stages 9 and 1 are the vegetative phase; 2-4 the reproductive phase; and 5-6 the grain-filling/ripening phase.
[b] Simulates growth, development, water balance, nitrogen balance, and phosphorus balance.

erences previously cited. Growth stages and environmental factors incorporated into the model are summarized in Tables 3 and 4.

Yield prediction

The most important simulation in the model is partitioning of biomass to the economic yield. Calculation of sink size is the most critical step in accurate yield prediction. In CERES-Maize the average rate of photosynthesis from silking to beginning of grain filling, together with a grain-number genetic coefficient, is used to determine grain numbers. Similarly, in CERES-Sorghum and CERES-Rice

Table 4. Information regarding factors of plant growth and development processes and their sensitivity to stresses.

	Growth		Development	
	Mass	Expansion	Phasic	Morphological
Principal environ-mental factor	Solar radiation	Temperature	Temperature Photoperiod	Temperature
Degree of variation among genotypes	Low	Low	High	Low
Sensitivity to plant water deficit	Low - stomata Moderate - leaf wilting and rolling	High - vegetative stage Low- grain filling stage	Low - delay in vegetative stage	Low- main stem High - tillers and branches
Sensitivity to nitrogen deficiency	Low	High	Low	Low- main stem High - tillers and branches

Source: Ritchie (1991).

models, the sink size is determined by the photosynthetic rate around anthesis, while in CERES-Wheat, the grain number is a function of the stem weight at anthesis.

The source of assimilates for grain growth comes from photosynthesis during the grain-filling period and also from potentially mobile assimilates or reserves in other plant organs (mainly stems). The latter supply becomes critical when sink demand exceeds the source. The reserve capacity ranges from 0.25 to 0.35 of the stem weight at anthesis. When the source is greater than the sink, excess assimilates are stored as reserve.

Grain growth is also controlled by the nitrogen source and sink size. This allows the model to accurately simulate grain N content and to avoid having grains with unrealistically low N content. The main source of grain N is remobilization of labile N from shoot and root.

Soil water balance

The soil water balance routines (Ritchie 1985) are common to the CERES, SUBSTOR, and GRO models. The input needed to operate the model with soil water balance option [level (b)] has been defined in Table 1. In the model, the soil is divided into vertical layers (a maximum of 15). Each layer contains water and root length density that change with time.

The characteristic limits of the soil are critical and should be measured in the field (IBSNAT, 1990b) or estimated from empirical functions of routinely measured soil properties (Ritchie et al. 1990).

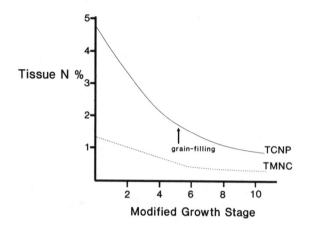

Figure 3. Relationship between critical and minimum tissue N concentration and modified growth stage.

The water balance routines use a modified SCS runoff curve number technique to simulate runoff (Williams et al. 1984). Runoff curve number is an input to the model (Table 1).

Evapotranspiration (ET) is simulated using procedures of Ritchie (1972). Potential evapotranspiration is calculated according to the Priestley-Taylor (1972) Model.

Soil nitrogen dynamics. The nitrogen balance component of the IBSNAT crop models simulates the processes of turnover of soil organic matter and crop residue (mineralization and immobilization of N). It also simulates hydrolysis of urea, nitrification (oxidation of ammonium), losses of N (leaching, ammonia volatilization, and denitrification), and the uptake and use of nitrogen by the crop. The nitrogen submodel can accommodate N applied as NO_3^-, NH_4^+, and urea.

Plant N uptake. The plant N uptake is determined from the lesser of plant N demand and N supply. The N submodel simulates N demand (ANDEM) as the sum of deficiency demand and new growth demand. The deficiency demand is calculated as the amount of N required to restore actual N concentration in the plant tops (TANC) to the critical plant top N concentration (TCNP) (Figure 3). New-growth N demand is based on the assumption that the newly formed tissues maintain critical N concentration.

CONCLUSIONS

Modeling is a continuing process, and development of the crop models is not complete. The IBSNAT models currently have no sensitivity to pests, weeds, and diseases, for example. Multiple cropping systems cannot be simulated in a satisfactory manner. Modeling work in the future will be concerned with such things, and refinements to the models are continually being made. Future modeling work will also cover such horticultural crops as sweetpotatoes, peppers, and bananas.

The next generation of IBSNAT crop models will be generic, multiple-crop simulation models. The generic models will be useful in the analysis and management of complex farming systems.

Despite limitations, crop simulation models are now at a stage of development where they can make a real contribution to the research and development process. The efficiency of research can be much enhanced through the use of models; large numbers of potential agrotechnology packages can be prescreened at the computer in an effort to ensure that only the most promising are actually tested in the field (with the expenditure of scarce research resources that this entails). In this way, models and field experimentation complement each other. Model applications at various levels are now in progress, and the development of integrated crop modeling-GIS packages has exciting implications for providing timely information for researchers, extension workers, and policymakers.

In the future, the IBSNAT models and network are expected to increase for the root crops—potatoes, sweetpotatoes and the aroids—because of their traditional and growing importance as a food source in developing nations.

REFERENCES

Boote, K.J., J.W. Jones, G. Hoogenboom, G.G. Wilkerson, and S.S. Jagtap. 1989. PNUTGRO V1.02: Peanut crop growth simulation model. User's guide. Florida Agr. Exp. Station J. No. 8420. Univ. of Florida, Gainesville, FL.

Bowen, W.T., J.W. Jones, and U. Singh. 1990. Simulation of green manure availability to subsequent maize crops. Page 14 in Agronomy Abstracts, ASA, Madison, WI.

Curry, R.B., R.M. Peart, J.W. Jones, K.J. Boote, and L.H. Allen. 1988. Simulation as a tool for analyzing crop response to climate change. Paper presented at the ASAE International Winter Meeting, Chicago, Dec. 13-16, 1988.

Curry, R.B., R.M. Peart, J.W. Jones, K.J. Boote, and L.H. Allen. 1989. Response of crop yield to predicted changes in climate and atmospheric CO_2 using simulation. ASAE Paper No. 894079. Paper presented at the ASAE International Summer Meeting, Quebec, Canada, June 25-28, 1989.

Godwin, D.C., J.T. Ritchie, U. Singh, and L. Hunt. 1990a. A user's guide to CERES-Wheat - V2.10. 2nd ed., International Fertilizer Development Center, Muscle Shoals, AL.

Godwin, D.C., U. Singh, R.J. Buresh, and S.K. De Datta. 1990b. Modeling of nitrogen dynamics in relation to rice growth and yield. Pages 320-325 in Trans. 14th Inter. Congress Soil Sci., Vol. IV: Commissions IV, Kyoto, Japan, August 12-18.

Godwin, D.C. and C.A. Jones. 1990. Nitrogen dynamics in soil-plant systems. Pages 287-321 in Modelling plant and soil systems, edited by J.T. Ritchie and H.J. Hanks. American Society of Agronomy, Monograph 31, Madison, WI.

Hodges, T., B.S. Johnson, and L.A. Manrique. 1989. SUBSTOR: A model of potato growth and development. Page 16 in Agronomy Abstracts, ASA, Madison, WI.

Hoogenboom, G., J.W. White, and J.W. Jones. 1989. A computer model for the simulation of bean growth and development. In Advances production. Publication No. 23, CIAT, Cali, Colombia.

Hoogenboom, G., J.W. Jones, and K.J. Boote. 1990. Modeling growth, development and yield of legumes: current status of the SOYGRO, PNUTGRO, and BEANGRO models. ASAE Paper No. 907060. Paper presented at the ASAE International Summer Meeting, Columbus, OH, June 24-27, 1990.

Hunt, L.A., J.W. Jones, J.T. Ritchie, and P.S. Teng. 1990. Genetic coefficients for the IBSNAT crop models. Pages 15-29 in Decision support system for agrotechnology transfer, Part I, Proceedings, IBSNAT Symposium, Las Vegas, NV, 16-18 Oct. 1989. Depart. Agron. Soil Sci., University of Hawaii, Honolulu, HI.

IBSNAT. 1986. Decision support system for agrotechnology transfer. Agrotechnology Transfer 2:1-5. International Benchmark Sites Network for Agrotechnology Transfer Project, University of Hawaii, Honolulu, HI.

IBSNAT. 1988. Experimental design and data collection procedures for IBSNAT: Minimum data set for systems analysis and crop simulation, 3rd ed., Tech. Report 1. Depart. Agron. Soil Sci., University of Hawaii, Honolulu, HI.

IBSNAT. 1990a. Documentation for IBSNAT crop model input and output files: For the decision support system for agrotechnology transfer (DSSAT V.2.1). Version 1.1, Tech. Report 5. Depart. Agron. Soil Sci., University of Hawaii, Honolulu, HI.

IBSNAT. 1990b. Field and laboratory methods for the collection of the IBSNAT minimum data set for the decision support system for agrotechnology transfer (DSSAT V.2.1). Tech. Report 2. Depart. Agron. Soil Sci., University of Hawaii, Honolulu, HI.

Jones, C.A., and J.R. Kiniry, eds. 1986. CERES-Maize: A simulation model of maize growth and development. Texas A&M University Press, College Station, TX.

Jones, J.W., K.J. Boote, S.S. Jagtap, G. Hoogenboom, and G.G. Wilkerson. 1989. SOYGRO V5.42. Soybean crop growth simulation model. User's guide. Florida Agr. Station J. No. 8304. University of Florida, Gainesville, FL.

Keating, B.A., D.C. Godwin, and J.M. Watiki. 1991. Optimising nitrogen inputs in response to climatic risk. Pages 329-358 in Climatic risk in crop production: Models and management for the semiarid tropics and subtropics, edited by Russell C. Muchow and Jennifer A. Bellamy. C.A.B. International, Oxon, UK.

Nix, H.A. 1980. Strategies for crop research. Proceedings, Agronomy Society of New Zealand 10, 107-110.

Otter-Nacke, S., D.C. Godwin, and J.T. Ritchie. 1986. Yield model development: Testing and validating the CERES-Wheat model in diverse environments, Agristars Publication No. YM-15-00407.

Peart, R.M., J.W. Jones, R.B. Curry, K.J. Boote, and L.H. Allen. 1988. Impact of climate change on crop yield in the Southeastern U.S.A.: A simulation study. Final Report. Institute of Food and Agricultural Sciences, University of Florida, Gainesville, FL.

Priestley, C.H.B., and R.J. Taylor. 1972. On the assessment of surface heat flux and evaporation using large-scale parameters. Mon. Weather Rev. 100: 81-92.

Ritchie, J.T. 1972. Model for predicting evaporation from a row crop with incomplete cover. Water Resour.Res.8(5):1204-1213.

Ritchie, J.T. 1985. A user-oriented model of the soil water balance in wheat. Pages 293-305 in Wheat growth and modeling, edited by W. Day and R.K. Atkin. Plenum Press, New York, NY.

Ritchie, J.T., and G. Alagarswamy. 1989. Simulation of sorghum and pearl millet phenology. Pages 24-26 in Modeling the growth and development of sorghum and pearl millet, edited by S.M. Virmani, H.L.S. Tandon and G. Alagarswamy. Res. Bull. No. 12. ICRISAT. Andhra Pradesh, India.

Ritchie, J.T., B.S. Johnson, S. Otter-Nacke, and D.G. Godwin. 1989. Development of a barley yield simulation model. Final progress report. USDA No. 86-CRSR-2-2867. Michigan State University, East Lansing, MI.

Ritchie, J.T., and D.S. NeSmith. 1991. Temperature and crop development. Pages 5-29 in

Modelling plant and soil systems, edited by J.T. Ritchie and H.J. Hanks. American Agronomy Society Monograph 31, Madison, WI.

Ritchie, J.T., D.C. Godwin, and U. Singh. 1990. Soil and water inputs for the IBSNAT crop models. Pages 31-45 *in* Decision support system for agrotechnology transfer, Part I: Proceedings, IBSNAT Symposium, Las Vegas, NV 16-18 Oct. 1989. Dept. Agron. and Soil Sci., University of Hawaii, Honolulu, HI.

Ritchie, J.T. 1991. Ideal model for predicting crop yields. Pages 97-122 *in* Climatic risk in crop production: Models and management for the semiarid tropics and subtropics, edited by Russell C. Muchow and Jennifer A. Bellamy. C.A.B. International, Oxon, UK.

Ritchie, J.T., U. Singh, D.C. Godwin, and L. Hunt. 1991a. A user's guide to CERES-Maize - V2.10. 2nd ed. International Fertilizer Development Center, Muscle Shoals, AL.

Ritchie, J.T., D.C. Godwin, and Otter-Nacke, S. 1991b. CERES-Wheat. A simulation model of wheat growth and development. Texas A&M University Press, College Station, TX.

Singh, U. 1985. A crop growth model for predicting corn performance in the tropics. Ph.D. diss., Agron. Soil Sci. Dept., University of Hawaii, Honolulu, HI.

Singh, U., D.C. Godwin, C.G. Humphries, and J.T. Ritchie. 1989. A computer model to predict the growth and development of cereals. Pages 668-675 *in* Proceedings, 1989 Summer Computer Simulation Conference, July 24-27, Austin, TX.

Singh, U., and D.C. Godwin. 1989. Phosphorus dynamics in IBSNAT crop models. Page 22 *in* Agronomy Abstracts. ASA, Madison, WI.

Singh, U., D.C. Godwin, and R.J. Morrison. 1990. Modelling the impact of climate change on agricultural production in the South Pacific. Pages 24-40 *in* Global warming-related effects on agriculture and human health and comfort in the South Pacific, edited by Philip J. Hughes and Glenn McGregor. Univ. of Papua New Guinea, Port Moresby.

Singh, U., D.C. Godwin, and J.T. Ritchie. 1992. A user's guide to CERES-Rice - V2.10. International Fertilizer Development Center, Muscle Shoals, AL.

Singh, U., J.T. Ritchie, G. Alagarswamy, and D.C. Godwin. A user's guide to CERES-Sorghum - V2.10. International Fertilizer Development Center, Muscle Shoals, AL (In press).

Wilkerson, G.G., J.W. Jones, K.J. Boote, K.T. Ingram, and J.W. Mishoe. 1983. Modeling soybean growth for crop management. Trans. ASAE 26(1): 63-73.

Williams, J.R., C.A. Jones, and P.T. Dyke. 1984. A modeling approach to determining the relationship between erosion and soil productivity. Trans. ASAE 27(1):129-144.

SECTION 4

FOOD TECHNOLOGY/ HUMAN NUTRITION

S. C. S. Tsou,[*] T. L. Hong[**]

The Nutrition and Utilization of Sweetpotato

Sweetpotato (*Ipomoea batatas*) is an important crop in many parts of the world. As a starchy root, it is not only an efficient producer of calories but also rich in many nutrients especially vitamins and minerals. Because it is rich in dietary fiber, sweetpotato is becoming a popular food in the modern diet. China contributes about 80% of the world's production of sweetpotato. It is generally produced on marginal land or rotated with other crops. It is used as food, feed and as an industrial raw material. Sweetpotato has also played a significant role in the diet in Japan, Taiwan and Korea, although production in these areas has declined sharply in the last 20 years. Changes in production systems and utilization patterns are needed to make sweetpotato a stronger competitor to other alternative crops. Improving dry matter yield and quality was identified as a major task for the sweetpotato improvement program at AVRDC. Significant progress has been made. The potential for improvement and results of quality evaluations are discussed. Properties of provitamin A, dietary fiber and starch are emphasized. It is concluded that sweetpotato has great potential, especially in developing countries. More research in varietal improvement, production technology, marketing systems and utilization is needed if the full potential of this important crop is to be realized.

Sweetpotatoes are used in many ways. The roots are used as a supplemental staple food, a vegetable, animal feed, and raw material for the starch and fermentation industries (Yang 1982). The tender tips are nutritious dark-green leafy vegetables, and the vines are a good source of green feed.

Although sweetpotato originated in the tropics, it is mainly grown in the temperate region and in the subtropics during the cool season. About 80% of world sweetpotato production is in China, and all of it is consumed domestically. In addition to food and feed, there are over 60 products that can be manufactured using sweetpotato as raw material (Shyong and Jou 1984). However, with the exception of a very few products, most of them can also be made from other raw materials. The potential of sweetpotato for feed and industrial use is basically determined by its price compared to other commodities. The major competitors of sweetpotato are corn and cassava. Yield, especially dry matter yield, could be the major attribute that impacts the utilization of sweetpotato. Significant improvement in dry matter yield has been achieved through breeding at AVRDC (Takagi and Opena 1988).

[*]Deputy Director General and Biochemist; [**]Principal Research Assistant, Analytical Laboratory, Asian Vegetable Research and Development Center, P.O. Box No. 42, Shanhua, Tainan 74199, Taiwan.

Table 1. Germplasm analysis of major chemical components in sweetpotato.

Components	Content range
Dry matter	12.74 - 41.20
Protein*	1.34 - 11.08
Sugar*	8.78 - 27.14
Starch*	44.59 - 78.02
Fiber*	2.70 - 7.60
β-carotene**	0.06 - 11.71
β-amylase activity**	8.89 -183.65

*% (dry wt. basis); **mg/100g fresh wt.; based on one year's data among 1600 accessions.

NUTRITIONAL VALUE OF SWEETPOTATO

Sweetpotato roots are rich in carbohydrates and generally low in fat and protein. Starch and sugars contribute over 60% of its dry matter. The addition of vegetable oil during preparation may improve the energy density of sweetpotato. Germplasm analyses of the major chemical components have been carried out at AVRDC (Table 1). The protein content of some lines can be higher than 10% on a dry weight basis. Cultural management, such as nitrogen fertilization, is an effective means to increase protein content. Results suggest that sweetpotato's nutritional value can be improved through effective breeding programs and appropriate field practices. Another possible approach is to complement a diet of sweetpotato (as a staple food) with legumes. Soybean would be ideal due to its high protein and oil content.

Estimation of the nutritional value of typical sweetpotato varieties is based on the relative nutrient cost of the Taiwanese diet (Tsou 1985). Nutritional values and cost of white-fleshed and orange-fleshed sweetpotatoes are compared to a few other commodities in Table 2. Energy contributes 10.5% and 2.5%, respectively, for total nutritional value of cultivars with white and orange flesh. Vitamin A in orange-fleshed cultivars accounts for 71.4% of total nutritional value. The nutritional value of sweetpotato tips is comparable to that of other green vegetables such as spinach.

The density of major nutrients of sweetpotato in relation to its food energy is presented in Figures 1a and 1b. In spite of its high energy content, sweetpotato is also a good source of vitamin C and iron. Orange-fleshed sweetpotato is an excellent source of provitamin A. Sweetpotato is also rich in potassium and other minerals, which makes it a biologically basic food and which gives it the potential to balance the acidity of other food items such as cereals and meats.

PROVITAMIN A IN SWEETPOTATO

Vitamin A deficiency is one of the major nutritional problems in the developing world with one-half million children suffering from blindness (De Luca et al. 1977). Orange-fleshed sweetpotato is rich in the provitamin A compound, β-carotene. The β-carotene content of some cultivars can be as high as 11 mg/100 g fresh weight (Table 1). Thus, one may obtain sufficient vitamin A from 200 g of orange-fleshed sweetpotato weekly.

Table 2. Comparison of nutritive value and market prices of selected commodities in Taiwan (1987).

Commodity	Nutrient value[1] (NT$/kg)	Taiwan price[2] (NT$/kg)
White-flesh sweetpotato	22.5	4.5
Orange-flesh sweetpotato	96.6	4.5
Sweetpotato tips	112.2	15.0
Rice (milled)	24.7	23.4
Wheat (whole)	64.8	20.0
Corn	43.8	25.0
Tomato	24.7	32.2
Onion	16.1	17.6
Cabbage	39.1	23.8
Spinach	170.3	40.3

[1]Nutrient Value (NV) $= \dfrac{\sum_{}^{n} RNC_j \times C_j}{n}$

n: Eight nutrients; C: Composition; RNC: Relative nutrient cost:

1) Energy: 0.0189 NT$/kcal   2) Protein: 0.63 NT$/g
3) Calcium: 0.099 NT$/g   4) Iron: 3.73 NT$/g
5) Vitamin A: 8 NT$/1000 IU   6) Vitamin B_1: 30.2 NT$/mg
7) Vitamin B_2: 48.75NT$/mg   8) Vitamin C: 0.40 NT$/mg

[2]US$ 1 = NT$27.3.

Figures 1a and 1b. Nutritional quality of orange-fleshed (top graph) and white-fleshed (bottom) sweetpotato based on relative nutrient density (nutrient content is percent of recommended daily allowance) in relation to food energy. Values (<0.5, 0.5-0.89, 0.9-4.9, 5.0-19.9, and >20) are respectively classified as poor, fair, adequate, good, and excellent. A different scale is used for Vitamins A and C.

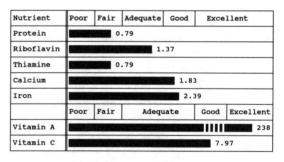

Table 3. Provitamin A availability of vegetables and fruits.

| Commodity | Availability* | Major carotenoids | |
		Provitamin A	Nonprovitamin A
Spinach	12.88 c	β-carotene	Xanthophylls
chlorophylls			
Water convolvulus	11.62 c	β-carotene	Xanthophylls
chlorophylls			
Field mustard	12.23 c	β-carotene	Xanthophylls
chlorophylls			
Sweetpotato (TN 66)	17.01 b	β-carotene	
Sweetpotato (1108-13)	14.86 bc	β-carotene	
Mango (Irwin)	17.79 b	β-carotene	Xanthophylls
Mango (Native)	16.34 b	β-carotene	Xanthophylls
Pumpkin	23.03 a	α-carotene	
		β-carotene	
Carrot	17.83 b	α-carotene	
		β-carotene	
Papaya	22.35 a	β-carotene	
		β-cryptoxanthin	Xanthophylls
Papaya (TN-2)	23.60 a	β-carotene	
		β-cryptoxanthin	Xanthophylls
β-carotene standard	21.20 a	β-carotene	
β-carotene standard	21.03 a	β-carotene	

*Different letter within column represents significant difference at 5% level by Duncan's Multiple Range Test.

A series of feeding experiments on rats was conducted at AVRDC to estimate the biological availability of vitamin A in various vegetables and fruits. In addition to a high content of provitamin A, the orange-fleshed sweetpotato is also high in its biological availability of provitamin A. The bioavailability of β-carotene in sweetpotato is significantly higher than that in other leafy vegetables (Table 3). The digestibility of β-carotene in sweetpotato, however, is not significantly different from other commodities tested. The higher bioavailability could be due to the lack of chlorophylls and other carotenoids. These compounds are found to be inhibitors of provitamin A absorption (Tsou and Kan 1985; High and Day 1952).

SWEETPOTATO STARCH

Sweetpotato is an important raw material for the starch industry in many Asian countries. The chemical and physical properties of sweetpotato starch have been studied extensively (Palmer 1982; Lii and Chang 1978). The sweetpotato starch granule is polygonal in shape with a diameter of 2 to 25 mm. It has an amylose content of about 18%. Its iodine affinity is 3.66% and its gelatinization temperature is 58-63-69°C. The chemical and physical properties, however, varied among the varieties tested. The DSC graph and Brabender viscograms of starch isolated from two sweetpotato clones are shown in Figures 2 and 3. The viscosity patterns suggested that they are both type-B starch.

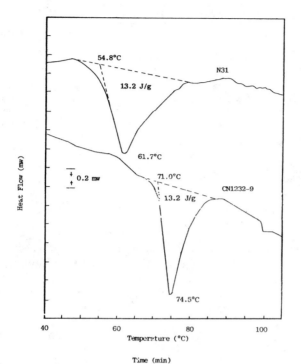

Figure 2. Differential scanning colorimetry (DSC) graph of sweetpotato starch.

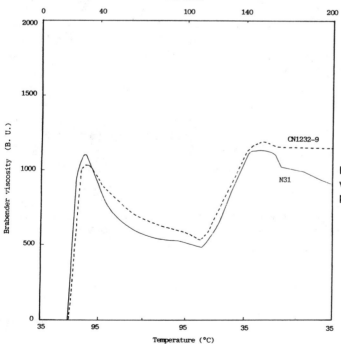

Figure 3. Brabender viscograms of sweetpotato starch.

Table 4. Estimated polysaccharide composition of selected sweetpotato clones.

Variety	Dry matter (%)	Pectin substance	Lignin	Cellulose	Hemicellulose
I367	17.34	0.49	8.16	7.28	12.69
CN1121-312	19.09	0.68	7.49	6.64	12.47
CN942-47	21.53	0.29	3.98	7.64	11.04
CN1229-16	38.46	0.53	1.57	14.29	17.49
CN1425-3	36.75	0.92	4.89	16.26	21.08
CN63-74	38.70	0.40	4.59	13.70	17.29
CN1219-1	29.01	0.55	6.44	9.12	14.27
CN1229-14	23.88	1.07	9.33	7.39	12.89
CN1232-9	27.90	0.50	6.53	12.69	18.27
TN57	31.70	0.44	4.75	11.95	16.77

Unit: g/100g total carbohydrate+lignin

Starch properties may be associated with the low protein digestibility of sweetpotato fed to pigs. However, the feeding efficiency can be improved either by cooking or by using clones that have easily digestible starch (Tsou and Hong 1988). Starch may also partially be responsible for the flatulence in sweetpotato. Proper cooking is essential in eliminating this undesirable property (Tsou and Yang 1984).

DIETARY FIBER IN SWEETPOTATO

The role of dietary fiber in human nutrition has attracted growing interest in recent years. Much research has been conducted on its physiological functions in the prevention of intestinal disorders, in absorption of minerals, serum cholesterol, and on their associated analytical methods (Mendeloff 1984; Vahouny et al. 1988). Crude fiber, which consists of only cellulose and lignin, does not adequately express the nutritional role of sweetpotato as a dietary fiber provider.

Most of the research programs carried out on sweetpotato are attempting to reduce the content of crude fiber for better eating quality. On the other hand, some consumers of sweetpotato direct their attention to the roughage characteristic of the commodity. Thus, a desired fiber pattern of sweetpotato is: low in cellulose and lignin and yet high in other components of dietary fiber, with smooth texture and good eating quality.The dietary fiber patterns of selected sweetpotato clones are presented in Table 4. The dry matter content of these clones varied from 17 to 31%. Variation in dietary fiber was also observed among the sweetpotato clones tested. These data suggest that it is possible to develop clones that are low in crude fiber and high in other dietary fiber content.

CONCLUSIONS

Sweetpotato, as a low-cost food, is rich in food energy, dietary fiber, minerals and vitamins. It can be used in many ways. However, effective research and promotion programs are needed in order to realize its full potential.

Sweetpotato can be a good low-cost supplemental staple food in areas where other staples are not readily available. Sweetpotato can be prepared either separately or by mixing with other staples. The processing industry in Taiwan has demonstrated that up to 15% of wheat flour can be replaced with sweetpotato without significantly affecting its physical properties. The present process of precooking the sweetpotato and then mixing it with wheat flour is labor-intensive. The development of a sweetpotato flour industry to provide large quantities of quality flour at low prices could be a means of increasing sweetpotato consumption. The model in China of using sweetpotato for both food and animal feed ensures a year-round supply of sweetpotato to the low-income population. Development of easily digestible sweetpotato clones can be very important in transferring this model to other developing countries.

Promoting sweetpotato as a health food has not yet being fully exploited. Orange-fleshed sweetpotatoes are not only a good source of provitamin A, but also rich in dietary fiber. Compositional analysis of selected sweetpotato clones suggests that it is possible to develop clones that are low in crude fiber yet high in other dietary fiber. These clones may have components that lead to improved eating quality with good nutritional value.

Sweetpotato tips can be used as green leafy vegetables (Tsou and Lee 1985; Villareal et al. 1982). Since they are often free from pests, they require little or no pesticide application. Improvements in yield, eating quality and postharvest properties are required in order to make this nutritious green vegetable more competitive.

REFERENCES

De Luca, L.M., J. Glover, J. Heller, J.A. Olson, and B. Underwood. 1977. Guidelines for the eradication of vitamin A deficiency and xerophthalmia. VI. Recent advances in the metabolism and function of vitamin A and their relationship to applied nutrition. A report of the International Vitamin A Consultative Group (IVACG).

High, E.G., and H.G. Day. 1952. Fate of lycopene in the rat and its effects on the utilization of carotene and vitamin A. Journal of Nutrition. 48: 369-372.

Lii, C.Y., and M.S. Chang. 1978. Studies on the starches in Taiwan. Pages 416-423 *in* Proceedings, National Science Council Vol. 2, No. 4, 1978, ROC.

Mendeloff, A.I. 1984. Dietary fiber and nutrient delivery. Bristol-Myers Nutrition Symposia. 3: 209-237.

Palmer, J.K. 1982. Carbohydrates in sweet potato. Pages 135-140 *in* Sweet potato, edited by R.L. Villareal and T.D. Griggs. Proceedings, The First International Sweet Potato Symposium, AVRDC (Asian Vegetable Research and Development Center), Shanhua, Tainan 74199, Taiwan, ROC.

Shyong, H.Y., and H.T. Jou. 1984. [Cultivation of sweet potato in China: General utilization of sweet potato] In Chinese. Shanhai Sci. Tech. Publishing, Shanhai. 378 pp.

Takagi, H., and R.T. Opena. 1988. Sweetpotato breeding at AVRDC to overcome production constraints and use in Asia. Pages 233-245 *in* Proceedings: Exploration, maintenance, and utilization of sweet potato genetic resources. CIP, Feb. 23-27. CIP, Lima, Peru.

Tsou, S.C.S. 1985. Relative nutrient costs and nutritional value. Pages 149-152 *in* Sweet potato products: a natural resource for the tropics, edited by J.C. Bouwkamp. CRC Press, Boca Raton, FL USA.

Tsou, S.C.S., and T.L. Hong. 1988. Digestibility of sweet potato starch. Pages 127-136 *in*

Proceedings: Improvement of sweet potato (*Ipomoea batatas*) in Asia. CIP, ICAR, CTCRI, 24-28 Oct 1988, ICAR, Trivandrum, India. Available from ICAR.

Tsou, S.C.S., and K.K. Kan. 1985. Availability of provitamin A in sweet potato. Pages 305-306 *in* Progress report 1985. AVRDC (Asian Vegetable Research and Development Center), Shanhua, Tainan 74199, Taiwan, ROC.

Tsou, S.C.S., and Y.Y. Lee. 1985. Composition of edible fiber in sweet potato tips. Pages 310-312 *in* Progress report 1985. AVRDC (Asian Vegetable Research and Development Center), Shanhua, Tainan 74199, Taiwan, ROC.

Tsou, S.C.S., and M.H. Yang. 1984. Flatulence factors in sweet potato. ACTA Horticulturae. 163:179-186.

Vahouny, G.V., S. Satchithanandam, I. Chen, S.A. Tepper, D. Kritchevsky, F. G. Lightfoot, and M.M. Cassidy. 1988. Dietary fiber and intestinal adaptation: effects on lipid absorption and lymphatic transport in the rat. American Journal of Clinical Nutrition. 201-205.

Villareal, R.L., S.C.S. Tsou, H.F. Lo., and S.C. Chiu. 1982. Sweet potato tips as vegetables. Pages 313-320 *in* Sweet potato, edited by R. L. Villareal and T.D. Griggs. Proceedings, The First International Sweet Potato Symposium, AVRDC (Asian Vegetable Research and Development Center), Shanhua, Tainan 74199, Taiwan, ROC.

Yang, T.H. 1982. Sweet potato as a supplemental staple food. Pages 31-34 *in* Sweet potato, edited by R.L. Villareal and T.D. Griggs. Proceedings, The First International Sweet Potato Symposium, AVRDC (Asian Vegetable Research and Development Center), Shanhua, Tainan 74199, Taiwan, ROC.

Sweetpotato Technology for the 21st Century. W.A. Hill, C.K. Bonsi and P.A. Loretan (Eds.) 1992. Tuskegee University, Tuskegee, AL

Jennifer A. Woolfe

The Contribution of Sweetpotato and Its Products to Human Diets

The sweetpotato as a food rich in starch, fiber and micronutrients is suitable for promotion by nutritionists to encourage healthy eating habits in both developing and developed countries. The increased use of yellow/orange-fleshed roots and the green tops of sweetpotato could be one important means of helping to prevent vitamin A deficiency, especially among small children and women in certain developing countries. Expanding means of utilization by processing could help to improve food security, promote a local resource, and improve nutritional status in many tropical developing countries. Some of the wide variety of products which can be made by using or incorporating sweetpotato are mentioned. Finally, some of the constraints to be overcome in implementing these possibilities are outlined.

INTRODUCTION

The sweetpotato was at one time a subsistence staple food of large population groups in many countries of the third world. In Asia, it kept famine and starvation from the door on frequent occasions of natural disaster and war. In its role as a staple it was the major, even the sole, item on the food plate accompanied with varying degrees of frequency or quantity by other minor food items. It still retains this role in a very few areas, notably parts of the Papua New Guinea Highlands, of Rwanda and Uganda in Africa and in poor, isolated and mountainous districts of China and other areas of Asia. More frequently nowadays it fulfills this role in a fall-back capacity, on a seasonal basis, when other preferred staples are in short supply or too expensive. Or it may be used as a co-staple, for example when rice and sweetpotato are cooked together in various Asian countries.

In some countries, the sweetpotato fulfills certain ceremonial, festive or social functions. In the United States it is an integral part of the meal served at Thanksgiving. In Nepal, it can be a sacred food prepared as an offering to God. The many forms of processed sweetpotato available in Japan are mostly luxury items given as gifts to friends and relatives or bought as tourist souvenirs.

People rarely think of sweetpotato as a special food. It has generally been stigmatized as a "poor man's food", but, as someone remarked at a recent sweetpotato workshop, "What on earth is wrong with that?" It has, for example, taken on the regular role of stomach filler for the lowest income groups in circumstances of

26, Westville Road, Thames Ditton, Surrey KT7 OUJ, England

financial hardship. Sweetpotato has kept hunger from the door in recent years for the urban poor of the central coast of Peru, because it is available at a lower price than potatoes or wheat-based products. This may, however, be a temporary phenomenon with consumption decreasing again if economic circumstances improve. There is evidence that, as people's incomes increase and their standard of living rises, their consumption of sweetpotato decreases (Tsou and Villareal 1982) as they turn to foods which provide greater variety of forms and more convenience in terms of preparation and cooking.

In recent decades with increasingly large migrations of the world's rural people to cities, and the consequent need to transport this easily damaged and highly perishable commodity long distances to urban markets, costs of sweetpotato to non-producer consumers have risen in relation to other foods and sweetpotato has increasingly moved from its role as staple to that of complementary vegetable food or snack. In some areas, sweetpotato is no longer affordable by the poorest consumers. Thus sweetpotato has to rise to a number of challenges so that it remains the food of those who need it most, while increasing its appeal to a wider range of income groups.

Some time ago, I was asked to write a rationale from my own perspective, i. e., that of a food scientist/nutritionist, which provided arguments justifying increased investment of resources in sweetpotato research. I entitled this "Why sweetpotato?" and set forth the advantages of sweetpotato as a food. However, afterwards I realized that many of the things I had written could be applied with equal justification to any number of other crops. Most people are able to choose their dietary items from a range of foods, however limited this may be. If we are serious about the importance of promoting sweetpotato as a valuable and nutritious food for all social groups we have to ask ourselves the question - what special features does sweetpotato have as a human food which distinguish it from other food crops. I suggest that outstanding among these features are the nutritional and sensory versatility of sweetpotato in terms of its micronutrient content and its wide range of colors, tastes and textures. Because of this versatility, sweetpotato can be compared in compositional and sensory terms not only with other roots and tubers, but with vegetables and fruits. These characteristics can be exploited to produce a whole spectrum of items into which sweetpotato can be processed. Thus it has an exciting potential for contributing increasingly to the diets of groups around the world.

FOOD FOR LARGE POPULATIONS

The nutritional qualities of the sweetpotato can be demonstrated in two ways, i.e., in terms of the total numbers of people that can be fed and as a food for the individual consumer. Table 1 shows that, even at the low yields still pertaining in some tropical countries, the sweetpotato produces more food per hectare per day than any of the other major crops listed. This is because it has a greater fresh weight yield than legumes or cereals and a shorter time to harvest than other roots and tubers. If the high yields, which have been shown experimentally—and already achieved on

Table 1. Number of people which one hectare of selected crops can support per day in terms of major nutrients.

	Energy	Protein	Vitamin A	Vitamin C	Iron
Sweetpotato roots (6 t ha^{-1})	20	20	0 - 1856	387	30
(30 t ha^{-1})	92	92	0 - 8565	1786	138
Leaves (13 t ha^{-1})	23	93	542	1444	325
Roots + Leaves (14 t ha^{-1} + 13 t ha^{-1})	63	63	542 - 4532	2276	390
Cassava	13	7	0	264	29
Beans	6	27	0	0	38
Soybeans	19	130	0	0	85
Rice	14	31	0	0	14
Maize	13	26	12	0	20

From: Woolfe 1989

farms in a few countries, could be more generally attained, then the sweetpotato is capable of feeding very large numbers of people.

A FOOD RICH IN NUTRIENTS FOR THE INDIVIDUAL CONSUMER

Malnutrition is widespread in the world today. It is now increasingly recognized that this can take several forms. Dietary deficiencies in terms of both quality and quantity of food are still the most pressing problems of malnutrition for large segments of the population in many tropical developing countries. The adverse health effects of "affluent" diets have only become apparent in recent decades and were thought to be confined mainly to the developed countries of the western world. However, chronic diseases such as cardiovascular diseases and cancer, which are associated with these diets, have recently been projected to become substantial health problems in virtually every country of the world by the year 2000 (WHO 1990). Any food, if eaten sensibly, can form part of a balanced diet. However, the sweetpotato is particularly well fitted to form part of any campaign designed to promote healthy eating whether in developing or developed countries.

Vitamin A (retinol) deficiency, leading to xerophthalmia and resulting some-times in complete blindness is still a serious problem among children in about 40 countries (WHO 1990). It has been calculated (Cohen et al. 1986) that in Bangladesh alone about 750,000 preschool children have some degree of xerophthalmia at any time and, of these, 12,000 are blind and about 45,000 have serious loss of sight in at least one eye. Lack of vitamin A also decreases resistance to infections and increases mortality in the young. In recognizing these factors, the International Consultative Group meeting in 1989 stressed the need to improve the diet and raise the level of vitamin A nutrition where a current intake is inadequate. The availability of vitamin A from foods is limited, especially if the diet is wholly or largely vegetarian. Plant foods do not contain the preformed vitamin, but a limited number, including the green tops and deep yellow or orange-fleshed roots of many sweetpotato cultivars are a good source of β-carotene, which is converted into vitamin A in the body (6 µg of β-carotene = 1 µg of retinol). Sweetpotato roots contain from trace to over 20 mg/100g [fresh weight basis (fwb)] of β-carotene; this corresponds to trace to greater than 3 mg/100g (fwb) retinol equivalents (RE) of vitamin A. The green tops contain about 3 mg/100g (fwb) of β-carotene (about 0.5 mg/100g (fwb) RE). Regular intakes (100 g per day) of yellow or orange-fleshed roots having moderate concentrations of β-carotene (for example 3 mg/100g (fwb) or of green tops or a mixture of the two in various proportions would provide more than 100% of recommended daily amounts of vitamin A for children. (The RDA will fulfill the dietary needs of all but a small proportion of a population).

Unfortunately, it is a sad fact that xerophthalmia is common in some environments where sweetpotato leaves are readily available. Yellow or orange-fleshed roots are rejected by adults in many developing countries in favor of white- or cream-fleshed types that have little or no provitamin A activity. The orange-fleshed cultivars are often the very moist mouth-feel, sweet-tasting lines with the least appeal for use as a staple food. It would seem unlikely that such adult prejudices extend to young children who love sweet, soft foods and might actually prefer the orange roots. Watson (1988) found that farmers she interviewed in one part of Indonesia certainly noted such a preference in their children who ate more sweetpotato than the adults. Although the adoption of the idea of "children's foods" is difficult in many tropical countries where a child is simply given part of the food from the family pot, carotene-rich cultivars could be promoted by extension workers for inclusion in backyards or home gardens for use as young children's snacks or between-meal fillers.

In many developing countries, adult men obtain the lion's share of the daily food with women and children coming a poor second, often to the severe detriment of their nutritional status. This may be particularly true if much of the food has to be purchased. Sweetpotato greens are an especially valuable item to include in backyard plots or home gardens which are often tended by women and the items grown there used for addition to their own and their children's meals. Since sweetpotato is adapted to the hot, humid tropics, it is easier to grow them in many tropical areas than to introduce western vegetables. Sweetpotato vines are more tolerant to extremes of drought or heavy rainfall than many other green leafy vegetables. They can also be harvested continuously over a number of weeks, not just once like many commercially grown vegetables. Their β-carotene content is accompanied by valuable quantities of protein (about 3% fwb), and riboflavin (vitamin B_2; see Table 2) which is often deficient in the rice based diets of Asia. A recent experimental introduction of pot-grown sweetpotato greens for urban slum dwellers (Villamayor 1991) holds the promise of increasing vegetable consumption even among the very poorest sections of urban society who have the minimum conditions necessary to cultivate their own food. Approximately 50 g of leaves can be harvested per pot every 10 to 15

Table 2. Protein, riboflavin and vitamin C in sweetpotato leaves and other leafy and non-leafy vegetables (per 100 g fresh)

Vegetable	Protein mg	Riboflavin mg	Vitamin C mg
Tropical leaves			
Sweetpotato	3.0	0.35	55 (20-136)
Amaranth	3.5	0.22	65
Cassava	7.0	0.27	300
Temperate leafy and non-leafy			
Cabbage	.9	0.05	45
Carrot	0.7	0.05	6
Onion	0.9	0.05	10
Lettuce	1.0	0.08	7
Spinach	3.2	0.17	46
Tomato	0.9	0.04	20

Data given by: Woolfe 1989.

days. Tentative estimates of the contribution which these 50 g of cooked leaves could make to the diet (Figure 1) indicate that 20% or more of the recommended daily allowance of vitamins A, C and riboflavin as well as the minerals Fe and Ca can be provided by these leaves. There are many uncertainties here including the acceptabil-

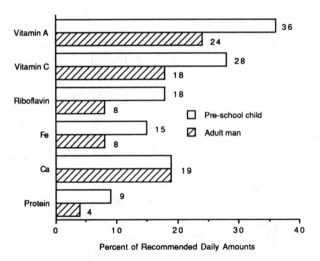

Percent of Recommended Daily Amounts

Figure 1. Percent recommended daily amounts of certain nutrients met by 50 g cooked sweetpotato leaves. Notes: Vitamin C may be very low in wilted, overcooked leaves; iron absorption may be less than 10% in diets of low bioavailability; calcium availability may be reduced by oxalate content. Sources: Nutrient levels in leaves from Woolfe (1992); Percent of RDAs calculated using recommended nutrient intakes from FAO (1988) for vitamin A and iron (assuming intermediate bioavailability of iron in the whole diet); Passmore et al. (1974) for vitamin C, riboflavin and calcium; FAO/WHO/UNU (1985) for protein.

Table 3. Proximate composition of sweetpotato roots, cooked or as flour (per 100 g)[a].

	Energy kcal	Protein g	Fat g	Carbohydrate* g	Dietary fiber g
Boiled	115	1.5	0.4	26.3	2.4
Baked	141	2.1	0.5	32.5	3.3[b]
Flour	337	3.3	0.6	78.3	ND

[a]Data from Woolfe 1992; [b]from Holland et al. 1991.
*Composed of about 80% starch, 20% sugars in raw
50% starch, 50% sugars in cooked;
(percentage of sugars much lower in low-sweet or
non-sweet cultivars)
ND = Not determined

ity of green leaves to small children, the distribution of food within the family, retention of nutrients with different cooking methods, and the influence of antinutritional compounds such as oxalate on the absorption of calcium and iron. Such factors should be studied in order to better assess the contribution sweetpotato could make to the prevention of nutritional deficiencies and to determine the most effective methods of promotion.

Leading causes of premature death in the developed world are chronic diseases such as coronary heart disease and cancer. The leading cardiovascular disorder in developing countries is stroke in which obesity, among other factors, plays a contributory role. Obesity is also related to the onset of diabetes. Constipation and other chronic disorders of the large intestine and dental caries are all prevalent in the developed world. Although causes of these diseases are multifactorial, an important component is diet, more particularly the energy-dense diet high in fat and added sugar and low in complex carbohydrates associated with the "affluent" society. Recent changes in diet in developing countries as a result of migrations from rural to urban areas and increased economic prosperity in some segments of the population have sometimes come to resemble those which took place earlier in the developed world with consequent increases in the incidence of chronic diet-related diseases. There is now renewed emphasis by nutrition scientists and practitioners, given endorsement by governments in some countries in the form of dietary guidelines, on the important role in a healthy diet of "starchy" foods and vegetables with their low fat content and hence moderate energy density, their dietary fiber components and their associated concentrations of micronutrients (vitamins and minerals). The sweetpotato is such a food (Tables 3 and 4). To my knowledge there has never been a report about the potential cariogenicity (ability to cause dental caries) of sweetpotato. Although sugar concentration, mainly in the form of maltose, increases with cooking, its extent of formation varies considerably with cultivar. Even in very sweet cultivars, sugar concentration after cooking is similar to that found in many fruits; fruits are considered to be of low cariogenicity in humans (Rugg-Gunn 1986).

Table 4. Content of some vitamins and minerals in cooked sweetpotato and other staple foods (per 100 g)[a].

	β-carotene mg	Thiamin mg	Niacin mg	Vitamin C mg	Ca mg	P mg	Fe mg
Sweetpotato (boiled)	0 ->20	0.10	0.6	17	32	39	0.7
Cassava[b] (boiled)	0	0.05	0.6	17	17	39	0.5
Potato (boiled)	0	0.09	1.5	16	7	53	0.6
Rice (white, boiled)	0	0.01	0.3	0	1	34	0.2
Maize (porridge)	Tr	0.06	0.5	0	4	ND	0.6
Bread (white)	0	0.21	1.7	0	110	91	1.6
Spaghetti (boiled)	0	0.01	0.5	0	7	44	0.5
Beans (boiled)	Tr	0.11	0.7	0	65	120	2.5

Sweetpotato also contains riboflavin, folic acid, pantothenic acid and vitamin B_6.
Data from: [a] Woolfe 1992; [b]Holland et al. 1991.

There is a great deal of interest at present in the antioxidant nutrients, β-carotene, ascorbic acid (vitamin C) and tocopherol (vitamin E). There is some evidence (as yet not substantiated) that these nutrients may help to prevent cancer [Williams and Dickerson 1990 (review)] and heart disease [Duthie 1990 (review)] by protecting the body's cells from the injurious effects of free radicals. These reactive molecules or molecular fragments, which are formed during metabolism in the body or taken in from exterior sources such as cigarette smoke, need hydrogen atoms to achieve stability. The hydrogen atoms can be removed from fatty acids, protein or DNA and so lead to damage to the structure and function of the cell. Antioxidants protect against injurious free radical reactions, for example, vitamin E can inhibit free radical-mediated lipid peroxidation in cell membranes (Duthie 1990). Nutrients such as ascorbic acid may manifest additional protective effects against cancer apart from their role as antioxidants (Williams and Dickerson 1990). If further investigations show that antioxidant nutrients can indeed protect significantly against the incidence of heart disease and cancer, there will be renewed interest in promoting foods such as sweetpotato that are rich in these nutrients (see Tables 5 and 6).

Table 5. Concentrations of β-Carotene, vitamin C and vitamin E in sweetpotato roots and other vegetables (per 100 g fresh).

Vegetable	β- carotene (mg)	Vitamin C (mg)	Vitamin E (mg)
Sweetpotato	1.8 - 16*	23	4.56
Carrots	4 - 11	6	0.56
Onions	0.01	5	0.31
Tomatoes	0.64	17	1.22
Peppers (green)	0.27	120	0.80
Pumpkin	0.45	14	1.06
Soybean sprouts	0.04	7	ND

Data from Holland et al. 1991; *Orange-fleshed lines; ND = Not determined.

Table 6. Composition of sweetpotato and certain fruits (per 100 g fresh basis).

Fruit/Root	β- carotene μg	Vitamin C mg	Vitamin E mg
Sweetpotato	1820 - 16000	23	4.56
Apricots	1000 - 2400	7	ND
Guavas (canned)	100	180	ND
Mangoes	1200	30	ND
Melons (canteloupe)	2000	25	0.1
Oranges	50	50	0.2
Papaya	500	15	ND
Peaches	250 - 1000	8	ND

*Orange-fleshed lines.
Data from: Holland et al. 1991.
ND = Not determined.

As a fresh item sweetpotato should be up to the challenge of providing sound nutrition combined with sensory delights. It is a food with a diversity of flesh color ranging from white through orange to deep purple, taste ranging from non-sweet to a dessert-type sweetness and a texture which varies from extremely dry to syrupy. If its popularity as a staple food is limited by its (generally) sweet taste, then new ways of presenting it should exploit that sweetness for healthy desserts and snack foods. It is suitable for a wide range of dishes including salads and soups. The development of low-sweet or non-sweet lines containing significant amounts of β-carotene would extend the range of possibilities even further.

PROMOTION

Researchers have found that, in general, the highest consumption levels of sweetpotato are found in the lowest income groups and that, as income rises, consumption of sweetpotato falls. However, in its nutritional value, we have a most valuable tool for promotion of sweetpotato among all income groups. During a small survey among 100 families in Japan (Woolfe 1992), one reason frequently mentioned for eating sweetpotato was its nutritional value, especially its fiber and vitamin content. The message should be strongly disseminated in other countries too. Community health and extension workers should be encouraged to adopt sweetpotato as an item for promotion in diet and and health education plans. Information should be given particularly to clinics, schools, hospitals, employees' cafeterias and other institutions. Nutrition information should include not only nutrient content per se but also value for money in terms of food value purchased. There could be training courses on sweetpotato aimed at health promotors or extension workers. School meal programs or cultivation of sweetpotato in school gardens or farms could promote good nutrition and enjoyment of sweetpotato among the young, and home economics classes could feature sweetpotato from time to time. Promotion of sweetpotato

Table 7. Contribution of 100 g of processed sweetpotato to the adult (male) recommended daily amounts of various nutrients (%).

RDA	Protein 37g	Vit A 600µg	Thiamin 1.2mg	Riboflavin 1.8mg	Niacin 19.8mg	Vit C 30mg	Iron 8-23mg
Flour	10	0 ->100	20	10	10	20	10-25
Flakes dry	10	0 ->100	5	10	10	150	10-30
prepared	<5	0 ->100	<5	<5	<5	40	<5-10
Steamed, sliced, dried	10	0 ->100	20	5	10	30	10-30
Candied	<5	0 ->100	<5	<5	<5	20	5-15
Dried "fruit-like" product	<5	>100	ND	ND	ND	25	ND

Notes: Nutrient levels in processed products from Woolfe (1992). Figures calculated to nearest 5% using recommended nutrient intakes from FAO/WHO/UNU (1985) for protein; FAO (1988) for vitamin A and iron (ranges reflect varying bioavailability of iron in the whole diet); Passmore et al. (1974) for thiamin, riboflavin, niacin and vitamin C.
< signifies less than; ND signifies not determined.

should start with the young to dispel any vestiges of the sweetpotato's image as a second class food.

PROCESSING

Processing of sweetpotato into forms which combine the advantages of diversity, nutritional value and convenience of use is a further means of promoting sweetpotato consumption among different strata of society. Processed products made from deep yellow- or orange-fleshed roots may stand a better chance of success than the fresh form in improving vitamin A status in regions where adults prefer white-fleshed roots or where there is a cultural resistance to the consumption of the green tops. Moreover, processing remains as a major key to preservation of a highly perishable, often highly seasonal commodity which is difficult and expensive to store in its fresh state. Although there is little detailed information at present on the nutrient content of processed forms of sweetpotato, data collected (Table 7) shows that processed sweetpotatoes can make significant contributions to RDAs for several nutrients.

Research has shown that care has to be exercised during processing to preserve nutrients such as β-carotene and ascorbic acid that are sensitive to heat and/or oxidation. Thermal processing can convert part of the biologically active all-*trans* form of β-carotene, which predominates in fresh roots, into less nutritionally active

Table 8. Isomerization of β-carotene in processed sweetpotatoes.

Product	Total β-carotene g/g dry wt.	All-trans %	Cis isomers %
Raw, fresh roots	440	95	5
Canned puree	390	83	17
Drum-dried	350	71	29
Microwaved	340	83	17

Based on: Chandler and Schwartz 1988.
Total losses of β-carotene approximately 25-30%.

cis isomers in processed products (Table 8), thus leading to a reduction in nutrient content. In tropical regions where leaves are acceptable in the diet, drying could be a solution to seasonal scarcities of vegetables that should provide essential nutrients. However, methods of drying which optimize nutrient retention should be researched (Table 9). Losses of β-carotene and ascorbic acid take place during storage of dehydrated products unless suitable packaging is used to prevent oxygen access. Any program aiming to introduce or expand processing so as to improve nutritional status in addition to other advantages should take nutrient losses into account.

In many tropical developing countries processing would not only be a source of income generation to farmers and traders, but could increase food security by cutting waste as well as expanding the seasonal supply. The increasing use of a local resource to partly replace imported cereal-based foods would represent a valuable saving of foreign exchange.

At present only a few countries have a significant part of their crop devoted to processing (Figure 2). The systems which prevail in parts of China are worthy of

Table 9. Carotene and ascorbic acid in fresh and dried sweetpotato leaves[a].

Treatment	Carotene mg/100 g (dwb)	Retention %	Ascorbic acid mg/100 g (dwb)	Retention %
Fresh leaves	49.6	100	1374	100
Dried leaves[b]:				
Enclosed solar drier (with shade)	16.9	34	22.5	2
Enclosed solar drier (without shade)	5.2	11	19.0	1
Open sunlight	2.1	4	30.7	2

[a]From Maeda and Salunkhe 1981.
[b]Blanched in boiling water 50 secs. before drying.

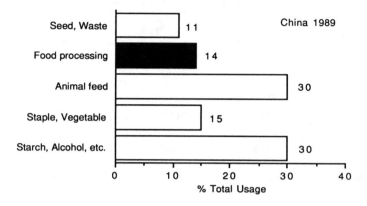

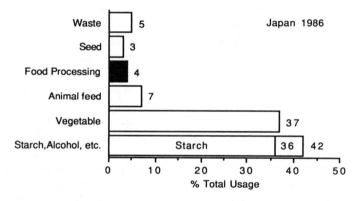

Figure 2. Distribution of sweetpotato use in China and Japan. Sources: (for China) Wiersema et al. 1989 (estimates); (for Japan) Duell 1989.

further study. A considerable number of small farmers convert roots into chips that are sun-dried in the field and then conveyed to large starch and alcohol plants or, where climate does not permit field drying, roots are processed directly at a home- or village level into starch, noodles and other food products (Table 10). Thus a stable source of energy which can be stored throughout the year is produced. In Peru, there are several small commercial bakeries making sweetpotato bread. One of these replaces about 50% of the wheat flour with raw grated sweetpotato, a very simple and practical technique which could be adopted elsewhere. Sweet breads are popular in parts of West Africa and the introduction of sweetpotato bread into such countries could be investigated. In southern Japan a small cooperative makes a high β-carotene sweetpotato paste which is being incorporated into bread that is served in schools as part of a meal service. The use of mashed sweetpotato in the form of croquettes for school lunches has also been suggested (I. Umemura 1989, Ibusuki Agriculture Experiment Station, personal communication.). Puréed or mashed roots are used as

Table 10. Sweetpotato processing units in Sichuan, China 1989.

Number of plants	Processing capacity Fresh roots per year per plant $(t \times 10^3)$	Final product	Total output per year $(t \times 10^3)$
17	0·3 - 15	Starch	93
> 200	0.1 - 0.3 (village scale)	Noodle & starch	67
> 2000	Less than 0.1 (family scale)	Mainly noodle	> 100

Source: Wiersema et al. 1989.

a stuffing in cakes and desserts in Japan, where they sometimes function as an inexpensive substitute for *marron glacé*. In the Philippines, researchers have focussed on converting orange-fleshed roots into fruity products. These include dried sweet and sour sweetpotato which can be eaten in the same way as dried fruits such as mangoes, apricots, peaches, etc. (and has a similar nutritional value), as well as catsup, jam and non-alcoholic beverages (Truong 1987; Truong and Fementira 1990). Orange-fleshed sweetpotato could also be a delicious and nutritious snack in the form of a "leather," crush or roll. In Taiwan, spaghetti-type noodles containing mashed orange sweetpotato to replace part of the wheat flour, or with sweetpotato greens added, in the same way that spinach is incorporated into pasta in Europe, have been produced experimentally. These attractive noodles could be eaten hot, as part of a main meal, or mixed with other vegetables and a dressing as a salad. Gelled blocks of sweetened sweetpotato, known as "dulces" are popular as desserts or snacks and are widely available in supermarkets in Argentina and Brazil. Orange- or purple-fleshed sweetpotato is added to ice cream for sale in shops and restaurants in some parts of Japan.

The range of products which have been or could be made from sweetpotato is very wide and has been exhaustingly reviewed elsewhere (Woolfe 1992). In quantitative terms these are dominated by the starch, alcohol- and starch-derived products originating mainly in China. A few others are produced commercially, by individuals or small businesses, in various countries. Most have never moved beyond the laboratory or pilot plant stage. The major reasons for this, at least when considering large-scale production, are unstable supplies of appropriate cultivars coupled with high production costs, making it impossible for sweetpotato to compete with other raw materials yielding similar end products. Efforts to increase processing possibilities should be synchronized with increases in production of suitable cultivars so that a void is not created at either end of the producer-processor chain which so often leads to a failure of promising market opportunities. Although technologies for processing at the home, village or factory level are already available, the transfer of these technologies from the technologist to the processor is often a further significant barrier to be overcome in translating potential into commercial reality.

There should be encouragement for the private sector to develop their own products by providing them with the necessary information about the processing characteristics of, and suitable technologies for, the sweetpotato. The very special food attributes of sweetpotato should prove an incentive to all researchers to overcome these problems so that sweetpotato can achieve its potential to make a valuable contribution to diets worldwide.

REFERENCES

Chandler, L.A., and S.J. Schwartz. 1988. Isomerization and losses of trans-β-carotene in sweet potatoes as affected by processing treatments. Journal of Agricultural and Food Chemistry 36 (1): 129-133.

Cohen, N., A. Jalil, H. Rahman, E. Leemhuis de Regt, J. Sprague, and M. Mitra. 1986. Blinding malnutrition in Bangladesh. Journal of Tropical Pediatrics 32:73-77.

Duell, B. 1989. Variations in sweet potato consumption in Japan. Journal of Tokyo International University 39:55-67.

Duthie, G.G. 1990. Antioxidant vitamins, free radicals and coronary heart disease. Nutrition and Health 92:32-36.

FAO (Food and Agriculture Organization of the United Nations) 1988. Requirements of vitamin A, iron, folate and vitamin B_{12}. Report of a joint FAO/WHO consultation, FAO Food and Nutrition Series 23, FAO Rome.

FAO/WHO/UNU. 1985. Energy and protein requirements. Report of a joint FAO/WHO/UNU Expert Consultation. WHO Tech. Rep. Ser. No. 724, WHO, Geneva.

Holland, B., I.D. Unwin, and D.H. Buss. 1991. Vegetables, herbs and spices. The fifth supplement to McCance and Widdowson's The Composition of Foods (4th edition), Royal Society of Chemistry, Cambridge.

Maeda, E.E., and D.K. Salunkhe. 1981. Retention of ascorbic acid and total carotene in solar dried vegetables. Journal of Food Science 46:1288-1290.

Passmore, R., B.M. Nicol, N.M. Rao, G.H. Beaton, and E.M. DeMaeyer. 1974. Handbook of human nutritional requirements. WHO Monograph Series 61, FAO/WHO Geneva.

Rugg-Gunn, A.J. 1986. Starchy foods and fresh fruits: their source of dental caries in Britain. Occasional Paper No. 3, London.

Truong, V.D. 1987. New developments in processing sweet potato for food. Paper presented at an International Sweet Potato Symposium, 20-26 May, Visayas State College of Agriculture, Baybay Leyte.

Truong, V.D., and G.B. Fementira. 1990. Formulation, consumer acceptability and nutrient content of non-alcoholic beverages from sweet potato. In: Tropical root and tuber crops changing role in a modern world, Proceedings of the Eighth Symposium of the International Society for Tropical Root Crops, 30 October-5 November, 1988, Bangkok.

Tsou, S.C.S., and R.L. Villareal. 1982. Resistance to eating sweet potato. Pages 37-44 in Sweet potato, edited by R.L. Villareal and T.D. Griggs, Proceedings of the First International Symposium, Asian Vegetable Research and Development Center, Shanhua, Tainan, Taiwan.

Villamayor, F.G. 1991. Camote tops pot gardens for the slum dwellers of Tacloban. Pages 135-148 in Sweet potato cultures of Asia and South Pacific, Proceedings of the Second Annual UPWARD International Conference, 2-5 April, Los Banos, Philippines.

Watson, G.A. 1988. Sweet potato in food systems. Home consumption: storage, processing and preferences. International Potato Center/Lembang Horticultural Research Institute. [Mimeo]

WHO (World Health Organization) 1990. Diet, nutrition and the prevention of chronic diseases. Report of a WHO study group. WHO Technical Report Series 797, WHO, Geneva.

Wiersema, S.G., J.C. Hesen, and B.F. Song. 1989. Report on a sweet potato postharvest advisory visit to the People's Republic of China, 12-27 January. International Potato Center, Lima. [Mimeo]

Williams, C.M., and J.W.T. Dickerson. 1990. Nutrition and cancer – some biochemical mechanisms. Nutrition Research Reviews 3:75-100.

Woolfe, J.A. 1989. Nutritional aspects of sweet potato roots and leaves. Pages 167-182 *in* Improvement of sweet potato (*Ipomoea batatas*) in Asia, International Potato Center (ed.). Report of the Workshop on Sweet Potato Improvement in Asia, ICAR, India, October 24-28, 1988.

Woolfe, J.A. 1992. Sweet potato – an untapped food resource. Cambridge University Press, Cambridge, England.

Sweetpotato Technology for the 21st Century. W.A. Hill, C.K. Bonsi and P.A. Loretan (Eds.) 1992. Tuskegee University, Tuskegee, AL

Barry R. Duell

Sweetpotato Product Innovations by Small Businesses in Kawagoe, Japan

One of the largest selections in Japan of products using sweetpotatoes has been developed by local small businesses in Kawagoe City. Helping encourage this phenomenon are the activities of the Kawagoe Friends of Sweetpotatoes, a grass-roots group that evolved from a 1982 community awareness project exploring the origins of Kawagoe's connections to sweetpotatoes. Annual sweetpotato activities now include a festival, symposium, publishing and, of course, cultivation and cooking. The mass media has spread a positive image of Kawagoe and sweetpotatoes and this free publicity has encouraged small businesses to create a variety of sweetpotato products including noodles, ice cream, sweets, and restaurant dishes. Evolution of these developments is explored in this paper.

SWEETPOTATO PRODUCTION/CONSUMPTION IN JAPAN

If the main islands of Japan were placed over the east coast of the United States, they would extend from Maine to southern Alabama. The main sweetpotato growing prefecture, Kagoshima, would overlap southern Alabama, and the other top growing prefectures, Ibaraki and Chiba, would overlap North Carolina. These three prefectures together account for two-thirds of sweetpotato production in Japan.

Sweetpotato developments in Kawagoe City, the subject of this paper, are taking place in Saitama Prefecture which is tenth in sweetpotato production or slightly more than one percent of total Japanese production (JMAFF 1990). Kawagoe has produced only about five percent of Saitama's production in recent years (KNK 1991).

Sweetpotato consumption has hovered near four kilograms per person per year since about 1970. Since then, national production has stayed fairly steady at about 1,400,000 metric tons. About one-third of production reaches the vegetable market, while about 30 percent is used for starch production. Sweetpotatoes are also converted into animal feed, alcohol, and processed foods (JMAFF 1990). The cultivars most favored for eating have red skin, dry meat, and light-yellow flesh.

SWEETPOTATOES and KAWAGOE

Kawagoe City has long had an image of sweetpotatoes associated with it (Duell 1984). However, until the early 1980s, there were few sweetpotato products sold in Kawagoe. Explored below is the development of the Kawagoe Friends of

Tokyo International University, Kawagoe City, Saitama Prefecture, Japan 350.

Sweetpotatoes (KFSP), a grassroots group formed in the early 1980s to promote the sweetpotato. [Much of the following section on the origins of the KFSP is adapted from Duell (1990).]

Just after World War II ended in 1945, the food shortage in Japan entered its most severe stages. The daily staple rice—in short supply—was replaced by sweetpotatoes, squash, and other foods (Duell 1986). These hard times may, to some degree, have spawned negative expressions about sweetpotatoes such as "sweetpotato girl," used to tease a girl for supposedly being a country hick, and other similar pejoratives.

The author's interest in sweetpotatoes began around 1981 while pursuing a master's degree in comparative culture at Sophia University in Tokyo. Ask a Japanese in Tokyo or one of the surrounding prefectures what comes to mind at the mention of Kawagoe, and they are likely to say "sweetpotatoes." This sparked an interest in exploring what brought about this image.

Writing a thesis on an anthropological look at sweetpotatoes (Duell 1983; Duell 1984) led to the meeting of many people interested in the crop and the eventual formation of the Kawagoe Sweetpotato Research Association to exchange sweet-potato information. The group prepared a special exhibit "Sweetpotato History in Kawagoe" in fall 1982 to celebrate the sixtieth anniversary of Kawagoe's incorporation as a city. This exhibit and a simultaneously-held community center course led to the networking of people interested in sweetpotato. The course included lectures on sweetpotato history, hands-on experience cultivating sweetpotatoes, and the learning of new ways to cook them (D/FCC 1982). Another course the following year led to the publication of an unexpectedly popular sweetpotato cookbook and Kawagoe's first Sweetpotato Festival (KCH 1983; KSPFOC 1983).

The Yambilee festival held every October in Opelousas, Louisiana, U.S.A. as well as one held annually on October 28 at Ryusenji Temple in Tokyo were the inspiration for starting a sweetpotato festival in Kawagoe. The first festival was held with themes of history and cooking. It received funding support from the beginning from the Kawagoe Farmer's Association, Fukuhara District Branch Office. Other features were added later. A sweetpotato haiku poetry contest was held for the '85 festival, followed by a sweetpotato song contest at the '86 festival (KFSP 1987).

By becoming a registered group of the Fukuhara Community Center, the KFSP was able to use center facilities free of charge but also could plan activities independently of the center's management. Center staff person Eiji Yamada became so engrossed in the sweetpotato courses he generated that he became the business manager (nonpaying position) of the fledgling KFSP. Yamada continued at the center, encouraging the KFSP on the side until 1989. In the spring of that year a sweetpotato museum was opened in Kawagoe through funds provided by a prosperous sweetpotato restaurant. Yamada had been involved since the planning stages in the museum project and switched jobs to become the museum's curator. Yamada continues as the able business manager of the KFSP.

The KFSP provides several community benefits. With Kawagoe being within commuting distance of Tokyo, it receives a constant influx of new residents looking for more affordable housing. Kawagoe's current population is about 300,000, roughly twice the figure of 1968 (KCH 1990). Helping newcomers think of Kawagoe not as a bed town for commuting to Tokyo, but as a town that has a culture to be proud of, is an important function of the KFSP. New residents who have joined the KFSP are able to make friends with local people while learning more about the community through sweetpotatoes. Through KFSP publications, sweetpotato products, cooking, history, etc. are introduced to the public. To a foreign resident like the author, KFSP activities offer a way to not only learn about the Japanese culture, but also to blend into it.

The members of KFSP have a varied background. Of the roughly 100 members, one-third are from outside Kawagoe. One-quarter of all members are from other prefectures, mostly sweetpotato producing areas. Members have no particular professional connection to sweetpotatoes. KFSP events are planned to tap the expertise of the heterogeneous membership in order to share with others.

The author, chairman of the KFSP, is the only non-Japanese KFSP member as of early 1991. Coming from a culture outside of Japan, it is the author's goal to continue trying to keep members' eyes open to the outside world. What began as an activity for exploring the sweetpotato's relation to Kawagoe has gradually expanded to include sweetpotato matters concerning Saitama Prefecture, Japan as a whole, and the world at large.

International Sweetpotato Exchange

Major opportunities for KFSP to engage in international sweetpotato exchange was made possible when the author presented a poster at the Seventh Symposium of the International Society for Tropical Root Crops held in 1985 in Guadeloupe (Duell 1985) and again in Bangkok in 1988 (Duell 1989).

KFSP members have had chances to meet several root crop researchers visiting Kawagoe from overseas. Dr. Jennifer Woolfe of England visited Japan in 1989 as part of a world search for materials to include in her book on sweetpotatoes (Woolfe 1992). KFSP members helped Dr. Woolfe gather material in Kawagoe and in so doing learned much about the status of root crops in the world (Hoku Hoku 1989). Dr. Truong Van Den visited Japan in 1989 to make a survey of postharvest utilization of sweetpotatoes. During his visit, KFSP members introduced him to sweetpotato processing in Kawagoe and learned much about his work in the Philippines (Kyuho 1989; Yomiuri Shinbun 1989).

Both Dr. Woolfe and Dr. Den have suggested that forming a grassroots group like the KFSP in other countries could lead to increased sweetpotato consumption in those areas (J.A. Woolfe 1989, Thames Ditton, England, personal communication; T.V. Den 1989, ViSCA, Baybay, Philippines, personal communication).

Overseas researchers visiting Kawagoe in 1990 were Dr. Lutgarda S. Palomar, Philippines, and Dr. Brad Swedlund, U.S.A. In addition to visitors from overseas, a number of Japanese researchers, business people, and others have visited Kawagoe small businesses processing sweetpotatoes and have exchanged information with KFSP members.

Since the start of activities promoting the sweetpotato in Kawagoe, there has been continuous coverage in the media of different aspects of this movement. Television, radio, newspapers, magazines, and other media, both local and national, have reported the activities from Kawagoe.

SWEETPOTATO PRODUCTS IN KAWAGOE

Until the early '80s, there were three sweetpotato products sold by a number of small Kawagoe businesses. "Imo senbei" or sweetpotato crisps are thin slices of roasted, sugar-coated sweetpotatoes. "Imo natto" are candied sweetpotato slices, and "imo karinto" are sweetpotatoes fried in deep-fat until crisp then sugar-coated (Tanaka 1982).

Though Kawagoe is a minor sweetpotato growing area and production continues to decline, the number of sweetpotato products sold in Kawagoe has been mushrooming since the 1980s. To show the commercial response to Kawagoe's growing sweetpotato image, businesses which have either developed their own sweetpotato products or brought in outside ones to sell or which market local sweetpotatoes are introduced below.

The Imozen Restaurant opened in 1982. Its name means "a dinner of sweetpotatoes." The founder, owner, and head chef Masahisa Kamiyama recounts that, when he held part-time work in Kawagoe restaurants as a college student, it made a lasting impression on him to hear customers complain that there was no restaurant serving sweetpotato meals even though Kawagoe was closely associated with sweetpotatoes.

Though there were few sweetpotato dishes on the menu at first, the most popular request now among the 100 or so customers that daily frequent the restaurant is for the full course sweetpotato dinner. All courses, including hors d'oeuvres, soup, salad, noodles, and ice cream, contain at least some sweetpotato. Due to the various ingredients used in combination with sweetpotato, and the variety of cooking methods used, one does not feel overwhelmed by sweetpotato.

Thirty to forty kilograms of sweetpotatoes are used daily. The cultivars chosen are red-skinned with light-yellow flesh that do not become off-color when cooked. Some dishes utilize the aesthetic value of the red skin by using unpeeled sweetpotatoes (M. Kamiyama 1991, Imozen, Kawagoe, personal communication). A portion of the above quantity includes sweetpotato flour for making sweetpotato noodles.

Imozen was one of the first businesses in Japan to make sweetpotato ice cream commercially available (Nihon Nogyo Shinbun 1984b). However, sweetpotato ice cream is also the main product of the Ichinokura Sweetpotato Coffee Shop. Located next to Imozen Restaurant, Fusako Hanamura, sister of Kamiyama, began this shop specializing in sweetpotato desserts in spring 1987. Though some is served in-house, most ice cream is packaged for carry-out customers or wholesaled to other shops in Kawagoe selling sweetpotato products. About thirty kilograms per day of sweetpotatoes are used for making three colors of ice cream using the cultivars 'Kokei 14,' 'Benihayato,' and 'Yamakawa Murasaki,' whose flesh colors are, respectively, yellow, orange, and purple.

Other products made in the shop include such sweetpotato desserts as cakes or puddings. About five kilograms per day of sweetpotatoes are used to make these items. One of Hanamura's dreams for the future is to attach a classroom to her shop where she can teach sweetpotato dessert-making to interested persons (F. Hanamura 1991, Ichinokura Coffee Shop, Kawagoe, Japan, personal communication).

Atsuo Watanabe is the second-generation manager of the family-run Ryuseido Crisps Shop making "imo senbei." These sweetpotato crisps are made by roasting thinly sliced sweetpotato between metal plates and then sugar coating them. This traditional product is eaten as a snack with Japanese green tea. Noting a trend for snack foods to become softer and less sweet than in times past, Watanabe is experimenting with unsugared crisps, a product that is 100 percent sweetpotato.

Other sweetpotato products with a relatively long shelf life, such as candy-coated sweetpotato sticks or candied sweetpotatoes, are also sold. The sticks are purchased from outside Kawagoe and are candy-coated by Watanabe's shop.

Ishi Hiramoto began her Roasted Sweetpotato Shop in 1947 and has the only such shop left in Kawagoe from those days. There used to be many shops in Kawagoe that roasted sweetpotatoes by linking them together with metal hooks and hanging the chains of sweetpotatoes into a large urn heated with coke. Hiramoto sells her product during the colder months, October to April. A customer receives a hot sweetpotato in a little bag Hiramoto has prepared in advanced from old newsprint. The product she offers has changed little since she started her shop, except for the cultivars used, and she expects to continue her single product line as is (I. Hiramoto 1991, Roasted Sweetpotato Shop, Kawagoe, Saitama, Japan, personal communication).

Toshiaki Tanaka's family runs a traditional sugar wholesale operation in Kawagoe that includes among its customers makers of sweetpotato products. Tanaka's fondness for buckwheat noodles prompted him to create a dried, sweetpotato buckwheat noodle which he began selling in 1986 at his shop Tanakaya. One of the noodle's ingredients is sweetpotato flour. Subsequent noodle types use mashed sweetpotatoes as an ingredient. Most Tanaka noodles are sold locally, but not all.

Shuichi Toda is the third generation owner of his family's noodle-making business. Toda's first sweetpotato noodles appeared in 1987. He wanted to make a noodle reflecting Kawagoe's sweetpotato image. Toda makes four different sweetpotato noodles varying in ingredients, noodle diameter, and/or noodle shape.

Most of the Toda business consists of making and delivering fresh noodles to high school and college cafeterias in Kawagoe and surrounding cities. No fresh sweetpotato noodles are made since they spoil more easily than regular noodles; mold easily forms if the noodles contain more than 15 percent moisture.

Dried noodle production accounts for about 20 percent of Toda's total noodle output, with sweetpotato noodles accounting for about 40 percent of the dried noodles sold. Monthly, 80 to 100 kg of sweetpotato flour are used in noodle making. Most of the sweetpotato noodles made are sold through area department stores. The remainder are sold in Toda's small retail shop or other businesses in Kawagoe.

A western-style restaurant with a long history in Kawagoe, Yoshitora has served sweetpotato pudding or soup from from the early 1980s. Chef/Owner Hideo Yoshizaki's restaurant has an established image in the minds of his regular customers so he has been cautious about meddling with his menu.

Yoshizaki devised a sweetpotato sherbet in 1984 that was inspired by a sweetpotato sherbet the author had created and introduced to Kawagoe restaurateurs to try to encourage them to develop frozen sweetpotato products (Nihon Nogyo Shinbun 1984b). Of Yoshizaki's sweetpotato creations, it is sweetpotato desserts such as sherbet or pudding that have proven most popular with his customers. This seems to have prompted Yoshizaki's current experimentation with sweetpotato pie.

Tomio Muro'oka began adding a variety of sweetpotato sweets to his shop in the latter half of the 1980s based upon sweetpotato paste. Muro'oka says he picks the cultivars used, and their production areas, according to the season in order to have the best color and taste for his products. He plans to continue most, if not all, of the sweetpotato products he now offers (T. Muro'oka 1991, Muro'oka Confectionery, Kawagoe, Japan, personal communication).

Hirohisa Ichikawa's shop sells mostly traditional Japanese sweets made largely from pounded glutinous rice and/or sweet bean paste. However, he began selling a sweet named "komochiimo" (sweetpotato with child) about 20 years ago. Though smaller than a sweetpotato, the sweet is shaped and colored like a well-roasted sweetpotato. Inside the thin dough covering is sweetened white bean paste. Inside the bean paste is a chunk of candied sweetpotato with its red skin still attached.

"Komochiimo" initially was wrapped in cellophane. This product is now wrapped in a heavy, clear, airtight plastic bag containing an oxygen absorbing packet in order to extend the product's shelf life.

Mitsuharu Kawano quit his company job in 1987 to work in his father's "dango"-making business (small rice dumplings sold on a skewer). Sweetpotato products currently sold are a baked bun filled with sweetpotato paste which debuted in 1988 and a deep-fat fried sweetpotato doughnut also filled with a paste that was introduced in 1989. The bun was developed in cooperation with an ingredients wholesaler that supplies the business. Kawano relates that such suppliers are in closer touch with current consumer trends than small retailers and offer advice to retailers on how to improve their product lines to increase business for both the wholesaler and retailer. Kawano designed the doughnut product himself.

Kawano plans to market two varieties of gelled sweetpotato paste which will be in cube form. In selling these various products, Kawano and other entrepreneurs are merely taking advantage of Kawagoe's association with sweetpotato (M. Kawano 1991, Maruwa Dango Shop, Kawagoe, Japan, personal communication).

Kawagoe Farmers' Association, Fukuhara Branch

Even though the Fukuhara District of Kawagoe is the main sweetpotato growing area of the city, other crops have more economic importance. In Kawagoe as a whole, sweetpotatoes rank eleventh in harvest tonnage (KCH 1990).

Kazuo Ochiai, a Kawagoe Farmers' Association official, indicates that KFSP sweetpotato activities have had a positive influence on increasing sales of boxed sweetpotatoes sold directly to customers. This influence has not only helped slow the decline in sweetpotato production, but has also caused the available stock to be sold out earlier each year. About 25 growers now take orders by mail or telephone and currently ship about 15,000 10 kg boxes per year. The average price is about 3300 yen per box (about $25.50 at an exchange rate of 130 yen/dollar). None of Kawagoe's sweetpotato crop goes to the fresh vegetable market. Most of it is sold directly to customers in boxed form or by customers digging them up themselves for recreation (K. Ochiai 1991, Kawagoe Farmers' Association, Kawagoe, Saitama, Japan, personal communication).

Sweetpotato Museum

A small museum devoted to sweetpotatoes opened in spring 1989. Eiji Yamada was the museum's first curator. The museum's exhibits help the KFSP to educate the public about various aspects of sweetpotatoes. Sweetpotato cultivars are displayed and their characteristics explained. The steps involved in growing sweetpotatoes are described. Products are on view to illustrate a broad range of usage. Other exhibits relate to history, cooking, or publications about sweetpotatoes.

Yamada has also created a shop attached to the museum which sells sweetpotato products gathered from various producers throughout Japan. Yamada also informally consults with small area businesses interested in developing new products. He hopes this will encourage merchants to continually update their marketing strategies. An example is his consultation with Imozen Restaurant to create a premixed, bottled sweetpotato cocktail and packaged sweetpotato-based rice seasoning. Besides helping create new products, Yamada also has introduced merchants to potential wholesalers of products that can be repackaged with a local label.

CONCLUSIONS

At the time a formal community movement began in Kawagoe in 1982 to learn more about the sweetpotato and improve its poor image, the number of sweetpotato products sold in Kawagoe was limited. As media coverage began of Kawagoe's sweetpotato movement, which evolved into the KFSP in 1984, small Kawagoe businesses handling sweetpotato products received publicity. This encouraged these businesses to develop new sweetpotato products or repackage existing products for sale in Kawagoe.

Establishment of a sweetpotato museum in Kawagoe has given the KFSP a base for providing information on various cultivars, consultation to Kawagoe businesses and finding new sources of or outlets for sweetpotato products. The museum also serves as an information center for visitors. What influence the recent increase in KFSP contact with overseas root crop researchers is having on Kawagoe businesses is not yet known, but this outside influence may give businesses new ideas for product development. Events in Kawagoe may also encourage formation of grassroots groups overseas for promotion of the sweetpotato.

REFERENCE LIST

D/FCC (Daito and Fukuhara community centers). 1982. [The abc's of sweet potatoes.] In Japanese. D/FCC, Kawagoe, Saitama, Japan. 81 pp.

Duell B. 1983. Anthropological problems connected with the introduction and diffusion of the sweet potato into Japan (I). Journal of the International College of Commerce & Economics, the Department of Commerce. 28:47-62.

Duell B. 1984. Anthropological problems connected with the introduction and diffusion of the sweet potato into Japan (II). Journal of the International College of Commerce & Economics, the Department of Commerce. 29:51-73.

Duell, B. 1985. Changing patterns in the consumption of sweet potatoes and potatoes in Japan following World War II. Page 97 *in* Abstracts, VIIth Symposium of the International Society for Tropical Root Crops, 1-6 Jul 1985, Pointe-à-Pitre, Guadeloupe. Institut National de la Recherche Agronomique, Guadeloupe.

Duell, B. 1986. The rice-substitute cooking contest of 1940. Pages 123-124 *in* Transactions, International Conference of Orientalists in Japan, no. XXXI. ICO, Tokyo, Japan.

Duell, B. 1989. [Barry Duell's report from Bangkok.] In Japanese. Pages 1-2 in the [Introduction to sweet potato series, no. 1]. Kawagoe Friends of Sweet Potatoes, Kawagoe, Saitama, Japan.

Duell, B. 1990. [Comparative culture of a local area sister city exchange and sweet potatoes in Kawagoe.] In Japanese. Jichi Kenkyu Saitama 10:12-23.

Hoku Hoku (Sweet Potato News). 15 Feb 1989. [Sweet potato researcher Dr. Jennifer Woolfe to visit Kawagoe from England.] In Japanese. Kawagoe Friends of Sweet Potatoes, Kawagoe, Saitama, Japan. 15:1.

JMAFF (Japan Ministry of Agriculture, Forestry, and Fisheries). 1990. [Data relating to the production and distribution of potatoes and sweet potatoes.] In Japanese. Hatasaku Shinkoka, JMAFF, Tokyo, Japan. 197 pp.

KFSP (Kawagoe Friends of Sweet Potatoes). 1987. [Kawagoe sweet potato song book.] In Japanese. KFSP, Kawagoe, Saitama, Japan. 18 pp.

KNK (Kanto Nosei Kyoku). 1991. [Annual agricultural statistics for the Iruma and Hiki districts.] In Japanese. Iruma/Hiki chiku norin tokei kyogikai, Sakado, Saitama, Japan. 94 pp.

KSPFOC (Kawagoe Sweet Potato Festival Organizing Committee). 1983. [Showa era sweet potato cookbook.] In Japanese. KSPFOC, Fukuhara Community Center, Kawagoe, Saitama, Japan. 74 pp.

Kyuho (Special Dispatch). 4 Nov 1989. [Sweet potato researcher Dr. Truong Van Den to visit Kawagoe from the Philippines.] In Japanese. Kawagoe Friends of Sweet Potatoes, Kawagoe, Saitama, Japan. 1 page.

Nihon Nogyo Shinbun (Japan Agricultural Newspaper). 7 Dec 1984b. [Increasing the repertoire of sweet potato cooking.] In Japanese. [What's to eat?: part 4 sweet potatoes, no. 29], 7981:5.

Tanaka, T. 1982. [Traditional sweet potato confections in Kawagoe.] In Japanese. Pages 24-25 in Kawagoe imo no rekishi. Kawagoe kurazukuri shiryokan, Kawagoe, Saitama, Japan. English summary.

Woolfe, J.A. 1992. Sweet potato—An untapped food resource. Cambridge University Press, Cambridge, England. 621 pp.

Yomiuri Shinbun (Yomiuri Newspaper). 14 Nov 1989. [Philippine agricultural researcher visits Kawagoe sweet potato museum/businesses.] In Japanese. 40749:26.

Truong Van Den

Sweetpotato Beverages: Product Development and Technology Transfer

Two types of beverage were developed from orange-yellow fleshed sweetpotato. The first was a fruity-sweetpotato beverage with a taste and appearance similar to fruit juice drinks. This product had a vitamin A and mineral content comparable or even superior to commercial fruit juices. It was rated with high sensory scores in consumer acceptability tests. Incorporation of fruit juices enhanced the aroma and acceptability scores of the sweetpotato beverage. The second was a vitamin A, energy-rich beverage powder consisting of sweetpotato and cocoa. The sweetpotato storage roots were processed into pre-cooked powder which was sieved and mixed with cocoa powder. The sweetpotato-cocoa (85:15) hot drink was rated with high scores for all sensory attributes. The technology of these sweetpotato beverages has been transferred to the private sector for pilot scale production. Experience and constraints in transfer of the developed technology are discussed.

Sweetpotato (*Ipomoea batatas*) is an important food crop in many countries. Over 114 million tons are produced on approximately 8 million hectares (FAO 1986). Sweetpotato has been the choice of many farmers in their cropping systems due to its high yielding ability, low input requirements, wide ecological adaptability and shorter growing period than other root crops.

Despite its importance, production and per capita consumption of sweetpotato have decreased in recent years (Alkuino 1983; Tsou and Villareal 1982). Such a decline is attributable mainly to, among other things, the inadequacy of processing technology. Development of the technology to convert raw sweetpotato storage roots into appealing processed products is thus recognized as one of the strategies to increase the utilization and market demand of the commodity.

To implement the strategy, a project was conceived to develop the technology to process sweetpotato storage roots into non-traditional food products which could compete with fruit-based products, thus increasing the economic value of the crop. Success in large scale production of such products would benefit: farmers with more markets for their crop, food processors with a relatively cheap and non-seasonal alternative to fruits and consumers with low-priced, nutritious products.

This paper presents the development of two types of sweetpotato beverages at the Visayas State College of Agriculture (ViSCA) and the transfer of the developed technology to end users in the Philippines.

Associate Professor, Department of Agricultural Chemistry and Food Science, Visayas State College of Agriculture (ViSCA), Baybay, 6521-A, Leyte, Philippines.

BACKGROUND/PRODUCT IDEA GENERATION

In the Philippines, sweetpotato is traditionally consumed after boiling, frying or cooking roots with other ingredients for snacks or vegetable dishes. Processed sweetpotato products such as fried chips and chunks, candies, flour and native delicacies are produced at the household level (Alkuino 1983; Alkuino et al. 1986; Truong and del Rosario 1986). Sweetpotato has also been processed into various products for commercial use (Table 1) in the Philippines and other countries.

Table 1. Summary of the uses and processing steps of commercial sweetpotato products.

Product	Use	Processing Operations	Home Scale	Intermediate	Large Scale
			Suitable (x) for		
Fried chips/strips	snack food	peeling, trimming, slicing, blanching (optional), deep frying, packaging	x	x	x
Dried chips/strips	food preparations	washing, peeling (optional), trimming, slicing, drying, packaging	x	x	x
Dried cubes	food preparations	washing, peeling, trimming, cubing, blanching, drying, packaging	x	x	x
Dehydrated flakes	breakfast food food preparations	peeling, trimming, blanching pureeing, flaking with drum dryers, grinding, packaging	x	x	x
Flour	baked products food preparations	grinding of good quality chips/strips, sieving, packaging	x	x	x
Starch	food (noodles, baked products, food preparations, etc.) industrial products (glucose, syrup, alcohol, textiles, medicines, chemicals, etc.)	washing, grinding in limed water (pH 8.6), sieving, setting, centrifugal dehydrating (large scale),drying	x	x	x
Canned/bottled products	food preparations, baby	peeling, sorting, trimming, blanching, grinding and formulating (for bottled products), filling, sealing, sterilizing			x
Frozen products (chunks/cubes/slices)	food preparations	peeling, trimming, size reduction, blanching, freezing			x
Fermented products	alcoholic drinks fuel alcohol	hydrolysis of starch by acid or enzymes, yeast fermentation, distillation	x	x x	x x
Specialty products (candies, sembei, "crackers," paste, pies, roasted SP, etc.)	snack food food preparation ice cream		x	x	x

Sources: Bouwkamp 1985; Duell 1988; Edmond and Ammerman 1971; Troung and del Rosario 1986; Winarno 1982.

These products were documented through a literature review and informal surveys as part of steps undertaken in 1985-86 during the initial phase of the project.

The inventory pointed to the need for strengthening the sweetpotato processing industry in the Philippines through (1) improvement of existing products and processes, (2) adoption of the technologies from other countries, and (3) development of new products with good marketability and growth potential. While the first and second approaches had been adapted in other research, we chose the third approach for this project.

Examination of chemical constituents of sweetpotato

Sweetpotato has been recognized for its high nutritive values. However, for a starchy commodity such as sweetpotato, development of new food products that would be different from traditional starch-based food items required a thorough examination of the chemical constituents of sweetpotato.

A tabulation of reported data from various published works indicated that the contents of vitamins and minerals in sweetpotato storage roots are comparable with various fruits (Table 2). One hundred grams of fresh roots can supply 25 to 50% of

Table 2. Nutrient composition of sweetpotato as compared with various fruits (per 100 grams edible).

CROP	Moisture %	Total Carbo-hydrate (g)	Fiber g	Ash mg	Ca mg	P mg	Fe mg	Vit. A I.U.	Ascorbic acid mg
Sweetpotato									
Yellow (boiled)	68.1	29.4	0.6	0.9	66	58	0.8	1,025	31
Orange (baked)*	-	-	-	-	45	-	1.0	9,184	2
Apricot**	85.3	12.8	-	-	17	23	0.3	2,700	10
Banana	73.2	24.4	0.6	0.8	23	36	0.9	340	32
Grapes	79.2	19.7	1.7	0.4	6	24	0.4	-	3
Lemon-Philippines (Kalamansi)	89.8	8.3	Tr	0.5	18	12	0.8	00	45
Mango	83.9	15.0	0.4	0.4	8	17	0.5	2,580	45
Orange	86.0	12.2	-	-	41	20	0.4	200	50
Papaya	86.4	12.2	0.6	0.6	23	10	0.7	425	89
Pineapple	86.0	13.0	0.4	0.4	19	9	0.2	15	21
Strawberry	91.3	7.2	1.6	0.5	34	21	1.2	15	107
Tomato	94.1	4.1	0.8	0.6	18	18	0.8	735	29

Sources: Food and Nutrition Research Institute (FNRI) 1980; *Anonymous 1980; **Salunkhe et al. 1974.

the Recommended Daily Allowance (RDA) of vitamin C (Anonymous 1980). The orange-fleshed sweetpotato also contains β-carotene (provitamin A) as high as in carrot and superior to other vegetables and fruits (Bureau and Bushway 1986).

The analogy between sweetpotato and fruits in terms of β-carotene, ascorbic acid and mineral content provided a basis for a hypothesis that sweetpotato can be processed into products which are traditionally made from fruits. Nevertheless, the high starch content of sweetpotato presented a problem in processing. Selection of varieties with low starch content and/or application of certain processing treatments could possibly overcome the above-mentioned problem.

Observations on commercial fruit products in the markets

Various local processed fruit products are available in the market. They are dried mango, dried papaya, dried pineapple, and other dried fruits, jam, and jelly, canned fruits, fruit juices and fruit drinks in cans, bottles, aluminum foil or tetrapacks. These products have good marketability and have been marketed for many years. However, due to the high cost and seasonality of fresh fruits, the products are expensive and mainly targeted for high income local consumers and export markets.

Sweetpotato is an inexpensive commodity which is non-seasonal and not as prone to damage caused by adverse weather. If sweetpotato can be processed into products similar in taste and appearance to fruit products, the production costs would be low enough to make it competitive with the latter. Thus a decision was made to proceed with the development of fruity-food products from sweetpotato.

Development of fruity-food products

Initially, the following products were developed: (1) dried sweetpotato with sweet and sour taste, (2) sweetpotato jam and (3) sweetpotato catsup. Results of the consumer acceptability tests on these products were very encouraging with over 80% respondents rating the products "like moderately" to "like very much" (Truong 1989). Some local food processors expressed their interest in adopting the developed technology. Thus the findings proved the stated hypothesis. The research then moved on to development of beverages from sweetpotato. Results on product development, evaluation and consumer acceptability of sweetpotato beverages and transfer of the technology to food processing companies are presented.

PRODUCT DEVELOPMENT: SWEETPOTATO (SP) BEVERAGES

Fruity Sweetpotato Beverage

Product formulation. A procedure for processing sweetpotato storage roots into a non-alcoholic and fruity beverage was developed. The processing steps involved washing, peeling, trimming to remove damaged parts, steaming, extracting and formulating with 12% w/v sugar, 0.20% w/v citric acid and 232 mg L^{-1} ascorbic acid as vitamin C fortification (Truong and Fementira 1988). The formulated beverage was bottled in 150 mL glass containers and pasteurized at 90 to 95°C.

Various sweetpotato (SP) varieties with root flesh colors varying from white, yellow, orange to purple were evaluated for suitability in processing into beverage. In general, the orange fruity-SP beverage was preferred to other colors. The beverage processed from VSP-1, a moist, orange fleshed variety which was developed at ViSCA, received the highest sensory scores on color and general acceptability.

Addition of juice or pulp of different fruits, e.g., guava, pineapple, Philippine lemon, to the SP beverage at concentrations of 0.6 to 2.4% w/v significantly improved the aroma scores of the product. Likewise, incorporation of artificial orange flavor also enhanced the aroma of the fruity-SP beverage (Truong 1989).

Comparison of the fruity-SP beverage with commercial fruit juices/drinks. The SP beverage has a pH of 3.2, total soluble solids of 13°Brix and insoluble solids of 9.4 mg/100 mL. These figures were found to be within the range of the values obtained from commercial fruit drinks. The appearance and color of the fruity-SP beverage were similar to that of the selected yellow-orange fruit juices and drinks available commercially. No significant difference in all sensory attributes was noted between the fruity-SP beverage and commercial products including orange juice and fruit drinks in tetrapacks/aluminum foil (Table 3). The SP beverage was given signifi-

Table 3. Color, vitamin A content and mean sensory scores of sweetpotato beverages and commercial fruit drinks/juices (Truong and Fementira 1988).

Sample	Color	Vit. A (I.U./100g)	Sensory Scores[1] Color	Aroma	General Acceptability
Group A - Commercial fruit drinks in tetrapacks/aluminum foil					
SP beverage (Formula I)	orange	1844.5	7.5[ns/]	7.5[ns/]	7.7[ns/]
Hi-C orange juice (*,**)	orange	39.5	7.1	7.0	7.0
Orange flavored (*,**)	yellow-orange	-	6.9	7.1	6.9
Mango juice (*)	golden yellow	621.1	8.0	8.1	8.2
Group B - Commercial fruit drinks in cans					
SP beverage (Formula I)	orange	1844.5	7.7 a	7.5 a	7.7 a
Orange juice w/sacks (**)	bright yellow	854.6	6.8 c	7.1 ab	7.2 ab
Papaya nectar	golden yellow	1077.8	7.4 ab	5.6 c	5.6 d
Pineapple-orange (*,**)	orange	1052.8	7.1 bc	6.5 b	6.4 c
Group C - Guava (G) flavored fruit drinks in cans					
SP-G beverage (Formula II)	orange	-	6.8[ns/]	7.6[ns/]	7.7[ns/]
Passion-G nectar (*,**)	pinkish orange	-	6.0	6.0	6.1
Pineapple-G drink (*)	light pink	-	6.3	6.2	6.0

(*) artificial color and (**) natural and/or synthetic color labelled.
[1]Hedonic scale with 9 = like extremely, 1 = dislike extremely.
Means in the same column within a group with common letter(s) are not significantly different at $p \leq 0.05$; ns = not significantly different at $p \leq 0.05$.

cantly higher scores for aroma and general acceptability than papaya nectar and pineapple orange drink. The SP beverage added with guava was rated with higher scores than guava flavored fruit nectar in cans.

It is interesting to note that artificial colors and flavorings were added to most commercial fruit juices as indicated on the labels of the products. The natural orange color, an indicator of high vitamin A content of the fruity SP beverage is an advantage over commercial fruit drinks in promotion of the product.

Consumer acceptability. Consumer acceptability of the fruity-SP beverage samples without flavorings (Formula I) and with added 0.6% w/v ripe guava (Formula II) was evaluated. For each formula, four groups of consumers belonging to different age brackets, i.e., 6 to 12 (pupils), 12 to 16 (high school students), 16 to 20 (college students) and 25 to 55 (adults) years old were requested to evaluate the products. Each group was composed of 145 to 150 randomly selected respondents in ViSCA and Tacloban City.

The "smiley" scale of 7 points (Mabesa 1986) was used for the first group while the others used the Hedonic scale (with 7 "like very much" and 1 "dislike very much") to evaluate the products. Each consumer was asked a series of questions regarding the preferred formula. These were included on the evaluation sheets.

A summary of consumer responses for both formulas is presented in Table 4. The results revealed that the authentic aroma of sweetpotato (VSP-1) in Formula I was not unpleasant. In fact, it was acceptable to the consumers as some respondents commented that the sweetpotato aroma was distinct but they rated the product with "like." The similarity in appearance and taste of the fruity-SP beverage to that of commercial fruit juices probably contributed to the positive response of consumers to the product. For the SP beverage with guava added as flavoring (Formula II), the percentage of respondents giving the "like" rating of the product increased in the four groups of consumers (Table 4) as compared to that of Formula I. The finding is in accordance to the judgment of the laboratory taste panel on the effect of guava on the aroma of the fruity-SP beverage.

Being aware of the fact that the beverage was processed from sweetpotato storage roots, some respondents expressed their apprehension about the flatulence problem after eating sweetpotato. It was hypothesized that flatulence occurring after a large intake of cooked sweetpotato is due to the undigested starch which escapes the small intestine (Truong et al. 1986). However, the starch content of the fruity beverage processed from VSP-1 variety was reported in the range of 0.8 to 1.0 gm/100 gm (Truong 1989), which is lower than the value of 1.0 to 3.7% in passion fruit juice (Pruthi 1963, as cited in Casimir et al. 1981). The absence of flatulence after consumption of the fruity-SP beverage was confirmed by ten volunteers who consumed an 8 oz. bottle of the beverage daily for a week (Truong 1989).

In comparing consumer acceptability of the fruity-SP beverage versus commercial fruit drinks, about 54% and 73% of the respondents from the four groups rated, respectively, that the developed products of Formula I and II are better than the commercial juices they commonly drink. The findings indicate a good opportunity for the fruity-SP beverage to compete for markets with commercial fruit juices.

Table 4. Summary of consumer responses (%) given to SP beverage without flavoring (Formula I) and with added ripe guava (Formula II).

Scale/Rating	Formula I				Formula II			
	Pupils	High School students	College students	Adults	Pupils	High School students	College students	Adults
A. Scale Rating								
7 - like very much	39.6	8.0	9.6	28.0	40.0	31.8	35.6	61.3
6 - like moderately	30.2	45.0	46.9	46.7	43.3	32.4	42.3	24.7
5 - like slightly	18.1	27.5	24.1	17.3	11.3	23.0	19.5	12.7
4 - neither like nor dislike	5.4	9.4	12.4	5.3	2.7	3.4	2.0	0
3 - dislike slightly	2.0	7.4	6.9	0	2.7	6.8	0	0.7
2 - dislike moderately	2.0	1.3	0	2.0	0	2	0.7	0.7
1 - dislike very much	2.7	1.3	0	0.7	0	0.7	0	0
Total number or respondents	149	149	145	150	150	148	149	150
B. Qualitative Rating								
a. Sample is much better than commercial fruit juices	36.2	12.8	9.0	26.7	44.7	18.2	30.9	56
b. Sample is slightly better than commercial fruit juices	33.2	32.2	38.0	38.7	22.7	41.2	46.3	30.7
c. No difference at all	8.0	12.0	6.0	6.0	17.3	10.8	6.0	6.0
d. Commercial fruit juices are slightly better than sample	14.8	30.8	39.6	24.7	11.3	18.2	15.4	6.7
e. Commercial fruit juices are much better than sample	8.7	12.0	7.6	4.0	4.0	11.5	1.3	0.7

Source: Truong and Fementira (1988).

Beverage-Type Sweetpotato Powder

Another type of beverage which is in the form of pre-cooked powder was also developed. The processing of the pre-cooked powder involved washing the storage roots (VSP-1 variety), peeling, trimming to remove damaged parts, cooking, grating, drying, grinding, and sieving. The SP powder was mixed with defatted cocoa powder for flavoring. For preparation of the drinks, the mixed powder (10 grams) and sugar (15 grams) were added to 150 mL hot water, and mixed thoroughly. The drinks were served to taste panelists for sensory evaluation. The SP-cocoa mix consisting of 85% SP powder and 15% cocoa powder were rated with "like moderately" to "like very much" category (7.0 to 8.0 score) for color and flavor. It was noted that the particle size of the SP precooked powder greatly affects the acceptability scores of the drink. The drink prepared from the SP precooked powder which was sieved through 100 and 200 mesh screens received high scores (7.0 to 8.0) for mouth feel and general acceptability. For use in the beverage formulation, the SP precooked powder should therefore be passed through at least a 100 screen mesh.

Nutrient content

The fruity-SP beverage processed from variety VSP-1 had a significantly higher content of vitamin A than commercial fruit drinks in cans and tetrapacks/aluminum foil (Table 3). Likewise, the product provided vitamin A at 41% and 48.5% of the RDA for adult men and women based on the respective RDA of 4,500 I.U. and 3,800 I.U. (Nutrition Research Committee, NRC 1976). An intake of 8 ounces (or 237 mL) of the VSP-1 beverage could provide the daily requirement of vitamin A for adults.

The fruity-SP beverage was also fortified with vitamin C—232 mg/L (55 mg/ 8 ounce serving). Fortification of commercial drinks with vitamin C is a common practice in fruit juice processing. Consumption of 8 ounces of the fruity-SP beverage could thus provide about 30 mg or 40% RDA for vitamin C (NRC 1976) assuming that 25 mg would be oxidized in the container (Phillips and Woodroof 1981).

Phosphorus and calcium content of the beverage particularly from VSP-1 were significantly higher than that of the Hi-C orange juice, mango juice drink and pineapple juice drink while the magnesium and potassium concentrations were within the range of values obtained with fruit drinks (Truong and Fementira 1988). The proximate analysis of the SP-cocoa powder (85:15) was the following: 93.12% dry matter, 3.10% fat, 7.57% protein, 41.93% starch, 31.84% total sugar and 2.95% ash. The vitamin A content of the beverage-type powder was 44,508 I.U. per 100 grams. The analysis indicated that the beverage prepared from the SP-cocoa powder mix is rich in energy and vitamin A and would be excellent as a breakfast drink.

TECHNOLOGY TRANSFER

In recognition of the originality of the developed process for the fruity-SP beverage, we filed a patent application at the Philippine Patent Office, Department of Trade and Industry. The technology was awarded with the Philippine Patent Number 23269 in May, 1989 (Truong and Fementira 1989). As a legal document, the patent protects the institutional right to the developed technology and serves as the basis for bargaining with private companies.

A strategy for technology transfer was formulated. The first step was information dissemination to the public through scientific reports, announcements in newspapers, and an investment forum. Display of actual products was also carried out in various science and technology fairs organized by government agencies and non-government organizations.

Because of the high vitamin A content of this product, a large Philippine food company expressed an interest in producing it. The product fit the company's current thrusts which are focused on using indigenous raw materials for production of nutritious, low priced food products on contractual arrangements with farmers to supply the raw material. Interestingly, the thrusts of the company matched the objectives of the project and, more importantly, the prime targeted clientele, root crop farmers. Moreover, adoption of the technology by a large food processor would help facilitate the penetration of the fruity-SP beverage into the markets.

With common interests, ViSCA and the company agreed in principle to the transfer of the processing technology for commercialization. In return, the company agreed to donate equipment to ViSCA for R & D in food processing. ViSCA and the company also agreed to undertake a joint project for scaling up the process for commercialization. An implementing team was formed composed of company personnel—a food product development specialist, a process development engineer, a marketing specialist, a fruit processing plant manager, an agricultural extension specialist—and the ViSCA inventor. The company provided funds and its existing fruit juice factories for pilot and semi-commercial production of the SP beverage.

Translation of ViSCA process to pilot scale operations

Product refinement and diversification. The SP beverage was prepared in the company's laboratory, following the process developed at ViSCA. The formulation was adjusted to meet the company's standards and the process was modified to make it fit the existing facilities of the company. Utilization of sweetpotato for other types of beverages was also explored.

Trial runs at the company's factories. Trial runs were conducted at the company's factories using both VSP-1 cultivar and sweetpotatoes purchased on the open market. Various factors affecting the process operations and product quality were determined. Beverage sensory attributes and shelf-life were evaluated. No major problems were encountered during the trial runs.

Product costing. The data obtained during the trial runs were used in pricing the whole process. The production cost of the SP beverage was analyzed in relation to fluctuations in the local price of sweetpotato storage roots.

Product testing and market plan. The beverage samples were subjected to consumer evaluation for market analysis. Several planning activities related to the production projection, profit estimation, product naming and product positioning were carried out.

Production of raw material. Since VSP-1 is a new sweetpotato variety, the company sought the assistance from ViSCA regarding the supply of planting materials, information on cultural management of the variety and postharvest handling and grading of the storage roots. To ensure regular supplies of the propagules to contracted farmers, the company collaborated with an agricultural school in the vicinity on propagation of VSP-1 cuttings. However, due to the need for scheduling the use of the company factories for sweetpotato processing which will be carried out only when there is no fruit processing, timing the production of VSP-1 storage roots by contracted farmers appears to be problematic.

For the precooked sweetpotato powder which can be used in the preparation of the SP-cocoa beverage and other products, the technology has been transferred to a food processor for pilot testing. However, because the pilot plant is located in an urban area, the cost of fresh sweetpotato storage roots is proving too high to make the project economically feasible.

CONCLUSION

It has been shown that sweetpotato can be processed into a fruity beverage with the nutrient content and sensory qualities being equal to or superior to commercial fruit juices and drinks. The process, developed in the laboratory, was successfully translated into a pilot scale operation. Some work needs to be done to develop an appropriate production scheme for raw materials and a marketing strategy before the fruity-SP beverage and its diversified forms can be marketed. Nevertheless, the generation and transfer of technology reported herein mark an important turning point in the use of sweetpotato as a raw material—in competition with expensive fruits—for commercial production of highly marketable food products. Likewise, the development of the beverage-type SP powder offers a possibility of increasing utilization of sweetpotato and providing consumers a low-priced and nutritious breakfast drink.

REFERENCES

Alkuino, J.M. Jr., Truong, Van Den, A.M. Suplico, G.B. Fementira, and F.C. Calub, Jr. 1986. Comparative cost and return analysis of indigenous technologies in rural processing of sweet potato and cassava, Terminal Report, IDRC-Funded project, ViSCA, Leyte, 87 pp.

Alkuino, J.M. Jr. 1983. An econometric analysis of the demand for sweet potato in the Philippines, Ph.D. Dissertation, Univ. of Hawaii, 144 pp.

Anonymous. 1980. Sweet potato quality. Southern Cooperative Series Bull. 249, S-101 Technical Committee, Univ. Georgia, Athens, USA.

Bouwkamp, J.C. 1985. Sweet potato products: A natural resource for the tropics, CRC Press, Boca Raton, FL USA.

Bureau, J.L., and R.J. Bushway 1986. HPLC determination of carotenoids in fruits and vegetables in the United States. J. Food Sci. 51:128-130.

Casimir, D.J., J.F. Kefford, and F.B. Whitfield. 1981. Technology and flavor chemistry of passion fruit juices and concentrates. Adv. Food Res. 27:243-290.

Duell, B. 1988. Ways of eating sweet potato in Japan. Paper presented at the Eighth Symposium of the International Society for Tropical Root Crops, Bangkok, Thailand, October 30-November 5, 1988.

Edmond, J.B., and C.R Ammerman. 1971. Sweet potato: Production, processing and marketing. AVI Publishing Co. Westport, Connecticut.

FAO. 1986. FAO Production Yearbook 1985. FAO, Rome, Italy.

Food and Nutrition Research Institute. 1980. Food Composition Table, Manila, Philippines.

Mabesa, L.B. 1986. Sensory evaluation of foods: principles and methods, College of Agriculture, Univ. of the Philippines at Los Banos, College, Laguna.

Nutrition Research Committee, National Nutrition Council. 1976. Philippine Recommended Dietary Allowances, Revision, Food and Nutrition Research Institute, Manila.

Phillips, G.F., and J.G. Woodroof. 1981. Beverage acids, flavors, colors and emulsifiers. Pages 152-207 in Beverages: carbonated and non-carbonated, J .G. Woodroof and G.F. Phillips, AVI Publishing Co., Westport, Conn., USA.

Salunkhe, D.K., S.K. Pao, and G.G. Dull. 1974. Assessment of nutritive value, quality and stability of cruciferous vegetables during storage and subsequent to processing. Pages 1-38 in Storage, processing and nutritional quality of fruits and vegetables, edited by D.K. Salunkhe. CRC Press, Ohio, USA.

Truong, Van Den. 1989. New developments in processing sweet potato for food.Pages 213-226 in Sweet potato research and development for small farmers, edited by K.T. Mackay, M.K. Palomar, R.R. Sanico, SEAMEO-SEARCA, College, Laguna, Philippines.

Truong, Van Den, and G.B. Fementira. 1989. Process for the production of non-alcoholic beverages and concentrates from sweet potato. Philippine Patent No. 23269.

Truong, Van Den, A.T. Sembrano, and G.B. Fementira. 1988. Process for preparing a dried sweet potato product with sweet and sour taste. Philippine Patent No. 22242.

Truong, Van Den, and G.B. Fementira. 1988. Formulations, consumer acceptability and nutrient content of non-alcoholic beverages from sweet potato. Paper presented at the Eighth Symposium of the International Society for Tropical Root Crops, Bangkok, Thailand, October 30-November 5, 1988.

Truong, Van Den, C.J. Biermann, and J.A. Marlett. 1986. Simple sugars, oligosaccharides and starch concentrations in raw and cooked sweet potato. J. Agric. Food Chem. 34:421-425.

Truong, Van Den, and E.J. del Rosario. 1986. Processing of sweet potatoes for food and industrial uses. Pages 38-47 in Philippine Council for Agricultural Resources and Development, State-of-the-Art-Sweet Potato Research, Los Banos.

Tsou, S.C.S., and R.L. Villareal. 1982. Resistance to eating sweet potato. Pages 37-44 in Sweet potato, edited by R.L. Villareal and T.D. Griggs. Proceedings of the First International Symposium on Sweet Potato, AVRDC, Taiwan.

Winarno, F.G. 1982. Sweet potato processing and by-product utilization in the tropics. Pages 373-384 in Sweet potato, edited by R.L. Villareal, and T.D. Griggs. Proceedings of the First International Symposium on Sweet Potato, AVRDC,Taiwan.

Sweetpotato Technology for the 21st Century. W.A. Hill, C.K. Bonsi and P.A. Loretan (Eds.) 1992. Tuskegee University, Tuskegee, AL

William M. Walter, Jr.*, Paul W. Wilson**

Frozen Sweetpotato Products

Frozen sweetpotato products, although available in many developed countries, account for only a small part of the total food use. Quality of this class of sweetpotato products is dependent upon processing operations. Peeling, the first processing step after washing, may be a heat-mediated process such as lye or steam peeling, or a mechanical procedure such as abrasive peeling. The roots are next comminuted or sliced, depending upon the target product, combined with other ingredients where applicable, heat-processed, and frozen. Various strategies can be employed at this stage to control flavor and textural attributes. Optimally the product should be rapidly frozen. The product may be packaged prior to or subsequent to freezing. Research has shown that properly frozen and packaged sweetpotato products maintain sensory properties and nutritional value during prolonged storage, provided they are held at or below -17.8°C (0°F).

For a number of years, per capita consumption of sweetpotato has been declining in many parts of the world. For the United States market, significant expansion of sweetpotatoes is dependent upon making nutritious, high-quality, and convenient processed products available to the consumer. With the suggestion by the American Cancer Society that beta carotene and complex carbohydrates may be beneficial in the diet, the time may be right to expand the market for sweetpotato products. However, to compete in the United States market, we will need to produce products that are of high quality and are convenient to use in addition to having nutritional advantages. Frozen sweetpotato products are in a position to satisfy increasing consumer demand.

A review of the literature indicates that a large number of frozen products have been developed. Table 1 lists a few of these. However, only a limited number of frozen sweetpotato products are currently being sold in the United States. They include candied sweetpotatoes, pies, patties, and a breaded form product.

In Japan a larger number of frozen products are commercially available. Table 2 presents the types and amounts of some Japanese frozen products. You will note there are several styles of blanched products, including random-cut, slices, a diced product, and puree or paste. There are also oil-fried products, some of which are coated with a sugary syrup. Others include baked sweetpotatoes, ice cream, and cakes.

*United States Department of Agriculture, Agricultural Research Service, and Department of Food Science, North Carolina State University, Raleigh, NC 27695-7624; and **Department of Horticulture, Louisiana State University, Baton Rouge, LA 70803.

Table 1. Frozen sweetpotato products.

Purees and Pie Fillings -	Woodroof and Atkinson 1944
	Turner and Danner 1957
	Hoover 1964
Slices and Pieces -	Hoover and Pope 1960
	Hoover 1964
Baked and Stuffed -	Hoover 1957
	Collins 1978
Patties -	Kimbrough and Kimbrough 1961
	Hoover et al. 1983
	Pak 1982
	Silva et al. 1989
French Fries, Dice, Strips -	Kelley et al. 1958
	Walter and Hoover 1986
	Chiang and Kao 1989

Table 2. Types and amounts of frozen sweetpotato products on the market in Japan.

Type	Name	Production (t)
Blanched		
Random-cut	Sweetpotato ran-giri	440
Slice-cut	Sweetpotato wa-giri	1,280
Stick-cut	Stick	30
Dice-cut	Satsuma dice	530
Puree	Paste or Imo-an	850
Fried		
Random-cut	Sweetpotato fry, ran-giri	340
Packed in sugary syrup	Daigaku-imo	1,000
Coated in sugary syrup	Chuuka-potato	60
Stick	Straight-cut, crinkled cut	170
Baked	Yaki-imo	250
Total		4,950

Data courtesy of Professor Tomonori Nagahama, Kagoshima University, Kagoshima, Japan.

There are a number of processing operations involved (Fig. 1) in producing high quality frozen sweetpotato products. When the roots are delivered to the processor, they must be washed to remove adhering soil. They are peeled and reduced in size by cutting, slicing, or pureeing. In some cases, it may be necessary to size the roots prior to size reduction. The potatoes are then heat-processed by blanching or cooking. They may be pureed prior to packaging or packaged after heat processing. They are then frozen.

Each of the processing operations will now be explained in more detail. Several peeling processes can be used, depending upon the end-product. There are heat-mediated operations such as lye-peeling, steam-peeling, and combination lye- and steam-peeling. In addition, abrasion-peeling can be employed. All of the peeling processes have limitations. Where lye is used, disposal of the waste is a problem since the high pH must be reduced. When the residue is neutralized, the high sodium content causes some limitations if the waste is to be used as animal feed. Steam-peeling eliminates the above problem in that the waste can be fed directly to animals, but steam-peeling alone is not as effective in removing deep blemishes. Some processors have found a short lye-peeling step, followed by a steam-peeling step, is a superior compromise. Abrasion-peeling is the least effective since the irregular shape and recessed lenticels greatly increase peeling losses. It is accepted by processors that sweetpotatoes should be peeled at least to below the cambial layer, a depth of about 2-3 mm. If blemishes are severe, deeper peeling is required. After peeling, some hand-trimming is required. Overall losses can run as high as 35%. Discoloration is also a problem in this step.

For some applications, the roots must be sized after peeling. For example, Woodroof and Atkinson (1944) found that the best quality puree was attained when roots were cooked in a steam atmosphere at 10 psi for varying periods of time, as dictated by their diameter. However, in most cases, sizing is not necessary.

Following peeling and sizing, the roots are cut, sliced, or pureed, depending upon the target product. Agents may be added to control discoloration and improve flavor and texture. For example, citric acid, lemon juice, or pyrophosphates can be used to retard discoloration. It is important that the freshly cut tissue not be held in contact with air for extended time periods.

After size reduction, the sliced or pureed material is heat-processed either by blanching or cooking. However, it is essential that the internal temperature reaches 88°C during heating so that detrimental enzyme systems are inactivated. Steam (both atmospheric and pressurized), water, and sucrose solutions have all been used both for blanching and cooking. During this phase of production, agents can also be added to improve flavor, color, and texture of the product. For example, sugars, raisins, and cinnamon have been used for stuffed sweetpotatoes. Texture can be modified by the use of firmness-retaining agents such as calcium, or softening agents such as amylases.

Since discoloration is a major problem for many frozen products, a great deal of effort has been exerted to understand the mechanisms and develop strategies to control it.

Discoloration of sweetpotatoes can be enzymatic or nonenzymatic. Generally, enzymatic discoloration is characterized by a brown, dark gray, or black color. It

PROCESSING STEPS

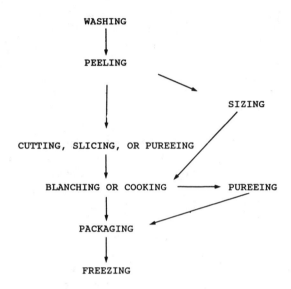

Figure 1. Processing steps.

occurs when the enzyme polyphenol oxidase catalyzes the oxidative polymerization of endogenous phenolics (mainly chlorogenic acid). Enzymatic discoloration occurs when natural barriers separating the enzyme and its substrate are disrupted either by mechanical means, as when roots are sliced, or by physical means, such as heat-mediated membrane disruption which occurs as a result of heat penetration from the lye peeling bath into tissue beneath the lye contact zone. This type discoloration can be prevented by lowering the pH with acidulants, by using inhibitors such as sulfite and ascorbic acid, or by heat-inactivation of the enzyme before significant reaction has occurred, such as by preheating the roots prior to lye- or steam-peeling.

Nonenzymatic discoloration is caused by phenolics complexing with metals. This discoloration may be gray, black, or green. Generally, the main culprit in this type of discoloration is iron. Iron-caused discoloration can be eliminated by the use of a mixture of sodium pyrophosphates. The pyrophosphate has a stronger affinity for the metal ions than do the phenolics, and, consequently, the phenolic-metal complex is destroyed. Pyrophosphates have been used effectively in the blanching medium (french fries) and added directly into several products.

After the cooking/blanching step, the product is drained (if necessary), cooled, and frozen. The best method of freezing most foods is quick-freezing to insure small ice crystal formation and, hence, less textural degradation. Four basic methods may be employed to quick-freeze food products: air blast- or tunnel-freezing; plate-freezing; immersion-freezing using alcohol, brine, or syrups; and cryogenic-freezing using liquid nitrogen or carbon dioxide applied as immersion, spray, or snow. Cryogenic-freezing is generally considered to be best, although the benefits may not outweigh the cost when compared to other methods.

Sweetpotato products may be frozen before or after packaging. Freezing products after packaging is more convenient and has the advantage of retarding dehydration during the freezing process, although any pieces within the package will be solidified into one mass. Freezing of the products prior to packaging allows somewhat faster freezing, but the product is subject to surface desiccation. This method is the only way to provide individual quick-freezing (IQF) of small pieces (i.e., french fries or cubes) which retain their identity after packaging and allows removal of portions from the package.

Plate freezers are normally used for products that are packaged prior to freezing (especially cartons), although some blast immersion, immersion, and cryogenic freezers can also be utilized in this manner. Air-blast, immersion, and cryogenic freezers are usually used for freezing products before packaging. Fluidized bed blast freezers and immersion freezers (conventional and cryogenic) are most applicable to IQF.

With all freezing methods, the products should be frozen quickly and solidly to below -30°C. Equally important or perhaps more important is the maintenance of frozen products at temperatures below -17.8°C (0°F) to inhibit deleterious chemical reactions (including oxidation) and recrystalization or ice crystal enlargement which destroys textural properties. Of all the factors involved in marketing frozen products, arguably, the one that contributes most to loss of product quality is temperature abuse during storage. This may occur in inventory, during distribution, at the retail level, or in the home.

Packaging is crucial in frozen foods because of the potential for dehydration and oxidative changes during frozen storage. The packaging material must have a low moisture vapor transmission rate which retards loss of moisture from the product. This barrier must also prevent entrance of moisture into the package which would cause internal frosting. The package should provide a gas barrier for control of oxidative deterioration and to reduce loss of volatiles and pickup of odors. The packaging material must maintain its integrity at low temperature, as low as -40°C for conventional freezing and as low as -195°C for cryogenic freezing. The package should be of size and shape to allow stacking and efficient use of frozen storage space. It should also resist abrasion and puncture and accept suitable printing inks without difficulty.

Packaging materials that in the past have provided most of the requirements for protection of frozen sweetpotato products include the paperboard carton with an interior liner of moisture-proof cellophane or an aluminum, foil-laminated overwrap. These types of cartons have been lately supplanted by cartons coated with hot-melt polyvinylidene chloride which provides somewhat better convenience and protection. Another type of container routinely used for frozen fruits and vegetables is the polyethylene film bag. This type bag accounts for nearly one-third of frozen vegetable packages at the retail level and is the predominant package for IQF products. For products that are frozen and cooked in the same container, the "boil-in-bag" is a polyethylene-coated polyester film bag usually packed in a folded paperboard carton. Additional packaging materials which have become useful in frozen foods are the insulation foams. Formed polystyrene sheets or molded forms have been used as outer containers to reduce temperature fluctuations of frozen products and retard deterioration of product quality.

Studies have reported on long-term, frozen storage of a french fry product (Schwartz et al. 1987), frozen sweetpotato-citron bars (Beauchamp de Caloni and Recio de Hernandez 1988), a stuffed sweetpotato-raisin-ham product (Collins 1978), and a frozen pureed product (Woodroof and Atkinson 1944). In all cases storage of up to six months had no detectable effect on sensory quality. Thus, frozen products would appear to have a long shelf life. Much less information is available on the effect of long-term storage on vitamins. One study on frozen french fries reported that significant loss of vitamin C occurred after 9 months of frozen storage, but that beta carotene was essentially unchanged.

In summary, we would like to emphasize the following points.

1. In the United States, development of high quality, nutritious (high beta carotene content) and convenient frozen sweetpotato products is essential if sweet-potato consumption is to increase.

2. Factors affecting most aspects of the quality of frozen sweetpotato products are well understood.

3. Frozen sweetpotato products can be stored for extended periods of time without causing serious quality deterioration.

REFERENCES

Beauchamp de Caloni, I., and E. Recio de Hernandez. 1988. Freezing and shelf life of sweet potato and citron bars. Journal of Agriculture of the University of Puerto Rico 72:171-172.

Collins, J.L. 1978. Flavor preference of selected food products from vegetables. Journal of Agricultural and Food Chemistry 26:1012-1015.

Hoover, M.W. 1957. Freezing sweet potatoes. Quick Frozen Foods 19:370.

Hoover, M.W. 1964. Preservation of the natural color in processed sweet potato products. Food Technology 18:1793-1796.

Hoover, M. W., and D. T. Pope. 1960. Effect of variety, curing and processing on carbohydrate content of precooked frozen sweet potatoes. Food Technology 14:227-230.

Hoover, M.W., W.M. Walter, Jr., and F G. Giesbrecht. 1983. Method of preparation and sensory evaluation of sweet potato patties. Journal of Food Science 48:1568-1569.

Kelley, E.G., R.B. Baum, and C.F. Woodward. 1958. Preparation of new and improved products from eastern sweetpotatoes: chips, dice, Juliene strips, and frozen French fries. Food Technology 12:510-513.

Kimbrough, R.L., and D.J. Kimbrough. 1961. Process of preparing a frozen food product from sweet potatoes. U. S. Patent No. 3,007,800.

Pak, P.K. 1982. Development of a frozen sweet potato patty suitable for restaurant handling. M.S. thesis, Mississippi State University, Mississippi State, Mississippi.

Schwartz, S.J., W.M. Walter, Jr., D.E. Carroll, and F.G. Giesbrecht. 1987. Chemical, physical and sensory properties of a sweet potato French fry-type product during frozen storage.

Journal of Food Science 52:617-619.

Silva, J.L., M.D. Yazid, M.D. Ali, and G.R. Ammerman. 1989. Effect of processing method on products made from sweetpotato mash. Journal of Food Quality 11:387-396.

Turner, J. L., and M.J. Danner. 1957. Acceptance of an improved frozen sweetpotato puree. Alabama Agricultural Experiment Station Circular No. 121. 14 pp.

Walter, W.M., Jr., and M.W. Hoover. 1986. Preparation, evaluation and analysis of a French fry-type product from sweet potatoes. Journal of Food Science 51:967-970.

Woodroof, J.G., and I.S. Atkinson. 1944. Freezing provides an answer to sweet potato problem. Food Industries :537-539.

Sweetpotato Technology for the 21st Century. W.A. Hill, C.K. Bonsi and P.A. Loretan (Eds.) 1992. Tuskegee University, Tuskegee, AL

Emma S. Data, Joni Jane A. Operario

Processing and Storage Characteristics of Sweetpotato Chips for Food

Processing operations of sweetpotato chip production slightly affected the physical and chemical constituents and microbial contamination of the product. Except for the moisture content which decreased with drying and the sugar content of the sweetpotato chips which decreased with chipping, all other chemical constituents (starch, ash and crude fiber) were not affected by processing operations. Microbial contamination also decreased with chipping and drying. No aflatoxin was detected in the chips during processing and storage. The physical and chemical constituents as well as the microbial contamination and insect infestation of dried chips were affected by the type of container and duration of storage. Polyethylene sacks were found to be the best packaging materials for six months' storage of sweetpotato chips.

INTRODUCTION

The problem of an inadequate food supply is worldwide. To cope with this problem, there is a need to augment the food supply by expanding production and reducing food losses that occur between harvest and consumption.

Root crops such as sweetpotato are perishable crops so they should be processed into forms with better storageability. Dried root crop products have been utilized in Africa, Asia and South America as food or feed (Ingram and Humphries 1972). There has been comparatively little research done on the storage of these products because Davies (1962) assumed that they are of relatively low commercial value and improved storage technology may be considered uneconomical.

One possible constraint to the adoption of technology that permits substitution of corn and wheat flour with root crop chips and root crop flour, respectively, is the limited knowledge on the processing and storage characteristics of root crop chips. Information is needed on the quality of chips produced by the different steps in the preparation of root crop chips as well as their behavior during storage. The lack of knowledge on the storageability of these dried materials may limit their utilization since there is no assurance that the processor can adequately store them with existing storage practices. Assessment of the chips' behavior and quality during processing and storage is necessary to determine the optimum processing and storage conditions required and the maximum length of storage possible to maintain the product in good quality. Identification of good packaging materials that could prevent or

Philippine Root Crop Research and Training Center, Visayas State College of Agriculture, Baybay, Leyte, Philippines.

Table A. Grading scale of color for sweetpotato 'V-11' chips for food.

Grade	Quality	Color of Chips
1	Excellent	Off-white with brown spots
2	Very Good	Off-white with dark spots
3	Good	Light brown
4	Fair	Brown
5	Poor	Grey-brown

minimize reabsorption of moisture from the atmosphere by the stored dried materials is also deemed necessary.

In this paper, the changes in the chemical constituents of sweetpotato during processing and storage using different packaging materials are reported. Microbial contamination and insect infestation as well as changes in color of the chips during storage are also discussed.

MATERIALS AND METHODS

Sweetpotato roots were harvested using a sweetpotato harvester and washed using the ViSCA modified washer. The roots were peeled manually and then chipped using the Malaysian chipper. The chips were dried in a mechanical dryer until the moisture content was below 10%. The dried chips were packed in different containers, namely, straw sacks, polyethylene sacks, jute sacks and crates. They were then stored in a storage house under ambient conditions. The temperature and relative humidity inside and outside the storage house were monitored daily for six months and varied from 26 to 32°C and 60 to 90% RH.

Sampling was done during each step of chip processing as well as every month during storage to monitor the changes in the chemical constituents (% starch, sugar, ash and crude fiber content) and the moisture content of the stored dried chips. Aflatoxin contamination was determined during processing and after the first, third and sixth month of storage. Microbial analyses using glucose yeast peptone agar (GYPA) for bacteria, maltose yeast agar (MYA) for yeast, and potato dextrose agar (PDA) for molds were done monthly using 100 g of dried sample. Insect infestation on the stored chips was assessed and changes in color were monitored monthly for six months using a grading scale for chips as food (Table A).

RESULTS AND DISCUSSION

Processing Characteristics of Sweetpotato Chips for Food

In general, the processing operations of root crop chip production slightly affected the physical and chemical constituents of the product. Except for the moisture content and sugar content which decreased significantly with drying and chipping, respectively, the other chemical constituents were not significantly affected by processing (Table 1). Drying of chips reduced the moisture content to a minimum

Table 1. Chemical constituents of sweetpotato roots at different stages of chip processing for food.[1]

Processing Operation	% Moisture	% Sugar	% Starch	% Ash	% Crude fiber
	Chemical Constituents				
Harvesting	69.73A	6.72A	68.09A	2.38A	3.31A
Washing	69.69A	7.22A	72.19A	2.15A	3.23A
Peeling[2]	68.03A	7.32A	76.24A	2.09A	3.35A
Peeling[3]	68.71A	6.05B	79.32A	1.99A	3.31A
Chipping	68.34A	3.31C	76.84A	2.29A	2.60A
Drying	5.70B	4.81BC	67.83A	2.20A	2.42A

[1]Values followed by a common letter are not significantly different at the 5% level of significance using Duncan's Multiple Range Test. [2]Freshly peeled; [3]soaked in water.

as a result of heat that came in contact with the chips which resulted in evaporation of the moisture present in the chips. The decrease in sugar content during chipping was attributed to pressure exerted by the chipper causing the sugar to be lost. Among the chemical constituents, sugar easily dissolves in water and thus can be readily dispersed.

Aflatoxin contamination was not detected in the different processing operations of chip production. The absence of aflatoxin could be attributed to the rapid processing of dried chips, thus avoiding rapid growth of molds causing aflatoxin production.

Processing did affect the microbial load of sweetpotato chips (Table 2). At harvest the chips contained many bacteria populations which decreased upon washing but tended to increase during the remainder of the processing. The decrease in the microbial load

Table 2. Microbial contamination of sweetpotato during processing .

Microbial Contamination	Processing Operations	Replication Group I	II	Mean
	Harvesting	3.4×10^3	3.2×10^3	3.3×10^3
	Washing	8.1×10^2	7.2×10^2	7.6×10^2
Bacteria	Peeling	9.6×10^2	8.7×10^2	9.1×10^2
	Chipping	1.2×10^3	1.3×10^3	1.2×10^3
	Drying	1.1×10^3	1.4×10^3	1.2×10^3
	Harvesting	2.7×10^3	2.8×10^3	2.7×10^3
	Washing	1.9×10^2	1.8×10^2	1.8×10^2
Molds	Peeling	1.6×10^2	1.9×10^2	1.7×10^2
	Chipping	2.0×10^3	2.3×10^3	2.1×10^3
	Drying	6.9×10^2	7.2×10^2	7.0×10^2
	Harvesting	1.7×10^2	1.5×10^2	1.6×10^2
	Washing	1.3×10^2	1.8×10^2	1.5×10^2
Yeasts	Peeling	1.8×10^2	1.9×10^2	1.8×10^2
	Chipping	1.8×10^2	2.0×10^2	1.9×10^2
	Drying	2.1×10^3	2.3×10^3	2.2×10^3

Table 3. Moisture content of sweetpotato for food during six months of storage[1].

Packaging Material	Months of Storage						
	0	1	2	3	4	5	6
Straw	5.70j	10.10h	10.83gh	12.50c-f	13.65b-d	14.67ab	14.67ab
Polyethylene	5.70j	8.17i	11.27f-h	11.83f-h	11.50e-g	12.00d-g	12.17d-g
Jute	5.70j	10.73g-h	12.17d-g	12.3c-f	14.00bc	14.50ab	14.50ab
Crate	5.70j	12.67c-f	12.67b-e	14.00bc	15.67a	16.00a	16.00a

[1] Values followed by a common letter are not significantly different at 5% level of significance using DMRT.

during washing could be due to the removal of impurities like soil from the roots or some of the peel. The increase in microbial load during peeling, chipping and drying may be attributed to exposure of the roots to the different pieces of equipment used in these processes which may not have been properly cleaned before being used.

Storage Characteristics of Sweetpotato Chips for Food

The physical and chemical constituents as well as the microbial and insect contents of dried sweetpotato chips were affected by the type of container or packaging material, kind of environment and duration of storage. There was an abrupt increase in moisture content of sweetpotato chips during the first month of storage (Table 3). This could have been due to the high relative humidity and low temperature in the storage house which allowed the dried chips to pick up the moisture from that environment. However, the rate of moisture uptake in the chips is influenced by the ability of the packaging materials to block moisture uptake. A slower rate of absorption of moisture occurs as storage progresses and as the dried chips have absorbed moisture close to the equilibrium point in the environment.

The chips stored in polyethylene sacks absorbed the least moisture followed by jute sacks. Jute sacks have holes while polyethylene sacks are sealed and prevent moisture from penetrating into the chips. The highest accumulation of moisture occurred in chips stored in open crates, but it was not significantly different from those stored in straw and jute sacks. The former had more surface area exposed to the atmosphere which obviously contributed to the increase in moisture.

The nutritive content of the chips stored in different containers varied with time in storage. There was no definite trend in the values obtained for the starch contents (Table 4) during the monthly sampling. However, the chips packaged in jute sacks exhibited a significant reduction in starch after 6 months of storage. There was a significant decrease in sugar content (Table 5) in chips stored in all containers by at least the fifth month of storage except for polyethylene bags. The ash content of sweetpotato chips increased with storage time but the increase was significant only after the fifth month of storage in some treatments (Table 6). The crude fiber content of

Table 4. Starch content of sweetpotato chips for food during six months of storage.[1]

Packaging Material	Months of Storage						
	0	1	2	3	4	5	6
Straw	64.17b-e	66.75a-d	76.29a	62.45c-f	60.59d-f	60.29d-f	63.00b-f
Polyethylene	64.17b-e	60.38d-f	72.68ab	62.59c-f	55.61ef	60.86d-f	62.11c-f
Jute	64.17b-e	67.13d-f	72.68ab	59.68d-f	64.96b-e	61.00d-f	54.00f
Crate	64.17b-e	71.00a-c	71.37a-c	67.42a-d	58.03d-f	62.57c-f	65.82d-f

[1]Values followed by a common letter are not significantly different at 5% level of significance using Duncan's Multiple Range Test.

Table 5. Sugar content of sweetpotato chips for food during six months of storage.[1]

Packaging Material	Months of Storage						
	0	1	2	3	4	5	6
Straw	6.32bc	6.62a-c	7.49ab	6.57a-c	5.50c-e	3.75e-g	4.10d-g
Polyethylene	6.32bc	6.29bc	8.70a	5.6c-e	5.48c-e	5.59bc	5.42c-e
Jute	6.32bc	5.71cd	8.06ab	6.26bc	5.28c-e	4.28d-g	3.40f-h
Crate	6.32bc	6.77a-c	8.37ab	5.64c-e	4.23d-g	1.83h	2.78gh

[1]Values followed by a common letter are not significantly different at 5% level of significance using Duncan's Multiple Range Test.

Table 6. Ash content of sweetpotato chips for food during six months of storage.[1]

Packaging Material	Months of Storage						
	0	1	2	3	4	5	6
Straw	2.07d-h	1.97g-h	2.03d-h	2.29b-f	2.11d-h	2.34a-d	2.28b-e
Polyethylene	2.07d-h	1.92g-h	1.95g-h	2.11d-h	1.84hi	2.33a-d	2.16c-g
Jute	2.07d-h	1.91g-h	2.08d-h	2.18c-g	2.00e-h	2.33a-d	2.59ab
Crate	2.07d-h	1.60i	2.07d-h	2.27b-f	2.22c-g	2.47a-c	2.56a

[1]Values followed by a common letter are not significantly different at 5% level of significance using Duncan's Multiple Range Test.

Table 7. Crude fiber content of sweetpotato chips for food during six months of storage.[1]

Packaging Material	Months of Storage						
	0	1	2	3	4	5	6
Straw	2.47f-i	3.37c-g	1.97g-i	3.03c-h	4.23a-d	2.43f-i	3.03c-h
Polyethylene	2.47f-i	2.43f-i	1.73h-i	3.40c-g	4.16a-d	4.30a-c	2.37f-i
Jute	2.47f-i	2.87d-i	2.07g-i	3.20c-h	3.53b-f	5.26a	3.27c-g
Crate	2.47f-i	2.63e-i	1.47i	2.37f-i	3.16c-h	4.86ab	4.40a-c

[1]Values followed by a common letter are not significantly different at 5% level of significance using DMRT.

the chips showed fluctuating values during storage (Table 7). However, after the sixth month of storage, chips stored in polyethylene sacks had the lowest crude fiber content while those stored in crates had the highest.

Microbial contamination and insect infestation in stored sweetpotato chips increased with storage time (Table 8). Chips stored in polyethylene sacks had the

Table 8. Microbial contamination and insect infestation of sweetpotato chips for food stored in different packaging materials.

Contamination/ Infestation	Packaging Materials	Month of Storage						
		0	1	2	3	4	5	6
Bacteria/mL	Straw	1.2×10^3	2.4×10^3	8.2×10^3	1.2×10^5	1.1×10^6	1.3×10^6	2.3×10^6
	Poly	1.2×10^3	5.7×10^3	6.6×10^4	1.2×10^4	3.2×10^5	3.3×10^5	3.9×10^5
	Jute	1.2×10^3	6.4×10^3	9.6×10^3	6.3×10^5	3.2×10^7	6.4×10^7	7.7×10^7
	Crate	1.2×10^3	7.9×10^3	8.4×10^5	1.5×10^6	1.8×10^6	1.9×10^6	4.2×10^7
Molds/mL	Straw	7.0×10^2	7.8×10^4	3.5×10^4	4.8×10^5	7.7×10^5	1.3×10^6	1.4×10^6
	Poly	7.0×10^2	5.1×10^3	5.7×10^3	1.0×10^4	1.1×10^4	3.1×10^4	2.0×10^5
	Jute	7.0×10^2	8.0×10^3	4.2×10^4	1.8×10^4	2.0×10^5	2.3×10^6	2.2×10^7
	Crate	7.0×10^2	9.4×10^4	7.7×10^4	7.0×10^5	2.5×10^6	5.9×10^7	4.2×10^7
Yeast/mL	Straw	2.2×10^3	4.0×10^5	8.2×10^5	1.1×10^6	2.0×10^5	4.0×10^7	5.9×10^7
	Poly	2.2×10^3	8.3×10^3	4.4×10^4	7.2×10^5	2.8×10^5	1.4×10^6	3.6×10^6
	Jute	2.2×10^3	1.0×10^4	4.8×10^4	1.6×10^5	1.9×10^6	2.1×10^6	2.9×10^7
	Crate	2.2×10^3	4.4×10^3	8.8×10^4	2.8×10^5	3.2×10^6	3.5×10^7	6.9×10^7
Insects/ 150g	Straw	0	0	0	4	8	8	7
	Poly	0	0	0	1	4	6	6
	Jute	0	0	3	8	14	14	17
	Crate	0	1	3	12	14	15	15

Table 9. Changes in color quality of stored sweetpotato chips.[1]

Packing Material	Months of Storage						
	0	1	2	3	4	5	6
Straw	1.00	1.00	1.33	1.33	1.66	1.66	2.00
Polyethylene	1.00	1.00	1.33	1.33	1.33	1.66	2.00
Jute	1.00	1.00	1.00	1.33	1.66	2.00	2.33
Crate	1.00	1.00	1.66	2.00	2.00	2.33	2.66

[1]Based on grading scale of 1 to 5; 1=excellent, 2=very good, 3=good, 4=fair, and 5 =poor.

lowest contamination in terms of bacteria, molds and yeasts, which were within the standard microbial limits set by the American Public Health Association (1976). Polyethylene sacks provided a modified microenvironmental condition of high CO_2 which was unfavorable to the growth of some microorganisms and insects. Chips stored in the other containers became unacceptable in terms of microbial load because of small holes and exposed areas. A higher moisture accumulation also favored the growth of microorganisms and insects. Insect infestation was least for chips stored in polyethylene sacks and greatest for those stored in jute sacks. The stored chips were attacked by insects belonging to the order Coleoptera but different families (Scaphidiidae, Pselephidae and Tenebrionidae). Aflatoxin contamination was not detected during the first, third and sixth month of storage in chips stored in any of the packaging materials.

Changes in color quality of sweetpotato chips were less for those chips stored in polyethylene sacks and straw sacks than those stored in jute sacks and in crates (Table 9). The rapid changes in color of chips in the latter containers could be due to higher moisture accumulation and rapid oxidation of the chips. The chips stored in the first two containers were still rated very good in color quality after six months of storage.

SUMMARY, CONCLUSION AND RECOMMENDATION

The physical and chemical qualities of sweetpotato storage roots are only slightly affected by the processing operations of chip production. The sugar content of the roots decreased starting with the peeling process and, of course, decreased markedly during drying. The microbial load of sweetpotato storage roots also decreased during processing.

The physical, chemical and microbial qualities of sweetpotato chips were also affected by the type of packaging material, duration of storage and the storage conditions. Polyethylene sacks were found to be the best packaging material among the containers used for storing chips, especially for storage over long periods of time. Slow degradation of the chemical constituents, lowest microbial contamination and lowest insect infestation occurred in chips stored in this container.

Improvement of the sampling method and further studies on how to reduce the damage to chips caused by insect infestation are recommended.

ACKNOWLEDGMENT

This project was funded by the International Development Research Center (IDRC) (Grant IDRC-RCU-3P- 86-0263 : Root Crop Utilization: Philippines), and their support of this research is appreciated.

LITERATURE CITED

American Public Health Association. 1976. Compendium of methods for the microbiological examination of foods. Washington, D.C.

Davies, J.C. 1962. Storage of agricultural produce. Dept. Agric., Uganda, 31 pp.

Ingram, J.S., and J.R.O. Humphries. 1972. Cassava storage: A review. Tropical Science 14(2):131-148.

Linda D. Johnson, Sharon K. Hunt,
Rhonda L. Colvin, Vonetta T. Moorman

Consumer Acceptability of Sweetpotato Yogurts

Consumer acceptability of sweetpotato yogurts was determined by means of a trained sensory panel comparison. The experimental sweetpotato yogurts were prepared using a basic vanilla yogurt base with several sweetpotato puree mixtures including apricots, apricots and lemon juice, and papaya and pineapple chunks. Microbial tests—carbohydrate fermentation and standard plate count—were used on the yogurts and showed that they contained no pathogenic microbes and were safe for human consumption. All the yogurt products were evaluated by a sensory panel and found to be as good as commercially prepared peach yogurt (the control) in appearance, taste, texture and sweetness.

The development of new and improved convenience products from sweetpotatoes is an excellent means of increasing the use of this high yielding, nutritious crop and reversing the decline in their consumption. Sweetpotatoes offer a wide range of flavor, color and textural properties which could contribute to new possibilities for food preparation. The convenience products developed from them, however, must appeal to the consumer. Changing food habits of Americans include a demand for low-calorie convenience products that are ready-to-eat or quickly microwaved or heated. Yogurts fit into that classification.

This study's goal was to develop a new, tasty and nutritious yogurt from sweetpotatoes. The specific objectives were to develop recipes for sweetpotato yogurts, to test them for potential contamination, and to determine the desirability of these products to consumers.

REVIEW OF LITERATURE

Sweetpotatoes are an excellent source of nutrients providing at least 90% of the recommended dietary allowance (RDA) for adults except protein and niacin (Bouwkamp 1985). Sweetpotatoes have been formulated into frozen pie mix (Marshall and Danner 1959), turnovers (Jaynes and Corley 1981), breakfast foods (Ware 1947), crackers (Bouwkamp 1985), candy (Van de Mare and Ware 1947; Lanham 1950), sweetpotato puree, chips, snacks and baby foods. Several products have displayed limited acceptance in specific regions of the world. Of the products

Fort Valley State College, Agricultural Research Station, Fort Valley, GA 31030-3298.

415

reviewed above, only baby food can be considered a commercial success in America. Several candy products are produced in Taiwan on a commercial scale but, overall, sweetpotato products have not received wide acceptance in the U.S.A.

Reichert (1989) experimented with sweetpotato yogurt and found it received very favorable scores from sensory panels. Sweetpotato works quite well in yogurt overcoming the harsh flavor of the sour milk and providing a portion of the thickener in the yogurt.

When current trends in product development were investigated, yogurt was found to be one of the 10 most popular foods in the age group 18 to 34 (Sills-Levy 1986). German and McLaughlin (1985) have reported that our aging population is demanding more fruit, fiber and unprocessed grains. Gerber (1989) stated that new products developed should appeal to the mature consumer, and that the health/nutrition equation should be considered. Such food will produce a larger and more successful crossover into mainstream food markets. Traditional foods such as meat and dairy products are major players in current food trends (Gerber 1989).

Combining sweetpotato with milk in a yogurt was considered to be in line with these trends. Sweetpotato along with other fruits or vegetables in yogurt could provide a better flavor and improved nutritional value. The deficiencies in protein and niacin in sweetpotatoes would be provided by the milk.

PROCEDURE

Formulation of recipe

A commercial plain yogurt containing an active, live culture was used in formulating the yogurt base for sweetpotato yogurts. Experimental yogurt was made with commercial yogurt, pasteurized, homogenized milk, dry milk powder and sugar. The milk mixture was heated to 82°C then cooled to 43°C. Vanilla flavoring and 30 mL of the commercial yogurt product was added. The mixture was poured into styrofoam containers, covered and incubated for 4 to 6 hours. After incubation, sweetpotato purees (15 mL) combined with 60 mL of the yogurt base and the mixture were refrigerated until served to a consumer panel.

The purees formulated included sweetpotato and sweetpotato/fruit purees. Sweetpotatoes were washed thoroughly, greased and baked in a conventional oven at 176°C (375°F) until done. Baked potatoes were blended and mixed with other ingredients to make purees. Three purees were prepared by blending: mashed sweetpotatoes, corn syrup, apricots, lemon juice and sugar (S/A[1]); sweetpotatoes, corn syrup, apricots and sugar (S/A[2]); and sweetpotatoes, papaya, pears, pineapple chunks and bananas (S/A[3]). These products were presented to sensory taste panelists after they were stirred to produce a uniform product.

Microbial tests

Standard plate count: Since dairy products serve as a vehicle for transmission of pathogenic microorganisms or other harmful agents, standard methods recommended by the American Public Health Association were utilized. Microbial examination was utilized to test for the presence and number of coliform microorganisms. The standard plate count method as described by Rohde (1969) was used. A Quebec colony counter was used to perform bacterial counts.

Fermentation tests: Fermentation tests were done on the yogurts and their components to determine any evidence of pathogenic microbes. Contamination of sweetpotato purees was not expected because of the sanitary procedures and cooking process used for their preparation. Techniques recommended for dairy products by the American Public Health Association were used (APHA 1985).

Carbohydrate fermentation test: The carbohydrate fermentation test was used to identify bacteria capable of anaerobic fermentation of carbohydrates and bacteria that are gram-negative. This is a prescriptive test.

EMB agar: Eosin methylene blue agar (EMB) was used for the isolation and differentiation of gram-negative enteric bacilli such as *Salmonella, Shigella,* and *Escherichia coli.* When grown on EMB, colonies of pathogenic enteric bacilli can be distinguished from other organisms capable of rapidly fermenting the lactose.

Hydrogen ion concentration

The sweetpotato yogurts produced in this study contained milk and sweetpotato, requiring the addition of acidulants (lemon juice, organic acids) for adequate pH control (Graham 1980). Measurements of pH were conducted on the yogurt base and purees in duplicate. Lower pH permits the outgrowth of certain organisms such as the coliforms, *Streptococci* and *Lactobacilli.* These organisms utilize the substrate lactose and, in doing so, lower the pH of milk from about 6.8 to about 5.0 when curdling occurs. The breakdown of proteins such as casein and formation of amines cause a rise in pH and then the pseudomonads, *Bacillus* spp. and other proteolytic organisms take over. These organisms continue to break down setting up anaerobic conditions. Such conditions permit the growth of *Clostridium* species and other anaerobic organisms to aid in the putrefactive process. With adequate pH control and sufficient heating, however, milk products are safe for human consumption.

Sensory evaluation

A trained sensory panel evaluated the acceptability of the sweetpotato yogurts. A commercially prepared peach yogurt was used as a control because of its visual similarity to the experimental yogurt. Using a 5-point scale (1, poor; 5,excellent), yogurts were screened for appearance, flavor, texture, sweetness and taste. Mean scores were evaluated separately and combined to determine significant differences among samples. Statistical analysis using the SPSS statistical package was performed. Data were analyzed and Duncan's Multiple Range Test was used to separate means.

RESULTS AND DISCUSSION

Microbial Tests

As expected, the results of the microbial tests confirmed the presence of aerobic and facultatively anaerobic gram-negative, non-sporeforming bacteria capable of

Table 1. Sensory ratings* for sweetpotato yogurts compared to commercial yogurts.

Product	Flavor	Appearance	Taste	Texture	Sweetness
			Parameter		
Standard	4.4a**	3.7ab	4.1a	4.0a	3.7a
With S/A[1]	3.6bc	3.9ab	3.6ab	4.0a	3.6a
With S/A[2]	3.9b	4.0a	3.7a	4.0a	3.7a
With S/A[3]	3.4c	3.3b	3.1b	3.1b	3.3a

*Mean value for 30 panelists; **Means in the same column with the same letter are not significantly different at 0.05 (DMRT).

fermenting carbohydrates. These microorganisms were not pathogenic and did not produce gas. Results of the standard plate count showed minimal growth, and the colony count was less than 30 per plate. Additionally, the results of the confirmed test (i.e., EMB agar slants) did not exhibit characteristics of *Escherichia coli* or other coliform organisms.

Hydrogen Ion Concentration

The pH of the control (commercially prepared peach yogurt) was 3.92 whereas the experimental yogurt bases (batch #1 and batch #2) had pH values of 6.36 and 5.54, respectively, before the sweetpotato purees were added. The pH of sweetpotato purees used were: S/A[1], sweetpotato puree with apricots and lemon juice, 4.41; S/A[2], sweetpotato puree with apricots, 4.93; and S/A[3], sweetpotato puree with papaya, 5.33. When these purees were combined with the yogurt base, the pH of the resulting sweetpotato yogurts decreased to 4.32, 4.54 and 4.57, respectively. This was not unexpected since lemon juice was added to S/A[1] and pineapple chunks were added to S/A[3].

Taste Panel

More than 60% of the panelists (N= 30) scored the experimental sweetpotato yogurts with apricots good to excellent for appearance and 46.6% of the panelists gave the same score to the sweetpotato yogurt with papaya. The control was rated highest for taste by 80% of the panelists.

A statistical comparison of sensory ratings of the sweetpotato and control yogurts was performed (Table 1). All of the sweetpotato yogurts scored just as high as the control yogurt in appearance. Sweetpotato yogurts with apricots (with [S/A[1]] and without [S/A[2]] lemon juice) were rated by the panelists as just as good as the control for appearance, taste, texture and sweetness. The sweetpotato yogurt containing the apricot puree (S/A[2]) was rated better than that containing papaya and pineapple chunks (S/A[3]). All the products were rated the same for sweetness. Some improvement would be necessary in the sweetpotato yogurts if they were to match the control in flavor.

IMPLICATIONS

This research has implications for incorporation of sweetpotato into traditional or ethnic foods. Yogurts produced with sweetpotato purees represent an attractive commercial possibility. Further tests need to be conducted to develop yogurts with the greatest market potential. The use of sweetpotatoes with a bland flavor could lend additional variety to new yogurt products.

ACKNOWLEDGEMENT

The authors express gratitude to Dr. Nathaniel Brown, Jr. for help in reviewing this manuscript and the Fort Valley State College Agricultural Research Station. The authors are also grateful for funding from USDA/CSRS, Project No. 4201.

REFERENCES

APHA. 1985. Standard methods for the examination of dairy products. New York.

Bouwkamp, J.C. (ed). 1985. Sweet potato products: A natural resource for the tropics. CRC Press, Inc., Boca Raton. 271 pp.

Gerber, J. 1989. How the aging will create new food trends. Food Technology 43(4):134-135, 150.

German, G.A., and E.W. McLaughlin. 1985. Supermarketing success. American Demographics (August): 34.

Graham, Horace D. 1980. The safety of foods. AVI Publishing Co., Westport, CT, pp. 17-18.

Jaynes, H.O., and D.T. Corley. 1981. Sweet potato turnovers. Tennessee Farm Home Science 120:11.

Lanham, B.T. 1950. Consumer reaction to Alayam candy. Alabama Agriculture Experiment Station Bulletin 271.

Marshall, W.W., and M.J. Danner. 1959. Consumer reaction to Presto-Pi. Alabama Agriculture Experiment Station Circular 134.

Meilgard, M., G.V. Civille, and B.T. Carr. 1987. Sensory evaluation techniques, Volume II. CRC Press, Inc., Boca Raton. 159 pp.

Riechert, B. 1989. The tuber whose time has come. UT Agriculture (Spring): 16.

Rohde, P.A. 1969. BBL manual of products and laboratory procedures, 5th ed. Becton and Dickinson Company, Cockeysville, MD.

Sills-Levy, E. 1986. U. S. food trends leading to the year 2000. Food Technology 43(4):128-132.

Van de Mark, M.S., and L.M. Ware. 1947. Candies from sweet potatoes. Sweet Potato Journal 3.

Ware, L.M. 1947. Nuggets, curls, waves, shreds: How you'll have your potatoes for breakfast this morning? Sweet Potato Journal 3.

Sweetpotato Technology for the 21st Century. W.A. Hill, C.K. Bonsi and P.A. Loretan (Eds.) 1992. Tuskegee University, Tuskegee, AL

Wayne J. McLaurin, Stanley J. Kays

Genetic Diversity in Sweetpotato Flavor

The sweetpotato, unlike most staple crops, has a very distinct and dominant flavor. In typical breeding programs, however, flavor is generally one of the last traits selected; thus the diversity of flavors present is often quite narrow. Based on increased interest in alternate sweetpotato flavor types, a polycross nursery was established to assess the level of diversity in the genepool. Approximately 600 clones were baked and submitted to taste panel analysis. A tremendous diversity and range of flavors was found within the sweetpotato germplasm tested. Eighty-nine clones representing a broad range in sweetness, flavor, aromatic properties, texture and color were selected for advanced trials. Distinct flavors detected were acidic, bland, baked potato, boiled potato, carrot, chalky, chemical, citrus, earthy, *Ipomoea*/terpene (described as a distinctive terpene odor that appeared to be expressed frequently in *Ipomoea batatas*), lemon, musty, pumpkin, salty, squash (winter type), starchy, sweet, sweetpotato (traditional), terpene, and turnip. Aromatic properties were likewise extremely diverse. Odors detected were baked and boiled potato, buttery, carrot, chalky, chemical, citrus, cooked corn, furfural, grassy/hay, *Ipomoea*/terpene, musty, pumpkin, squash, sweetpotato, and a number of distinct off-odors. Sweetness ranged from very sweet (i.e., significantly greater than conventional cultivars) to non-sweet. Textures varied from very dry to very moist. Of the lines tested, 46.6% were classed as dry, while 44.9% were classed as moist. Fiber content also varied widely, with 39.7% of the lines exhibiting some fiber. The results indicate that the genetic diversity for flavor present in sweetpotato germplasm will allow making substantial changes in the flavor of new cultivars, thus potentially opening previously unexploited or under-exploited markets.

INTRODUCTION

The acceptability of a food is a combination of its flavor, visual appeal, and texture. Flavor is considered to be the overall sensation caused by the impact of food on the chemical receptors in the nose and mouth. It can be divided into two components, taste and odor. Taste, perceived in the mouth by the taste buds, is thought to be made up of four primary sensations: sweet, sour, salt, and bitter. Odor, in contrast, is detected by the olfactory epithelium in the nose (Moncrieff 1967). The human olfactory system can detect up to 10,000 distinct odors. Furthermore, humans have thousands of taste receptors as compared to millions of odor receptors.

Department of Horticulture, University of Georgia, Athens, Georgia 30602.

Therefore, odor represents a critical part of the overall flavor perceived and, due to the vast number of odors possible, provides a virtually unlimited diversity to flavor.

Foods can be categorized into four general groups based on their characteristic flavor volatiles (Nursten 1978): (1) those whose aroma is composed primarily of one character impact compound; (2) those whose aroma is due to a mixture of a small number of compounds, of which one may be a character impact compound; (3) those whose aroma is due to a large number of compounds and with a careful combination of these components the odor can be reproduced; (4) those whose aroma is made up of an unreproduceable complex mixture of compounds. The volatiles emanating from cooked sweetpotatoes represent a diverse array of compounds, including hydrocarbons, acids, alcohols, aldehydes, esters, furans, ketones, and nitrogen-containing compounds (Kays 1988). While the character impact compound has not been ascertained for the sweetpotato, cooked sweetpotatoes are known to give off a number of compounds. For example, from the cultivar 'Morado' the following compounds have been identified: pentene-2, acetone, 2,3-butanedione, hexane, pentane-2-one, methylbenzene, 2-pentanol, methylacetate, dimethylbenzene, pyridine, 2-phenyl-2-methylbutane, furfural, 2-acetylfuran, benzaldehyde, 2-propenylfuran, 2-methyl-6-ethylpyridine, α-terpineol, heptylbenzene (isomer), hexadecanol, heptadecanol, 1-isopropyl-4-isopropenyl benzene, tetradecanol, a monoterpene, and 4-sesquiterpenes (Kays and Horvat 1984). Unlike the volatiles of other cooked products, no pyrazines were detected in sweetpotato volatiles (Purcell et al. 1980). According to Constantin et al. (1966), there may be differences in yet unidentified aroma precursors which, once identified, may enhance selection of sweetpotato cultivars with consistently good flavor.

Flavor has a direct impact on food use. For example, food staples with low intensity flavor are thought to be more acceptable in that they can be prepared in more varied ways than staples with strong flavors (Kays 1988). Such staples are more readily adaptable to an indigenous cuisine and, as a consequence, may be more readily introduced into regions where they have not been used before. To bland staples can be added characteristic combinations of flavors called "flavor principles" (Rozin 1973, 1977). Low flavor products such as rice, wheat, cassava, and white potatoes typically act as flavor carriers to which flavor is added (Kays 1988).

It has been proposed that the very dominant flavor of the sweetpotato limits its popularity and has been one of the factors responsible for the progressive decline in the consumption of sweetpotato worldwide (Kays 1985). A survey characterizing the utilization of sweetpotatoes by consumers has indicated high acceptance (82.8%) but low use frequency (10.4%)(Law 1977), suggesting that even where a food is culturally accepted, factors such as flavor can limit its utilization. The principal taste of most sweetpotato cultivars is sweetness, which is the result of various combinations of maltose and sucrose, as well as smaller amounts of glucose and fructose (Kays 1988). When the sweetpotato is cooked, sweetness increases substantially due to the disaccharide maltose, formed *via* starch hydrolysis. Sugar content, contrary to general opinion, may actually decrease the appeal of a staple crop by intensifying flavor. Villareal (1982) describes the sugar content of most staple crops as low, e.g., rice less than 1%, wheat and white potato approximately 2%, as compared to sweetpotato with 8-40% sugar. If other traits are equal, a low-sugar sweetpotato has a much lower intensity flavor than does its high-sugar counterpart.

Low-sugar cultivars have the potential to increase the acceptability of sweetpotatoes as a staple crop for human consumption. Therefore, there may be a potential market for a low-flavor sweetpotato that could be introduced as a second, complementary type. Breeding for such a sweetpotato is already underway and several cultivars that do not sweeten during cooking are available (Dukes et al. 1987; Hashimoto 1988). These early successes, however, underscore the need for a better understanding of the operative mechanism(s) giving low starch conversion during the cooking of the non-sweet selections (Kays 1985). A greater understanding will enhance the development of new cultivars with maximum phenotypic stability for low sugar.

Breeding is important to improving acceptance and utilization of sweetpotatoes (Martin and Jones 1986); however, it is complicated by the fact that the flavor and preference for existing cultivars is known to vary widely (Lin et al. 1983). In the southeastern United States, preferred quality includes intense orange color, moist texture, and a very sweet taste (Anon. 1980). In other areas of the world, many people dislike the flavor of deep orange sweetpotatoes, describing it as strong, oily, or carrot-like. However, the flavor associated with intense orange color in sweetpotato is of considerable importance in the United States. The occurrence of orange pigmentation does not in itself appear to contribute appreciably to the flavor, though certain flavor compounds may be produced as a result of the increased flow of carbon through the terpene synthesis pathway. Many people in tropical regions who use sweetpotato as a staple prefer a dryer mouthfeel and less sweet flavor. White or yellow-flesh types, known as *boniatos* in Cuba, are likely to be consumed daily in some areas of the Caribbean (Rodriquez-Nodales 1970; Baynes 1972). In Puerto Rico, for example, people show a preference for one of two types: the orange, moist, sweet type, or the white or yellow, dry, low-sweet or bland type (Martin and Rodriguez-Sosa 1985). In Puerto Rico, a good flavor is likely to be described as "rico" or rich. In other areas, desirable flavor characteristics may include blandness and the absence of bitterness or "off" flavors. In West Africa, the preferred flavor is yam-like and is similar to that of *Dioscorea*, the true yams (IITA 1981). In staple foods, little or no sweetness is considered desirable (Villareal 1982), but this is a relatively uncommon trait in indigenous sweetpotato clones. Individual quality characteristics, therefore, need to be defined for each region according to local preferences (Martin 1983).

The development of new flavor types for commercial use requires considerable flavor diversity within the gene pool; however, the extent of the flavor diversity present within sweetpotato germplasm has not been explored. As many tropical root and tuber crops have an almost universal phenotype, breeding in the past has concentrated on "all-purpose" lines. Greater specialization of phenotype based on intended product use is becoming more common in breeding programs today, e.g., roots for alcohol production, high quality french fries, and baking. In addition to selecting for flavor and specialized uses, breeding programs select for disease resistance, root color and size, and a number of agronomic traits. The usual method of selection leaves only about 1% of the seedling lines initially grown by the end of the first year, necessitating a large initial number of progeny (Jones et al. 1976; MacKay, 1987; Kays 1988). In breeding programs, most selection is for agronomic traits rather than flavor, though flavor is considered a top priority (Martin and Jones 1986).

Breeding goals should be based on knowledge of the potential of the crop, as well as immediate needs. In the case of sweetpotato, a breeding program should not be initiated until a survey has been conducted to determine the uses of the crop in an area, preferred flavor types, environmental and cultural constraints, pests, and diseases. A survey of 26 countries and territories by Lin et al. (1983) identified the major uses of sweetpotatoes that would influence breeding goals. In Asia and the Pacific, the characteristics that require improvement by breeding are eating quality (flavor and other attributes) and nutritional components.

Flavor preference is highly subjective, varying widely between individuals. Therefore, the preferred flavor could involve blandness, richness, sweetness or any other characteristic. Flavor analysis is needed: (1) to determine what the preferred flavor is for a particular target population of consumers; and (2) to screen advanced lines for that preferred flavor in the breeding program. Edmond and Ammerman (1971) recommend including individuals on panels for flavor assessment who have a vital interest in sweetpotatoes, such as sweetpotato researchers, extension specialists, and shippers. This insures continuation of the existing flavor type, the assumption being that it is what the general population wants. However, when alternative or new flavor types are sought, it is doubtful that such a panel will be able to function adequately.

An analytical measure of flavor (aroma and taste) has been proposed as a basis for flavor selection in breeding programs (Kays 1983). This involves: (1) identifying the critical flavor compounds; (2) ascertaining their optimum concentration; and (3) developing a rapid but accurate assay for quantifying these compounds. Use of an analytical approach to selection for flavor traits would allow selecting for a number of different preferences simultaneously (Kays 1988), thus maximizing the effectiveness and international impact of a breeding program. This paper represents an initial assessment of the flavor diversity of the sweetpotato.

MATERIALS AND METHODS

Six lines and two cultivars 'HiDry' (Hamilton et al. 1985) and 'Sumor' (Dukes et al. 1987) exhibiting a range in flavor, sweetness levels, and dry matter were selected for a polycross nursery. The parent lines were grafted on *Ipomoea carnea*, Jacq. ssp. *fistulosa* (Mart. ex. Choisy) D. Austin, cultivar 'Inducer' and grown at the Attapulgus Extension Research Center, Attapulgus, GA in 1989. Seeds were harvested when dry and stored.

Seeds were placed in concentrated sulfuric acid for 30 min (agitated every 10 min). After removal, the seeds were rinsed in distilled water and then covered with an aqueous sodium bicarbonate solution to neutralize the remaining acid. After rinsing, the seeds were germinated in a flat of soilless mix under a mist system in the greenhouse. When the second true leaves were formed, the plants were transferred to 5 inch pots. Cuttings were taken from these plants and grown at the University of Georgia Horticulture Farm (1990) using standard sweetpotato production practices (Granberry et al. 1990). At harvest, the storage roots from each line were placed in individual plastic mesh bags, cured for 7 days (29°C, 90% RH), and stored at 15.5°C (85% RH).

After one month of storage, an individual root of each line was selected for evaluation. The root was washed, cut cross-sectionally in 2 pieces of equal size and the distal end wrapped in aluminum foil and baked at 20°C for 75 min. After removal from the oven, the roots (25 per session) were placed on a laboratory bench and allowed to cool for 5 min. The foil was sequentially removed from each root and the root immediately sliced lengthwise and evaluated for aromatic properties. After all 25 roots had been evaluated in this manner, they were then evaluated for sweetness (level), flavor (description and intensity), flesh color (color, uniformity, and distribution), flesh optical properties (opaque vs translucent), and fiber content. In contrast to a conventional breeding program where approximately 99% of the progeny are discarded before any quality attributes are assessed, all of the lines were screened for the preceding quality attributes. Lines were selected to be saved based on the uniqueness of their flavor rather than desirability since the objective was to obtain an estimate of the diversity of the flavor in the sweetpotato genepool.

RESULTS AND DISCUSSION

A tremendous diversity and range of flavors was found within the sweetpotato germplasm tested. Inasmuch as the sweetpotato by name is expected to taste sweet, it was of considerable interest to find that sweetness ranged from very sweet (<1%), sweet (13.4%), non-sweet/slightly sweet (68.8%) to non-sweet (16.9%). It is doubtful, however, that this distribution would be typical of most breeding programs since the parent lines selection process was biased in favor of non-sweetness. It was evident, though, that the lack of sweetness is a trait that can be readily transferred to subsequent generations.

A number of unique flavors were found among the lines tested. Out of the eight parents (two cultivars and six lines) there were 20 distinct flavors detected. There were varying degrees of expression of these traits in the seedling population, as well as mixtures of flavors. Distinct flavors detected were acidic, bland, baked potato, boiled potato, carrot, chalky, chemical, citrus, earthy, *Ipomoea*/terpene (described as a distinctive terpene odor that appeared to be expressed frequently in *Ipomoea batatas*), lemon, musty, pumpkin, salty, squash (winter type), starchy, sweet, sweetpotato (traditional), terpene, and turnip. The *Ipomoea*/terpene flavor occurred in approximately 13% of the population. The trait did not appear to be consistently tied to any particular flavor, since it was found in sweet lines as well as those with tart or acidic tastes, indicating that it possibly represents compounds that are expressed independently. Sweetness was associated with 29.3% of the lines tested and was the most common flavor trait detected within the seedling population. This attribute was found across virtually all types of other minor flavors and odors.

The standard North American sweetpotato flavor (typical of the moist-type/orange-fleshed sweetpotato) occurred in 17.7% of the lines sampled. It was the second most pronounced flavor after sweetness. The caramel/cooked sugar flavor was grouped in with the sweetpotato flavor, although in the white fleshed lines, the odor appeared to be less intense. When the sweet flavor and sweetpotato flavors are grouped together, they account for 47% of the population.

Many of the descriptors for flavor were also used to characterize the odor of the cooked roots. The most common was the *Ipomoea*/terpene odor. The second most common was the sweetpotato/cooked caramel odor (typical of North American orange-fleshed sweetpotatoes). Within a particular odor type, there were varying degrees of intensity, ranging from very slight to extremely strong. The more common odors tended to cross over all of the flavor categories; an exception would be the characteristic North American sweetpotato odor which tended to be associated with sweetness. Other odors detected were baked and boiled potato, buttery, carrot, chalky, chemical, citrus, cooked corn, furfural, grassy/hay, musty, squash, and pumpkin and a number of distinct off-odors.

The optical properties described consisted of degrees of opaqueness or translucence of the cooked root tissue. Translucent tissue resembled the water soaked appearance commonly seen with fleshy tissue that has been frozen and then thawed (Kays 1991). Of all of the lines tested, only one was found to be highly translucent. The majority were either predominately translucent (28.9%) or opaque (31.5%). A large number of the lines displayed a mixture of opaque and translucent areas which gave an undesirable visual appearance. Mixtures were found as spots or streaks of translucence in the opaque roots and opaque spots and streaks within the translucent roots. The spots occurred in patterns around the outside of the roots and also at random within the roots. Differences in optical properties may be related to the moisture content, water holding potential of the cellular constituents (e.g., starch), or the degree of degradation of the cell wall and membranes upon cooking. The degree of cell breakdown upon cooking is known to vary with cultivar (Sterling and Aldridge 1977).

Fiber was detectable in 39.7% of the lines tested. It was not detected in the majority of the roots; however, the roots were sampled in a manner that may not have been conducive to precise fiber detection (i.e., the analysis was subjective). The physical characteristics and amount of the fibers varied. Some lines exhibited very short fibers while others had long fibrous strands.

The texture of the flesh ranged from very moist to very dry. Of the lines tested, 46.6% were classed as dry while 44.9% were rated as moist. The remaining lines were very dry (6.9%) while 1.2% were classed as very moist. Other descriptors used were pasty, slick, and soupy. The high frequency of dry-fleshed lines was most probably a function of the number of high dry matter parent lines used. For example, 'HiDry' has a dry matter content of over 40% (Hamilton et al. 1985).

It was evident from this initial survey that there is tremendous genetic diversity for flavor and other quality traits present in the sweetpotato genepool. The selection protocol utilized in conventional breeding programs is not conducive to seeing this diversity. In addition, most unique flavor lines that make it through to the quality assessment stage of selection are readily discarded in conventional programs. The tremendous genetic diversity in flavor present in the germplasm poses the question: If additional flavor types are to be selected, what flavors are the best? Determining the best flavor for a staple product has a number of difficulties. For example, it was found that, when testing the flavor of a non-sweet line with traditional sweetpotatoes and using a taste panel that knew they were tasting sweetpotatoes and were familiar with the flavor of traditional North American sweetpotatoes, the non-sweet line was always ranked very low (Lyon et al. 1985). Thus a different testing protocol is required for testing low consumption volume products vs high consumption volume products (staple type sweetpotatoes). Also, there are a variety of different ways in which the roots could be prepared for testing consumer preference, e.g., in traditional dishes or simply cooked and served unaltered with other ingredients.

It is evident that the genetic potential is present in the germplasm that will allow making substantial changes in the flavor of sweetpotatoes, thus potentially opening the door to previously unexploited or under-exploited markets. Determining the appropriate flavor types to select may pose a more difficult problem than the actual selection of the lines.

LITERATURE CITED ·

Anon. 1980. Sweet potato quality. Southern Cooperative Series Bull. 249, Russell Research Center, Athens, Georgia. 51 pp.

Baynes, R.A. 1972. Sweet potato varieties in the Eastern Caribbean. Caribb. Agr. 3:20-21.

Constantin, R.J., T.P. Hernandez, J.C. Miller, and H.L. Hammett. 1966. Inheritance of baking quality in the sweet potato, *Ipomoea Batatas*. Proc. Amer. Soc. Hort. Sci. 88:498-500.

Dukes, P.D., M.G. Hamilton, A. Jones and J.M. Schalk. 1987. 'Sumor', a multi-use sweet potato. HortScience 22:170-171.

Dukes, P.D., A. Jones, and J.M. Schalk. 1990. 'Inducer', a tree morning glory rootstock cultivar for use in breeding sweetpotatoes. HortScience 25:238-239.

Edmond, J. B., and C.R. Ammerman. 1971. Sweet potatoes: Production, processing, marketing. AVI Publishing Company, Inc., Westport, Connecticut, USA. 334 pp.

Granberry, D.M., Wayne J. McLaurin, and W.O. Chance. 1990. Sweetpotato, commercial vegetable production. Univ. of GA Coop. Ext. Ser., Athens, Georgia. Bull. 677, 8 pp.

Hamilton, M.G., P.D. Dukes, A. Jones, and J.M. Schalk. 1985. 'HiDry' sweet potato. HortScience 20:954-955.

Hashimoto, K. 1988. New summer crop cultivars registered by the Ministry of Agriculture, Forestry, and Fisheries in 1987: (1) paddy rice, sweet potato, potato and soybean. Jpn. J. Breeding 38:108-116.

IITA. 1981. Annual Report for 1980. International Institute of Tropical Agriculture, Ibadan, Nigeria.

Jones, A., P.D. Dukes, and F.P. Cuthbert, Jr. 1976. Mass selection in sweet potatoes; breeding for resistance to insects and diseases and for horticultural characteristics. J. Amer. Soc.

Hort. Sci. 101:701-704.

Kays, S.J. 1985. Formulated sweet potato products. Pages 205-218 *in* Sweet potato products: A natural resource for the tropics, edited by J.C. Bouwkamp. CRC Press, Boca Raton, FL.

Kays, S.J. 1988. Strategies for selecting conventional and new flavor types of tropical root and tuber crops to increase consumer acceptance and use. Pages 178-188 *in* Eighth Symposium, International Society of Tropical Root Crops, edited by R.H. Howeler. Bangkok, Thailand.

Kays, S.J. 1991. Postharvest physiology of perishable plant products. Van Nostrand Reinholt, N.Y. 532 pp.

Kays, S.J., and R.J. Horvat. 1983. Insect resistance and flavor chemistry: Integration into future breeding programs. In: Breeding New Sweet Potatoes for the Tropics, edited by F.W. Martin. Amer. Soc. Hort. Sci. Trop. Reg. 27 (B):97-106.

Kays, S.J., and R.J. Horvat. 1984. A comparison of the volatile constituents and sugars of representative Asian, Central American and North American sweet potatoes. Pages 577-586 *in* Proceedings, 6th Symposium, International Society of Tropical Root Crops, International Potato Center, Lima, Peru.

Law, J.M. 1977. Factors affecting the purchase and use of sweet potatoes. Louisiana St. Univ. Agric. Expt. Sta. Bul. 706, 36 pp.

Lin, S.S.M., C.R. Peet, D.M. Chen, and J.F. Lo. 1983. Breeding goals for sweet potato in Asia and the Pacific—a survey of sweet potato production and utilization. Pages 42-60 *in* Breeding new sweet potatoes for the tropics, edited by F.W. Martin, Proc. Am. Soc. Hort Sci., Tropical Region.

Lyon, B.G., R.J. Horvat, and S.J. Kays. 1985. Sensory responses to five cultivars of sweet potatoes. HortScience 20:1107-1108.

MacKay, G.R. 1987. Selecting and breeding for better potato cultivars. Pages 181-196 *in* Improving vegetatively propagated crops, edited by A.J. Abbott and R.K. Atkin. Academic Press, NY.

Martin, F.W. 1983. Goals in Breeding the Sweet Potato for the Caribbean and Latin America. Pages 61-71 *in* Breeding new sweet potatoes for the tropics, edited by F.W. Martin Proceedings, Amer. Soc. Hort. Sci. Tropical Region.

Martin, F.W., and A. Jones. 1986. Breeding sweet potatoes. Plant Breed Rev. 4:313-345.

Martin, F.W., and E.J. Rodriguez-Sosa. 1985. Preference for color, sweetness and mouthfeel of sweet potato in Puerto Rico. J. Agr. Univ. Puerto Rico 69:99-106.

Moncrieff, R.W. 1967. Introduction to symposium. Pages 3-22 *in* Symposium on foods: The chemistry and physiology of flavors, edited by H. W. Schultz, E.A. Day and L.M. Libbey. AVI Publishing Company, Inc., Westport, CN.

Nursten, H.E. 1978. Why flavor research? How far have we come since 1975 and where now? Pages 337-335 *in* Progress in flavour research, edited by D.G. Land and H.E. Nursten. Proc. 2nd Weurman Flavour Res. Symp., Applied Science Pub., London.

Purcell, A.E., D.W. Later, and M.J. Lee. 1980. Analysis of the volatile constituents of baked 'Jewel' sweet potatoes. J. Agri. Food Chem. 28:939-941.

Rodriguez-Nodales, A. 1970. Estudio comparative de variedades selectas de boniato, *Ipomoea batatas* (L.) Lam. en diversas condiciones edaficas y ambientales. Bol. de Divulgacion Equipo Tecnico Agricola, Ano 3, No. 20. La Habana, Cuba.

Rozin, R. 1973. The Flavor Principle Cookbook, Hawthorn, NY. 277 pp.

Rozin, P. 1977. The use of characteristic flavorings in human culinary practice. Pages 101-127 *in* Flavor: Its chemical, behavioral and commercial aspects, edited by C.M. Apt. Proc. A. D. Little Flavor Symp., Westview Press, Boulder, CO.

Sterling, C., and M.L. Aldridge. 1977. Mealiness and sogginess in sweet potato. Food Chem. 2:71-76.

Villareal, R. L. 1982. Sweet potato in the tropics-progress and problems. Pages 1-15 *in* Sweet potato, edited by R.L. Villareal and T.D. Griggs. Proceedings, 1st International Symposium, AVRDC75, Shanhua, Taiwan.

Tomonori Nagahama, Toshihiko Suganuma, Kotaro Matsukubo*

Chemical and Physical Properties of Sweetpotato Shochu Distillatory Slops and Treatment of Them

In Southern Kyushu, most sweetpotatoes produced are used for manufacturing starch (107,000 t) and "shochu" (62,000 kL), a special liquor characterized by its distinct taste. The shochu distillatory slops, which are drained away after distillation of the fermented mash, contain about 3.5% suspended solids. Most of this suspended material consists of cellular residue from sweetpotato and must be removed before the slop can be disposed of. Common chemical or physical treatments do not precipitate them. However, treatments with cellulolytic enzymes, especially those with avicelase activity, caused them to precipitate. Thus, water held inside seems to become movable through the thinned cell walls.

In Southern Kyushu, sweetpotato is an important root crop because it is resistant to frequent typhoons and intense droughts, and it grows well on the volcanic soils characteristic of this area. Sweetpotato production in this area amounts to 630,000 t, half of the production in Japan. Differing from other areas, most of the sweetpotato, 370,000 t and 65,000 t, respectively, are used for manufacturing starch (107,000 t) and "shochu" (62,000 kL).

Shochu is a local liquor distilled by a pot still. In the brewing process, starchy materials are saccharified with "Koji," which provides enzymatic sources produced by spreading *Aspergillus kawachii* on ordinarily cooked rice. Alcohol fermentation proceeds in the presence of citric acid produced by the fungus. Commonly, such starchy materials as barley, sweetpotato, buckwheat, or rice are used for shochu distilling, and the total production of shochu amounts to 200,000 kL a year, corresponding to about 24% of all distilled liquors in Japan (Yano 1990).

Sweetpotato shochu is produced in Southern Kyushu, especially in Kagoshima, and is one of the most important sweetpotato products in this area. However, sweetpotato shochu distillatory slops are too pulpy for recycling or discarding, in contrast to other shochu slops. In this study, chemical and physical properties of sweetpotato shochu distillatory slops were investigated so as to consider how to recycle or dispose of them. Proposed steps for treatment of the slops are also reviewed.

MATERIALS AND METHODS

Shochu distillatory slops

The distillatory slops were taken in heat-resistant plastic containers (20-liter)

Faculty of Agriculture, Kagoshima University, Kagoshima 890, and &*Kagoshima Prefectural Institute of Industrial Technology, Kagoshima 899-1, Japan.

and stored at 5°C just after draining away from the still pots in five shochu distilleries in Kagoshima. Most of the work was performed on the slops from one distiller, Komasa Jozo Co.

Enzyme preparations

Pectinases: Abbreviation, APG is "Pectinase G" from *Asp. pulverulentus* by Amano Pharmaceutical Co., Ltd.; RMZ, "Macerozyme R-10" from *Rhizopus* spp. by Yakult Biochemical Co., Ltd.

Cellulases: ANA is "Cellulase A" from *Asp. niger* by Amano Pharmaceutical Co., Ltd.; ANC, "Cellulosin AC-15" from *Asp. niger* by Ueda Kagaku Kogyo Co., Ltd.; TVO, "Cellulase Onozuka R-10" from *Trichoderma viride* by Yakult Biochemical Co., Ltd.; TVM, "Meiji cellulase TP60" from *T. viride* by Meiji Seika Kaisha Ltd.; TVT, "Cellulase T" from *T. viride* by Amano Pharmaceutical Co., Ltd.

Spectrophotometric determination of sugars and glycerol

For determining reducing sugars, Somogyi-Nelson's method was used. Total sugars were determined directly by the phenol-sulfuric acid H_2SO_4 method without hydrolysis or by Somogyi-Nelson's method after hydrolysis with 2M TFA at 100°C for 5 hr. Uronic acids were determined by Galambos' method (Galambos 1967). Glycerol was determined by "F-kit Glycerol" (Boehringer Mannheim Yamanouchi K.K.) which contains the enzyme system of glycerokinase, pyruvate kinase and lactate dehydrogenase.

Determination of nitrogenous components

Nitrogen content was determined by the Kjeldahl method, and protein content by Lowry's method.

Chemical analysis of cellular residues

Southgate's method (Southgate 1969) was partly modified: most of the procedure was done in a centrifuge tube (50-mL) without transferring the sample to other vessels, and Termamyl 120L (NOVO INDUSTRI A/S) instead of Takadiastase was used to hydrolyze residual starch just after gelatinization of starch by boiling.

Estimation of separability of insoluble residues

The volume of supernatant from 40 mL of slop was measured after centrifugation at 1500 rpm for 5 min. The filtration rate was followed by measuring the time required for 50 mL of slops to pass through a folded filter (Toyo No.2, 11 cm) set on a funnel (7 cm). Separability was represented by mL per 100 mL.

Chromatography

The following chromatographic analyses were performed to determine and identify organic acids, polyols and saccharides.

Thin layer chromatography (TLC): Carbohydrates were run on Silica gel 60 TLC Plates (Merck & Co., Ltd.) with (A) a mixture of EtOAc:iso-PrOH:0.05M sodium acetate (65:25:10) or (B) EtOAc:AcOH:H_2O (10:5:6), and revealed with 25% H_2SO_4 or 0.2% $KMnO_4$ in 1N NaOH. Data were represented by R_{Glc} or Rf.

High performance liquid chromatography (HPLC): Saccharides and polyols were analyzed by use of Nihon Bunko BIP-1 equipped with a system of an RI detector and a column of Shodex KS 801 (8 x 300mm, Showa Denko K.K.). The mobile phase was water, at 60 or 70°C. Organic acids were monitored at 211 nm by use of a column of Shodex S-801. The mobile phase was 0.1% H_3PO_4 at room temperature. Retention time was represented by RT_{PrOH} or RT.

Carbon column chromatography: The sample was applied on a column of active carbon (17 x 930mm)(Wako Pure Chemical Industries Ltd.) and was eluted with H_2O and then with a gradient system of H_2O-10%EtOH. Each tube of the eluates was analyzed for carbohydrates by the phenol-H_2SO_4 method and by TLC.

Gradient chromatography on a column of DEAE Cellulofine AL (18 x 130mm)(Seikagaku Co.) with 0.1M acetate buffer (pH 5.0) and 1M NaCl was used for analyzing distribution of neutral and acidic saccharides. Chromatography on Sephadex G25 (19 x 450mm)(Pharmacia Fine Chemicals) with 0.1M acetate buffer (pH 5.0) was used for analyzing distribution of mono-, oligo- and poly-saccharides.

Enzyme activities

Assay for cellulolytic activities was done essentially according to Okada et al. (1968), and all assays except for polygalacturonase were carried out at pH 4.0 at 40°C.

Filter paper disintegrating activity: Two pieces (Toyo No. 2, 2 x 2 cm) of filter paper suspended in an enzyme solution (0.1M acetate buffer) were shaken in an L-shaped tube, and the time needed to complete disintegration of the filter paper was measured. The activity was represented by a reciprocal of hour per mL of 1.0% solution of the enzyme.

Avicel or carboxymethylcellulose(CMC) saccharifying activities: A suspension of 0.5% Avicel SF (Funakoshi Co.) or CMC (Taiyo Kako K.K.) in 0.1M acetate buffer solution containing 0.05% enzyme was shaken in an L-shaped tube. After 10 min or 100 min incubation, the reducing sugar produced per min per mL of the solution was determined by Somogyi-Nelson's method.

Salicinase: A mixture of 0.5% salicine (Nacalai Tesque Inc.) and enzyme was incubated and determined as above. Polygalacturonase: A mixture of 0.02% pectic acid (Nacalai Tesque Inc.) and enzyme in 0.005M citrate buffer solution was incubated at 30°C for 30 min and galacturonic acid formed was determined by Galambos' (1962) method. The enzyme activity was represented as above.

430

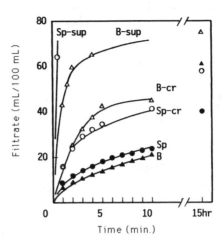

Figure 1. Filtration rate of shochu distillatory slops. The insoluble part of shochu distillatory slops was separated and washed out on a sieve (200 mesh) and suspended in 0.6% citric acid solution. Filtration rate was determined by measuring filtrates through filter paper (Toyo No. 2, 11 cm). SP = sweetpotato shochu distillatory slops; B = barley shochu distillatory slops; sup= supernatant of slops; cr = cellular residues.

EXPERIMENTAL RESULTS

Separability of the insoluble matter from the slops

In contrast to barley shochu distillatory slops, sweetpotato shochu distillatory slops are kept in a stable pulpy suspension for a long time, and it is harder to separate the water from the suspension. To elucidate the cause of difficult separability of the sweetpotato slops, they were centrifuged, the pellet was resuspended in 0.6% citric acid solution, and their filtration rates were estimated. As shown in Figure 1, the filtration rate of the artificial slops from barley shochu was faster than that of the whole slops in the early fermentation stage, and those of the whole and artificial slops from barley shochu were faster than those of both the slops from sweetpotato shochu in the later stages. On the other hand, the supernatant of the sweetpotato slops passed through a filter paper faster than that of the barley slops. This fact suggests that, for sweetpotato slops, suspended material is responsible for its poor separability.

Compositions of insoluble and soluble parts

The insoluble part of the slops was fractionated by sieving, and the cellular residues were washed with water on a screen. The fine residues passing through a 200-mesh screen, mainly cells of yeast, were collected by centrifugation.

As shown in Table 1, the suspended matter in the barley slops consisted of a coarse mass which is readily separated, and the supernatant was found to contain twice as much dry matter as the sweetpotato slops. Carbohydrates in the supernatant were found by Sephadex and DEAE column chromatography to be mostly neutral polysaccharides and sugars. On the other hand, the suspended residue from sweetpotato slops, identified under a microscope, was found to be sweetpotato cells with their cell walls remaining intact.

Table 1. Composition of insoluble parts in shochu distillatory slops.

Sieving	Sweetpotato Shochu			Barley Shochu		
	Appearance	Yield, %		Appearance	Yield, %	
		fresh	dry		fresh	dry
> 16 mesh	Peel, fibers	3.6	0.33	Husk	10.2	1.45
> 60	Cellular residues	32.9	1.51	Bran	3.5	0.31
>200	Cellular residues	26.0	1.02	Tissue pieces	18.6	1.99
Centrifuge	Yeast	1.8	0.57	Yeast	2.3	0.29
Insolubles	Watery mass	64.3	3.43	Coarse mass	34.6	4.04
Supernatant	Clear, thin	(96.6)	(3.52)	Turbid, thick	(96.0)	(7.24)

The insoluble part on sieve consisted of mainly the residues coming from sweetpotato or barley and also a little of residual mycelia.

The supernatant was concentrated in vacuo and fractionated successively with addition of EtOH into three fractions: precipitates, intermediates and solutes. Each was analyzed in detail for carbohydrates. These results are shown in Table 2.

Table 2. Composition of soluble material in sweetpotato shochu distillatory slops.

Fractionation with EtOH	Chemical components in soluble part (content per whole slops, 100mL)		
Solutes	Polyols	1130 mg	
2.03 g	Glycerol	730	
	Mannitol, Erythritol, Inositol	400	
	Saccharides (DS/UA/TS)	205/68/479[3]	
	Trehalose, Glc-oligomer		
	Et β - D-Galactoside		
	Oligosaccharides		Glc, Gal, Man, GalUA[2]
	Organic acid	585	
	Citric acid	488	
	Crude protein	250	
Intermediates	Oligosacch. (DS/UA/TS)	80/220/169[3]	Glc, Gal, Man, Rham,
1.00 g			GalUA[2]
	Crude protein	34	
Precipitates	Polysacch. (DS/UA/TS)	18/203/256[3]	Glc, Gal, Man, Rham,
0.36g			GalUA[2]
	Crude protein	10	
Soluble part	Saccharides (DS/UA/TS)	324/498/920[3]	
total	Polyols	1130	
3.40 g	Organic acids	585	
	Amino acids	82	Ala, Gly, Arg, Glu, Lys[1]
	Crude protein	296	
	Ashes	520	K, P[1]

[1]: Matsukubo et al. (1991)
[2]: Oligo- and polysaccharides were hydrolyzed with 2M TFA at 100°C for 5 hr, and the constituents were analyzed by HPLC and TLC.
[3]: Reducing sugars (DS) and total sugars (TS) were determined by Somogyi-Nelson's method, and were represented as glucose. Uronic acid (UA) was determined directly by a modified Galambos (1967) method.

EtOH-solutes were concentrated and further fractionated by use of a carbon column chromatography. Larger amounts of polyols were found in those fractions eluting first. These polyols were identified to be glycerol ($RT_{PrOH}0.72$; $R_{Glc}0.68$ (B)), erythritol ($RT_{PrOH}0.67$; $R_{Glc}0.61$(B)), mannitol ($RT_{PrOH}0.61$; $R_{Glc}0.52$(B)), and m-inositol ($RT_{PrOH}0.67$; $R_{Glc}0.42$(B)) by use of HPLC and TLC. Enzymatic analysis for glycerol gave the same result. From 4-5% EtOH fractions, ethyl β-D-galactoside (RT_{PrOH},0.58; R_{Glc},1.80(A)) and trehalose (RT_{PrOH}, 0.48; R_{Glc},0.46(A)) were isolated and identified with authentic standards using HPLC and TLC.

Polyols are common by-products of yeast, and it is thought that trehalose is released from yeast during distillation and that the galactoside occurs by enzymatic transglycosylation during fermentation. M-inositol may come from sweetpotato.

Oligosaccharides eluted with higher concentrations of EtOH were hydrolyzed, and the major component was found to be glucose. Uronic acid was found as a component of the intermediates and precipitates. The major neutral sugar components of these fractions found after hydrolysis were glucose (RT_{PrOH},0.61; R_{Glc},1.00(A)) in the former and mannose (RT_{PrOH},0.65; R_{Glc},1.17(A)) in the latter. Galactose and rhamnose (RT_{PrOH},0.65,0.62; R_{Glc},0.78,2.18(A), respectively) were also detected in both fractions. These facts suggest that oligosaccharides and polysaccharides come from hemicellulose and/or pectic substances.

Citric acid (RT 21 min) was the major component of the organic acids.

General properties of slops

In order to examine the pH dependence of the filtration rate of the slops, they were adjusted to regular pH intervals, and the filtrates were measured after 5, 10, 30 and 120 min. In the first 10 min, the filtration volume of these slops from sweetpotato and from the barley showed 23.6 mL and 31.0 mL at the original pH 4.0 and 3.6, respectively. The pH values showing the fastest filtration were observed to be 3.0 (26.3 mL) for sweetpotato and 5.0 (38.2 mL) for barley. The rate decreased in the higher ranges of pH in both cases. However, the filtration volume after 120 min was about 39 mL for sweetpotato slops and 64-68 mL for barley slops.

In order to examine the temperature dependence, filtrates from the slops after 10 min were measured at 8, 20, 50 and 80°C. As to the barley slops, the filtrates amounted to 21-22 mL at 8 and 20°C and also 30 mL at 50°C, 37 mL at 80°C. On the other hand, for sweetpotato slops, the filtrates after 10 min amounted to 23 mL at 8-20°C and to 31 mL at 50-80°C, increasing no more after that.

Treatments with aluminum chloride, ferric sulfate, calcium hydroxide and carbon dioxide, chitosan, zeolite, and hydrolysis with diluted mineral acids failed to facilitate sedimentation.

Enzymatic treatments and their effect on separability

The sweetpotato slops were treated with commercial enzyme preparations at 40°C for 9 hr and the resultant supernatants measured after centrifugation. As shown

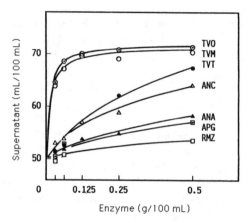

Figure 2. Effect of enzyme preparations on separability of insoluble parts from sweetpotato shochu distillatory slops. Sweetpotato shochu distillatory slops were treated with the enzyme preparations at 40°C for 9 hr and then centrifuged at 1500 rpm for 5 min. ANA, ANC, TVM, TVO, TVT: the enzyme preparations of cellulase; APG, RMZ: the enzyme preparations of pectinase. Refer to text for the enzyme preparations.

in Figure 2, such pectinases as APG and RMZ slightly increased supernatant volume; the cellulases TVO and TVM at 300-600 ppm significantly increased precipitation of the cellular residues. Moreover, a model of the slops, 2.5% suspensions of the cellular residues in 0.1% citrate buffer solution (pH 4.3), was treated with APG, RMZ ANC, and TVM in the same way. In this case too, TVM was the most effective preparation for separation of cellular residues by both centrifugation and filtration.

Activities of enzyme preparations

Among the enzyme preparations, TVM, TVO, or TVT evidently affected separability as seen in Figure 2.

To elucidate the specific action of the enzyme preparations, their enzymatic activities toward filter paper, avicel, CMC, salicine, and pectic acid were measured at pH 4.0. As shown in Table 3, such cellulases as TVM, TVO, and TVT from *Trichoderma viride* showed relatively higher activities toward avicel and filter paper, and ANA and ANC from *Aspergillus niger* relatively higher activities toward CMC. The separabilities shown in Figure 2 seem to depend on avicel saccharifying activity rather than activities toward filter paper and CMC, because RMZ, having relatively higher activity toward filter paper and both ANA and ANC having higher CMC-activity, had less effect on the separability of the cellular residues.

Change in cellular residues by enzymatic treatment

The cellular residues of the sweetpotato slops, 4.8% on a dry basis, were suspended in citrate solution (pH 4.3) and were incubated with 0.125% of TVM at 40°C.

Table 3. Activities of enzyme preparations.

Enzyme[1] & Origin	Pectinase		Cellulases				
	Asp.	Rhiz.	Asp.niger		Trich.viride		
Activities[2]	APG	RMZ	ANA	ANC	TVM	TVO	TVT
Avicel saccharifying $\times 10^2$	0.42	0.07	0.10	0.15	5.0	3.0	0.45
CMC saccharifying	0.14	0.06	0.22	0.34	0.57	0.39	0.06
Filter paper disintegrating [3]	null	2.0	<0.25	<0.25	4.3	3.0	0.77
Salicinase	0.84	0.01	0.02	0.09	0.06	0.07	0.01
Poly- galacturonase	0.12	0.17	n.d.	0.13	0.01	0.33	n.d.

[1]Commercial enzyme preparations were used. Refer to text for abbreviations.
[2]Activities were represented by reducing sugar, μmole formed by enzymic reaction/min/mL of 0.05% solution of enzyme preparation at 40°C, pH 4.0.
[3]Activity was represented by reciprocal of hour/mL of 1.0% solution of enzyme.

The reaction mixtures were analyzed for sugar composition of the supernatant and the residues at intervals of 3 h for 12 h.

Total sugars in the supernatant increased from 0 to 1.2% during the first 3 h but no more after that period. The major saccharide occurring was cellobiose (RT_{Glc}, 0.83). With time, cellobiose was gradually converted into glucose. Weight loss of the cellular residues corresponded to sugar formation in the supernatant.

Changes in weight and chemical composition of the cellular residues after 9 h are shown in Figure 3. The enzyme clearly digested the cellulose portion of the cellular residues, and most of the other portions remained intact.

DISCUSSION

There are some problems peculiar to processing of sweetpotatoes. One of them is troublesome handling of the distillatory slops. This laboratory was asked to find an effective way to precipitate the suspended material so that the residues can be recycled or discarded.

Separability of cellular residues from the distillatory slops

Sweetpotato shochu distillatory slops consist of watery residues and a thin supernatant, differing from the barley slops which consist of coarse residues and a thick supernatant (Table 1). When the supernatants of these two slops were exchanged with citrate solution, the cellular residues of the sweetpotato slops still showed little separability (Fig.1).

The outer structure of most of the sweetpotato cells remains intact (Fig. 4, left). The cells do not turn red with 0.1% ruthenium red dye solution, differing from cells of just cooked sweetpotato, but ruthenium red affects them strongly when I_2-KI

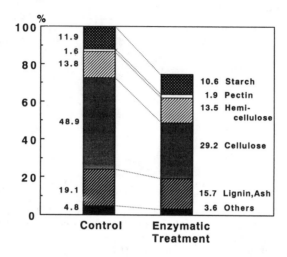

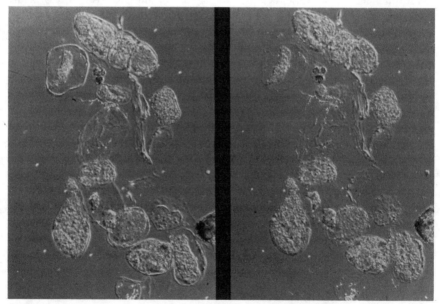

Figure 3. Changes in chemical composition of cellular residues of sweetpotato shochu by the enzymatic treatment. Cellular residues (4.8% on a dry basis) separated from sweetpotato shochu distillatory slops were suspended in 0.1% citric acid solution (pH 4.3) and treated with 0.125% of TVM at 40°C for 12 hr. The residues were analyzed according to Southgate (1969).

Figure 4. Microphotographs of enzymatic action on cellular residues in sweetpotato shochu distillatory slops. Cellular residues were treated with 0.4% of TVM at 40°C under a microscope (x 125 on film). Left: 0 min.; right: 10 min.

solution containing $ZnCl_2$ is used. These facts suggest that the cell walls remain intact but lose pectic substances. There are not even common precipitants which will separate the cellular residues. Thus, the cellular residues from sweetpotato are considered to behave as cellular bags holding water inside, and this is responsible for the poor separability of the slops.

The supernatant includes small amounts of polysaccharides (Table 2), which seem to have little effect on the separability of the cellular residues (Fig.1).

Characteristic action of cellulase on cellular residues

The enzyme preparations examined here showed different action patterns on cellulosic and pectic substances, depending on their origin (Table 3). Among them, the cellulase preparations from *T. viride* were distinctively effective for our purpose (Fig. 2). These enzymes evidently attacked the cellulosic portion of the cellular residues causing a decrease in the cellulose content (Fig. 3) and an increase in supernatant cellobiose. Under a microscope, their cell walls appeared to become thinner after the enzymatic treatment (Fig. 4, right).

These cellulase preparations, TVM and TVO, include multiple components of cellulolytic enzymes which convert CMC or crystalline cellulose such as avicel into glucose or cellobiose with different substrate specificities (Okada et al. 1968; Okada 1975). The avicel saccharifying component from TVO has been named avicelase (Berghem et al. 1973).

It has not yet been shown which component of avicelase from *T. viride* is responsible for improving the separability. However, our results suggest that water held inside each of the cellular residues is released through the thinned cell wall after this enzymatic treatment. Our finding will be applicable to handling of the slops and also processing of sweetpotato.

Presently, trials for recycling of shochu slops are being conducted. The slops are nutritious (Matsukubo et al. 1991) and a considerable part of them has been used for feeding hogs and steers. It has been reported that vitamin E coming from sweetpotato is concentrated in the flesh of hogs, which keeps the flesh fresh (Kawaida et al. 1990). Also, a system of fractionation of the slops and utilization of each fraction is being tried: for example, the supernatant is used for production of yeast to feed fish, and the residues for dietary fibers, emulsion stabilizer, and cultivation of mushrooms (Okizono et al. 1991). Our enzymatic treatment will be available to promote these fractionating processes. A hybrid from Koji-fungus and cellulolytic fungus has been reported and may be used to clarify the slops (Furukawa et al. 1990).

ACKNOWLEDGMENTS

This study was performed as a part of the Project on Development of a New Production and Recycling System in the Food Industry with the financial support of Kagoshima Prefecture and the Ministry of International Trade and Industry. The distillatory slops were mainly supplied by Komasa Jozo Co. Some of the commercial enzyme preparations were donated by Meiji Seika Co., Ltd. and Amano Pharmaceutical Co., Ltd. A part of this study was done in cooperation with Dr. Shigeo Fujimoto, a former associate professor of Kagoshima University, and also Messrs. Akio Kawabata, Kouki Yamamoto, Shigeru Hinaga, Chihiro Nakazono, Kenji Hamada, and Toyokadu Sonoda. The authors wish to express their thanks to all concerned.

REFERENCES

Berghem, L.E.R., and L.G. Pettersson. 1973. Mechanism of enzymic cellulose degradation. Purification of a cellulolytic enzyme from *Trichoderma viride* active on highly ordered cellulose. European Journal of Biochemistry 37:21-30.

Galambos, J.T. 1967. The relation of carbazole with carbohydrates I. Effect of borate and sulfamate on the carbazole color of sugars. Analytical Biochemistry 19:119-132.

Kawaida, H., T. Fukunaga, S. Ueyama, K. Matsumoto, M. Yanase, and T. Horinouchi. 1990. Studies on the feeding and the meat quality of the strain and the strain-cross swines. Kagoshima Prefectural Animal Husbandry Experiment Station 22:63-67.

Matsukubo, K., A. Haseba, K. Mizumoto, I. Tabata, H. Ito, and I. Shinmura. 1991. General properties and utilization of shochu distillatory slops. *In* Report of the project on development of a new production and recycling system in the food industry, Kagoshima Prefecture.

Murao, S., M. Arai, and R. Sakamoto. 1987. Cellulose. Kodan-sha. 162 pp.

Nagahama, T., S. Fujimoto, T. Suganuma, K. Yamamoto, and A.Kawabata. Studies on utilization of sweet potato shochu distillatory slops. 1. On carbohydrate components in the soluble part. Page 15 *in* Abstracts of Annual Meeting, Japan Society for Bioscience, Biotechnology, and Agrochemistry, 10 Oct 1987, Yamaguchi, Japan.

Nagahama, T., S. Fujimoto, T. Suganuma, and K. Hamada. 1990. Studies on utilization of sweet potato shochu distillatory slops. 3. Composition of insoluble part. Page 15 *in* Abstracts of Annual Meeting, Japan Society for Bioscience, Biotechnology, and Agrochemistry, 31 March 1990, Fukuoka, Japan.

Furukawa, K., J. Inoue, T. Hidaka, and K. Ogawa. 1991. Hybrid formation between koji-fungus and cellulolytic fungus by using their protoplasts. Page 41 *in* Abstracts of Annual Meeting, Japan Society for Bioscience, Biotechnology, and Agrochemistry, 20 Oct 1990, Kumamoto, Japan.

Okada, G., K. Nishizawa, and H. Suzuki. 1968. Cellulase components from *Trichoderma viride*. Journal of Biochemistry (Tokyo) 63:591-609.

Okada, G. 1975. Enzymatic studies on a cellulase system of *Trichoderma viride*. II. Purification and properties of two cellulases. Journal of Biochemistry (Tokyo) 77:33-42.

Okizono, K., and I. Maeda. *In* Report of the project on development of a new production and recycling system in the food industry, Kagoshima Prefecture.

Southgate, D.A.T. 1969. Determination of carbohydrates in foods. II.Unavailable carbohydrates. Journal of the Science of Food and Agriculture 20:331-335.

Yano, I. (ed). 1990. Nihon Kokusei Zue. Kokusei-sha. 606 pp.

Poster Presentations

NUTRITIVE COMPOSITION OF SWEETPOTATOES GROWN IN NFT WITH DIFFERENT NUTRIENT SOLUTION APPLICATION PROTOCOLS

P. Grant, J. Lu, D. Mortley, P. Loretan, C. Bonsi, W. Hill, C. Morris
George Washington Carver Agricultural Experiment Station, Tuskegee University, Tuskegee, AL 36088.

The sweetpotato cultivar 'TI 155' was grown for 120 days at 28/22°C day/night temperatures in a greenhouse using the nutrient film technique (NFT) and a modified half-Hoagland solution. During the growth period, the nutrient solution was changed every 2 days (C_1), every 2 weeks (C_2) or every 4 weeks (C_3). Storage root yield, moisture, protein, fat, ash, P, K, Na, Ca, Mg and vitamin B_1 were higher for the C_1 than the C_2 and C_3 treatments. Vitamin B_2, starch, ascorbic acid and beta-carotene were higher for the C_3 and C_2 than the C_1 treatment. Results showed that nutrient solution manipulation greatly influenced the yield and nutrient composition of the sweetpotato.

It has been demonstrated that sweetpotatoes can grow and develop storage roots in nutrient film systems (Hill et al. 1990; Loretan et al. 1990; Morris et al. 1989). The nutrient film technique (NFT) provides an excellent method for determining the effect of environmental factors on sweetpotato growth, yield and nutrient composition. In a previous study with sweetpotatoes using NFT, analysis of the nutrient solution every 2 days beginning four weeks after planting showed that N was depleted in 2 days whereas K was depleted in 7 to 10 days (Mortley, unpublished data). It was speculated that, if these nutrients were replenished, storage root yield and nutritional content (especially protein) would be increased. The objective of this study was to determine the effect of frequency of nutrient solution change on yield and nutritive composition of sweetpotatoes grown in NFT.

MATERIALS AND METHODS

The sweetpotato cultivar 'TI 155' was grown in a greenhouse using the nutrient film technique (NFT) as previously described by Morris et al. (1989), Hill et al. (1989), Loretan et al. (1989). Experimental treatments involved changing the nutrient solution every 2 days (C_1), every 2 weeks (C_2) and every 4 weeks (C_3). Each treatment channel was planted with four 'TI 155' cuttings spaced 15 cm apart. The composition of the nutrient solution used is described in Bonsi et al. (1992). The plants were grown for 120 days at 28/22°C (day/night temperatures). At harvest, storage roots per plant were counted and weighed to determine yield.

Percent moisture, protein, fat and ash were determined by AOAC procedures (AOAC 1980). Percent starch was determined by enzyme analysis (Lu et al. 1989). Amino acid analysis was determined with an amino acid analyzer from Medallion Laboratories (Minneapolis, Minnesota). An atomic absorption spectrometer (Perkin

Table 1. Total yield[1] of hydroponically grown 'TI-155' sweetpotatoes as affected by frequency of nutrient solution change.[2]

Treatment[3]	Storage root yield
C^1	1688.43 $\pm$466.39a
C^2	769.16 $\pm$135.42b
C^3	613.71 $\pm$ 41.18b

[1]Yield in grams
[2]Means and standard errors based on 4 values. Means with the same superscript are not significantly different at the 5% level of probability using Duncan's Multiple Range Test.
[3] Frequency of nutrient solution change: C_1 - every 2 days; C_2 - every 2 weeks; C_3 - every 4 weeks.

Elmer, Model No. 1100B, Perkin Elmer Corp., Norfolk, Conn.) was used to determine K, Na, Ca and Mg content. A colorimetric method (Davis and Kramer 1973) was used for P determination. Vitamins B_1 and B_2 were determined by a fluorometer; ascorbic acid was determined by titration with 2,6,dichlorophenolindophenol (AOAC 1980) and total carotenoids were determined by a spectrophotometric method (Reddy and Sistrunk 1980).

Analysis of variance was used to determine the difference among treatment means and Duncan's Multiple Range Test to compare means at the 5% level.

RESULTS AND DISCUSSION

Table 1 shows storage root yield per plant. The results show that frequency of nutrient solution change had a profound impact on production of storage roots. The yield of C_1 was about twice that of C_2 and nearly three times higher than for C_3. In previous studies, C_2 was the method used to grow sweetpotato in NFT (Mortley 1990).

Table 2 shows the macro-composition of storage roots. The results indicate that the moisture content of C_1 was higher than for C_2 and C_3, and C_2 was higher than

Table 2. Composition of hydroponically grown 'TI-155' sweetpotatoes at different frequencies of nutrient solution change.[1]

Treat-ment[3]	Moisture	Dry Matter	Starch[2]	Protein[2]	Fat[2]	Ash[2]
			%			
C_1	84.45$\pm$0.50a	15.55$\pm$0.50a	39.90$\pm$2.48a	16.11$\pm$2.44a	5.60$\pm$0.71a	6.64$\pm$0.51a
C_2	81.38$\pm$0.71b	18.62$\pm$0.76b	53.79$\pm$3.82b	7.46$\pm$0.35b	2.78$\pm$1.14b	5.59$\pm$0.58a
C_3	79.28$\pm$0.42c	20.72$\pm$0.42c	52.76$\pm$3.10b	4.93$\pm$0.29c	1.11$\pm$0.12b	3.24$\pm$0.15b

[1]Means and standard errors based on 6 values. Means with the same superscript are not significantly different at the 5% level of probability using Duncan's multiple range test.
[2]Dry weight basis.
[3]Frequency of nutrient solution change: C_1 - every 2 days; C_2 - every 2 weeks; C_3 - every 4 weeks.

Table 3. Amino acid composition of hydroponically grown 'TI-155' sweetpotatoes at different frequencies of nutrient solution change.

Amino acid	% (dry weight basis)			g/16g N		
	C_1	C_2	C_3	C_1	C_2	C_3
Asp	3.05	1.27	0.53	17.67	16.41	10.33
Thr	0.52	0.23	0.12	3.04	2.98	2.43
Ser	0.60	0.24	0.11	3.47	3.12	2.23
Glu	0.93	0.51	0.33	5.39	6.64	6.48
Pro	0.30	0.19	0.14	1.74	2.44	2.63
Gly	0.36	0.20	0.18	2.11	2.58	3.44
Ala	0.76	0.43	0.23	4.40	5.56	4.46
Val	0.51	0.33	0.16	2.98	4.20	3.04
Met	0.13	0.07	0.04	0.74	0.95	0.81
Le	0.33	0.18	0.11	1.92	2.31	2.23
Leu	0.34	0.28	0.11	1.98	2.31	2.23
Tyr	0.22	0.11	0.07	1.30	1.36	1.42
Phe	0.43	0.21	0.14	2.48	2.71	2.63
His	0.14	0.05	0.05	0.81	0.68	1.01
Lys	0.20	0.12	0.08	1.18	1.49	1.62
Arg	0.29	0.14	0.06	1.67	1.76	1.22
NH_3	0.30	0.13	0.05	1.74	1.63	1.01

Frequency of nutrient solution change: C_1 - every 2 days; C_2 - every 2 weeks; C_3 - every 4 weeks.

C_3. Conversely, the % dry matter of C_2 was higher than for C_2, and C_2 was higher than for C_1. Starch is a major component of sweetpotato. Starch content generally ranges from 50 to 70% depending upon cultivar, harvest and storage conditions (Collins and Walter 1985). The C_1 treatment resulted in a lower starch content than C_2 and C_3. These findings suggest an inverse relationship between moisture content and starch content. The storage root protein content was the highest with the C_1 treatment and the lowest with the C_3 treatment. Protein content of sweetpotatoes generally ranges from 2 to 5% (Bradbury and Holloway 1988) although some cultivars have been reported to contain 10 to 11% protein (Walter and Catignani 1981). With a protein content of 10% or higher, sweetpotato can provide substantial amounts of dietary protein in addition to carbohydrates, vitamins and minerals. The crude protein content of 16.11% resulting from the C_1 treatment also included substantial amounts of non-protein nitrogen (NPN) compounds such as amino-N, NO_3-N, peptides and ammonia-N as indicated in Table 3. Fat and ash content followed the same trend as crude protein where C_1 was highest, followed by C_2, then C_3 (Table 2).

The % amino acid in storage roots decreased in the order of C_1, C_2 and C_3 (Table 3). The C_1 treatment had the highest amino acid content of 9.11% while C_2 had 4.46% and C_3, 2.38%. The amino acid pattern was similar for the three treatments except

Table 4. Some vitamins[1] in hydroponically grown 'TI-155' sweetpotatoes at different frequencies of nutrient solution change.[2]

Treatment[3]	Total carotenoid mg/100g	B_1 mg/100g	B_2 µg/g	Ascorbic acid mg/100g
C_1	32.55±2.73a	0.25±0.03a	6.87±0.85a	99.48±8.17a
C_2	36.93±3.25a	0.14±0.02b	2.88±0.26b	65.03±5.05b
C_3	33.76±0.94a	0.14±0.01b	9.11±1.69a	115.99±5.29a

[1] Percent dry weight.
[2] Means and standard errors based on 5 values. Means with the same superscript are not significantly different at the 5% level of probability using Duncan's Multiple Range Test.
[3] Frequency of nutrient solution change: C_1 - every 2 days; C_2 - every 2 weeks; C_3 - every 4 weeks.

that the % aspartic acid was greater for C_1 and C_2 than for C_3. The major amino acids found were aspartic acid, glutamic acid and alanine. The most limiting essential amino acid was methionine. Sulfur containing amino acids have been identified as the limiting amino acids in field-grown sweetpotatoes (Purcell et al. 1972). The results of this study showed that methionine, histine and lysine content of 'TI 155' were limiting.

Sweetpotato is a rich source of beta-carotene and ascorbic acid (Lu et al. 1986). Orange-flesh sweetpotatoes contain substantial amounts of carotenoids in which the major percent is beta-carotene, a precursor of vitamin A (Collins and Walter 1985). Sweetpotato also contains appreciable amounts of vitamins B_1 and B_2. Table 4 shows the vitamin content of storage roots for the C_1, C_2 and C_3 treatments. No difference in total carotenoids was observed among the three treatments, but C_1 had a higher B_1 content than C_2 and C_3. The vitamin B_2 and ascorbic acid contents were lower for C_2 than for C_1 and C_3. The difference may reflect some variation in metabolic rate of the storage roots at different stages of growth. In general, the effect of frequency of nutrient solution changeout was greater for macronutrient than for vitamin content.

Phosphorous and K are important elements that are closely related to the development of storage roots (Jones 1983). Table 5 indicates that P and K were the major minerals in sweetpotato storage roots. The C_1 treatment resulted in the highest P and K contents in the storage roots and the C_3 treatment the lowest. The C_1 treatment had higher Na, Ca and Mg contents than C_2 and C_3. This result agreed with the previous observation (Table 2) that the ash content was much higher for C_1 than for C_2 and C_3.

CONCLUSION

It was concluded from this study that manipulation of environmental factors such as frequency of nutrient solution change has a significant effect on sweetpotato

Table 5. Mineral content[1] in hydroponically grown 'TI-155' sweetpotatoes at different frequencies of nutrient solution change.[2]

Treatment[3]	P	K	Na	Ca	Mg
C_1	1.68±0.12a	4.01±0.39a	0.15±0.02a	0.24±0.03a	0.24±0.04a
C_2	0.91±0.01b	3.09±0.23C	0.12±0.01ab	0.12±0.01b	0.14±0.01b
C_3	0.77±0.04b	1.55±0.13b	0.08±0.01b	0.16±0.02b	0.12±0.01b

[1]Percent dry weight.
[2]Means and standard errors based on 5 values. Means with the same superscript are not significantly different at the 5% level of probability using Duncan's Multiple Range Test.
[3]Frequency of nutrient solution change: C_1 - every 2 days; C_2 - every 2 weeks; C_3 - every 4 weeks.

growth, storage root production and nutrient composition and that treatment C_1 resulted in a higher storage root yield and nutrient content than C_2 and C_3.

REFERENCES

AOAC. 1980. Official methods of analysis. 13th ed., Association of Official Analytical Chemists, Washington D.C.

Bradbury, J.H., and W.D. Holloway (eds.). 1988. Chemistry of tropical root crops: significance for nutrition and agriculture in the pacific. Australian Centre for International Agricultural Research, ACLAR Canberra. 201 pp.

Collins, W.W., and W.M. Walter. 1985. Fresh roots for human consumption. Pages 153-174 *in* Sweet potato products: a natural resource for the tropics, edited by J.C. Bouwkamp. CRC Press, Boca Raton, Fla.

Davis, C.A., and A. Kramer. 1973. Methods of nutrient analysis. Pages 468-506 *in* Quality control for the food industry, edited by A. Kramer and B.A. Twigg. The AVI Publishing Company, Westport, Connecticut.

Hill, W.A., P.A. Loretan, C.K. Bonsi, C.E. Morris, J.Y. Lu, and C. Ogbuehi. 1989. Utilization of sweet potatoes in closed ecological life support systems (CELSS). Adv. Space Res. 9, #8, 29-41. Pergamon Press PLC, Oxford.

Hill, W.A., D.G. Mortley, C.L. Mackowiak, P.A. Loretan, T.W. Tibbits, R.M. Wheeler, C.K. Bonsi, and C.E. Morris. 1990. Growing root, tuber and nut crops hydroponically for CELSS. Adv. Space Res. 12(5):125-131.

Jones, J.B. 1983. A guide for the hydroponic and soilless culture grower. Timber Press, Portland, Oregon.

Loretan, P.A., W.A. Hill, C.K. Bonsi, C.E. Morris, J.Y. Lu, C.R. Ogbuehi, and D.G. Mortley. 1989. Sweet potatoes for Closed Ecological Life Support Systems (CELSS) using the nutrient film technique. NASA/CELSS Pl Meeting, February, Orlando, FL.

Lu, J.Y., P.K. Biswas, and R.D. Pace. 1986. Effect of elevated CO_2 growth conditions on the nutritive composition and acceptability of baked sweet potatoes. Food Science 51(2): 358-359, 539.

Lu, J.Y., P. Miller, and P.A. Loretan. 1989. Gamma radiation dose rate and sweet potato quality. Food Quality 12:369-376.

Purcell, A.C., H.E. Swaisgood, and D.T. Pope. 1972. Protein and amino acid content of sweet potato cultivars. J. Am. Soc. Hortic. Sci. 97:30-33.

Reddy, N.N., and W.A. Sistrunk. 1980. Effect of cultivar, size, storage, and cooking method on carbohydrates and some nutrients of sweet potato. J. Food Sci. 45:682-687.

Splittstoesser, W.E. 1984. Vegetable growing handbook. 2nd Ed. Principles and procedures for producing an abundance of quality vegetables. Van Nostrand Reinhold Company, New York, N.Y. 298 pp.

Walter, W.M., and G.L. Catignani. 1981. Biological quality and composition of sweet potato protein fractions. J. Agric. and Food Chem. 29:797-799.

SENSORY PROFILES OF THREE SWEETPOTATO CULTIVARS GROWN USING THE NUTRIENT FILM TECHNIQUE

Dana M. Greene, John Y. Lu

Tuskegee University, Tuskegee, AL 36088.

Karen Crippen

USDA-Southern Regional Research Center, New Orleans, LA 70130.

A sensory evaluation was conducted of three sweetpotato cultivars ('TI-155', 'Georgia Jet', and 'TI-70357') grown for 120 days using the nutrient film technique (NFT) system. A trained taste panel characterized the flavor profiles of the three cultivars in comparison to that of sweetpotatoes available commercially. A lexicon of descriptive terminology for sweetpotatoes was developed by the panel. The organoleptic tests showed that 'Georgia Jet' storage roots grown using NFT compared most favorably for flavor and acceptability to conventionally-grown sweetpotatoes purchased in the supermarket.

INTRODUCTION

Sweetpotato (*Ipomoea batatas*) ranks seventh in production among world food crops (Collins 1982). It can offer a significant contribution to the diet. It is an excellent source of energy and contains at least 90% of all nutrient requirements excluding niacin and protein (Bouwkamp 1985). Its nutritive qualities as well as its cultural habits and ease in food preparation have made it an ideal candidate for use as a food source in long-term manned space missions (Hill et al. 1984). Sweetpotatoes grown hydroponically using the nutrient film technique have the same nutritive quality as those grown conventionally (Hill et al. 1989), but to date studies have not been carried out to indicate that their taste is comparable. Sensory evaluation of the sweetpotato storage roots grown in this fashion is essential. Lu et al. (1986) used a consumer taste panel to evaluate the acceptability of sweetpotatoes grown under elevated CO_2 growth conditions, but they used neither a trained taste panel nor a descriptive analysis for the product.

Descriptive analysis provides a "flavor" profile of the specific food being tested, dividing each individual taste, flavor or mouthfeel of the food into a separate component (Johnsen 1986; Johnsen et al. 1987). It is necessary to develop an acceptable lexicon or list of terms for each food for panelists to use in order to provide a comprehensive and precise descriptive analysis of flavor (Johnsen and Civille 1986; Lyon 1987). These terms (a lexicon) are based on the underlying order or structure from within the product frame of reference (Civille 1987). No such lexicon is presently available for sweetpotato panelists to use.

The purpose of this study was to prepare a lexicon of descriptors which can be utilized to assess the palatability of sweetpotatoes and to use this to conduct a sensory evaluation of sweetpotatoes (cultivars 'TI-155', 'Georgia Jet', and 'TI-70357') grown using the NFT system compared to those conventionally grown.

MATERIALS AND METHODS

Sensory Evaluation Panel

A nine member sensory evaluation panel was selected. Each panelist chosen had been previously trained to detect differing intensities in a variety of foods. They had, through repetition, been orientated in the utilization of the Spectrum Reference Intensity Scale, a universal scale in which 1 represents the lowest intensity and 15 the highest in taste, flavor, and mouthfeel (Meilgaard et al. 1987).

Descriptive Analysis System

The sensory profile of the sweetpotato storage roots in this study was developed by using a standardized descriptive language for evaluating the flavor of sweetpotatoes also known as "Descriptive Analysis." In order to establish this descriptive analysis system for sweetpotatoes a selection of appropriate terms was made by panelists. Descriptive terminologies which characterized the flavor components of the sweet-potato were chosen. The list of descriptors was arrived at by the consensus of the panel members who were experienced tasters for sweetpotatoes and its various flavors. These panelists had to develop a descriptor list or lexicon for all tastes, flavors and mouthfeels perceived in a store-bought sweetpotato sample. Store purchased sweetpotatoes were used for preparation of this list since they were considered to be consumer acceptable. Samples were randomly chosen from stores throughout the New Orleans Metropolitan area. The following protocol was used to prepare sweetpotato storage roots for testing by panelists:

Sweetpotatoes were baked at 190°C for 90 minutes (Lanier and Sistrunk, 1979; Lu et al. 1986). They were peeled and mashed (until texture was smooth and without lumps-approximately 2-3 minutes) using a large stainless steel spoon. For each panelist, a 28 g sample of the mashed sweetpotato was placed in a DAZEY, 1/2 pint, seal-a-meal bag, already labeled with a randomized 3 digit sample code number to eliminate bias among samples (Rao et al. 1975). The bag was sealed for 4 seconds with a heating element. The prepared samples were placed in a refrigerator at 37°F (3°C) overnight or until needed. Sample presentation order was randomized. When needed, the sample bags were removed from the refrigerator and a small puncture was made in the corner of each bag. They were microwaved (high setting) for one minute prior to serving. Samples were then served immediately to panelists.

Sweetpotato Descriptor Panels

The first panel was devoted to developing descriptor names for all tastes that could be perceived in each sweetpotato sample as described above.

A second panel was dedicated to tasting references that corresponded with the descriptor names developed in panel one. Reference trays were prepared that contained the following food products:

white squash	brown sugar	yellow squash
caramel	carrots	collard greens
bran flakes	grape nuts	pecans
almonds	corn starch	0.1% alum solution
white potato	oranges	lemons
diacetyl	jasmine	MIB (methylisoborneol)

All the vegetables on the reference tray were steamed, except the collard greens and white potatoes which were boiled. The corn starch used was composed of corn starch and enough water to make a paste. The grape nuts, bran flakes, caramels, pecans, almonds, and brown sugar were served dry (from the box). The oranges and lemons were sliced and served with peeling still attached. A 0.1% alum solution was prepared from 0.1 g of alum and 100 mL of water. The MIB, jasmine and diacetyl were placed in bottles and sniffed by the panelists.

A sample which was considered to be a "good sweetpotato sample" was tasted by each panelist. Following the sampling each panelist tasted products from two of the aforementioned reference trays. These references were compared in flavor to that in the sweetpotato sample. After sampling was complete, a general list of those references that were applicable to sweetpotato taste and flavor was compiled by the panelists. This was the first descriptor list that could contribute to a final lexicon.

Finally, two more sweetpotato samples were presented for tasting, and they too were compared to the references.

A discussion followed each sampling, and the list containing the descriptors that were applicable to sweetpotato taste and flavor was again considered. This list became more accurate and precise as the samplings progressed until it was finalized. The definitions were prepared for each descriptive term, and the list was made available for the panelists to use when tasting samples in succeeding panels.

Sweetpotato Sensory Panels

The next series of panels focused on specifically tasting various sweetpotato samples. The first of these panels analyzed samples that were randomly chosen from different stores throughout the New Orleans Metropolitan area. Panelists used paper ballots to record all tastes, flavors and mouthfeels perceived using previously determined descriptors.

The next panel centered around scoring the intensities of each descriptor for individual sweetpotato samples. Here, intensity refers to a number score for each taste, mouthfeel, or chemical feeling factor perceived using the aforementioned Spectrum Reference Intensity Scale. The panelists used a light pen computer program and computers to enter their scores for each attribute in individual samples. Sample numbers and sample presentation order were randomized again.

Finally, an extensive series of panels followed for the purpose of scoring intensities on actual experimentally grown sweetpotatoes. For each of these panels, five sweetpotato samples were presented, and NFT-grown sweetpotatoes were incorporated into the comparison. This allowed a direct comparison between the NFT-grown sweetpotato storage roots and store-bought sweetpotatoes. Intensity scores were obtained for each descriptor for each individual sample in all remaining panels.

Statistics

A comparison was conducted on the grand means of the sensory data obtained from all four treatments of sweetpotato storage roots that were tasted. Each flavor descriptor was analyzed for each individual treatment followed by a mean comparison (LSD) to indicate the differences among treatments in relation to their descriptors.

RESULTS AND DISCUSSION

A lexicon of descriptive terminology was constructed by a trained taste panel reporting all the flavors, tastes, and mouthfeels associated with eating sweetpotatoes. The final compilation of the aforementioned descriptive terms is listed in Table 1 including the descriptor, its abbreviation and its definition. The descriptors are classified according to aromatics, basic tastes and chemical feeling factors. Some of these descriptors are the same as those identified by Syraief et al. (1985).

Table 1. Lexicon of sweetpotato flavors.

Aromatics

Brown sugar/caramel (BSC): the sweet aromatics associated with heated sugars such as cooked caramel, brown sugar or molasses.

Buttery (BTY): the aromatic associated with dairy lipid products or sweet cream butter.

Citrus (CIT): a sharp tart aromatic caused by acids or alcohols resembling that of citrus fruits, i.e., oranges, or lemons.

Earthy (ETY): an aromatic which resembles the odor of earth or soil.

Malt (MLT): aromatic which resembles grape nuts, malt, and nuts (pleasant).

Nutty (NTY): the pleasant malty aromatic which resembles nuts other than oilseed nuts, i.e., pecans.

Starchy (SHY): the aromatic associated with uncooked starch.

Vegetable (VEG): aromatic associated with the odor and taste of cooked vegetables having the distinct flavor of cooked carrots, squash, or greens.

White Potato (WTP): the aromatic associated with cooked potatoes.

Basic Tastes

Sweet (SWT): taste on the tongue associated with sugars.

Sour (SOR): taste on the tongue associated with acids.

Bitter (BIT): taste on the tongue associated with bitter agents such as caffeine, quinine, etc.

Salty (STY): taste on the tongue associated with sodium ions.

Chemical Feeling Factors

Astringent (ATR): the chemical feeling factor on the tongue described as puckering/dry and associated with tannin or alum.

The panelists also determined that out of the descriptors that contribute to the overall taste of a sweetpotato certain characteristic tastes and flavors were disagreeable. These negative attributes included earthy, starchy, bitter, and astringent flavors. The lower the intensity of these descriptors, the better the sweetpotato as determined by

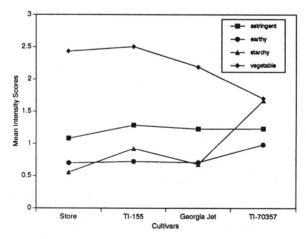

Figure 1. Mean intensity ratings for negative sweetpotato flavor descriptors.

Table 2. Mean intensity ratings of lexicon descriptors for standard sweetpotato samples and sweetpotato samples grown using NFT for individual descriptors.

Attribute	Mean Intensity Scores			
	Store Purchased (standard)	'TI-155'	'Georgia Jet'	'TI-70357'
Vegetable	2.433	2.505	2.19	1.700*
Brown sugar/caramel	2.104	1.185*	1.646*	0.700*
Nutty	0.925	0.661*	0.957	0.600
Malt	0.646	0.414	0.600	0.369
Citrus	1.178	0.920	0.950	0.169
Buttery	1.439	1.055*	1.153	0.715*
Earthy	0.697	0.720	0.703	0.984
Starchy	0.554	0.920*	0.676	1.669*
White Potato	1.129	1.502*	1.453	1.884*
Sweet	2.505	1.217*	1.923*	1.123*
Sour	1.012	1.182	1.146	0.892
Bitter	0.873	1.132*	0.973	0.861
Salty	0.753	0.914	0.946	0.984
Astringent	1.080	1.285	1.226	1.230

*Indicates that the mean intensity rating differed significantly from the standard mean intensity rating in the same row using LSD at the 5% level.

the panel. Also, a vegetable flavor intensity rating less than 2.4 led to a less desirable sweetpotato than store-purchased samples. The mean intensities for these attributes for all four treatments are shown in Figure 1. Several factors may contribute to the different intensity ratings listed here and later for all intensities in Table 2. First of all, the sweetpotatoes grown using NFT were not cured after harvest while the samples purchased in the supermarkets were. Also, the 'TI-70357' cultivar is a white-fleshed sweetpotato while the other cultivars were orange-fleshed.

Based on statistical analyses of the intensity ratings for each descriptor, it was determined that the brown sugar/caramel, butter and nutty flavors, in combination with a sweet taste, made a sweetpotato desirable and acceptable. Within this combination a balance between the intensities of these attributes was needed to maintain the desirability of these flavors when experienced together. It was seen that within the balance there were the following ranges of intensities: sweet – 1.25 to 2.5; nutty – 0.50 to 1.00; buttery – 0.75 to 1.5; and brown sugar – 0.75 to 2.10. The mean intensities of these positive flavors as perceived in the store-purchased sweetpotato samples as compared to those samples grown in NFT are shown in Figure 2. The comparisons seen in this figure show that 'TI-70357' storage roots varied the most from the store-purchased sweetpotatoes and 'Georgia Jet' corresponded most closely. The other descriptors defined in the lexicon provide characteristic sweet-potato tastes and contribute to their overall flavor, but they do not necessarily contribute to what makes a storage root "good" in relation to taste and flavor. The

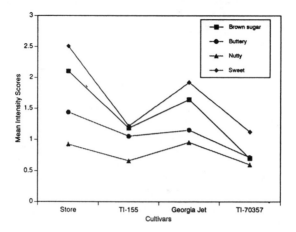

Figure 2. Mean intensity ratings for positive sweetpotato flavor descriptors.

overall mean intensities for all descriptors, including those that are not designated as positive or negative are shown in Table 2.

CONCLUSIONS

A trained taste panel was able to generate a lexicon of descriptor terms for sweetpotatoes. Using these terms, the panelists were able to conduct sensory evaluations of three sweetpotato cultivars grown using an NFT system as compared to store-bought sweetpotatoes. This series demonstrated that of the three cultivars, 'Georgia Jet' storage roots were the most palatable in that they more closely resembled a store-bought sweetpotato according to their total sensory profile.

Furthermore, the tests also revealed the qualities that contribute to the negative tastes and flavors in sweetpotato, these being the starchy, earthy, and vegetable flavors, and the astringent mouthfeel. It was concluded that the positive flavor attributes of sweetpotatoes were the sweet taste, and the nutty, brown sugar/caramel, and buttery flavors.

ACKNOWLEDGEMENT

The authors gratefully acknowledge the assistance of Edwin Martinez and Dr. Desmond G. Mortley in growing the sweetpotatoes used in this study. This research was supported by funds from the U. S. National Aeronautics and Space Administration (Grant No. NAG10-0024) and USDA/CSRS (Grant No. ALX-SP-1). The sensory evaluation panels were carried out at the USDA/SRRC Center in New Orleans, and their support of the research is also greatly appreciated.

REFERENCES

Bouwkamp, J.C. (ed). 1985 Sweet potato products: A natural resource for the tropics, CRC Press, Inc., Boca Raton, FL.

Civille, G.V. 1987. Development of vocabulary for flavour descriptive analysis. Page 357 *in* Flavour Science and Technology, edited by M. Martens, G. Dalen and H. Russwurm John Wiley and Sons, Ltd. Chichester, England.

Collins, W.W., and W.M. Walter Jr. 1982. Potential for increasing the nutritional value of sweet potatoes. Page 355-363 *in* Sweet potato, edited by R. L. Villareal and T. D. Griggs, Proceedings of the First International Symposium, AVRDC, Shanua, Tainan, Taiwan, China.

Hill, W.A., P.A. Loretan, and C.K. Bonsi (eds). 1984. The sweet potato for space missions. Tuskegee University, AL, 64 pp.

Hill, W.A., P.A. Loretan, C.K. Bonsi, C.E. Morris, J.Y. Lu, and C.R.A. Ogbuehi. 1989. Utilization of sweetpotatoes in controlled ecological life support systems. Advances in Space Research 9(8):29-41.

Johnsen, P.B. 1986. A lexicon of peanut flavor descriptors.USDA, Agricultural Research Service publication ARS-52. 7 pp.

Johnsen, P.B., G.V. Civille, and J.R. Vercellotti. 1987. A lexicon of pond-raised catfish flavor descriptors. J. Sen. Studies. 2:85-91.

Johnsen, P.B., and G.V. Civille. 1986. A standardized lexicon of meat WOF descriptors. J. Sen. Studies. 1:99-104.

Lanier, J.J., and W.A. Sistrunk. 1979. Influence of cooking method on quality attributes and vitamin content of sweet potatoes. J. of Food Science. 44(2):374-376,380.

Lu, J.Y., P.K. Biswas, and R.D. Pace. 1986. Effect of elevated CO_2 growth conditions on the nutritive composition and acceptability of baked sweet potatoes. J. of Food Science. 51(2):358-359.

Lyon, B.G. 1987. Development of chicken flavor descriptive attribute terms aided by multivariate statistical procedures. J. of Sens. Studies. 2:55-67.

Meilgaard, M., G.V. Civille, and B.T. Carr. 1987. Sensory evaluation techniques, Volume I., CRC Press, Boca Raton, Florida..

Meilgaard, M., G.V. Civille, and B.T. Carr. 1987. Sensory evaluation techniques, Volume II, CRC Press, Boca Raton, Florida..

Rao, V.N.M., D.D. Haman, and E.G. Humphries. 1975. Apparent viscosity as a measure of moist mouthfeel of sweet potatoes. J. of Food Science. 40:97-100.

Steel, R.G.D., and J.H.Torrie. 1980. Principles and procedures of statistics: A biometrical approach. McGraw-Hill Book Company, New York, New York.

Syarief, H., F.G. Hamann, F.G. Giesbrecht, C.T. Young, and R.J. Monroe. 1985. Interdependency and underlying dimensions of sensory flavor characteristics of selected foods. J. of Food Science. 50:631-638.

SWEETPOTATO α-and β-AMYLASES: RAPID PURIFICATION AND KINETIC STUDIES WITH ENDOGENOUS INHIBITORS

Vital Hagenimana, Ronald E. Simard

Departement de Sciences et Technologie des Aliments, Universite Laval, Ste-Foy, Qc, GIK 7P4.

Louis P. Vezina

Station de recherche, Agriculture Canada, 2560 Bvd. Hochelaga, Ste-Foy, Qc, GIV 2J3.

In order to optimize the direct hydrolysis of starch in sweetpotato mashes by endogenous amylases, α- and β-amylases were purified 662- and 24-fold, respectively. The purification steps involved ammonium sulfate precipitation, affinity chromatography (cycloheptaamylose and cyclohexaamylose) and gel filtration. These purified enzyme preparations were used in kinetic studies in which purified sweetpotato starch was used as a substrate and in which ascorbate, oxalate, total endogenous phenolics, phytate and sweetpotato extracts were assayed for their potential inhibitory activity. A 0.08 mM concentration of ascorbate strongly inhibited the β-amylase activity. The addition of oxalate, phytate, phenolics, and two types of sweetpotato extract (chloroform and methanol-water soluble) had no influence on the activity of this enzyme. The α-amylase activity was reduced by 0.2 mM ascorbate up to 70%; Na oxalate and Na phytate moderately inhibited this last enzyme. Furthermore, phenolics and sweetpotato extracts had no influence on its activity.

Heating at 70°C for 10 min improves the rheological properties of sweetpotato mashes and sweetens their taste (Hoover 1967; Walter et al. 1975). However, such treatment fails to adequately hydrolyze the native starch of sweetpotato despite the high endogenous amylase activity of the tissue. Walter et al. (1975) found large differences in the percentage of starch converted to sugars among baked roots of four sweetpotato cultivars; these differences however, were not closely correlated with measured β-amylase activity of the tissue, which also varied erratically. McArdle (1983) observed that diluted sweetpotato amylases appear to act more efficiently on corn mashes than on sweetpotato mashes. He concluded that other biochemical phenomena, such as differences in the nature of the starch fraction or enzyme inhibition might be involved. The objective of the present work was to purify α- and β-amylase from sweetpotato and to identify the various intrinsic inhibitors of these amylases.

MATERIAL AND METHODS.

'Regal' sweetpotato storage roots were provided by William M. Walter, Jr. (North Carolina State University at Raleigh).

Extraction of the enzymes

Sweetpotato storage roots were thoroughly washed in water and sliced. A 150 g amount of sliced sweetpotato was homogenized in a Waring blender for 1 min with

450 mL of cold 20 mM Na phosphate buffer (pH 6.0) containing 0.3% NaC1 (w/v), 0.2% CaCl$_2$ (w/v) and 0.005 M β-mercaptoethanol, and then filtered through cheesecloth. This extract was centrifuged in a refrigerated Sorvall RC-5B centrifuge for 10 min at 13,200g. The supernatant was taken as a crude extract and placed on ice.

Ammonium sulfate precipitation

Ammonium sulfate was slowly added to the crude extract with constant stirring at 0 to 4°C until 20% saturation, and then centrifuged in the cold (0 to 4°C) for 20 min at 13,200g. After discarding the precipitate, the ammonium sulfate concentration was very carefully increased to 80% saturation. After centrifugation in the cold at 13,200g for 20 min, the precipitate was collected and dissolved in Na phosphate buffer (pH 6.0), and centrifuged again for 15 min at 15,000g. The supernatant was desalted by passage through a Sephadex G-50 column previously equilibrated with 50 mM Na acetate buffer, pH 5.0 (β-amylase buffer), or with 50 mM Na acetate buffer (pH 6.0) containing 1 mM CaCl$_2$ and 0.04% NaCl for α-amylase purification.

Affinity chromatography

For β-amylase purification, the Sephadex G-50 column extract was applied to a Cyclohexaamylose (CHA)-Sepharose affinity chromatography column prepared as described by Vretblad (1974). The loaded column of CHA-Sepharose was washed with β-amylase buffer until the effluent was protein free. Bound protein was eluted with β-amylase buffer containing 10 mg/mL CHA. The CHA was then removed by applying the enzyme solution on a Sepharose 4B column after having been concentrated by ultrafiltration.

Purification of α-amylase was carried out by affinity chromatography on Cycloheptaamylose (Cha)-Sepharose as described by Silvanovich and Hill (1976), using a column previously equilibrated with α-amylase buffer. Eluted α-amylase was concentrated and the Cha removed on a Sepharose 4B column.

Protein quantification

Total proteins were quantified by the method of Bradford (1976) with BSA as standard.

α-amylase assay

α-amylase was assayed by the method of Hall et al. (1970) and detection based on hydrolysis of amylose azure (20 mg/mL), prepared in 20 mM Na phosphate buffer (pH 6.0) containing 2 mM CaCl$_2$ and 0.005 M β-mercaptoethanol. Assays were conducted at 40°C for 10 min and the reaction was stopped with 18% acetic acid (v/v). A standard curve of α-amylase preparation (No. A 2771, Sigma, St. Louis, MO) was made with amylose azure suspension and used to correct sweetpotato α-amylase activity units. One unit (U) of activity was defined as the amount of enzyme liberating a quantity of colored, soluble material corresponding to 2.5 absorbance units at 595 nm from 54 mg of amylose azure under defined assay conditions.

β-amylase assay

β-amylase activity was assayed as described by McCleary and Codd (1989). Aliquots of 0.2 mL of the extract (or dilution in 100 mM Na malate buffer, pH 5.5) containing Na_2 EDTA (1 mM), BSA (1 mg/mL) and NaN_3 (3 mM) were incubated with 0.2 mL of substrate mixture [p-nitrophenyl maltopentaoside (PNPG5), 5 mM and α-glucosidase (20 U), in distilled water] at 40°C for 10 min. The reaction was terminated and color developed by adding 1% (w/v) Trizma base (3.0 mL), and the absorbance at 410 nm measured. A unit (U) of enzyme is defined as the amount of enzyme which releases 1 μmole of p-nitrophenol/min under defined assay conditions.

Gel electrophoresis

SDS-PAGE was conducted using the buffer system of Laemmli (1970) with a 12.5% polyacrylamide separating gel and a 4.65% stacking gel.

Kinetic studies

The effect of polyphenols, phytate, oxalate and ascorbate on purified sweet-potato amylases was studied by treating enzyme solutions with the specific reagents. The amylase activity inhibition was measured by the method of Bernfeld (1955), using sweetpotato starch purified by the procedure of Thurber and Paine (1934), and then washed with 70% ethanol as substrate. All reagent solutions capable of changing the pH of the buffered enzyme were adjusted prior to their addition to the reaction mixture. Sweetpotato polyphenolic extracts were prepared by the method of Walter and Purcell (1979); phytate, oxalate and ascorbate were reagent grade. Possible endogenous inhibitory compounds in sweetpotato were also identified. Total hydrophilic and lipophilic low-molecular weight compounds were separated from sweetpotato roots by the following method: 200 g of sliced fresh sweetpotato were blended in a Waring blender for 3 min with 800 mL of chloroform-methanol-water (5:3:1) solution. This was then filtered and the two fractions obtained by phase separation were concentrated by evaporation, and then used in inhibitory studies with the amylases.

RESULTS AND DISCUSSION

Cycloamylose affinity chromatography (CAC) was the most effective step in the purification of sweetpotato amylases, resulting in a 417-fold and 6.5-fold purification of α- and β-amylases, respectively, in pooled fractions. The recovery of amylase activity after CAC, as a percentage of total activity, was 42% for α-amylase (Table 1) and only 2.4% for β-amylase (Table 2). One peak was observed in the elution of α- or β-amylase (Fig. 1). Fraction 7 (Fig. 1A) had a specific activity of 168.5 units/mg protein for α-amylase, and fraction 12 (Fig. 1B) had the highest β-amylase activity with 1529 units/mg protein. However, these measured activities were inaccurate because the amylases were in the presence of cycloamyloses known to be amylase inhibitors (Nomura et al. 1986). The low recovery of β-amylase was due to saturation of the CAC column with β-amylase.

Table 1. Purification of α-amylase

Purification Steps	Total volume (mL)	Activity (U/mL)	Protein (mg/mL)	Specific Activity (U/mg prot.)	Total Activity (U)	Yield (%)	Purifi- cation
Crude extract	400	0.296	1.247	0.237	118.40	100	1
20-80% Ammonium sulfate precipitation	40	2.598	4.169	0.623	103.92	87.8	2.62
Affinity Chromatography (pooled fractions)	7.5	6.627	0.067	98.910	49.70	42.0	417.4
Sepharose 4B (pooled fractions)	15	2.825	0.018	156.944	42.38	35.8	662.1

Cycloamyloses were removed from samples by Sepharose 4B gel filtration. Gel filtration of sweetpotato amylases also resulted in significant increases in purity. In fact, SDS-PAGE analysis of amylase preparations from the CAC column showed 2 small bands in addition to the amylase bands (data not shown) that were eliminated by gel filtration. Ultimately, sweetpotato α-amylase was purified 662-fold while β-amylase was purified 24-fold.

The high degree of purity attained is evident from the SDS-PAGE (Fig.2), which showed a single band for α-amylase as well as for β-amylase. The ability to hydro-lyze amylose azure is specific to α-amylase (Doehlert and Duke 1983), while p-nitrophenyl-maltopentaoside is specific to β-amylase (McCleary and Codd 1989). In addition, none of these purified amylase preparations hydrolyzed p-nitrophenyl-glycoside substrate (Table 3). These results indicated that these enzymes do not belong to the α-glucosidase group.

Kinetic studies

Polyphenolic compounds are known to inhibit enzymes (Golstein and Swain, 1965), particularly trypsin and lipase (Milic et al. 1968) but sweetpotato polyphe-nolic compounds, which are principally chlorogenic and isochlorogenic acids (Walter et al. 1979), had no effect on sweetpotato amylases.

Table 2. Purification steps for β-amylase.

	Total Volume (mL)	Activity (U/mL)	Protein (mg/mL)	Specific Activity (U/mg) prot.)	Total Activity (U)	Yield %	Purifi- cation
Crude extract	350	506.7	3.447	147.01	177,345	100	1
20-80% $(NH_4)_2SO_4$ precipitation	35	3,811.6	10.601	359.55	133,406	75.2	2.44
Sephadex G-50	50	2,383.0	5.513	432.20	119,150	67.2	2.93
Affinity Chromatography (pooled fractions)	8	545.9	0.570	357.71	4,367	2.4	6.51
Sepharose 4B (pooled fractions)	10	822.9	0.230	3577.80	8229	4.6	24.33

455

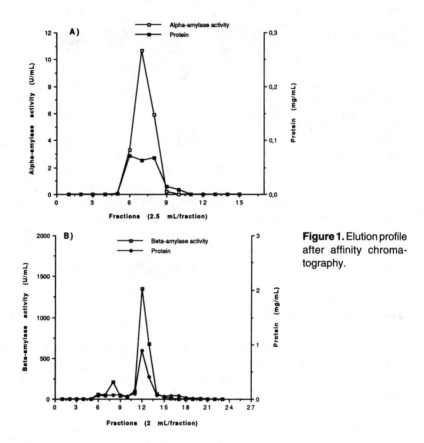

Figure 1. Elution profile after affinity chromatography.

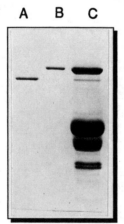

Figure 2. SDS-PAGE analysis of sweetpotato amylase preparations. Lane A, α-amylase preparation (5 μg); lane B, β-amylase preparation (5 μg); lane C, 20-80% ammonium sulfate precipitate (20 μg).

Table 3. Sweetpotato amylase substrate specificity.

Substrate	α-amylase	β-amylase
Amylose azure	+	o
Boiled sweetpotato starch[a]	+	+
P-nitrophenyl-glycoside	o	o
P-nitrophenyl-maltopentaoside	o	+
Soluble potato starch	+	+
Sweetpotato starch granules [b]	o	o

[a]Starch granules were maintained for 3 min at 100°C before assaying with sweetpotato amylase preparations.
[b]Incubated for 1 h at 40°C.

At a concentration of 0.08 mM, K-ascorbate inhibited β-amylase activity by 85% (Fig. 3). Ascorbates are known to inhibit β-amylase by reduction of copper ions and formation of an inactive cuprous enzyme (Rowe and Weill 1962). On the other hand, ascorbates are not reported to have any inhibitor effect on α-amylase; it is interesting to observe that 0.2 mM K-ascorbate reduced the α-amylase activity by 70% (Fig. 3). Since Bradbury (1988) reported the average content of sweetpotato vitamin C to be 24mg/100g, ascorbates may play an important role in the prevention of direct hydrolysis of sweetpotato starch, and it will be of interest to evaluate the effect of ascorbic acid on amylases during sweetpotato storage.

Five mM Na oxalate reduced the sweetpotato α-amylase activity by 46% (Fig. 4), but β-amylase was not sensitive to this compound. Oxalate ions have been reported to inhibit some Ca-requiring enzymes by forming compounds with the prosthetic groups (Belfanti et al. 1935). One one-hundreth molar or a concentration

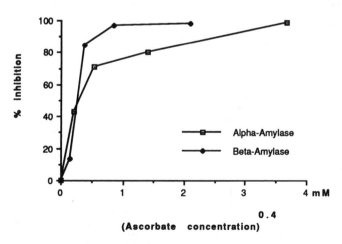

Figure 3. Effect of ascorbate on sweetpotato α- and β-amylase at 40°C, pH 6.0, after 10 min. reaction. (Ascorbic acid solution was adjusted to pH 6.0 with 1 M KOH before adding to sweetpotato starch mixture or to α-amylase solution).

of 10^{-2} M oxalate has also been observed to inactivate the *Bacillus subtilis* amylase by 69%, although no evidence of a prosthetic group has been found (Di Carlo 1947).

A 0.406 mM concentration of Na phytate inhibited α-amylase by 50% (Fig. 5), but the enzyme was relatively insensitive to further increases in phytate concentration, up to 10 mM. Amylase inhibition by phytates was found by Cawley and Mitchell (1968) and Deshpande and Cheryan (1984) to be related to complexation of the Ca^{2+}.

The concentrations of phytate and oxalate used in this study were based on values found by Oboh et al. (1989) in most sweetpotato varieties. At these concentrations it appears that phytate and oxalate influence the direct hydrolysis of

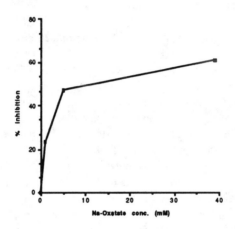

Figure 4. Effect of Na-oxalate on sweetpotato α-amylase at 40°C, pH 6.0, after 10 min. reaction. The enzyme was first incubated with oxalate for 30 min.

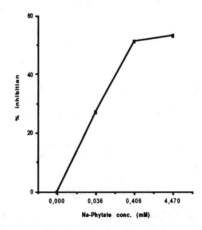

Figure 5. Effect of phytates on sweetpotato α-amylase at 40°C, pH 6.0, after 10 min. reaction. The enzyme was first incubated with phytate for 30 min.

sweetpotato starch. However, no inhibitory effect was observed on α- or β-amylase in sweetpotato fraction soluble in chloroform or in methanol-water.

Also, sweetpotato amylases were unable to hydrolyze native sweetpotato starch granules after 1 h of incubation at different temperatures. However, boiled starch granules were hydrolyzed at rates similar to those found when soluble starch served as the substrate. Raw potato starch is known to be less susceptible to enzymatic digestion than, for example, raw cereal starch (Dreher et al. 1981; Walker and Hope 1963). The content of bound phosphorus is generally higher in roots and tubers than in cereal starch (Greenwood 1970), but sweetpotato starch contains only about one fifth the organic phosphorus of white potato starch (Takeda et al. 1986). In addition to amylases, phosphorylase is probably vital for the degradation of raw sweetpotato starch.

REFERENCES

Belfanti, S., A. Contardi, and A. Ercoli. 1935. The influence of some electrolytes on the phosphatases of animal tissue. Phosphatases of the liver, kidney, serum and bones of the rabbit. Biochem. J. 29:517-527.

Bernfeld, P. 1955. Amylases, α- and β-. Page 149 in Methods in enzymology, edited by S.P. Colowick and N.O. Kaplan, Academic Press, New York, Vol. 1.

Bradbury, J.H. 1988. The chemical composition of tropical root crops; ASEAN Food J. 4:3-13.

Bradford, M.M. 1976. A rapid and sensitive method for the quantitation of microgram quantities of protein utilizing the principle of protein-dye binding. Anal. Biochem. 72:248-254.

Cawley, R.W., and T.A. Mitchell. 1968. Inhibition of wheat α-amylase by bran phytic acid. J. Sci. Food Agric. 19:106-108.

Deshpande, S.S., and M. Cheryan. 1984. Effects of phytic acid, divalent cations, and their interactions on α-amylase activity. J. Food Sci. 49:516-519.

Di Carlo, F.J., and S. Redfem. 1947. α-amylase from Bacillus subtilis. II. Essential groups. Arch. Biochem. 15:343-350.

Doehlert, D.C., and S.H. Duke. 1983. Specific determination of α-amylase activity in crude plant extracts containing β-amylase. Plant Physiol. 71:229-234.

Dreher, M.L., J.C. Scheerens, C.W. Weber, and J.W. Berry. 1981. Nutritional evaluation of buffalo gourd root starch. Nutr. Rep. Intern. 23:1-8.

Golstein, J.L., and T. Swain. 1965. The inhibition of enzymes by tannins. Phytochemistry 4: 185-192.

Greenwood, C.T. 1970. Starch and glycogen. Page 471 in The carbohydrates. The chemistry and biochemistry, edited by W. Pigman, D. Horton and A. Herp. Academic Press Inc., New York.

Hall, F.F., T.W. Culp, T. Hayakawa, C.R. Ratliff, and N.C. Hightower. 1970. An improved amylase assay using a new starch derivative. Amer. J. Clin. Path. 53:627-634.

Hoover, M.W. 1967. An enzyme activation process for producing sweetpotato flakes. Food Technol. 21:322-325.

Laemmli, U.K. 1970. Cleavage of structural proteins during the assembly of the head of bacteriophage T_4. Nature 227:680-685.

McArdle, R.N. 1983. The use of endogenous amylase to produce fermentable saccharides in Ipomoea batatas (L.) Lam. and Zea mays L. Ph.D. Thesis Dissertation. University of Maryland.

McCleary, B.V., and R. Codd. 1989. Measurement of β-amylase in cereal flours and commercial enzyme preparations. J. Cereal Sci. 9:17-33.

Milic, B., S. Stojanovic, N. Vucurevic, and M. Turcuc. 1968. Chlorogenic and quinic acids in sunflower meal. J. Sci. Fd. Agric. 19:108-113.

Nomura, K., B. Mikami, and Y. Morita. 1986. Interaction of soybean β-amylase with glucose. J. Biochem. 100:1175-1183.

Oboh, S., A. Ologhobo, and O. Tewe. 1989. Some aspects of the biochemistry and nutritional value of the sweetpotato *(Ipomoea batatas)*. Food Chem. 31:9-18.

Rowe, A.W., and C.E. Weill. 1962. The inhibition of β-amylase by ascorbic acid. II. Biochim. Biophys. Acta. 65:245-251.

Silvanovich, M.P., and R.D. Hill. 1976. Affinity chromatography of cereal alpha-amylase. Anal. Biochem. 73:430-433.

Takeda, Y., N.Tokunaga, C. Takeda, and S. Hizukuri. 1986. Physicochemical properties of sweetpotato starches. Starch/Starke. 38:345-350.

Thurber, F. H., and H.S. Paine. 1934. Purification of sweet and white potato starches. Ind. Eng. Chem. 26:567-569.

Vretblad, P. 1974. Immobilisation of ligands for biospecific affinity chromatography via their hydroxyl groups. The cyclohexaamylose α-amylase system. FEBS Letters 47:86-89.

Walker, G.J., and P.M. Hope. 1963. The action of some α-amylases on starch granules. Biochem. J. 86:452-462.

Walter, W.M., Jr., and A.E. Purcell. 1979. Evaluation of several methods for analysis of sweetpotato phenolics. J. Agric. Food. Chem. 27:942-946.

Walter, W.M., Jr., A.E. Purcell, and G.K. McCollum. 1979. Use of high-pressure liquid chromatography for analysis of sweetpotato phenolics. J. Agric. Food. Chem. 27:938-941.

Walter, W.M., Jr., A.E. Purcell, and A.M. Nelson. 1975. Effects of amylolytic enzymes on "moistness" and carbohydrate changes of baked sweetpotato cultivars. J.Food Sci. 40:793-796.

THE USE OF SWEETPOTATO IN BREAD MAKING

Zosima Huaman

International Potato Center, Apartado 5969, Lima, Peru.

The importance of sweetpotato as a food is based on its high carbohydrate content or as a source of starch. However, this root crop is also an excellent source of vitamins A and C. It also contains small amounts of vitamin B, calcium, iron, and sodium as well as a considerable amount of protein of good nutritive quality.

Many countries of Latin America, Asia and Africa have insufficient wheat production. They spend much of their hard currency to import wheat to produce the flour used in bread making. However, in these countries sweetpotato could substitute for a considerable percentage of wheat flour and other starch sources. In many of these countries the price of sweetpotato is several times cheaper than wheat flour.

Since 1975, the Agrarian University of LaMolina in Peru has produced a biscuit using mashed sweetpotato for up to 15% of the wheat flour. This technology has been extended to other commercial bakeries in Peru which substitute ground sweetpotato to produce a widely-accepted bread similar to pure wheat bread.

In Lima, the bakery Nova Pan is producing sweetpotato bread with 30% raw sweetpotato substituted for wheat flour. A small machine grates the sweetpotato into fine threads that are easily incorporated into the dough.

The El Progreso bakery in Carabayllo uses a very simple, large hand grater to grind the sweetpotato. Their recipe calls for 5 kg of wheat flour, 2 kg ground sweetpotato, 600 g sugar, 80 g salt, 150 g yeast, 500 g fat, 60 g dough conditioner and 2.6 L water and makes 350 pieces of bread. The dough conditioner, commercially available under several brand names, is made of glycerine esters, multiprotein complex, dehydroascorbic acid, azodicarbonamide, potassium bromate, calcium salts and wheat flour.

The advantages of producing sweetpotato bread in countries importing large quantities of wheat are: (1) bakeries will reduce production costs because sweetpotato is cheaper than wheat; (2) the country will save badly needed hard currency; and (3) the farmers will have a secure market for large amounts of sweetpotato.

UTILIZATION OF SWEETPOTATOES IN THE SOUTHERN DISTRICT OF THE PEOPLE'S REPUBLIC OF CHINA

Machiko Ono and Toshiaki Hirano

Nagoya Women's University Nagoya, Aichi, Japan 467.

China alone produces about 80 percent of the world's sweetpotatoes. Though an important food source, few reports are available on how sweetpotatoes are consumed at home. During three visits between 1986 and 1989 the authors investigated the use of sweetpotatoes in Guizhou, Guangdong, and Fujian provinces in southern China.

The Miao and Gujia minorities of Guizhou Province are basically self-sufficient in food. Both minorities use 50 to 60 percent of their sweetpotatoes for food and the remainder for animal feed. Harvested once a year, sweetpotatoes are stored in cellars or dried to make them available for use throughout the year.

In Nanhai District in Guangdong Province, sweetpotatoes are used mainly for pig feed, in preparing processed foods, and for starch and alcohol production. Sweetpotatoes were a staple food there until the 1950s but are now rarely eaten. In Fujian Province sweetpotatoes have much the same use. However, in Huian District where little rice is grown, sweetpotatoes are a preferred food and so are available throughout the year in fresh or dried form.

In all areas, sweetpotatoes are usually steamed, boiled, or baked, and there is little variety in preparation. Processed food products include dried sweetpotatoes, flour, and fried chips. Though it was observed that young sweetpotato leaves and stems are sometimes eaten as food, the above-ground portions of the sweetpotato are mostly utilized as animal feed.

PEROXIDASE AND POLYPHENOLOXIDASE ACTIVITY IN BLANCHED, FROZEN SWEETPOTATO SLICES

J.L. Silva, S.X. Ma, N. Abbas, J.O. Garner, Jr.*, J.O. Hearnsberger

Department of Food Science and Technology and *Department of Horticulture, Mississippi State University, Mississippi State, MS 39762.

Whole sweetpotato slices made from green and cured 'Centennial' and 'Jewel' storage roots were blanched at different time/temperature combinations and individually quick frozen. The slices were analyzed for enzymatic activity, phenolics, and discoloration after 1 and 12 months of storage at -18°C. Phenolics were higher in slices from 'Centennial' but decreased in both cultivars after 12 months of frozen storage. Polyphenoloxidase (PPO) activity was minimal after 3 min blanching at 100°C or 5 min. at 94°C. On the average, peroxidase (POD) activity was lower than PPO. Acceptable visual color scores were recorded on slices blanched for 3 min at 100°C. Results of this study suggest that PPO and not POD should be used as the indicator of adequate blanching in sweetpotato products.

INTRODUCTION

Sweetpotato [*Ipomoea batatas* L. (Lam.)] products which are not completely cooked or blanched are subject to degradation by enzymatic reactions. Polyphenoloxidases (PPO) and peroxidases (POD) are used as convenient indicators of adequate blanching. According to Williams et al. (1986), the temperature and time required for adequate blanching depend on the type of substrate. The POD is inadequate especially at low pH's as an indicator of PPO inactivation. Work by Ma et al. (1992) showed that inactivation of PPO resulted in adequate blanching of the slices.

The objectives of this work with frozen sweetpotato slices were: (1) to examine the effect of cultivar, curing, blanching temperature and time, and storage time on total phenolics, POD, and PPO residual activity of frozen sweetpotato slices; (2) to establish an optimum blanching temperature/time combination for the product; and (3) to determine the relationship between darkening, phenolics and PPO residual activity.

MATERIALS AND METHODS

Whole sweetpotato storage roots from 'Centennial' and 'Jewel' cvs. were treated as depicted in the flow chart (Fig. 1). The experiment was a complete 2 x 2 x 2 x 3 x 2 factorial with 3 replications in a completely randomized design (Fig. 2). Data were analyzed using SAS (1985). Means for blanched slices were compared to controls (not blanched) by using the Least Significant Difference (LSD) method with significance at P<0.05 (Steel and Torrie 1980).

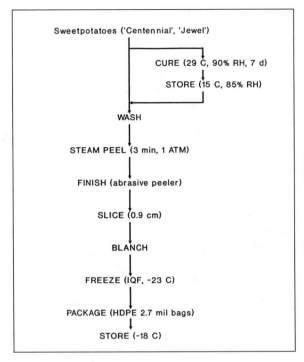

Figure 1. Sample preparation for sweetpotato slices.

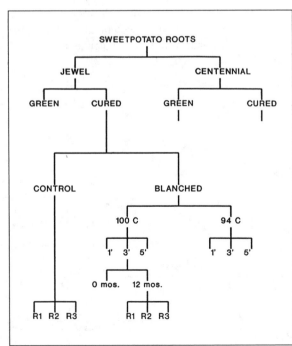

Figure 2. Statistical experimental design for evaluation of sweetpotato slices.

463

Table 1. Mean phenolics content for blanched sweetpotato slices from two cultivars at 0 and 12 months frozen storage.

Frozen Storage Time (months)	Total Phenolics (mg/1009)	
	Cultivar	
	'Jewel'	'Centennial'
0	42.2a*	61.9a
12	27.2b	47.9b

*Means within column not followed by same letter differ (P < 0.05).

Sample analyses were conducted using the following methods:
1. Phenolics - Rosenblatt and Peluso (1941);
2. POD Activity - Modification of Ngo and Lenhoff 1980 (Abbas 1991);
3. PPO Activity - Modification of Coseteng and Lee 1987 (Ma 1988);
4. Discoloration - 7 point scale (Ma 1988); and
5. Color - Hunter 'L' (Abbas 1991).

RESULTS AND DISCUSSION

Total phenolics were higher in slices analyzed just after freezing (0 mos.) than in those stored for 12 months (Table 1). This may account for lower residual PPO activity after 12 months of storage (Figs. 3 and 4). 'Centennial' had a higher concentration of PPO substrate (phenolics) than 'Jewel' but, when blanched, both cultivars showed the same trend.

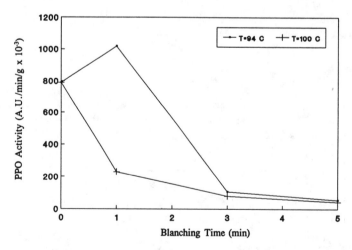

Figure 3. Residual polyphenoloxidase (PPO) activity in frozen sweetpotato slices stored 5 days (0 months) as a function of blanching temperature and time.

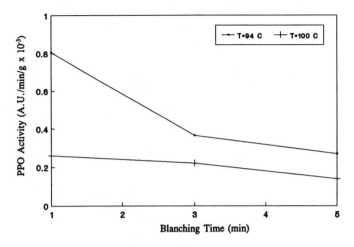

Figure 4. Residual polyphenoloxidase (PPO) activity in frozen sweetpotato slices stored 12 months as a function of blanching temperature and time.

PPO activity was higher after 1 min blanching than in unblanched controls but decreased thereafter reaching insignificant levels after 5 min of blanching (Fig. 3). Blanching for 3 min at 100°C and 5 min at 94°C resulted in similar PPO activity for slices analyzed just after freezing (0 mo). When PPO activity was analyzed after 12 mo frozen storage, the residual activity was very low as compared to the freshly frozen product (Fig. 4). When POD was measured after 12 mo frozen storage (Fig. 5), its residual activity was low even after 1 min blanching. Compared to PPO activity, POD appears more heat sensitive and thus should not be the choice indicator enzyme for adequacy of blanching sweetpotatoes.

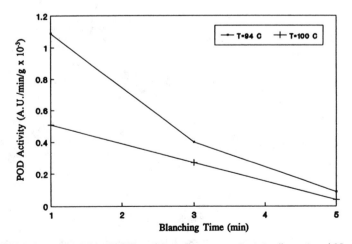

Figure 5. Residual peroxidase (POD) activity in frozen sweetpotato slices stored 12 months as a function of blanching temperature and time.

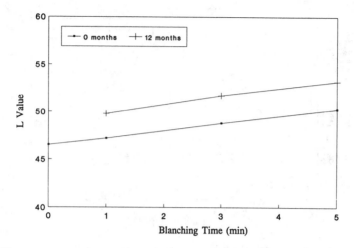

Figure 6. Hunter 'L' values in frozen sweetpotato slices as a function of blanching time and frozen storage time.

Hunter 'L' (lightness) values were used as an objective measure of discoloration with higher values indicating less discoloration. Hunter 'L' values increased with increased blanching time (Fig. 6) and were higher after 12 mo frozen storage. This confirms PPO activity data in that, at lower activity levels, there is less discoloration. Color scores as measured by sensory panelists ('1' being brown and '7' being absent of discoloration) showed increased scores with increased blanching time (Fig. 7). A score of '5' or higher was acceptable. Lower scores for slices stored for 12 mo may be the result of different panelists used in the initial and final evaluation. However, the trends were the same.

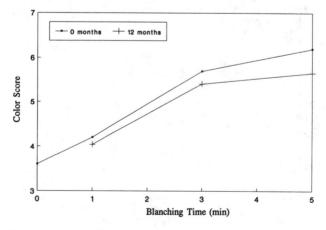

Figure 7. Visual color scores ('7' being absence of discoloration) in frozen sweetpotato slices as a function of blanching time and storage time.

466

CONCLUSIONS

It appears that PPO and not POD should be used as the indicator enzyme in blanched sweetpotato products. Blanching in water for either 3 min at 100°C or for 5 min at 94°C appears to be sufficient to inactivate PPO in sliced sweetpotatoes.

Visual color scores confirm that an acceptable product is produced by blanching the slices for at least 3 min.

ACKNOWLEDGMENTS

This paper is Journal Article PS-8089 of the Mississippi Agricultural and Forestry Experiment Station, Mississippi State, MS 39762.

REFERENCES

Abbas, N. 1991. The effect of cultivar, curing, blanching, and frozen storage on biochemical and physical properties of frozen sweetpotato slices. M.S. Thesis. Mississippi State University, MS.

Coseteng, M.Y., and C.Y. Lee. 1987. Change in apple polyphenoloxidase and polyphenol concentrations in relation to degree of browning. J. Food Sci. 52:985.

Ma, S.X. 1988. The effect of cultivar, curing, blanching temperature and time on phenolic content, ascorbic acid, polyphenoloxidase activity, color and texture of frozen sweet potato (*Ipomoea batatas* (L.) Lam) slices. M.S. Thesis, Mississippi State University, MS.

Ma, S.X., J.L. Silva, J.O. Hearnsberger, and J.O. Garner, Jr. 1992. Effect of cultivar, curing, and blanching on polyphenoloxidase and color of sweetpotato slices. J. Agric. Food Chem. 40:864-867.

Ngo, T.T., and H.N. Lenhoff. 1980. A sensitive and chromogenic assay for peroxidase-coupled reactions. Analyt. Biochem. 105:389.

Potter, N.N. 1986. Vegetable and fruits. Pages 500-531 *in* Food Science, 4th ed. AVI/VNR, Florence, KY.

Rosenblatt, M., and J.V. Peluso. 1941. Determination of tannins by photocolorimeter. Assoc. of Agric. Chem. 24(1):170.

SAS. 1985. Statistical Analysis System. SAS Institute, Cary, NC.

Steel, R.G.O., and J.M. Torrie. 1980. Principles and Procedures of Statistics. McGraw-Hill Book Co., New York.

Williams, D.C., M.H. Lim, A.O. Chen, R.M. Pangborn, and J.R. Whitaker, Jr. 1986. Blanching of vegetables for freezing—which indicator enzyme to choose. Food Technol. 42(6):130.

Sweetpotato Technology for the 21st Century. W.A. Hill, C.K. Bonsi and P.A. Loretan (Eds.) 1992. Tuskegee University, Tuskegee, AL

PROCESSING OF SWEETPOTATO VERMICELLI IN INDIA

Annavi Susheela Thirumaran and D. Malathy Ravindran
Tamil Nadu Agricultural University, Coimbatore - 641 003 India.

Sweetpotato, though high in many essential nutrients, plays only a minor role in the Indian diet. It can be processed into sweetpotato flour. If mixed with wheat flour it can be extruded into vermicelli spaghetti. The incorporation of legume flours— greengram, blackgram or defatted soy flour—raises the protein level in the product. The vermicelli was rated acceptable by a taste panel with the addition of up to 20% legume flour. Other processed products may also raise the level of sweetpotato in the Indian diet.

INTRODUCTION

Sweetpotato, *Ipomoea batatas* L. (Lam), is a versatile root crop in its adaptibility to different environments; it is grown in all parts of the tropical and subtropical world. The sweetpotato storage roots are a major source of carbohydrates. They are consumed without being processed in India. The fresh storage root is boiled, or steamed and consumed directly. In terms of productivity in a limited time period, sweetpotato exceeds many tropical crops. It is valued for its short growing period (90 to 120 days), 25 metric ton per hectare output, and its nutritive components. Specifically, the nutritive components of sweetpotato (on a 100 g basis) include: carbohydrates - 28.2 g and energy of 120 kcal, protein -11.2 g, fat - 0.3 g, minerals - 1.0 g, fiber - 0.8 g, calcium - 46 mg, phosphorus - 50 mg, carotene - 6 mg, vitamin C - 24 mg, niacin - 0.7 mg, iron - 0.8 mg, thiamin - 0.08 mg and riboflavin - 0.04 mg (Gopalan et al. 1985). For three local varieties, 'Co-1,' 'Co-2' and 'Co-3,' the respective starch and sugar contents were: 12.42 and 9.19, 17.65 and 9.29, and 19.53 and 9.23 g/100g (Jansi Rani 1985). Analyses of 15 U.S. cultivars found total solids range from 24 to 34.6%, total phenols (ortho, meta and para isomers of the aromatic compounds) were 22.0 to 76.0 mg/100g fresh weight and ortho phenols (only ortho isomers) were 10.4 to 36.4 mg/100g fresh weight. Sweetpotatoes can also be made into industrial products including preparations of syrup, flour and starch.

Despite having many essential nutrients, the role of sweetpotato in many Indian diets is minor. A study conducted to assess the food consumption patterns and nutrient intake of 350 rural farm families in three income brackets in seven villages near Tamil Nadu Agricultural University compared that intake by category (Table 1) to food and nutrient allowances recommended by the Indian Council of Medical Research (ICMR). The top six categories are all below the recommended levels in every income bracket. For the top three food items, a conversion of intake to energy needs met by the rural diet (3.5 kcal/g for cereals and millets and 1.29 kcal/g for roots and tubers) (Table 2) indicates how small a portion of energy needs are met by roots and tubers—less than 5% for those in the poorest income bracket. Ways must be found to increase consumption of sweetpotato in the common man's diet.

Table 1. Per capita food and nutrient intake* of Indian families in Tamil Nadu region.

| | Monthly income range | | | |
Food item	Rs.500 & below	Rs.501-1000	Rs.1001- above	RDA by ICMR
Cereals	229.2	201.0	192.0	410
Millets	35.8	24.8	27.3	
Roots and tubers	36.8	36.8	55.5	75
Green leafy vegetables	13.0	10.5	15.8	125
Other vegetables	43.9	46.0	59.9	75
Fruits	14.7	13.4	27.7	30
Nuts & oil seeds	55.7	31.0	43.2	40
Animal foods	29.1	31.8	42.5	30
Mllk and milk products	159.4	67.4	98.0	100
Sugar and jaggery	46.3	47.1	53.4	35

*grams; 30 Rs. = $1 (November, 1992 rate).

To be eaten fresh, however, sweetpotatoes must be able to be stored. In India, sweetpotato is grown on over 225 thousand hectares with a total production of 1.3 million metric tons. Storage of sweetpotato storage roots without deterioration is usually difficult because of heavy infestation by the sweetpotato weevil, *Cylas formicarius* (Jayaramaiah 1975). The usual practice of storage is to keep the harvested storage roots exposed in the godown. Control of the weevil is very often difficult as most life stages (egg, larva, and pupa) take place inside the roots. Fumigating the storage roots and treating the bags containing them with 5% DDT can reduce weevil infestation. Storage of storage roots in sand also prevented infestation (Cheriyan 1945). However, storage in gunny bags even with insecticides was not effective beyond one month. Sweetpotato storage roots heaped on the floor and covered with red earth and wood ash were found to be free from weevil infestation and dehydration for two months (Rajamma 1984). There is presently no way to store the roots much beyond this time.

Table 2. Ratio of energy met by the rural diet according to monthly income range.

| | Energy (kcal) | | |
Source	Rs. 500 & below	Rs. 501-1000	Rs. 1001 & above
Cereals	802.3	703.5	671.9
Millets	123.8	85.8	94.4
Roots and Tubers	47.4	47.5	71.6
Total	973.5	836.8	838.0

Table 3. Vermicelli preparations incorporating legume flour.

Product	Weight of refined wheat flour + sweetpotato flour mix (%)	Weight of pulse flour (%)	Moisture level (%)	Salt
Control	79	—	20	1
Greengram/ blackgram/ soyflour/flour incorporated				
10%	59	10	30	1
20%	49	20	30	1
30%	39	30	30	1

The objective of this paper is to examine the possibility of introducing the sweetpotato into Indian diets as processed vermicelli, made partially with sweetpotato flour, and to study its shelf life and acceptability.

MATERIALS AND METHODS

Processing of sweetpotato flour into vermicelli

White flesh sweetpotato varieties were used for processing into flour. Sweetpotatoes were washed, peeled, treated with 0.1% sulphur dioxide, dried and milled into flour. Preliminary trials were conducted to obtain the right formula for sweetpotato flour-based, ready-to-use food mixes. The nutritive composition of the final preparation was analyzed using methods of AOAC (1985).

Vermicelli was prepared by extrusion using 50% each of sweetpotato flour and refined wheat flour maida. This was the control in the study. Trials were made of extruded vermicelli incorporating 10, 20 and 30% levels (Table 3) of legume flours like greengram, blackgram and defatted soyflour to enhance the protein content of the product. A flow diagram (Fig. 1) describes the processing steps involved in the preparation of the vermicelli. The nutritive content of the basic mix (control and each of the legume flour additives) was also analyzed using AOAC methods (1985).

A mean drying temperature of 35.5°C was used for 18 hours of tempering and drying over an 18 hour period. A final moisture content of 11.5% was adopted for the control and all the treatments.

The extrusion behavior of each treatment was studied for the uniformity in the flow of strands and external appearance. A panel of 10 judges was selected to study the physical characteristics of processed vermicelli for fineness, shape, length, tensile strength and packaging possibilities using a score card.

Figure 1. Flow diagram for vermicelli extrusion.

Table 4. Nutritive composition of sweetpotato flour.

Moisture	Ash (minerals)	Calories	Protein	Calcium	Iron	Reducing sugar	Total sugar
(g)	(g)	(kcal)	(g)	(mg)	(mg)	(g)	(g)
9.5	2.1	366.4	2.4	96.8	2.9	2.7	3.1

Fifty gram samples of the sweetpotato vermicelli were cooked with 200 mL of boiling water and the time was noted (Bradbury and Holloway 1988). The end point was tested by pressing cooked samples between two glass slides with the absence of uncooked starch indicating a fully cooked sample. The amount of water absorbed for cooking was recorded.

For sensory evaluation of the vermicelli, a recipe for 'Payasam,' a very popular Indian delicacy, was selected. It was prepared with vermicelli processed with the incorporation of greengram, blackgram and defatted soyflour and was evaluated by a panel of 10 judges for its acceptability characteristics. Scoring was on the basis of a 1 to 9 point scale with 9 being the highest.

In order to determine storage characteristics, greengram, blackgram and defatted soyflour-incorporated vermicelli and the control were also packed in 200 gauge polyethylene bags, sealed and studied during storage in order to ascertain their shelf life.

RESULTS AND DISCUSSION

The nutritive analysis of sweetpotato flour (Table 4) indicates the high level of energy available from sweetpotato but also the low level of protein. The protein content of extruded vermicelli can be improved by the addition of any of the three legume flours; greengram, blackgram or defatted soyflour (Table 5).

The physical characteristics in terms of fineness, shape, length, tensile strength and packaging possibilities of the extruded vermicelli were rated highly acceptable for all three types of legume flour at a 20% level of incorporation. The flow of strands

Table 5. Nutritive value of a basic sweetpotato flour mix for vermicelli and selected legume flour additives on a 100 gram basis.

Products	Calories (kcal)	Protein (g)	Calcium (mg)	Iron (mg)	Phosphorus (mg)
Basic mix	234.0	6.1	34.5	1.5	85.5
Selected legume flours:					
Greengram	184.3	7.9	31.9	1.5	122.9
Blackgram	184.0	7.8	47.7	1.5	118.9
Defatted soyflour	196.7	14.2	64.9	2.8	42.0

was also uniform at this level. The shelf-life of the vermicelli product packed in polyethelene bags was found to be more than 60 days.

Sensory evaluation scores of the 10% greengram, 10% blackgram and 10% defatted soyflour ranged from 7.2 to 8.3, 7.9 to 8.2 and 6.6 to 8.5 respectively. When 20% of each of the legume flour additives were incorporated, the score ranges dropped to 6.9 to 7.9, 6.5 to 8.0 and 6.5 to 7.5. With incorporation of 30% legume flours, the scores were 6.4 to 7.4, 6.3 to 7.0 and 5.9 to 6.9. Incorporation at the 20% level was considered acceptable.

Thus, sweetpotatoes can be introduced into the basic Indian diet as part of a nutritious extruded vermicelli product also incorporating up to 20% legume flour. The product would use processed sweetpotatoes—avoiding the need for fresh storage—and would have a shelf life of two months. Use of sweetpotato vermicelli would decrease the reliance of the population on wheat flour. Other products, e.g., starch, candy and a beverage, can also be derived from the sweetpotato and brought into the diet.

ACKNOWLEDGEMENT

The authors wish to express their thanks to Dr. S. Jayaraj, Vice Chancellor and Director of Research, Tamil Nadu G. D. Naidu Agricultural University in Coimbatore. The authors also thank Dr. I. Irulappan, Dean and the staff of the College of Horticulture for providing the storage roots for the study from the college fields and for all the help rendered during the course of the study.

REFERENCES

AOAC. 1985. Official methods of analysis. Association of official analytical chemists (AOAC) 12:3, 71-74, 535, Washington, D. C.

Bradbury, J. H., and D.H. Holloway. 1988. Chemistry of tropical root crops: Significance for nutrition and agriculture in the Pacific. Australian Centre for International Agricultural Research, Canberra.

Cheriyan, M. 1945, Report on the operation of the Department of Agriculture, Madras Presidency. 46:15.

Gopalan, C., B.V. Ramasastri, and S.C. Balasubramanian. 1985. Nutritive value of foods, NIN, Hydersabad, p. 75.

Jansi Rani, P. 1985. Evaluation of sweetpotato (*Ipomoea batatas* Lam.) clones for biometrical characters and biochemical constituents. M. Sc. Thesis (Hort) to the Tamil Nadu GD Naidu Agricultural University, Coimbatore - 641 003.

Jayaramaiah, M. 1975. Bionomics of sweet potato weevil *Cylas formicarius* (Fabricius) (*Coleoptera curculionidae*), Mysore J. Agric. Sci. 9:99.

Rajamma, P. 1984. Control of *Cylas formicarius* during storage of sweet potato (*Ipomoea batatas*) tubers, J. of Fd. Sci. and Tech. 21(3):183-185.

Thompson, D. P. 1984. Composition of sweet potato cultivars at harvest time. J. of Fd. Sci. and Tech. 21(1):43-44.

Walter, W. M. Jr., and A.E. Furcell. 1979. Evaluation of several methods for analysis of sweet potato phenolics, J. Agric. Fd. Chem. 27:942.

PROMOTING SWEETPOTATO THROUGH RECIPES

Jack S. J. Tsay, Mei-chin C. Cheng and Chiu-O Chen
Tainan County Farmer's Association, No. 5, Ming Tse Road, Hsinying, Tainan County, Taiwan.

There are farmers associations organized in every county and township in Taiwan. Their objectives are to protect farmers' interests and upgrade the quality of life for farm families through modernization of farming technology and improvement of the rural economy. The major functions of the associations are to provide agricultural extension services, to assist with marketing agricultural produce, and to assure availability of farm machinery, credit services and insurance.

In view of the important role of rural women in agriculture, education in home economics has been a major program of every farmers association since their founding. Improvements have been made in areas such as the rural environment, nutrition education and household management. In order to apply knowledge of food science and nutrition to people's daily lives, a series of sweetpotato recipes (See Appendix) was published by the Tainan County Farmers Association.

Sweetpotato is an important crop in Tainan county. It was consumed traditionally as a supplemental staple to rice. Due to recent economic development, consumption patterns regarding sweetpotato have changed. It is now consumed mainly for its nutrients rather than for energy. Recipes today partially reflect this tendency. They also demonstrate that the art of Chinese dishes is in combining several materials in their right proportion to enrich appearance, flavor and taste. If this principle is applied, unlimited dishes can be created by combining sweetpotato with many other food items.

There are two popular varieties available in Taiwan markets—Taiwan 57 and Taiwan 66. Both of them have good eating quality and an attractive appearance. They can be produced year round under subtropical environments with a yield of around 60 tons per hectare. The fresh roots are suitable for salads and can be cooked with other vegetables. Mashed sweetpotatoes are used as stuffing. The idea of preparing sweetpotato dishes is not limited to appearance nor to taste; principles of nutrition are also incorporated.

One way to use sweetpotato as a supplemental staple food is to fortify wheat flour with sweetpotato. This adds vitamin A to the wheat flour and makes the resulting flour more nutritionally balanced. The amount of sweetpotato can be varied according to the properties of the food items. Our experience has shown that sweetpotato-fortified flour can be used in preparing other food items such as bread, noodles, cookies and even cakes.

Orange-fleshed sweetpotato is very rich in vitamin A. It is important to maintain this vitamin in designing new recipes. Studies have shown that high temperature/short-time cooking is an effective way of retaining provitamin A in sweetpotato. Stir frying is one recommended method. The addition of salad oil is another way to enhance the availability of beta-carotene. Fried sweetpotatoes incorporate this idea as do sweetpotato salads using mayonaisse or oil.

473

Sweetpotato leaves are cooked as a traditional dish in Chinese diets. However, they are not considered a high quality leafy vegetable due to their high fiber content. New cultivars specific for tip use have been developed. These are generally low in fiber and remain green in color after cooking. Blanching prior to sauteing has been found to be a useful practice in improving the eating quality of sweetpotato leaves. As a dish it is gaining popularity in Taiwan because the leaves are free from pesticides. It is particularly popular during the summer season when other green leafy vegetables are difficult to grow.

The importance of dietary fiber to the human digestive system has been recognized in recent years. Sweetpotato is recommended by nutritionists for its high fiber content. It is not only good as a vegetable side dish but also as a healthy snack food. Sweetpotato chips and sweetpotato jello are only two examples among many products of this nature. Candied sweetpotatoes is a sweet dish generally served as part of a meal. Skill, technique and the correct raw materials are key in preparing this dish.

In summary, sweetpotato is nutritious, but it is the good recipe or food product which will make people want to eat it. We hope more people not only try sweetpotatoes but also develop more new recipes to make sweetpotato a popular vegetable not only in Taiwan but also in other parts of the world.

(Editors' note: The recipes of the Tainan County Farmers Association of Taiwan can be found in Section 6 along with other recipes distributed at the symposium from Japan, India, the United States, Ghana in Africa and Guyana in South America.)

SECTION 5

INTERFACING NEW TECHNOLOGIES WITH CONVENTIONAL BREEDING

Sweetpotato Technology for the 21st Century. W.A. Hill, C.K. Bonsi and P.A. Loretan (Eds.) 1992. Tuskegee University, Tuskegee, AL

Melvin R. Hall*, Don R. La Bonte**, Conrad K. Bonsi***

New Techniques and Conventional Breeding of Sweetpotato

Successful breeding methodologies have been developed to overcome inherent difficulties arising from poor flowering, sterility, and incompatibility in sweetpotato [*Ipomoea batatas* (L.)]. Even with a narrow gene base, significant improvements in yield and pest resistances have been developed. However, strategies successfully used in the past will need to be augmented to achieve equivalent rates of success in the future. Identifying sources of resistance and the transfer of resistance to elite germplasm have relied heavily on traits for which screening can be conducted easily and quickly under natural conditions. A combination of strategies will be required to develop control methods for most insect pests and pathogens for which only partial genetic resistances are currently known. These strategies may include, but are not limited to, the development of protocols for screening under controlled environmental conditions, identifying sources of resistance in related species and subsequent interspecific transfer, nonpreference (antixenosis) and antibiosis. The added time and expense required to achieve results using these methods will put further constraints on breeding programs. Individual programs will have to increasingly rely on exchange of germplasm for desired traits developed in other programs, and this interdependence will require a greater need for worldwide communication not only to identify germplasm but to reduce duplication of efforts. Advances in computer technology will also enable breeders to more efficiently manage data and to make breeding-related decisions. In addition, there are possibilities for merging technologies directly related to genetic improvement with other technologies usually not associated with conventional breeding, for example the development and selection of clones specifically designed for growth during long-term space missions. The challenge to the sweetpotato breeder in the 21st century will be to successfully combine new and emerging technologies with already proven practices of conventional breeding to provide improved cultivars for both conventional agriculture and for newly identified uses.

INTRODUCTION

Great strides in sweetpotato technology have been made in the 20th century, but where do we go from here? Sustained scientific effort in the past 70 years has resulted in high yielding, multiple pest resistant cultivars. These tremendous gains have

---

*Horticulture Dept., University of Georgia Coastal Plain Experiment Station, Tifton, GA.

**Horticulture Dept., Louisiana State University Agricultural Center, Baton Rouge, LA.

***George Washington Carver Agricultural Experiment Station, Tuskegee University, Tuskegee, AL 36088.

enabled sweetpotato to maintain its prominence as an important staple crop in the diet of much of the developing world. Our past accomplishments may still foreshadow our future as we integrate new technologies with already proven techniques.

It is fitting that we are holding this conference in a place where nearly 100 years ago a dynamic but humble man also probably asked, "Where do we go from here?" George Washington Carver arrived at Tuskegee in 1896. Could he have foreseen the technological changes that would occur in his lifetime? Could he have imagined that in just seven years the Wright Brothers would make their now famous motorized flight at Kitty Hawk, North Carolina, and that someday people would commonly travel by air? Perhaps—experimental airplanes were invented in 1896 and people were already familiar with hot air balloons. Could he have imagined the changes that would occur in sweetpotato breeding?

CONVENTIONAL BREEDING

The term "conventional breeding" suggests unchanging methods. However, just as we gradually adopt new technologies in our daily lives, sweetpotato breeders employ new techniques in their breeding programs. Let us first look at the evolution of conventional sweetpotato breeding through three general stages and then attempt to answer the question, "Where do we go from here?"

Sweetpotato is a hexaploid with 90 chromosomes and demonstrates both self- and cross-incompatibility and sterility (Edmond 1971; Martin 1965), so breeding programs for sweetpotato were slower to develop than for crops with simpler genetic systems. Modest improvements were made to existing germplasm by selecting superior spontaneous mutations (Edmond 1971; Kukimura 1986). For example, 'Beniaka', selected for improved red skin color in 1898 from 'Yatsubusa', has remained a popular Japanese cooking type (Kukimura 1986). Miller's breeding program in Louisiana (U.S.A.) began in the mid-1930's with intensive selection for superior mutants of 'Porto Rico' (Miller 1931; 1936). Variants for shape, yield, and carbohydrate content were selected and released as cultivars. Miller's most important selection was 'Unit 1 Porto Rico,' a high-yielding strain which had an important impact on the sweetpotato industry in the United States (Edmond 1971). Spontaneous mutations have been augmented with mutations produced by irradiation and chemical mutagens. Kukimura (1986) described the integration of mutation breeding into practical breeding programs in Japan. These induced mutants may be used directly or as parents in a crossing program.

Breeders successfully overcame barriers in sweetpotato crossing and, even with a narrow gene base, significantly improved yield and pest resistances by cross breeding. Several early workers demonstrated flowering and seed production in sweetpotato both in the tropics and in the continental U.S. Both characteristics were at one time considered rare or nonexistent in many locations (Edmond 1971). In the 1930's, Miller (1939) developed a system for inducing flowers and seed set at relatively low cost with equipment available at most experiment stations. He also initiated the first systematic efforts in the U.S. for controlled genetic recombination of sweetpotato. Other breeding programs soon followed. From throughout the world germplasm was collected for crossing, but Puerto Rico and Cuba were particularly important sources. Recombination of germplasm was first by hand pollination using the pedigree method and later by open pollination as fertility increased in the germplasm. Understanding that inheritance in sweetpotato is best described in quantitative terms led to mass selection as an effective way of combining favorable characters in parental types (Jones 1965; Jones 1986; Jones et al. 1986). Mass selection improves the mean performance of successive generations and provides higher levels of performance than in the base population. In contrast with pedigree breeding, where the same parental clones may be crossed year after year, mass selection and polycrossing constantly develops a whole set of improved parental clones. Today's sweetpotato breeder usually combines pedigree breeding and mass selection while always watching for spontaneous mutations or in some cases inducing mutations.

Along with maintaining yield and quality, a major achievement in sweetpotato breeding has been the introduction of multiple pest resistances into modern cultivars (Jones et al. 1986). Identifying sources of resistance and transferring it to elite germplasm have relied heavily on traits for which screening can be conducted easily and quickly under natural conditions. For example, insect damage is identified by visual evaluations and scoring of holes or other damage on the storage roots. Nematode damage is evaluated by visually counting and scoring galling of fibrous roots and by visible infestation or other damage, depending on nematode species, of the storage root. Disease infection is evaluated by degree of plant and/or root damage. Breeders have continually developed better cultivars because they have continued to incorporate new technology into their conventional breeding programs.

NEW TECHNIQUES

Unlike today, pioneers in sweetpotato breeding had few options available to address seemingly overwhelming problems. The breeder of today has the opportunity to choose among approaches to address specific problems. Some new techniques, particularly those in molecular biology, can be imposing to traditional breeders, but symposia and books such as this one help to move these techniques out of the realm of basic science and into everyday applications. Many of the chapters in this book (Dodds et al. 1992; Nakamura 1992; Prakash and Varadarajan 1992; Cantliffe 1992; Jarret et al. 1992; Carelli et al. 1992; Ozias-Akins and Perera 1992; etc.) present information on the new technologies which may be interfaced with conventional breeding. Let us speculate on three areas in which new technologies may be used in conventional breeding: (1) transfer of genetic information; (2) communication and management of technical information; and (3) merging technologies of genetic improvement with technologies usually not associated with conventional breeding.

First, let us discuss the transfer of genetic information. Conventional sweetpotato breeding includes three stages: (1) identification and selection of mutations, the primary method of sweetpotato improvement up through the 1930's; (2) pedigree breeding of selected parental clones, which began in the 1930's and remained the primary innovation for at least twenty years; and (3) the current stage of quantitative genetics, which best describes inheritance in sweetpotato, and mass selection. It seems impossible not to deduce that the fourth evolutionary stage of conventional sweetpotato breeding is now in process. This stage is the era of genetic engineering/ biotechnology. Just as each of the previous three stages was incorporated into conventional sweetpotato breeding, so shall these new tools be incorporated into our concept of conventional sweetpotato breeding. Simply stated, breeders will learn how to transfer genetic information in ways which complement selection of mutations, pedigree breeding, and mass selection. A combination of strategies will be required to develop control methods for most insect pests and pathogens, for which only partial genetic resistances are currently known. These strategies may include, but are not limited to, the development of protocols for screening under controlled environmental conditions, the identification of sources of resistance in related species and subsequent interspecific transfer, nonpreference (antixenosis) and antibiosis. These new methods will require added time and expense to achieve results, which will further constrain our breeding programs. Individual programs will have to increasingly rely on exchange of germplasm for desired traits developed in other programs, and this interdependence will demand greater worldwide communication, not only to identify germplasm but to reduce duplication of efforts.

Sweetpotato breeding programs rely increasingly on interaction and cooperation among entomologists, plant pathologists, food scientists, social scientists and molecular biologists. Close ties with extension specialists and growers are also imperative to identify strengths and weaknesses in our programs and to maintain a focus on problems that can be addressed through genetic improvement. A cooperative spirit among members of the team is the most important ingredient, and modern technology can facilitate communication among such interdisciplinary teams. The overwhelming amount of information generated while screening the myriad of traits must be organized and summarized for members of the group to make informed decisions. Computer databases are particularly useful in this capacity. Some databases are general in nature (Hess 1987), and some are specifically designed for sweetpotato (Yoshida 1984; St. Amand and LaBonte 1990). Added decision-making power is achieved if the database can summarize accumulated data over years.

The idea of information management can be taken one step further. Sweetpotato breeders need to familiarize themselves with other sweetpotato breeding programs. Sweetpotato breeders work in many countries, but only indirectly is information communicated through journal articles, symposia, and professional meetings. The isolation developed through distance and language barriers prevents most breeders from benefiting from research conducted elsewhere. One solution to this problem could be the development of a cooperative newsletter in which contributors can present preliminary findings, test hypotheses, and make germplasm available to the breeding community at large. Numerous crops such as corn, tomato and cucurbits have such newsletters; the time may be right for sweetpotato. Databases may also facilitate information transfer between breeding programs. Information can be stored on diskettes and shared with all breeders seeking germplasm useful to their programs. Conceptually this sharing could: (1) minimize duplication of efforts to develop complex traits; and (2) facilitate exchange of germplasm with resistance to potentially 'new' diseases or insects not currently present in an area.

Plant breeders have always employed two strategies to help solve increasing food demands of an ever-increasing world population: deciding what crops to grow and how to most effectively and efficiently breed the chosen crops. We have entered the space age. As we approach the 21st century, plant breeders must develop new methods to meet the new challenges ahead. They have the challenging task of anticipating the kinds of changes likely to take place in food demands and in ecological changes in various farming systems. Plant breeders must be cognizant of energy resources, population shifts, land availability and resources, and the necessity to improve the human diet (Christian and Lewis 1982; Rubenstein et al. 1980; Blixt and Vose 1984; Sinha and Swaminathan 1984). Sweetpotato breeders must face the challenge of developing cultivars suitable for nonconventional uses and production systems.

George Washington Carver could have traveled by airplane during his lifetime. But could anyone have imagined that in 1959, just 16 years after Carver's death, an unmanned spacecraft would orbit the Earth and in 1969 a human being would actually walk on the moon! Carver imagined and accomplished many things, and it might not have surprised him that those at Tuskegee University today would be working on the development of systems for growing sweetpotatoes for long-term, manned space missions. However, growing sweetpotatoes in outer space is not closely associated with conventional sweetpotato breeding. The challenge of producing food for humans during space flight—like producing food in sustainable agricultural systems on earth—demands a merging of conventional technologies for genetic improvement with the newest technologies for transfer of genetic information and other technologies which breeders have not traditionally used. Breeding programs increasingly use techniques such as tissue culture, protoplast culture, and protoplast fusion. Callus embryos have been developed and direct manipulation of DNA is now possible (Agricultural Biotechnology 1987; Mabry 1987; Rubenstein et al. 1980). Undoubtedly, these approaches will become part of the conventional breeding of sweetpotatoes in the 21st century as breeders seek such goals as rapid screening for pest resistance, pesticide tolerance, understanding of the mechanisms of gene regulation and expression, transfer of specific genes, and maintenance and preservation of germplasm. These possibilities raise many questions, including how to best incorporate new knowledge into a practical breeding program, how to determine if new techniques offer better possibilities of achieving breeding objectives, whether new techniques are faster than the old methods and if they are economical enough to use in a practical breeding program.

A very important change in outlook for sweetpotato breeders in the next century relates to the concept of developing methods which consider a total system for growing sweetpotatoes for storage roots and for diverse use of every plant part. In this regard, as well as other considerations already mentioned, it is likely that sweetpotato breeders will encounter increasing numbers of situations where they will merge previously unrelated technologies with conventional breeding. Therefore, as we enter the 21st century we cannot overemphasize the importance of an interdisciplinary approach in merging new technologies with conventional sweetpotato breeding.

CONCLUSION

George Washington Carver died on January 5, 1943, after gaining international fame for his work at Tuskegee. He was inducted into the Inventors Hall of Fame in April, 1990. Among Carver's many discoveries were over 100 products from sweetpotato. Would he be surprised at the successes of sweetpotato researchers who have followed him in time, including those of us attending this meeting and those who have preceded us in sweetpotato research? Would he be surprised at sweetpotato technology for the 21st century? He might be surprised, but probably not. Carver expected progress and must have liked a challenge, as he once said, "No individual has any right to come into the world and go out of it without leaving behind him distinct and legitimate reasons for having passed through it" (Charles 1991). The challenge to the sweetpotato breeder in the 21st century will be to leave the world a better place by successfully combine new and emerging technologies with already proven practices of conventional breeding and provide improved cultivars for conventional and newly identified uses.

REFERENCES

Agricultural Biotechnology. Strategies for National Competitiveness. 1987. National Academy Press, Washington, D.C. 205 pp.

Blixt, S., and P.B. Vose. 1984. Breeding towards an ideotype. Aiming at a moving target? Pages 414-426 *in* Crop breeding: A contemporary basis, edited by P. B. Vose and S. G. Blixt, Pergamon Press, New York.

Charles, L.A. 1991. Carver legacy remembered. The Iowa Stater 17(3):1,6&7. Iowa State University, Ames, Iowa.

Christiansen, M.N., and C.F. Lewis (eds). 1982. Breeding plants for less favorable environment. John Wiley & Sons, New York. 459 pp.

Edmond, J.B. 1971. Genetics, breeding behavior, and development of superior varieties. Pages 58-80 *in* Sweet potatoes: production, processing, marketing, edited by J.B. Edmond and G.R. Ammerman, AVI Publishing Company, Westport, Connecticut.

Hess, P.J. 1987. Vartest: a computer program package for variety trials. Applied Agricultural Research 2:196-202.

Jones, A. 1965. A proposed breeding procedure for sweetpotato. Crop Science 5:191-192.

Jones, A. 1986. Sweet potato heritability estimates and their use in breeding. HortScience 21:14-17.

Jones, A., P.D. Dukes, and J.M. Schalk. 1986. Sweet Potato Breeding. Pages 1-35 *in* Breeding vegetable crops, edited by M. Bassett. AVI Publishing Company, Westport, Connecticut.

Kukimura, H. 1986. Mutation breeding in root and tuber crops—a review. Gamma Field Symposia, No. 25:109-130. Institute of Radiation Breeding, NIAR, MAFF, Ohmiya-machi, Ibaraki-ken, Japan.

Mabry, T.J. (ed). 1982. Plant biotechnology. Research bottlenecks for commercialization and beyond. $1C^2$ Institute, The University of Texas at Austin. 203 pp.

Martin, F.W. 1965. Incompatibility in the sweet potato. A review. Economic Botany 19:406-415.

Miller, J.C. 1931. A study of mutations of the Porto Rico sweet potato. Proceedings of the American Society for Horticultural Science 27:343-346.

Miller, J.C. 1936. Further studies of mutations of the Porto Rico sweet potato. Proceedings of the American Society for Horticultural Science 33:460-465.

Miller, J.C. 1939. Further studies and technic used in sweet potato breeding in Louisiana. Journal of Heredity 30:485-492.

Rubenstein, I., G. Gengenbach, R.L. Phillips, and C.E. Green (eds). 1980. Genetic improvement of crops. Emergent techniques. University of Minnesota Press, Minneapolis. 241 pp.

St. Amand, P.C., and D.R. La Bonte. 1990. Database for sweetpotato breeding programs. HortScience 25:855 (abstr.).

Sinha, S.K., and M.S. Swaminathan. 1984. New parameters and selection criteria in plant breeding. Pages 1-21 *in* Crop breeding: a contemporary basis, edited by P.B. Vose and S.G. Blixt, Pergamum Press, New York.

Yoshida, T. 1984. Data processing system in sweet potato breeding. Japan. Journal of Breeding 34:373-378.

Sweetpotato Technology for the 21st Century. W.A. Hill, C.K. Bonsi and P.A. Loretan (Eds.) 1992. Tuskegee University Tuskegee, AL

Christopher A. Clark*, Don R. La Bonte**

Disease Factors in Breeding and Biotechnology for Sweetpotato

Development of disease-resistant cultivars by traditional breeding has been one of the most effective strategies for controlling sweetpotato diseases despite the fact that breeders have had access to only a small proportion of the world's sweetpotato germplasm. As access to new sources of germplasm increases, traditional breeding will continue to have a dominant role in the development of disease-resistant sweetpotatoes. The recent development of tissue culture and indexing procedures for producing pathogen-tested plants will foster greater international exchange of germplasm. It is not clear yet whether these techniques will be profitable if used in routine propagation of the crop for avoidance of systemic and root-borne pathogens. Eventually, a number of approaches, such as *in vitro* screening, somaclonal variation, and transformation with recombinant DNA may be used in conjunction with traditional breeding for development of disease-resistant sweetpotatoes. A mixed models statistical approach will allow greater efficiency and flexibility in dealing with multi-location or multi-year tests in assessing disease resistance and other characteristics of sweetpotato genotypes developed by either traditional or recombinant techniques.

INTRODUCTION

Importance of diseases

Although many of the nonviral diseases which affect sweetpotato in developed countries have been described in the literature (Clark and Moyer 1988), some of the viruses have yet to be fully characterized (Moyer and Salazar 1989). Relatively little information is available on the geographic distribution or extent of losses caused by any sweetpotato disease. There is a definite need to determine the distribution and effects of diseases on sweetpotatoes in different regions of the world and for international communication among sweetpotato pathologists. However, it is clear that the importance of specific diseases varies greatly from continent to continent and according to the method of propagation. For example, soil rot or pox, caused by *Streptomyces ipomoea*, is very serious in the United States and Japan, but there are few reports of its occurrence in other countries; virus diseases limit production in

*Department of Plant Pathology and Crop Physiology, Louisiana Agricultural Experiment Station, Louisiana State University Agricultural Center, Baton Rouge, LA 70803-1720, USA.
**Department of Horticulture, Louisiana Agricultural Experiment Station, Louisiana State University Agricultural Center, Baton Rouge, LA 70803-2120, USA.

484

much of Africa, but their effect is subtler and difficult to measure in other countries; leaf and stem scab, caused by *Elsino batatas*, and witches broom, caused by a mycoplasma-like organism (MLO), are serious in southeast Asia and some Pacific islands, but they do not occur in most other sweetpotato growing areas. In temperate sweetpotato growing regions, storage diseases are very important while in tropical regions, where sweetpotato can be grown throughout the year, they are often not even considered because sweetpotatoes are not stored for long. The variation in disease problems around the world makes it difficult to focus control efforts on specific diseases except at the local level.

In addition to those diseases mentioned above, there are a number of others which merit attention: bacterial stem and root rot, caused by *Erwinia chrysanthemi*; bacterial wilt in China, caused by *Pseudomonas solanacearum*; black rot, caused by *Ceratocystis fimbriata*; root rot, caused by *Plenodomus destruens*; root-knot nematode, *Meloidogyne* spp.; reniform nematode, *Rotylenchulus reniformis*; the storage rots caused by *Rhizopus stolonifer, Fusarium solani*, and *Lasiodiplodia theobromae*; and the viruses, especially sweetpotato feathery mottle virus (SPFMV) and the virus complex that occurs in Africa (Clark and Moyer 1988).

Traditional breeding and disease resistance

Use of disease-resistant cultivars has been the most effective means of controlling most sweetpotato diseases. It has virtually eliminated some diseases (e.g. Fusarium wilt and internal cork in the USA) as constraints to economic production and has contributed to reductions in losses due to many other diseases (Clark et al. 1991). In some cases, breeding programs have made it a priority to develop lines resistant to specific diseases such as root knot, Fusarium wilt, internal cork, soil rot, vine and leaf scab and others (Clark 1988; Clark et al. 1991; Jones et al. 1976; Takagi and Opeña 1988). In other cases, breeders have not used reaction to diseases such as bacterial root and stem rot, Fusarium root rot, vine and leaf scab as selection criteria. However, subsequent screening indicated cultivars varied in reaction to these diseases even though they were not specifically selected for resistance (Clark et al. 1991; Takagi and Opeña 1988).

Breeding strategies for disease resistance rely heavily on quantitative theory, but only four heritability estimates have been made: Fusarium wilt, root-knot nematode (*Meloidogyne incognita, M. javanica*), and a sweetpotato virus disease in Africa (Jones 1986). Fusarium wilt resistance is evidence to the success of breeding for quantitative resistance. Heritability estimates for Fusarium wilt resistance consistently have been greater than 0.70, and results of heritability studies suggest—and experience has proven—that gains in Fusarium wilt resistance can be rapid and substantial (Jones 1969; Collins 1977). Resistance to the development of internal cork symptoms appears to be controlled by dominant genes (Hammett et al. 1982). As a result, a high proportion of seedlings in U.S. breeding programs are resistant to Fusarium wilt and internal cork, and resistance to both is considered essential for any new cultivar.

It has been proposed that wild species of *Ipomoea* would be useful in sweetpotato breeding programs as a source of resistance to the sweetpotato weevil. Although it has been reported that *I. littoralis* has resistance to black rot, caused by *C. fimbriata* (Iwanaga 1988), these species have not been investigated adequately as potential sources of disease resistance. Otherwise, there is little published information on disease resistance of other *Ipomoea* spp.

It is important to remember that much of the progress in developing disease-resistant cultivars occurred before the relatively recent intensification of efforts to collect, exchange, and maintain sweetpotato germplasm. Thus, individual breeding programs accomplished much while having access to only a small proportion of the world's sweetpotato germplasm. Greatly increased germplasm collection and maintenance activities during the past 5 to 10 years will provide sweetpotato breeders access to a more diverse array of germplasm. Furthermore, there are several important diseases for which there have been no sustained attempts to identify sources of resistance (e.g., Rhizopus soft rot). Therefore, it seems likely that traditional breeding will continue to play a dominant role in disease control in sweetpotato. Success of these efforts will depend in part on international cooperation and communication. Specifically, there is a need to collect and share information regarding the disease resistance of sweetpotato germplasm held in different collections. It also may be worthwhile to screen *Ipomoea* species related to *I. batatas* for resistance to those diseases for which resistance has not yet been identified in sweetpotato. In addition, screening for certain diseases can only be conducted in those regions where the diseases occur. This will require cooperation in evaluation of disease resistance of available sweetpotato germplasm.

Unresolved disease problems

There are a few sweetpotato diseases for which adequate control programs have not yet been developed. For some other diseases, control relies on the use of pesticides, which are potentially subject to regulatory removal in some countries. Research is needed to develop new or alternative controls for these diseases.

Reniform nematode is widely distributed in the tropics and subtropics and can reduce substantially both yield and quality of sweetpotatoes (Clark and Wright 1983). Damage by this nematode may be reduced by use of nematicides. However, since the nematode often develops unusually large populations, the proportion of the population surviving nematicide treatment may still be damaging. Some of the germplasm available in the USA has been screened for reaction to *R. reniformis*. Although variation in reaction was observed, no useful levels of resistance or tolerance were identified (Clark and Wright 1983). Thus, there is currently no entirely effective means for reducing losses to this pest. Resistance would be the preferred method of control of this nematode. A more extensive effort to identify resistance in sweetpotato is justified.

Rhizopus soft rot is one of the most widespread and serious storage rots of sweetpotato. In the USA, it is controlled primarily by application of the fungicide dichloronitroaniline to the storage roots when they are packed for shipment to market (Clark and Moyer 1988). In addition to regulatory actions which restrict use of pesticides, consumers in some countries have begun to express a preference for pesticide-free produce. Thus, there is good reason to seek an alternative method of controlling Rhizopus soft rot. While it has been suggested that commercial sweetpotato cultivars may vary in reaction to Rhizopus soft rot, to our knowledge there has never been a sustained attempt to develop screening methods or identify sources of resistance to this disease.

Resistance can be used to reduce losses to the virus disease complex that occurs in Africa (Hahn et al. 1981). However, there is a lack of published information on sources of resistance to specific viruses, such as the ubiquitous sweetpotato feathery mottle virus (SPFMV).

A common concern raised about the use of resistant cultivars for disease control is the possibility that they will select for new races of the pathogen that are virulent on the previously resistant cultivars. While this problem has developed with certain diseases on some crops, there are no examples of this having occurred on sweetpotato. Fusarium wilt and internal cork resistance have held up in commercial production for 40 to 50 years. Although populations of *Meloidogyne* spp. vary in their virulence on different cultivars, it appears that this variability predates the release of root knot-resistant sweetpotato cultivars (Clark et al. 1991). In contrast, use of new cultivars may have contributed to emergence of some new diseases. For example, Fusarium root rot and bacterial stem and root rot were not recorded on sweetpotato in the USA until the release of 'Jewel' and 'Georgia Red,' respectively (Clark et al. 1991). Although new cultivars have not yet been observed to select new pathogen races, this does not preclude the possibility that this may eventually happen. Thus, continued efforts to identify new and diverse sources of resistance, either through traditional breeding approaches or through molecular transformation, are justified.

Analyzing data on disease resistance and other traits

New approaches to disease resistance should also include new approaches to data analysis. Breeders and pathologists alike have depended heavily on statistical methods based on variations of regression, the analysis of variance (ANOVA), or covariance (ANCOV). These methods strictly classify model parameters into fixed and random effects. Mixed models are a generalization of the same linear model theory which embodies these more familiar forms of analysis. Mixed models do not rigidly classify model parameters into fixed and random effects. This flexibility permits a more appropriate match of assumptions about the experiment and results in greater efficiency. Numbers of replications can be reduced, power and ease in dealing with multi-locations and multi-year testing is enhanced, and recovery of interblock information in incomplete block designs (treatments or selections missing from blocks) is possible. One can also predict using the mixed model approach.

A mixed model approach is useful when data is collected from multiple locations and years. Locations, years, and even selections can be considered as random depending on the judgment of the researcher. For instance, variances at two locations may not be pooled due to heterogeneity. In this case, considering location effects as random, intra-location variance components for blocks and experimental error are used to predict values of selections absent at a given location, but present at other locations. Standard error can also be reduced depending on classification of the model parameters (i.e., blocks or locations as random).

As another example, treatment means in incomplete block designs are based on the block into which a given selection is placed. Bias results when a selection in a superior block (i.e., yield as a measure of resistance) is compared to other selections in more average blocks. The mixed model approach adjusts mean yield by considering blocks as random and basing means on interblock analysis.

Treating selections (i.e., diverse germplasm) as random utilizes information about the distribution among entries such as the variance between and within selections, the mean of the populations and the selection itself. However, model assumptions require treating selections as fixed when the number of selections is small and the pedigree is unknown. A thorough discussion of the topic is covered by Stroup (1989) and others. Computer programs to aid in analysis are also discussed in this Southern Cooperative Series Bulletin.

TISSUE CULTURE FOR PATHOGEN ELIMINATION OR AVOIDANCE

After resistance, sanitation, which includes the use of 'disease-free' propagating material, has been one of the most widely employed principles of disease control in sweetpotato. Tissue culture techniques that allow production of 'disease-free' or 'pathogen-tested' plants may provide opportunities to improve approaches to disease control by sanitation. An important reason for producing pathogen-tested plants is to reduce the risk of pathogen dissemination during international exchange of sweetpotato germplasm. The value of tissue culture as a means of avoiding systemic and root-borne pathogens during production of certified propagating material or routine propagation of the crop has not been determined. A possible added benefit to tissue culture propagation may be to avoid the somatic mutations that arise when sweetpotatoes are propagated from the adventitious buds formed on storage roots (De Klerk 1990; Klekowski and Kazarinova-Fukshansky 1984).

A review of the development of methods for detection and identification of viruses and of tissue culture techniques to produce plants free of virus diseases of sweetpotato could consume several chapters in this book. We will not attempt to cover this subject in depth since it has been well covered elsewhere (Green 1988; Green and Lo 1989; Love et al. 1987; Moyer et al. 1989; Moyer and Salazar 1989). Meristem-tip culture is a well-established technique for eliminating viruses from vegetatively propagated plants including sweetpotato (Love et al. 1987). Meristem-tip culture alone or in combination with thermotherapy or chemotherapy has been successfully employed to produce sweetpotatoes apparently free of the viruses associated with the crop (Green 1988; Green and Lo 1989; Moyer et al. 1989). Great progress has been made in the last five years in developing procedures for detection and identification of sweetpotato viruses, and an international set of guidelines has been developed for this purpose (Love et al. 1987; Moyer and Salazar 1989; Moyer et al. 1989). Not as much is known regarding elimination of the witches' broom microplasma-like organism, but it appears that meristem-tip culture is also useful for this purpose (Moyer et al. 1989). Sweetpotato is also affected by another unusual systemic disease: chlorotic leaf distortion (CLD) caused by the fungus *Fusarium lateritium* (Clark et al. 1990). Meristem-tip culture can also be employed to produce CLD-free sweetpotato plants (Clark et al. 1990).

It is clear from the literature that meristem-tip culture alone or in combination with thermotherapy or chemotherapy can be used to produce plants free of several systemic pathogens and that sensitive, accurate detection techniques are or soon will be available for these pathogens. However, two significant questions remain: 1) what effect do these pathogens have on quality and yield of the crop? and 2) what is the best approach to exploit our present technological capabilities in controlling these diseases?

Virus diseases such as russet crack and internal cork have an obvious effect on quality of the crop since they produce lesions on or in the storage roots (Clark and Moyer 1988). However, this loss of quality is already controlled in most countries by use of cultivars that are resistant to development of symptoms, even though they may support virus replication. It is evident that the virus disease complex that occurs in Africa has a pronounced effect on yield of the crop (Hahn 1979). Although sweetpotatoes appear to be universally infected with one virus or another, usually SPFMV (Moyer and Salazar 1989), their effects on yield have in most cases not been accurately assessed. In many situations, it is possible that breeding programs have unknowingly selected for clones with a degree of tolerance to the viruses present by selecting for high-yielding types (Moyer and Salazar 1989). In any event, there is little data available to provide a basis for speculation on what gains in production could be expected by propagating the crop from pathogen-tested plants. Furthermore, since these plants would be subject to reinfection when planted in the field, the possible acute effects of new virus infections during the season must be considered in determining the influence of viruses on yield. Thus, alternative approaches such as transforming virus-tested plants with viral coat protein genes to induce a cross protection-like phenomenon may prove more attractive (Beachy 1992).

Once an approach has been chosen (i.e., use of pathogen-tested planting material or transformed plants), there remains the question of how to deliver the product to the farmer. Fortunately, sweetpotato is amenable to propagation by a variety of methods including use of both vine cuttings and storage roots. Thus, approaches to increasing planting material are limited only by the imagination and the availability of tissue culture, greenhouse or screenhouse, and field facilities. As an example, workers in Kyushu, Japan have reported that, using their methods, it should be possible to increase sweetpotato from a single shoot tip to more than 2 million plants in a single year (Takahashi et al. 1988). The use of *in vitro* embryogenesis as a method of clonal regeneration has been studied by Cantliffe et al. (1987). Somatic embryos (artificial seed) were directly sown in the field using fluid gel techniques, and normal plants were obtained. These studies were initiated as a cost-efficient way to use sweetpotato for biomass production.

BIOTECHNOLOGY AND DISEASE RESISTANCE

It is not possible to accurately predict what the technology developing in the area of genetic transformation of plants will allow in the future. We will attempt to suggest some capabilities that are presently lacking in developing disease resistance in sweetpotatoes in the hopes that these techniques may some day be brought to bear on these problems. In many cases, these may be impractical pipe dreams, but it is not possible to direct our efforts if we do not first attempt to define our desires. Several aspects might be addressed: (1) improving the efficiency and/or accuracy of screening germplasm for disease resistance; (2) developing resistance for diseases for which no resistance has been found within available sweetpotato germplasm; and (3) combining resistance to multiple diseases and insects into individual genotypes.

Improving efficiency of screening

In vitro screening, which involves subjecting cells, calli, or plantlets to some selection pressure, has been suggested as a means to increase the number of individuals that can be screened in a limited amount of space. It has been used to select for resistance to stresses, including pathogens. While there is a report in which this approach was used to screen for salt-resistant sweetpotatoes, we are not aware of any report where it has been used for selection for disease resistance (Salgado-Garciglia et al. 1985). Sweetpotato breeding differs from many crops in that considerable effort is required to produce a relatively small number of 'true' seed from which to evaluate and select. A further constraint is the inherent difficulty in manipulating germplasm for given traits due to self-incompatibility, sterility and poor flowering. Thus, with relatively small numbers of seedlings, it is usually possible to establish a hierarchy of traits that allows screening all the seedlings produced for disease resistance at some stage in the evaluation process. Furthermore, *in vitro* screening generally relies on knowledge of the mechanisms of pathogenicity for specific diseases. For example, it is more effective when screening can be done with a toxin that is known to be a primary determinant of pathogenicity (Wenzel 1985). Such basic information is almost totally lacking for sweetpotato pathogens which have not been subjected to the same intensive investigation as pathogens on other crops. However, culture filtrates from *Fusarium* spp. pathogenic to potato have been useful in *in vitro* screening of potato, and it is possible that the same methods could be employed for *F. solani* and/or *F. lateritium* on sweetpotato. At present, the only advantages of *in vitro* screening techniques on sweetpotato are that they could improve the selection of somaclonal variants or might allow screening of trans- formed plants that cannot be screened in the field because of regulatory restrictions.

It is sometimes not practical or possible to screen progeny for resistance to certain diseases of interest. A genetic map of sweetpotato would enable screening for resistance to "new" pathogens where inoculation with the pathogen is not possible. Genetic maps have been developed for a number of crop species including the tetraploid potato (*Solanum tuberosum*) using restriction fragment length polymorphism (RFLP). Specific traits can be directly selected for by linkage to detectable RFLP markers. What makes this concept particularly appealing is to extend analyses to include genetic loci [quantitative trait loci (QTL)] underlying a quantitative trait. Efficiencies would be gained screening germplasm for any number of diseases as well as screening wild non-root-forming relatives without interspecific combination (Tanksley et al. 1989).

Recombinant DNA and disease resistance

Recombinant DNA technology is already having a major impact on plant disease diagnosis, especially in the use of nucleic acid probes for detection and identification of viruses. We will not cover diagnostic applications here. This technology also may prove useful for assessing quantitative resistance (Wenzel 1985). For example, cDNA may be used to quantify virus titer in lines being screened for resistance.

There is great interest in the possibilities of using recombinant DNA technology to transform many crop plants including sweetpotato. It may be possible to use a variety of techniques to insert foreign DNA into the sweetpotato genome. While there may yet be a number of technical hurdles to overcome in making this process routine for sweetpotato, it appears that the greatest question concerns identifying what genes to use. There are many complications involved and few genes, natural or synthetic, have been identified or isolated (Wenzel 1985).

One area where preliminary success has been achieved in transforming plants with foreign genes is the system using virus coat protein genes to induce resistance to specific viruses. This is the subject of another chapter in this book (Beachy 1992), and we refer readers to that for an in-depth treatment of this subject.

Until it is possible to precisely identify the location of resistance genes in plant genomes, transforming plants with genes for resistance to specific diseases from unrelated plants will be limited. However, should that capability be realized, there are potential applications for sweetpotato. One in particular involves reniform nematode. As indicated above, a source of resistance to this nematode has not been identified in the limited sweetpotato germplasm that has been evaluated. Reniform nematode-resistant lines and cultivars have been developed in several other crop plants including soybeans, cotton, potato and others (Clark and Wright 1983).

Combining multiple pest resistance and horticultural traits

Perhaps the greatest challenge in breeding for disease resistance in sweetpotato is to combine resistance to all the important diseases and insects into horticulturally acceptable cultivars. Even the most widely grown cultivars are susceptible to one or more of the most important diseases. In the process of sexual reproduction of the hexaploid sweetpotato, breeders are not able to manipulate germplasm as freely as for other crops in which specific traits can be transferred using inbred lines. Tremendous benefits could be realized if a method was found to improve the one or two undesirable traits in widely accepted cultivars whose traits are for the most part desirable.

Somaclonal variation might be exploited for such improvements. The goal would be to take a cultivar with generally desirable characteristics but lacking resistance to an important disease and improve it by selecting a disease-resistant variant that retained the other desirable characteristics. However, procedures to select somaclonal variants can be exhausting and most variants will likely be undesirable (Larkin and Scowcroft 1981; Wenzel 1985). Sweetpotato clones vary in the frequency of overall variation during vegetative propagation and may or may not mutate with respect to the specific disease resistance of interest. Therefore, it is important to select the sweetpotato clone to be used and the character for which variation is sought to increase the probability of obtaining a desirable variant.

Another approach might be to transform sweetpotatoes with genes that confer broad-spectrum resistance. A gene for a broad-spectrum antimicrobial compound might in theory confer resistance to many diseases. This is being pursued with genes for peptides which cause lysis of bacteria (Destefano-Beltran et al. 1990).

Broad-spectrum resistance might also be attained by tying transformations to natural plant processes that affect disease development. For example, sweetpotato storage rot pathogens all require a wound for entry into the plant and subsequent disease development (Clark and Moyer 1988). When wound healing occurs before an infection can become established, disease does not develop. Plants, including sweetpotato, have a number of genes that are expressed in response to wounding such as those for polyphenol production, synthesis of phenylalanine ammonia lyase (PAL), and other enzymes (Bolwell et al. 1986; Uritani 1982). It may be possible to target transformations to sections of the plant genome that are activated in response to wounding, such as the gene for PAL synthesis. Thus, if genes can be inserted that enhance wound healing or that are induced by wounding to produce inhibitors of microbial growth, it may be possible to confer a broad-spectrum resistance. In potato tubers incubated under hypoxic conditions, which favor bacterial soft rot, the normal wound response does not occur. However, a distinct set of proteins is produced in response to hypoxia (Vayda and Schaeffer 1988). For bacterial soft rot resistance, it may therefore be necessary to couple transformation to the hypoxia-induced responses.

CONCLUSIONS

The accomplishments of traditional sweetpotato breeding have in many ways paved the way for consideration of biotechnological approaches to improving disease control. By developing cultivars with a combination of many desirable horticultural and disease and insect resistance characteristics, it has created an opportunity to use somaclonal variation to put finishing touches on certain cultivars. The increased availability of diverse sweetpotato germplasm will give new and greater opportunities for improving disease resistance by traditional breeding and screening approaches. The cultivars which have been developed also provide a solid genetic foundation on which recombinant DNA technology could conceivably build. However, for any improvements which may result from this technology to be implemented in sweetpotato production and storage, they must be integrated into a breeding program. There will be a continued need for cooperative efforts of pathologists and breeders in traditional approaches to improving sweetpotato disease resistance. A similar cooperative effort will be needed to integrate and take full advantage of all the available techniques for controlling sweetpotato diseases.

REFERENCES

Beachy, R.N., C. Malpica, and G. Clark. 1992. Coat protein mediated resistance: Strategy for genetic engineering virus resistance in sweetpotatoes. Pages 507-513 *in* Sweetpotato technology for the 21st century, edited by W.A. Hill, C.K. Bonsi and P.A. Loretan, Tuskegee University, Tuskegee, AL.

Bolwell, G.P., C.L. Cramer, C.J. Lamb, W. Schuch, and R.A. Dixon. 1986. L-Phenylalanine ammonia-lyase from *Phaseolus vulgaris*: modulation of the levels of active enzyme. Planta 169:97-107.

Cantliffe, D. J., J.R. Liu, and J.R. Schultheis. 1988. Development of artificial seeds of sweet potato for clonal propagation through somatic embryogenesis. Pages 183-195 *in* Methane from biomass - A systematic approach, edited by W. H. Smith, Elsevier, New York.

Clark, C.A. 1988. Principal bacterial and fungal diseases of sweet potato and their control. Pages 275-289 *in* Exploration, maintenance, and utilization of sweet potato genetic resources, Report of the First Sweet Potato Planning Conference 1987. Centro Internacional de la Papa, Lima, Peru.

Clark, C.A., and J.W. Moyer. 1988. Compendium of sweet potato diseases. APS Press, St. Paul, MN. 74 pp.

Clark, C.A., P.D. Dukes, and J.W. Moyer. 1992. Diseases. Pages 88-105 *in* Fifty years of collaborative sweetpotato research 1939-1989, edited by A. Jones and J.C. Bouwkamp, Southern Cooperative Series Bulletin No. 369.

Clark, C.A., R.A. Valverde, J.A. Wilder-Ayers, and P.E. Nelson. 1990. *Fusarium lateritium*, causal agent of sweetpotato chlorotic leaf distortion. Phytopathology 80:741-744.

Clark, C.A., and V.L. Wright. 1983. Effect and reproduction of *Rotylenchulus reniformis* on sweet potato selections. J. Nematol. 15:197-203.

Collins, W.W. 1977. Diallel analysis of sweet potatoes for resistance to *Fusarium* wilt. J. Amer. Soc. Hort. Sci. 102:109-111.

De Klerk, G. -J. 1990. How to measure somaclonal variation. Acta Bot. Neerl. 39:129-144.

Destefano-Beltran, L., P.G. Nagpala, M.S. Cetiner, J.H. Dodds and J.M. Jaynes. 1990. Enhancing bacterial and fungal disease resistance in plants: application to potato. Pages 205-221 *in* The molecular and cellular biology of the potato, edited by M.E. Vayda and W.D. Park. C.A.B. International, Wallingford, UK.

Green, S.K. 1988. AVRDC virus elimination and indexing procedures for international exchange of sweet potato germplasm. Pages 311-317 *in* Exploration, maintenance, and utilization of sweet potato genetic resources, Report of the First Sweet Potato Planning Conference, Centro Internacional de la Papa, Lima, Peru.

Green, S.K., and C.Y. Lo. 1989. Elimination of sweet potato yellow dwarf virus (SPYDV) by meristem tip culture and by heat treatment. Z. Pflanzenkrank. Pflanzenschutz 96:464-469.

Hahn, S.K. 1979. Effects of viruses (SPVD) on growth and yield of sweet potato. Exp. Agric.

15:1-5.

Hahn, S.K., E.R. Terry, and K. Leuschner. 1981. Resistance of sweet potato to virus complex. HortScience 16:535-537.

Hammett, H.L., Teme P. Hernandez, W.J. Martin, and C.A. Clark 1982. Breeding sweet potato for disease resistance. Pages 321-329 in Sweet potato, edited by R.L. Villareal and T.D. Griggs, Proceedings, First International Symposium. Asian Vegetable Research and Development Center, Shanhua, Taiwan, ROC.

Iwanaga, M. 1988. Use of wild germplasm for sweet potato breeding. Pages 199-210 in Exploration, maintenance, and utilization of sweet potato genetic resources, Report of the First Sweet Potato Planning Conference 1987. Centro Internacional de la Papa, Lima, Peru.

Jones, A. 1969. Quantitative inheritance of Fusarium wilt resistance in sweet potatoes. J. Amer. Soc. Hort Sci. 94:207-208.

Jones, A. 1986. Sweet potato heritability estimates and their use in breeding. HortScience 21:14-17.

Jones, A., P.D. Dukes, and F.P. Cuthbert. 1976. Mass selections in sweet potato: breeding for resistance to insects and diseases and for horticultural characteristics. J. Amer. Soc. Hort. Sci. 101:701-704.

Klekowski, E.J., Jr., and N. Kazarinova-Fukshansky. 1984. Shoot apical meristems and mutation: Selective loss of disadvantageous cell genotypes. Amer. J. Bot. 71:28-34.

Larkin, P.J., and W.R. Scowcroft. 1981. Somaclonal variation - a novel source of variability from cell culture for plant improvement. Theoret. Appl. Genet. 60:197-214.

Love, S.L., B.B. Rhodes, and J.W. Moyer. 1987. Meristem-tip culture and virus indexing of sweet potatoes. International Board for Plant Genetic Resources, Rome. 46 pp.

Moyer, J.W., G.V.H. Jackson and E.A. Frison, eds. 1989. FAO/IBPGR technical guidelines for the safe movement of sweet potato germplasm. Food and Agriculture Organization of the United Nations, Rome/ International Goard for Plant Genetic Resources, Rome. 29 pp.

Moyer, J. W., and L. F. Salazar. 1989. Viruses and viruslike diseases of sweet potato. Plant Dis. 73:451-455.

Salgado-Garciglia, R., F. Lopez-Gutierrez, and N. Ochoa-Alejo. 1985. NaCl-resistant variant cells isolated from sweet potato cell suspensions. Plant Cell Tissue Organ Culture 5:3-12.

Stroup, W.W. 1989. Why mixed models? Pages 1-8 in Applications of mixed models in agriculture and related disciplines. Southern Coop. Series Bull. 343.

Takagi, H., and R.T. Opena. 1988. Sweet potato breeding at AVRDC to overcome production constraints and use in Asia. Pages 233-245 in Exploration, maintenance, and utilization of sweet potato genetic resources, Report of the First Sweet Potato Planning Conference 1987. Centro Internacional de la Papa, Lima, Peru.

Takahashi, K., K. Ichi, M. Karube and A. Shinya. 1988. Production of virus-free sweet potato plants. International Working Group on Sweet Potato Viruses Newsletter 1:8-9.

Tanksley, S.D., N.D. Young, A.H. Paterson, and M.W. Bonierbale. 1989. RFLP mapping in plant breeding: new tools for an old science. Bio/Technology 7:257-264.

Uritani, I. 1982. Postharvest physiology and pathology of sweet potato from the biochemical viewpoint. Pages 421-428 in Sweet potato, edited by R.L. Villareal and T.D. Griggs, Proceedings of the First International Symposium, Asian Vegetable Research and Development Center, Shanhua, Taiwan, ROC.

Vayda, M.E., and H.J. Schaeffer. 1988. Hypoxic stress inhibits the appearance of wound-response proteins in potato tubers. Plant Physiol. 88:805-809.

Wenzel, G. 1985. Strategies in unconventional breeding for disease resistance. Annu. Rev. Phytopathol. 23:149-172.

Sweetpotato Technology for the 21st Century. W.A. Hill, C.K. Bonsi and P.A. Loretan (Eds.) 1992. Tuskegee University, Tuskegee, AL

Richard K. Jansson*, Kandukuri V. Raman**

Applications of New Technologies to Integrated Pest Management in Sweetpotato

Concepts and practices of sweetpotato IPM have begun to mature, especially during the last five years. Technological changes in research and development result in significant changes in crop improvement. Considerable advances have been achieved recently in several aspects of sweetpotato IPM including: an improved understanding of the taxonomy of *Cylas* weevils; the development of a synthetic sex pheromone for *C. formicarius* (Fabricius); the development of IPM programs for *C. formicarius* in Asia; the use of entomopathogens for control of *C. formicarius* and the West Indian sweetpotato weevil, *Euscepes postfasciatus* (Fairmaire); the potential use of *Agrobacterium*-mediated gene transfer to produce pest resistant sweetpotato plants; the development of phytochemical methods to assess resistance of sweetpotato to insects, especially *C. formicarius*; the development of several cultivars with resistance to pest complexes; and improved methods for managing vectors, viruses, and plant-parasitic nematodes of sweetpotato. However, more research and development is needed internationally in sweetpotato IPM, especially in developing countries.

Historically, sweetpotato pest management has been a neglected research topic worldwide, especially in the developing world (Jansson & Raman 1991b). Its lack of attention is due to several factors. The most concentrated research on this topic has been in the United States, where the crop is of minor importance (0.6 million MT; $160 million; USDA 1989). In regions of the world where the crop is a major staple and losses due to insects are high, funding for integrated pest management (IPM) research is minimal. Worldwide, the crop has been seriously underfunded (Gregory et al. 1990; TAC 1985). In addition, certain IPM methods, such as improved germplasm, biological control agents, etc., are not available in developing countries. For this reason, approaches for managing pests of sweetpotato have relied on the use of remedial measures on a pest-by-pest basis and, in most cases, management has relied exclusively on cultural practices. This is most apparent with the management of sweetpotato weevils, *Cylas* spp. and *Euscepes postfasciatus* (Fairmaire).

Also, few specialists are present in the National Agricultural Research Systems (NARS) of developing countries, and these specialists often lack an understanding of IPM. Many of these countries lack trained entomologists, nematologists, virologists, and plant pathologists. Also, mechanisms for technology transfer, such as training, on-farm research, and human resource development, are limited (Jansson and Raman 1991b).

*University of Florida Institute of Food and Agricultural Sciences, Tropical Research and Education Center, Homestead, Florida 33031 USA
**International Potato Center, P. O. Box 5969, Lima Peru.

Concepts and practices of sweetpotato IPM have begun to mature, especially during the last five years. Technological changes in IPM research and development may result in significant changes in crop improvement. Sweetpotato IPM is no exception. Considerable advances have been achieved in several aspects of sweetpotato IPM, including: an improved understanding of the taxonomy of *Cylas* weevils; the development of a synthetic sex pheromone for the sweetpotato weevil, *C. formicarius* (Fabricius); the development of IPM programs for *C. formicarius* in Asia; the use of entomopathogens for control of *C. formicarius* and the West Indian sweetpotato weevil, *E. postfasciatus;* the potential use of *Agrobacterium*-mediated gene transfer to produce pest resistant sweetpotato plants; the development of phytochemical methods to assess resistance of sweetpotato to insects, especially *C. formicarius;* the development of several cultivars with resistance to pest complexes; and improved methods for managing vectors, viruses, and plant-parasitic nematodes of sweetpotato. However, considerably more research and development is needed internationally to counteract the lack of research attention given to sweetpotato IPM, especially in developing countries. A major cooperative program is needed to provide leadership in the following areas: (1) a global needs assessment for sweetpotato IPM research and development; (2) preservation of sweetpotato germplasm; (3) research in priority areas, such as host plant resistance to insects, nematodes, and diseases, and the use of sex pheromones and biological, biotechnological, and cultural methods for managing these pests; (4) training, documentation, and information exchange; and (5) increased crop promotion and public awareness.

A recent book reviewed the status of research on the biology and management of the most important insect, nematode, and virus pests of sweetpotato worldwide (Jansson and Raman 1991a). Pests included were: sweetpotato weevils, *C. formicarius, C. puncticollis, C. brunneus* (Fabricius), and *E. postfasciatus;* sweetpotato vine borers, *Omphisa anastomosalis* Guenee and *Megastes grandalis* Guenee; wireworms, *Conoderus* spp.; cucumber beetles, *Diabrotica* spp.; flea beetles, *Systena* spp.; viruses and their associated vectors; and plant-parasitic nematodes. The present paper briefly reviews the new technologies available in sweetpotato IPM and presents the major gaps in their knowledge and technology.

Taxonomy of pests

Wolfe (1991) reviewed the taxonomy of the genus *Cylas,* which comprises the major weevil pest species of sweetpotato in the world. A previous problem plaguing researchers of *Cylas* spp. was uncertainty in nomenclature between *Cylas formicarius elegantulus* (present in the Western Hemisphere) and *C. f. formicarius* (present in Asia, South Pacific, and parts of Africa). Wolfe (1991) considered these two species designations to be junior synonyms of *C. formicarius.* Despite this, however, there is still an increasing need to solve the systematic problems involving the members of *C. formicarius* and especially the *C. puncticollis* species complexes. Future systematic work on these species should include biochemical, karyological, and molecular analyses, such as DNA fingerprinting (rDNA) for more conclusive answers. Examination of mitochondrial DNA may help to elucidate parental lines and similarity of different weevil populations. Such information may help plant breeders target development and subsequent distribution of resistant plant varieties.

Sex pheromone of *C. formicarius*

The history and use of a female-produced sex pheromone, (Z)-3-dodecen-1-ol (E)-2-butenoate, that attracts only male weevils for monitoring and managing *C. formicarius* has been reviewed (Heath et al. 1991; Jansson et al. 1991). This sex pheromone has good potential for integrating into current weevil management programs worldwide. A pheromone-trap monitoring system developed in the U.S. (Jansson et al. 1991a) is currently being marketed in the southern U.S. by AgriSense (Fresno, California) and Great Lakes IPM (Vestaburg, Michigan). The sex pheromone has already been integrated into weevil management programs in several developing countries and is currently being used by the International Potato Center (CIP) to develop monitoring systems for *C. formicarius* worldwide. One of the major factors limiting the use of this technology in developing countries has been the availablity of the pheromone at a cost that developing countries can afford. In order to overcome this problem, synthetic chemists in certain developing countries have investigated the possibility of synthesizing the pheromone using locally available resources. Several countries are currently interested in producing this pheromone by the use of less expensive synthetic methods. Both Taiwan and India have synthesized this pheromone. However, quality control of pheromone synthesis is central to pheromone efficacy (Heath et al. 1991; Jansson et al. 1991a), and pheromone synthesized by alternative methods should be analyzed by HPLC, NMR, and mass spectroscopy to confirm its chemical structure and purity (Heath et al. 1991; Jansson et al. 1991a). In addition, field studies that use standardized protocols are needed to compare the efficacy and attractiveness of pheromone produced by alternative methods with that produced in the U.S.

In most developing countries, sweetpotato is grown in small fields rarely exceeding 1 ha. Thus, pheromone has good potential for managing *C. formicarius* populations by mass trapping and/or mating disruption in these small plantings. Recent studies showed that the pheromone was efficacious as a mass trapping and mating disruption tool during the cool winter months in southern Florida (Mason et al. 1992). Studies are needed to assess its potential at managing this insect under a wide variety of geographic, climatic, and agronomic conditions. Determination of the management potential of this pheromone is central for integrating the pheromone with other management tactics, especially cultural practices and the use of biological control agents.

The two most efficacious and efficient traps at collecting *C. formicarius,* the plastic funnel trap, which was developed in the U.S. Virgin Islands and later modified in Florida, and the commercially available Universal moth trap (available from Great Lakes IPM, Vestaburg, Michigan), are too costly for many developing countries. The cost of a trapping system may also be prohibitive in certain regions of the United States (Jansson et al. 1991a). For example, the North Carolina Department of Agriculture continues to use and recommend the screen-cone boll weevil trap in its monitoring program for *C. formicarius* in North Carolina despite the poor efficacy and efficiency of this trap. Although this trap is inferior to other traps that were tested, it is considerably less expensive than the Universal moth trap. For these reasons, alternative, inexpensive traps that are efficient at collecting this weevil are needed in both developing and developed countries. Additionally, in developing countries, traps are needed that can be constructed from locally available materials at minimal cost. Prototypes are currently being tested by CIP and cooperating national agricultural scientists in several countries.

Considering current domestic and international restrictions on trade and movement of sweetpotato and associated plant parts, this pheromone also has great potential for use in regulatory entomology. Studies are needed to modify the existing monitoring system for regulatory purposes and develop a detection system for this weevil in sweetpotato storage facilities.

Sex pheromones of other weevil species, such as *C. puncticollis* (Boheman), *C. banneus* and *E. postfasciatus,* have not been recognized to date. Preliminary studies are currently underway in Kenya to determine if *C. puncticollis* produces a sex pheromone. The availability of pheromone for *C. puncticollis* would help to improve the management of this weevil in Africa.

Biological control of sweetpotato weevils

There are numerous natural enemies of sweetpotato weevils (Jansson 1991, Raman and Alleyne 1991). Of these, entomopathogens, such as entomopathogenic nematodes and fungi, are most promising for control of these weevils. Concerning biological control of *Cylas* spp. with entomopathogenic nematodes, there are indications that locally-adapted, tropical or subtropical isolates of these nematodes may be more virulent to *C. formicarius* than those from temperate zones. Surveys are needed to isolate these nematodes from tropical soils. A survey for these nematodes is currently underway in the Caribbean basin, and several isolates have been found in Puerto Rico, Jamaica, and the U.S. Virgin Islands (Jansson, R.K., R.R. Gaugler, and W. Figueroa, unpublished data). Also, the potential of these nematodes during the dry season in the tropics needs to be assessed. Other factors, such as soil edaphic characteristics and environmental parameters, that may affect the success of these nematodes as biological control agents of *Cylas* spp. were presented earlier (Jansson 1991) and need considerably more research. The potential of these nematodes at managing populations of *E. postfasciatus* also needs to be determined. Research on identification, virulence, and efficacy of improved strains of fungi, such as *Beauveria bassiana* (Bals.) Vuill., *B. brongniartii (= B. tenella),* and *Metarhizium anisopliae* (Metchnikoff) Sorikin, and bacteria *Bacillus thuringiensis* var. *tenebrionis (= morrisoni)* should be accorded high priority (Jansson 1991). Consideration should be given to the development of cottage industries in certain developing countries to produce entomopathogens for use against these weevils and other insect pests of agronomic importance. In addition to entomopathogenic nematodes and fungi, parasitoids of these weevils also have potential. Insect parasitoids that achieve high levels of parasitism in the center of origin of *Cylas* species (i.e., Africa) and of *C.*

formicarius (i.e., India) should be exchanged and introduced and their establishment assessed in areas of introduction.

Breeding for resistance to insects

Breeding programs for resistance to insect pests of sweetpotato have been reviewed (Collins et al. 1991). Progress in the area of host-plant resistance to sweetpotato weevils has been slow. In spite of over 50 years of research, no cultivars with high levels of resistance are available. Low levels of resistance to weevils have been reported in several pools of sweetpotato germplasm. The International Institute for Tropical Agriculture (IITA) and the Asian Vegetable Research Development Center (AVRDC) tried to increase levels of resistance to weevils by using conventional plant breeding techniques; however, they had little success.

There is potential to develop cultivars with higher levels of resistance in the future. Numerous reports indicate that different levels of weevil damage occur in certain populations of sweetpotato. However, several problems have complicated interpretations of the results from some of these studies. For example, the experimental design used to assess levels of resistance in the field has often consisted of the use of small, single-row plots with few replications. These tests relied on either natural infestations and/or artificial infestations of weevils and lacked consistency in their methodology. Additionally, various methods have been used to assess weevil damage in the field thereby reducing the possibilities for comparative analyses among tests. For these reasons, standardized protocols for evaluating germplasm for resistance in the field are needed worldwide. The use of such methods may enhance the ability to select for resistant clones, especially for a trait of low heritability.

Many of the wild species of *Ipomoea* and primitive cultivars maintained in the world collection of sweetpotato germplasm at CIP need to be evaluated for levels of resistance. Preliminary studies at CIP and AVRDC showed that a wild species, *I. trifida* (HBK) Don, may contain valuable genes for resistance to *C. formicarius*. Some success has been achieved in crossing *I. trifida* ($4x$ form) with cultivated sweetpotato ($6x$), and in producing *I. trifida* that are more compatible with *I. batatas*. Other forms of *I. trifida* ($2x$, $4x$) are also known. Further studies are needed to make genes of *I. trifida* more available for conventional plant breeding programs so that the potential value of this and other wild species of *Ipomoea* can be assessed (Collins and Mendoza 1991). Based on previous studies, resistance to sweetpotato weevils is a quantitatively inherited trait with a low heritability (Collins and Mendoza 1991; Collins et al. 1991). This type of trait is usually difficult to evaluate in a selection and breeding program. Restriction fragment length polymorphism (RFLP) markers have been associated with quantitative trait loci (QTL's) in other crops. Specific RFLP patterns must be determined in sweetpotato to link genes which control QTL's for weevil resistance. Direct selection for RFLP marker loci associated with weevil resistance may result in a correlated increase in the frequency of favorable alleles for resistance (Collins and Mendoza 1991). Other approaches that may be useful to increase levels of resistance in sweetpotato germplasm were reviewed (Collins 1992).

Biochemical and biotechnological techniques which may lead to a better understanding of the weevil and the resistance mechanisms of sweetpotato are improving rapidly. Oviposition and other volatile stimulants/attractants have been studied (Starr et al. 1991; Wilson et al. 1991). Studies are needed to correlate the quantitative and/or qualitative relationships between phytochemicals in storage roots and the expression of resistance to weevils in the field. An analytical approach based on the levels of kairomones in storage roots, which affect oviposition of *C. formicarius,* could be an important tool for plant breeders.

Progress in developing resistant cultivars for other pests, such as *Conoderus* spp., *Diabrotica spp.,* and *Systena* spp., has promise. Several cultivars with multiple resistance to these pests are now available in the United States (Collins et al. 1991; Schalk et al. 1991). These pests are of major importance in many countries of South America. For this reason, studies are needed to transfer genes from these cultivars to germplasm that is adapted to the tropics.

Development of transgenic sweetpotato plants

Several laboratories have successfully transformed sweetpotato plants (Dodds et al. 1991a,b; Prakash 1991). Both *Agrobacterium*-mediated gene transfer and particle gun transformation methods have been shown to have potential. Approaches such as those from *B. thuringiensis,* protease inhibitors (e.g., cowpea trypsin inhibitor), or chitinases, that govern toxicity to pests will have potential to transfer genes to sweetpotato plants, to increase levels of resistance to insect pests and subsequently to improve pest management programs on sweetpotato in the future (Dodds et al. 1991b). However, at present, no information is available on the toxicity of any of the candidate toxins to sweetpotato weevils. Currently, a potential gene of interest, cowpea trypsin inhibitor, is being bioassayed for toxicity to *C. formicarius, C. puncticollis,* and *E. postfasciatus* (K.V. Raman, personal communication). Additional studies on the toxicity and eventual integration of genes for *B. thuringiensis* var. *tenebrionis* are planned in Florida and Alabama. Central to this research is the development of a suitable bioassay for evaluating the toxicity of *B. thuringiensis var. tenebrionis* to the cryptic immatures. Caution is advised in this area of research, however, because recently several insects, such as Indianmeal moth, *Plodia interpunctella* (Hubner), diamondback moth, *Plutella xylostella (L.),* Colorado potato beetle, *Leptinotarsa decemlineata* (Say), almond moth, *Cadra cautella* (Walker), tobacco budworm, *Heliothis virescens* (Fabricius), and others developed resistance to *B. thuringiensis.* Thus, the development of transgenic sweetpotato plants with genes from *B. thuringiensis* var. *tenebrionis* that encode for toxicity to sweetpotato weevils may enhance development of weevil resistance to these toxins.

Plant volatiles

Preliminary work demonstrated that *C. formicarius* is attracted to host plant volatiles from a variety of *Ipomoea* species (Starr et al. 1991). More work is needed to isolate, identify, bioassay, and synthesize the volatile(s) that are important in attracting these weevils to their host plants. Such an attractant might ultimately be useful for attracting female *C. formicarius* to traps. Currently, only male *C. formicarius* are caught in traps baited with a synthetic sex pheromone similar to that produced by female weevils. Integration of a female attractant in traps might help to manage this weevil in the future.

IPM program for weevils

An IPM program for *C. formicarius* described by Talekar (1991) is simple and is readily adaptable for controlling other major sweetpotato weevil species, such as *C. puncticollis* and *E. postfasciatus*. Cultural practices are essential to the success of this program. In many regions of the world, however, some of its component strategies, such as the removal of wild *Ipomoea* spp. from the near vicinity of sweetpotato fields and the use of isolated planting of the crop, are not possible. For this reason, this program will need to be modified and adapted to local growing conditions in various parts of the world. Modified IPM programs should be flexible to allow for integration of new technologies in the future. Both international and national programs should encourage farmer participation in the evaluation and use of these approaches.

Management of the Wireworm-*Diabrotica-Systena* complex

Schalk et al. (1991) and Chalfant and Seal (1991) reviewed the biology and management of the major insect pests of sweetpotato in the southern U.S., with the exception of *C. formicarius*. From their reviews, it is apparent that more studies are needed to better understand the biology of these pests on sweetpotato in the the U.S. and the tropics. A sex pheromone for *D. balteata* (LeConte) has been synthesized and should help to improve IPM programs for this pest worldwide; however, considerably more work will be needed to better understand the dynamics of this pheromone system. Biological control agents, such as the new strains of bacteria, entomopathogenic fungi, and entomogenous nematodes, which are effective against coleopterous pests, may have potential for managing these pests as part of an integrated control program in the future. Because of reductions in the numbers of chemical insecticides available for use against these pests, cultural and biological control strategies that are sustainable will need to be developed and implemented to provide adequate control of these pests in the future.

Management of vine borers

Vine borers, *Omphisa anastomasalis* (Guenee) and *Megastes grandalis* (Guenee), are important pests of sweetpotato in Asia and the Caribbean, and the biology and management of these pests have been reviewed (Talekar and Pollard 1991). Little research has been conducted on these pests, especially in recent years, considering their importance in these regions. Studies have identified resistance to both of these species in sweetpotato. These sources of resistance should be incorporated into an active breeding program. There are also indications that adult females of *O. anastomasalis* produce a sex pheromone that attracts males. Research is needed to identify, bioassay, and synthesize the active component(s) of this pheromone.

The diverse complex of egg and larval parasitoids of these pests should also be investigated more fully. Studies are needed to develop and determine the impact of classical biological control programs for these pests in regions where they occur. Additional studies should determine if parasitoids of one vine borer species may also attack the other species. If crossover of parasitoids occurs and high levels of parasitism can be achieved, then exchange and introduction of these parasitoids for management of these vine borer species is encouraged.

Management of vectors and associated viruses

Moyer and Larsen (1991) reviewed the viruses and vectors that attack sweetpotato worldwide, and presented potential management approaches. However, at present, there are few management programs that were specifically developed for vectors and viruses of sweetpotato. More work is needed to develop such programs for this crop.

Fourteen virus diseases and one mycoplasmalike disease are known to attack sweetpotato (Moyer and Larsen 1991). Characterization of some of these disorders, such as sweetpotato virus disease in Africa, Georgia mosaic and yellow dwarf in the United States, sweetpotato veinclearing virus in Israel, and sweetpotato leaf curl disease is still unclear. Thus, considerable work is needed to classify these diseases.

A continuing problem facing many sweetpotato improvement programs worldwide is the production and movement of pathogen-tested germplasm. CIP has concentrated on establishing phytosanitary standards for pests and pathogens for the distribution of both true seed and *in vitro* cultures of *Ipomoea*. The major constraints for developing such standards are the space and labor needed to index germplasm for virus detection. Newer methods of virus detection and testing, which require fewer resources, such as *in vitro* assay procedures which are now being used on potato, need to be studied further for sweetpotato. Recently, J.W. Moyer and coworkers cloned the capsid protein gene for viral RNA for sweetpotato feathery mottle virus (J.W. Moyer, personal communication). Such an advancement allows for the development of probes for detecting viral RNA and viral proteins in sweetpotato germplasm. Further studies are needed to clone capsid protein genes for other virus diseases of sweetpotato.

The status of the major vector of sweetpotato virus diseases, sweetpotato whitefly, *Bemisia tabaci* (Gennadius), needs to be assessed. The pest status of this insect recently accelerated in the Western Hemisphere. Because *B. tabaci is* a very polyphagous insect, holistic management programs that consider the surrounding, previous, and subsequent cropping systems and other surrounding vegetation are needed to successfully manage this insect and the diseases that it vectors. Studies are also needed to determine the importance of various alternate hosts as reservoirs for vectors, their associated viruses, and their natural enemies. Additional studies are needed to develop improved IPM programs for virus vectors and viruses on sweetpotato.

Lastly, there is good potential to develop sweetpotato plants with resistance to viruses. Beachy et al. (1992) illustrates the development and application of coat protein-mediated resistance to viruses by genetic engineering. Such strategies have been used in potato and will have great potential for virus management in the future.

Management of plant-parasitic nematodes

Jatala (1991) reviewed the biology and management of plant-parasitic nematodes that attack sweetpotato. In general, very little research has also been conducted on these pests, especially in developing countries. More research is needed to improve the management of plant-parasitic nematodes. Host plant resistance to plant-parasitic nematodes has been identified in wild and cultivated accessions, and is currently maintained in the world collection of sweetpotato germplasm at the International Potato Center (CIP). Studies are needed to incorporate resistance to these nematodes with resistance to other important pests and pathogens. Improved IPM programs need to be developed for these nematodes and integrated with management programs for other pests.

CONCLUSIONS

IPM programs for sweetpotato pests have a promising future. The future of *C. formicarius* management is exciting and points towards a greater emphasis on the use of biological, parabiological and biotechnological approaches (e.g., see Dodds et al. 1991a, Jansson 1991, Jansson et al. 1991a). These approaches are well suited for low input agricultural systems.

Successful development and implementation of new IPM technologies requires an integrated program of research with an interdisciplinary perspective. Central to this approach is the need for an improved understanding of the relationships between cultural practices and pest severity (O'Hair 1991). In addition, the role of sweetpotato in farming and cultural systems must be better understood. More recently, it has become clear that, in addition to farmers, the perspectives and needs of consumers, processors, and market agents must also be considered in designing, testing, and implementing new technologies in sweetpotato IPM (Horton and Ewell 1991). Additionally, the socioeconomic constraints of the farming system in which the technologies will operate must be understood in order for IPM to operate effectively. More information is needed on each of these aspects so that appropriate IPM systems are developed and utilized by growers worldwide. Based on this, we must select management approaches that are compatible with the limitations of the agricultural systems in which the crop is grown. We must recognize that research on sweetpotato IPM focuses on a commodity in a food system and not only on a crop in a production system. In many regions of the world, sweetpotato is considered a low-status crop. The way in which the crop will be used is clearly linked to its image, and much remains to be done with regard to public awareness of its potential (Jansson et al. 1991a).

CIP is currently developing an international network for sweetpotato IPM in developing countries. The objective of this network is to focus research on the components of IPM (host plant resistance, cultural control practices, biological control agents, sex pheromones, and the judicious use of chemical insecticides), and develop more holistic and integrated approaches for managing pests on sweetpotato. Sweetpotato IPM programs will become a reality in developing countries when these technologies are developed, implemented, adapted to local conditions, and accepted by farmers. Pest surveys and on-farm demonstration research will help to facilitate this process. National and international agricultural research and development programs in these countries should encourage such activities.

In the United States, IPM programs for pests of sweetpotato are more advanced; however, considerably more research and extension efforts are needed to develop and implement improved IPM programs. For example, although cultivars with resistance to multiple pests have been developed for the United States, they are not widely grown. The sweetpotato industry is reluctant to change to new cultivars despite their potential benefits (i.e., reduced pesticide use, reduced production costs) (Chalfant et al. 1990). Efforts are needed to educate the producers, marketing specialists, and consumers to increase acceptance of cultivars with pest resistance.

The development of new conventional, chemical insecticides to replace those removed from use on sweetpotato by the Environmental Protection Agency, and those that have lost their effectiveness over time is unlikely. Sweetpotato is considered a minor crop in the United States and, thus, it lacks the importance (i.e., market size) needed to justify development of new insecticides (Chalfant et al. 1990).

The reduced levels of acceptance of cultivars with resistance to pests and the reduced availability of effective chemical pesticides will undoubtedly trigger additional research on developing other alternative tactics for managing pests of sweetpotato. In the future, sweetpotato will probably be well represented in the surge in research on agro-ecology and sustainable agriculture along with other crops. Also, considerable research is expected to occur on the development and application of biotechnology for use in sweetpotato pest management programs as we enter the 21st century.

ACKNOWLEDGMENTS

This paper is based, in part, on information from two previous publications (Jansson, R.K. and K.V. Raman. 1991. Sweetpotato pest management: a global overview, pp. 1-12 *In* R.K. Jansson and K.V. Raman (eds.). Sweetpotato pest management: a global perspective, Westview Press, Boulder, Colorado and London; and R.K. Jansson, K.V. Raman and O.S. Malamud. 1991. Sweet potato pest management: future outlook, pp. 429-437. (*In* Same volume). Parts of this paper were reprinted with permission from Westview Press, Boulder, Colorado. This is Florida Agricultural Experiment Station Journal Series No. R-01673.

REFERENCES

Beachy, Roger N., Carlos Malpica, and Gregg Clark. 1992. Coat protein mediated resistance: Strategy for genetic engineering virus resistance in sweetpotato. Pages 507-513 *in*

Sweetpotato technology for the 21st century, edited by W.A. Hill, C.K. Bonsi and P.A. Loretan. Tuskegee University, Tuskegee, AL.

Chalfant, R.B., and D.R. Seal. 1991. Biology and management of wireworms on sweet potato. Pages 303-326 *in* Sweet potato pest management: a global perspective, edited by R.K. Jansson and K.V. Raman. Westview Press, Boulder, Colorado and London.

Chalfant, R.B., R.K. Jansson, D.R. Seal, and J.M Schalk. 1990. Ecology and management of sweet potato insects. Annu. Rev. Entomol. 35:157-180.

Collins, Wanda W. 1992. Practical applications of biotechnology for sweetpotato improvements. Pages 514-520 *in* Sweetpotato technology for the 21st century, edited by W.A. Hill, C.K. Bonsi and P.A. Loretan. Tuskegee University, Tuskegee, AL.

Collins, W.W., and H.A. Mendoza. 1991. Breeding sweet potato for weevil resistance: future outlook. Pages 399-406 *in* Sweet potato pest management: a global perspective, edited by R.K. Jansson and K.V. Raman. Westview Press, Boulder, Colorado and London.

Collins, W.W., A. Jones, M.A. Mullen, N.S. Talekar, and F.W. Martin. 1991. Breeding sweet potato for insect resistance: a global overview. Pages 379-398 *in* Sweet potato pest management: a global perspective, edited by R.K. Jansson and K.V. Raman. Westview Press, Boulder, Colorado and London.

Dodds, J.H., J. Benavides, F. Buitron, F. Medina, and C. Siguenas. 1992. Biotechnology applied to sweetpotato improvement. Pages 7-19 *in* Sweetpotato technology for the 21st century, edited by W.A. Hill, C.K. Bonsi and P.A. Loretan. Tuskegee University, Tuskegee, Alabama.

Dodds, J.H., C. Merzdorf, V. Zambrano, C. Siguenas, and J. Jaynes. 1991. Potential use of Agrobacterium-mediated gene transfer to confer insect resistance in sweet potato. Pages 203-220 *in* Sweet potato pest management: a global perspective, edited by R.K. Jansson and K.V. Raman. Westview Press, Boulder, Colorado and London.

Gregory, P., M. Iwanaga, and D.E. Horton. 1990. Sweet potato: global issues. Pages 462-468 *in* Proceedings of the 8th Symposium of the International Society of Tropical Root Crops, edited by R.H. Howeler. International Center of Tropical Agriculture (CIAT), Bangkok, Thailand.

Heath, R.R., J.A. Coffelt, F.I. Proshold, R.K. Jansson, and P.E. Sonnet. 1991. Sex pheromone of *Cylas formicarius:* history and implications of chemistry in weevil management. Pages 79-96. *in* Sweet potato pest management: a global perspective, edited by R.K. Jansson and K.V. Raman. Westview Press, Boulder, Colorado and London.

Horton, D.E. 1989. Constraints to sweet potato production and use. Pages 219-223 *in* Improvement of sweet potato *(Ipomoea batatas)* in Asia. International Potato Center, Lima, Peru.

Horton, D.E., and P.T. Ewell. 1991. Sweet potato pest management: a social science perspective. Pages 407-428 *in* Sweet potato pest management: a global perspective, edited by R.K. Jansson and K.V. Raman. Westview Press, Boulder, Colorado and London.

Jansson, R.K. 1991. Biological control of *Cylas* spp. Pages 169-201 *in* Sweet potato pest management: a global perspective, edited by R.K. Jansson and K.V. Raman. Westview Press, Boulder, Colorado and London.

Jansson, R.K., and K.V. Raman (eds.). 1991a. Sweet potato pest management: a global perspective. Westview Press, Boulder, Colorado and London. 458 pp.

Jansson, R.K., and K.V. Raman. 1991b. Sweet potato pest management: a global overview. Pages 1-12 *in* Sweet potato pest management: a global perspective, edited by R.K. Jansson and K.V. Raman. Westview Press, Boulder, Colorado and London.

Jansson, R.K., L.J. Mason, and R.R. Heath. 1991a. Use of sex pheromone for monitoring and managing *Cylas formicarius.* Pages 97-138 *in* Sweet potato pest management: a global perspective, edited by R.K. Jansson and K.V. Raman. Westview Press, Boulder, Colorado and London.

Jansson, R.K., K.V. Raman, and O.S. Malamud. 1991b. Sweet potato pest management: future outlook. Pages 429-437 *in* Sweet potato pest management: a global perspective, edited by R.K. Jansson and K.V. Raman. Westview Press, Boulder, Colorado and London.

Jatala, P. 1991. Biology and management of plant-parasitic nematodes on sweet potato. Pages 359-378 *in* Sweet potato pest management: a global perspective, edited by R.K. Jansson and K.V. Raman.Westview Press, Boulder, Colorado and London.

Mason, L.J., R.K. Jansson, and R.R. Heath. 1992. Potential of mass trapping in combination with mating disruption for managing sweetpotato weevil *(Cylas formicarius)* (Coleoptera: Apionidae). J. Econ.Entomol. (In review).

Moyer, J.W., and R.C. Larsen. 1991. Management of insect vectors of viruses infecting sweet potato. Pages 341-358 *in* Sweet potato pest management: a global perspective, edited by R.K. Jansson and K.V. Raman. Westview Press, Boulder, Colorado and London.

O'Hair, S.K. 1991. Growth of sweet potato in relation to attack by sweet potato weevils. Pages 59-78 *in* Sweet potato pest management: a global perspective, edited by R.K. Jansson and K.V. Raman. Westview Press, Boulder, Colorado and London.

Prakash, C., and Usha Varadarajan. 1992. Genetic transformation of sweetpotato. Pages 27-37 *in* Sweetpotato technology for the 21st century, edited by W.A. Hill, C.K. Bonsi and P.A. Loretan. Tuskegee University, Tuskegee, Alabama.

Raman, K.V., and E.H. Alleyne. 1991. Biology and management of the West Indian sweet potato weevil, *Euscepes postfasciatus. Pages* 263-281 *in* Sweet potato pest management: a global perspective, edited by R.K. Jansson and KV. Raman. Westview Press, Boulder, Colorado and London.

Schalk, J.M., A. Jones, P.D. Dukes, and J.K. Peterson. 1991. Approaches to the control of multiple insect problems in sweet potato in the southern United States. Pages 283-301 *in* Sweet potato pest management: a global perspective, edited by R.K. Jansson and K.V. Raman. Westview Press, Boulder, Colorado and London.

Starr, C.K., R.F. Severson, and S.J. Kays. 1991. Volatile chemicals from sweet potato and other *Ipomoea:* effects on the behavior of *Cylas formicarius.* Pages 235-246 *in* Sweet potato pest management: a global perspective, edited by R.K. Jansson and K.V. Raman. Westview Press, Boulder, Colorado and London.

TAC (Technical Advisory Committee, Consultative Group on International Agricultural Research). 1985. TAC review of CGIAR priorities and future strategies. FAO, Rome.

Talekar, N.S. 1991. Integrated control of *Cylas formicarius.* Pages 139-156 *in* Sweet potato pest management: a global perspective, edited by R.K. Jansson and K.V. Raman. Westview Press, Boulder, Colorado and London.

Talekar, N.S., and G.V. Pollard. 1991. Vine borers of sweet potato. Pages 327-339 *in* Sweet potato pest management: a global perspective, edited by R.K. Jansson and K.V. Raman. Westview Press, Boulder, Colorado and London.

USDA. 1989. Crop production 1988 summary. U.S. Department of Agriculture, National Agricultural Statistics Service and Agricultural Statistics Board, Washington, D.C.

Wilson, D.D., R.F. Severson, and S.J. Kays. 1991. Oviposition stimulant for *Cylas formicarius* in sweet potato: isolation, identification, and development of analytical screening method. Pages 221-234 *in* Sweet potato pest management: a global perspective, edited by R.K. Jansson and K.V. Raman. Westview Press, Boulder, Colorado and London.

Wolfe, G.W. 1991. The origin and dispersal of the pest species of *Cylas* with a key to the pest species groups of the world. Pages 13-43 *in* Sweet potato pest management: a global perspective, edited by R.K. Jansson and K.V. Raman. Westview Press, Boulder, Colorado and London.

Sweetpotato Technology for the 21st Century. W.A. Hill, C.K. Bonsi and P.A. Loretan (Eds.) 1992. Tuskegee University, Tuskegee, AL

Roger N. Beachy, Carlos Malpica, Gregg Clark*

Coat Protein Mediated Resistance: Strategy for Genetic Engineering Virus Resistance in Sweetpotatoes

Of the several different strategies employed to produce virus resistance in transgenic plants, coat protein (CP) mediated resistance has been the most widely applied. The strategy of CP mediated resistance is to introduce a gene encoding a capsid protein of the virus against which resistance is desired. Transgenic plants that express the viral capsid protein gene are resistant to the virus from which the CP was taken and to closely related viruses, but not to viruses belonging to different virus groups. To date this strategy has been successfully used to produce resistance against viruses from eleven different groups in a variety of transgenic plants, including tomato, tobacco, potato, alfalfa, and cucumbers. Among the common viruses that cause significant symptoms and yield reductions in sweetpotato are members of the potyvirus group, including sweetpotato feathery mottle virus. Through collaboration with Jim Moyer (North Carolina State University) we have obtained cloned cDNAs from several strains of sweetpotato feathery mottle virus. Using site-directed mutagenesis and PCR, we isolated the CP coding sequences. We are currently testing the expression of these sequences in a transient assay in plants. The CP sequences were also ligated with the enhanced P 35S promoter from cauliflower mosaic virus and were introduced into tobacco plants by   mediated transformation. The results of these experiments to test open reading frames will be discussed. Although we have initiated studies in sweet-potato tissue culture, it has yet to be demonstrated that these genes will function in sweetpotato plants. The goal of our research is to create transgenic sweetpotato plants that express capsid protein genes of sweetpotato feathery mottle potyvirus and other potyviruses in order to develop resistance suitable for controlling the diseases caused by these viruses.

Through classical plant breeding plant varieties have been developed that possess substantial resistance against a variety of pathogens, including viruses, bacteria, nematodes, and fungi. In many other examples, however, classical plant breeding has not identified useful sources of genetic resistance for all pathogenic races or strains. This is especially the case with plant viruses, and there are a number of virus strains of pathogens that overcome most types of resistance in virtually every major agricultural crop.

The complete situation with virus disease resistance in sweetpotato is unclear because there is limited information about the distribution of viruses in sweetpotato

Department of Cell Biology, MRC-7, The Scripps Research Institute, 10666 North Torrey Pines Road, La Jolla, CA 92037 and *Department of Biochemistry, St. Louis University, St. Louis, MO.

inside or outside of the U.S. It is known, however, that a number of plant viruses cause substantial economic losses in parts of Africa and Asia, including sweetpotato feathery mottle virus (SPFMV), sweetpotato mild mottle virus (SPMMV), and sweetpotato latent virus (SPLV). In cases where virus disease resistance is not available, biotechnologists have taken a number of approaches to produce disease resistance in transgenic plants. The major strategies for engineering resistance against plant viruses include: (1) expression of genes that produce antisense RNAs, i.e., RNAs that are complimentary to the viral genome (Cuozzo et al. 1988; Hemenway et al. 1988; Powell et al. 1989) and the use of ribosomes to enhance the activity of the antisense RNAs; (2) expression of satellite RNAs to decrease the severity of the disease caused by the helper virus; (3) the expression of other sequences such as a fragment of the replicase cistron of tobacco mosaic virus (Golemboski et al. 1990); and (4) the expression of capsid protein genes (reviewed by Beachy et al. 1990).

Since 1985, when coat protein mediated resistance was first described for resistance in tobacco against tobacco mosaic virus, a number of examples of such resistance have been described in the literature and at research conferences. A current list of successes are given in Table 1.

Included within the list are several potyviruses. Since the major viral pathogens of sweetpotato are members of the potyvirus group, we have initiated a project to isolate the coat protein gene of sweetpotato feathery mottle virus for the purpose of introducing it into sweetpotato cells by transformation, and to regenerate intact plants to develop disease resistant varieties of sweetpotato. In this paper we will review coat protein mediated resistance and briefly describe our preliminary results on the isolation and characterization of a gene for sweetpotato feathery mottle virus.

COAT PROTEIN MEDIATED RESISTANCE: A summary of examples.

Coat protein mediated resistance is a general term given to describe the expression of a viral coat protein gene in transgenic plants to produce resistance against the virus. The strategy employed for the isolation of the coat protein gene has been previously described (Beachy et al. 1987). In brief, the approach is to isolate from the viral genomic RNA or DNA the sequences that encode the viral coat protein. This, of course, requires an understanding of genome organization and mechanisms of gene expression of the virus in question. Once the coding region for the capsid protein is isolated, it is ligated to an appropriate transcriptional promoter and a transcription terminator with polyadenylation signal. In most of the successful examples of coat protein mediated resistance to date, the promoters have caused the expression of the capsid protein in all or most cell types throughout the life cycle of the plant, i.e., a constitutive promoter. The most commonly used promoter is that which encodes the 35S transcript of cauliflower mosaic virus (CAMV). Other promoters have been used as well but less frequently than the 35S promoter. After the chimeric gene is produced, it is used in the production of transgenic plants, generally through the use of disarmed strains of *Agrobacterium tumefaciens* and the

Table 1. Examples of coat protein-mediated resistance in transgenic plants (from Fauquet and Beachy).

Virus group	CP Gene	Transgenic Plant	Virus Resistance	Reference
Tobamovirus	TMV	tobacco	TMV	(Powell et al. 1984)
	"	"	ToMV	(Nelson et al. 1988)
	"	"	PMMV	(Nejidat et al. 1990).
	"	"	TMGMV	"
	"	"	HRSV	"
	"	"	ORSV	"
	"	tomato	TMV	(Nelson et al. 1988)
	"	"	ToMV	"
	ToMV	tomato	ToMV	(Sanders et al. 1990)
Tobravirus	TRV	tobacco	TRV	(van Dun et al. 1988)
	"	"	PEBV	"
Carlavirus	PVM	potato	PVM	(Wefels et al. 1990)
	PVS	tobacco	PVS	(McKenzie et al. 1990)
Potexvirus	PVX	tobacco	PVX	(Hemenway et al.1988)
	"	potato	PVX	(Lawson et al. 1990)
Potyvirus	PVY	potato	PVY	"
	SMV	tobacco	PVY	(Stark et al. 1989)
	"	"	TEV	"
	ZYMV	tobacco	ZYMV	(Namba et al. 1990)
	WMV II	tobacco	WMV II	"
	PRSV	tobacco	PRSV	(Ling et al. 1990)
	"	"	TEV	"
Furovirus	BNYVV	beet (protoplast)	BNYVV	(Kallerhoff et al. 1990)
AlMV group	AlMV	tobacco	AlMV	(Loesch-Fries et al. 1987)
	"	"	"	(Tumer et al. 1987)
	"	"	"	(van Dun et al. 1987)
	"	tomato	"	(Tumer et al. 1987)
	"	alfalfa	"	(Hill et al. 1990)
Cucumovirus	CMV	tobacco	CMV	(Cuozzo et al. 1988)
	"	"	"	(Nakayama et al. 1990)
	"	tomato	CMV	(Cuozzo et al. 1988)
Ilarvirus	TSV	tobacco	TSV	(van Dun et al. 1988)
Luteovirus	PLRV	potato	PLRV	(Tumer et al. 1990)
	"	"	"	(Kawchuk et al. 1990)

Abbreviations: AlMV, alfalfa mosaic virus; BNYVV, beet necrotic yellow vein virus; CMV, cucumber mosaic virus; ORSV, Ondontoglossum ringspot virus; PEBV, pea early browning virus; PMMV, pepper mild mosaic virus; PRSV, papaya ringspot virus; PVM, potato virus M; PVS, potato virus S; PVX, potato virus X; PVY, potato virus Y; TEV, tobacco etch virus; TMGMV, tobacco mild green mosaic virus; TMV, tobacco mosaic virus; ToMV, tomato mosaic virus; TRV, tobacco rattle virus; TSV, tobacco streak virus; WMV II, watermelon mosaic virus II; ZYMV, zucchini yellow mosaic virus.

now-common leaf disc transformation and regeneration system (Horsch et al. 1985).

Plants that are regenerated after transformation are characterized with respect to the presence and expression of the gene and level of accumulation of the viral capsid protein. Plants that accumulate detectable levels of capsid protein (i.e., generally by an antibody reaction such as ELISA or Western immunoblot), seeds are collected from the parent plant. Those R_0 plants give rise to R_1 seedlings, which are then used in virus inoculation experiments. In assays for resistance, populations of plants are inoculated with the virus from which the gene was taken and the degree of resistance is determined either by quantitating the amount of virus that accumulates or the rapidity with which symptoms appear.

In 1986 we first reported that tobacco plants that expressed the coat protein (CP) gene of tobacco mosaic virus (TMV) are resistant to infection by TMV (Powell-Abel et al. 1986). Subsequent experience with transgenic tomato plants that express the coat protein gene of TMV were likewise successful (Nelson et al. 1988). These initial successes were quickly followed by other viruses, including alfalfa mosaic virus (Tumer et al. 1987; Cuozzo et al. 1988) and potato virus X (Hemenway et al. 1988). Since that time, a large number of examples have been described, and viruses that belong to a variety of virus classifications have been tested in similar assays. This led to the conclusion that coat protein mediated resistance would provide protection against a wide variety of viruses in a number of different types of plants.

FIELD TESTING OF COAT PROTEIN MEDIATED RESISTANCE

To date there have been several reports of field tests of coat protein mediated resistance with transgenic tomatoes, potatoes, and tobacco plants. Nelson et al. (1988) transplanted R_1 tomato (cv 'VF36') seedlings (in a split-plot design) that expressed the TMV coat protein gene, and later mechanically inoculated the plants with the common strain of TMV: checks included non-inoculated plants and non-transgenic plants that were inoculated. Inoculated plants that did not contain the CP gene [CP(-)] became diseased in the expected period of time and developed classical symptoms of infection. Many of the non-inoculated checks eventually became infected as well, presumably through mechanical transmission that occurred during the hoeing and weeding, throughout the season. By contrast, most of the plants that expressed the TMV CP gene [CP(+)] escaped infection; symptoms did not develop on the plants and no virus accumulated in the upper leaves of the plant. Those plants that became infected developed symptoms substantially later than did the CP(-) plants, the symptoms were generally more mild on the CP(+) plants than on the CP(-) plants, and the level of virus accumulation was significantly lower in the CP(+) plants than in the CP(-) plants. Furthermore, there was no effect of CP gene expression on the yield of CP(+) tomato fruits, whereas virus infected CP(-) plants suffered 25-30% reduction in yield.

Kaniewski et al. (1990) field tested cuttings of transgenic Russet Burbank potato plants that expressed the CP genes of potato virus X (PVX, a potexvirus) and potato virus Y (PVY, a potyvirus). The test, which included four lines, involved mechanical inoculations with PVX and PVY and comparisons of the levels of resistance following the quantitation of PVX and PVY in each plant. Each of the four lines were resistant to PVX, but only line 303 was resistant to both PVX and PVY. Tuber yields of all lines except 303 were remarkably lower than in the non-inoculated checks, presumably due to infection by PVY; yields from line 303 were maintained at those of the non-inoculated checks. Other studies demonstrated that line 303 was also resistant to infection by viruliferous aphids carrying PVY (Kaniewski et al. 1990).

More recent studies with tomato mosaic virus (ToMV), a virus closely related to TMV, and transgenic tomato plants that contain the ToMV CP gene were reported by Sanders et al. (in progress). These workers found that the CP gene of ToMV gave better protection, in tomato, against ToMV than against TMV; the inverse was also true, that is, the TMV CP gene gave greater resistance, in this field experiment, against TMV than against ToMV.

The tests with tobacco plants that express the CP gene of alfalfa mosaic virus (AlMV) were similar (Krahn et al. unpublished data). Plants that contained the CP gene were much less likely to become infected by AlMV than CP(-) plants (9% vs 93%). Furthermore, CP(+) plants accumulated much less AlMV than did the CP(-) plants. Other experiments that are ongoing by seed companies (unpublished) have indicated that there is field level resistance in transgenic plants that express a variety of capsid protein genes. To date, however, there has been no commercial use of these plants, and approval will be dependent upon the review process of agencies of the federal government.

COAT PROTEIN MEDIATED RESISTANCE AGAINST POTYVIRUSES

There have been several reports in the literature of coat protein mediated resistance against potyviruses. Potyviruses are a group of plant viruses that includes sweetpotato feathery mottle virus and sweetpotato mild mottle virus that are generally born by aphids and can cause severe damage. The viruses contain a long viral RNA (approximately 9.5 to 10.0 kb in length) encapsidated by a single capsid protein (Dougherty and Hiebert 1985). Because of the organization of potyviruses, there are special considerations that must be maintained to isolate the capsid protein gene for expression in transgenic plants, as described for the creation of the chimeric gene for soybean mosaic virus (Eggenberger et al. 1989). Furthermore, these authors subsequently demonstrated that the expression of this gene in transgenic tobacco plants provided resistance against tobacco etch virus and potato virus Y, and raised the possibility that a single coat protein gene can provide resistance against a variety of distantly related potyviruses (Stark and Beachy 1989).

Sweetpotato feathery mottle virus (SPFMV) has been worked on extensively by James Moyer and colleagues (North Carolina State University) who described a variety of isolates with material collected and maintained by the International Potato Center in Peru (Moyer and Kennedy 1978; Clark and Moyer 1988). Some of these virus isolates were further characterized by cDNA cloning and DNA sequence analysis (Jorge Abad 1991., Ph.D. Thesis, North Carolina State University).

cDNA clones representing a portion of the SPFMV genome were made available to our laboratory for the current work. The DNA sequence for the capsid protein gene was modified by site directed mutagenesis to introduce convenient endonuclease restriction sites, and appropriate sequences for the initiation of protein sequences. The cloned cDNA was further analyzed to confirm that the coat protein gene was functional. Concurrently, the 35S promoter from cauliflower mosaic virus was attached to the cloned gene encoding the coat protein, and was subsequently introduced by transformation into *Nicotiana benthamiana,* a host for a mechanically transmitted strain of SPFMV. At the current time, plants are being regenerated and the level of expression will be confirmed by immunochemical analyses (C. Malpica and R.N. Beachy, unpublished data).

An important concern when dealing with coat protein mediated resistance against potyviruses is reflected by the results that we and others have experienced with the potyviruses. Stark (1989, Ph.D. Thesis, Washington University) transformed and regenerated a large number of transgenic tobacco plant lines that express the capsid protein gene of soybean mosaic virus. Some of these plant lines expressed protein levels as high as 0.25% (w/w). A number of lines were also tested for their resistance against infection by potato virus Y and tobacco etch virus—while many lines had low levels of resistance, others had little or no resistance, and a very few lines (about 1 in 25) had high levels of resistance. Resistance was similar to the protection against TMV in tobacco and tomato in that CP(+) plants either escaped infection or had diminished symptoms and a lower level of virus. Unlike CP mediated resistance against TMV (Powell et al. 1989), however, the level of potyvirus coat protein accumulation did not correlate with the level of virus disease resistance. On the other hand, the levels of resistance were effective under high levels of virus inoculum. Resistance was exhibited by reduced numbers of plants that were infected and a reduced amount of virus accumulation in inoculated leaves, and in leaves above the inoculated leaf (Stark et al. 1989). Kaniewski et al. (1990) reported similar results for CP mediated resistance against PVY in Russet Burbank potato.

At this time it is unclear why the level of coat protein and the level of disease resistance are not tightly correlated, but it is postulated that the level of resistance is influenced by the levels of coat protein expression in specific cell types during specific times of plant development. Since it is not known what determines the levels and timing of gene expression, there remains a great deal of work yet to determine how the phenotype is expressed.

CONCLUSIONS

We and others have concluded that genetic transformation to produce coat protein mediated resistance is a viable strategy to develop new lines of virus resistant plants. The usefulness of such new plant lines in plant breeding remains to be demonstrated for vegetatively propagated plants such as potato and sweetpotato, but we remain hopeful that there will develop an integral relationship between the "classical" and "molecular" plant breeders to develop novel and useful germplasm.

REFERENCES

Beachy, R.N., S. Loesch-Fries and N.E. Tumer. 1990. Coat-protein-mediated resistance against virus infection. Annu. Rev. Phytopathol. 28:451-474.

Beachy, R.N., S.G. Rogers and R.T. Fraley. 1987. Genetic transformation to confer resistance to plant virus disease. Pages 229-247 *in* Genetic engineering, Vol. 9, edited by Jane K. Setlow, Plenum Press, New York, NY.

Clark, C.A., and J.W. Moyer. 1988 *in* Compendium of sweet potato diseases. American Phytopathology Society Press, St. Paul, MN.

Cuozzo, M., K.M. O'Connell, W. Kaniewski, R.-X. Fang, N-H. Chua and N.E. Tumer. 1988. Viral protection in transgenic tobacco plants expressing the cucumber mosaic virus coat protein or its antisense RNA. Bio/Technology 6:549-557.

Dougherty, W.G., and E. Hiebert. 1985. Genome structure and gene expression of plant RNA viruses. Pages 23-82 *in* Molecular plant virology. Replication and gene expression, edited by J. W. Davies. CRC Press, Inc., Boca Raton, FL.

Eggenberger, A.L., D.M. Stark and R.N. Beachy. 1989. Nucleotide sequence and expression of the SMV coat protein coding region in *Escherichia coli* and tobacco callus. J. Gen. Virology 70:1853-1860.

Golemboski, D.B., G.P. Lomonossoff and M. Zaitlin. 1990. Plants transformed with a tobacco mosaic virus nonstructural gene sequence are resistant to the virus. Proc. Natl. Acad. Sci. 87:6311-6315.

Hemenway, C., R.X. Fang, W.K. Kaniewski, N.H. Chua and N.E. Tumer. 1988. Analysis of the mechanism of protection in transgenic plants expressing the potato virus X coat protein or its antisense RNA. EMBO J. 7:1273-1280.

Horsch, R.B., J.E. Fry, N.L. Hoffman, D. Eicholtz, S.G. Rogers and R.T. Fraley. 1985. A simple and general method for transferring genes into plants. Science 227:1229-1231.

Kaniewski, W.K., C. Lawson, B. Sammons, L. Haley, J. Hart, X. Delanney, and N.E. Tumer. 1990. Field resistance of transgenic Russet Burbank potato to effects of infection by potato virus X and potato virus Y. Bio/Technology 8:750-754.

Moyer, J.W., and G.G. Kennedy. 1978. Purification and properties of sweet potato feathery mottle virus. Phytopathology 68:998-1004.

Nelson, R.S., S.M. McCormick, X. Delannay, P. Dube, J. Layton, E.J. Anderson, M. Kaniewska, R.K. Proksch, R.B. Horsch, S.A. Rogers, R.T. Fraley and R.N. Beachy. 1988. Virus tolerance, plant growth, and field performance of transgenic tomato plants expressing coat protein from tobacco mosaic virus. Bio/Technology 6:403-409.

Powell, P.A., P.R. Sanders, N. Tumer and R.N. Beachy. 1990. Protection against tobacco mosaic virus infection in transgenic plants requires accumulation of capsid protein rather than coat protein RNA sequences. Virology 175:124-130

Powell, P.A. et al. 1989. Protection against tobacco mosaic virus in transgenic plants that express TMV antisense RNA. Proc. Nat. Acad. of Science.

Powell-Abel, P.A., R.S. Nelson, B. De, N. Hoffmann, S.G. Rogers, R.T. Fraley and R.N. Beachy. 1986. Delay of disease development in transgenic plants that express the tobacco mosaic virus coat protein gene. Science 232:738-743.

Sanders, P.R., B. Sammons, W.K. Kaniewski, L. Haley, J. Layton, B.J. LaVallee, X. Delannay and N. Tumer. Field resistance of transgenic tomatoes expressing the tobacco mosaic virus or tomato mosaic virus coat protein genes. Phytopath. 82:683-690.

Stark, D.M., and R.N. Beachy. 1989. Protection against potyvirus infection in transgenic plants: Evidence for broad spectrum resistance. Bio/Technology 7:1257-1262.

Tumer, N.E., K.M. O'Connell, R.S. Nelson, P.R. Sanders and R.N. Beachy. 1987. Expression of alfalfa mosaic virus coat protein gene confers cross-protection in transgenic tobacco and tomato plants. EMBO J. 6:1181-1188.

Sweetpotato Technology for the 21st Century. W.A. Hill, C.K. Bonsi and P.A. Loretan (Eds.) 1992. Tuskegee University, Tuskegee, AL

Wanda W. Collins

Practical Applications of Biotechnology to Sweetpotato Improvement

Sweetpotato improvement using traditional breeding methods has been tremendously successful. However, lack of efficient evaluation methods and inadequate genetic variability have resulted in lack of improvement in some needed traits. The advent of biotechnological tools for increased efficiency of selection and for creating new genetic variability in the species could provide exciting new potential for sweetpotato improvement. Gene transfer, marker aided selection using RFLPs or RAPDs in conjunction with isozyme and morphological markers, and cell culture appear to be the most promising biotechnological methods for practical application to sweetpotato breeding in the near future. While there is no doubt that these methods may provide means of sweetpotato improvement in traits for which improvement has been minimal, the minor status of the crop in the US and lack of funding for applied plant breeding may preclude widespread use of the more highly technical and expensive methodologies. However, expanded emphasis on the utilization of sweetpotato internationally could result in increased funding for practical applications in developing countries.

INTRODUCTION

Sweetpotato improvement through traditional breeding methods has been tremendously successful over the past 30 years. Much of this success has been due to the increased power and efficiency of selection through the development and use of quantitative genetic methodology which is ideally suited for a hexaploid, highly heterozygous crop such as sweetpotato. Yields have been increased, multiple disease and insect resistances have been incorporated, plant architecture has been changed, and nutritional content and quality have been improved. The level of heterozygosity and range of variability in cultivated sweetpotatoes also insures that levels of most desirable traits can continue to be increased through the application of proper breeding and selection methodologies. The recent dramatic increase in interest in sweetpotatoes has generated systematized collection efforts of both sweetpotato and its wild relatives throughout the world. This provides sweetpotato breeders with the potential for an even wider range of variability for many traits with which to work.

Department of Horticultural Science, Box 7609, North Carolina State University, Raleigh, North Carolina 27695-7609, USA.

However, breeding programs, regardless of the power and sophistication of the statistical methodologies available, are no better than (1) the efficiency of the selection procedures and (2) the type and level of genetic variability of desirable traits. For example, resistance to Fusarium wilt is a highly heritable character (h2 = .85 to .90) with high levels of resistance available; evaluation is consistent and reliable from test to test. Consequently, Fusarium wilt resistance has been increased to near immunity levels in commercial cultivars. In contrast, evaluation methods for resistance to sweetpotato weevil, the major worldwide pest of sweetpotatoes, are unreliable and inconsistent from test to test and from year to year. Genetic variability appears to be low although very little actual genetic analysis has been done with this trait because of the lack of efficient evaluation methodology. Consequently, field resistance has not been developed and is not available in commercial cultivars.

The development of biotechnological methods for application to plant improvement could provide sweetpotato breeders with extremely sophisticated and precise evaluation methodologies, increase the level of genetic variability for certain desired traits, increase the precision and ease with which desired genes for some of those traits can be located and subsequently transferred through sexual hybridization, or introduce new traits directly into commercial cultivars. Some uses of biotechnological processes will not be directly applicable by breeders but will serve to build basic information about the species and its close relatives; other uses should be directly applicable and usable by plant breeders.

POTENTIAL APPLICATIONS OF BIOTECHNOLOGY METHODS TO SWEETPOTATO IMPROVEMENT

Increasing Variability by Gene Transfer

Gene transfer involves direct insertion of DNA constructs into a genome. This can be accomplished in a number of ways including bacteria or viral mediated transfer, absorption, electroporation or bombardment—among others. This offers a powerful technique for inserting suitable genes from any species into a target crop such as sweetpotato to provide some needed trait such as insect resistance. Use of this technique at present is limited in sweetpotatoes. As was reported earlier in this book, researchers at the International Potato Center have inserted the HEAAE (high essential amino acid) gene into sweetpotatoes through *Agrobacterium*-mediated transfer. Researchers at Tuskegee University are currently working to perfect both *Agrobacterium*-mediated transfer and particle bombardment transformation. They have successfully transformed sweetpotatoes with the GUS gene (Prakash and Varadarajan 1991) using the particle bombardment method.

This method of providing new variability probably holds the most potential in future biotechnological efforts with sweetpotato for transfer of genes from other species. Any gene which can be identified and isolated can potentially be transferred regardless of the species from which it comes. This can offer many single gene traits such as the cowpea trypsin inhibitor genes (CpTI) for insect resistance, the HEAAE genes for protein content and quality, *Bacillus thuringiesis* (Bt) toxin genes for insect resistance, virus resistance genes, and others.

One tremendous advantage of transferring genes is that existing pleiotrophic or linkage relationships may be bypassed. For example, dry matter content and protein content have been negatively correlated in many populations of sweetpotato. The insertion of a foreign gene for high protein could bypass the linkage or pleiotrophy.

Gene transfer is certainly not without problems to be overcome before it can be practically applied to sweetpotato improvement. Some aspects to be considered are:

1. A reliable and efficient regeneration system is absolutely necessary for production of transformed plants. This has always been a problem in sweetpotatoes because of low regeneration rates. However, several groups are working on regeneration protocols which may alleviate the problem or at least raise regeneration rates to acceptable levels (Komaki and Kukimura, 1989; Ozias-Akins and Perera, 1990). Much effort is needed to increase our knowledge of the physiology of sweetpotato and genetic regulation of events important in regeneration.

2. Most commercially important traits in sweetpotato are not under single gene control but are quantitatively inherited. The number of traits which can be improved will be limited to those single genes discovered in other species which offer certain desired traits. Traits such as yield which are controlled by many genes will not be immediately affected although it is possible in the future that genes with major regulatory effects on yield may be isolated and transferred.

3. Important single gene traits which might be transferred to sweetpotato may be located in close relatives which to date have received very little research attention. For example, *I. trifida* possesses some resistance to sweetpotato weevil (International Potato Center 1989). The genetic basis for that resistance is not known. In fact, the presence and genetic bases of potentially desirable genes in *I. trifida* and other close relatives is unknown because of the lack of genetic research efforts in those species. These species could contain major genes that are not available anywhere else and might be of regional or worldwide importance to sweetpotato breeders. Efforts to study the related species and their potential should be increased now that adequate collections are available.

Marker Aided Selection and Evaluation

Restriction Fragment Length Polymorphisms (RFLPs). RFLPs offer a powerful accessory to plant breeders for a number of activities. As markers to aid in selection, RFLPs can increase precision when selection is not efficient and increase expediency when large numbers of plants are involved. They can also allow easy determination of allelic frequencies and thus aid in determining allelic changes with selection. RFLPs increase precision and expedience by allowing breeders to determine genotype without progeny testing and ultimately screen and select by genotype in the preliminary stages of testing. Because the genotype is only one component of the final phenotypic response, plants will still require field testing to evaluate the environmental and genotype x environmental components of phenotype. However, parental plants could be selected quite early in the life cycle and used in crosses to transfer marked loci before field testing.

As most commercial traits in sweetpotato are quantitatively inherited, one of the most powerful uses of RFLPs for plant breeders would be in marking quantitative trait loci (QTLs) for selection. The problems associated with that usage are not minor. Tremendous numbers of markers are needed to saturate the genome. Adding markers to a genome is a time-consuming, expensive effort. After markers are added, correlations must be made to QTLs requiring exhaustive and extensive field testing. However, once the work is done, it need never be repeated for that specific trait. As long as the chosen RFLPs and QTLs are tightly linked and testing has been properly conducted, the uncertainties of environments and genotype x environment interactions are removed.

Prime candidates for RFLP marker aided selection would be regionally specific disease and insect resistances. If QTLs can be associated with specific RFLP patterns, then germplasm can be screened in any program in the world to be supplied for a specific regional need. Tolerance to abiotic stresses would also be major candidates; however, at present we lack sufficient knowledge of the physiological responses of sweetpotato to abiotic stresses to consider that a viable short-term reality.

The development of RFLP technology in sweetpotatoes is still in its infancy. There are few labs actively engaged in RFLP work in sweetpotato and those labs are now involved in developing the technology. DNA extraction is essential and procedures have been defined (Varadarajan and Prakash 1991a) but reliable, applicable RFLP technology is probably still a few years away. Hexaploid species also introduce greater problems in data interpretation and are more difficult to work with than diploid species.

Random Amplified Polymorphic DNA (RAPDs). RAPD markers may offer much more short-term potential to applied plant breeders than RFLPs. RAPD marking is non-radioactive and can easily be automated. RAPDs mark only dominant homologous loci—they are allele specific and no multiple alleles are delineated. This means that a hexaploid pattern such as might be observed with sweetpotato would be changed to a diploid pattern. RAPDs are also not sensitive to genome contamination so the entire genome does not have to be saturated such as is more desirable with RFLPs. RAPD markers are much easier to incorporate into a genome than RFLPs. A researcher simply targets the specific section which has been selected phenotypically. RAPDs would be used in F_2 populations when a trait exists that one can select for with confidence, such as a disease resistance locus. By inference, it is most practical for simply inherited traits but can be extended to quantitative traits especially if genes can be shown to have major effects.

RAPD markers have advantages and disadvantages. They are simpler to use and can access DNA which is not accessible to RFLPs because of repetitive sequences. A universal set of primers can be used and there is no need for a cDNA library or nucleotide sequences to be established. They are more limiting than RFLPs because they are dominant markers. However, RFLPs are limiting to the plant breeder because of the cost, technology involved and potential difficulty in interpretation with a hexaploid species. At present, RAPD technology does not exist for sweetpotato. Researchers at Tuskegee have just begun to explore this method of genome marking.

Isozyme and Morphological Markers. Isozyme and morphological markers perform the same function as DNA markers. Morphological markers have not been established in sweetpotato and its related species because most traits of interest are quantitatively inherited and not controlled by single genes. Isozyme markers of sweetpotato and its related species have also been rarely studied. However, when suitable isozyme markers do exist, they are preferable to RFLP markers because they are much less expensive and quicker to score. Reliable methods for isozyme analysis of *Ipomoea* species have been developed (Kennedy and Thompson 1991; Reyes 1991). It appears that isozyme polymorphism in sweetpotatoes and some related species is low compared to many other crops such as maize. It has been suggested that protein and DNA variability might serve as a useful index to predict RFLP variability (DeVerna and Alpert 1990). If so, RFLP variability may also be limited in these species.

The use of isozyme markers should receive more attention because of the advantages they have over DNA markers and the lack of knowledge about them in *Ipomoea* species. They do have distinct disadvantages in that they are subject to environmental effects—they mark genes indirectly by a product instead of directly at the DNA level. However, their potential should be further explored.

Germplasm Identification

Kennedy and Thompson (1991) reported resolution of nine cultivars using isozyme analysis and indicated that this tool has good potential for clonal identification. The International Potato Center (1990) also routinely uses isozyme analysis for duplicate identification. The major disadvantage of protein markers for clonal identification has already been mentioned: a gene product is represented rather than the actual DNA. It is therefore subject to environmental influences. RFLPs can be used as markers for clonal identification but have limitations also already mentioned. Hypervariable minisatellite DNA probes offer more potential for clonal identification; these probes have been shown to detect DNA variation in sweetpotato and related species (Varadarajan and Prakash 1991b) and are now being investigated further by researchers at Tuskegee University.

Cell Culture

Procedures for cell culture of sweetpotato using various explant sources are available. Regeneration rates are usually low. Several regeneration papers in this book present the latest information available on somatic embryogenesis and regeneration from protoplasts. The importance of regeneration in transformation has been discussed. The development of consistent cell culture and high frequency regeneration techniques would stimulate studies of *in vitro* cell selection for simple, easily scored traits as well as more complex traits such as abiotic stresses. Development of *in vitro* selection techniques would immensely benefit plant breeders, most of whom have easy access to tissue culture facilities.

RELATED RESEARCH IN OTHER DISCIPLINES

There are many uses of biotechnological methods in other disciplines (physiology, plant pathology, food science, etc.) which would be of long-term benefit to plant breeders. For example, basic research has been underway for some time at N. C. State University to identify and characterize viruses. The capsid protein gene for sweetpotato feathery mottle virus has been cloned and sequenced (Dr. J. W. Moyer, 1991, N. C. State University, personal communication). Work continues on sequencing capsid protein genes for other sweetpotato viruses. Other researchers are beginning to work on incorporating virus resistance through transformation.

All research efforts which seek to clarify basic aspects of gene action and interactions of sweetpotato and its related species, and especially those dealing with disease resistance, will aid plant breeders in understanding and evaluating genetic responses at the whole plant level.

SUMMARY

Biotechnology methods offer plant breeders a powerful tool to augment traditional methods of plant breeding. In crops where research efforts and inputs are at high levels, plant breeders are beginning to benefit from the development of these methods (e.g., tomato, maize, soybean). However, in crops where research efforts and relative inputs are low, such as sweetpotatoes, the practical application of these methods may be as much as a decade away. The exceptions will probably be in the area of gene transfer, where new genes can be inserted into the sweetpotato genome and made available to plant breeders very quickly, and cell culture techniques, where facilities are already available to most sweetpotato breeders. With more sophisticated technology such as RFLP analysis, the practical application will depend on several factors. Among these are: (1) relatively low cost of assays; (2) development of "user-friendly" adaptations of technology; and (3) close cooperation in team efforts of plant breeders and biotechnologists to identify proper research objectives and to implement the technology to achieve those objectives. Walton (1990) has reviewed the application of RFLP technology to applied plant breeding programs and concluded that its utility will depend upon the cooperation between RFLP labs and individual breeding programs and the ability of the lab to supply cost-efficient data of high quality and volume in a timely manner. Practical use of RAPD analysis will depend on the same factors but may be more quickly used because of lower level of sophistication necessary for application.

Much of the practical application of biotechnology may occur outside the United

States because of the lack of importance of sweetpotato in the overall agriculture of the U.S. compared with the increased emphasis on its importance as a world food crop in developing countries. In the U.S. it is a minor crop and funding is severely limited, especially for applied types of research. James (1990) has collected data showing that an increasing number of minor crops will not be improved even with conventional plant breeding in future years. A major reason for this decreased emphasis on minor crops is lack of funding opportunities for applied plant breeding efforts. While sweetpotatoes are not specifically mentioned, the number of U.S. sweetpotato breeding programs has declined. A grassroots effort is underway at this moment to secure a stable, consistent funding program for sweetpotatoes from the US government which would include biotechnology research at both the basic and applied levels. It is also encouraging that USAID has targeted biotechnology research for developing countries as a high priority and has, through a panel conducted by the National Research Council (1990), prioritized several specific applied areas of research. Funding will likely be made available in those areas.

LITERATURE CITED

DeVerna, Joseph W., and Kevin B. Alpert.1990. RFLP technology. Plant Biology 11:347-261.

International Potato Center. 1990. Annual Report CIP 1990, Lima, Peru. 258 pp.

International Potato Center. 1989. Annual Report CIP 1989, Lima, Peru. 178 pp.

James, Norman I. 1990. A survey of public plant breeding programs in the U.S., 1989. Diversity 6:32-22.

Kennedy, Larry S., and Paul G. Thompson. 1991. Identification of sweetpotato cultivars using isozyme analysis. HortScience 26:300-302.

Komaki, K., and H. Kukimura. 1989. Establishment of regeneration techniques from proto-plasts. Annual Report of Sweet Potato Breeding, Kyushu National Agricultural Experi-ment Station, MAFF, Japan. p. 12.

National Research Council. 1990. Plant biotechnology research for developing countries. National Academy Press, Washington, D.C., 44 pp.

Ozias-Akins, Peggy, and Srini Perera. 1990. Organogenesis in cultured adventitious root segments and in protoplast-derived callus of sweetpotato. HortScience 25:1121 (Abstr.)

Prakash, C.S., and U. Varadarajan. 1991. Genetic transformation of sweetpotato by microprojectile bombardment. Plant Cell Reports 11:53-57.

Reyes, Luz Marina. 1991. Isozyme analysis of sweetpotato and related Ipomoea species. Ph.D. thesis. North Carolina State University, Raleigh, North Carolina. 144 p.

Varadarajan, G. S., and C. S. Prakash. 1991a. A rapid and efficient method for the extraction of total DNA from the sweetpotato and its related species. Plant Mol. Bio. Rptr. 9:6-12.

Varadarajan, G. S., N.K. Sinha, and C. S. Prakash. 1992. Analysis of genomic variation in the sweetpotato through DNA fingerprinting. Pages 92-97 in Sweetpotato technology for the 21st Century, edited by W.A. Hill, C.K. Bonsi and P.A. Loretan. Tuskegee University, Tuskegee, Alabama.

Walton, Mark. 1989. Application of RFLP technology to applied plant breeding. Plant Biology 11:335-346.

Sweetpotato Technology for the 21st Century. W.A. Hill, C.K. Bonsi and P.A. Loretan (Eds.) 1992. Tuskegee University, Tuskegee, AL

Edward E. Carey, Enrique Chujoy, Tulsir Dayal, Haile M. Kidanemariam, Humberto A. Mendoza, Il-Gin Mok

Helping Meet Varietal Needs of the Developing World:The International Potato Center's Strategic Approach to Sweetpotato Breeding

Sweetpotato was added to CIP's mandate in 1986, and CIP's sweetpotato breeding program is being developed within a strategic approach that involves global collaboration with partners in the developing world. To meet the varietal needs of national research systems and achieve maximum local impact, the strategy stresses: (1) needs assessment and priority setting through meetings, surveys, and in-depth field studies; (2) a decentralized breeding effort in response to regional differences in needs; (3) the evaluation and utilization of genetic resources, including wild species; (4) virus indexing, international distribution, and testing of important varieties from many areas, as well as promising clones and advanced seed populations; (5) research on the genetics of priority traits and on breeding methodologies; and (6) training and information exchange to build capacities of national programs.This paper presents work to date on assessment of needs, establishment of priorities, and implementation of CIP's sweetpotato breeding program.

INTRODUCTION

The International Potato Center (CIP), an international agricultural research center, has worked on potato since the center was founded in 1971 and on sweetpotato since 1986. This paper presents work to date on needs assessment, establishment of priorities, and implementation of CIP's sweetpotato breeding program.

THE ASSESSMENT OF NEEDS FOR SWEETPOTATO RESEARCH IN THE DEVELOPING WORLD

The approaches to assess needs for sweetpotato research in the developing world have included surveys, conferences, workshops, and in-depth field studies. This work has involved scientists from national programs of developing and developed countries, other international centers, such as the Asian Vegetable Research and Development Center (AVRDC) and the International Institute of Tropical Agriculture (IITA), as well as farmers and marketers (Achata et al. 1990; CIP 1988abc, 1989ab, 1990ab; Gregory et al. 1990; Horton 1989; Horton et al. 1989; Lin et al. 1983; Mackay et al. 1990).

In some countries, this assessment—including that for breeding—has been hampered by a lack of sweetpotato researchers and of previous research on the crop.

The International Potato Center, P.O. Box 5969, Lima, Peru.

Table 1. Sweetpotato production, area and yield in developing countries by regions, 1986-88[1,2]

Region	Production (000 t)	Area (000 ha)	Yield (t/ha)
China	108,063 86.6%	6,306 70.2%	17.1
Asia + Oceania (except China)	8,198 6.6% (49.0%)	1,175 13.1% (43.9%)	7.0
Africa	6,264 5.0% (37.4%)	1,202 13.4% (44.9%)	5.2
Latin America + Caribbean	2,284 1.8% (13.6%)	298 3.3% (11.1%)	7.7
Total	124,809	8,981	13.9
(Total without China)	(16,746)	(2,675)	

[1]Adapted from Scott (1991).
[2]Percent figures are relative to totals, or to totals excluding China (in parentheses).

Data on sweetpotato production and utilization in many countries are often poor or nonexistent. However, there are a few notable exceptions, with well-established research programs and a good record of technology development and transfer.

Findings relevant to sweetpotato breeding are presented below.

Global distribution of production and recent production trends

China, which accounts for over 80% of production, is the world's principal producer of sweetpotato (Table 1). The remainder is produced in more than 100 countries. Within and among countries, there are large differences in the importance of sweetpotatoes for food security and income generation. Countries also differ widely in recent trends in production, area, and yield, as illustrated in Table 2. Researchers in countries with declining production generally expressed the need to focus on new forms of utilization and other ways to increase demand.

The distribution of diseases and pests

Principal diseases and pests of sweetpotato vary markedly across large geographic regions, as illustrated in Table 3. Overall, weevils are the single most severe constraint to sweetpotato production in the tropics, but species vary with region.

Table 2. Sweetpotato production in the top fifteen developing countries.

Countries	1986-88			1986-88 vs. 1973-75		
	Production (000 t)	Area (000 ha)	Yield (t/ha)	Production	Area (Percent Change)	Yield
China	108,063	6,306	17.1	-13.1	-31.8	27.5
Indonesia	2,087	243	8.6	-14.1	-28.6	20.3
Viet Nam	1,913	325	5.9	74.0	48.7	17.0
Uganda	1,698	388	4.4	2.5	-20.1	28.3
India	1,385	172	8.1	-21.4	-22.9	1.9
Rwanda	940	131	7.2	64.7	61.6	1.9
Brazil	734	74	9.9	-56.1	-51.6	- 9.5
Philippines	711	150	4.8	-12.6	-13.8	1.5
Burundi	619	85	7.3	48.4	27.1	16.8
Korea Rep .	596	27	21.7	-64.7	-69.6	16.2
Bangladesh	573	53	10.8	-16.1	-17.0	1.1
Kenya	523	40	13.1	93.9	26.3	53.5
Korea DPR	492	34	14.6	55.0	44.3	7.5
Papua New Guinea	471	104	4.5	17.1	15.7	1.2
Madagascar	467	92	5.1	76.6	59.1	11.0

Adapted from Scott (1991).

The substantial regional differences in pests and diseases highlight the importance of decentralization of sweetpotato germplasm evaluation and breeding to effectively select for resistances to regionally important diseases and pests.

Drought, excess moisture, low soil fertility, and cold have been identified as the principal environmental stresses, and other stresses such as shade or soil salinity may be locally important. Principal environmental stresses are not confined to large geographical regions as are diseases and pests. Rather, environmental stresses occur within specific climatic or agroecological zones worldwide. For example, cold stress occurs at higher altitudes and latitudes, and drought and low soil fertility tend to be problems on nonirrigated uplands.

Important agronomic and quality traits

Earliness is one of the most important traits desired in new sweetpotato varieties worldwide. Early varieties are desired by farmers in both commercially-oriented production systems and subsistence systems. In subsistence systems, varieties also must be able to produce well during a prolonged harvest season.

Increased dry matter content of roots is another widely-desired characteristic. High dry matter content is related to good eating quality in many areas where sweetpotato is consumed as a staple. It also contributes to product yields, where roots are processed by drying, or extraction of starch.

Table 3. Distribution and relative importance of key sweetpotato diseases and pests by region.[1]

Disease or Pest	Region			
	China	Asia + Oceania (except China)	Africa	Latin America + Caribbean
Weevils				
Cylas formicarius	** (S. China)	***	*2	*** (Caribbean + Venezuela)
Cylas puncticollis			***	
Cylas brunneus			***	
Euscepes postfasciatus		**		**(Caribbean + S. America)
Nematodes				
Meloidogyne spp.	**	**	*	**
Ditylenchus destructor	***			
Scab				
Elsinoe batatas	* (S. China)	***(except India)		
Anthracnose[3]			**(Zaire-Nile ridge)	
Black Rot				
Ceratocystis fimbriata	***			
Virus diseases[4]				
SPFMV	**	**	**	**
SPMMV		*	**	
Complex		*	***	

[1] Number of asterisks indicates degree of severity across regions.
[2] Some reports of *C. formicarius* in Africa may be due to misidentification (Parker et al. 1990).
[3] Reported to be caused by *Alternaria solani* (Simbashizweko and Perreaux 1988).
[4] Work on the identification of virus diseases in East Africa is underway (Wambugu et al. 1990). SPFMV seems to be important in all complexes (Moyer and Salazar 1989).

THE ROLE OF CIP'S SWEETPOTATO BREEDING PROGRAM TO HELP MEET NEEDS

Breeding as a component of research and development

Assessment of needs for sweetpotato research shows differences among and within regions in production, utilization, and in the distribution of principal biotic and abiotic constraints. Breeding can play an important role in combating a number of these constraints. However, other measures such as the use of improved cultural practices can also make important contributions. Breeding efforts are therefore viewed as one of the components in CIP's multidisciplinary research efforts.

There is a strong need for new uses for sweetpotato, particularly where production is stagnant or declining. Breeding can play a role in providing materials with characteristics appropriate for new uses, but this must go hand-in-hand with the development and promotion of the new forms of utilization.

Priority traits for CIP's breeding program

The priorities for CIP's breeding work vary across regions and are shaped by the findings of the needs assessment work. Thus, in most locations, top priority is being given to selection for earliness and increasing root dry matter content. The principal abiotic stresses are being addressed through the use of selected experimental environments where these occur. The use of host plant resistance to control most of the important biotic constraints has been reported (Wilson et al. 1990; Hahn et al. 1989; Jones and Dukes 1980). Each of these regionally important biotic constraints has a high priority in regions where it occurs. Research is under way to determine the extent to which breeding can contribute to the control of weevils and sweetpotato feathery mottle virus (SPFMV).

Development of novel traits that could lead to expanded utilization of sweetpotato is a high priority. For example, use of nonsweet sweetpotatoes (lacking β-amylase) may have potential for increasing the use of sweetpotato as a staple in some places. Elimination of trypsin inhibitor from roots and selection of types with easily digestible starch could lead to an expansion in use of raw sweetpotatoes as animal feed. Increased digestibility might also be beneficial to humans, if it led to a reduction in flatulence.

Priority locations for CIP's breeding program

Specific needs in different locations around the world have driven the decentralization of CIP's sweetpotato breeding effort. Thus, breeders and resources have been allocated to strategic locations in Asia, Africa, and Latin America.

CIP now has sweetpotato breeders as members of regional research teams in India, Indonesia, Philippines, Kenya, Egypt, and at headquarters in Peru. Research

525

teams in the regions also include pathologists, entomologists, agronomists, and social scientists. This allows CIP scientists to work closely with national program colleagues to help strengthen national programs and to develop or adapt new technologies to local conditions.

The model being followed for CIP's sweetpotato breeding program is that of a network among individual breeding efforts. Headquarters serves as the overall coordinator of global efforts. In addition to its global role, headquarters works closely with national programs in Latin America and the Caribbean.

The roles of CIP and the national programs

Ideally, there is a complementarity between the roles of CIP breeders and national program researchers. The national programs focus on the specific tasks of selecting varieties for national and local needs, and CIP breeders concentrate on longer-term problems of regional importance, and the development of parental materials for use by national programs.

However, national programs are often poorly supported, and variety selection systems have not been developed. Thus, in some cases, CIP breeders are helping to establish or strengthen varietal selection systems of national programs, as well as promote simple methods for testing and rapid distribution of varieties, with farmer involvement.

OPERATIONAL STEPS: THE IMPLEMENTATION OF THE BREEDING PROGRAM

Germplasm evaluation and utilization

Breeding programs at the national level (particularly in Asia) use crosses between standard selected parents. Reliance on a limited number of parents, as well as use of the same parent during subsequent generations, may have led to a narrowing of the genetic base of their populations, and to a degree of inbreeding in newer varieties. In recent years, genetic gains appear to have become more difficult to achieve.

Broadening of the genetic base through introduction of new germplasm, as well as establishment of population improvement programs using recurrent selection, will maximize genetic gain and continued breeding progress.

As part of an effort to conserve sweetpotato genetic resources, new sources of germplasm are being collected by CIP in the primary center of genetic diversity (Latin America and the Caribbean), and in secondary centers of diversity (such as the highlands of Papua New Guinea and Iryan Jaya, Indonesia, and northern Luzon, Philippines). This germplasm is being evaluated by CIP breeders in collaboration with national programs and will broaden genetic bases in some countries and contribute specific traits to breeding programs.

The wild relatives of sweetpotato may serve as a source of new traits for breeding programs. The limited work done to date indicates that wild relatives may serve as sources of increased dry matter content, resistance to weevils, and increased yield potential (Iwanaga 1988).

Current CIP research focuses on developing methods for efficient evaluation and utilization of the closest relatives of sweetpotato, which do not generally produce storage roots and have ploidy levels different from sweetpotato. Germplasm, as well as methods for using it, will be made available to interested national programs.

The distribution and evaluation of pathogen-tested germplasm

Distribution of pathogen-tested germplasm is a key strategy in CIP's breeding effort. Research to develop adequate virus elimination and testing procedures has been necessary to permit safe distribution of germplasm.

In vitro clones in the process of clean-up, or available for distribution, include important varieties from different countries, as well as advanced materials from breeding programs such as those of IITA, AVRDC and CIP. Seed is also an excellent means of germplasm distribution.

These advanced sources of germplasm make a great contribution to breeding programs in the developing world, but feedback on performance of introduced materials in different countries is crucial to increase the effectiveness of this effort. For this reason, field books for data collection are distributed with germplasm. CIP regional staff also provide direct follow-up on the performance of introduced materials.

Agroclimatological approach for site selection

For germplasm evaluation and breeding, sites are chosen that have key sets of stresses representative of larger production areas. For example, separate highland (cool) and lowland (hot) sites are used for evaluation of germplasm in the Philippines and Peru.

Further research is underway to select the most appropriate sites for breeding work. Work is needed for the definition of key environmental factors to define broad agroecological zones for sweetpotato. For example, the influence of photoperiod on yields and earliness is not well-investigated and could be important in selecting sites at low versus high latitudes.

Research on the genetics of priority traits

Progress in breeding requires genetic variation for the traits being selected as well as reliable screening procedures for identifying desired genotypes. Rapid progress is anticipated for some traits such as higher dry matter content and root knot nematode resistance because genetic variability is great and screening methods are straightforward. Experience so far also indicates that rapid progress in selection for earliness will be possible.

Breeding for resistance to weevil *(Cylas* spp.) is one of the greatest challenges. While resistance to weevils has been reported in sweetpotato, there is still controversy as to whether it exists and at what levels. Evaluation methods are generally unreliable, and there has been no long-term effort at recurrent selection to increase gene frequencies for resistance. Research is now underway to develop reliable methods for evaluating host-plant resistance. This in turn should permit recurrent selection programs to be effective in increasing resistance. Varieties with increased resistance would then be used as one component of an integrated pest control effort.

Cooperation with other organizations to extend geographic reach and to carry out specific work

One of CIP's key strategies is to cooperate with other organizations working on sweetpotato, to extend geographic coverage, or to conduct specific work in which CIP does not have a comparative advantage.

CIP's work with China is an example of cooperation with a strong national program in a developing country. Research contracts have been developed for germplasm management and breeding with two of the premier sweetpotato research institutes in China, the Xuzhou Institute for Sweet Potato, and the Guangdong Academy of Agricultural Sciences. These institutes, in turn, subcontract some work on germplasm evaluation for specific traits to other institutes in locations where particular biotic or abiotic stresses are important. These contracts have also served to introduce new germplasm to China and to promote export of Chinese materials to other countries.

Cooperation with programs in developed countries include a research contract with North Carolina State University in the U.S. to take advantage of advanced materials selected with a range of root quality characteristics likely to be acceptable in developing countries. CIP also has a contract with Mississippi State University to develop reliable weevil screening methods, as well as resistant germplasm.

Biotechnological applications for sweetpotato breeding are another area of cooperation with programs in developed countries. Collaborative efforts are underway to use genetic engineering for traits including resistances to weevils and viruses, as well as for application of RFLP and other techniques to sweetpotato breeding (Dodds et al. 1992).

Training and information exchange

Training and information activities complement CIP's collaborative research efforts in building national program capabilities. Training approaches include individual and group training, workshops, and formal degree education.

Universities in both developing and developed countries play a strong role, especially for advanced degree training. Arrangements are encouraged that allow students to do their course work at universities and at least a part of their research in breeding projects in the developing world.

CIP's information services unit maintains an up-to-date database of sweetpotato literature, and this information is available to researchers in the developing world.

EXAMPLES OF WORK UNDERWAY

Evaluation and utilization of the sweetpotato germplasm collection in Peru

Figure 1 illustrates the current set-up of sweetpotato germplasm evaluation and utilization at CIP headquarters in Peru. Germplasm is evaluated for specific criteria by researchers of several disciplines.

Evaluations for environmental adaptation and breeding for multiple traits are conducted at experiment stations in three agroclimatic zones of Peru. Materials are moved among sites to evaluate broad adaptation. A high priority is given to determining the value of these selection sites for evaluating germplasm for various target environments of the developing world.

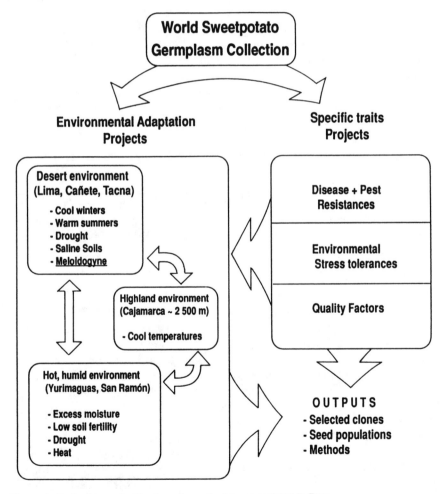

Figure 1. Evaluation and utilization of sweetpotato germplasm in Peru.

Quarantine restrictions and the slow process of virus testing have so far limited availability of many non-Peruvian clones to breeders in Peru. Quarantine restrictions on seed introductions are less strict than for clones, so breeders have introduced advanced germplasm from a number of breeding programs via seed. Comparison of the characteristics of introductions (quality as well as agronomic characteristics) with each other and with Peruvian germplasm, at the Peruvian selection sites, is helping to determine strengths and weaknesses of materials from different sources, as well as appropriateness of the selection sites for different target environments.

Regional projects

In India, breeding work is conducted in collaboration with the Central Tuber Crops Research Institute with emphasis on selection for early types for integration into the intensive cropping cycles found in this highly populated region. Selection for high dry matter content and improved storage potential under ambient conditions is also emphasized. Successful materials developed in this project may also be beneficial in Bangladesh, Sri Lanka, and China.

In Indonesia, CIP's work is conducted in collaboration with the Central Research Institute for Food Crops and is focusing on evaluation and selection of newly-collected germplasm for resistance to weevil and scab and tolerance to low soil fertility. Selected materials will be available for international distribution and will be used for further breeding.

In the Philippines, newly-collected germplasm is being evaluated for adaptation to highland and lowland environments, yield, earliness, dry matter content, and resistance to weevil and nematodes *(Meloidogyne)*.

In East Africa, the initial work of CIP is building on the the work of IITA and is focusing on evaluation of local germplasm for priority traits in each of a number of countries. Work is conducted in collaboration with Kenya, Tanzania, Uganda, Rwanda, Burundi, and Ethiopia.

EXPECTED IMPACT

We expect that within a short time the strategy of introducing already existing advanced varieties will pay off with the release and adoption of new varieties in a number of countries around the world. In the medium-term we expect that the focus on developing materials suitable for new forms of utilization will contribute to increasing demand for sweetpotato in countries where production has been declining. Additionally, the focus on breeding for resistance to key biotic and abiotic constraints will contribute to the increased production of sweetpotato in many countries.

ACKNOWLEDGMENTS

The authors would like to thank Peter Gregory, Wanda Collins, K.V. Raman, Gordon Prain, Zosimo Huaman, Jim Bemis, and Kristine Keenan for valuable contributions to this manuscript.

REFERENCES

Achata, A., H. Fano, H. Goyas, O. Chiang, and M. Andrade. 1990 [Sweet potato in the food system of Peru. The case of the Canete valley.] In Spanish. International Potato Center, Lima, Peru. 63 pp.

CIP (International Potato Center). 1988a. Exploration, maintenance, and utilization of sweet potato genetic resources Report of the First Sweet Potato Planning Conference, 1987, 369 pp.

CIP (International Potato Center). 1988b. Improvement of sweet potato *(Ipomoea batatas)* in East Africa, with some references of other tuber and root crops. Report of the Workshop on Sweet Potato Improvement in Africa, ILRAD, Nairobi, September 28 - October 2, 1987. (UNDP Project CIAT-CIP-IITA). 208 pp.

CIP (Centro Internacional de la Papa). 1988c. Mejoramiento de la batata *(Ipomoea batatas)* en Latinoamerica. Memorias del Seminario sobre mejoramiento de la batata *(Ipomoea batatas)* e Latinoamerica. CIP, Lima, Junio 9-12, 1987. 277 pp.

CIP (International Potato Center). 1989a. Improvement of sweet potato *(Ipomoea batatas)* in Asia. Report of the Workshop on Sweet Potato Improvement in Asia, ICAR, India, October 24-28, 1988. 256 pp.

CIP (International Potato Center). 1989b. Annual Report CIP 1989. Lima, Peru. 194 pp.

CIP (International Potato Center) l990a. Recommendations of the Workshop on Sweet Potato Germplasm Utilization, Los Banos, Philippines, March 5 to 14, 1990. Lima, Peru.

CIP (International Potato Center) l990b. Annual Report CIP 1990. Lima, Peru. 258 p.

Dodds, J.H., J. Benavides, F. Buitron, F. Medina, and C. Siguenas. 1992. Biotechnology applied to sweetpotato improvement. Pages 7-19 *in* Sweetpotato technology for the 21st century, edited by W.A. Hill, C.K. Bonsi and P.A. Loretan. Tuskegee University, Tuskegee, AL.

Gregory, P.M., M. Iwanaga, and D.E. Horton. 1990. Sweet potato: global issues. Pages 462-468 *in* Proceedings, 8th Symposium of the International Society of Tropical Root Crops, edited by R.H. Howeler. CIAT, Bangkok, Thailand.

Hahn, S.K., J.G.G. Isoba, and T. Ikotun. 1989. Resistance breeding in root and tuber crops at the International Institute of Tropical Agriculture (IITA), Ibadan, Nigeria. Crop Protection 8:147-168.

Horton, D. 1989. Constraints to sweet potato production and use. Pages 219-224 *in* Improvement of sweet potato *(Ipomoea batatas)* in Asia. Report of the Workshop on Sweet Potato Improvement in Asia, CIP (International Potato Center), held at ICAR, India, October 24-28, 1988.

Horton, D., G. Prain, and P. Gregory. 1989. High-level investment returns for global sweet potato research and development. CIP Circular 17:(3).

Iwanaga, M. 1988. Use of wild germplasm for sweet potato breeding. Pages 199-210 *in* Exploration, maintenance, and utilization of sweet potato genetic resources, Report of the First Sweet Potato Planning Conference, CIP (International Potato Center).1987.

Jones, A., and P.D. Dukes 1980. Heritabilities of sweet potato resistances to root knot caused by *Meloidogyne incognita* and *N. javanica*. J. Amer. Soc. Hort. Sci. 105:154-156.

Lin, S.M., C.C. Peet, D-M. Chen, and H-F. Lo. 1983. Breeding goals for sweet potato in Asia and the Pacific: A survey on sweet potato production and utilization. Pages 42-60 *in* Breeding new sweet potatoes for the tropics. Proceedings of the American Society of Horticultural Science, Tropical Region. Vol 27, Part B, edited by F.W. Martin.

Mackay, K.T., M.K. Palomar, R.T. Sanico, eds. Sweet potato research and development for small farmers. SEAMEO-SEARCA. 391 pp.

Moyer, J. W., and L. F. Salazar. 1989. Virus and viruslike diseases of sweet potato. Plant Disease 73:451-455.

Parker, B.L., N. Smit, and A. Abubaker. 1990. The sweet potato weevil with references to studies in Tonga and Kenya. Paper presented at 2nd Triennial Conference of the African Potato Association, Mauritius.

Scott, G.J. 1991. Sweet potatoes as animal feed in developing countries: present patterns and future prospects. Paper presented at the FAO experts' consultation on The use of roots, tubers, plantains and bananas in animal feeding, CIAT, Cali, Colombia, 21-25 January, 1991.

Simbashizweko, A., and D. Perreaux. 1989. L'anthracnose de la patate douce *(Ipomoea batatas* (L) Lam) au Burundi: Description de l'agent causal et mise au point d'une methode de criblage. Pages 115-120 *in* Improvement of sweet potato *(Ipomoea batatas)* in East Africa, with some references to other tuber and root crops. Report of the Workshop on Sweet Potato Improvement in Africa, CIP (International Potato Center), ILRAD, Nairobi, September 28 - October 2, 1987. (UNDP Project CIAT-CIP-IITA). .

Wambugu, F.M., A.A. Brunt, and E.M. Fernandez-Northcote. 1990. Viruses and virus disease of sweet potato *(Ipomoea batatas)* in Kenya and Uganda. Paper presented at 2nd Triennial Conference of the African Potato Association, Mauritius.

Wilson, J.E., P. Taufatofua, F.S. Pole, and N.E.J.M Smit 1990. Breeding leaf scab resistant sweet potatoes in Tonga. Pages 491-499 *in* Proceedings, 8th Symposium, edited by R.H Howeler. ISTRC, CIAT, 1988, Bangkok, Thailand.

Sweetpotato Technology for the 21st Century. W.A. Hill, C.K. Bonsi and P.A. Loretan (Eds.) 1992. Tuskegee University, Tuskegee, AL

Katsumi Komaki, Osamu Yamakawa, Masaru Yoshinaga, Misao Hidaka

New Wave of Sweetpotato Breeding in Japan

Sweetpotato has been predominantly used for starch production and table consumption in Japan. However, gradually its value has been reduced because domestic starch made from sweetpotato costs more to the consumer than imported starch and also there have been changes in diet. In order to develop new demands for sweetpotato and stabilize farmers' income, various types of sweetpotato cultivars are required such as those with low β-amylase activity, low polyphenol content and high starch content for food processing, high flesh pigmentation for colorant production, and high starch content and fascinating flavor for distilling sweetpotato shochu. We have just started programs to develop new cultivars to meet these various demands. This paper describes research work at the Sweetpotato Breeding Laboratory, Kyushu National Agricultural Experiment Station and new promising breeding lines developed here.

INTRODUCTION

Among food crops in Japan, sweetpotato [*Ipomoea batatas* (L.) Lam.] ranks seventh in production acreage (MAFF 1990). Sweetpotato can convert solar energy to carbohydrates efficiently and tolerates environmental extremes, such as drought and typhoons, which cause significant losses of upland crop production in the southwestern part of Japan. Therefore, it has been one of the most important upland crops in Japan.

Between five to seven million tons of sweetpotato were produced on 350,000 to 450,000 ha annually during 1945 to 1960. However, the production acreage and quantity have been decreasing gradually due to the higher price of domestic over imported sweetpotato starch and changes in diet. Sweetpotato production in 1989 was approximately 1.3 million tons on 63,000 ha (Figure 1). As shown in Figure 2, about 30% is used for starch production, 30% is consumed through the fresh market, and the rest is used as animal feed, farmers' food and material for fermentation products including alcohol and "sweetpotato shochu", which is a distilled alcoholic beverage made from sweetpotato.

Domestic sweetpotato starch has been protected for the last 20 years by a policy of a tie-in sale with imported corn starch. Free trade of agricultural products is a general tendency in the world, and sweetpotato starch would lose protection. If the political protection is repealed in the future, the demand for sweetpotato will be

Kyushu National Agricultural Experiment Station, 6644 Yokoichi-cho, Miyakonojo, Miyazaki 885, Japan.

533

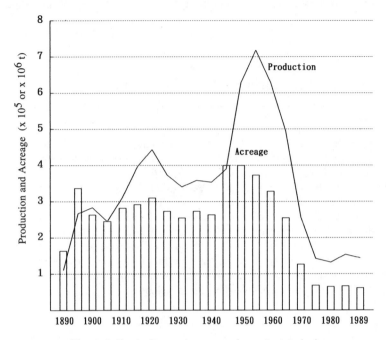

Figure 1. Production and acreage of sweetpotato in Japan.

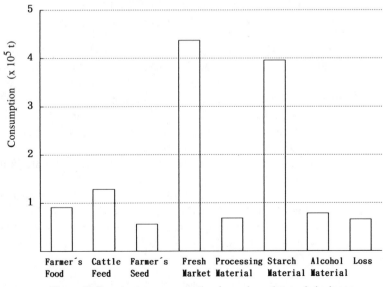

Figure 2. Sweetpotato consumption for various demands in Japan.

reduced by about 30%. This reduction could bring the decline of upland farming in the southwestern part of Japan, where sweetpotato is an indispensable crop because of low soil fertility and an irregular summer rainfall distribution.

Fortunately, sweetpotato has a wide range of variation in sweetness, anthocyanin content, carotene content, polyphenol content and so on. The potential of sweetpotato far exceeds its current utilization. There might be many ways of using sweetpotato that are yet unknown.

We have started new breeding programs to meet new demands, such as for food processing, colorant and sweetpotato-shochu. This paper describes our research work and new breeding lines released during the realization of this program.

BREEDING FOR FOOD PROCESSING

Sweetpotato has been traditionally used for "Daigaku-Imo" and "Imo-Karinto"— both are fried and sweetened by sugar addition. It has been also used as a paste called "Imo-An." Since no special quality of sweetpotato is required for these products, cultivars for these purposes have not been developed in Japan. However, recent life style changes favor snack foods, such as fried chips and french fries. Consequently, market demands are increasing for snack raw materials, such as flakes and granules. In these cases, low color degradation is indispensable during processing. Oxidation of polyphenols and sugars have been suggested to contribute to color degradation. In order to use sweetpotato for processing extensively, such traits urgently need to be improved.

Low Oxidation

Oxidation of root flesh after cutting results in the deterioration of snack product quality through browning of the flesh color. When polyphenol oxidase acts on the sweetpotato root, polyphenol oxidation occurs causing the browning.

We can evaluate oxidation rate according to Jones' method (1972). After dipping the cut roots in a 0.25M catechol solution for 5 minutes, the degree of oxidation is coded on a 1 to 5 scale with 1 representing no appreciable darkening and 5 representing complete blackening. Our breeding materials and registered cultivars have a wide variation in oxidation rate. 'Shiroyutaka' is expected to be suitable for producing low oxidation material in our breeding program. In addition, we need to select low oxidation genotypes in our sweetpotato germplasm.

Low Sweetness

When sweetpotato roots are cooked, the starch is hydrolyzed to maltose by β-amylase and the sweetness increases dramatically. Sugars, including maltose, degrade the quality of fried chips and french fries, changing their color to brown after cooking. Until recently, all sweetpotatoes were assumed to have β-amylase in the roots, which caused increased sugar content during cooking. However, Martin

(1987) reported non-sweet sweetpotatoes, and our experiment station released 'Satsumahikari' (Kukimura et al. 1989), a new sweetpotato cultivar, with no or low β-amylase activity. 'Satsumahikari' produces little or no maltose during cooking (Baba et al. 1987).

Kumagai et al.(1990) analyzed segregation of root β-amylase activity and concluded that breeding sweetpotato with low β-amylase activity would be relatively easy. In our research program, non-sweet genotypes sometimes appear in the crosses between normal sweet cultivars. 'Satsumahikari' has a relatively low starch content, which leads to a low yield of granules and flakes. Therefore, cultivars with high dry matter content as well as low β-amylase activity are required. We have a new breeding line, 'Kyushu 108,' with a higher starch content and a low sugar content after cooking.

Low Polyphenol Content

Flesh darkening through the action of polyphenol oxidase as well as darkening after cooking are undesirable for food processing. In potato, flesh darkening after cooking is caused by polyphenol in association with ferric ion in the tubers (Talburt and Smith 1975). Since flesh darkening has been considered to occur in the same manner in sweetpotato (Baba 1990, Kagoshima Prefecture Laboratory of Agriculture, personal communication), low polyphenol content in roots is required to reduce flesh darkening after cooking. Polyphenol content varies remarkably among genotypes (KPAES 1984). We have been screening a great number of genotypes by visual judgment of darkening of steamed root flesh in order to develop cultivars with low polyphenol content. However, since judgment is influenced by the original flesh color, a more reliable method for polyphenol content evaluation must be developed.

Since polyphenol in flesh is oxidized in association with ferric ion, polyphenol content was determined by adding ferric chloride to the steamed roots. The degree of darkening is coded on a scale of 1 to 5 with 1 representing no appreciable darkening and 5 representing complete darkening, after dipping the steamed roots in 1% ferric chloride solution for 5 minutes. Genotypes coded below 3 in the degree of darkening are selected to be as low polyphenol content lines. We have already selected breeding lines with low polyphenol content.

BREEDING FOR COLORANT PRODUCTION

Anthocyanins from various sources, such as purple corn and red cabbage, have been reported as potential colorants, but they have a common problem in stability. Bassa and Francis (1987) suggested that the anthocyanins in sweetpotato roots are more stable than others and acyl groups give stability to the pigments. Most sweetpotato genotypes produce white to yellow-fleshed roots; however, storage roots of some genotypes contain anthocyanins. 'Yamagawamurasaki' produces the most intensely purple-fleshed roots in our germplasm. We have been using it and other less purple genotypes as parents in our breeding program. Both the visual observation of root flesh and the color value based on the absorption coefficient are used for assessing the amount of anthocyanins in the roots. The color value is determined by general methods (FAO 1983).

The color value of roots of 'Yamagawamurasaki' is around 2.0, but root yield is extremely low. Thus, it is not suitable for colorant production because of its low color amount (the color value x root yield), and new cultivars are needed for this purpose. Breeding lines derived from the crosses between 'Yamagawamurasaki' and high yielding cultivars range in the color value from 1.7 to 12.5 (Odake 1990, Sanei Kagaku Co. Ltd., Osaka, personal communication). We have selected a breeding line, 'Kyushu-109,' with higher root yield and color value than 'Yamagawamurasaki.' And, some breeding lines exceed 'Yamagawamurasaki' in the color value and other important traits, such as root yield and dry matter content.

Anthocyanins from natural sources have problems of stability to light and heat. Color retention can be evaluated by the decrease in color value after sweetpotato extracts are placed in a sunny room. In order to develop new cultivars containing highly stable anthocyanins, we need to select for not only high color value but also high color retention.

BREEDING FOR SWEETPOTATO SHOCHU PRODUCTION

Sweetpotato shochu is a popular distilled alcoholic beverage in Japan. However, its market share among alcoholic beverages is low due to its unpleasant aroma. It has been suggested that the flavor of sweetpotato shochu is influenced by terpenic alcohols, such as linalool (Ohta 1989, National Research Institute of Brewing, Tokyo, Japan, personal communication), but detailed research on factors controlling the flavor have not yet been conducted. The flavor of shochu and steamed roots have been investigated for a number of breeding lines and introduced cultivars in cooperation with some sweetpotato shochu distilleries. Based on these investigations, new cultivars with high yield, high dry matter content and an attractive flavor will be developed for sweetpotato shochu production in the near future.

NEW BREEDING LINES FOR NEW DEMANDS FROM KYUSHU NATIONAL AGRICULTURAL EXPERIMENT STATION

'Kyushu-108,' a cross between 'Kyushu-76' and 'Kyushu-89,' is a breeding line for food processing. Both parents are nematode-resistant lines with high dry matter content. The storage root is fusiform with white skin and flesh. Outstanding characteristics of 'Kyushu-108' include non-sweetness and high dry matter content. These characteristics assure that 'Kyushu-108' is suitable as a material for various processing industries. Moreover, the polyphenol content in cooked roots and the oxidation rate of fresh roots are relatively low. Although it yields less than 'Koganesengan', a leading cultivar for starch production, we believe that 'Kyushu-108' will play an important role in food processing.

Table 1. Proposed purposes and characteristics to be improved in the sweetpotato breeding program.

Root characteristics	Purpose					
	Granules and flakes	Salad or snacks	Colorant	Shochu	Starch	Fresh consumption
Low oxidation	x	x				x
Low polyphenol content	x	x				x
Non-sweetness	x	x				
High starch content	x			x	x	
Low starch content		x				
High yielding ability				x	x	
High anthocyanin			x			
High carotene			x			
Fascinating flavor				x		x
Whiteness of starch					x	
Red skin and yellow flesh of roots						x
Uniform and good shape of roots	x	x				x
Good taste						x
Insect and disease resistance	x	x	x	x	x	x
Storageability	x	x	x	x	x	x

'Kyushu-109,' a cross between 'Chiranmurasaki' and 'Yamagawamurasaki,' is a breeding line for anthocyanin production. Both parents are indigenous cultivars with purple fleshed roots. Roots of 'Kyushu-109' are elongated fusiform with dark purple skin and flesh. A distinctive characteristic of 'Kyushu-109' roots is an extremely high anthocyanin content—4.0 to 6.0 in the color value, which exceeds one of the parents, 'Yamagawamurasaki,' by 200%. The root yield is two to three times higher than that of 'Yamagawamurasaki', though it is still below that of 'Koganesengan.' Colorant production industries have suggested that sweetpotato is a good source of anthocyanin because of its stable productivity under different cultural conditions compared to red cabbage. 'Kyushu-109' could be a promising breeding line for colorant production due to its high ability to accumulate high anthocyanins in the roots.

CONCLUSION

Characteristics required for food processing and other expected uses for sweetpotato have been described. Table 1 shows characteristics improved for various purposes. Recent breeding objectives for starch types have been high yielding ability and high dry matter content. Breeding objectives for table types have been bright red skin, yellowish-white flesh, good shape and good taste. Storageability, pest and insect resistance have been sought for both uses. Though market demand for table consumption is still very high, that for food processing and other industrial uses is expected to occupy a larger part of sweetpotato consumption in the near future. Presently, we pay attention to traits connected with root quality, such as polyphenol content, polyphenol oxidase activity, β-amylase activity and pigment content. With the new quality demands, the selection process becomes more complicated than it has been previously. Breeding programs for colorant and sweetpotato shochu production are carried out in cooperation with private companies. We try to develop simple selection methods to achieve characteristics required in the new wave of sweetpotato breeding.

The importance of sweetpotato as a crop cannot be estimated solely on the basis of the past or present production and utilization statistics. It is the most important upland crop in Japan, especially in the southwestern part where cultural conditions are so severe for other crops that they cannot take the place of sweetpotato. We are convinced that sweetpotato, which has been gradually decreasing in production acreage, has to be recovered with breeding efforts and new tactics for utilization.

REFERENCES

Baba, T., H. Nakama, Y. Tamaru, and T. Kono. 1987. Changes in sugar and starch contents during storage of new type sweet potato (low β–amylase activity in roots). In Japanese. Nippon Shokuhin Kogyo Gakkaishi 34(4):249-253. English summary.

Bassa, I.A., and F. J. Francis. 187. Stability of anthocyanins from sweet potatoes in a model beverage. Journal of Food Science 52(6):1753-1754.

FAO (Food and Agriculture Organization of the United Nations). 1983. FAO Food and Nutrition Paper No. 5, Revision 1. Rome, Italy.

Jones, A. 1972. Mass selection for low oxidation in sweetpotato. Journal of the American Society for Horticultural Science 97(6):714-718.

KPAES (Kagoshima Prefectural Agricultural Experiment Station). 1984. Varietal difference of availability for processing. Pages 114-117 in KPAES (Annual reports of marketing and processing division, 1983], KPAES, Kagoshima, Japan. In Japanese.

Kukimura, H., T. Yoshida, K. Komaki, S. Sakamoto, S. Tabachi, Y. Ide, and O. Yamakawa. 1989. ["Satsumahikari": A new sweetpotato cultivar]. In Japanese. Bulletin of the Kyushu National Agricultural Experiment Station 25(3):225-250. English summary.

Kumagai, T., Y. Umemura, T. Baba, and M. Iwanaga. 1990. The inheritance of β–amylase null in storage roots of sweetpotato, Ipomoea batatas (L.) Lam. Theoretical Applied Genetics 79:369-376.

MAFF (Ministry of Agriculture, Forestry and Fisheries). 1990. The 65th statistical yearbook 1988-1989. Tokyo, Japan. 705 pp.

Martin, F. W. 1987. Non-sweet or staple type sweet potatoes. HortScience 22(1):160.

Talburt, W.F., and O. Smith. 1975. Potato processing. Third ed. AVI Publishing, Westport, Connecticut. 705 pp.

Marilyn Z. Oracion,* Itaru Shiotani**

Cytology and Fertility of Sweetpotato *X* Diploid *Ipomoea trifida* F1 Hybrids and Their Potential in Analytic Breeding of Sweetpotato

Metaphase I chromosome configurations of the F1 hybrids generally showed high bivalent formation, few or several quadrivalents and rare trivalents and univalents. Anaphase I and metaphase II appeared normal, but incomplete separation of chromosomes at anaphase II followed by restitution nucleus formation was observed in some hybrids. The pollen mother cell showed above 70% tetrads, the rest being varying amounts of monads, dyads, triads and polyads with or without microcytes. Unreduced pollen estimates varied from zero to 6.4%; well-strained pollen varied from 31 to 63% among the hybrids. Crossability test data showed that, when the hybrids were used as male, seed set ranged from 0.6 to 48% while the reciprocal crosses also showed a wide range of seed set from 1.2 to 37.9%. The probable causes of sterility and the potential of the F1 hybrids in the analytic breeding scheme using diploid gene sources are presented.

Species that cross with sweetpotato *Ipomoea batatas* L. are valuable to broaden the sweetpotato germplasm for breeding. At present, only the *Ipomoea trifida* species can cross with sweetpotato and therefore be utilized for crop improvement. Utilization of hexaploid *I. trifida* for sweetpotato improvement has been successfully carried out in Japan (Kobayashi and Sakamoto 1987; Kobayashi and Miyazaki 1976; Kukimura et al. 1988; Sakamoto 1976). Moreover, the potential of $4x$ interspecific hybrids between sweetpotato cultivars and $4x$ *I. trifida* has also been studied and found promising (Iwanaga et al. 1987). These reports are encouraging the use of *I. trifida* germplasm in sweetpotato improvement. However, an effective and specific gene transfer from a polyploid wild relative to cultivated sweetpotato may be complicated by the following reasons: (1) it is very difficult to identify and locate a gene or genes at the polyploid level due to its highly buffered genetic system; and (2) when a given number of genes are involved, selection of the ideal genotype out of segregated genotypes would require progenies which may be too large for the breeder to handle. Analytic breeding for polyploid crop species has been proposed by Chase (1963; 1964). Because of the two reasons mentioned above, it has been suggested (Shiotani 1987a) that an analytic breeding plan using a gene in diploid state, i.e., reconstruction of hexaploid sweetpotato by using diploids having a known gene or genes, may provide important genetic sources for breeding. This reconstruction can take place

---

*Department of Plant Breeding and Agricultural Botany, Visayas State College of Agriculture, Leyte 6521-A Philippines.
**Faculty of Bioresources, Mie University, Tsu 514, Japan.

540

when tetraploid hybrids between sweetpotato and the diploid gene source are fertile enough to reproduce their progeny. It is fortunate that the *I. trifida* complex as proposed by Kobayashi (1984) also includes diploids that may be of importance to sweetpotato improvement. The use of 2x *I. trifida* as a source for gene transfer to sweetpotato is therefore studied in the present work. This attempt could thereby constitute the first of the two main steps in the presently proposed enhancement scheme for sweetpotato. These steps are: (1) to produce tetraploid hybrids from crosses between sweetpotato and the diploid gene source; and (2) to reconstruct hexaploid lines for breeding purposes.

MATERIALS AND METHODS

The 2288 parental strains of diploid *I. trifida* were clones selected from progenies of sexual plants produced from seeds collected at Salina Cruz, Oaxaca, Mexico, and the 2232 strains of tetraploid *I. trifida* were clones obtained from seeds collected at Santa Elena, Guatemala. These seed materials comprised the Kyoto University's "Expedition Cientifica a la America Latina" collection during 1972 to 1973 (Muramatsu and Shiotani 1974). The sweetpotato cultivars used as parents were 'Tamayutaka' (TY), 'Minamiyutaka' (MY) and 'Kyukei 15-2120' (K 15-2120). The TY is a variety derived from crosses between existing sweetpotato cultivars; the MY is a leading variety produced by backcrossing a sweetpotato x hexaploid *I. trifida* hybrid twice to sweetpotato (Kobayashi and Sakamoto 1987). The breeding line K15-2120 is a selected F1 hybrid between sweetpotato and hexaploid *I. trifida*.

Meiotic chromosome behavior in PMCs was determined in two diploid *I. trifida* parents (2288-36 and 2288-64), two sweetpotato parents (TY and MY), and ten F1 tetraploid hybrids (A48 and A65 from the 2x X 6x crosses and A100, A101, A106, A110, A111, A112, A113 and A115 from the 6x X 2x crosses). In addition, two tetraploid *I. trifida* strains (2232-33 and 2232-34) were examined by the following methods. Root tips were pretreated in 0.002 mol 8-hydroxyquinoline at 12°C for 3 h. Root tips and buds were fixed in modified Newcomer's fixative, i.e., 12:5 Newcomer's fluid-glacial acetic acid solution. Hydrolysis was done in 0.7 N hydrochloric acid for 10 min at 42°C for buds and 1 h at 40°C for root tips. The materials were then rinsed in distilled water for a few minutes and transferred to Schiff's reagent for 1/2 to 2 h. Slides were prepared using the iron-acetocarmine squash technique. In more difficult PMC materials after prolonged storage, pre-mordanting of anthers in about 1% ferric acetate solution overnight followed by the iron-acetocarmine squash technique proved satisfactory.

For sporad analysis, buds at the appropriate stage were fixed in modified Newcomer's fixative for at least 30 min. About 3 to 4 anthers each from different buds were rinsed briefly in distilled water, squashed in 0.5% lactphenol cotton blue and left overnight prior to scoring of sporad types and microcytes. Data were taken based on 120 PMCs for hybrids and a minimum of 500 PMCs for natural tetraploids. Counting two unreduced (2n) pollen in the dyad and one in the triad, the frequency in 2n pollen grains was estimated using the equation $(2x2 + x3)/(2x2 + 3x3 + 4x4)$

where $x2$, $x3$ and $x4$ are the number of dyads, triads and tetrads, respectively. To investigate the development of sporads, mature pollen from buds 2 days before anthesis were prepared in a manner similar to the sporads. More than 1,000 pollen grains were examined for each hybrid.

RESULTS AND DISCUSSION

Cytology

Fifteen bivalents were regularly observed in the diploid parents while the sweetpotato cultivars showed means of 23.8 to 25 bivalents, 4.4 to 4.5 quadrivalents, 3.4 to 3.5 hexavalents, 1.0 to 1.3 univalents, 0.1 trivalents and 0.1 to 0.2 pentavalents. Their Fl hybrids showed highly normal pairing with grand means of 21.05 (18.8 to 24.0) bivalents, 3.92 (2.6 to 5.0) quadrivalents, 1.48 (0.04 to 5.8) univalents and 0.32 (0.1 to 1.0) trivalents, respectively (Table 1). These data suggest a high degree of

Table 1. Mean chromosome configuration in sweetpotato 2x *I. trifida* F1 hybrids and 4x *I. trifida*.

| Hybrid or Clone | Chromosome configuration at Metaphase I | | | | No. of PMCs |
	Univalent	Bivalent	Trivalent	Quadrivalent	
2x *I. trifida* x sweetpotato F1					
A48	3.8	20.9	0.0	3.6	18
	(0-6)	(15-25)		(2-6)	
A65	2.6	18.8	0.2	4.8	30
	(0-8)	(13-24)	(0-2)	(3-7)	
Sweetpotato x 2x *I. trifida* F1					
A100	0.4	20.4	0.1	4.6	62
	(0-6)	(12-26)	(0-2)	(2-9)	
A101	0.7	21.1	0.1	4.7	37
	(0-4)	(13-27)	(0-2)	(2-9)	
A106	0.4	24.0	0.4	2.6	25
	(0-2)	(18-30)	(0-1)	(0-5)	
A110	0.0	23.6	0.0	3.2	52
		(18-30)		(0-6)	
A111	0.7	20.4	0.3	3.7	36
	(0-4)	(17-24)	(0-1)	(2-5)	
A112	0.4	22.4	0.6	3.0	29
	(0-1)	(13-29)	(0-1)	(0-8)	
A113	0.04	19.1	1.0	5.0	23
	(0-1)	(15-25)	(0-1)	(2-7)	
A115	5.8	19.8	0.5	4.0	35
	(3-9)	(15-23) ·	(0-2)	(2-5)	
Grand Mean	1.484	21.05	0.32	3.92	
4x x *I. trifida*					
2232-33	0.1	24.1	0.0	2.9	35
	(0-2)	(20-28)		(1-5)	
2232-34	0.0	23.2	0.0	3.4	46
		(20-26)		(2-5)	

Range is given in parentheses.

pairing between the diploid *I. trifida* genome and at least one of the sweetpotato genomes indicating close homology between them. Moreover, the presence of 3.92 quadrivalents normally suggests a certain degree of homology among the four chromosome complements, i.e., one from diploid *I. trifida* and three from sweetpotato. More important to the sweetpotato breeder, however, is the implication that the pairing of *I. trifida* chromosomes with the sweetpotato chromosomes allows gene transfer from *I. trifida* to sweetpotato.

Most cells at anaphase I and metaphase II stages were observed to be normal in the hybrids. However, some anaphase II plates showed abnormality during separation of chromosomes to opposite poles. Instead of full travel to opposite poles, the daughter chromosomes either travel only halfway or remain scattered near the equatorial plate in an apparently disoriented state, a situation that could lead to the formation of a restitution nucleus in the next meiotic stages (i.e., the nuclear membrane reassembles to form only one nucleus that encloses within it all the chromosomes thereby forming one diploid microspore instead of two haploids). This observation was in agreement with the sporad analysis wherein dyads and triads were among the sporad types recorded (Table 2). In this case, dyads represent PMCs

Table 2. Percents of tetrads with and without microcytes, monads, dyads, triads, polyads and unreduced pollen estimates in sweetpotato - 2x *I. trifida* F1 hybrids and 4x *I. trifida*.

Hybrid or Clone	Tetrad w/out microcytes	Tetrad with microcytes	Monad	Dyad	Triad	Polyad	Unre-duced pollen (%)
			(with or without microcytes)				
2x *I. trifida* x sweetpotato F1							
A48	36.7	45.8	-	6.7	10.8	-	6.4
A65	46.7	25.0	21.6	0.8	4.2	1.7	1.9
Sweetpotato x 2x *I. trifida* F1							
A100	23.3	67.5	1.7	-	6.7	0.8	1.8
A101	57.5	20.8	10.8	3.3	6.7	0.8	3.9
A106	20.8	71.7	-	-	0.8	6.7	0.2
A110	89.2	4.2	4.2	-	1.7	0.8	0.5
A111	98.3	1.7	-	-	-	-	-
A112	96.7	3.3	-	-	-	-	-
A113	85.8	10.0	2.5	-	0.8	0.8	2.2
A115	56.7	38.3	-	-	5.0	-	1.3
4x x *I. trifida*							
2232-33	97.1	2.9					
2232-34	98.9	1.1					

where both daughter cells after meiosis I would form a restitution nucleus each, while a triad could represent PMCs where only one of the two daughter cells would form a restitution nucleus. The estimated amount of unreduced pollen per hybrid was computed, and it can be seen that this varied from zero to 6.4%. It is important for the sweetpotato breeder to know the presence of both reduced and unreduced pollen in the gametic pool of the tetraploid Fl hybrid population.

Fertility-sterility

We had pointed out earlier that reconstruction of hexaploid sweetpotato from Fl tetraploid hybrids having a gene or genes from a wild diploid can take place when the Fl hybrids are fertile. The pollen viability (measured as % stainable pollen) showed a range of 30.7% to 63%, thereby showing a fair degree of pollen fertility. However, when the hybrids were used as pollen sources in crosses with two highly fertile natural tetraploid *I. trifida* testers, the results showed variable degrees of fertility with a range of 0.6 to 48% seed set, but one hybrid (A101) had nondehiscent anthers and two hybrids (A48 and A115) were cross-incompatible (i.e., no pollen germination took place due to sporophytic type of incompatibility) when crossed with 2232-34. On the other hand, all the hybrids set seeds when used as female in the crosses. The results of the meiotic analysis, the sporad analysis and pollen staining all show probable contributing factors to the reduction in seed set of hybrids. The causes may be summarized as follows: (1) the presence of univalents, trivalents and quadrivalents that could lead to irregular chromosome distribution giving rise to unbalanced aneuploid daughter cell types; (2) abnormalities in sporad formation exhibited by monads, dyads, triads, polyads and tetrads with microcytes; (3) reduced frequency of stainable pollen, showing a mean range of 30.7 to 63% among the hybrids as compared to above 90% stainable pollen in the natural tetraploid strains; and (4) probably maternal or cytoplasmic influence as indicated by the difference in reciprocal crosses in some hybrids. A more detailed analysis of some of the causes has been reported (Oracion et al. 1990).

Analytic Breeding Scheme

The reported successful resynthesis of hexaploid sweetpotato using diploids of thickening root types (Shiotani 1987a) and some hexaploids synthesized from diploid and tetraploid wild relatives of sweetpotato (Shiotani and Kawase 1987) were all achieved by chromosome manipulation through colchicine treatment. The present proposed scheme makes use of new experimental evidence presented in this paper. This alternative route at resynthesis of hexaploid sweetpotato involves two main steps, namely: (1) crosses between sweetpotato and selected diploid gene sources to produce tetraploid breeding lines; and (2) utilization of the reduced and unreduced gametic pool of the tetraploid breeding population either by controlled crosses or the open polycross method to reconstruct hexaploid sweetpotato for use in conventional breeding work.

In this proposed pathway of sweetpotato resynthesis, the first step has been experimentally tested; the second remains to be tested. Recent work done on derived hexaploids regarded as hybrids from union of 2n egg and 2n pollen in triploid *I. trifida* intercrosses (Shiotani and Kawase 1989) suggests a high probability of success in step 2 of this proposed route. Shiotani (1987b) discussed the advantages of sweetpotato synthesized by gametic doubling over sweetpotato synthesized by colchicine treatment.

ACKNOWLEDGMENTS

We acknowledge the research funding provided by the Matsumae International Foundation and Mie University (Japan).

REFERENCES

Chase, S. S. 1963. Analytic breeding in *Solanum tuberosum* L.—a scheme utilizing parthenotes and other diploid stocks. Canad. J. Genet. Cytol. 5:359-363.

Chase, S. S. 1964. Analytic breeding of amphipolyploid plant varieties. Crop Sci. 4:334-337.

Iwanaga, M., J. Y. Yoon, N. S. Talekar, and Y. Umemura. 1987. Evaluation of the breeding value of 5x interspecific hybrids between sweet potato cultivars and 4x *I. trifida*. Pages 57-65 *in* Sweet potato research and development for small farmers, edited by K. T. Mackay, M. K. Palomar and R. T. Sanico. SEAMCO-SEARCA, College, Laguna, The Philippines.

Kobayashi, M. 1984. The *Ipomoea trifida* complex closely related to sweet potato. Paper presented at Sixth Symp., Intl. Soc. Trop Root Crops, Lima Peru.

Kobayashi, M., and S. Sakamoto. 1987. Utilization of exotic gerplasm in sweet potato breeding. Paper presented at the International Workshop on Crop Genetic Resources of East Asia held at Tsukuba, Japan.

Kobayashi, M., and T. Hirazaki. 1976. Sweet potato breeding using wild related species. Pages 53-57 *in* Proceedings, Sixth Symp., Intl. Soc. Trop. Root Crops, Lima, Peru.

Kukimura, H. , K. Komaki and H. Yoshinaga. 1988. Current progress of sweet potato breeding in Japan. Paper presented at the Eighth Symp., Intl. Soc. Trop. Root Crops held in Bangkok, Thailand.

Muramatsu, M., and I. Shiotani. 1974. Closely related wild *ipomoea* species of sweetpotato in Mexico and Guatemala Rep. Plant Germplasm Inst. Fac. Agr. KyotoUniv. 1:9-13, 19-30.

Oracion, H.Z., K. Niwa, and I. Shiotani. 1990. Cytological analysis of tetraploid hybrids between sweet potato and diploid *Ipomoea trifida* (H. B. K.) Don. Theor. Appl. Genet. 80:617-624.

Sakamoto, S. 1970. Utilization of related species on breeding of sweetpotato in Japan. Japan Agr. Res. Quarterly 5(4):1-4.

Sakamoto, S. 1976. Breeding of new sweet potato variety, Minamiyutaka, by the use of wild relatives. Japan Agr. Res. Quarterly 10:184-186.

Shiotani, I. 1987a. Sweetpotato evolution. Pages 5-15 *in* Sweet potato research and development for small farmers, edited by K. T. Mackay, M. K. Palomar and R. T. Sanico. SEAMCO-SEARCA, College, Laguna, The Philippines.

Shiotani, I. 1987b. Genomic structure and the gene flow in sweet potato and related species Pages 61-73 *in* Exploration, maintenance and utilization of sweet potato genetic resources Report of the First Sweet Potato Planning Conf., CIP, 1987, Lima, Peru.

Sweetpotato Technology for the 21st Century. W.A. Hill, C.K. Bonsi and P.A. Loretan (Eds.) 1992. Tuskegee University, Tuskegee, AL

Gisella Orjeda, Masaru Iwanaga[*], Rosanna Freyre[**]

Use of *Ipomoea trifida* Germplasm for Sweetpotato Improvement: Evaluation of Storage Root Initiators

Wild relatives of sweetpotato (*Ipomoea batatas*) do not produce storage roots big enough for evaluating storage-root related traits, such as dry-matter content and eating qualities, which are important for sweetpotato improvement. The cultivated species is hexaploid ($6x$) and all other wild relatives are either diploid ($2x$) or tetraploid ($4x$); these ploidy differences act as a reproductive barrier to obtaining sufficient progeny in hybridization programs. Thus, the use of storage-root initiators, that is, $4x$ clones capable of producing progenies with adequate yields when crossed with wild relatives, was proposed as a way of evaluating those wild relatives for storage-root related traits. A total of 190 tetraploid interspecific hybrids between sweetpotato cultivars ($6x$) and $2x$ accessions of *I. trifida* were produced. Those $4x$ hybrids were crossed with many accessions of $2x$ and $4x$ *I. trifida* in order to assess their crossability, and to check if the hybrids produce storage roots. A total of 25,550 hand pollinations were made in five crossing combinations. The number of plants obtained per 100 pollinations varied from 1.23 to 22.68 among the five combinations. Of 1,374 hybrid progenies between the $4x$ hybrids and *I. trifida* accessions evaluated in the field, only 3.3% produced more than 200 g of storage root per plant. Further improvement of the storage-root initiators ($4x$ hybrids) for fertility and capability for storage root induction is needed.

Introduction

Most of the important objectives in sweetpotato breeding are related to its storage roots: earliness, yield, eating quality, nutritive value, storageability, and insect resistance (Iwanaga 1988). There are two main constraints in using wild species for sweetpotato breeding: first, none of the wild species of the *Batatas* section produces sizable storage roots. For this reason, they cannot be directly evaluated for desirable characteristics related to storage roots. Second, there are different ploidy levels between wild ($2x$ and $4x$) and cultivated species ($6x$). These differences act as a reproductive barrier to obtaining sufficient progeny with which the wild parent can be evaluated through progeny testing.

We therefore propose an alternative scheme for evaluating wild sweetpotato species in general, and $2x$ or $4x$ *I. trifida* in particular, for characteristics related to storage roots (Orjeda et al. 1991). This alternative scheme aims, firstly, to develop a $4x$ population which produces storage roots and is able to induce the formation of

The International Potato Center (CIP) P.O. Box 5969, Lima, Peru; present addresses: [*]Deputy Director General, IBPGR, Via delle Sette Chiese 142, 00145 Rome, Italy; [**]Department of Crop and Soil Sciences, Michigan State University, East Lansing, MI 48824 USA.

storage roots in their progeny with $2x$ and $4x$ wild species. Such a $4x$ population could be obtained by crossing *I. batatas* with $2x$ *I. trifida*. Secondly, the scheme aims to use this population as storage root initiators with many different $2x$ and $4x$ wild species accessions. Finally, it aims to evaluate by progeny testing hybrids between initiators and wild accessions which need to be evaluated.

More than 28,000 pollinations were carried out between five *Ipomoea batatas* and 41 diploid *I. trifida* accessions of diverse origins to obtain $4x$ interspecific hybrids. From the resultant 730 seeds, 248 plants were finally obtained. Ploidy level determination of the progeny showed that 190 of the 248 plants were $4x$. Most $4x$ progenies did not produce storage roots or had very poor yields; nonetheless, and despite their cultivated parents' poor yields, eight genotypes yielded between 0.81 and 1.50 kg/plant (Orjeda et al. 1991).

The success of the alternative scheme depends on two factors: first, the fertility and crossability of the $4x$ hybrids (storage root initiators) with $2x$ and $4x$ *I. trifida* accessions, and second, their capability to induce storage root formation in their hybrid progenies with $2x$ and $4x$ *I. trifida* accessions. The experiments described here were therefore conducted to not only ascertain the hybrids' ability to fulfil the two factors, but also to interbreed hybrids so as to produce a new $4x$ population which would perform better than the original $4x$ hybrid population.

MATERIALS AND METHODS

Crosses between $4x$ interspecific hybrids and $2x$ and $4x$ *I. trifida* accessions (HT and TH families)

From January to July 1989, a total of 17,100 hand pollinations were performed on $4x$ interspecific hybrids and $2x$ and $4x$ accessions of *I. trifida* in four different combinations (Table 1). We used 45 of the 190 tetraploid interspecific hybrids, and seven $4x$ interspecific hybrids obtained from Dr. I. Shiotani of Mie University, Japan, as well as 23 diploid and six $4x$ *I. trifida* accessions obtained from the Kyushu National Agricultural Experiment Station (KNAES). All the genotypes which were used as females were tested for self-incompatibility with the fluorescent method (Martin 1959).

Table 1. Combinations in which $4x$ *Ipomoea* hybrids and *I. trifida* were crossed.

Group	Female	Male
HT	$4x$ hybrids	$2x$ *I. trifida*
HT	$4x$ hybrids	$4x$ *I. trifida*
TH	$2x$ *I. trifida*	$4x$ hybrids
TH	$4x$ *I. trifida*	$4x$ hybrids
HH	$4x$ hybrids	$4x$ hybrids

Seeds were harvested one month after pollination and classified into one of three categories: class A, plump with a normal shape and therefore viable; class B, intermediate shape between class A and C; and class C, empty or deformed as a result of abnormalities in development and hence probably not viable.

Crosses among 4x interspecific hybrids (HH families)

Crosses were made among 4x interspecific hybrids. A total of 8,450 hand pollinations in 213 different families were performed on 41 of the 4x hybrids under greenhouse conditions. Of these 41 tetraploid genotypes, 36 were chosen from the 4x interspecific hybrids generated by our laboratory and the other five were obtained from Dr. I. Shiotani. These plants were selected because they were flowering at the time and showed self-incompatibility. The seeds produced were also harvested and classified into the three classes according to their appearance.

Germination

Only class A seeds were scarified, that is, they were cut on the opposite side to the helium after disinfection in three successive solutions of HCl 1N, soap, and 70% ethanol. After scarification, the seeds were placed in petri dishes, lined with filter paper soaked in sterilized water and kept at 30°C for 2 or 3 days until germination.

Yield observation trials

HT and TH families. To obtain an estimate of the 4x hybrids' potential as storage root initiators they were planted together with their progenies (HT and TH) in two observation fields. One field was at San Ramón, a mid-altitude tropic area at 11° 08' S latitude, with an altitude of 800 m, a minimum mean temperature of 14.5°C, and a maximum mean of 31°C. The other field was at Cañete, a temperate area with a mean temperature of 22.3°C, an altitude of 40 m and at latitude 13° 09' S.

The fields were planted in spring (September in San Ramón and October in Cañete) and were harvested after 200 and 176 days, respectively. The plot size was 1 m in length and 10 cuttings per genotype were planted in each plot. It was not possible to plant repetitions because of the large number of genotypes and the lack of cuttings. After harvest, the progenies were grouped into three classes: no storage roots, with less than 200 g of storage roots per plant, and with 200 g or more of storage roots per plant.

HH families. HH families were developed by intercrossing 4x interspecific hybrids. These families were planted in two observation fields at San Ramón and Cañete. The plot size was 1 m in length and 10 cuttings per genotype were planted in each plot. Again, because of the large number of genotypes, only one repetition was planted.

Pollen stainability

Percentage of pollen stainability was measured both in the 4*x* interspecific hybrids and their HH progenies. Two environments were used for the 4*x* interspecific hybrids: San Ramón and La Molina, a dry temperate area at latitude 12° 05'S, and an altitude of 240 m, and with a maximum mean temperature of 28.6°C and minimum mean temperature of 19.3°C (the crossing blocks for this work were carried out at this site). Because of lack of space, pollen stainability of the HH progeny was determined only at San Ramón.

From the 190 tetraploid interspecific hybrids obtained, only 140 genotypes were examined for their pollen stainability in La Molina. The rest did not flower or flowered in a different season. At San Ramón, only 116 interspecific hybrids were examined for the same reasons. The HH genotypes had a slightly better flowering rate. From 209 individuals of HH families, 174 flowered at the time.

The flower buds were collected one day before anthesis, put in vials containing water, and placed within screenhouse to avoid contamination with alien pollen carried by bees. The next day, pollen samples were prepared by using Marks (1954) acetic-carmine glycerol jelly method. The percentage of pollen stainability was obtained by dividing the number of stained pollen grains by the total number of pollen grains in the sample.

2n pollen

2n pollen grains were found to be 30% bigger than normal (data not shown), and were easily distinguishable from normal n pollen grains under 100x magnification. The pollen samples used to estimate pollen stainability were also used to identify 2n pollen producers and calculate their individual frequencies of production. The frequency of 2n pollen production in each individual was calculated by dividing the number of giant pollen grains by the total number of grains in the sample, stained and unstained.

RESULTS AND DISCUSSION

Crossability between the 4*x* interspecific hybrids and 2*x* and 4*x* accessions

The total number of pollinations, seeds produced and percentage of class A seeds per 100 pollinations are shown in Table 2. The most successful combination was that of 4*x* hybrids as the female and 4*x* *I. trifida* as the male, even though the number of seeds obtained was much lower than that resulting from normal intraspecific intraploidy crosses between *I. trifida* clones (data not shown). In this type of combination 1,528 seeds were produced, of which 30.7 class A seeds per 100 pollinations were obtained. Similar seed set results were reported by Oracion et al. (1990). This was lowered to 26 when 2*x I. trifida* clones were used as the male parent; only 1,380 class A seeds were produced from 5,307 pollinations indicating, as expected, that

549

Table 2. Seed set in crosses between 2x and 4x *Ipomoea trifida* and 4x interspecific hybrids.

Combination[a]		Pollinations	No. of seeds in class			No. of class A seeds per 100
Female	Male		A	B	C	
4x H	4x T	4,977	1,528	80	199	30.70
4x H	2x T	5,307	1,380	96	110	26.00
4x T	4x H	1,529	312	100	106	20.41
4x H	4x H	8,450	799	97	119	9.46
2x T	4x H	5,287	193	304	524	3.65

[a]4x H = 4x interspecific hybrids; 4x T = 4x *I. trifida*; 2x T = 2x *I. trifida*.

ploidy level differences form a crossing barrier, which, nevertheless, is not suffi-ciently strong to inhibit gene flow between 2x and 4x gene pools.

The next successful combination was 4x *I. trifida* as the female and 4x hybrids as the male, resulting in 312 class A seeds obtained from 1,529 pollinations (20.41 seeds per 100 pollinations). In this combination, there are no ploidy differences, meaning therefore that the decrease in number of seeds produced cannot be attributed to ploidy differences. Assuming *I. trifida* does not have fertility problems stemming from its wild nature and mainly sexual reproduction, it is probable that the 4x hybrids have low fertility because of their interspecific nature and that their male fertility is more affected than their female fertility.

From the 8,450 pollinations performed on the 4x interspecific hybrids (HH group), 1,015 seeds were produced. When these seeds were classified into the three categories based on their appearance, 799 seeds were selected as class A. This means 9.46 seeds were potentially viable from every 100 pollinations (Table 2). This combination, despite the fact that the parents had the same ploidy level, was not particularly successful, indicating problems of male and female fertilities in the hybrids.

Finally, the least successful combination was that of 2x *I. trifida* as the female and 4x hybrids as the male. This combination produced only 193 class A seeds from 5,287 pollinations. The very low seed set (3.65 Class A seeds per 100 pollinations) may be seen as the result of three negative factors acting together: interploidy barriers, low male fertility, and the female plant having the lower ploidy level. This result confirms empirical data indicating that the plant with the lower ploidy level should be used as the male in the interploidy crosses.

The three least successful combinations have 4x interspecific hybrids as the male, thus indicating that male fertility is more affected than female fertility. Our hypothesis is that an abnormal meiosis resulting from aberrations of chromosome pairing is the cause of the fertility reduction. Oracion et al. (1990), performing a cytological analysis of 4x interspecific hybrids of *I. batatas* crossed with 2x *I. trifida*, reported several abnormalities in meiosis. The causes underlying these aberrations were attributed to univalent formation, multivalent formation, and disturbances in the spindle, among others. By studying the formation of male and female gametophytes,

550

we would understand, at least partly, why male fertility is more affected than female fertility by an abnormal meiosis. The low female and male fertilities of the 4x interspecific hybrids reduce their efficiency for seed production in crosses with 2x and 4x wild *Ipomoea* accessions. Further improvement of the 4x hybrid population for increased male and female fertilities is crucial to make the scheme successful.

The lowest seed set was obtained when the 2x *I. trifida* was used as the female. This combination was not only the least successful in terms of number of class A seeds per 100 pollinations (3.65%), but also showed the highest production of class B and C seeds. The presence of a large number of poor quality seeds (aborted embryos, collapsed endosperm, etc.) may indicate that, although fertilization occurs, a harmonious development of the seed is lacking. This combination also presented the poorest germination rate in class A seeds (see next section), which may indicate the presence of underdeveloped embryos or even lack of embryos in class A seeds.

Germination

From 4,212 class A seeds, 1,737 seeds were scarified to assess germinability; the other seeds belonged to specific families selected for a later experiment. The germination rate varied, depending on the parental combination. Table 3 shows the number of seeds scarified and germinated, and the number and percentage of plants obtained. The number of plants obtained from 100 pollinations was also calculated by using the data from Table 2. Again, the least successful combination was 2x *I. trifida* crossed with 4x hybrids in which only 37 plants were obtained from 110 scarified seeds (33.64%). Furthermore, only 1.23 plants were obtained from 100 pollinations.

In the reciprocal combination, 4x hybrids crossed with 2x *I. trifida*, 614 seeds were scarified. From these only 509 germinated and 435 plants were finally obtained, which means that 70.85 plants were obtained from 100 scarified seeds. We obtained 26 class A seeds from 100 pollinations, the actual number of plants per 100 pollinations was 18.42, that is, we need to pollinate 6 flowers to obtain one plant.

The next combination in increasing order was 4x hybrids x 4x *I. trifida* with 396 plants produced from 536 class A scarified seeds (73.88 %). In this case, the number of plants expected from 100 pollinations was 22.68 which means 5 pollinations are needed to obtain a plant.

Comparing these numbers with those obtained from the interploidy crosses between 6x *I. batatas* and 2x *I. trifida* reported by Orjeda et al. (1991) shows the clear advantage of working with less difference in ploidy levels. The numbers of plants expected from 100 pollinations in crosses between 6x sweetpotato and 2x I. *trifida,* and 4x interspecific hybrids and 2x I. *trifida*, were 0.88 and 18.42, respectively. Therefore, the 4x interspecific hybrids were 21 times more efficient than sweetpotato cultivars in producing hybrids with 2x *I. trifida*. Thus, as we anticipated, the reduction of ploidy levels from 6x to 4x greatly improved the efficiency in hybrid production with 2x *I. trifida* which is the wild germplasm targeted for sweetpotato improvement.

Table 3. Germination percentages and number of plants obtained from 100 pollinations in each combination of crosses in *Ipomoea* spp.

Combination[a]		Seeds			Plants obtained	Plants obtained from 100 seeds	Plants per 100 pollinations
Female	Male	Scarified (no.)	Germinated (no.)	(%)	(no.)	(no.)	(no.)
4*x* H	4*x* H	279	238	85.3	209	74.91	7.09
4*x* H	4*x* T	536	462	86.2	396	73.88	22.68
4*x* H	2*x* T	614	509	82.9	435	70.85	18.42
4*x* T	4*x* H	198	111	56.1	81	40.91	8.40
2*x* T	4*x* H	110	45	40.9	37	33.64	1.23

[a]4*x* H = interspecific hybrids; 4*x* T = 4*x I. trifida*; 2*x* T = 2*x I. trifida*.

The most successful combination for germination used 4*x* hybrids as both female and male parents. From the 799 class A seeds produced in this combination only 279 were scarified, 238 germinated and finally 209 (74.91%) plants grew. The number of plants expected per 100 pollinations was 7.07. This means 15 pollinations are needed to obtain a plant. This combination had the second most successful germination rate, which indicates that, when produced, the seeds had no major abnormalities and were normally viable, even though they had female and male fertility problems.

A large difference in seedling survival rates was observed between those combinations having the 4*x* interspecific hybrids and those having *I. trifida* as the female parent (Table 3). When the 4*x* interspecific hybrids were used as the female, the seedling survival rates were normal (ranging between 74.91% and 70.85%), whereas the rates decreased considerably (40.91% and 33.64%) when *I. trifida* was used as the female. It seems that the low seed sets in the first three combinations (4*x* interspecific hybrids as females) resulted from reduced fertilization or seed abortion at a very early stage. In contrast, in the combinations involving *I. trifida* as the female parent the seeds appeared healthy, but the seeds had either no embryos or underdeveloped embryos. Despite the fact that it is difficult to explain these data without proper cytological analysis, our hypothesis is that there is a physiological imbalance between *I. trifida* and the 4*x* hybrids for hybrid seed development. The lower ploidy level of the female parent makes this process more acute, affecting both germination rate and seed set.

Yield observation trials

The main objective of these trials was to test the hypothesis of storage root initiators. In other words, we needed to determine if the progenies from 4*x* hybrids x *I. trifida* really produce storage roots big enough for evaluation as a result of genetic input from the 4*x* hybrids.

A total of 626 progenies from 24 tetraploid hybrids were examined in San Ramón and 748 in Cañete. The summary for each testing site is shown in Tables 4 and 5.

Table 4. Yields[a] of 4x interspecific hybrids and yield distribution of their progeny with 2x and 4x *Ipomoea trifida*, Cañete, Peru, 1990.

4x hybrid parent (Code No.)	Yields (g/plant)	No. of progenies for each yield class		
		0	0-200	>200
9.1	340	60	21	3
33.3	0	59	38	8
40.1	0	3	0	0
41.1	120	14	5	0
41.2	525	27	13	0
42.3	243	25	15	0
46.1	156	6	2	0
49.1	275	9	11	0
51.5	563	36	26	3
57.1	489	2	4	1
57.2	478	7	3	3
58.1	900	1	10	0
58.2	657	1	1	0
78.2	417	3	2	1
80.6	0	198	12	0
82.11	0	27	0	0
91.2	213	1	0	0
96.2	320	6	2	0
97.10	200	46	5	0
100.6	980	3	2	0
100.5	1480	10	5	1
100.2	1567	2	1	3
100.19	675	0	0	0
100.27	200	1	0	0
Total		547	178	23

[a] 200 days in the field.

Only 23 genotypes from the 626 evaluated in San Ramón and the same number from the 748 evaluated in Cañete produced more than 200 g of storage roots per plant (the minimal yield considered necessary for further evaluation on storage roots). Hence, percentages of progenies with acceptable yield were only 3.1 and 3.7 in Cañete and San Ramón, respectively. These were unacceptably low values for the 4x hybrids to be called storage root initiators. If we combine these figures with seed set and germinability, 175.4 pollinations would be necessary to obtain 1 progeny with acceptable yields from the crosses between initiators and 2x *I. trifida* accessions. If we assume that at least 10 progenies with yields of 200 g per plant are needed for a proper evaluation of a 2x *I. trifida* accession, we need to make 1754 pollinations.

Improvement of the 4x interspecific hybrid population

Though the observation trials showed that it is possible to obtain progenies with storage-root production from 4x hybrids x *I. trifida* crosses, better root initiators are

Table 5. Yields[a] of 4x interspecific hybrids and yield distribution of their progeny with 2x and 4x *Ipomoea trifida*, San Ramón, Peru, 1990.

4x hybrid parent (Code no.)	Yields (g/plant)	No. of progenies for each yield class		
		0	0-200	>200
9.1	1280	35	37	4
33.3	233	45	53	3
40.1	200	2	1	0
41.1	80	17	4	0
41.2	1233	12	3	0
42.3	78	20	3	4
46.1	37	3	1	0
49.1	143	10	3	0
51.5	1267	17	13	1
57.2	340	11	0	2
57.1	562	3	4	1
58.1	571	4	7	1
78.2	140	3	4	0
80.6	89	177	24	0
82.11	25	25	1	0
91.2	243	2	0	0
96.2	829	5	3	0
97.1	333	19	3	0
100.2	380	1	5	4
100.5	843	12	5	0
100.6	917	0	4	1
100.19	1750	1	0	0
100.27	480	1	0	0
Total		425	178	23

[a]200 days in the field.

needed to improve two important traits: yields (or storage root initiation capability) and crossability with 2x and 4x *I. trifida*. It was necessary to establish a new breeding and selection program at the 4x level with the objective of accumulating genes for yield and improved fertility.

Yield

Although the field trial of the HH families was only an observation trial without replications, it was clear that HH families were improved, compared with their original interspecific parents. In Cañete, 12.65% of the genotypes evaluated yielded from more than 600 g to 1,330 g per plant (Table 6). In San Ramón, 18.02% yielded from more than 600 g to 2,080 g per plant. These are high yields considering the ploidy level and origin of this material.

Table 6. Yield distribution of (HH) progeny of breeding among 4*x* interspecific *Ipomoea* hybrids in Cañete and San Ramón, Peru.

Location	Percentages of individuals in each yield class (kg/plant)								
	0	0-0.2	0.2-0.4	0.4-0.6	0.6-0.8	0.8-I.0	1.0-1.5	>1.5	Total
Cañete	8.86	38.60	25.95	13.92	8.23	1.26	3.16	0	158
S. Ramón	4.91	42.07	20.76	14.20	7.10	2.73	6.55	1.64	183

Some 4*x* interspecific parents were crossed with 4*x* individuals obtained from Dr. I. Shiotani. It was noticed that families coming from these crosses had good yields, suggesting the presence of heterosis. Our working hypothesis is that 4*x* storage root initiators with higher yields would have progenies with higher yields when crossed with 2*x* or 4*x* *I. trifida* accessions. This hypothesis should be tested by comparing the original 4*x* hybrid with the newly developed 4*x* population for frequencies of progenies with yields of more than 200 g.

Pollen stainability

Pollen stainability was used as an estimate for male fertility. In La Molina, of 140 tetraploid interspecific hybrids examined, 20.7% produced pollen grains that were all sterile and not stainable (Table 7). Only 10.7% of individuals had pollen with more than 50% stainability and were considered fertile. In San Ramón, pollen stainability percentages were somewhat better, indicating a slight environmental effect for this characteristic. Of the 116 individuals examined, only two genotypes (4.3%) had pollen grains with no stainability and 19.8% had stainability percentages greater than 50%. These percentages indicate, as expected with interspecific hybrids, male fertility problems in this group of material.

Table 7. Comparative pollen stainability percentages among 4*x* interspecific *Ipomoea* hybrids and their progenies, La Molina and San Ramón, Peru.

Population[a] (location)	Percentages of individuals with different pollen stainability (%)						
	0	0-1	1.1-5	5.1-10	10.1-20	20.1-50	>50
4*x* (LM)	20.7	0.7	2.1	7.9	21.4	36.4	10.7
4*x* (SR)	4.3	0.9	2.6	5.2	25.9	41.4	19.8
HH (SR)	2.9	0.0	0.6	1.7	5.2	22.4	67.2

[a]Numbers of genotypes examined for the three populations (4*x* LM, 4*x* SR, and HH SR) are 140, 116, and 174, respectively.

The comparative pollen stainability percentages between the 4x interspecific hybrids and their HH progenies is shown in Table 7. From 209 HH individuals only 174 were examined. In contrast with their 4x interspecific parents, only 2.9% produced pollen grains with no stainability; 7.5% had pollen stainability percentages equal or smaller than 20%; and 67.2% of the population examined had pollen stainability percentages higher than 50%.

The pollen stainability percentages showed a dramatic improvement in only one generation (Table 7). Although the parental 4x interspecific generation had only 19.8% of its individuals producing more than 50% of stained pollen grains, their progeny population (HH) showed 67.2% of its individuals with the same or higher stainability percentages: a threefold increase of genotypes considered to be fertile. It is expected that improved stainability means improved fertility and crossability with 2x and 4x *I. trifida*.

The improved stainability can be explained by two reasons. As reported by Oracion et al. (1990), some of the 4x hybrids are very likely to be aneuploids that naturally have fertility problems. Passing through one sexual cycle probably reduces the involvement of aneuploid gametes; thus, resultant progenies would have a higher frequency of euploid progeny than the original population. The second possible reason is that the meiotic products of the original hybrids have experienced chromosome pairing between genomes of the two species, and therefore the resultant progenies (HH families) have chromosomes with chromosome segments of both species. This is expected to result in improved pairing and higher fertility in the HH progenies.

2n pollen

From 140 individuals examined in La Molina, 24 produced 2n pollen grains in frequencies that ranged from 0.23 to 10.12%. In San Ramón, 16 of 116 individuals were found to produce 2n pollen grains. The 2n pollen frequencies ranged from 0.15 to 9.36%. When the HH population was examined in San Ramón it was found that 14 individuals out of 174 produced frequencies of 2n pollen that ranged from 0.16 to 5.06%. The 2n pollen producers were not always the same in both environments, suggesting that a genotype-environment interaction influences this character. Nevertheless, 2n pollen production was confirmed in 4x populations checked in three different environments.

The finding of 2n pollen production in 4x individuals of *Ipomoea* opens new possibilities for gene transfer between different ploidy levels and also between wild and cultivated germplasm. There are several indications that 2n gametes exist in the genus *Ipomoea* (Eckenwalder and Brown 1986; Freyre et al. 1991; Jones 1990; Oracion et al. 1990; Orjeda et al. 1990). The 2n gametes are gametes with the sporophytic rather than the gametophytic chromosome number. Thus, they allow polyploidization and interploidy crosses between different populations.

The 2n pollen in 4x individuals permits the production of 6x plants by crossing 4x individuals, one of which produces 2n gametes. This finding makes the introgression of genes from wild germplasm to the 6x sweetpotato much easier. It also agrees with Kobayashi's concept (Kobayashi 1978) of an *I. trifida* complex which includes populations of different ploidy levels sexually interconnected by means of 2n gametes.

CONCLUSIONS

The results discussed indicate that the 4x interspecific hybrids can indeed induce storage root formation in their progenies with 2x and 4x *I. trifida*. However, there existed a crossability barrier between the initiators and 2x *I. trifida*, requiring a large number of pollinations to obtain a sufficient number of viable progenies. Moreover, frequencies of progenies with yields sufficient for progeny testing were extremely low. Because of this low crossability and low frequency of progenies with sufficient yields, the present initiators are not amenable for practical purposes.

The results obtained with the new HH plants strongly support the possibility of improvement of the 4x population to develop more efficient storage root initiators. It was possible to develop 4x sweetpotato genotypes with high yields and fertility. It is planned to develop new 4x interspecific hybrids involving 2x *I. trifida* and high-yielding sweetpotato varieties. Special consideration will be given to geographic origin of such sweetpotato cultivars to widen the genetic base of the 4x population.

Our results also suggest the possibility of having 4x sweetpotato cultivars through further improvement at the 4x level. The advantages of a 4x sweetpotato cultivar over a hexaploid cultivar would be its tetrasomic inheritance, earliness because of their lower ploidy level, and easier introgression of "wild" genes. Having a wider genetic background in the 4x population would be key to the success for continuous improvement.

REFERENCES

Eckenwalder, J.E., and B.P. Brown. 1986. Polyploid speciation in hybrid morning glories of *Ipomoea* L. sect. Quamoclit Griseb. Can. J. Genet. Cytol. 28:17-20.

Freyre, R.Y. 1989. Producción de Hexaploides Sintéticos de *Ipomoea trifida* (H.B.K.) G. Don. M.Sc. Thesis. Universidad Nacional Agraria, Lima, Peru.

Freyre, R., M. Iwanaga, and G. Orjeda. 1991. Use of *Ipomoea trifida* (H.B.K.) G. Don germ plasm for sweet potato improvement. 2. Fertility of synthetic hexaploids and triploids with 2n gametes of *I. trifida,* and their interspecific crossability with sweet potato. Genome 34:209-214.

Iwanaga, M. 1988. Use of wild germplasm for sweet potato breeding. Pages 199-210 *in* Exploration, maintenance, and utilization of sweet potato genetic resources. Report of the First Sweet Potato Planning Conference.. International Potato Center (CIP), Lima, Peru.

Iwanaga, M., R. Freyre, and G. Orjeda. 1991. Use of *Ipomoea trifida* (H.B.K.) G. Don germplasm for sweet potato improvement. 1. Development of synthetic hexaploids of *I. trifida* by ploidy-level manipulations. Genome 34:201-208.

Jones, A. 1990. Unreduced pollen in a wild tetraploid relative of sweetpotato. J. Am. Soc. Hort. Sci. 115: 512-516.

Kobayashi, M. 1978. Sweet potato breeding method using wild relatives in Japan. Trop. Agric. Res. Ser. 11: 1-8.

Ling, C.P. 1984. Genetic variability in interspecific F1 hybrids between *Ipomoea batatas* L. and *I. littoralis*. M. Sc. Thesis, Chinese Academy of Agricultural Sciences, Beijing, 45 pp.

Marks, G.E. 1954. An acetocarmine glycerol jelly for use in pollen fertility counts. Stain Tech. 29:277.

Martin, F.W. 1959. Staining and observing pollen tubes in the style by means of fluorescence. Stain Tech. 34:125-128.

Oracion, M.Z., K. Niwa, and I. Shiotani. 1990. Cytological analysis of tetraploid hybrids between sweet potato and diploid *Ipomoea trifida* (H.B.K.) Don. Theor. Appl. Genet. 80:617-624.

Orjeda, G., R. Freyre, and M. Iwanaga. 1990. Production of 2n pollen in diploid *Ipomoea trifida*, a putative wild ancestor of sweet potato. J. Hered. 81:462-467.

Orjeda, G., R. Freyre, and M. Iwanaga. 1992. Use of *Ipomoea trifida* germplasm for sweet potato improvement. 3. Development of 4x interspecific hybrids between *I. batatas* Lam. (2n=6x=90) and *I. trifida* (H.B.K) G. Don (2n=2x=30) as storage root initiators for wild species. TAG 83:159-163.

Sweetpotato Technology for the 21st Century. W.A. Hill, C.K. Bonsi and P.A. Loretan (Eds.) 1992. Tuskegee University, Tuskegee, AL

Poster Presentations

DATA MANAGEMENT IN SWEETPOTATO BREEDING PROGRAMS

P. C. St. Amand, D. R. LaBonte
Department of Horticulture, Louisiana State University Agricultural Center, Louisiana State University Experiment Station, Baton Rouge, LA 70803-2120, USA and Department of Horticulture, North Carolina State University, Box 7609, Raleigh, NC 27695, USA, respectively.

Detailed records are essential for a plant breeder to make timely decisions concerning the retention of breeding lines and progress towards desired breeding objectives. A database program can assist in achieving these goals by facilitating storage, retrieval and manipulation of data (Brown 1984).

This database is written in the FoxBASE+ database language for IBM-compatible personal computers. The database program allows users with limited computer knowledge and instruction to quickly use the program's various features. The database framework consists of 5 pull-down menus (TEST, FIELD PLANS, REPORTS, UTILITIES, and DATAFORMS), each containing one or more options (Table 1). Each option has prompts (print, escape, save, etc.) to direct the user.

The main purpose of the sweetpotato database program is to allow assemblage of pertinent data on individual selections (lines) using various test options. An ancillary role is to maintain a comprehensive record of all aspects of the breeding program.

By using the ADD/EDIT SELECTIONS option available in the TEST menu, a breeder can assemble a record for any given selection. This option asks the user for the parentage, release name (if applicable), maturity, seed production, total carotenoids, and percent dry matter. Root and canopy descriptors adapted from Huaman (1987) are also included in this option. A powerful feature of the database program is its capacity to summarize test data for individual lines and to list the plant descriptors in a printout by selecting the PRINT ALL INFORMATION option in the REPORTS main menu. For example, yield data entered into the Test menu YIELD option is presented as an overall mean and standard deviation for each market grade for all yield tests in which the line has been entered. Yield data are also presented on a percentage basis with respect to three user-specified check cultivars. A similar summary is given for the following self-descriptive TEST menu options: BEDDING EVALUATION, BAKING, CANNING, FUSARIUM ROOT ROT, FUSARIUM WILT, INTERNAL CORK, JAVA BLACK ROT, ROOT KNOT NEMATODE, SOIL ROT/CIRCULAR SPOT, BACTERIAL SOFT ROT, GRUB, BANDED CUCUMBER BEETLE, AND FLEA BEETLE. All test options are based on those commonly employed by members of the National Sweetpotato Collaborators Group in the United States. This format provides a breeder with a performance profile over different environments and years. This is particularly useful since genotype x

559

Table 1. Main menus and options available in the sweetpotato breeding database program and references upon which these evaluations are based.

MAIN MENUS	OPTIONS	
TEST	ADD/EDIT SELECTIONS YIELD (National Sweetpotato CollaboratorsGroup) BEDDING EVALUATION (National Sweetpotato Coll. Group) BAKING (National Sweetpotato Collaborators Group) CANNING (National Sweetpotato Collaborators Group) CHLOROTIC LEAF DISTORTION (Clark et al. 1990) FUSARIUM ROOT ROT (Clark et al. 1986) FUSARIUM WILT (Collins and Nielson 1976) INTERNAL CORK (Nielson and Pope 1960) JAVA BLACK ROT (Lo 1986) ROOT KNOT NEMATODE (Lawrence 1986) SOIL ROT/CIRC. SPOT (FIELD) (Martin et al. 1975) SOIL ROT (LAB) (Moyer et al. 1984) BACTERIAL SOFT ROT (Clark et al. 1989) GRUB (Rolston and Barlow 1980) FLEA BEETLE BANDED CUCUMBER BEETLE (Rolston et al. 1979)	
FIELD PLANS	TEST PLOTS BEDDING PLOTS	
REPORTS	LIST ALL SELECTION NAMES LIST ALL TEST NAMES PRINT ALL INFORMATION FOR ONE SELECTION LIST ALL SELECTIONS PLANTED LIST SELECTIONS TO MAINTAIN PRINT LINEAGE OF ONE SELECTION CUSTOM QUERY LIST ALL PLOT PLANS	
UTILITIES	RENAME SELECTIONS QUIT PROGRAM BACKUP DATA RESTORE DATA FROM BACKUP DELETE TESTS IMPORT DATA CHANGE CHECKS CREATE ASCII FILES	
DATA FORMS	INDIVIDUAL SELECTION BED EVALUATION CANNING BACTERIAL SOFT ROT CHLOROTIC LEAF DISTORTION INTERNAL CORK ROOT KNOT NEMATODE SOIL ROT/CIRCULAR SPOT (FIELD)	YIELD BAKING INSECT FUSARIUM ROOT ROT FUSARIUM WILT JAVA BLACK ROT SOIL ROT (LAB)

environmental interactions for yield and a number of quality factors are commonplace in sweetpotato (Collins et al. 1987).

All statistical applications are based on Fisher's unprotected least significant difference (LSD) procedure (P=0.05) for a randomized complete block design. Raw data are analyzed by the method of least squares. If missing data are present, a generalized inverse is computed using the G2SWEEP operator as described by Goodnight (1979). Least significant differences and rankings are printed in a publication-ready table. Test size is constrained by the number of replications and selections in concert. As the number of replications decrease, a greater number of selections can be evaluated. A typical test plot with 4 replications can have up to 26 lines entered. Eight replications is the maximum allowed. Some options in the TEST menu do not have statistical applications, namely BEDDING EVALUATION, CHLOROTIC LEAF DISTORTION, INTERNAL CORK and JAVA BLACK ROT. These options record relative reactions to checks.

Preparation of trials for the growing season is aided by recording plot plans through the TEST PLOT and BEDDING PLOT options within the FIELD PLANS menu. A file for a given plot plan is opened, or edited if it already exists, by specifying a test name, location, and year. The user is subsequently queried as to various dimensions of the plot, planting date, number of replications, and number of days to harvest. Any additional pertinent information (i.e., pesticide applications, fertilization practices) can be recorded in a note section. A printout is available as the user exits the file. To further aid the user, location, planting date, and calculated harvest date for all trials in a given year are provided through the LIST ALL TEST NAMES option in the REPORTS menu. All variables specified in a plot plan are transferred to the appropriate file in the TEST menu if the same trial name, location, and year are used when opening the file. Data collected on forms available in the DATAFORMS menu facilitate data entry into respective options in the TEST menu.

The REPORTS menu has several options associated with record-keeping. The LIST SELECTIONS TO MAINTAIN and LIST ALL SELECTIONS PLANTED options, respectively, permit the user to identify extant lines, and identify which lines are entered into what tests for a given year. The PRINT LINEAGE option reports the pedigree of a line. The CUSTOM QUERY option permits the user to screen the database for lines which meet certain criteria for any number of user specified variables (i.e., soil rot resistance, yield, maturity). Individual factors can be set to be greater than, equal to, or less than any quantitative variable, or equal to or not equal to a qualitative variable.

Options within the UTILITIES menu produce and restore a copy of the data, delete unwanted tests, and rename selections. The IMPORT DATA option permits data transfer through diskettes between different computer terminals. This allows all collaborative researchers to have the same data set. Another useful feature is the CREATE ASCII FILES option. All data in the database can be put into a subdirectory for further manipulation by a word processor, spreadsheet or statistical software.

Diskettes of the database language and a user's guide are available for a nominal charge.

LITERATURE CITED

Brown, J. 1984. A new data base computer package for plant breeders. Euphytica 33:935-942.

Clark, C.A., R.A. Valverde, J.A. Wilder-Ayers, and P.E. Nelson. 1990. *Fusarium lateritium* causes sweetpotato chlorotic leaf distortion. Phytopathology 80:741-744.

Clark, C.A., W.M. Randle, and C.S. Pace. 1986. Reactions of sweet potato selections to fusarium root and stem canker caused by *Fusarium solani*. Plant Disease 70:869-871.

Clark, C.A., J.A. Wilder-Ayers, and V. Duarte. 1989. Resistance of sweet potato to bacterial root and stem rot caused by *Erwinia chrysanthemi*. Plant Disease 73:984-987.

Collins, W.W., L.J. Wilson, S. Arrendell, and L.F. Dickey. 1987. Genotype x environment interactions in sweet potato yield and quality factors. J. Amer. Soc, Hort. Sci. 112:579-583.

Collins, W.W., and L.W. Nielson. 1976. Fusarium wilt resistance in sweetpotatoes. Phytopathology 66:489-493.

Goodnight, J.H. 1979. A tutorial on the SWEEP operator. American Statistician. 33:149-158.

Huaman, Z. 1987. Descriptors for the characterization and evaluation of sweet potato genetic resources. Pages 331-355 *in* Exploration, maintenance, and utilization of sweet potato genetic resources. International Potato Center, Lima, Peru.

Lawrence, G.W., and C.A. Clark 1986. Infection and morphological development of *Meloidogyne incognita* in roots of susceptible and resistant sweet potato cultivars. Plant Disease 70:545-547.

Lo, J.Y. 1986. Sources of inoculum and factors favoring infection of sweet potato by the java black rot pathogen, *Diplodia gossypina*. Ph.D. Diss., Louisiana State University, Baton Rouge.

Martin, W.J., Travis P. Hernandez, and Teme P. Hernandez. 1975. Development and disease reaction of Jasper, a new soil rot-resistant sweetpotato variety from Louisiana. Plant Disease Reporter 59:388-391.

Moyer, J.W., C.L. Campbell, E. Echandi, and W.W. Collins. 1984. Improved methodology for evaluating resistance in sweet potato to *Streptomyces ipomoea*. Phytopathology 74:494-497.

National Sweetpotato Collaborators Group. 1989. *In* National Sweetpotato Collaborators Group Progress Report 1989, edited by W.J. McLaurin. Athens, GA.

Nielson, L.W., and D.T. Pope. 1960. Resistance in sweet potato to the internal cork virus. Plant Disease Reporter 44:342-347.

Rolston, L.H., and T. Barlow. 1980. Insecticide control of a white grub (*Phyllophaga ephilida* Say, Coleoptera:Scarabaeidae) on sweet potato. Journal of the Georgia Entomological Society. 15:445-449.

Rolston, L.H., T. Barlow, Teme Hernandez, and S.S. Nilakhe. 1979. Field evaluation of breeding lines and cultivars of sweet potato for resistance to the sweet potato weevil. HortScience 14:634-635.

ETIOLOGY OF SWEETPOTATO GALLS IN CHIAPAS, MEXICO

M. Santos-Ojeda, L. Fucikovsky

Centro de Fitopatologia, Colegio de Postgraduados. Montecillo, Edo. de Mexico. C.P. 56230.

Different size galls were found on stems at the soil level and also on storage roots at 5 to 10 cm depths of sweetpotato plants in Villaflores, Chiapas, Mexico. Plants affected had from one to ten galls. The incidence of plants infected was estimated at 30%. Plants with galls had lower storage root yields and quality than plants without galls. Selected predominant and purified bacterial isolates obtained from infected plants in the field were inoculated on healthy sweetpotato, sunflower and tomato plants in the glasshouse. All these plants produced fleshy galls after 21 days. When reisolated from the galls, the bacteria produced white colonies on PDA medium and was characterized as *Agrobacterium tumefaciens*. This is the first report of this kind in Mexico and, as far as is known, has not been reported elsewhere.

The sweetpotato (*Ipomoea batatas* L.) is a storage root that is grown in tropical and subtropical regions. Sweetpotato is used in the preparation (enhancement) of certain sweets and traditional meals. Sweetpotato is an excellent source of carbohydrates and, to a lesser extent, a source of proteins for humans and animals (Folquer 1978).

In the state of Chiapas, Mexico the sweetpotato is cultivated on a semi-commercial basis and is sold in the local market. Sweetpotatoes provide supplemental income for small farmers that, with little investment and little care, nets him high returns.

Like all cultivated plants, the sweetpotato is affected by biotic factors. In Villaflores, Chiapas, galls of different (varying) sizes were observed on roots at ground level and also on roots at 5 to 10 cm depths. During the harvest of sweetpotatoes in 1988, a 30% incidence of plants with one to 10 galls per plant was detected. These galls reduced the yield and the quality of the roots and in this manner reduced the plant's commercial value.

MATERIALS AND METHODS

The causative agent for the galls was isolated by placing small pieces of the tops of the galls in the middle of plates with PDA medium and incubating at 28°C for 48 hours. Three bacterial colonies with different morphological characteristics were obtained: the first with cream color; the second with clear yellow color; and the third and most abundant of the isolates with a whitish color and rapid growth. Once purified, cell suspensions of the three bacterial types were made for pathogenicity testing.

Sweetpotato, sunflower and tomato were injected with each bacterial suspension at 3 x 10 cells/mL using a sterile hypodermic syringe. Twenty days after the inoculation was complete, a comparison of the galls obtained and the original galls was made. Biochemical proofs were applied to 10 stocks with the same organoleptic characteristics for the specific identification of the pathogenic organism.

563

Table 1. Characteristics of bacteria in comparison with *Agrobacterium tumefaciens* Biovar 1*.

Characteristics	Isolates from Sweetpotato	Agrobacterium tumefaciens Biovar 1
Fluid increase	+	+
White colony	+	+
Gram positive	-	-
Oxidase	+	+
Ketolactose	+	+
Ammonium iron citrate	+	+
Reaction at 37°C	+	+
Reaction in 2% NaCl	+	+
Acid Production:		
Melesitose	+	+
Sucrose	+	+

*Kerr and Panagopoulos 1977; Dhanvantari 1978; Schaad 1988.

RESULTS AND DISCUSSION

All plants that were inoculated with cells from the white colored colonies had gall formation 20 days after inoculation. After 26 days the galls were of an appreciable size. The other two bacteria types that were isolated did not induce any change in the inoculated plants.

The characteristics of the isolations (pathogenic) are presented in Table 1. On the basis of results obtained and compared with Kerr and Panagopoulos (1977), Dhanvantari (1978), and Schaad (1988), it is certain that the galls on the sweetpotato were caused by *Agrobacterium tumefaciens* Biovar. This is the first report of this bacteria affecting the sweetpotato in this manner.

REFERENCES

Dhanvantari, B.N. 1978. Characterization of *Agrobacterium* isolates from stone fruits in Ontario. Can.J. Bot. 56:2309-2311.

Folquer, F. 1978. La batata (camote) estudio de la planta y su produccion comercial. Edit. Hemisferio Sur. Buenos Aires, Argentina. 144 pp.

Kerr, A., and O.B. Panagopoulos. 1977. Biotypes of *Agrobacterium radiobacter* var. *tumefaciens* and their biological control. Phytopathol. Z. 90:172-179.

Schaad, N.W. 1988. Laboratory guide for identification of plant pathogenic bacteria. 2a. ed. American Phytopathological Society, St. Paul, Minn. 165 pp.

HERITABILITY FOR SWEETPOTATO WEEVIL RESISTANCE

Paul G. Thompson, John C. Schneider, Boyette Graves[*]
Mississippi State University, Mississippi State, MS 39762; [*]Beaumont Unit, South Mississippi Branch Experiment Station, Beaumont, MS 39423.

A breeding population including parents with known moderate levels of sweetpotato weevil (*Cylas formicarius elegantulus*) resistance was evaluated for resistance in a field experiment. Plants with roots intact were harvested and evaluated for stem diameter at the soil line, depth of first root, number and weight of injured and noninjured roots. Narrow sense heritabilities were estimated by parent offspring regression and correlations among traits were analyzed. There was indication of a negative correlation between stem diameter and percentage noninjured roots. Heritabilities for percentage noninjured roots and stem diameter were 34% and 32%, respectively. Selection and intermating should increase resistance levels. A selection technique using family, in combination with individual selection within families, will result in the most rapid gain in resistance.

INTRODUCTION

Sources of resistance to sweetpotato weevils (*Cylas formicarius* and *C. puncti- collis*) have been identified and resistance transferred through selection and intermating (Hahn and Leuschner 1982; Mullen et al. 1985). In addition, Mullen et al. (1985) reported a reduction in percentage root damage from 45 to 17% in their breeding population for the period 1980 to 1984, showing that the resistance level was increased by breeding. Therefore, usable genetic variability for resistance to the most destructive pest of sweetpotato is available and its use in breeding should result in higher resistance levels.

We initiated a breeding program in 1990 to increase weevil resistance levels in combination with yield, quality, and other disease and insect resistance. Cooperative work with the International Potato Center (CIP) will include screening foreign germplasm for additional sources of genes for resistance and other traits. Those genes, once identified, will be introduced into breeding populations.

To optimally increase resistance levels through breeding and also increase or maintain other desirable traits, additional information is needed on the inheritance and relationship between those characters. Broad sense heritability for resistance to *C. puncticollis* was estimated to be 0.73 (Hahn and Leuschner 1981). Broad sense heritability, the ratio of total genotypic variance to phenotypic variance, is useful in the vegetatively propagated sweetpotato to estimate the probability of selecting improved clones in the immediate generation. However, total genotypic variance includes dominance variance which is unstable following one cycle of sexual reproduction. Therefore, broad sense heritability is not useful for predicting gains in population means by intermating selected genotypes. Narrow sense heritability, the ratio of additive genetic variance to phenotypic variance is the estimate needed to

565

determine expected population improvement over generations of sexual reproduction combined with selection. Additive genetic variance and covariance estimates are also needed to determine genetic correlations between traits. Results of a study conducted during 1990 to estimate narrow sense heritability (heritability) for resistance to the sweetpotato weevil *Cylas formicarius elegantulus* (Summers) is presented here. Discussion on plans for future research in the program is also included.

MATERIALS AND METHODS

Plant Materials

Seventeen parents from a polycross and their seedling progenies were evaluated. The polycross contained 30 genotypes with all clones originating from U.S. breeding programs (Table 1). Entries with the highest resistance levels in evaluations by Mullen et al. (1985) (e.g., 'W226,' 'Resisto,' and 'Regal') were included. Two additional families from the last polycross for weevil resistance development at the U.S. Vegetable Laboratory (Mullen et al. 1985) and 4 checks gave a total of 40 entries. The checks and their resistance levels were: 'Centennial'-susceptible, 'Jewel'-intermediate, 'Regal'-moderate, and 'W226'-moderate.

Insects

Weevils were collected at six Mississippi locations and cultured on storage roots in 1.1 liter glass jars. Wild weevils were pooled over a period of 3 generations, after which 20 males and 20 females were taken from different jars to oviposit in roots for a 7 day period. Weevils from those roots were used for field infestation.

Resistance Evaluation

Field evaluations were conducted at the Beaumont unit of the South Mississippi Branch Experiment Station. Beaumont is in a weevil infested area, but naturally occurring weevil numbers were low because sweetpotatoes had not been grown for many years.

A randomized complete block design with 5 plant plots of each entry replicated 8 times was used. One female and one male weevil were applied to the crown of each plant 70 days after transplanting. Extra plants of each entry were dug to determine root size at time of infestation. Average storage root length by diameter was 92 x 38 mm at time of weevil application. Soil cracking was present around all plants the date weevils were released. Average crack width was 15 mm and storage roots on some plants were visible through the cracks.

Plants with storage roots intact were harvested 145 days after transplanting by mowing vines 15 cm above the soil surface. Measurements made were: stem diameter, depth from soil line to first storage root attachment, presence or absence of stem damage by weevils, number and weight of injured and noninjured roots. Data were recorded by individual plant.

Heritabilities were estimated by parent-offspring regression. The sweetpotato is hexaploid, but predominately bivalent chromosomal pairing has been observed

(Jones 1965). Also, unpublished phenotypic segregation ratios of qualitative traits have agreed with diploid ratios (Jones 1969). Assuming bivalent pairing and recombination, the parent-offspring regression coefficients (b) were used to estimate heritabilities (h^2):

$$b = (1/2)VA/VP$$
$$\text{and } h^2 = 2b = VA/VP$$

where VA and VP are additive genetic variance and phenotypic variance, respectively. To estimate the amount of nonadditive variance, broad sense heritabilities (H) were estimated by variance component analyses of parental data:

$$H = \frac{VC}{VP}$$

where VC is among clone variance and contains total genotypic variance.

Since parents and offspring were evaluated at one location, genotype x environment variance was included in the h^2 and H estimates. The within parental clone variance was entirely environmental and was deducted from VC to remove G x E from H. The within parental clone variance as a percentage of total genetic variance was deducted from the regression coefficients for h^2 estimates. Since h^2 is the ratio of VA to VP, the environmental variance as a percentage of total genetic variance overcompensated and should result in a conservative estimate of h^2.

Genetic correlations among measured traits were estimated by the formula:

$$r_{Gxy} = COV_{Axy}/(VA_x \cdot VA_y)^{1/2}$$

where COV_{Axy} was the additive covariance component between traits and VA_x and VA_y were additive variance components.

RESULTS

No evidence of above ground feeding or oviposition was observed. Lack of leaf or stem feeding was probably due to extensive soil cracking which allowed ready access to storage roots. Weevils were observed to enter cracks immediately after release, and the day following application no weevils were observed on above-ground parts.

Mean percentage uninjured root numbers ranged from 25 to 85 (Table 1) indicating that detection of moderate and low levels of resistance was possible with this level of weevil. Ranking of most lines based on weevil injury was as expected since the USDA lines selected for resistance were near the highest. 'US-1' (2nd) was from the latest USDA weevil polycross and clone 'W226' (4th) exhibited the highest resistance in the last USDA evaluation (Mullen et al. 1985). The fact that 'Regal' and 'Resisto' (moderate resistance levels) were near the mid range, 63% and 55%, and no higher than 'Jewel' (intermediate check) was not expected. The susceptible check 'Centennial' (37th) was at the low end of resistance.

Genetic correlations between most traits were low and smaller than standard errors. There was indication of a relationship between stem diameter (X) and percentage noninjured roots (Y). Regression and correlation coefficients approached

Table 1. Storage root injury by the sweetpotato weevil.

Noninjured roots (%)			Noninjured roots (%)			Noninjured roots (%)		
Entry[z]	No.	Wt.	Entry	No.	Wt.	Entry	No.	Wt.
W244	85	80	P MS1631	68	64	P MS2137	59	55
US-1	81	80	W263	68	63	MS1631	57	54
P Resisto	78	77	P MS105	67	63	Resisto	55	53
W226	76	73	P Excel	66	60	MS2137	49	48
P NC902	74	72	P MS1012	65	61	MS121	48	43
P MS114	73	68	P MS211	64	58	MS741	48	44
US-2	73	67	P Beau.	63	60	P MS49	45	43
W250	72	65	Beau.	63	60	P MS121	44	39
P W250	72	71	Excel	63	57	NC 902	43	39
W873	72	71	P W873	63	60	Cent.	42	38
P W244	71	69	Regal	63	55	MS114	35	31
P MS741	71	68	Jewel	63	59	MS49	29	29
P W263	70	67	MS1012	59	56	MS105	25	20
MS211	69	64						
LSD (0.05)	24	25						

[z]All codes are parent identifications. P preceding code = Progeny; US-1 & 2 were seedling families from latest USDA weevil resistance polycross. MS = Mississippi, NC = North Carolina. W lines are from U.S. Vegetable Lab.

significance (P=0.08). The probability was too high for even a preliminary conclusion, but worthy of additional observation.

Broad sense heritability estimates for percentage noninjured root numbers and weight were 0.65 and 0.59, respectively. Heritability estimates, followed by standard errors, based on half-sib family means were 0.34 ± 0.20 and 0.36 ± 0.22 for the same traits, respectively. Heritability estimates based upon individual plants were 0.27 ± 0.16 and 0.28 ± 0.18 for those traits, respectively. The differences between broad sense and narrow sense heritabilities indicate that nonadditive variance is sizable for weevil resistance. In choosing between family and individual plant selection for determining plants to include in crossing blocks for recombination, the higher heritabilities (even though differences were smaller than standard errors) would tend to favor among family selection. A combination of among family followed by individual plant selection within highest performing families should be efficient. Additive variance among half-sib families as well as within (1/4 VA + 3/4 VA, respectively) will contribute to selection gain using this technique. No additional time is required to complete a recombination cycle using this method over individual plant selection.

In summary, the 0.34 and 0.36 heritability estimates for percentage noninjured roots are in the low-to-moderate range and indicate that reasonable gain in weevil resistance can be expected. Inclusion of additional sources of resistance into the breeding population should increase heritabilities and rate of progress in resistance improvement.

PLANS FOR FUTURE WORK

The 1990 evaluation will be repeated in 1991 to estimate and remove additional G x E from heritability estimates. Additional germplasm including as many clones with reported resistance as possible will be included in polycrosses and evaluations.

Resistance to Different Species

An important topic for future research will be the determination of common genetic controls for weevils of different species and genera, and also for weevils and insects from other families. There is some evidence that resistance to *C. puncticollis* was also effective against *C. formicarius* (Ralston et al. 1979). The weevil *Euscepes postfasciatus* is seldom mentioned but is a problem in some Caribbean, Central and South American countries. If funding can be obtained, plans should include cooperative work with CIP to determine if resistances to *Cylas* and *Euscepes* are controlled by common genes.

There are also indications that resistance due to a common genetic control is effective in reducing injury by several species of insects belonging to different families: wireworms, cucumber beetles and *C. formicarius* (Cuthbert and Davis 1970; Jones et al. 1982). The determination of common genetic controls for resistance to different insect species will facilitate development of total insect resistance.

Improvements are needed in evaluation techniques. Different methods have been used for rating resistance levels [discussed by Talekar (1982)] and the most effective and efficient method needs to be identified. Optimum field plot technique including plot size and shape and replication number needs to be determined. Especially critical is the need to increase precision of field evaluations. Experimental errors were high in the 1990 evaluations as shown by the LSD values (Table 1) and few significant differences resulted. Mullen et al. (1985) also observed few significant differences. Hahn and Leuschner (1981), however, found more differences in root damage among genotypes, especially when averaged over seasons and years. Whether the increased precision was due to method of evaluating injury, differences in sweetpotato genotypes or weevil species, field plot technique, and/or evaluation over more environments needs to be determined.

The identification of weevil oviposition stimulants and quantification of that stimulant reported by Son et al. (1991) should facilitate progress in breeding for resistance. Field evaluation will continue to be important for confirming resistance levels. The extent that laboratory techniques can effectively replace field evaluations needs to be determined. We plan to address some of those needs as time and facilities permit.

CONCLUSION

Previous research and our 1990 investigations show that development of weevil resistance can be achieved with continued research. The success in development of resistance to other soil-inhabiting insects injurious to sweetpotato supports that conclusion (Jones et al. 1987; Thompson and Hurley 1989). Increased levels of resistance will be useful as a part of overall control programs and should always be considered for use in combination with other control measures. Immunity to injury is not a realistic expectation, but economical production with reduced pesticide use is.

ACKNOWLEDGMENT

This research was partially funded by the International Potato Center.

LITERATURE CITED

Cuthbert, F.P., Jr., and B.W. Davis. 1970. Resistance in sweet potatoes to damage by soil insects. Journal of Economic Entomology. 63:360-361.

Hahn, S.K., and K. Leuschner. 1981. Resistance of sweet potato cultivars to African sweet potato weevil. Crop Science 21:499-503.

Hahn, S.K., and K. Leuschner. 1982. Breeding sweet potatoes for weevil resistance. Pages 331-336 in Sweet potato, edited by R. L. Villareal and T. D. Griggs. Proceedings of the First International Symposium, AVRDC, Shanhua, Taiwan.

Jones, A. 1965. Cytological observations and fertility measurements of sweetpotato. Proceedings of the American Society for Horticultural Science 86:527-537.

Jones, A. 1969. Quantitative inheritance of ten root traits in sweetpotatoes. Journal of the American Society for Horticultural Science 94:271-275.

Jones, A., J.M. Schalk, and P.D. Dukes. 1982. Progress in selection for resistance in sweet potato to soil insects of the WDS complex. Pages 337-343 in Sweet potato, edited by R. L. Villareal and T. D. Griggs, Proceedings of the First International Symposium, AVRDC, Shanhua, Taiwan.

Jones, A., J. M. Schalk, and P. D. Dukes. 1987. Control of soil insect injury by resistance in sweet potato. Journal of the American Society for Horticultural Science 112:195-197.

Ralston, L. A., T. Barlow, T. Hernandez, and S.S. Nilakhe. 1979. Field evaluation of breeding lines and cultivars of sweet potato for resistance to the sweet potato weevil. HortScience 14:634-635.

Son, K.C., R.F. Severson, and S.J. Kays. 1991. A rapid method for screening sweetpotato genotypes for oviposition stimulants to the sweetpotato weevil. HortScience 26:409-410.

Talekar, N.S. 1982. A search for sources of resistance to sweetpotato weevil. Pages 147-156 in Sweet potato, edited by R.L. Villareal and T.D. Griggs, Proceedings of the First International Symposium, AVRDC, Shanhua, Taiwan.

Thompson, P.G., and R.M. Hurley. 1989. Marketable yields of insect-resistant sweet potato cultivars. Mississippi Agricultural and Forestry Experiment Station Research Report. 14:1-3.

SECTION 6

PHOTO JOURNAL / RECIPES

Group photo of participants at International Symposium on Sweetpotato Technology for the 21st Century held June 2-6, 1991 at Montgomery and Tuskegee, Alabama.

Roger Beachy

Jennifer Woolfe and Truong Van Den

Marikis Alvarez and Walter A. Hill

Phil Loretan, Da Peng Zhang, Conrad Bonsi and Qi Han Xue

Lynda Wickham and Stan Kays

Tom Nakashima, Audrey Trotman, Gordon Osuji

Jimmy Henderson and Simon Lyonga

Artist Eiji Yamada of Kawagoe, Japan prepared these posters for the symposium showing the versatility and other unique features of "supersweetpotato."

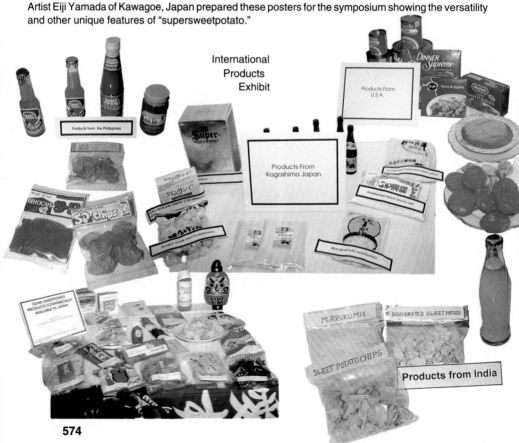

574

Curried sweetpotato and chicken (p. 577)

weetpotato was an ingredient in each of the dishes served uring the Chinese food demonstration and luncheon.

Sauteed sweetpotato leaves (p. 578)

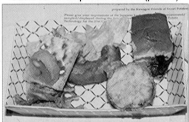

JSDA official monitors opening of Japanese varieties used n cooking demonstration. From left: Barry Duell, Eiji Yamada, plant protection official, Mei-chin Cheng, Samson Tsou, Eunice Bonsi, Chiu-O Chen, and Jack Tsay.

Japanese sweetpotato sampler: Tempura or fritter (p. 589), burger (p. 590), dough-nut (p. 588), fruit salad on cracker (p. 590).

Candies, noodles and snack foods from Taiwan with Western- and Chinese-style cookies (p. 589) in forefront.

Eriko Kanao, Kyoko Hara and Machiko Ono demon-strate sweetpotato preparation Japanese-style.

575

Photographs by Walter Scott, J.H.M. Henderson, Marie Loretan, the Tainan County Farmers Association, the Kawagoe Friends of Sweetpotato, and Tamil Nadu Agricultural University.

Sweetpotato Meat Soup (p. 582)

Sweetpotato Squares (p. 583)

Sweetpotato Vermicelli (p. 584)

Chappathi (p. 585)

Sweetpotato Pie (p. 594)

Sweetpotato Muffins (p. 596)

Chinese Sweetpotato Recipes[1*]

CURRIED SWEETPOTATOES

WITH CHICKEN	Metric	U.S.
One half chicken	450 g	1 pound
Onion	110 g	1 medium
Sweetpotato	250 g	1 small
Carrot	225 g	3 medium
Curry powder	15 g	2 tbsp.
Salt	8 g	1 tsp.
Monosodium glutamate (MSG)	2 g	1/2 tsp.
Cooking oil	30 mL	2 tbsp.
Water	480 mL	2 cups

Peel and cut the sweetpotato and carrot into large chunks. Cut the onion and chicken into large pieces also. Heat curry powder in oil until fragrant. Add sweetpotato, carrot, chicken and onion and stir fry for 2 minutes over high heat. Add water and cook until ingredients are tender. Season with salt and MSG. Serve hot.

CANDIED SWEETPOTATOES

Sweetpotato	1350 g	3 medium
White sesame seeds	40 g	1/2 cup
Sugar	120 mL	1/2 cup
Cooking oil		

Peel and cut sweetpotatoes into large chunks. Fry until golden brown and set aside. Heat oil, add sugar and boil into a syrup. Add sweetpotato chunks and sesame seeds. Dip the syrup-coated chunks in cold water to make the coating crispy. Serve hot.

SWEETPOTATO CHIPS

Sweetpotato	700 g	1 large
Salt	2 g	1/4 tsp
Sugar, fine	1 g	1/4 tsp
Vegetable oil		

Thinly slice peeled sweetpotatoes into chips and place in cold water for about 4 hours, changing water 3 or 4 times. Drain well and set aside. Deep fat fry until golden brown. Place on paper towel to absorb excess oil; season with salt and sugar.

---

* These recipes from the Tainan County Farmers Association in Taiwan are followed by recipes from Ghana, Guyana, India, Japan and the United States. Footnotes are at the end of each set of recipes.

SWEETPOTATO CAKES (Patties)	Metric	U.S.
Sweetpotato	700 g	1 large
Pork, ground	100 g	1/5 pound
Carrot	225 g	3 medium
Vegetable oil		
All purpose flour	120 mL	1/2 cup
Soy sauce	30 mL	2 tbsp
Corn starch	7 g	1 tbsp
Salt	10 g	1/2 tbsp

Peel and chop carrots into fine pieces. Cook sweetpotatoes in boiling water, peel and mash. Mix ground pork, soy sauce, corn starch and salt; cook in 2 tablespoons oil, stirring frequently; drain oil. Combine carrot, mashed sweetpotatoes and cooked pork, and shape them into 12 patties. Coat with flour and fry until golden brown.

SAUTÉED SWEETPOTATO NOODLES

Sweetpotato noodles	300 g	2/3 pound
Sweetpotato leaf noodles (green)	300 g	2/3 pound
Fresh mushroom	225 g	1/2 pound
Pork	225 g	1/2 pound
Carrot, peeled	150 g	2 medium
Onion, peeled	110 g	1 medium
Salt to taste		
Monosodium glutamate (MSG)	2 g	1/2 tsp
Sugar	2 g	1/2 tsp
Cooking oil	30 mL	2 tbsp

Cook noodles according to directions. Wash with cold water, drain well and arrange on a serving plate. Cut the mushroom, carrot, pork and onion into thin strips about 2 in. (5 cm) long. Saute with salt, sugar and MSG in cooking oil and pour over noodles. Serve warm. **Note:** The noodles are available in some Asian food stores.

SAUTÉED SWEETPOTATO LEAVES

Sweetpotato leaves	700 g	1 1/2 pounds
Chili powder	0.5 g	1/4 tsp
Garlic, peeled, crushed	2 to 3 cloves	
Cooking oil	30 mL	2 tbsp
Salt	8 g	1 tsp
MSG	2 g	1/2 tsp

Boil leaves in water until tender; drain. Stir fry the leaves with all the other ingredients.

FRIED SWEETPOTATOES   Metric   U.S.

Orange flesh sweetpotato, peeled	700 g	1 large
Garlic, peeled	1 or 2 cloves	
Celery	2 stalks	

Cut the sweetpotato, celery and garlic into thin strips about 2 inches (5 cm) long. Saute all the ingredients in oil until tender.

SWEETPOTATO COLD PLATE

Sweetpotato	450 g	1 medium
Ham	100 g	1/5 pound
Agar	1/2 stick	
Cucumber	225 g	1
Cooking oil		
Soy sauce	30 mL	2 tbsp
Sesame oil	5 mL	1 tsp
Monosodium glutamate	1 g	1/4 tsp
Salt	4 g	1/2 tsp

Cut the agar into 2 inch thin strips, soak in cold water for 30 minutes, drain well and set aside. Peel and cut the sweepotato into thin strips, fry until golden brown. Slice the ham into strips also. Peel cucumber, remove the portion with seeds, and cut into thin strips. Salt the cucumber for about 3 minutes, remove excess salt by washing and draining. Mix the sweetpotato, agar, ham and cucumber. Add the soy sauce, sesame oil and MSG, and mix again. Refrigerate and serve cold. **Note: The agar** is available in some Asian food stores as foot-long dried sticks (1 x 1 inch) colored white. Cooked agar does not soften at room temperature even after 2 hours.

SWEETPOTATO SALAD

Sweetpotato	700 g	1 large
Carrot	300 g	4 medium
Cucumber	225 g	1 piece
Egg, hard boiled	60 g	1 large
Mayonnaise	240 mL	1 cup
Salt	8 g	1 tsp

Peel the sweetpotato and carrot. Steam until tender and cut into small cubes (about 1/2 inch or 1 cm cubes). Cut egg and cucumber (without portion containing seeds) into cubes also. Salt cucumber for 10 minutes, rinse excess salt with water and drain well. Mix the ingredients with mayonnaise, refrigerate and serve cold.

CHINESE-STYLE COOKIE	Metric	U.S.
All purpose flour	720 mL	3 cups
Sweetpotato flour	320 mL	1 1/3 cups
Shortening	40 g	3 tbsp
Salt	4 g	1/2 tsp
Baking powder	8 g	2 tsp
Egg	180 g	3 large
Sugar, fine	240 mL	1 cup
White sesame seeds	40 g	1/4 cup

Beat eggs, adding sugar slowly while beating. Sift flour and baking powder. Mix all ingredients except sesame seeds. On a floured board, roll dough into 2.5 cm (1 inch) balls. Coat with sesame seeds. Deep fat fry for about 3 minutes until golden brown.

WESTERN-STYLE COOKIE

Butter	450 g	1 pound
Shortening	300 g	1 1/3 cups
Sugar, fine	240 mL	1 cup
Icing or confectioners' sugar	240 mL	1 cup
Salt	10 g	1 1/4 tsp
Egg	240 g	4 large
Milk	120 mL	1/2 cup
Vanilla	5 mL	1 tsp
All purpose flour	1260 mL	5 1/4 cups
Sweetpotato, cooked and mashed	450 g	1 medium

Whip butter, shortening, and both sugars until fluffy. Add eggs slowly, beating constantly. Add milk and vanilla; blend well. Sift flour; mix thoroughly with mashed sweetpotato and other ingredients. Shape dough into half inch balls; flatten into round or oblong cookies. To get a corrugated effect, score in parallel lines with a fork dipped in flour. Bake at 190°C (375°F) for about10 minutes or until golden brown.

CHINESE-STYLE COOKIE (SA-JI-MA)

All purpose flour	320 mL	1 1/3 cups
Sweetpotato flour	180 mL	3/4 cup
Egg	180 g	3 large
Baking soda	5 g	1 tsp
Syrup:		
Sugar, fine	320 mL	1 1/3 cups
Malt	120 g	6 tbsp
Water	80 mL	1/3 cup

Blend all the ingredients for the dough. Add a few teaspoons of water and knead to a soft dough. Flatten the dough to 0.2 to 0.3 cm (1/8 inch) thick and slice into long strips. Fry in oil for about 1 minute and cool. Heat ingredients for the syrup and stir until thick. Arrange the fried slices in a greased pan and pour the syrup over it. Compress lightly, cool for 1 hour and cut into bars. **Note: Sweetpotato flour** may be purchased from some Asian food stores. It can also be prepared by slicing peeled sweetpotato into thin chips, drying the chips under the sun or in the oven at 65°C (150°F), and milling the dried chips into flour using a blender.

SWEETPOTATO PIE	Metric	U.S.
Egg	180 g	3 large
Sugar	120 mL	1/2 cup
Brown sugar	120 mL	1/2 cup
Salt	4 g	1/2 tsp
Cinnamon powder	4 g	1 tsp
Nutmeg powder	1 g	1/4 tsp
Ginger powder	1 g	1/4 tsp
Clove powder	1 g	1/4 tsp
Mixed spice powder	1 g	1/4 tsp
Milk	80 mL	1/3 cup
Sweetpotato	700 g	1 large
Butter, melted	15 mL	1 tbsp
Pie shell, 8 inch diameter	1	1

Boil, peel and mash sweetpotato. Mix with all other ingredients except butter. Brush the unbaked pie shell with butter and pour in mixture. Bake at 210°C (410°F) for 10 minutes; reduce to 180°C (360°F) and bake 20 more minutes or until lightly brown.

SWEETPOTATO JELLO

Sweetpotato, cooked, mashed	1200 g	3 medium
Agar	1 stick	1 stick
Sugar	320 mL	1 1/3 cups
Water	720 mL	3 cups

Wash the agar, and soak in water until tender. Blend in the other ingredients. Cook over low flame, stirring constantly until thick. Pour into mold(s), refrigerate and serve cold as dessert. **Note:** See note about agar on page 577.

---

[1]Sweet potato recipes. 1991. Tainan County Farmers Association, Taiwan, R.O.C. See page 473 for further background information on the association, Chinese cooking and the nutrition of sweetpotato.

Sweetpotato Recipes from Ghana

SWEETPOTATO TIP STEW[1]	Metric	U.S.
Vegetable oil	30 mL	2 tbsp
Beef, lean pork, shrimp or fish	450 g	1 pound
Ground fresh ginger	10 mL	2 tsp
Onion, chopped	60 g	1 small
Fresh garlic, minced	1 mL	1/4 tsp
Sweetpotato leaf tips, chopped	300 g	4 cups
Coconut milk	240 mL	1 cup
Pepper or ground chili and MSG	1 g each	1/4 tsp each
Bouillon cubes	2	2

Saute' meat, onion, garlic and ginger in oil. Add sweetpotato leaves, cover and simmer until half cooked (about 15 minutes). Add coconut milk. Season with pepper, bouillon cubes and MSG. Cover and simmer until sauce thickens. Serve hot with boiled rice, potatoes or noodles. Makes 11 servings (120 mL or 1/2 cup). Note: Prepare coconut milk by adding 2 cups (480 mL) water to 1 cup (120 mL) grated fresh coconut meat. Soak for about 5 minutes; squeeze water from the pulp while straining.

SWEETPOTATO MEAT SOUP[2]

Ground beef	110 g	1/4 pound
Onion, medium (110 g), chopped	110 g	1 medium
Tomato paste or puree	15 mL	1 tbsp
Chili powder	1 g	1/2 tsp
Ginger, ground dry or minced fresh	5 g	1 tsp
Beef bouillon cube	1	1
Thyme and sage, ground	1 g each	1 tsp each
Sweetpotato, peeled and diced	900 g	2 medium
Carrots, minced	30 mL	2 tbsp
Green peas	60 mL	1/4 cup

Brown meat in a skillet; then add onion, tomato, bouillon cube and the spices. Stir and simmer for 10 min. Add 3 cups (720 mL) water. When boiling, add sweetpotatoes. Simmer until sweetpotatoes are cooked and the liquid thickens. Add carrots and peas and cook for 5 more min. Makes 10 servings (1/2 cup or 120 mL).

---

[1]Bonsi, Eunice. 1988. *In* Sweet potato, recipes and nutritional information, edited by R. Pace, E. Bonsi, and J. Lu. George Washington Carver Agricultural Experiment Station, Tuskegee University, Tuskegee, Alabama.

[2]Mkhonta, Christabel, and Eunice Bonsi. 1988. *In* Sweet potato, recipes and nutritional information, edited by R. Pace, E. Bonsi, and J. Lu. George Washington Carver Agricultural Experiment Station, Tuskegee University, Tuskegee, Alabama.

Sweetpotato Recipes from Guyana

SWEETPOTATO SQUARES	Metric	U.S.
Sweetpotato, grated	250 g	1 1/2 small
Margarine	170 g	12 tbsp
Sugar	120 mL	1/2 cup
Flour	60 mL	1/4 cup
Eggs	180 g	3 large
Cornmeal (optional)	60 mL	1/4 cup
Baking powder	4 g	1 tsp
Nutmeg	3 g	1 tsp
Ground cloves	2 g	1/2 tsp
Ground cinnamon	1 g	1/2 tsp
Salt	2 g	1/4 tsp
Vanilla or almond extract	10 mL	2 tsp
Raisins	230 g	1/2 pound

Mix ingredients (in the above order) well. Place in 9 x 13 inch (approx. 23 x 33 cm) pan. Bake at 340°F (170°C) for 20 to 30 min. Cool slightly and cut into 12 squares.

SWEETPOTATO ROOT DRINK (FLY)

Sweetpotato, grated	1400 g	2 large
Granulated sugar (fine)	2 1/4 kg	5 pounds
Egg whites	2	2
Water	5.7 L	1 1/2 gal
Lemon or lime juice, strained	120 mL	1/2 cup
Ground mace	6 g	1 tbsp
Ground cinnamon	1 g	1/2 tsp
Whole cloves	12	12

Use a large glass or plastic container (3 gal or 12 liters) with cover; do not use metal as it might leach. Put grated sweetpotato in a muslin cloth, then into a collander and hold under running water until all the starch is removed. Squeeze gently. Put washed sweetpotato, water, lemon juice, mace, cinnamon and cloves into the container. Whip egg white stiff and add to mixture. Sweeten to taste. The entire amount of sugar indicated above does not have to be used. Cover tightly and leave for 5 days. Strain and chill.

In Sweet potato, recipes and nutritional information. 1988. R. Pace, E. Bonsi, and J. Lu (eds.). George Washington Carver Agricultural Experiment Station, Tuskegee University, Tuskegee, Alabama.

Sweetpotato Recipes from India

SWEETPOTATO MASH	Metric	U.S.
Sweetpotato, cooked and mashed	200 g	1 cup
Vegetable oil	30 mL	2 tbsp
Mustard	1 g	1/4 tsp
Powdered black gram dhal*	5 mL	1 tsp
Onion, chopped	30 mL	2 tbsp
Green chili, chopped	5 mL	1 tsp
Salt to taste		

Heat oil, then add mustard, black gram dhal, onion, green chili and salt, stirring continuously until slightly brown. Add sweetpotato mash and mix thoroughly. Serve hot. **Note:** ***Black gram** is a small bean about the size of a mung bean. ***Dhal** is any split bean without a seed coat. Blanching or soaking overnight or, if the bean is small and has a thin coat, slight roasting helps seed coat removal.

WEANING FOOD MIX

Sweetpotato flour,* roasted	120 mL	1/2 cup
Bengal gram flour,* roasted	60 mL	1/4 cup
Sugar	10 g	2 tsp
Cardamon powder	1 g	1/2 tsp

Mix all the ingredients well. Sift through a size 60 mesh (250 µm) sieve. The food mix can be stored in an air-tight container. To reconstitute, add 30 mL (2 tablespoons) of the food mix to 1 cup of milk. Mix thoroughly, boil for 3 minutes and serve at desired temperature. (To roast flour, heat 30 mL (2 tablespoons) vegetable oil, add flour and stir constantly to prevent lumping until brown.) **Note:** See page 579 about the preparation of ***Sweetpotato flour**. (Browning can be prevented by soaking sweetpotato in water after cutting or treating with a sulfite solution which also prevents microbial growth). **Bengal gram flour** is prepared from split peas with seed coats removed.

SWEEETPOTATO VERMICELLI

Sweetpotato flour (see above)	120 mL	1/2 cup
Wheat flour	320 mL	1 1/2 cups
Pulse flour*	10 g	2 tbsp
Salt	8 g	1 tsp

Mix all ingredients with water to make dough. Pass through extruder, dry and pack. **Note:** ***Pulse** is the edible seeds of plants with pods like peas, beans and lentils.

CHAPPATHI MIX	Metric	U.S.
Sweetpotato flour	420 mL	1 3/4 cups
Wheat flour	240 mL	1 cup
Salt	To taste	To taste

Mix all ingredients and add water to make a soft dough. Knead well and set aside for 10 minutes. Divide into 5 cm (2 inch) balls. Roll into flat, round sheets about a quarter inch (1/2 cm) thick. Fry each side of the chappathi and serve hot.

SWEETPOTATO VERMICELLI PAYASAM

Sweetpotato vermicelli	100 g	1/4 pound
Ghee*	15 mL	1 tbsp
Broken cashew nuts	15 mL	1 tbsp
Raisins	150 g	1 cup
Sugar	240 mL	1 cup
Milk	480 mL	2 cups
Water	240 mL	1 cup
Cardamon powder	1 g	1/2 tsp
Rose essence	1 drop	1 drop

Roast vermicelli in melted ghee until golden brown. Then cook in boiling water. Add sugar, boil for another minute and cool. Simmer milk and add. Roast cashew nuts and raisins in small amount of ghee and add along with cardamon and rose essence; mix. Serve either hot or cold. **Note: *Ghee** is clear melted butter. It is prepared by melting cream from churned milk.

SWEETPOTATO POLI

Sweetpotato, cooked, mashed	240 mL	1 cup
Powdered jaggery* or sugar	90 g or 120 g	1/4 cup
Cardamon powder	1 pinch	1 pinch
Vegetable oil	30 mL	2 tbsp
Maida (wheat flour)	60 g	1/2 cup
Water	15 to 30 mL	1 to 2 tbsp
Banana leaves	Several	Several

Mix sweetpotato mash, sugar and cardamon, and shape into 2.5 cm (1 inch) balls. Add water to the flour and knead into thick dough. Divide into 5 cm (2 inches) balls. Roll each maida ball into flat circles. Place sweetpotato ball on center and wrap. Transfer to oiled banana leaf. Flatten into 1 cm (about 1/2 inch) thick chappathi. Fry each side until golden brown. **Note: *Jaggery** is solidified sugar cane juice which has turned brown during concentration by boiling and intermittent stirring.

PAL KOLUKATTAI

	Metric	U.S.
Sweetpotato flour	60 g	1/2 cup
Milk	480 mL	2 cups
Vanilla	3 drops	3 drops
Salt and sugar to taste		

Mix salt and flour, and add water to make a thick paste. Shape into 1cm (half inch) balls and flatten with fork to make kolukattai. Simmer milk, add sugar, stirring to dissolve. Add kolukattai to the milk and cook for 10 minutes. Cool and add vanilla. Chill and serve as a dessert.

IDIAPPAM (Steamed breakfast items)

Sweetpotato flour	420 mL	1 3/4 cups
Oil	10 mL	2 tsp
Mustard powder	1 g	1/4 tsp
Powdered black gram dhal	5 mL	1 tsp
Cashew nuts, broken	15 mL	1 tbsp
Onion, chopped	30 mL	2 tbsp
Green chili, chopped	15 mL	1 tbsp
Salt to taste		
Lime juice	15 mL	1 tbsp

Add water to flour and make a thick dough. Steam for 7 minutes. Press through idiappam mold (which is made of two pans, one fitting inside the other so as to force dough through the larger pan which has a detachable bottom containing disks with various size and shape perforations). Season with oil, mustard, black gram dhal, cashew nuts, onion, green chili and salt. Sprinkle lime juice and serve hot.

PAKODA MIX

Sweetpotato flour	160 mL	2/3 cup
Bengal gram flour	160 mL	2/3 cup
Garlic powder	5 g	3 1/2 tsp
Asafoetida powder*	1 g	1/8 tsp
Chili powder	3 g	2 1/2 tsp
Vegetable oil	30 mL	2 tbsp

Mix all ingredients with water (and salt as desired) to make a thick paste. Form into a ribbon (pakoda) using the idiappam mold and disk with inch-long slits. Press the dough ribbon into heated oil and fry until slightly brown and serve. Pakoda can be stored for about 15 days in an air-tight container. **Note: *Asafoetida** is a tree resin which comes as powder or chunks. A small amount is used for flavor and aroma.

586

MURUKKU MIX	Metric	U.S.
Sweetpotato flour	1020 mL	4 1/4 cups
Bengal gram or blackgram flour	240 mL	1 cup
Vanaspathi or margarine	100 g	1/2 cup
Salt	10 g	2 1/4 tsp
Red chili powder	5 g	2 1/2 tsp
Cumin powder	7 g	3 1/2 tsp
Asafoetida powder	3 g	3/8 tsp

Mix ingredients well, adding water to make thick paste. Press through idiappam mold using disk with star shaped hole. Swirl while pressing to make round form with 3 inch (7.5 cm) diameter. Deep-fat fry until golden brown.

SWEETPOTATO LADDU

Sweetpotato flour	480 mL	2 cups
Sugar	240 mL	1 cup
Ghee	180 mL	3/4 cup
Broken cashew nuts	60 mL	1/4 cup
Raisins	20 g	1/8 cup

Roast sweetpotato flour for 2 minutes; mix in sugar. Roast cashews and raisins slightly in ghee and add. Mix and shape into one inch balls while mixture is warm.

HALWA MIX

Sweetpotato flour	420 mL	1 3/4 cups
Powdered sugar	420 mL	1 3/4 cups
Cardamon powder	2 g	2 tsp
Food coloring		
Ghee or vegetable oil	60 mL	4 tbsp

Mix flour, sugar and cardamon powder to prepare Halwa mix. Stir 3/4 cup water to 1 cup Halwa mix. Add any food coloring, the amount depending on the desired color intensity. Cook for 5 minutes with constant stirring over a low flame. Add ghee or vegetable oil; continue cooking until the excess water evaporates and oil oozes out. Transfer the cooked mass into a greased plate or pan. Cool, then cut to desired size. Garnish with cashew nuts and raisins.

Recipes provided by Annavi Susheela Thirumaran and D. Malathy Ravindran, Tamil Nadu Agricultural University, Coimbatore - 641 003, India.

Sweetpotato Recipes from Japan

YAM DOUGHNUTS[1]

	Metric	U.S.
Pastry flour	240 mL	1 cup
Baking powder	3 g	3/4 tsp
Corn flour	30 g	4 tbsp
Egg	60 g	1 large
Brown sugar	15 g	4 tsp
Sweetpotato (orange flesh), mashed	50 g	1/4 cup
Milk	60 mL	1/4 cup
Candied lemon peel	20 g	1/6 cup
Salad oil for deep-fat frying		

Sift flour, baking powder, and corn flour together. Beat egg in another bowl; adding sugar while beating. Add cooked, mashed sweetpotato. Gradually mix in milk, then sifted flour and candied lemon peel. With rubber spatula, place the dough into a pastry bag. Squeeze into doughnut shapes. Deep-fat fry at 175°C (350°F) for 3 minutes or until golden brown. Makes 15 small doughnuts. **Variation:** Replace orange-fleshed sweetpotato with 30 grams (2 tablespoons) of light yellow, dry-fleshed cultivar, and 30 grams (2 tablespoons) of dry-fleshed winter squash. Increase milk to 100 milliliters (2/5 cup).

SWEETPOTATO CASSEROLE[1]

Sweetpotato, light yellow, dry-fleshed cultivar	2100 g	3 large
Onion	225 g	1 large
Button mushrooms	10 pieces	10 pieces
Small shrimp	225 g	1/2 pound
Salt	8 g	1 tsp
Pepper to taste		
Butter	30 g	2 tbsp
White wine	30 - 60 mL	1/8 - 1/4 cup
Béchamel Sauce		
Milk	1000 mL	4 cups
Bouillon (beef broth)	100 - 200 mL	2/5 - 4/5 cup
Butter	100 g	1/4 pound
Flour	240 mL	1 cup
Salt and pepper to taste		
Topping:		
Grated cheese	15 g	1/6 cup
Butter	10 - 20 g	1 - 1 1/2 tbsp
Green pepper, medium (75 g)	1 piece	1 piece

Peel sweetpotatoes, cut into 1.5 cm (approximately half inch) cubes, boil and drain. Cut onion into long, thin sticks. Slice mushrooms thinly. Peel shrimp and remove dark spinal thread. Melt butter in fry pan, sauté onion and mushroom. Add shrimp and sauté. Add wine and season to taste with salt and pepper.

Make Béchamel Sauce by melting butter in another pan. Add flour and stir well until cooked, taking care that no lumps form. Slowly mix in warm milk. When sauce has thickened, mix in bouillon, and season to taste with salt and pepper.

In a casserole dish, spread out vegetable mixture, add cubed sweetpotatoes, and top with Béchamel Sauce. Put on top green pepper rings, butter and grated cheese. Bake at 220°C (430°F) for about 10 minutes until browned. Serves 10.

TEMPURA[2]	Metric	U.S.
Vegetables:		
Sweetpotato, light yellow,		
dry-fleshed cultivar	250 g	1 small
Celery with leaves	1 stalk	1 stalk
Green pepper	100 g	1 large
Carrot	75 g	1 medium
Parsley sprigs	3	3
Batter:		
Pastry flour	200 mL	4/5 cup
Egg	60 g	1 large
Water	150 mL	3/5 cup
Sauce:		
Japanese consommé (clear soup)	200 mL	4/5 cup
Soy sauce	45 mL	3 tbsp
Sugar	30 mL	2 tbsp
For deep-fat frying:		
Salad oil		

Slice unpeeled sweetpotato crosswise into 1 cm (approx. 1/2 inches) thick sections. Cut celery leaves into 5 cm (2 inch) length pieces and the stalk into similar length thin sticks. Cut green pepper in half, then cut further into bite-sized pieces after removing seeds. Divide carrot into 2 portions; cut one half into 5 cm (2 inch) long thin sticks; finely grate the other half. Gradually add egg and water to the flour while mixing slowly. Add finely chopped parsley and grated carrot to the batter to make it more nutritious. Dip bite-sized portions of each of the vegetables in batter and deep-fat fry at 170°C (340°F). Mix sauce ingredients and warm before serving. Dip fried vegetables into the sauce before eating. Serves 8.

SWEETPOTATO BURGER[2]

	Metric	U.S.
Sweetpotato, orange-fleshed	750 g	3 small
Raw squid	160 g	1/3 pound
Raw shrimp	160 g	1/3 pound
Egg, large (60 g)	1/2	1/2
Bread crumbs	100 mL	2/5 cup
Salt, pepper, mixed spice to taste		
Hamburger buns	10	10
Ketchup, steak sauce, salad oil		
Butter	100 g	1/4 pound

Peel sweetpotatoes, grate finely, and squeeze out excess liquid. Peel squid, mince with knife. Peel shrimp, remove dark spinal thread, and mince finely with squid in food processor. Mix minced seafood, egg and bread crumbs with sweetpotatoes. Add salt, pepper and spice to taste. Mix and form into patties. Fry on both sides in salad oil and butter. Serve on buns with butter, ketchup and steak sauce. Serves 10.

SWEETPOTATO OSHIZUSHI[2]

Sweetpotato, light yellow dry-fleshed cultivar	250 g	1 small
Sweetpotato, orange-fleshed cultivar	250 g	1 small
Rice, short-grained, Japonica type	960 mL	4 cups
Vinegar	100 mL	2/5 cup
Sugar	60 mL	1/4 cup
Salt	10 mL	2 tsp

Wash rice 2 or 3 times with water and drain well. Cook rice in 1920 mL (8 cups) water. Peel sweetpotatoes, slice thinly and parboil. Dissolve sugar and salt in vinegar. Pour over cooked rice and mix well. Pack alternate layers of sweetpotato and rice into a sushi form, firmly compressing. Remove and cut into 8 easy-to-eat pieces.

SWEETPOTATO FRUIT SALAD[2]

Sweetpotato	750 g	3 small
Sugar	60 mL	1/4 cup
Pineapple, canned	2 slices	2 slices
Pineapple juice	50 mL	1/5 cup
Water	50 mL	1/5 cup
Apple	225 g	1/2 medium
Kiwifruit	1	1

Peel sweetpotatoes thickly, soak in water, and drain. Boil until soft, drain, and mash. Add sugar, pineapple juice, and water; stir over low heat. When cool, add small pieces of pineapple. Cut apple and peeled kiwifruit into 5 mm (approximately 1/4 inch) cubes. Mix fruit into sweetpotato mixture. Serves 8.

SWEETPOTATO FRUIT SHERBET[2]	Metric	U.S.
Sweetpotato fruit salad (prepared above)	300 g	2/3 pound
Plain yogurt	200 mL	4/5 cup
Egg whites from large (60 g)	2	2
Sugar	70 - 100 g	1/3 - 2/5 cup
Lemon juice	30 - 45 mL	2 - 3 tbsp

Beat egg whites until stiff, adding sugar 1/3 at a time. Add beaten egg whites and lemon juice to yogurt and add gradually to sweetpotato fruit salad. Mix in small pieces of additional fruit if desired. Pour mixture into a form, then freeze. Before serving, remove from form and cut as desired. Serves 8.

---

[1]Prof. Machiko Ono, Nagoya Women's College, Japan.
[2]Kyoko Hara, Apron Tei Restaurant, Kawagoe, Japan.

Sweetpotato Recipes from the United States

**HONEYED CHICKEN
AND SWEETPOTATOES[1]**

	Metric	U.S.
Chicken breasts, deboned	4	4
Heavy cream	240 mL	1 cup
Honey	30 mL	2 tbsp
Salt	8 g	1 tsp
Ground nutmeg	1 g	1/2 tsp
Ground allspice	1 g	1/2 tsp
Ground cloves	pinch	pinch
Butter	30 g	2 tbsp
Sweetpotato	2800 g	4 large

Cook sweetpotatoes in boiling water and remove skin. Arrange deboned chicken breasts, skin side up, in a shallow baking dish. Mix cream, honey, salt and spices and pour over chicken. Dot with butter. Bake for 30 minutes at 350°F (175°C), basting with cream mixture. Remove from oven and arrange sweetpotatoes around chicken. Bake 30 minutes longer or until chicken is tender. Yield: 8 servings.

SOUTHERN SWEETPOTATO BREAD[1]

Butter	60 g	1/4 cup
Brown sugar, firmly packed	120 mL	1/2 cup
Eggs, beaten	120 g	2 large
Sweetpotatoes, cooked, mashed, fresh or canned	240 mL	1 cup
Milk	45 mL	3 tbsp
Orange rind, grated	5 mL	1 tsp
Self-rising flour, sifted	480 mL	2 cups
Ground nutmeg	1 g	1/4 tsp
Ground allspice	1 g	1/4 tsp
Chopped nuts	120 mL	1/2 cup

Heat oven to 350°F (175°C). Grease a 9 x 5 x 3 inch (approx. 23 x 13 x 8 cm) loaf pan. Cream butter; add brown sugar and beat until light and fluffy. Add eggs, sweetpotatoes, milk and orange rind. Beat with mixer until thoroughly combined. Add flour, nutmeg, allspice and nuts to sweetpotato mixture. Mix until smooth. Pour batter into prepared pan. Bake 45 to 50 min. Cool in the pan for 10 minutes, remove and place on cake rack. Cool before slicing. Serve with: Orange Cream Spread: blend 1 tablespoon (15 mL) orange juice and 1 teaspoon (5 mL) grated peel with one ounce (30 g) of cream cheese. **Note:** If using plain flour, sift 3 teaspoons (12 g) baking powder and 1 teaspoon (7 g) salt with flour.

592

SWEETPOTATO SOUFFLE[1]	Metric	U.S.
Sweetpotato, mashed	480 mL	2 cups
Margarine, softened	60 g	1/4 cup
Sugar	60 mL	1/4 cup
Apple juice	60 mL	1/4 cup
Egg, beaten	60 g	1 large
Salt	1 g	1/8 tsp

Mix all ingredients, mixing until fluffy. Put in greased baking dish; sprinkle with nuts, if desired. Bake 30 minutes at 350°F (175°C). Yield: 5 to 6 servings.

SWEETPOTATO SOUFFLE[2]

Sweetpotato, cooked and mashed	720 mL	3 cups
Corn, cream style*	480 mL	2 cups or 17 oz. can
Corn muffin mix**	200 g	7 oz. package
Eggs	180 g	3 large
Garlic powder	3 g	1/2 tsp
Vegetable oil	80 mL	1/3 cup
Sharp Cheddar cheese, grated	40 mL	1/4 cup

Mix sweetpotatoes with all ingredients except cheese. Beat for 5 minutes. Pour into greased baking dish and sprinkle cheese on top. Bake for 20 to 25 minutes at 350°F (175°C) or until inserted knife comes out clean and top is slightly browned. Makes 14 half cups (120mL). **Note:** *Substitute canned corn with 2 1/2 cups (600 mL) corn cut from ear and simmered until tender in 1 cup (240 mL) milk. **Corn muffin mix: Sift together 3/4 cup (180 mL) wheat flour, 2 1/2 teaspoons (10 g) baking powder, 1 to 2 tablespoons (15 to 30 g) sugar and 3/4 teaspoon (5 g) salt. Add 1 1/4 cups (300 mL) corn meal.[3]

SWEETPOTATO BAKE SUPREME[2]

Sweetpotato, cooked and mashed	1200 mL	5 cups
Butter or margarine	30 g	2 tbsp
Milk	120 mL	1/2 cup
Ground nutmeg	1 g	1/4 tsp
Salt	2 g	1/4 tsp
Ground cinnamon	1 g	1/4 tsp
Marshmallows, miniature	240 mL	1 cup

Add butter, nutmeg and salt to mashed sweetpotatoes. Transfer to a greased baking dish and sprinkle the top with cinnamon. Spread marshmallows and push down into the mixture. Bake at 350°F (175°C) for 20 to 25 minutes or until marshmallows are browned. Makes 12 half cup (120 mL) servings.

SWEETPOTATO BISCUITS[1]	Metric	U.S.
All-purpose wheat flour	300 mL	1 1/4 cups
Baking powder	12 g	3 tsp
Salt	4 g	1/2 tsp
Shortening	45 mL	3 tbsp
Sweetpotato, cooked, mashed and cooled	240 mL	1 cup
Milk	About 60 mL	About 1/4 cup

Sift together flour, baking powder and salt. Mix in the shortening until mixture resembles a coarse meal. Add sweetpotatoes; mix well. Add only enough milk to make a soft dough. Knead the dough a few strokes. Roll on floured surface to 1/2 inch (approximately 1 cm) thick sheet. Cut into 2 inch (5 cm) round pieces and place on a baking sheet. Bake at 450°F (220°C) for 12 to 15 minutes. Serve hot with butter. Yield: 18 biscuits.

SOUTHERN SWEETPOTATO PIE[1]

Butter	75 g	1/3 cup
Sugar	180 mL	3/4 cup
Eggs, beaten	120 g	2 large
Evaporated milk	180 mL	3/4 cup
Sweetpotatoes, cooked and mashed (If using canned sweetpotato, do not use those packed in syrup.)	480 mL	2 cups
Vanilla extract	5 mL	1 tsp
Salt	2 g	1/4 tsp
Pie shell, unbaked, 9-in. (ca. 23 cm)	1	1

Preheat oven to 375°F (190°C). Cream butter and sugar together. Add eggs and stir. Add sweetpotatoes and mix well. Stir in milk, vanilla and salt, making sure all ingredients are thoroughly mixed. Pour into pie shell and bake 40 min. When using a commercially frozen pie shell, use a 9-inch deep dish shell. **Note:** This is a plain sweetpotato pie with the flavor of sweetpotatoes accented only by vanilla. For extra flavor, add 1/2 teaspoon (1 g) each of ground cinnamon and nutmeg, or 1 tablespoon (15 mL) of grated lemon rind and 2 tablespoons (30 mL) of lemon juice.

This pie can also be made without a crust. Pour ingredients into a buttered 9 inch pie plate and bake 40 minutes at 375°F (190°C) or until knife inserted in center comes out clean.

SWEETPOTATO PECAN PIE[1]

	Metric	U.S
Sweetpotatoes, cooked and mashed	960 mL	4 cups
Sugar	240 mL	1 cup
Egg yolks	3	3
Chopped pecans	240 mL	1 cup
Margarine	110 g	1/4 pound
Vanilla extract	5 mL	1 tsp
Pie shell, unbaked, 9-inch (ca. 23 cm)	1	1
Topping:		
Egg whites	3	3
Vanilla extract	5 mL	1 tsp
Cream of tartar	1 g	1/4 tsp
Sugar	20 g	2 tbsp
Shredded coconut	10 mL	2 tsp

Mix the first 6 ingredients and pour into the pie shell. Bake at 350°F (175°C) for 10 to 12 minutes. Beat egg white, vanilla and cream of tartar. Gradually add sugar, beating until stiff and glossy peaks form and sugar is dissolved. Spread topping on hot filling and bake at the same temperature for 10 minutes more. Sprinkle with coconut and bake for 5 minutes. Cool before serving. Makes 14 half cup servings.

SWEETPOTATO COOKIES[4]

	Metric	U.S
All-purpose wheat flour, sifted	300 mL	1 1/4 cups
Sweetpotato flour, sifted	240 mL	1 cup
Baking soda	5 g	1 tsp
Salt (optional)	8 g	1 tsp
Butter or margarine	225 g	1 cup
Sugar	300 mL	1 1/4 cups
Vanilla extract	5 mL	1 tsp
Eggs	120 g	2 large
Chopped raisins or chocolate chips		
(optional)	360 mL	1 1/2 cups

Combine wheat and sweetpotato flour, baking soda and salt. Cream softened butter and sugar with a beater or electric mixer. Gradually add the flour mix, beating continuously. Fold in chopped raisins or chocolate chips using a spatula. Add a small amount of water if batter is too thick. Drop a level teaspoon of batter on lightly greased cookie sheets. Bake at 375°F (190°C) for 9 to 11 minutes.

SWEETPOTATO CAKE[4]

	Metric	U.S.
All-purpose wheat flour, sifted	360 mL	1 1/2 cups
Sweetpotato flour, sifted	240 mL	1 cup
Ground nutmeg	2 g	1/2 tsp
Salt	4 g	1/2 tsp
Baking powder	10 g	2 1/2 tsp
Vanilla extract (optional)	5 mL	1 tsp
Butter	220 g	1/2 pound
Sugar	360 mL	1 1/2 cups
Eggs	300 g	5 large
Water	About 120 mL	About 1/2 cup

Combine wheat and sweetpotato flour, baking powder, nutmeg and salt. Cream butter and sugar. Beat in eggs. Gradually add the flour mix while beating continuously. Add vanilla extract; beat again. Pour into a greased, floured pan (9 x 5 x 3 in. or approx. 23 x 13 x 8 cm) and bake at 350°F (175°C) for 50 minutes or until done.

SWEETPOTATO MUFFINS[5]

Sugar, granulated	750 mL	3 1/8 cups
Shortening	370 g	1 5/8 cups
Eggs	360 g	6 large
Sweetpotato, baked and mashed	480 mL	2 cups
All-purpose wheat flour	1020 mL	4 1/4 cups
Baking soda	18 g	3 1/2 tsp
Salt	10 g	1 1/2 tsp
Ground cinnamon	4 g	1 1/2 tsp
Ground ginger	5 g	1 tsp
Vanilla extract	15 mL	1 tbsp

Cream sugar and shortening using a flat beater at medium speed. Add eggs and beat thoroughly. Add sweetpotatoes and continue beating for another 10 minutes. Combine wheat flour, baking soda, salt, cinnamon and ginger. Add to the sweetpotato mixture and blend at low speed. Add vanilla and mix again. Pour batter into muffin pans. Bake at 350°F (175°C) for 35 to 40 min. Yield: 50 muffins.

---

[1] Kinlaw, R.K., and L.G. Wilson. Cooking with sweet potatoes, 3rd ed., Sweet Potato Council of U. S., Inc., P.O. Box 14, McHenry, MD 21541.

[2] Pace, R., E. Bonsi and J. Lu (eds.). 1988. Sweet potato, recipes and nutritional information George Washington Carver Agricultural Experiment Station, Tuskegee University, Tuskegee, Alabama.

[3] I.S. Rornbauer and M.R. Becker, 1964. Joy of Cooking, New York, American Library.

[4] Lu, J.Y., Department of Home Economics, Tuskegee University.

[5] Bonsi, Eunice, District Agent, Tuskegee University Cooperative Extension Program.

Index

abscisic acid, 234–235
acids, 226
Acraea spp., 144
ADPG pyrophosphorylase activity, 325–331
aeroponic production, 126–132
affinity chromatography, 453–461
Africa
    cropping systems, 133–142, 167–170
    diseases in, 485, 489, 502, 508, 524
    insect pests, 144-147, 496
    marketing, 141, 167, 407
Agrius cingulata, 144
Agrius convolvuli, 144
Agrobacterium rhizogenes, 9–11, 13, 69–70
Agrobacterium tumefaciens, 7–14, 23–24, 28, 53
    and crown galls, 30-31, 563
    as vector, 27–34, 52–59, 67–70, 495, 500, 508, 515
alcohol
    production, 156, 377, 381, 422
alcoholic beverages
    and enzymatic treatments, 428–430, 433–437
    see also shochu
alcohols, 226
aldehydes, 226
allelopathy, 263, 267–268
allopolyploidy, 88
almond moth, 500
α-amylases
    inhibitors of, studies, 452–459
amino acids, 209–262, 441–442
amylopectin, 204-205
amylose, 204-205
Angola, 135
animal feed, 165, 364, 381, 525
    in China, 155-159, 461
anthocyanins, 222-223, 536
antioxidants, 219, 373
aphids, 144

Argentina, 179, 378
aroma, 226–227, 420–426, 447–448
ascorbic acid, 157, 229–230, 274, 373–376, 391–392
    see also vitamin C
Asia, 215, 367, 370, 407,
    breeding program, 526
    diseases, 485, 524
    insect pests, 143–152
Asian Vegetable Research and Development Center (AVRDC), 7, 146–150, 359–362, 499, 521–532
Aspergillus kawachii, 428
Aspergillus niger, 434
autopolyploidy, 88
autoradiographic imaging, 93–96
auxin, 234–235, 284

Bacillus thuringiensis (Bt), 5, 10, 18, 498, 500, 516
bacterial stem and root rot, 485, 487
bacterial wilt, 158, 485
Bangladesh, 369, 523, 530
batatas-related species, 47–51, 72
'Beauregard', 321
Beauveria bassiana, 498
Beauveria brongniartii, 498
Bedellia spp., 144
'Beniaka', 478
'Benihayato', 384
β-amylase, 211–212, 525, 535–536
    gene expression of, 20–26
    inhibitors of, studies, 452–459
β-carotene, 220–222, 360–362, 369–377, 392
β-glucoronidase, 11, 22–24, 29–32, 35–36, 52–59, 515
beverages, 389-398
    consumer response to, 394–395
    fruity, 392-394
    nutrient content, 396
    sweetpotato powder, 396